CHILDREN OF IMMIGRANTS

Health, Adjustment, and Public Assistance

Committee on the Health and Adjustment of
Immigrant Children and Families

Donald J. Hernandez, *Editor*

Board on Children, Youth, and Families

National Research Council
and
Institute of Medicine

NATIONAL ACADEMY PRESS
Washington, D.C.

National Academy Press • 2101 Constitution Avenue, N.W. • Washington, D.C. 20418

NOTICE: The project that is the subject of this report was approved by the Governing Board of the National Research Council, whose members are drawn from the councils of the National Academy of Sciences, the National Academy of Engineering, and the Institute of Medicine. The members of the committee responsible for the report were chosen for their special competences and with regard for appropriate balance.

This study was supported by the U.S. Department of Health and Human Services through the Office of the Assistant Secretary for Planning and Evaluation under contract number 282-95-0020 and the National Institute for Child Health and Human Development under cooperative agreement number NO1-HD-6-3253, by the Office of Educational Research and Improvement in the National Institute on Early Childhood Development and Education of the U.S. Department of Education, by the Carnegie Corporation of New York under grant number B6347, by the W.T. Grant Foundation under grant number 94160394, by the Rockefeller Foundation under grant number SI9522, and by the California Wellness Foundation under grant number 9700139. Any opinions, findings, conclusions, or recommendations expressed in this publication are those of the author(s) and do not necessarily reflect the views of the organizations or agencies that provided support for this project.

Library of Congress Cataloging-in-Publication Data

Children of immigrants : health, adjustment, and public assistance / Donald J. Hernandez, editor ; Committee on the Health and Adjustment of Immigrant Children and Families, Board on Children, Youth, and Families, National Research Council and Institute of Medicine.

p. cm.

Includes bibliographical references.

ISBN 0-309-06545-3 (pbk. : alk. paper)

1. Children of immigrants—United States—Social conditions. 2. Children of immigrants—United States—Economic conditions. 3. Children of immigrants—Health and hygiene—United States. I. Hernandez, Donald J. II. Committee on the Health and Adjustment of Immigrant Children and Families (U.S.)

HV741 .C536157 1999

362.7'086'91—dc21

99-6624

Suggested citation:
National Research Council and Institute of Medicine (1999). *Children of Immigrants: Health, Adjustment, and Public Assistance.* Committee on the Health and Adjustment of Immigrant Children and Families, Donald J. Hernandez, editor. Board on Children Youth and Families. Washington, DC: National Academy Press.

Additional copies of this report are available from: National Academy Press, 2101 Constitution Avenue, N.W., Washington, D.C. 20418. Call 800-624-6242 or 202-334-3313 (in the Washington Metropolitan Area).

This report is also available online at http://www.nap.edu

Printed in the United States of America

COMMITTEE ON THE HEALTH AND ADJUSTMENT OF IMMIGRANT CHILDREN AND FAMILIES

Evan Charney *(Chair)*, Department of Pediatrics, University of Massachusetts Medical Center
Kathleen Gainor Andreoli, Rush-Presbyterian-St. Luke's Medical Center, Rush University
E. Richard Brown, School of Public Health, University of California, Los Angeles
Donald J. Cohen, Child Study Center, Yale University
Janet Currie, Economics Department, University of California, Los Angeles
Michael Fix, Population Studies Center, The Urban Institute
Bill Ong Hing, School of Law, University of California, Davis
Arthur Kleinman, Harvard Medical School, Harvard University
Alan Kraut, Department of History, American University
Nancy S. Landale, Department of Sociology, Pennsylvania State University
Antonio McDaniel, Population Studies Center, University of Pennsylvania
Fernando S. Mendoza, School of Medicine, Stanford University
Victor Nee, Department of Sociology, Cornell University
Mary L. de Leon Siantz, School of Nursing, University of Washington
David R. Smith, Health Sciences Center, Texas Tech University
Alex Stepick, Department of Anthropology and Sociology, Florida International University
Sylvia Fernandez Villarreal, Department of Pediatrics, University of California, San Francisco General Hospital

David Featherman *(Liaison)*, Institute for Social Research, University of Michigan
Fernando Guerra *(Liaison)*, Board on Children, Youth, and Families

Donald J. Hernandez, *Study Director*
Katherine Darke, *Research Assistant*
Nancy Geyelin Margie, *Research Assistant*
Karen Autrey, *Senior Project Assistant*
Ronné Wingate, *Project Assistant*

BOARD ON CHILDREN, YOUTH, AND FAMILIES

Acknowledgments

The authors of the papers presented in this volume are to be commended for their intellectual contributions and their diligence in completing this enormously valuable set of studies, which together constitute a major contribution to the knowledge base about contemporary children in immigrant families. These commissioned papers were essential to informing the work of the Committee on the Health and Adjustment of Immigrant Children and Families, which was established in 1996 by the Board on Children, Youth, and Families of the Commission on Behavioral and Social Sciences and Education of the National Research Council (NRC) and the Institute of Medicine. In 1998 the committee released the report *From Generation to Generation: The Health and Well-Being of Children in Immigrant Families*, which contains its main findings and conclusions. This companion volume contains the detailed background papers that the committee commissioned along the way.

The papers in this volume have been reviewed in draft form by individuals chosen for their diverse perspectives and technical expertise, in accordance with procedures approved by the NRC's Report Review Committee. The purpose of this independent review is to provide candid and critical comments that will assist the institution in making the published volume as sound as possible and to ensure that it meets institutional standards. The review comments and draft manuscript remain confidential to protect the integrity of the deliberative process.

We wish to thank the following individuals for their participation in the review of this report: Kathleen Gainor Andreoli (Rush-Presbyterian-St. Luke's Medical Center), E. Richard Brown (University of California, Los Angeles), Larry Bumpass (University of Wisconsin), Evan Charney (University of Massachusetts Medical Center), Donald J. Cohen (Yale University), Janet Currie (University of California, Los Angeles), David L. Featherman (University of Michigan), Michael Fix (The Urban Institute), Fernando Guerra (San Antonio Public Health District), Bill Ong Hing (University of California, Davis), Arthur Kleinman (Harvard University), Alan Kraut (American University), Nancy S. Landale (Pennsylvania State University), Antonio McDaniel (University of Pennsylvania), Fernando S. Mendoza (Stanford University), Victor Nee (Cornell University), Mary L. de Leon Siantz (University of Washington), David R. Smith (Texas Tech University), Alex Stepick (Florida International University), and Sylvia Fernandez Villarreal (San Francisco General Hospital). Although these individuals provided constructive comments and suggestions, it must be emphasized that responsibility for the final content of this report rests entirely with the authoring committee and the institution.

We also wish to thank Deborah Phillips, director of the Board on Children, Youth, and Families, for conceiving the need and obtaining funding for this study and for contributing her intellectual insights throughout the course of the project. Our thanks also go to Barbara Torrey, executive director of CBASSE, for her guidance and encouragement; Faith Mitchell for her important managerial support; Karen Autrey and Ronné Wingate for outstanding administrative support; Katherine Darke and Nancy Geyelin Margie for research assistance; and Barbara Bodling for editorial review.

Financial support was provided by the Public Health Service, the Office of the Assistant Secretary for Planning and Evaluation (OASPE), and the National Institute of Child Health and Human Development (NICHD) of the U.S. Department of Health and Human Services. Our project officers were especially helpful; David Nielsen of OASPE and Rose Li of NICHD provided guidance and technical support and contributed to the development of ideas for the research. Support was also provided by the Office of Educational Research and Improvement of the National Institute on Early Childhood Development and Education of the U.S. Department of Education, the Carnegie Corporation of New York, the W.T. Grant Foundation, the Rockefeller Foundation, and the California Wellness Foundation.

The Institute for Social Research at the University of Michigan, with the leadership of its director, David L. Featherman, provided necessary resources to conduct new data analyses. The Population Studies Center at the University of Michigan provided access to computing facilities and to census data that were essential, and Lisa Neidert of the Population Studies Center provided invaluable technical assistance.

It was a pleasure working with the many people who contributed to the creation and publication of this volume.

Evan Charney, *Chair*
Donald J. Hernandez, *Study Director*
Committee on the Health and Adjustment of Immigrant Children and Families

The National Academy of Sciences is a private, nonprofit, self-perpetuating society of distinguished scholars engaged in scientific and engineering research, dedicated to the furtherance of science and technology and to their use for the general welfare. Upon the authority of the charter granted to it by the Congress in 1863, the Academy has a mandate that requires it to advise the federal government on scientific and technical matters. Dr. Bruce M. Alberts is president of the National Academy of Sciences.

The National Academy of Engineering was established in 1964, under the charter of the National Academy of Sciences, as a parallel organization of outstanding engineers. It is autonomous in its administration and in the selection of its members, sharing with the National Academy of Sciences the responsibility for advising the federal government. The National Academy of Engineering also sponsors engineering programs aimed at meeting national needs, encourages education and research, and recognizes the superior achievements of engineers. Dr. William A. Wulf is president of the National Academy of Engineering.

The Institute of Medicine was established in 1970 by the National Academy of Sciences to secure the services of eminent members of appropriate professions in the examination of policy matters pertaining to the health of the public. The Institute acts under the responsibility given to the National Academy of Sciences by its congressional charter to be an adviser to the federal government and, upon its own initiative, to identify issues of medical care, research, and education. Dr. Kenneth I. Shine is president of the Institute of Medicine.

The National Research Council was organized by the National Academy of Sciences in 1916 to associate the broad community of science and technology with the Academy's purposes of furthering knowledge and advising the federal government. Functioning in accordance with general policies determined by the Academy, the Council has become the principal operating agency of both the National Academy of Sciences and the National Academy of Engineering in providing services to the government, the public, and the scientific and engineering communities. The Council is administered jointly by both Academies and the Institute of Medicine. Dr. Bruce M. Alberts and Dr. William A. Wulf are chairman and vice chairman, respectively, of the National Research Council.

Contents

1 Children of Immigrants: Health, Adjustment, and Public Assistance — 1
Donald J. Hernandez

2 Socioeconomic and Demographic Risk Factors and Resources Among Children in Immigrant and Native-Born Families: 1910, 1960, and 1990 — 19
Donald J. Hernandez and Katherine Darke

3 Access to Health Insurance and Health Care for Children in Immigrant Families — 126
E. Richard Brown, Roberta Wyn, Hongjian Yu, Abel Valenzuela, and Liane Dong

4 The Health and Nutritional Status of Immigrant Hispanic Children: Analyses of the Hispanic Health and Nutrition Examination Survey — 187
Fernando S. Mendoza and Lori Beth Dixon

5 Immigration and Infant Health: Birth Outcomes of Immigrant and Native-Born Women — 244
Nancy S. Landale, R.S. Oropesa, and Bridget K. Gorman

6 The Health Status and Risk Behaviors of Adolescents in Immigrant Families — 286
Kathleen Mullan Harris

7 Educational Profile of 3- to 8-Year-Old Children of Immigrants 348
Christine Winquist Nord and James A. Griffin

8 Psychological Well-Being and Educational Achievement Among Immigrant Youth 410
Grace Kao

9 Passages to Adulthood: The Adaptation of Children of Immigrants in Southern California 478
Rubén G. Rumbaut

10 Receipt of Public Assistance by Mexican American and Cuban American Children in Native and Immigrant Families 546
Sandra L. Hofferth

11 Receipt of Public Assistance by Immigrant Children and Their Families: Evidence from the Survey of Income and Program Participation 584
Peter David Brandon

12 Children in Immigrant and Nonimmigrant Farmworker Families: Findings from the National Agricultural Workers Survey 620
Richard Mines

Other Reports from the Board on Children, Youth, and Families 659

CHILDREN OF IMMIGRANTS

CHAPTER 1

Children of Immigrants: Health, Adjustment, and Public Assistance

Donald J. Hernandez

The children of today are the citizens, workers, and parents of America's future, and no group of American children is expanding more rapidly than those in immigrant families. During the seven years from 1990 to 1997, the number of children in immigrant families grew by 47 percent, compared to only 7 percent for children of native-born parents, and by 1997 nearly one of every five children (14 million) was the child of an immigrant (Hernandez and Charney, 1998). Most of the growth in the number of children during the next three decades also will occur through immigration and births to immigrants and their children. Mainly because the majority of children in immigrant families are of Hispanic or Asian origin, the proportion of children in the United States who are non-Hispanic whites is projected to drop from 69 percent in 1990 to only 50 percent in 2030 (Day, 1996).[1] Meanwhile, as the baby boom generation reaches retirement ages, the vast majority (about 75 percent) of elderly persons also will be non-Hispanic whites. Thus, as the predominantly non-Hispanic white baby boom generation ages, it will depend increasingly for its economic support on the productivity,

[1]These projections assume continued high fertility among Hispanics. If fertility among Hispanics declines in the future, growth in the Hispanic population will be lower than indicated by these projections.

health, and civic participation of adults who are members of racial and ethnic minorities, many of whom lived in immigrant families as children.

Because of the burgeoning importance of children in immigrant families to the vitality of this nation, the Committee on the Health and Adjustment of Immigrant Children and Families was appointed to assess the state of scientific knowledge about the circumstances, health, and development of children in immigrant families in the United States and about the delivery of health and social services to these children and families. The committee was struck, as it began deliberating, by the paucity of research on these issues. To supplement existing knowledge, the committee commissioned new research presented in the 11 papers in this volume. Nearly a dozen federal agencies conduct or fund data collection and research efforts that constitute the core of the nation's system for monitoring and understanding the physical and mental health of children in the United States, their exposure to risk and protective factors, and their access to and use of public benefits.[2] Yet few studies of children in immigrant families have been conducted using these data. Thus, the studies presented in this book are among the first to address critical issues about the current circumstances and future prospects of this country's most rapidly expanding population of children through detailed analyses of nationally or regionally representative surveys and censuses that constitute a large share of the national system for monitoring the health and well-being of the U.S. population.

The research presented in this book was made possible by support from the committee's sponsoring agencies within the U.S. Department of Health and Human Services—the Public Health Service, the Office of the Assistant Secretary for Planning and Evaluation, and the National Institute of Child Health and Human Development. Additional funding was provided by the Na-

---

[2]These agencies include the Centers for Disease Control and Prevention, the National Center for Health Statistics, the National Institute of Child Health and Human Development, the National Institute on Drug Abuse, the Bureau of Justice Statistics, the National Center for Education Statistics, the Bureau of the Census, the National Science Foundation, the Health Care Financing Administration, and the Food and Nutrition Service.

tional Institute on Early Childhood Development and Education in the U.S. Department of Education, the Carnegie Corporation of New York, the W.T. Grant Foundation, the Rockefeller Foundation, and the California Wellness Foundation. In developing the research for this book, the chapter authors met three times as a group, first to elaborate a guiding conceptual framework and outline complementary analyses, next to review and comment on first drafts of all papers, and then (with the parent committee) to develop plans for extending and refining the analyses presented in second drafts. David L. Featherman, director of the Institute for Social Research at the University of Michigan, was especially helpful in providing both access to the institute's resources and intellectual guidance during the first meeting of the group.

To answer key scientific questions regarding the relationships linking immigration to the health and well-being of children (ages 0 to 17), chapter authors were asked to distinguish children, insofar as possible, along three major dimensions. First, to assess the extent and nature of assimilation that occurs from one generation to the next, children were identified as being first-generation (foreign-born), second-generation (native-born with at least one foreign-born parent), or third-generation (native-born with native-born parents) offspring (but see individual chapters for the precise approach used in each). Second, because countries around the world differ enormously in social, economic, and cultural conditions, children were identified according to their specific countries of origin. Third, because life chances differ greatly according to race and ethnicity in the United States, and because the racial and ethnic composition of immigrants to this country has shifted markedly during recent decades toward a larger representation of Hispanic and nonwhite minorities, the studies herein compare the situations of children in immigrant families (first or second generations) to those in native-born families (third and later generations) who are white, black, Hispanic, Asian, or American Indian.

Among the best-documented relationships in epidemiology and child development are that children and youth are at risk of negative health, developmental, and educational outcomes if their family incomes are below the poverty threshold, their parents have low educational attainments, only one parent or many siblings are in the home, or they live in overcrowded housing.[3] In Chapter 2, Hernandez and Darke report analyses of 1990 decennial census data indicating that children and adolescents in immigrant families are, on average, less likely than children in native-born families to live with only one parent but somewhat more likely to have a family income below the official poverty threshold (despite high rates of fathers' labor force participation for most countries of origin), to have parents with very low educational attainments, to have many siblings, and to live in overcrowded housing. These socioeconomic risk levels differed enormously, however, by country of origin. Children with origins in two dozen particular countries, for example, had poverty rates below those for non-Hispanic whites in native-born families, while children with origins in 12 other countries that account for close to half of all children in immigrant families had a poverty rate of 35 percent and elevated risks along several additional socioeconomic dimensions. Many officially recognized refugees come from five of these 12 countries (the former Soviet Union, Cambodia, Laos, Thailand, and Vietnam), and immigrants from four of these countries have fled homelands experiencing war or political instability (El Salvador, Guatemala, Nicaragua, and Haiti). Two are small countries sending many labor migrants (Honduras and the Dominican Republic). The twelfth country is Mexico, which currently sends the largest number of both legal and illegal labor immigrants and which has been a major source of unskilled labor for the U.S. economy throughout the twentieth century.

Children in immigrant families may experience additional risk factors associated with their families' immigration. Lack of English fluency and other cultural differences may not pose enormous difficulties for immigrants in communities with a large number of individuals from the same country of origin, but they

[3]The research in this volume often uses the federal government's poverty threshold as a measure of low income because it approximates the income level used to determine eligibility for many public benefits programs. Outcomes for children may be related to their families' income level more generally, regardless of whether they happen to have an income slightly above or below the poverty threshold.

can limit their effective functioning in the broader society in health care facilities, schools, and other settings that provide essential resources to children and youth in immigrant families. Children and youth from the 12 countries noted above with especially high socioeconomic risks are highly likely to live in linguistically isolated households in which no one over age 13 speaks English exclusively or very well. Hernandez and Darke (Chapter 2, this volume) found from 1910 census data that the overall proportion of children with non-English-speaking parents today is similar to that at the turn of the century. Nevertheless, about one-half of first-generation children and four-fifths of second-generation children speak English exclusively or very well.

The physical and mental health of children and youth in immigrant families and the extent to which they adjust successfully to U.S. society are the subjects of Chapters 3 through 8. Along a number of important dimensions, children and adolescents in immigrant families appear to experience better health and adjustment than do children and youth in native-born families—results that are counterintuitive in light of the racial or ethnic minority status, the overall lower socioeconomic status, and the higher poverty that characterize many immigrant children and their families.

Access to health care services, particularly for children, is essential to ensure that preventive services are provided as recommended, acute and chronic conditions are diagnosed and treated in a timely manner, and health and development are adequately monitored so that minor health problems do not escalate into serious and costly medical emergencies. Access, in turn, is facilitated by health insurance coverage and having a usual source of care. In Chapter 3, Brown et al. present analyses of access to health insurance and health care based on the 1996 Current Population Survey and the 1994 National Health Interview Survey.

Immigrant children and youth are three times as likely, and citizen children and youth with immigrant parents are twice as likely, compared to those in native-born families to lack health insurance coverage, mainly because of its high cost and lack of employer coverage. Even among children whose parents work full time year-round, those in immigrant families are less likely to be insured than those in native-born families with U.S.-born parents. Hispanic children and youth are the most likely of all immigrant groups studied to lack health insurance. Medicaid has played an important role in reducing the risk of not having health insurance among immigrant children and youth, with about one in four receiving their coverage through this source. Moreover, in large part because of the automatic eligibility of refugees for Medicaid, Southeast Asian children exhibit very low rates of not being covered by health insurance despite their very low socioeconomic status.

Immigrant children and youth—regardless of whether they are Hispanic, Asian, or non-Hispanic white—are considerably less likely than U.S.-born children and youth with either immigrant or U.S.-born parents to have had at least one doctor's visit during the previous 12 months. They are also less likely to have a usual health care provider or source of health care. Children and adolescents in immigrant families who are not insured are less likely to have a connection to the health care system than those with Medicaid or private or other coverage. Those who are uninsured and have no usual source of care have the lowest probability of having seen a doctor.

Analyses reported elsewhere (Hernandez and Charney, 1998) that were commissioned by the committee and conducted by Brown et al. (1998) using the 1994 National Health Interview Survey indicate that, according to the reports of parents of children in immigrant families, such children experience fewer acute and chronic health problems than children in native-born families, including infectious and parasitic diseases; acute ear infections; acute injuries; chronic respiratory conditions such as bronchitis, asthma, and hay fever; and chronic hearing, speech, and deformity impairments. In Chapter 4, Mendoza and Dixon report additional estimates for children of Mexican origin using the 1996 National Health and Nutritional Examination Survey, which also relied on parent reports. They found that first- and second-generation children have fewer acute injuries and poisonings and fewer major activity limitations than third- and later-generation children. Although these differences are not always statistically significant because of the limited sample sizes of available datasets, they are quite consistent.

Two commonly used indicators of infant health are the rate of low birthweight (less than 2,500 grams) and infant mortality (deaths in the first year of life; Institute of Medicine, 1985; U.S. Department of Health and Human Services, 1986). In Chapter 5, Landale, Oropesa, and Gorman report analyses using the national Linked Birth/Infant Death Data Sets for a wide range of immigrant groups, including Mexicans, Cubans, Central/South Americans, Chinese, Filipinos, and Japanese. They found that children born in the United States to immigrant mothers are less likely to have low birthweights and to die in the first year of life than are children born to native-born mothers from the same ethnic group, despite the generally poorer socioeconomic circumstances of immigrant mothers from many specific countries of origin. These results confirm and extend earlier analyses for the Mexican American population. The nativity differentials in birthweight and infant mortality in other groups are often smaller than they are for Mexican Americans, however, and are sometimes consistent with expectations based on socioeconomic differences between immigrant and native-born women. Differences in rates of cigarette smoking are one important determinant of the differences in low birthweight and infant mortality between immigrant and native-born women.

In Chapter 6, Harris reports on health status and risky behaviors, using the National Longitudinal Survey of Adolescent Health (Add Health) for children in grades 7 through 12 in 1995 with origins in Mexico, Cuba, Central/South America, China, the Philippines, Japan, Vietnam, Africa/Afro Caribbean, and Europe/Canada. Among adolescents overall and for most of the specific countries of origin studied, immigrants were less likely than native-born adolescents with immigrant or native-born parents to consider themselves in poor health or to have school absences that were due to health or emotional problems. First-generation immigrant adolescents also reported that they were less likely to engage in risky behaviors, such as first sexual intercourse at an early age, delinquent or violent behaviors, and use of cigarettes and substance abuse. Yet immigrant adolescents living in the United States for longer periods of time tend to be less healthy and to report greater prevalence of risky behaviors. By the third generation, rates of most of these behaviors approach or exceed those of native-born non-Hispanic white adolescents.

These estimates raise the intriguing possibility that immigrant children and youth are somewhat protected, albeit temporarily, from deleterious health consequences that typically accompany poverty, minority status, and other indicators of disadvantage in the United States. However, not all of the conclusions that can be drawn about the health of immigrant children are favorable. Mendoza and Dixon (Chapter 4) found, for example, that children in immigrant families from Mexico are more likely to be reported by their parents as having teeth that are in only poor to fair condition and those over age 6 are reported as being much more likely to have ever had anemia and, especially for those ages 12 to 16, to have vision problems. In addition, epidemiological evidence as well as physician reports indicate that children of recently arrived immigrants, particularly those from selected high-risk countries, are at elevated risk of harboring or acquiring tuberculosis, hepatitis B, and parasitic infections and of having unsafe levels of lead in their blood (Hernandez and Charney, 1998).

In Chapter 7, Nord and Griffin report on analyses using the National Education Household Survey (NEHS) pertaining to family and school experiences that influence children's educational accomplishments. Family members can foster school success by engaging in various activities with their young children, including teaching them letters and numbers, reading to them, and working on projects with them. In 1996 children in immigrant families were equally or only somewhat less likely than non-Hispanic white children in native-born families to have parents who engaged in seven different activities of this type during the past week. Among children in immigrant families, the proportions were usually higher for second-generation children than for the first generation, and the proportions tended to be somewhat lower for Hispanic children than for Asians. Parents can also foster school achievement by taking their children on a variety of educational outings. Estimates of the proportion of immigrant and native-born children whose parents took them on six different types of outings in 1996 did not vary systematically between first-, second-, third-, and later-generation immigrants or between Hispanic and Asian children in immigrant families.

The involvement of parents in their children's schools is a

third set of activities that foster successful school achievement. Children in immigrant families were about as likely as children in native-born Hispanic and black families to have parents who reported themselves as being highly involved in their children's schools. Although children in immigrant families were somewhat less likely than children in non-Hispanic white families to have parents who were highly involved in school, most of the difference was accounted for by the higher proportion with a moderate level of parental involvement. Parental involvement was somewhat greater for the second generation than the first and for Asian children in immigrant families compared to corresponding Hispanic children.

Also in the NEHS, children in immigrant families were less likely to be enrolled in prekindergarten childhood programs, which help children prepare for school, than were children from native-born families of various racial and ethnic groups. The second generation was more likely than the first to attend such programs, and Hispanic children in immigrant families were slightly less likely than Asians to do so.

Children are able to learn better if the schools they attend are well disciplined. Parental participation can be encouraged by a variety of school practices that foster such involvement. In parental ratings of children's schools along 10 dimensions, these proportions varied substantially but not usually in any specific direction in comparisons across racial, ethnic, and immigrant groups.

Kao presents new estimates of psychological adjustment in Chapter 8 using the National Educational Longitudinal Survey (NELS) of 1988 for eighth graders from China, the Philippines, Mexico, and other Hispanic countries as does Harris in Chapter 6 (see above using Add Health). The Add Health survey measured psychological distress and psychological well-being; the NELS measured feelings of having control over the direction of one's life (self-efficacy), self-esteem, and feelings of being unpopular among school peers (alienation).

Kao found that first- and second-generation adolescents had significantly lower feelings of self-efficacy and higher feelings of alienation from their schoolmates compared with children in native-born families. In contrast, adolescents in immigrant and native-born families did not differ in self-esteem. Harris also found no differences between youth in immigrant and native-born families in psychological well-being and psychological distress. Taken together, these results suggest that adolescents in immigrant families may be able to maintain positive feelings about themselves and their general well-being despite perceiving that they have relatively less control over their lives and that they are less well accepted by their school peers.

Important differences among adolescents in immigrant families emerge, however, in analyses distinguishing youth by country of origin and racial and ethnic group and when controls for socioeconomic status are added. In the NELS data, lower levels of feeling control over their own lives occurred among first- and second-generation Mexican-origin and other Hispanic-origin adolescents and among first-generation Chinese, Filipino, and black adolescents but not among the second generations of the latter groups or among first- or second-generation white youth in immigrant families. Alienation among adolescents in immigrant families, compared to youth in native-born families, was found specifically among first- and second-generation Mexican and Chinese youth but not among other groups. Although adolescents in immigrant families do not experience greater psychological distress according to the Add Health data than those in native-born families, first- and second-generation Mexican and Filipino youth overall are more likely to feel such distress than are non-Hispanic white adolescents.

Once controls for socioeconomic status are added, the NELS data continue to show relatively lower self-efficacy and greater feelings of alienation among most of the Hispanic, Asian, and black generational groups experiencing these disadvantages, compared to non-Hispanic whites in native-born families. Socioeconomic controls have little effect on the magnitude of the disadvantage for Asian youth (both Chinese and Filipino), but 40 to 60 percent of the disadvantage for Hispanic and black youth is accounted for by their lower parental education and income. Moreover, the lower self-esteem of first- and second-generation Mexican adolescents, compared to non-Hispanic whites in native-born families, is accounted for entirely by the lower socioeconomic status of the Mexican-origin youth.

When controls for socioeconomic influences such as family

poverty and disadvantaged neighborhood circumstances are introduced in the Add Health data, these factors were found to be very influential predictors of psychological distress for all adolescents, especially Mexican-origin youth. This pattern of results suggests, with the noteworthy partial exception of Mexican youth, a protective influence of immigrant status for adolescents who, because of exposure to poverty and inner-city neighborhoods, would be expected to show poor psychological health.

Kao also assesses educational accomplishments among adolescents in Chapter 8. First- and second-generation adolescents in immigrant families nationally have slightly higher grades and math test scores than adolescents in native-born families, but the reading test scores of first-generation adolescents are somewhat lower than those of youth in native-born families. The relationship is not uniform for adolescents in immigrant families but varies by country of origin.

First-, second-, and higher-generation Mexican adolescents are similar in grades and in math test scores, although there is a tendency, especially for reading test scores, toward improvement across generations. Mexican adolescents of all generations have substantially lower educational achievements than non-Hispanic white adolescents in native-born families; most of the difference for each generation is explained by lower levels of parental education and lower family income among Mexican adolescents.

Chinese adolescents in immigrant families, especially the second generation, exceed Chinese adolescents in native-born families in grades and math test scores. However, only the second generation exceeds the third and higher generations in reading test scores. Chinese first- and second-generation adolescents also exceed non-Hispanic white adolescents in native-born families in grades and math test scores. The second generation has higher reading scores as well. The superior grades and math test scores of first-generation Chinese are not explained by socioeconomic status, psychological well-being, or other school experiences. For the second generation, however, one-third to one-half of the superior performance is explained by these factors, particularly parental education and family income.

Among Filipino adolescents, the second generation also achieves better grades and math and reading test scores than the first or third and higher generations. Compared to non-Hispanic white adolescents in native-born families, first- and second-generation Filipino adolescents achieve higher grades. One-half to three-fourths of the Filipino advantage in math and reading test scores, compared to non-Hispanic white adolescents in native-born families, is accounted for by differences in parents' education and family income.

The Children of Immigrants Longitudinal Study (CILS), conducted in Southern California (San Diego) and South Florida (Miami and Fort Lauderdale), is the first large-scale survey of changes in the family, community, and educational experiences of youth in immigrant families from 77 countries of origin, mainly in the western hemisphere and Asia (see Portes, 1995, 1996; Portes and MacLeod, 1996; Portes and Rumbaut, 1996; Rumbaut, 1994a, 1994b, 1995, 1997a, 1997b). Although it does not provide nationally representative estimates for children from these countries of origin and does not include comparative data from native-born families, the survey is a rich source of psychological data and provides insights into the processes that might underlie patterns in the psychological well-being of immigrant youth.

Rumbaut uses these data in Chapter 9 in analyses of San Diego youth who were originally from Mexico, the Philippines, Vietnam, Cambodia, or Laos. This research assessed possible risk and protective factors for low self-esteem and depressive symptoms, including gender, country of origin, intra- and extrafamily contexts and stressors, educational aspirations and achievement, language preference and skills, and physical looks and popularity with the opposite sex.

The study found that low self-esteem and high depressive symptoms were more frequent among female immigrants and children experiencing high parent-child conflict, low family cohesion, recent serious illness or disability in the family, a high proportion of English only spoken in the neighborhood, a school perceived as unsafe, dissatisfaction with physical looks, and lack of popularity with the opposite sex. Seven additional factors associated with higher depression were a later age at arrival in the United States, a nonintact family, a recent worsening of the family's economic situation, perceptions of poor teaching quality or unfairness, experience with stress in school, a high proportion of friends not planning to attend college, and experience with racial or ethnic discrimination. Also associated with low self-esteem were such factors as being of Filipino or Vietnamese origin, a recent family move to another home, low grades and educational aspirations, limited English proficiency (LEP), and LEP status in 1991. The NELS data discussed above also revealed the importance of language factors and school experiences in feelings of self-efficacy among Hispanic and black immigrant youth but not for Asian immigrant youth. Of course, it is important to know that the direction of causation may often operate in the opposite direction (e.g., lower self-esteem may lead to the perception that one's neighborhood is unsafe).

In the San Diego study, Rumbaut found that adolescents in immigrant families had higher grades at every grade level than the districtwide average and lower school dropout rates, even among Mexican-origin adolescents, despite significant socioeconomic and linguistic handicaps. Factors contributing to these outcomes are the amount of time spent doing homework, time spent watching television, and the educational aspirations of the adolescents and their parents.

Prior to passage of the Personal Responsibility and Work Opportunity Reconciliation Act of 1996 (PRWORA), eligibility rules for most health and welfare programs were nearly identical for legal immigrants, refugees, and native-born citizens. Under welfare reform, the extremely restrictive eligibility rules for many programs that applied historically only to illegal immigrants are now also applied to legal immigrants who arrived after August 22, 1996 (when PRWORA became law), unless they become citizens, and to refugees beginning five to seven years after arrival in the United States. In addition, the focus of decisions affecting immigrant children's eligibility for many benefits has shifted from the federal government to the states. Specific provisions of welfare reform are subject to change as the legislation evolves, but it is clear that the law's potential impact on immigrant children and youth derives in large part from the programmatic reach of the new restrictions on immigrants' eligibility for public benefits, which go far beyond welfare as conventionally known to encompass benefits programs, including Medicaid, Supplemental Security Income, food stamps, and noncash services.

Benefits and services provided by health and social programs, whether from public or private sources, represent important investments in and critical resources for all children and youth, including but not restricted to those in immigrant families. Analyses of the extent to which first-, second-, and third- and later-generation children live in families that receive assistance from important federal programs are presented by Hofferth in Chapter 10 using the Panel Study of Income Dynamics (PSID) and by Brandon in Chapter 11 using the Survey of Income and Program Participation (SIPP).

Prior to welfare reform, children and adolescents in immigrant families were about as likely as, or only slightly more likely than, children and youth in native-born families to live in families that received public assistance, particularly noncash assistance. Most of the differences that existed reflected higher participation rates for first-generation children.

The comparatively high rates of reliance on public assistance among first-generation families are largely attributable to their disadvantaged socioeconomic and demographic characteristics, not their immigrant status per se. When comparisons are made between immigrant and native-born families with adjustments for these characteristics, the differences either disappear or, in the case of children and youth in Mexican immigrant families, the differences indicate less reliance on the public assistance programs for which they are eligible. In addition, the special refugee status of many immigrants from Southeast Asia and the former Soviet bloc countries appears to involve comparatively high participation rates for the first generation, while children and youth in Mexican immigrant families are less likely than those in native-born families at the same socioeconomic level to live in families that rely on both cash and noncash public assistance.

In Chapter 12, Mines uses the National Agricultural Workers Survey to portray the situation of a small but highly disadvantaged population of children in immigrant (and native-born) families—those living with a migrant farmworker parent. Mines documents the extraordinarily high proportions of U.S.-based children of migrant farmworkers who have a parent who completed less than eight years of schooling (60 percent) and who live in poverty (more than 67 percent).

Prior to the new studies presented in this book, few of the datasets represented here had been used to assess the circumstances of children in immigrant families. These new studies made every effort to draw on available measures to correctly identify and present estimates for children by generation and immigrant status, country of origin, and race and ethnicity. But because few national information systems currently collect the full array of data needed on country of origin and immigrant status and because few have samples large enough to support conclusions for more than three or four specific countries of origin, the results derived in these studies should be viewed as the best-available first step in assessing the circumstances of children in immigrant families. The approaches used to classify children differ somewhat from study to study, and the reader is encouraged to consult the individual chapters for detailed descriptions of data and procedures.

Examples of the important limits imposed by current measurement in the datasets that provide the foundation for this book are to be noted here, however. None explicitly identify undocumented children and parents, and although some undocumented persons may be included in most samples, estimates of undercoverage of the undocumented population in these data systems are not available. Many datasets do not ascertain detailed country of birth for foreign-born persons. Hence, information on race and ethnicity (e.g., Chinese, Filipino, Mexican) is used as a proxy, leading to a misclassification of country of birth for some children or parents. Because the 1990 census and most other datasets do not ask country of birth of parents, birthplaces can be ascertained for parents living in the child's home but not for parents living elsewhere. Hence, second-generation children who have only one foreign-born parent and who do not have that parent in the home are misclassified as third-generation children. More generally, because virtually no information is available regarding the characteristics or circumstances of parents not living in a child's home, most estimates pertaining to children's parents exclude parents not in the home. Also, available data do not allow most third- and higher-generation children to be classified by country of origin, except through the use of race and ethnicity data.

Another caveat regarding inferences drawn from these studies is that differences between first, second, and later generations may reflect changes brought about through the process of intergenerational assimilation; but differences between the generations may, alternatively, reflect changes over years or decades in the characteristics of successive waves of immigrants. For example, among the four Central American countries with high U.S. child poverty rates and for which information is available in the 1990 census not only for the first two generations but also for later-generation children, poverty is substantially lower among third- and later-generation children than among second-generation children. Although this might be due to intergenerational socioeconomic assimilation, a more plausible interpretation is that poverty is lower among the later generations because the grandparents of the third- and later-generation children entered the United States in earlier times with much higher socioeconomic status than did the parents of second-generation children who immigrated more recently. Results presented by Hernandez and Darke (Chapter 2) suggest that such a change in the characteristics of immigrants from these countries did, in fact, occur; the parental educational attainments of children in immigrant families from these four countries in 1960 were much higher than in 1990. The characteristics of successive waves of immigrants to the United States from several other countries of origin, including Cuba and Vietnam, also have changed greatly over time.

Finally, trajectories of health, development, assimilation, and adjustment occur across periods of years or decades for children, and the nature of individual outcomes depends on the timing and sequencing of specific personal, family, neighborhood, and historical events in a child's life. These are best measured and analyzed through longitudinal data collection and research that follow the same individuals over extended periods. Only the study by Rumbaut (Chapter 9) using the CILS undertakes analyses that follow children across two periods of time, although several of these datasets (Add Health, NELS, PSID, SIPP) provide such an opportunity for future research.

Despite the limitations of the studies presented in this book, they represent some of the very best and most extensive research efforts to date on the circumstances, health, and development of children in immigrant families and the delivery of health and social services to these children and their families. These analyses, therefore, expand enormously on existing knowledge about these children and families and point toward future research. Overall, the findings suggest that despite the greater exposure of children in immigrant families, especially first-generation children, to socioeconomic risks that tend to lead to negative outcomes for children generally, despite the predominance of racial and ethnic minorities among children in immigrant families, and despite a lack of feeling in control of their own lives, it appears that these children have physical health that is better than or equal to children in native-born families and that their academic achievement is often at least as good, if not better, than children in native-born families. These advantages appear to diminish over time and across generations. It is important to not overgeneralize, however, for there is enormous variability among children in immigrant families with various countries of origin.

REFERENCES

Brown, E.R., R. Wyn, H. Yu, A. Valenzuela, and L. Dong

1998 Special tabulations prepared from the 1994 National Health Interview Survey by the University of California at Los Angeles Center for Health Policy Research with support from the Robert Wood Johnson Foundation.

Day, J.C.

1996 *Population Projections of the United States by Age, Sex, Race, and Hispanic Origin: 1995 to 2050.* U.S. Bureau of the Census, Current Populations Reports, P25-1130. Washington, D.C.: U.S. Government Printing Office.

Hernandez, D.J.

1997 Child development and the social demography of childhood. *Child Development* 68:149-169.

Hernandez, D.J., and E. Charney, eds.

1998 *From Generation to Generation: The Health and Well-Being of Children in Immigrant Families.* Committee on the Health and Adjustment of Immigrant Children and Families, National Research Council and Institute of Medicine. Washington, D.C.: National Academy Press.

Institute of Medicine

1985 *Preventing Low Birthweight.* Washington, D.C.: National Academy Press.

Portes, A.

1995 Children of immigrants: Segmented assimilation and its determinants.

Pp. 248-279 in *The Economic Sociology of Immigration: Essays on Networks, Ethnicity, and Entrepreneurship*, A. Portes, ed. New York: Russell Sage Foundation.

1996 *The New Second Generation*. New York: Russell Sage Foundation.

Portes, A., and D. MacLeod

1996 Educational progress of children of immigrants: The roles of class, ethnicity, and school context. *Sociology of Education* 69:255-275.

Portes, A., and R.G. Rumbaut

1996 *Immigrant America: A Portrait*. Second edition. Berkeley: University of California Press.

Rumbaut, R.G.

1994a The crucible within: Ethnic identity, self-esteem, and segmented assimilation among children of immigrants. *International Migration Review* 28:748-794.

1994b Origins and destinies: Immigration to the United States since World War II. *Sociological Forum* 9:583-621.

1995 The new immigration. *Contemporary Sociology* 24(4):307-311.

1997a Ties that bind: Immigration and immigrant families in the United States. Pp. 3-46 in *Immigration and the Family: Research and Policy on U.S. Immigrants*, A. Booth, A.C. Crouter, and N. Landale, eds. Mahwah, N.J.: Lawrence Erlbaum Associates.

1997b Paradoxes (and orthodoxies) of assimilation. *Sociological Perspectives* 40(3):483-511.

U.S. Department of Health and Human Services

1986 *Report of the Secretary's Task Force on Black and Minority Health, Volume VI, Infant Mortality and Low Birthweight*. Bethesda, Md.: National Institutes of Health.

CHAPTER 2

Socioeconomic and Demographic Risk Factors and Resources Among Children in Immigrant and Native-Born Families: 1910, 1960, and 1990

Donald J. Hernandez and Katherine Darke

All children share the same basic needs. Children in immigrant families are no different from others in the United States in their need for food, clothing, shelter, physical safety, psychological nurturing, health care, and education. They also share a dependence on adults—family members, communities, government—to assure their healthy development. Despite the similar needs of children in immigrant families, many have recently been denied equal access to publicly funded health and social benefits, or decisions regarding eligibility for such benefits have been devolved from the federal to state governments.

Although the basic needs of all children are similar, children in immigrant families may also have special needs, or special access to resources, because of their current circumstances or conditions associated specifically with immigration. Historical trends in the numbers and socioeconomic and demographic circumstances of children in immigrant families, compared to children in native-born families, reflect key conditions that influence the needs and resources of these children.

The purpose of this chapter is to provide historical perspective on the changing experiences of children in immigrant families in the United States, compared to those in native-born families, and on differences across first-, second-, and later-generation children in 1990 regarding socioeconomic and family risk factors and resources and potential risks specific to children in immigrant families. The 1990 decennial census provides the best and most recent source of information on risk factors for children with origins in a large number of countries. Historical changes are assessed in this study using the 1910, 1960, and 1990 decennial censuses to allow an examination of risk factors following the decade of peak immigration to the United States (1901 to 1910), the subsequent era of very low immigration (1931 to 1960), and the most recent decades of increasing immigration for which census data are available (1970 to 1990).

This assessment is the first to use decennial census data with children as the unit of analysis to study long-run historical changes in the lives of children in immigrant and native-born families. The assessment draws on analytical approaches to identifying first-, second-, and later-generation children developed in recent years (Hernandez, 1993; Jensen and Chitose, 1997; Oropesa and Landale, 1995, 1997a, 1997b; Landale et al., 1997). As defined here, the first generation is children ages 0 to 17 who were born in a foreign country, the second generation is children born in the United States to at least one foreign-born parent, and later-generation children are native-born children with native-born parents. Conclusions from decennial census data concerning socioeconomic and demographic assimilation across various generations must be treated as preliminary for reasons discussed in Appendix 2A.

NUMBER AND COUNTRIES OF ORIGIN OF CHILDREN IN IMMIGRANT FAMILIES

Immigrants from various countries of origin may differ enormously in their socioeconomic and demographic characteristics, their language and culture, and their racial and ethnic composition. The number and countries of origin of children in immigrant families have changed greatly during the twentieth century.

The number of children in immigrant families living with at least one parent dropped from 9.3 million in 1910 to 3.7 million in 1960 and then jumped to 8.2 million in 1990, nearly returning to the level of 1910. But the total population of children was rising as well. Hence, children in immigrant families as a proportion of all children plummeted from 28 percent in 1910 to only 6 percent in 1960, but the subsequent rise to 13 percent in 1990 represented only one-half the level of 1910.

Turning to country of origin, among children in immigrant families (first- or second-generation children) in 1910 who lived with at least one parent, most had origins in Europe (87 percent) or Canada (10 percent). The Northwestern European countries of Germany, Scandinavia, Ireland, and the United Kingdom accounted for the largest proportions, at 20, 11, 10, and 9 percent, respectively. Southeastern European countries of origin for many children included Italy, Poland, and Austria, at 9, 7, and 6 percent, respectively. Russia and Hungary each accounted for an additional 3 percent. Immigrants speaking Yiddish or Jewish have been a focus of recent research on ethnicity and country of origin using the 1910 census (Watkins, 1994). Adopting the same approach here, children identified as Jewish, based on their own or their parents' mother tongue, accounted for 7 percent of children in immigrant families in 1910, most in families emigrating from Russia.

At the turn of the century, perceived differences in culture and race separating Southern and Eastern European immigrants from native borns were viewed as enormous. In the massive government study of the time, the Joint U.S. Immigration Commission (popularly known as the Dillingham Commission) drew sharp distinctions between the "old" Northern and Western European immigrants and the "new" Southern and Eastern European immigrants (U.S. Immigration Commission, 1911). Anthropologists, scientists, and policy makers of the era shared the public sentiment that the new immigrants were likely to dilute both the racial and cultural purity of native-born Americans with a mainly Northwestern European heritage. Despite these concerns, however, a comprehensive assessment using 1980 census data found that, while white ethnic groups maintain some distinctive patterns, differences on many measures have disappeared, including fertility rates and socioeconomic measures such as educational attainment. A high degree of assimilation among white ethnic groups also is reflected in high levels of intermarriage across ethnic lines (Lieberson and Waters, 1988).

By 1960 children with European or Canadian origins accounted for a substantially smaller proportion of children in immigrant families with at least one parent in the home than they did in 1910, only 71 percent, at 56 and 15 percent, respectively. The largest numbers from Europe had origins in Germany, the United Kingdom, and Italy, at 10 or 11 percent each, followed by Poland, Scandinavia, Ireland, and the former Soviet Union, at 3 percent each. By 1990 only 18 percent of children in immigrant families with at least one parent in the home had origins in Europe or Canada, with only Germany, the United Kingdom, and Canada accounting for as much as 2 or 3 percent each (Table 2A-1a).

Corresponding increases have occurred since 1910 among sending countries in Latin America and Asia. The proportion of children in immigrant families from Central or South America, Mexico, or the Caribbean jumped from only 2 percent in 1910 to 18 percent and then to 55 percent in 1960 and 1990, respectively, with most having origins in Mexico, at 2, 13, and 31 percent, respectively, during these years. Meanwhile, the proportion of children in immigrant families from Asia jumped from 1 to 7 percent between 1910 and 1960 and then to 25 percent in 1990. The most important sending countries in Asia as of 1990 were China, India, Korea, the Philippines, and Vietnam, but each accounted for only 2 to 5 percent of children in immigrant families with at least one parent (Table 2A-1a).

Since the beginning of the twentieth century, then, the countries of origin of children in immigrant families have become increasingly diverse, as reflected in the shrinking number of countries that individually account for substantial proportions of children and in the broadening global distribution of these countries, with increasing numbers from Latin America and Asia. The lone partial exception to this generalization is Mexico, which has rapidly increased as a source of children in immigrant families, accounting for one-third of all such children in 1990. Associated with these shifts in country of origin are rising proportions of children in immigrant families who are classified according to the racial and ethnic stratification system of the United States as Hispanic or Asian minorities.

A final indicator of diversity in 1990 is suggested by the fact that children in immigrant families from 34 different countries each amounted to at least 50,000 (Table 2A-1a). Given that 50,000 persons is the minimum size for a city to be officially classified by the federal government as a metropolitan area, these estimates indicate that if the children in immigrant families from each of these countries of origin were concentrated in a single city the number of children in immigrant families is large enough that they could be classified as constituting 34 separate metropolitan areas representing 34 different countries of origin.

RISK FACTORS AMONG CHILDREN GENERALLY

The extent to which the risks and needs of children in immigrant and native-born families differ depends, at least in part, on the extent to which they are similar or different in certain family circumstances. These circumstances include poverty, parental educational attainments, paid work by various family members, living in a one- or a two-parent family, living with a small or a large number of siblings, and exposure to overcrowded housing conditions.

One of the best-documented relationships in epidemiology and child development is that social and economic inequality has negative consequences for health and other important outcomes for persons of low socioeconomic status—that is, persons experiencing poverty, job insecurity or unemployment, and limited educational attainment (U.S. Department of Health and Human Services, 1981; Starfield, 1982, 1991, 1992; Hill and Duncan, 1987; Newacheck and Starfield, 1988; Montgomery et al., 1996; Wilkinson, 1996; Duncan and Brooks-Gunn, 1997). Parents of children living in poverty do not have enough money to purchase necessary goods and services, such as housing, food, clothing, and health care.

Parental educational attainments are important not only because they influence parental occupation and income as well as current parental values in socializing but also because they influence the levels of education and income that children achieve when they, in turn, become adults (Blau and Duncan, 1967; Kohn, 1969; Sewell and Hauser, 1975; Featherman and Hauser, 1978; Sewell et al., 1980; Kohn and Schooler, 1983; Alwin, 1984). Thus, children whose parents have completed relatively few years of school are disadvantaged compared to children with more highly educated parents because their parents are less likely to have paid jobs that provide access to health insurance and to the income required to buy other important goods and services and because these children are less likely to complete high school or college themselves and hence are less likely to achieve economic success in adulthood.

Because paid work by parents is the primary source of family income for most children, the number of parents who work for pay and whether they work part time or full time are key determinants of whether children live in poverty, in middle-class comfort, or in luxury. Father's paid work has been the primary factor determining trends in child poverty since the Great Depression, but mother's paid employment has become increasingly important (Hernandez, 1993, 1997).

Children who live with only one parent are at risk for a variety of current and long-term negative life outcomes because children with two parents in the home have greater access, potentially, to parents as personal caregivers and as economic providers than do children living with one parent and because children in one-parent families often experience greater personal or parental stress (Featherman and Hauser, 1978; Kominski, 1987; Sewell and Hauser, 1975; Kohn, 1969; Kohn and Schooler, 1983; Blau and Duncan, 1967; Hetherington et al., 1978; Sewell et al., 1980; Alwin, 1984; Hernandez, 1997; Wallerstein et al., 1988; Wallerstein and Kelly, 1989; Cherlin et al., 1991; McLanahan and Sandefur, 1994).

Many children in one-parent families live in poverty partly because their fathers' incomes may not be available in the home and partly because low socioeconomic status strongly influences both family disruption and out-of-wedlock childbearing. Poverty has major effects on child outcomes that are independent of family structure; but children living with only one parent are also at risk of negative life outcomes, beyond the effects of poverty (Elder, 1974; Conger et al., 1990; Hernandez, 1993; Conger and Elder, 1994; McLanahan and Sandefur, 1994).

Most children live not only with one or two parents but also with one or more brothers or sisters who are potential sources of lifelong loving companionship, as well as potential competitors for the scarce time and economic resources parents can devote to their children. Although research has found that the number of siblings has little effect on a child's psychological well-being in adulthood, children in families with five or more siblings tend to complete fewer years of schooling than children from smaller families and therefore are less likely as adults to enter high-status occupations with high incomes (Featherman and Hauser, 1978; Glenn and Hoppe, 1982; Blake, 1981, 1985, 1987, 1989). In addition, overcrowded housing conditions often associated with low family income can facilitate the transmission of communicable diseases (Hernandez and Charney, 1998).

Poverty and Income Inequality

Children in immigrant families in the 1990 census experienced a somewhat greater risk of living in poverty (in 1989) than did children in native-born families (22 versus 17 percent; Table 2A-1a). Most of the difference was accounted for by the high poverty rate among the first generation (33 percent), while the second generation was only slightly more likely (19 percent) to be poor than children in native-born families (17 percent; Tables 2A-1a and 2A-2a). In the 1960 census the opposite was true, overall, because children in immigrant families were less likely to be poor (in 1959) than those in native-born families (19 versus 26 percent), although, as in the 1990 census, the risk was greater for the first generation than for the second in the 1960 census (23 versus 19 percent).

Poverty rates differed enormously in both the 1960 and the 1990 censuses among children in immigrant families with various countries of origins and among children in native-born families by race and ethnicity. For example, in the 1990 census the poverty rate for non-Hispanic white children in native-born families was only 11 percent but was three to four times greater for black, Hispanic, and American Indian children in native-born families, at 40, 31, and 38 percent, respectively (Figure 2-1, Table 2A-1a).

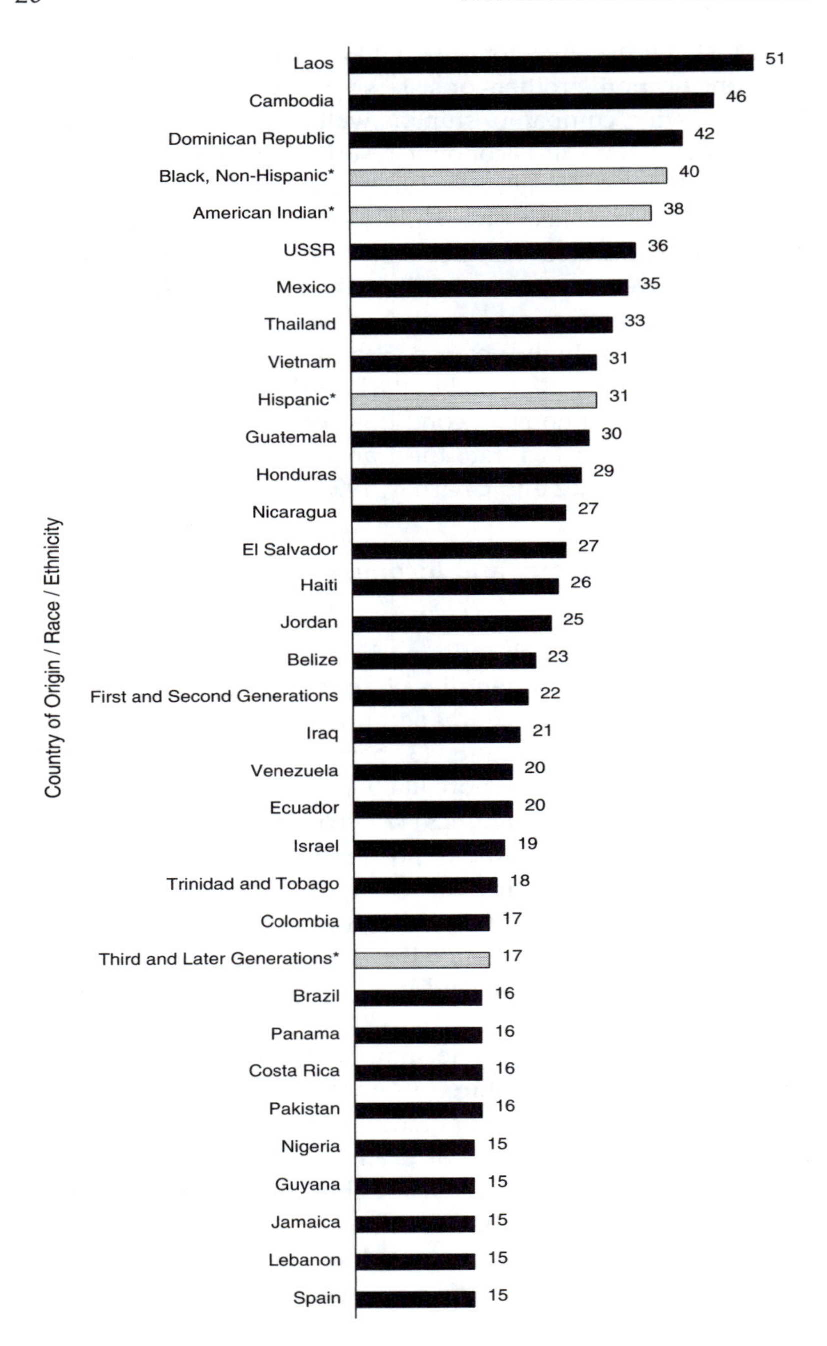
Country of Origin / Race / Ethnicity
Laos 51
Cambodia 46
Dominican Republic 42
Black, Non-Hispanic* 40
American Indian* 38
USSR 36
Mexico 35
Thailand 33
Vietnam 31
Hispanic* 31
Guatemala 30
Honduras 29
Nicaragua 27
El Salvador 27
Haiti 26
Jordan 25
Belize 23
First and Second Generations 22
Iraq 21
Venezuela 20
Ecuador 20
Israel 19
Trinidad and Tobago 18
Colombia 17
Third and Later Generations* 17
Brazil 16
Panama 16
Costa Rica 16
Pakistan 16
Nigeria 15
Guyana 15
Jamaica 15
Lebanon 15
Spain 15

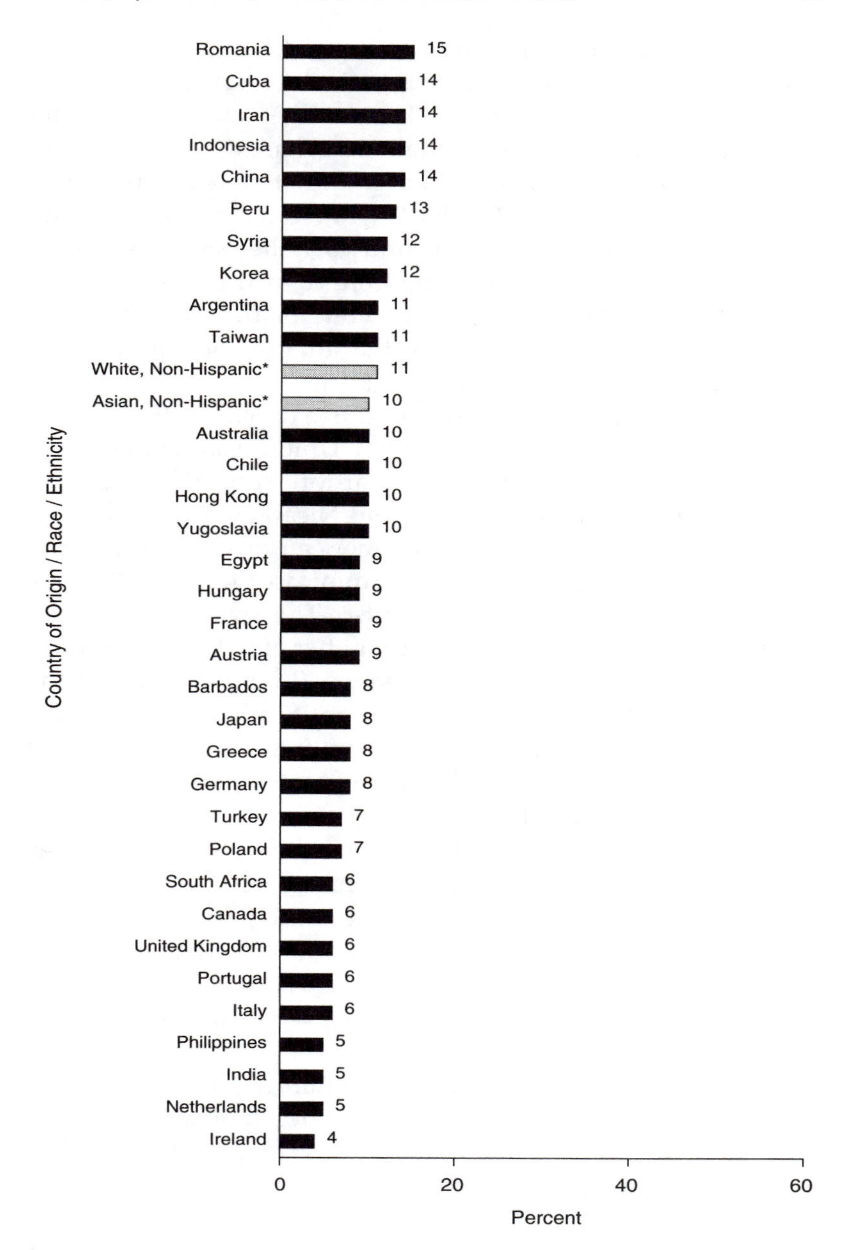

FIGURE 2-1 Percentage of children ages 0 to 17 in immigrant and native-born families in official poverty, 1990. * indicates third- and higher-generation children in native-born families.

Similarly, among children in immigrant families from about two dozen countries spread across Latin America and the Caribbean, Asia, Europe, the Middle East, and Africa, poverty rates were about equal to, or substantially less than, the rate of 11 percent for non-Hispanic white children in native-born families in the 1990 census (Figure 2-1, Table 2A-1a). But for children in immigrant families from 12 other countries in the 1990 census, poverty rates were quite high, ranging from 26 to 51 percent depending on the country of origin. In view of the negative risks associated with poverty generally, the situation of children from these 12 countries is of particular concern.

Five of the 12 countries are the source of many officially recognized refugees (the former Soviet Union, Cambodia, Laos, Thailand, and Vietnam); three are war-torn countries in Central America (El Salvador, Guatemala, and Nicaragua); and three are small and impoverished Central American or Caribbean countries (Honduras, Haiti, and the Dominican Republic) that are sources of unskilled labor migrants. The twelfth country is Mexico, which has sent the largest number of both legal and illegal unskilled laborers to the U.S. economy (Romo, 1996; Rumbaut, 1996). Within the racial and ethnic stratification system of the United States, most children from 11 of these 12 countries, with the former Soviet Union as the sole exception, are classified as Hispanic, Asian, or black.

Children with origins in these 12 countries accounted for 46 percent (3.9 million) of all children in immigrant families in 1990 (8.4 million), but they accounted for about 80 percent of the children in immigrant families who lived in poverty. Moreover, Mexico alone accounted for 31 percent (2.6 million) of all children in immigrant families but 50 percent of those officially classified as poor in the 1990 census.

In fact, the number of children in immigrant families, especially those from Mexico, who live in poverty is at least somewhat higher. Additional analyses commissioned by the Committee on the Health and Adjustment of Immigrant Children and Families (Mines, this volume) using the National Agricultural Workers Survey indicate that more than 67 percent of U.S.-based children in migrant farmworker families lived in poverty in each year from 1993 to 1995—that is, more than 590,000 of the 880,000 in total. Insofar as a substantial portion of migrant farmworker families and their children, especially those of Mexican origin who account for 69 percent of the U.S.-based children in the survey, are not enumerated in the decennial census, the total number (and percentage) of children in immigrant families, especially of Mexican origin, who were living in poverty is higher, perhaps by several hundred thousand (and several percentage points), than indicated by the decennial census data.

Poverty rates for children in immigrant families in the 1990 census were lower, sometimes much lower, for second-generation children than for the first generation for nearly all countries of origin, including most of the 12 countries with the highest poverty rates. But for children with origins in Mexico, which accounts for about two-thirds of the children in immigrant families from these 12 countries, poverty rates for the second and later generations were quite similar, at 32 and 28 percent, respectively, which is two and one-half to three times greater than for non-Hispanic white children in native-born families (Tables 2A-2a and 2A-3a).

Among children with origins in the four Central American countries (El Salvador, Guatemala, Honduras, and Nicaragua) for which information is available for all three generations (Tables 2A-2a and 2A-3a), the decline in poverty from the second to later generations is somewhat larger than for Mexican children, and the levels for the poverty rates for the later generations is 14 to 17 percent, only somewhat greater than for non-Hispanic white children in native-born families (11 percent). This might reflect greater intergenerational assimilation of children from these four countries than from Mexico. But a plausible alternative explanation derives from the possibility that immigrants from these countries during the past two decades, especially those escaping war-torn conditions in El Salvador, Guatemala, and Nicaragua, may have had substantially lower socioeconomic status, on average, than did immigrants from the same countries during earlier decades. For example, among children in immigrant families with Central American origins in 1960, the proportions with fathers in the home who graduated from high school were 61 and 69 percent, respectively, for the first and second generations, compared to 51 percent for non-Hispanic white children in native-born families. Thus, the apparent improvement between the second and later generations of children in 1990 from these Central American countries may reflect differences in the socioeconomic status of parents as they entered the United States rather than intergenerational socioeconomic assimilation.

Children in immigrant families with origins in the Dominican Republic and Haiti also had very high poverty rates in the 1990 census, but their rates were nearly the same for the first and the second generations (41 and 42 percent, respectively, for the Dominican Republic; 30 and 24 percent for Haiti), and available data for the Dominican Republic indicate no change for the later generation (40 percent).

The continuing high poverty rates of second- and later-generation children from these Caribbean countries and Mexico suggest that black and Hispanic children from these countries may be subject to racial and ethnic stratification that greatly limits their opportunities, even in the case of Mexican-origin children after many generations. For Mexicans the pattern has been quite consistent since at least 1960, when the poverty rates for the first, second, and later generations were 58, 48, and 53 percent, respectively—that is, about two and one-half to three times greater than the rate of 19 percent for non-Hispanic white children in native-born families. Thus, in both the 1960 and the 1990 censuses, the poverty rate for third- and later-generation children of Mexican origin was 70 to 80 percent as high as among black and American Indian children.

Although official poverty rates declined by approximately two-fifths between the 1960 and 1990 censuses for children in native-born families belonging to each of these racial and ethnic groups, Mexican-origin, black, and American Indian children all have continued to experience highly elevated risks of poverty, compared to non-Hispanic white children. This continuity of economic deprivation among children belonging to these racial and ethnic minorities raises the following question for the new Central American immigrant populations of Hispanic origin: Will they tend to assimilate socioeconomically to the level of non-Hispanic whites or to the level of Mexican-origin Hispanics?

Of course, it is possible that a substantial portion of children in native-born families with a Mexican-origin parent or grandparent also have a non-Mexican-origin parent or grandparents and that such children tend not to be reported as being of Mexican origin and tend to have lower poverty rates than children with two Mexican-origin parents of four Mexican-origin grandparents. But as of 1990, only 9 percent of children in native-born families who were identified as being of Mexican origin, or as having at least one Mexican-origin parent, had a Mexican-origin parent but were not themselves identified as being of Mexican origin. Hence, the exclusion of these children from the poverty estimates above cannot affect the poverty rates of third- and later-generation Mexican-origin children by more than a percentage point or two. Additional research is required to assess the possible effect of outmarriage by Mexican-origin grandparents or great-grandparents on the identification of children as Mexican origin and on poverty. Available evidence suggests, however, that the lack of change in the pattern of very high poverty rates across generations for Mexican-origin children, compared to non-Hispanic whites, between 1960 and 1990 may reflect the continuing power of racial and ethnic stratification in determining the life chances of children of Mexican origin, as has been the case historically for minority black and American Indian children.

Alternative measures of "relative poverty" and of income inequality are valuable for historical and international comparisons because they take into consideration changes in the real standard of living that occur through time and that exist across countries (Smith, 1776; Galbraith, 1958; Fuchs, 1965; Rainwater, 1974; Expert Committee on Family Budget Revisions, 1980; Ruggles, 1990; Hernandez, 1993; Smeeding and Torrey, 1995; Citro and Michael, 1995). These "relative" measures (taking family composition into account in a fashion similar to the official poverty measure) are defined as follows: relative poverty is an income that is less than 50 percent of the median family income during a given year; near-poor frugality is at least 50 percent but less than 75 percent of the median family income; middle-class comfort is at least 75 percent but less than 150 percent of the median family income; and luxury-level income (listed as "Very Well-Off Financially" in the tables) is 150 percent or more of the median family income level (Hernandez, 1993).

The relative and official poverty rates were quite similar in the 1960 census, but by the 1990 census relative poverty rates were substantially higher. Among children in immigrant families from the 12 countries of origin with the highest official child poverty rates, the relative poverty rates were about three- to six-tenths higher than the official poverty rates (Table 2A-1a). Hence, the official poverty rates ranged from 26 to 51 percent for these countries, compared to 39 to 65 percent using the relative poverty measure. Overall, the relative poverty rate for children in immigrant families was 33 percent, compared to 24 percent for children in native-born families in the 1990 census. The patterns of relative poverty across the first, second, and later generations were similar to the patterns in official poverty but at generally higher levels. For example, the relative poverty rates for the second generation were somewhat greater than for the third and later generations, at 29 and 24 percent, respectively, but enormously larger at 47 percent for the first generation (Tables 2A-1a and 2A-2a).

At the other end of the income distribution, middle-class or luxury-level family incomes represent important resources for children. Although poverty rates for children in immigrant families exceeded those for children in native-born families by 5 and 9 percentage points, respectively, using the official and relative measures, the proportion with luxury-level incomes was nearly as high for children in immigrant families as for children in native-born families, at 19 and 22 percent, respectively (Table 2A-1a). In fact, among children from 36 of the 62 countries of origin that each accounted for at least 15,000 children in immigrant families in 1990, the proportions living in luxury were 25 percent or more—that is, at a level at least equal to or exceeding the 26 percent rate for non-Hispanic white children in native-born families. These 36 countries included 13 of 14 European countries, 10 of 14 Asian countries, three of six Middle Eastern countries, four of the eight South American countries, Egypt, South Africa, Australia, and Canada but only one Caribbean country (Cuba) and no Central American countries.

Among children in immigrant families from most of these countries, the combined proportion with middle-class or luxury-level family incomes also equaled or exceeded the proportion for non-Hispanic white children in native-born families (68 percent). Thus, children in immigrant families from more than half of the countries of origin accounting for at least 15,000 children in 1990 experienced family economic resources at least as great as non-Hispanic white children in native-born families.

Across the income spectrum, then, children in immigrant families were much more likely than those in native-born families to have family incomes below the relative poverty threshold in 1989 (1990 census) but only slightly less likely to have incomes at the luxury level. Hence, children in immigrant families experience substantially greater economic inequality than children in native-born families. Moreover, children in immigrant families from various countries are extremely diverse with respect to economic resources. Children in immigrant families from about a dozen countries experience levels of economic deprivation similar to those of black, Hispanic, and American Indian children in native-born families, and most of the children from these countries are Hispanic, black, or Asian. At the opposite extreme, children in immigrant families from more than two dozen countries experience economic resources similar to or greater than those of non-Hispanic white children in native-born families; these countries are in all regions of the world except Central America and, with one exception, the Caribbean.

Parents' Education

First-, second-, and later-generation children in families with fathers in the home were about equally likely in 1990 to have fathers who had graduated from college (24 to 26 percent), and the various generations in families with mothers in the home were about equally likely to have mothers who had graduated from college (16 to 18 percent; Table 2A-1d). In addition, in 1990 among children in immigrant families from about two dozen countries, 35 percent or more had a father in the home who had graduated from college—higher than the 28 percent recorded for non-Hispanic whites in native-born families. For a similar number of countries, 25 percent or more had a mother in the home who had graduated from college, notably higher than the 20 percent for non-Hispanic whites in native-born families. All of these proportions with parents graduating from college were two to three times greater than the corresponding rates for black, Hispanic, and American Indian children in native-born families.

But children in immigrant families, overall, were also much more likely than children in native-born families to have parents with very low educational attainments, and this was especially true for the 12 countries of origin with children at greatest risk of living in poverty, with the sole exception of the former Soviet Union (Tables 2A-1a and 2A-1d). For example, among children living with their fathers, the overall proportions with fathers not graduating from high school were two to three times greater for the first and second generations than for the later generations, at 49, 36, and 15 percent, respectively, and this difference is accounted for mainly by differences in the proportions with fathers completing no more than eight years of schooling, which for the three generations were 34, 23, and 3 percent, respectively. Patterns in mothers' education were quite similar (Tables 2A-1a, 2A-1d, 2A-2a, and 2A-2d).

Generational differences in parental education followed a similar pattern in 1960, although differences in the proportions with very low educational attainments were substantially smaller than in 1990. The only measure of educational attainments available in the 1910 census is the illiteracy rate. Second and later generations of children were similar in their chances of having a parent in the home who was illiterate, at 9 to 14 percent, respectively, but the first generation was substantially more likely to have an illiterate father (22 percent) or mother (34 percent).

As with poverty, parental educational attainments vary enormously by country of origin for children in immigrant families and by race and ethnicity among children in native-born families (Tables 2A-1a and 2A-1d), both historically and today. In 1990 children in immigrant families from the 12 countries with the highest poverty rates were also, with the exception of the former Soviet Union, somewhat to enormously more likely than non-Hispanic whites in native-born families to have parents in the home who had not graduated from high school or elementary school.

Among children from these 11 countries, parental educational attainments generally increased substantially from the first to the second to the third generations. Most third-generation children from the countries for which estimates are available had parents who had completed nine or more years of schooling, but few had parents who had completed college, largely a result of the high proportion of these children with origins in Mexico (Table 2A-3e). Moreover, the proportion of Mexican-origin children in native-born families with parents not graduating from high school remained in the range of 30 to 34 percent, similar to the level for black children in native-born families and for American Indian children (26 to 29 percent) and two to three times greater than for non-Hispanic white children in native-born families (12 percent) (Table 2A-3a).

The disadvantage in parental educational attainments for Mexican-origin children, compared to non-Hispanic whites, has remained large throughout the twentieth century, at a level similar to that for black and American Indian children. For example, in 1960 among Mexican-origin children living with a father, the proportion with a father who had completed no more than eight years of schooling was 76 to 79 percent for first- and second-generation children in immigrant families and for later-generation Spanish-surname children in the five southwestern states. Although some third- and later-generation Mexican-origin children lived outside the five southwestern states in 1960, and some Spanish-surname children in these five states were not of Mexican origin, the estimates for these children are, no doubt, approximately equal to the proportion for third- and later-generation Mexican-origin children throughout the United States at that time. These educational attainments are somewhat less than the corresponding proportions of 61 to 64 percent, respectively, for blacks and American Indians in 1960. But each of these minority groups was about two and one-half to three times more likely than non-Hispanic white children (26 percent) to have a father with this little education.

Similarly, at the upper end of the education distribution, the proportions with fathers in the home who had completed 12 years of schooling were only 13 to 19 percent for first- and second-generation Mexican-origin children, third- and later-generation Spanish-surname children in the five southwestern states, and blacks and American Indians. The corresponding proportion for non-Hispanic white children was more than two and one-half times greater at 51 percent.

Parental illiteracy rates are the only measure in the 1910 census reflecting parental educational accomplishments. Among children with a father in the home, the illiteracy rate was 66 percent for first-generation Mexican-origin children and 37 to 39 percent for second- and later-generation Mexican-origin children as well as for black and American Indian children. The corresponding father's illiteracy rate for white children was about one-sixth as great, at only 6 percent.

Between the early and mid-twentieth century, then, the relative educational attainments of fathers in the homes of Mexican-origin, black, and American Indian children may have improved compared to non-Hispanic whites. Since then educational attainments have improved for all groups, and the absolute gaps between these minorities and non-Hispanic whites have narrowed. But the relative disadvantage has remained about the same, and children from all three racial and ethnic groups—Mexican-origin, black, and American Indian—have experienced fairly similar levels of disadvantage. Patterns of educational attainment across these groups and across the century for mothers in the home have been generally similar to those for fathers in the home.

Parents' Labor Force Participation

Throughout the twentieth century the overwhelming majority of children in both immigrant and native-born families with fathers in the home have had fathers who worked in the labor force. Among first-, second-, and later-generation children the proportions were 95 to 96 percent in 1910; 96 to 97 percent in 1960; and, as of 1990, 88 percent for the first generation and 94 to 95 percent for the second and later generations. The combined proportion for the first and second generations in 1990 was 93 percent, only slightly less than the 95 percent for the third and later generations (Tables 2A-1c, 2A-2c, and 2A-3c). Differences in labor force participation among fathers in the homes of immigrant children cannot, therefore, account for most of the poverty differences between the two in the 1960 and 1990 censuses. Even among children in immigrant families from the 12 countries of origin with very high poverty rates, the proportions with fathers in the home who were not in the labor force exceeded 11 percentage points for only five countries (Cambodia, Laos, Thailand, Vietnam, and the former Soviet Union) (Table 2A-1c).

Despite high levels of employment among fathers in the homes of children in immigrant families, overall and for most specific countries of origin, many fathers worked less than full time year-round in 1990 (Table 2A-1c). Little difference existed between children in immigrant and native-born families in 1960 in their chances of having a father in the home who worked full time year-round (72 to 73 percent), but by 1990 the difference had expanded to 10 percentage points (69 versus 79 percent). In fact, it is the lack of full-time year-round work among fathers in the home, along with the fathers' very low educational attainments and linguistic isolation from English-speaking culture, that are especially common among children from the 12 countries of origin with very high poverty rates.

Although children in immigrant families from an additional 16 countries in 1990 had very high proportions of fathers who did not work full-time year-round, children from most of these 16 countries had two advantages compared to children from the 12 very high poverty countries of origin. Most did not have high proportions with very low parental educational attainments, and most had at least one person in the household, no doubt often a parent, who spoke English exclusively or very well. Thus, very high poverty rates for children in immigrant families tended to occur among children from countries with very low parental educational attainments (eight years of schooling or less), fathers who could find full-time year-round work, and parents who did not speak English exclusively or very well. These results suggest that the combination of very limited father's educational attainments and linguistic isolation of the household are key factors that make it difficult for fathers in immigrant families to obtain full-time year-round work that pays well enough to lift the family out of poverty (Tables 2A-1a, 2A-1c, and 2A-1d).

Of course, many mothers also contribute to family income by working for pay. Among children with mothers in the home, historical trends in mothers' labor force participation have been broadly similar for those in immigrant and native-born families, rising from 6 and 12 percent, respectively, in 1910 to 27 percent in 1960, and 58 and 66 percent, respectively, in 1990. Full-time year-round employment rates for mothers have also been similar, rising from 9 percent for children from immigrant and native-born families in 1960 to 28 and 31 percent, respectively, in 1990.

As of 1990, of the 12 countries of origin with high proportions (50 percent or more) of children with mothers who were not in the labor force, seven had high proportions (68 to 80 percent) with fathers working full time year-round. Children in immigrant families from the remaining five countries were among the 12 with very high poverty rates, and they had comparatively high proportions with fathers not working full time year-round (38 to 68 percent), but they also had high proportions with mothers not graduating from high school (55 to 76 percent), and four had high proportions with five or more siblings in the home (14 to 35 percent) (Tables 2A-1a and 2A-1c). This pattern suggests that among mothers with very low educational attainments large family size may often be inconsistent with mother's employment outside the home, perhaps because of a trade-off between mother's work and providing care for children in the home.

One-Parent Families

The proportion of children living with only one parent was smaller for the second generation than for the first generation overall and for most countries of origin in 1990. Risk levels for both generations were similar to or less than the risk for native-born non-Hispanic white children, except for children with origins in Cambodia, Vietnam, and most Central American and Caribbean countries. For most countries of origin with available data, the third and later generations were much more likely than the second generation to live in a one-parent family in 1990, with levels at least twice as great as the 18 percent recorded for native-born non-Hispanic white children. For third- and later-generation children with origins in most countries of Central and South America and the Caribbean, these proportions sometimes reach or exceed the level of 62 percent for black children in native-born families (Tables 2A-2a and 2A-3a).

Focusing on children in immigrant families from the 12 countries of origin with very high poverty rates in the 1990 census, those from Cambodia and the six Central American and Caribbean countries (Dominican Republic, El Salvador, Guatemala,

Haiti, Honduras, and Nicaragua) were substantially more likely to live in one-parent families (26 to 48 percent) than were non-Hispanic white children in native-born families (18 percent). Children from these countries tended to have smaller proportions with five or more siblings in the home than children from those high-poverty countries with higher proportions in two-parent families, and they tended to have higher proportions with mothers in the labor force (Tables 2A-1a and 2A-1c). Thus, children in immigrant families from the 12 countries of origin with very high poverty rates in the 1990 census tended to live in families with a large number of siblings and comparatively few working mothers or they tended to live in one-parent families but not both.

Overall, first-, second-, and later-generation children in 1960 were about equally likely to live in one-parent families. First-generation children from Mexico, Central America, and the Caribbean were, however, substantially more likely to live in one-parent families (16 to 17 percent versus 9 to 10 percent), although the differences disappeared for children from Mexico and Central America by the second generation. One-fourth of black children in native-born families lived in one-parent families in 1960. First-, second-, and later-generation children were about equally likely to live in one-parent families in 1910, although black children in native-born families were substantially more likely than others to live in one-parent families, at 19 percent versus 8 to 10 percent.

Families with Many Siblings

The pattern of change across generations in 1990 for the risk of living in a family with a large number of siblings was quite different from the pattern of change for one-parent family living. In 1990 the proportion of children living in families with five or more siblings dropped steadily across generations from 17 to 9 to 4 percent, respectively, between the first, second, and later generations (Tables 2A-1a and 2A-2a). For many specific countries of origin, not only did the second generations in 1990 have smaller proportions in large families than first-generation children from the same countries, the proportions usually were similar to native-born non-Hispanic white children, at 4 percent or less for the second generation. Risk levels for third- and later-generation children also were similar, overall, to native-born non-Hispanic whites.

Nonetheless, among children in immigrant families from the 12 countries of origin with very high poverty rates, four of the five that did not have high proportions in one-parent families (excluding only the former Soviet Union) had high proportions with large numbers of siblings, and children in immigrant families from three countries experienced elevated risks of both living with one parent only and with a large number of siblings (Cambodia, Haiti, and Nicaragua).

In 1960 and 1910, first-, second-, and later-generation children were about equally likely to live in families with many siblings, at 17 to 21 percent in 1960 and 38 to 43 percent in 1910. In both 1910 and 1960 an extraordinary 51 percent of first-generation children with Mexican origins lived in large families, but the proportion declined sharply from 61 to 48 percent between 1910 and 1960 for the second generation and from 59 to 40 percent for the third and later generations. Meanwhile, the proportion of black children in families with five or more siblings remained about constant at 45 to 48 percent.

By 1990 the proportions of children with five or more siblings were much smaller for all groups. Among first-, second-, and later-generation Mexican-origin children, 19, 12, and 6 percent, respectively, lived in families with five or more siblings. Thus, among children in native-born families, those of Mexican origin were somewhat less likely than blacks to live in large families, at 6 versus 7 percent, respectively, and somewhat more likely than non-Hispanic whites to live in such families (4 percent) (Tables 2A-2a and 2A-3a).

Overcrowded Housing

In 1990 only 12 percent of third-generation children lived in overcrowded housing with more than one person per room compared to elevated risks of 38 percent for the second generation and 62 percent for the first generation (Tables 2A-1b and 2A-2b). Children in immigrant families from most specific countries of origin in 1990 also had elevated risks of living in overcrowded housing, although children in immigrant families from the 12 countries with very high poverty rates were much more likely than most to live in such conditions. For children from most of these 12 countries, declines in overcrowding are substantial across the first and second generations and, where measurable, to the third and later generations. But third and later generations continued to experience high levels of overcrowding, especially Mexican-origin children at an extraordinary 31 percent, which is similar to the 26 and 34 percent experienced, respectively, by black and American Indian children and is more than four times greater than the 7 percent experienced by white, non-Hispanic children in native-born families (Tables 2A-2b and 2A-3b).

Overall levels of overcrowding were much higher among children in 1960 than in 1990 but were about equal for first-, second-, and later-generation children at 31 to 36 percent. However, 75 percent of first- and second-generation Mexican-origin children and 69 to 70 percent of black children and third- and later-generation children of Mexican origin lived in overcrowded conditions in 1960.

POTENTIAL RISK FACTORS SPECIFIC TO CHILDREN IN IMMIGRANT FAMILIES

Children in immigrant families from countries where English is not the native language or is not widely taught may be at special risk, compared to children in native-born families, because they may not themselves speak English well or they may live with parents who do not speak English well. A lack of English fluency can limit effective communication and functioning in health care facilities, schools, and other settings that provide essential resources to children and their families.

Children who are undocumented are not eligible for most public benefits and services, and under the Personal Responsibility and Work Opportunity Reconciliation Act of 1996 children who are legal immigrants but not citizens may also be ineligible for important medical and social services (Hernandez and Charney, 1998). Equally important, native-born children in immigrant families who are eligible for such services may not receive them because immigrant parents who are not themselves eligible for services may not be aware that their children are or may fear contact with the government agencies that administer services. Because legal immigrants and U.S. citizens experienced essentially the same welfare eligibility requirements prior to the welfare reform legislation of 1996, for legal immigrants not being a U.S. citizen has become a potential risk factor for immigrant children and families only recently.

The devolution of responsibilities, under welfare reform, from the federal government to the states also implies that eligibility for and access to publicly funded health, medical, and social services by children in immigrant families will depend increasingly on decisions and investments by state and local governments (Hernandez and Charney, 1998). Because children in immigrant families are concentrated in a few states, and a small number of states have comparatively high proportions of children from immigrant families, the eligibility rules in those states will be critical both to these children and to state expenditures.

English-Language Fluency

In 1990 at least 60 percent of children in immigrant families from most countries of origin spoke a language other than English at home. Among the exceptions were English-speaking countries of origin as well as Austria, Egypt, France, Germany, Hungary, Indonesia, Italy, Japan, the Netherlands, and Panama (Table 2A-1e). But for only 13 countries of origin did the proportion of children in immigrant families not speaking English exclusively or very well reach the substantial risk level of 30 percent or more. Eleven of these countries are among the 12 with children at highly elevated risk of living in poverty (excluding only Haiti), and the remaining two were China and Hong Kong.

Generational differences are large, however, as the proportion who speak English exclusively or very well rises from only 55 percent for the first generation to 81 percent for the second (Tables 2A-2e and 2A-3d). For children in immigrant families from the 12 countries with very high poverty rates, the range is 35 to 53 percent for the first generation but rises to 65 to 91 percent for the second generation for 10 of 12 countries (excluding Cambodia and Laos).

Lack of English fluency may not pose enormous difficulties

for immigrants in communities that have a large number of residents from their home country, but it does isolate immigrants from mainstream American society. The U.S. Bureau of the Census defines a linguistically isolated household as one in which no person age 14 or over speaks English either exclusively or very well. Among children in immigrant families in 1990, 26 percent lived in linguistically isolated households. But for children from each of the 12 countries of origin with children at high levels of socioeconomic risk, the proportions in linguistically isolated households were 34 to 38 percent for three countries, 41 to 46 percent for seven countries, and 60 percent for two (Laos and Cambodia). Children from only five additional countries had 30 percent or more in linguistically isolated households (China, Hong Kong, Taiwan, Korea, and Colombia) (Table 2A-1a).

No language information was collected in the 1960 census, but historical changes are best measured by comparing "mother tongue" data for 1910 to "language spoken at home" in 1990. In 1910 the proportions of children in immigrant families for whom English was not the mother tongue for either the father or the mother were 84 to 85 percent, and for 79 percent of children in immigrant families with two parents in the home, neither parent had English as a mother tongue. In 1990 the proportions of children in immigrant families who lived with a mother or father who did not speak English at home were 76 to 78 percent. In households with both mother and father at home, the proportion was 70 percent. Although these measures of language are not identical, they are similar, and the similarity of results for 1910 and 1990 suggests that historical differences in the proportion of children in immigrant families with parents speaking or not speaking English were about the same at the end of the century as at the beginning.

U.S. Citizenship

Of the 8.4 million children in immigrant families in the United States in 1990, 75 percent were U.S. citizens by birth, 4 percent were naturalized citizens, and 21 percent (1.7 million) were not U.S. citizens. Of the U.S. citizen children, 54 percent (3.6 million) had at least one parent in the home who was not a U.S. citizen;

thus, approximately two-thirds of children in immigrant families in 1990 were either themselves not U.S. citizens or lived with a noncitizen parent (Hernandez and Charney, 1998). Welfare eligibility exclusions are most important for children with family incomes below or near the official poverty level. In the 1990 census the official poverty rate for noncitizen children was 34 percent, and the rate for children who were not citizens or had at least one noncitizen parent was 28 percent.

Children in immigrant families from nine of the 12 countries of origin with high levels of poverty were especially likely to be noncitizens, at 29 percent or more. The proportion was 21 to 23 percent for the remaining high-risk countries (the Dominican Republic, Mexico, and Haiti). Three additional countries had 29 percent or more of children who were noncitizens and poverty rates that were greater among native-born non-Hispanic whites (Venezuela, Romania, and Guyana). For children in immigrant families with origins in two of the 12 countries with high poverty rates, 62 or 63 percent were not U.S. citizens or had at least one parent in the home who was not a U.S. citizen; this rose to 73 to 78 percent for five of these countries and 81 to 89 percent for the remaining five countries. The figure was 50 percent or more for 18 of the other 27 countries of origin with child poverty rates at least as high as for native-born non-Hispanic whites (11 percent). Thus, eligibility rules that exclude noncitizens from public benefits and services may have important consequences for children with many different countries of origin.

State of Residence

California accounted for 35 percent of all children in immigrant families in 1990, followed by New York, Texas, Florida, Illinois, and New Jersey, at 12, 11, 7, 5, and 4 percent, respectively, for a total of 74 percent in six states (Figure 2-2). An additional six states had at least 2 percent of children in immigrant families (Arizona, Massachusetts, Michigan, Pennsylvania, Virginia, and Washington). Three less populous states also had comparatively high proportions (higher than the national average of 14 percent) of children in immigrant families (Hawaii, Rhode Island, and Ne-

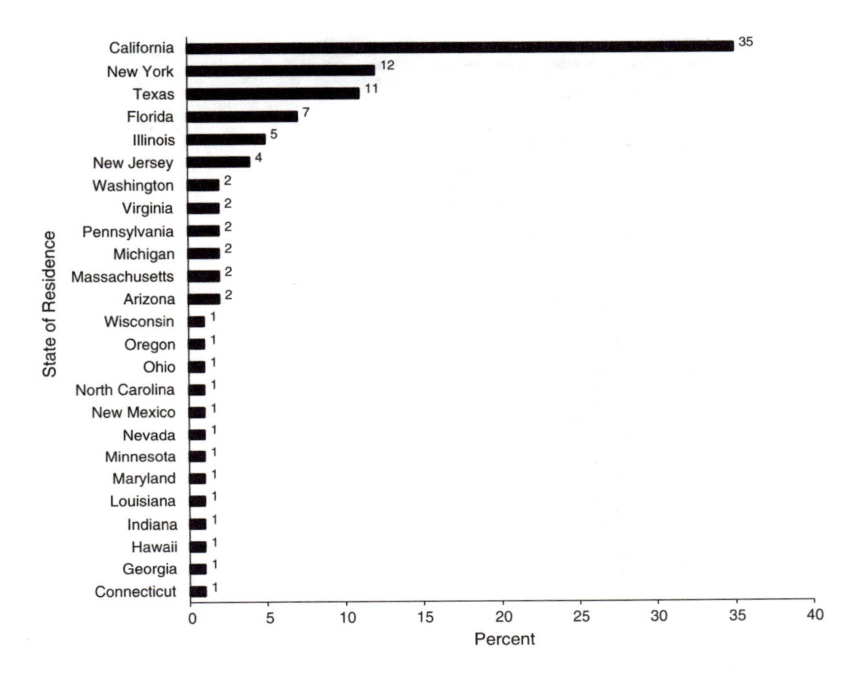

FIGURE 2-2 Percentage of first- and second-generation immigrant children (ages 0 to 17) by state, 1990 (for states with ≥ 1%).

vada; Figure 2-3). These 15 states accounted for 84 percent of all children in immigrant families.

SUMMARY

Children generally have been found to be at risk of negative health or educational outcomes if they have family incomes below the poverty threshold, parents with low educational attainments, only one parent in the home, five or more siblings in the home, or overcrowded housing conditions. Children in immigrant families in 1990 were, overall, less likely than children in native-born families to have only one parent in the home, but they were somewhat more likely to live in poverty or in families with many siblings and much more likely to have parents with very

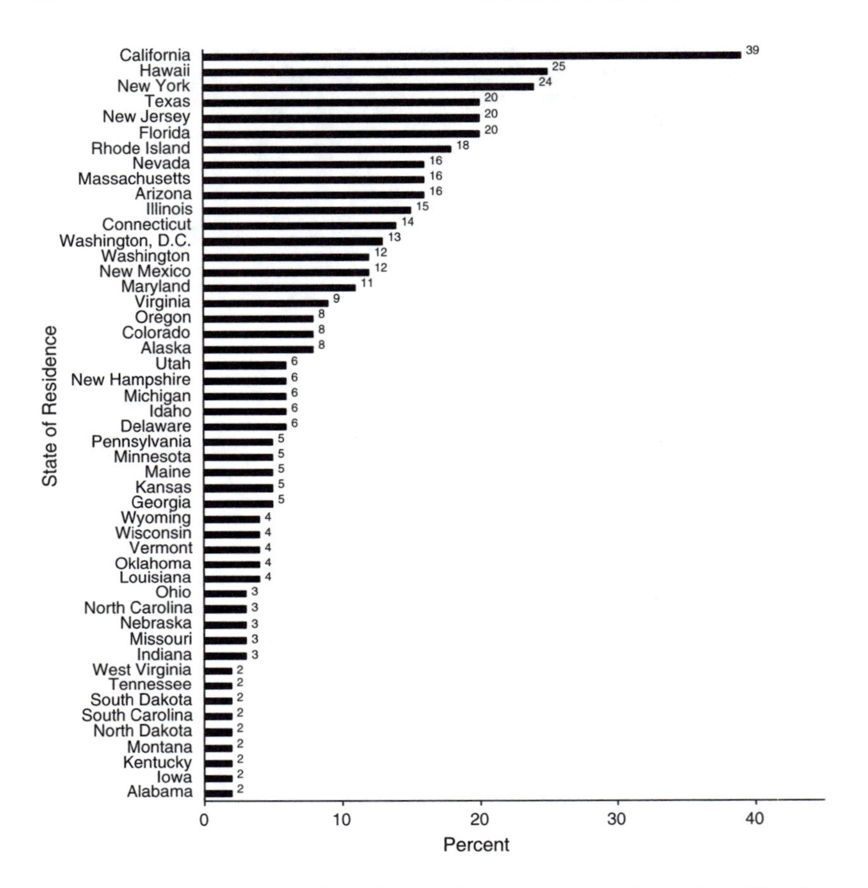

FIGURE 2-3 Percentage of total state child population (ages 0 to 17) who are first- or second-generation immigrants, 1990.

low educational attainments (eight years of schooling or less) and to live in overcrowded housing.

Children from 12 countries of origin, however, experienced extremely high risks of living in poverty. Five are the source of many officially recognized refugees (the former Soviet Union, Cambodia, Laos, Thailand, and Vietnam); three are war-torn countries in Central America (El Salvador, Guatemala, and Nicaragua); three are small impoverished Central American or Caribbean countries that are strong sources of unskilled labor migrants (Honduras, Haiti, and the Dominican Republic) for the United

States; and the twelfth (Mexico) is the largest source of both legal and illegal unskilled labor migrants. Children in immigrant families from 11 of these 12 countries (excepting only the former Soviet Union) experience very high risks of having parents with less than eight years of schooling, of living in overcrowded housing, and of living in either a one-parent family or a family with many siblings.

Risk levels decline for most of these factors between the first and the second generations for most countries of origin. However, data available for selected countries suggest that for third- and later-generation children with origins in Mexico and the Dominican Republic, and perhaps to a lesser extent for children with origins in Central American countries, the risks of living in poverty with parents who have not graduated from high school, in overcrowded housing conditions, and with only one parent remain quite high. Thus, racial and ethnic stratification may limit the opportunities for children from these countries to assimilate into the mainstream middle class (Lieberson and Waters, 1988; Lalonde and Topel, 1991). These risks for third- and later-generation children from Mexico and the Dominican Republic approach or exceed the high levels experienced by black and American Indian native-born children. In fact, third- and later-generation Mexican-origin children have experienced disadvantaged circumstances at or near the level of black and American Indian children throughout the twentieth century.

It should be remembered, however, that children in immigrant families from about two dozen other countries spread across Latin America and the Caribbean, Asia, Europe, the Middle East, and Africa have poverty rates about equal to or substantially less than the rate of 11 percent for non-Hispanic white children in native-born families, and many experience levels of risk along other dimensions that are less than those for children in native-born families, including non-Hispanic white children.

Children in immigrant families may experience additional risk factors growing out of their immigrant circumstances. Lack of English fluency can limit effective communication and functioning in health care facilities, schools, and other settings that provide resources essential to children and their families. Most children in immigrant families from most countries speak a language other than English at home, but the vast majority (73 percent) of children in immigrant families speak English exclusively or very well, and language assimilation occurs rapidly across generations, as reflected in the rise from 55 to 81 percent between the first and second generations.

Not being a U.S. citizen became a potentially important risk factor with the passage of federal welfare reform legislation in 1996 for noncoverage by public health and social benefits programs. One-fourth of children in immigrant families in this country are not U.S. citizens, but two-thirds of children in immigrant families are not U.S. citizens *or* have at least one parent in the home who is not a U.S. citizen. Thus, a large majority of children in immigrant families may be ineligible for important benefits or have parents who are ineligible and who therefore are hesitant to secure benefits on behalf of their children. Moreover, reductions in the benefits available to such families will reduce overall resources within families.

Not only are children in immigrant families from the 12 countries with the highest poverty rates especially likely to experience the socioeconomic risk factors of low parental education, living with one parent or many siblings, and overcrowding, they also often have the highest risk of not speaking English exclusively or very well, of living in a linguistically isolated household, and of not being U.S. citizens or having a parent in the home who is not a U.S. citizen.

The devolution of responsibilities under welfare reform from the federal government to the states also implies that eligibility for and access to publicly funded health and social services may vary greatly across states, making state of residence a potentially important risk factor. Eighty-four percent of children in immigrant families live in 15 states. The largest is California (with 35 percent), followed by New York, Texas, Florida, Illinois, and New Jersey (with 12 to 4 percent each), and Arizona, Massachusetts, Michigan, Pennsylvania, Virginia, and Washington (with 2 percent each). Three additional states have proportions with immigrant children higher than the national average of 14 percent (Hawaii, Rhode Island, and Nevada).

Overall, children in immigrant families experience moderately elevated socioeconomic and demographic risks along a variety of dimensions; these risks tend to decline across generations (with the exception of increases in one-parent families). But there are enormous differences among children with various countries of origin. Children in immigrant families from about two dozen countries have moderate to low levels of risk that are often no greater or even smaller than levels experienced by non-Hispanic white children in native-born families.

In striking contrast, children in immigrant families fleeing the former Soviet Union, the war-torn countries of Southeast Asia and Central America, or impoverished countries in Central America and the Caribbean, and Mexico experience highly elevated risks along virtually all of the dimensions reviewed here: poverty, low parental education, families with only one parent or many siblings in the home, lack of English fluency, and not being a U.S. citizen or having a parent in the home who is not a U.S. citizen.

ACKNOWLEDGMENTS

The authors thank the Population Studies Center at the University of Michigan for providing access to computing facilities and Public Use Microdata Samples and Integrated Public Use Microdata Samples datasets, without which this research would not have been possible. We are especially indebted to Lisa Neidert for providing invaluable technical assistance in conducting analyses for this study.

REFERENCES

Alwin, D.F.

1984 Trends in parental socialization values: Detroit, 1958-1983. *American Journal of Sociology* 90(2):359-382.

Blake, J.

1981 Family size and the quality of children. *Demography* 18:321-342.

1985 Number of siblings and educational mobility. *American Sociological Review* 50:84-94.

1987 Differential parental investment: Its effects on child quality and status attainment. Pp. 351-375 in *Parenting Across the Life Span: Biosocial Dimensions*, J.B. Lancaster et al., eds. New York: Aldine de Gruyter.

1989 *Family Size and Achievement.* Berkeley: University of California Press.

Blau, P.M., and O.D. Duncan

1967 *The American Occupational Structure*. New York: Wiley.

Cherlin, A.J., F.F. Furstenburg, P.L. Chase-Lansdale, K.E. Kiernan, P.K. Robins, D.R. Morrison, and J.O. Teitler

1991 Longitudinal studies of the effects of divorce on children in Great Britain and the United States. *Science* 252:1386-1389.

Citro, C.G., and R.T. Michael, eds.

1995 *Measuring Poverty: A New Approach*. Committee on National Statistics, National Research Council. Washington, D.C.: National Academy Press.

Conger, R.D., and G.H. Elder

1994 *Families in Troubled Times: Adapting to Change in Rural America*. Hawthorne, N.Y.: Aldine de Gruyter.

Conger, R.D., G.H. Elder, Jr., F.O. Lorenz, K.J. Conger, R.L. Simons, L.B. Whitbeck, J. Huck, and J.N. Melby

1990 Linking economic hardship and marital quality and instability. *Journal of Marriage and the Family* 52:643-656.

Duncan, G.J., and J. Brooks-Gunn, eds.

1997 *Consequences of Growing Up Poor*. New York: Russell Sage Foundation.

Elder, G.H., Jr.

1974 *Children of the Great Depression: Social Change in Life Experience*. Chicago: University of Chicago Press.

Expert Committee on Family Budget Revisions

1980 *New American Family Budget Standards*. Madison, Wisc.: Institute for Poverty Research.

Featherman, D.L., and R.M. Hauser

1978 *Opportunity and Change*. New York: Academic Press.

Fuchs, V.F.

1965 Towards a theory of poverty. Pp. 79-91 in *The Concept of Poverty*. Washington, D.C.: U.S. Chamber of Commerce.

Galbraith, J.K.

1958 *The Affluent Society*. Boston: Houghton Mifflin.

Glenn, N.D., and S.K. Hoppe

1982 Only children as adults: Psychological well-being. *Journal of Family Issues* 5:363-382.

Hernandez, D.J.

1986 Childhood in sociodemographic perspective. *Annual Review of Sociology* 12:159-180.

1993 *America's Children: Resources from Family, Government, and the Economy*. New York: Russell Sage Foundation.

1997 Poverty trends. Pp. 18-34 in *Consequences of Growing Up Poor*, G.J. Duncan and J. Brooks-Gunn, eds. New York: Russell Sage Foundation.

1998 The well-being of immigrant children, native-born children with immigrant parents and native-born children with native-born parents. Pp. 421-543 in Office of the Assistant Secretary for Planning and Evaluation, *Trends in the Well-Being of America's Children and Youth*. Washington, D.C.: U.S. Department of Health and Human Services.

Hernandez, D.J., and E. Charney, eds.
1998 *From Generation to Generation: The Health and Well-Being of Children in Immigrant Families*. Committee on the Health and Adjustment of Immigrant Children and Families, National Research Council and Institute of Medicine. Washington, D.C.: National Academy Press.

Hetherington, E.M., M. Cox, and R. Cox
1978 The aftermath of divorce. In *Mother-Child, Father-Child Relations*, J.J. Stevens, Jr., and M. Matthews, eds. Washington, D.C.: National Association for the Education of Young Children.

Hill, M.S., and G.J. Duncan
1987 Parental family income and the socioeconomic attainment of children. *Social Science Research* 16(1):39-73.

Jensen, L., and Y. Chitose
1997 Immigrant generations. Pp. 47-62 in *Immigration and the Family: Research and Policy on U.S. Immigrants*, A. Booth, A.C. Crouter, and N.S. Landale, eds. Mahwah, N.J.: Lawrence Erlbaum Associates.

Jacobs, J.A., and M.E. Greene
1994 Race and ethnicity, social class, and schooling, in *After Ellis Island: Newcomers and Natives in the 1910 Census*, S.C. Watkins, ed. New York: Russell Sage Foundation.

Kohn, M.L.
1969 *Class and Conformity*. Homewood, N.J.: Dorsey Publishing.

Kohn, M.L., and C. Schooler
1983 *Work and Personality*. Norwood, N.J.: Ablex Publishing.

Kominski, R.
1987 *What's It Worth? Educational Background and Economic Status*. Current Population Reports, Series P-70, No. 21. Washington, D.C.: U.S. Government Printing Office.

Lalonde, R.J., and R.H. Topel
1991 Labor market adjustments to increased immigration. Pp. 167-199 in *Immigration, Trade, and the Labor Market*, J. Abowd and R.B. Freeman, eds. Chicago: University of Chicago Press.

Landale, N.S., R.S. Oropesa, and D. Llanes
1997 Schooling, Work and Idleness Among Mexican and Non-Latino White Adolescents. Unpublished manuscript, Population Research Institute, Pennsylvania State University.

Lieberson, S., and W.C. Waters
1988 *From Many Strands: Ethnic and Racial Groups in Contemporary America*. New York: Russell Sage Foundation.

McLanahan, S., and G. Sandefur
1994 *Growing Up with a Single Parent: What Hurts, What Helps*. Cambridge, Mass.: Harvard University Press.

Montgomery, L.E., J.L. Kiely, and G. Pappas
1996 The effects of poverty, race, and family structure on US children's

health: Data from the NHIS, 1978 through 1980 and 1989 through 1991. *American Journal of Public Health* 86:1401-1405.

Newacheck, P.W.

1994 Poverty and childhood chronic illness. *Archives of Pediatric and Adolescent Medicine* 148:1143-1149.

Newacheck, P.W., and W.J. Jameson

1994 Health status and income: The impact of poverty on child health. *Journal of School Health* 65:229-233.

Newacheck, P.W., and B. Starfield

1988 Morbidity and use of ambulatory care services among poor and nonpoor children. *American Journal of Public Health* 78:927-933.

Oropesa, R.S., and Nancy S. Landale

1995 Immigrant Legacies: The Socioeconomic Circumstances of Children by Ethnicity and Generation in the United States. Working Paper 95-01R, Population Research Institute, Pennsylvania State University.

1997a Immigrant legacies: Ethnicity, generation, and children's familial and economic lives. *Social Science Quarterly* 78(2):399-415.

1997b In search of the new second generation: Alternative strategies for identifying second generation children and understanding their acquisition of English. *Sociological Perspectives* 49(3):429-455.

Rainwater, L.

1974 *What Money Buys: Inequality and the Social Meanings of Income.* New York: Basic Books.

Romo, H.

1996 "The Newest Outsiders": Educating Mexican migrant and immigrant youth. Pp. 61-91 in *Children of La Frontera*, J. Flores, ed. Charleston, W.Va.: ERIC Clearinghouse on Rural Education and Small Schools.

Ruggles, P.

1990 *Drawing the Line.* Washington, D.C.: The Urban Institute.

Ruggles, S., and M. Sobek

1995 Integrated public use microdata series: Version 1.0. Minneapolis: Social History Research Laboratory, University of Minnesota.

Rumbaut, R.G.

1996 Origins and destinies: Immigration, race, and ethnicity in contemporary America. Pp. 21-42 in *Origins and Destinies: Immigration, Race, and Ethnicity in America*, S. Pedraza and R.G. Rumbaut, eds. Belmont, Calif.: Wadsworth.

Sewell, W.H., and R.M. Hauser

1975 *Education, Occupation, and Earnings.* New York: Academic Press.

Sewell, W.H., R.M. Hauser, and W.C. Wolf

1980 Sex, schooling, and occupational status. *American Journal of Sociology* 83(3):551-583.

Smeeding, T., and B.B. Torrey

1995 Revisiting Poor Children in Rich Countries. Unpublished manuscript.

Smith, A.

1776 *Wealth of Nations.* London: Everyman's Library. Cited in *Alternative*

Measures of Poverty, staff study prepared by the Joint Economic Committee, U.S. Congress, October 18, 1989.

Starfield, B.

1982 Family income, ill health, and medical care of U.S. children. *Journal of Public Health Policy* 3:244-259.

1991 Childhood morbidity: Comparisons, clusters, and trends. *Pediatrics* 88:529-526.

1992 Effects of poverty on health status. *Bulletin of the New York Academy of Medicine* 68(1):17-24.

U.S. Department of Health and Human Services (DHHS)

1981 *Better Health for Our Children: A National Strategy.* Report of the Select Panel for the Promotion of Child Health to the United States Congress and the Secretary of Health and Human Services, Executive Summary. Washington, D.C.: DHHS.

U.S. Immigration Commission

1911 *Report of the Immigration Commission, Vol. 4. Emigration Conditions in Europe.* Washington, D.C.: U.S. Government Printing Office.

Wallerstein, J.S., and J.B. Kelly

1980 *Surviving the Breakup: How Children and Parents Cope with Divorce.* New York: Basic Books.

1989 *Second Chances: Men, Women, and Children a Decade After Divorce.* New York: Ticknor & Fields.

Wallerstein, J.S., S.B. Corbin, and J.M. Lewis

1988 Children of divorce: A 10-year study. Pp. 197-214 in *Impact of Divorce, Single Parenting, and Stepparenting on Children,* E.M. Hetherington and J.D. Arasteh, eds. Hillsdale, N.J.: Lawrence Erlbaum Associates.

Watkins, S.C.

1994 *After Ellis Island: Newcomers and Natives in the 1910 Census.* New York: Russell Sage Foundation.

Wilkinson, R.G.

1996 *Unhealthy Societies: The Afflictions of Inequality.* London: Routledge.

APPENDIX 2A

Data Sources. Estimates in this paper were derived from the Integrated Public Use Microdata Samples files for the 1910 and 1960 censuses (Ruggles and Sobek, 1995) and the 1990 census Public Use Microdata Samples 5 percent sample.

Generation. Children ages 0 to 17 were identified as first generation if foreign born, as second generation if native born with at least one foreign-born parent, and as third generation if native born with native-born parents. In 1990 parents' birthplaces could be ascertained only for parents living in the child's home, with the result that some second-generation children were misclassified as third-generation offspring because their parents' status as foreign born was not reported in the decennial census.

Country of Origin. First-generation children were classified by their own country of birth. Second-generation children were classified by their parents' country of birth or, if the parents were foreign born in different countries, by the mother's country of birth. In 1910 the mother tongue of a child or parent(s) was also used to identify certain countries of birth, in accordance with procedures used by Jacobs and Greene (1994). In 1990 the countries of origin for third- and later-generation children were approximated by using the race or Hispanic origin of each child as a proxy for the country of birth, leading to misclassification of family country of origin for some children.

Parental Characteristics. Other than country of birth in 1910 and 1960, parental characteristics (e.g., labor force participation, educational attainments) were available only if the parent was present in the household. Hence, all estimates of father's or mother's characteristics are based on only those children who have the indicated parent in the household.

Poverty. In 1960 poverty was calculated by using the federal government's U.S. poverty definition as of 1980. Poverty years are designated according to the year of data collection, rather than the year during which income was obtained. Thus, in this paper 1990 poverty is reported by the Census Bureau as 1989 poverty from the 1990 decennial census.

Parental Labor Force Participation. Full-time year-round work is defined as 48 or more weeks worked last year and 35 or more hours worked last week.

Siblings. The number of siblings in a child's home is estimated as the number of children ever born to the child's mother. Thus, estimates are available only for children living with their mothers.

Major Limitations to Inferences. Beyond the limitations to inferences cited above in the context of specific variables, it is essential to note that differences between generations may be due to intergenerational assimilation; alternatively, they may be due to changes in the characteristics of immigrants through time. For example, the 1990 poverty rate declined from 27 to 17 percent between the second and the third and later generations of Guatemalan-origin children. If parental educational attainments of Guatemalan immigrants had been constant for 30 years, this decline could be attributed to intergenerational increases in parental educational attainments. But parental educational attainments for first- and second-generation Guatemalan-origin children were much higher in 1960 than in 1990, suggesting that the decline in parental educational attainments between 1960 and 1990 may account for poverty differences between the second and later generations.

TABLE 2A-1a Social and Economic Risk Factors for First- and Second-Generation Children by Country of Origin, for First and Second Generations Combined, and for Third- and Later-Generation Children by Race and Ethnicity: 1990

	Number of children (thousands)	Children in official poverty (percent)	Children in relative poverty (percent)	Children in middle-class comfort (percent)
All First and Second Generations	8,373	22	33	31
All Third and Later Generations	52,685	17	24	39
Third and Later Generations by Race and Ethnicity:				
White, Non-Hispanic	40,201	11	17	42
Black, Non-Hispanic	8,031	40	51	25
Asian, Non-Hispanic	329	10	14	38
American Indian	562	38	51	24
Hispanic	3,489	31	42	31
First and Second Generations by Country of Origin:				
Laos	113	51	65	16
Cambodia	64	46	62	19
Dominican Republic	179	42	55	24
USSR	62	36	42	23
Mexico	2,618	35	52	22
Thailand	69	33	42	29
Vietnam	226	31	42	29
Guatemala	101	30	46	24
Honduras	52	29	46	26
El Salvador	203	27	44	26
Nicaragua	74	27	43	28
Haiti	105	26	39	30
Jordan	19	25	35	31
Belize	16	23	31	35
Iraq	20	21	30	39
Ecuador	64	20	31	36

Children very well-off financially (percent)	Children in one-parent families (percent)	Children whose fathers have less than a high school education (percent)	Children whose mothers have less than a high school education (percent)	Children with 5 or more siblings (percent)	Children who live in linguistically isolated households (percent)
19	17	39	42	8	26
22	26	15	16	4	1
26	18	12	12	4	0
9	62	26	29	10	0
37	25	7	9	6	1
7	40	28	29	10	4
11	42	30	35	8	9
2	15	54	73	35	60
4	26	57	76	18	60
5	48	49	55	5	41
26	10	20	18	5	46
4	19	74	74	14	38
16	13	34	56	17	42
13	19	39	54	11	45
7	28	56	61	5	43
8	31	42	44	5	34
5	31	61	65	6	46
8	27	34	40	8	43
10	36	38	43	8	34
14	7	25	31	13	10
12	29	29	29	6	4
17	5	32	42	10	16
14	24	34	35	3	29

continued on next page

TABLE 2A-1a (Continued)

	Number of children (thousands)	Children in official poverty (percent)	Children in relative poverty (percent)	Children in middle-class comfort (percent)
Venezuela	22	20	25	37
Israel	60	19	25	31
Trinidad and Tobago	52	18	28	37
Colombia	117	17	27	37
Pakistan	39	16	23	36
Costa Rica	23	16	26	38
Panama	40	16	25	37
Brazil	31	16	24	39
Romania	26	15	22	32
Spain	27	15	21	39
Lebanon	36	15	23	34
Jamaica	132	15	25	37
Guyana	46	15	22	41
Nigeria	34	15	27	35
China	131	14	24	30
Indonesia	17	14	19	37
Iran	76	14	19	32
Cuba	211	14	22	38
Peru	61	13	25	37
Korea	231	12	19	38
Syria	15	12	21	33
Taiwan	97	11	15	33
Argentina	35	11	19	38
Yugoslavia	44	10	16	42
Hong Kong	56	10	16	33
Chile	21	10	18	37
Australia	18	10	16	32
Austria	21	9	14	41
France	41	9	13	34
Hungary	25	9	14	35
Egypt	29	9	15	36
Germany	258	8	14	40

Children very well-off financially (percent)	Children in one-parent families (percent)	Children whose fathers have less than a high school education (percent)	Children whose mothers have less than a high school education (percent)	Children with 5 or more siblings (percent)	Children who live in linguistically isolated households (percent)
25	12	14	15	2	19
32	5	16	19	16	12
20	37	23	19	5	1
16	23	29	30	2	31
27	6	8	18	6	13
17	19	28	31	3	17
23	23	12	16	3	7
25	14	20	20	3	22
30	8	25	25	18	21
27	14	23	26	3	12
24	6	28	29	8	11
21	36	27	22	4	0
18	31	25	28	4	1
15	16	2	5	7	4
30	9	31	35	2	41
31	8	8	11	3	21
37	9	6	11	1	18
27	21	28	27	2	16
19	18	18	19	3	25
26	9	6	18	0	34
29	4	22	25	4	17
42	10	5	8	1	36
29	11	21	20	2	15
27	10	30	32	3	11
37	8	24	29	1	35
28	15	14	17	3	18
44	9	8	11	7	1
38	8	8	8	10	2
41	11	9	9	5	6
39	9	14	13	9	10
39	6	4	8	5	10
32	11	8	11	3	2

continued on next page

TABLE 2A-1a (Continued)

	Number of children (thousands)	Children in official poverty (percent)	Children in relative poverty (percent)	Children in middle-class comfort (percent)
Greece	68	8	16	42
Japan	100	8	12	37
Barbados	15	8	16	47
Poland	80	7	12	45
Turkey	15	7	13	32
Italy	179	6	11	45
Portugal	77	6	11	51
United Kingdom	209	6	10	38
Canada	263	6	11	39
South Africa	15	6	10	25
Netherlands	38	5	11	39
India	175	5	9	35
Philippines	399	5	10	45
Ireland	44	4	7	41

NOTE: Countries are listed from highest to lowest official poverty rate for first and second generations combined.

Children very well-off financially (percent)	Children in one-parent families (percent)	Children whose fathers have less than a high school education (percent)	Children whose mothers have less than a high school education (percent)	Children with 5 or more siblings (percent)	Children who live in linguistically isolated households (percent)
25	6	39	32	1	12
41	7	4	7	1	28
21	39	25	21	8	0
32	10	19	15	1	22
38	8	18	18	2	11
30	6	34	29	2	7
22	8	61	58	1	23
41	10	6	9	3	0
39	9	10	10	5	1
57	5	2	7	1	1
38	7	7	6	6	1
47	4	7	12	1	11
32	12	8	13	3	9
39	8	15	14	4	0

TABLE 2A-1b Household and Housing Risk Factors for First- and Second-Generation Children by Country of Origin, for First and Second Generations Combined, and for Third- and Later-Generation Children by Race and Ethnicity: 1990

	Number of children (thousands)	Children in households with no car or truck (percent)
All First and Second Generations	8,373	11
All Third and Later Generations	52,685	8
Third and Later Generations by Race and Ethnicity:		
White, Non-Hispanic	40,201	3
Black, Non-Hispanic	8,031	30
Asian, Non-Hispanic	329	4
American Indian	562	14
Hispanic	3,489	17
First and Second Generations by Country of Origin:		
Laos	113	17
Cambodia	64	29
Dominican Republic	179	54
USSR	62	23
Mexico	2,618	10
Thailand	69	15
Vietnam	226	13
Guatemala	101	18
Honduras	52	22
El Salvador	203	15
Nicaragua	74	13
Haiti	105	24
Jordan	19	8
Belize	16	19
Iraq	20	4
Ecuador	64	24
Venezuela	22	6
Israel	60	13
Trinidad and Tobago	52	29
Colombia	117	13
Pakistan	39	7
Costa Rica	23	14

Children with no telephone in their homes (percent)	Children living in houses built before 1950 (percent)	Children in crowded homes (percent)
7	24	44
8	24	12
5	23	7
18	27	26
3	18	21
32	17	34
15	25	30
4	28	78
4	31	74
19	50	52
2	32	40
15	23	69
3	24	49
1	19	58
9	33	67
9	26	56
8	29	75
10	24	71
10	33	53
2	23	31
7	35	44
1	17	34
8	41	43
4	18	30
1	28	27
7	39	30
6	27	42
2	17	35
4	28	33

continued on next page

TABLE 2A-1b (Continued)

	Number of children (thousands)	Children in households with no car or truck (percent)
Panama	40	16
Brazil	31	7
Romania	26	8
Spain	27	8
Lebanon	36	4
Jamaica	132	22
Guyana	46	30
Nigeria	34	10
China	131	18
Indonesia	17	4
Iran	76	4
Cuba	211	6
Peru	61	11
Korea	231	3
Syria	15	2
Taiwan	97	3
Argentina	35	6
Yugoslavia	44	6
Hong Kong	56	9
Chile	21	6
Australia	18	5
Austria	21	5
France	41	5
Hungary	25	8
Egypt	29	4
Germany	258	3
Greece	68	4
Japan	100	3
Barbados	15	29
Poland	80	5
Turkey	15	4
Italy	179	4
Portugal	77	4
United Kingdom	209	3
Canada	263	2

Children with no telephone in their homes (percent)	Children living in houses built before 1950 (percent)	Children in crowded homes (percent)
6	25	25
2	24	24
2	32	31
3	28	20
2	26	20
5	30	29
4	40	36
3	18	50
1	33	39
1	16	29
1	12	21
3	17	28
4	26	36
1	13	33
0	20	23
0	11	24
2	20	24
1	31	16
1	26	34
2	21	28
0	23	9
0	27	11
1	29	11
2	26	14
1	24	20
3	22	8
1	26	9
1	15	12
4	41	22
1	32	10
1	22	16
1	31	7
2	43	14
2	22	7
2	20	8

continued on next page

TABLE 2A-1b (Continued)

	Number of children (thousands)	Children in households with no car or truck (percent)
South Africa	15	4
Netherlands	38	2
India	175	5
Philippines	399	3
Ireland	44	4

NOTE: Countries are listed from highest to lowest official poverty rate for first and second generations combined.

Children with no telephone in their homes (percent)	Children living in houses built before 1950 (percent)	Children in crowded homes (percent)
1	20	7
1	23	8
1	13	24
1	15	38
1	38	8

TABLE 2A-1c Parents' Labor Force Participation for First- and Second-Generation Children by Country of Origin, for First and Second Generations Combined, and for Third- and Later-Generation Children by Race and Ethnicity: 1990

	Number of children (thousands)	Children with fathers not in the labor force (percent)	Children with fathers not working full-time, year-round (percent)	Children with mothers not in the labor force (percent)
All First and Second Generations	8,373	7	31	42
All Third and Later Generations	52,685	5	21	34
Third and Later Generations by Race and Ethnicity:				
White, Non-Hispanic	40,201	4	19	34
Black, Non-Hispanic	8,031	11	34	33
Asian, Non-Hispanic	329	4	18	29
American Indian	562	14	46	40
Hispanic	3,489	8	30	43
First and Second Generations by Country of Origin:				
Laos	113	48	68	66
Cambodia	64	41	60	65
Dominican Republic	179	11	38	52
USSR	62	21	54	46
Mexico	2,618	7	38	50
Thailand	69	30	46	53
Vietnam	226	19	42	46
Guatemala	101	5	31	41
Honduras	52	8	37	41
El Salvador	203	5	32	34
Nicaragua	74	5	32	31
Haiti	105	8	36	22
Jordan	19	11	30	68
Belize	16	9	33	31
Iraq	20	10	30	61
Ecuador	64	4	30	39
Venezuela	22	8	28	47
Israel	60	7	26	54
Trinidad and Tobago	52	8	34	25

TABLE 2A-1c (Continued)

	Number of children (thousands)	Children with fathers not in the labor force (percent)	Children with fathers not working full-time, year-round (percent)	Children with mothers not in the labor force (percent)
Colombia	117	4	28	38
Pakistan	39	4	26	60
Costa Rica	23	8	31	38
Panama	40	6	27	29
Brazil	31	6	28	47
Romania	26	9	26	46
Spain	27	5	26	40
Lebanon	36	9	27	61
Jamaica	132	6	29	17
Guyana	46	6	28	26
Nigeria	34	6	38	26
China	131	5	27	31
Indonesia	17	10	29	41
Iran	76	8	28	46
Cuba	211	4	22	34
Peru	61	4	27	35
Korea	231	6	26	39
Syria	15	8	32	58
Taiwan	97	6	23	40
Argentina	35	3	21	44
Yugoslavia	44	6	26	42
Hong Kong	56	6	21	31
Chile	21	3	19	38
Australia	18	4	16	49
Austria	21	4	19	35
France	41	3	20	43
Hungary	25	5	20	41
Egypt	29	4	23	42
Germany	258	3	18	37
Greece	68	6	26	46
Japan	100	4	20	58
Barbados	15	5	23	20
Poland	80	4	21	34
Turkey	15	4	20	48

continued on next page

TABLE 2A-1c (Continued)

	Number of children (thousands)	Children with fathers not in the labor force (percent)	Children with fathers not working full-time, year-round (percent)	Children with mothers not in the labor force (percent)
Italy	179	5	21	47
Portugal	77	5	27	29
United Kingdom	209	3	17	38
Canada	263	3	18	38
South Africa	15	4	17	48
Netherlands	38	2	14	39
India	175	2	19	35
Philippines	399	5	22	18
Ireland	44	4	18	42

NOTE: Countries are listed from highest to lowest official poverty rate for first and second generations combined.

TABLE 2A-1d Parents' Education for First- and Second-Generation Children by Country of Origin, for First and Second Generations Combined, and for Third- and Later-Generation Children by Race and Ethnicity: 1990

	Number of children (thousands)	Children with fathers who have 8 or fewer years of education (percent)	Children with mothers who have 8 or fewer years of education (percent)	Children whose fathers have four or more years of college education (percent)	Children whose mothers have four or more years of college education (percent)
All First and Second Generations	8,373	25	26	24	16
All Third and Later Generations	52,685	3	3	26	18
Third and Later Generations by Race and Ethnicity:					
White, Non-Hispanic	40,201	3	2	28	20
Black, Non-Hispanic	8,031	6	4	12	9
Asian, Non-Hispanic	329	1	1	40	31
American Indian	562	8	6	9	7
Hispanic	3,489	9	10	12	7
First and Second Generations by Country of Origin:					
Laos	113	41	60	7	3
Cambodia	64	42	60	6	2
Dominican Republic	179	27	30	9	5
USSR	62	8	6	41	36
Mexico	2,618	55	52	4	2
Thailand	69	25	45	24	13
Vietnam	226	21	32	18	8
Guatemala	101	35	38	9	5
Honduras	52	23	24	13	7
El Salvador	203	37	40	6	4
Nicaragua	74	17	17	21	11
Haiti	105	14	17	14	10
Jordan	19	11	12	29	11
Belize	16	10	7	14	7
Iraq	20	13	21	25	16

continued on next page

TABLE 2A-1d (Continued)

	Number of children (thousands)	Children with fathers who have 8 or fewer years of education (percent)	Children with mothers who have 8 or fewer years of education (percent)	Children whose fathers have four or more years of college education (percent)	Children whose mothers have four or more years of college education (percent)
Ecuador	64	14	13	18	9
Venezuela	22	6	5	45	28
Israel	60	5	6	41	32
Trinidad and Tobago	52	7	5	18	12
Colombia	117	11	12	22	13
Pakistan	39	3	8	65	41
Costa Rica	23	11	12	20	13
Panama	40	2	3	26	17
Brazil	31	9	10	40	29
Romania	26	9	10	38	31
Spain	27	12	12	29	19
Lebanon	36	14	12	35	21
Jamaica	132	8	5	19	15
Guyana	46	6	8	23	12
Nigeria	34	0	2	80	45
China	131	18	20	39	28
Indonesia	17	2	4	54	34
Iran	76	2	3	68	39
Cuba	211	12	9	25	16
Peru	61	5	6	29	17
Korea	231	2	7	43	28
Syria	15	10	11	41	19
Taiwan	97	3	4	73	52
Argentina	35	9	7	34	25
Yugoslavia	44	18	19	18	14
Hong Kong	56	13	14	43	30
Chile	21	5	5	33	22
Australia	18	3	1	50	33
Austria	21	2	1	45	37
France	41	4	2	49	36
Hungary	25	6	3	39	29
Egypt	29	1	2	67	44
Germany	258	2	2	35	22

TABLE 2A-1d (Continued)

	Number of children (thousands)	Children with fathers who have 8 or fewer years of education (percent)	Children with mothers who have 8 or fewer years of education (percent)	Children whose fathers have four or more years of college education (percent)	Children whose mothers have four or more years of college education (percent)
Greece	68	23	19	21	17
Japan	100	2	2	55	32
Barbados	15	8	4	18	14
Poland	80	7	5	30	23
Turkey	15	10	9	41	32
Italy	179	19	16	19	14
Portugal	77	43	39	7	5
United Kingdom	209	1	1	43	26
Canada	263	3	2	40	26
South Africa	15	0	1	68	40
Netherlands	38	2	1	41	26
India	175	2	4	76	59
Philippines	399	3	6	39	46
Ireland	44	5	3	31	19

NOTE: Countries are listed from highest to lowest official poverty rate for first and second generations combined.

TABLE 2A-1e Children's Language Use and Citizenship for First- and Second-Generation Children by Country of Origin, for First and Second Generations Combined, and for Third- and Later-Generation Children by Race and Ethnicity: 1990

	Number of children (thousands)	Children who do not speak English at home (percent)
All First and Second Generations	8,373	67
All Third and Later Generations	52,685	6
Third and Later Generations by Race and Ethnicity:		
White, Non-Hispanic	40,201	3
Black, Non-Hispanic	8,031	3
Asian, Non-Hispanic	329	8
American Indian	562	18
Hispanic	3,489	43
First and Second Generations by Country of Origin:		
Laos	113	96
Cambodia	64	93
Dominican Republic	179	93
USSR	62	84
Mexico	2,618	91
Thailand	69	66
Vietnam	226	87
Guatemala	101	90
Honduras	52	79
El Salvador	203	94
Nicaragua	74	89
Haiti	105	75
Jordan	19	62
Belize	16	18
Iraq	20	69
Ecuador	64	85
Venezuela	22	70
Israel	60	65
Trinidad and Tobago	52	6
Colombia	117	84
Pakistan	39	72

Children who do not speak English exclusively or very well (percent)	Children not U.S. citizens (percent)	Children who are not U.S. citizens, or who have at least 1 parent in the home who is not a citizen (percent)
27	21	65
2	N/A	N/A
1	N/A	N/A
1	N/A	N/A
3	N/A	N/A
7	N/A	N/A
15	N/A	N/A
61	39	89
59	42	85
39	23	73
45	51	62
40	21	78
39	48	75
44	34	63
40	31	81
31	29	73
44	34	83
46	51	83
29	22	75
11	9	38
5	16	72
11	12	44
24	17	76
23	31	76
19	18	42
1	18	71
23	21	70
19	20	55

continued on next page

TABLE 2A-1e (Continued)

	Number of children (thousands)	Children who do not speak English at home (percent)
Costa Rica	23	68
Panama	40	42
Brazil	31	67
Romania	26	73
Spain	27	64
Lebanon	36	71
Jamaica	132	6
Guyana	46	7
Nigeria	34	23
China	131	81
Indonesia	17	41
Iran	76	68
Cuba	211	81
Peru	61	81
Korea	231	65
Syria	15	61
Taiwan	97	80
Argentina	35	69
Yugoslavia	44	61
Hong Kong	56	79
Chile	21	74
Australia	18	13
Austria	21	26
France	41	46
Hungary	25	43
Egypt	29	56
Germany	258	18
Greece	68	70
Japan	100	54
Barbados	15	3
Poland	80	66
Turkey	15	55
Italy	179	37
Portugal	77	75
United Kingdom	209	7

Children who do not speak English exclusively or very well (percent)	Children not U.S. citizens (percent)	Children who are not U.S. citizens, or who have at least 1 parent in the home who is not a citizen (percent)
18	16	68
13	12	48
25	28	76
23	33	47
15	17	65
16	15	40
2	24	66
2	31	62
7	12	82
36	22	46
18	23	50
20	28	67
18	11	47
26	26	67
23	23	55
15	12	43
28	27	52
17	24	60
10	9	44
35	24	39
17	19	64
3	18	76
9	4	29
10	15	56
13	9	27
13	10	34
4	5	36
11	3	36
29	31	73
1	17	58
15	18	54
8	15	51
8	3	39
16	14	63
2	13	64

continued on next page

TABLE2A-1e (Continued)

	Number of children (thousands)	Children who do not speak English at home (percent)
Canada	263	11
South Africa	15	12
Netherlands	38	13
India	175	63
Philippines	399	35
Ireland	44	5

NOTE: Countries are listed from highest to lowest official poverty rate for first and second generations combined.

Children who do not speak English exclusively or very well (percent)	Children not U.S. citizens (percent)	Children who are not U.S. citizens, or who have at least 1 parent in the home who is not a citizen (percent)
3	11	62
3	30	58
3	5	43
14	22	68
11	15	44
1	8	48

TABLE 2A-2a Social and Economic Risk Factors for First- and Second-Generation Children by Country of Origin for First and Second Generations Separately: 1990

	Number of children (thousands)	Children in official poverty (percent)	Children in relative poverty (percent)	Children in middle-class comfort (percent)
All First-Generation Children	2,084	33	47	24
All Second-Generation Children	6,288	19	29	33
Third and Later Generations by Race and Ethnicity:				
White, Non-Hispanic	40,201	11	17	42
Black, Non-Hispanic	8,031	40	51	25
Asian, Non-Hispanic	329	10	14	38
American Indian	562	38	51	24
Hispanic	3,489	31	42	31
First- and Second-Generation Children by Country of Origin:				
Laos - 1st Generation	49	51	64	16
Laos - 2nd Generation	64	50	65	15
Cambodia - 1st Generation	30	52	68	14
Cambodia - 2nd Generation	34	41	57	23
Dominican Republic - 1st Generation	48	41	57	21
Dominican Republic - 2nd Generation	131	42	54	25
USSR - 1st Generation	38	51	60	17
USSR - 2nd Generation	24	11	14	32
Mexico - 1st Generation	643	44	63	14
Mexico - 2nd Generation	1,975	32	49	24
Thailand - 1st Generation	36	59	73	12
Thailand - 2nd Generation	33	5	10	46
Vietnam - 1st Generation	99	42	54	23
Vietnam - 2nd Generation	33	23	32	35
Guatemala - 1st Generation	35	36	54	19
Guatemala - 2nd Generation	66	27	42	27

Children very well-off financially (percent)	Children in one-parent families (percent)	Children whose fathers have less than a high school education (percent)	Children whose mothers have less than a high school education (percent)	Children with 5 or more siblings (percent)	Children who live in linguistically isolated households (percent)
11	23	49	54	17	41
21	15	36	38	9	21
26	18	12	12	4	0
9	62	26	29	10	0
37	25	7	9	6	1
7	40	28	29	10	4
11	42	30	35	8	9
1	17	60	75	29	55
2	13	50	72	39	63
3	27	65	80	19	58
6	25	50	73	17	63
2	51	63	65	6	49
7	47	44	52	4	38
14	11	26	23	7	64
45	10	11	10	2	19
2	23	83	85	19	52
5	18	71	71	12	33
3	16	63	76	33	67
29	9	6	36	1	15
7	23	51	64	15	46
19	15	30	47	9	44
3	32	66	73	6	53
9	26	52	55	5	38

continued on next page

TABLE 2A-2a (Continued)

	Number of children (thousands)	Children in official poverty (percent)	Children in relative poverty (percent)	Children in middle-class comfort (percent)
Honduras - 1st Generation	17	37	59	19
Honduras - 2nd Generation	35	25	40	29
El Salvador - 1st Generation	77	32	50	21
El Salvador - 2nd Generation	126	25	41	29
Nicaragua - 1st Generation	39	36	55	20
Nicaragua - 2nd Generation	35	18	29	37
Haiti - 1st Generation	28	30	49	25
Haiti - 2nd Generation	77	24	36	32
Jordan - 1st Generation	2	47	54	26
Jordan - 2nd Generation	17	22	33	31
Belize - 1st Generation	3	23	39	30
Belize - 2nd Generation	12	23	28	36
Iraq - 1st Generation	4	34	46	34
Iraq - 2nd Generation	17	19	27	40
Ecuador - 1st Generation	12	26	40	30
Ecuador - 2nd Generation	52	19	28	38
Venezuela - 1st Generation	8	33	39	27
Venezuela - 2nd Generation	15	13	18	41
Israel - 1st Generation	13	23	30	35
Israel - 2nd Generation	46	18	24	30
Trinidad and Tobago - 1st Generation	12	30	43	27
Trinidad and Tobago - 2nd Generation	41	14	23	39
Colombia - 1st Generation	29	19	34	33
Colombia - 2nd Generation	88	16	24	39
Pakistan - 1st Generation	11	24	34	32
Pakistan - 2nd Generation	28	13	18	38
Costa Rica - 1st Generation	4	29	40	36
Costa Rica - 2nd Generation	19	14	23	38
Panama - 1st Generation	6	27	39	39
Panama - 2nd Generation	33	15	23	36
Brazil - 1st Generation	9	21	35	33
Brazil - 2nd Generation	21	13	20	42

Children very well-off financially (percent)	Children in one-parent families (percent)	Children whose fathers have less than a high school education (percent)	Children whose mothers have less than a high school education (percent)	Children with 5 or more siblings (percent)	Children who live in linguistically isolated households (percent)
2	41	49	56	8	49
10	27	39	39	3	26
3	36	69	75	8	48
7	29	57	60	5	45
3	30	40	46	11	54
14	24	28	34	5	30
5	39	49	57	10	39
12	35	35	38	8	32
8	16	36	40	11	23
15	6	24	30	13	8
11	34	40	42	6	10
13	27	26	26	6	3
10	6	46	59	14	14
18	5	29	38	9	16
7	32	43	49	4	42
16	22	32	32	3	26
15	19	21	23	2	36
30	9	10	12	2	10
23	7	15	17	12	22
35	5	17	20	18	9
10	46	37	33	4	2
23	35	20	16	5	0
9	32	34	42	3	44
18	21	27	27	1	27
13	10	10	20	6	21
32	4	7	17	6	10
6	26	41	36	5	34
20	17	26	30	2	14
9	34	15	22	3	19
26	21	11	14	2	5
16	19	24	23	2	45
29	12	18	19	4	11

continued on next page

TABLE 2A-2a (Continued)

	Number of children (thousands)	Children in official poverty (percent)	Children in relative poverty (percent)	Children in middle-class comfort (percent)
Romania - 1st Generation	11	18	27	33
Romania - 2nd Generation	15	13	18	31
Spain - 1st Generation	6	37	47	28
Spain - 2nd Generation	22	9	15	42
Lebanon - 1st Generation	8	25	39	22
Lebanon - 2nd Generation	28	12	18	37
Jamaica - 1st Generation	40	18	30	36
Jamaica - 2nd Generation	92	14	23	37
Guyana - 1st Generation	18	18	28	38
Guyana - 2nd Generation	28	13	19	43
Nigeria - 1st Generation	5	28	37	29
Nigeria - 2nd Generation	29	13	25	36
China - 1st Generation	34	25	42	28
China - 2nd Generation	97	10	18	30
Indonesia - 1st Generation	4	45	50	22
Indonesia - 2nd Generation	13	4	9	43
Iran - 1st Generation	24	27	34	29
Iran - 2nd Generation	52	8	12	33
Cuba - 1st Generation	27	27	40	30
Cuba - 2nd Generation	184	13	19	39
Peru - 1st Generation	18	22	39	27
Peru - 2nd Generation	43	10	19	41
Korea - 1st Generation	67	20	29	33
Korea - 2nd Generation	163	9	15	40
Syria - 1st Generation	2	28	41	41
Syria - 2nd Generation	13	9	18	31
Taiwan - 1st Generation	32	19	26	35
Taiwan - 2nd Generation	65	7	10	31
Argentina - 1st Generation	10	18	32	30
Argentina - 2nd Generation	26	9	14	41
Yugoslavia - 1st Generation	5	12	19	44
Yugoslavia - 2nd Generation	39	10	15	42

Children very well-off financially (percent)	Children in one-parent families (percent)	Children whose fathers have less than a high school education (percent)	Children whose mothers have less than a high school education (percent)	Children with 5 or more siblings (percent)	Children who live in linguistically isolated households (percent)
21	9	32	32	19	34
36	7	21	21	17	13
12	19	43	43	3	29
31	12	20	23	3	8
18	11	47	47	8	21
26	5	23	24	8	9
13	44	37	31	5	0
25	33	24	18	4	0
10	36	38	40	5	2
23	28	17	21	4	1
7	22	4	8	16	7
16	15	2	5	6	4
9	10	45	53	3	59
37	9	26	28	1	35
12	15	20	29	3	48
38	6	5	6	3	11
24	14	13	19	1	34
43	6	3	7	1	10
9	25	60	60	2	39
29	21	24	22	2	13
12	21	19	23	3	42
22	16	18	18	2	19
19	11	12	18	0	48
29	9	4	18	0	28
4	5	32	39	4	40
34	4	20	22	4	12
24	17	9	13	1	47
51	6	3	6	1	31
18	13	32	32	1	32
33	10	17	15	3	9
19	11	31	35	3	27
28	10	30	31	3	9

continued on next page

TABLE 2A-2a (Continued)

	Number of children (thousands)	Children in official poverty (percent)	Children in relative poverty (percent)	Children in middle-class comfort (percent)
Hong Kong - 1st Generation	17	26	35	31
Hong Kong - 2nd Generation	39	3	8	35
Chile - 1st Generation	5	19	28	33
Chile - 2nd Generation	17	8	15	38
Australia - 1st Generation	3	13	17	27
Australia - 2nd Generation	14	10	16	33
Austria - 1st Generation	1	33	42	30
Austria - 2nd Generation	20	7	12	42
France - 1st Generation	7	11	14	30
France - 2nd Generation	34	8	13	35
Hungary - 1st Generation	3	17	20	33
Hungary - 2nd Generation	22	8	13	35
Egypt - 1st Generation	5	20	29	42
Egypt - 2nd Generation	25	7	12	35
Germany - 1st Generation	16	25	32	31
Germany - 2nd Generation	243	7	12	41
Greece - 1st Generation	3	16	24	44
Greece - 2nd Generation	65	8	15	42
Japan - 1st Generation	32	11	13	26
Japan - 2nd Generation	68	6	11	41
Barbados - 1st Generation	3	6	25	36
Barbados - 2nd Generation	11	8	14	51
Poland - 1st Generation	18	14	22	42
Poland - 2nd Generation	62	5	9	45
Turkey - 1st Generation	3	11	23	20
Turkey - 2nd Generation	12	6	11	35
Italy - 1st Generation	8	14	20	36
Italy - 2nd Generation	171	6	11	45
Portugal - 1st Generation	14	11	17	50
Portugal - 2nd Generation	64	5	10	51
United Kingdom - 1st Generation	31	10	13	31
United Kingdom - 2nd Generation	178	5	9	39

Children very well-off financially (percent)	Children in one-parent families (percent)	Children whose fathers have less than a high school education (percent)	Children whose mothers have less than a high school education (percent)	Children with 5 or more siblings (percent)	Children who live in linguistically isolated households (percent)
14	15	49	57	3	54
47	5	14	17	1	26
17	18	21	28	0	37
31	14	13	14	4	12
45	11	9	14	2	3
43	9	8	10	9	1
13	18	23	26	16	24
40	7	7	7	10	0
48	11	10	14	1	24
39	11	9	9	5	3
26	8	18	21	13	37
41	9	14	12	8	6
19	12	5	10	4	27
43	5	4	8	5	7
25	22	10	18	4	11
33	11	8	10	3	1
17	10	45	51	0	33
26	6	39	31	1	11
52	3	3	4	1	63
36	9	5	8	1	12
13	54	33	35	7	0
24	35	24	17	8	0
23	15	18	15	1	44
35	8	19	15	1	16
36	4	18	23	0	16
38	9	18	17	2	9
25	10	45	48	4	23
30	6	34	28	2	6
14	12	82	83	2	37
24	7	56	53	1	20
45	16	8	15	1	2
41	9	6	8	3	0

continued on next page

TABLE 2A-2a (Continued)

	Number of children (thousands)	Children in official poverty (percent)	Children in relative poverty (percent)	Children in middle-class comfort (percent)
Canada - 1st Generation	33	9	14	31
Canada - 2nd Generation	230	6	11	40
South Africa - 1st Generation	5	7	11	23
South Africa - 2nd Generation	10	6	9	27
Netherlands - 1st Generation	2	14	19	24
Netherlands - 2nd Generation	36	5	11	40
India - 1st Generation	45	10	17	39
India - 2nd Generation	130	3	6	33
Philippines - 1st Generation	83	9	15	48
Philippines - 2nd Generation	316	4	8	44
Ireland - 1st Generation	4	12	14	38
Ireland - 2nd Generation	40	4	7	42

NOTE: Countries are listed from highest to lowest official poverty rate for first and second generations combined.

Children very well-off financially (percent)	Children in one-parent families (percent)	Children whose fathers have less than a high school education (percent)	Children whose mothers have less than a high school education (percent)	Children with 5 or more siblings (percent)	Children who live in linguistically isolated households (percent)
47	12	11	13	2	5
38	8	11	10	5	1
58	7	1	6	1	2
56	5	2	8	1	0
42	18	5	7	3	3
38	7	7	6	6	1
27	13	5	23	1	18
53	5	95	8	1	9
20	12	88	15	6	16
35	7	93	13	2	7
26	24	76	23	7	3
41	14	86	13	4	0

TABLE 2A-2b Household and Housing Risk Factors for First- and Second-Generation Children by Country of Origin for First and Second Generations Separately: 1990

	Number of children (thousands)	Children in households with no car or truck (percent)
All First-Generation Children	2,084	17
All Second-Generation Children	6,288	9
Third and Later Generations by Race and Ethnicity:		
White, Non-Hispanic	40,201	3
Black, Non-Hispanic	8,031	30
Asian, Non-Hispanic	329	4
American Indian	562	14
Hispanic	3,489	17
First- and Second-Generation Children by Country of Origin:		
Laos - 1st Generation	49	18
Laos - 2nd Generation	64	17
Cambodia - 1st Generation	30	32
Cambodia - 2nd Generation	34	27
Dominican Republic - 1st Generation	48	60
Dominican Republic - 2nd Generation	131	51
USSR - 1st Generation	38	32
USSR - 2nd Generation	24	8
Mexico - 1st Generation	643	15
Mexico - 2nd Generation	1,975	8
Thailand - 1st Generation	36	27
Thailand - 2nd Generation	33	2
Vietnam - 1st Generation	99	18
Vietnam - 2nd Generation	33	10
Guatemala - 1st Generation	35	20
Guatemala - 2nd Generation	66	17
Honduras - 1st Generation	17	26
Honduras - 2nd Generation	35	21
El Salvador - 1st Generation	77	16
El Salvador - 2nd Generation	126	15
Nicaragua - 1st Generation	39	17
Nicaragua - 2nd Generation	35	8

Children with no telephone in their homes (percent)	Children living in houses built before 1950 (percent)	Children in crowded homes (percent)
10	26	62
6	24	38
5	23	7
18	27	26
3	18	21
32	17	34
15	25	30
4	29	78
4	27	79
5	31	76
4	30	73
22	49	63
18	51	48
3	35	54
0	28	17
21	24	83
13	23	64
4	34	79
1	14	16
2	21	67
1	17	50
10	32	79
8	34	61
12	27	71
8	25	49
8	28	82
7	30	71
13	25	84
6	22	57

continued on next page

TABLE 2A-2b (Continued)

	Number of children (thousands)	Children in households with no car or truck (percent)
Haiti - 1st Generation	28	30
Haiti - 2nd Generation	77	21
Jordan - 1st Generation	2	15
Jordan - 2nd Generation	17	7
Belize - 1st Generation	3	33
Belize - 2nd Generation	12	16
Iraq - 1st Generation	4	10
Iraq - 2nd Generation	17	3
Ecuador - 1st Generation	12	34
Ecuador - 2nd Generation	52	22
Venezuela - 1st Generation	8	11
Venezuela - 2nd Generation	15	4
Israel - 1st Generation	13	11
Israel - 2nd Generation	46	13
Trinidad and Tobago - 1st Generation	12	40
Trinidad and Tobago - 2nd Generation	41	25
Colombia - 1st Generation	29	17
Colombia - 2nd Generation	88	11
Pakistan - 1st Generation	11	10
Pakistan - 2nd Generation	28	6
Costa Rica - 1st Generation	4	18
Costa Rica - 2nd Generation	19	13
Panama - 1st Generation	6	25
Panama - 2nd Generation	33	15
Brazil - 1st Generation	9	10
Brazil - 2nd Generation	21	6
Romania - 1st Generation	11	10
Romania - 2nd Generation	15	7
Spain - 1st Generation	6	10
Spain - 2nd Generation	22	7
Lebanon - 1st Generation	8	9
Lebanon - 2nd Generation	28	3
Jamaica - 1st Generation	40	29
Jamaica - 2nd Generation	92	19
Guyana - 1st Generation	18	42
Guyana - 2nd Generation	28	23
Nigeria - 1st Generation	5	19
Nigeria - 2nd Generation	29	9

Children with no telephone in their homes (percent)	Children living in houses built before 1950 (percent)	Children in crowded homes (percent)
13	34	68
9	33	47
9	15	46
1	24	29
7	35	59
6	35	40
3	31	47
1	14	31
11	46	60
7	40	39
4	21	50
5	16	20
2	25	32
1	29	26
9	45	43
6	37	26
9	29	59
5	26	36
2	20	49
2	16	29
11	22	52
3	30	28
3	28	46
7	25	22
2	24	38
3	25	18
5	37	41
0	29	23
4	31	31
3	27	17
1	32	34
2	24	16
5	33	39
5	28	25
3	46	49
5	36	28
4	18	62
3	18	48

continued on next page

TABLE 2A-2b (Continued)

	Number of children (thousands)	Children in households with no car or truck (percent)
China - 1st Generation	34	36
China - 2nd Generation	97	12
Indonesia - 1st Generation	4	11
Indonesia - 2nd Generation	13	2
Iran - 1st Generation	24	8
Iran - 2nd Generation	52	3
Cuba - 1st Generation	27	12
Cuba - 2nd Generation	184	6
Peru - 1st Generation	18	13
Peru - 2nd Generation	43	10
Korea - 1st Generation	67	5
Korea - 2nd Generation	163	2
Syria - 1st Generation	2	6
Syria - 2nd Generation	13	2
Taiwan - 1st Generation	32	4
Taiwan - 2nd Generation	65	2
Argentina - 1st Generation	10	6
Argentina - 2nd Generation	26	6
Yugoslavia - 1st Generation	5	13
Yugoslavia - 2nd Generation	39	5
Hong Kong - 1st Generation	17	19
Hong Kong - 2nd Generation	39	5
Chile - 1st Generation	5	8
Chile - 2nd Generation	17	5
Australia - 1st Generation	3	6
Australia - 2nd Generation	14	5
Austria - 1st Generation	1	20
Austria - 2nd Generation	20	4
France - 1st Generation	7	5
France - 2nd Generation	34	5
Hungary - 1st Generation	3	16
Hungary - 2nd Generation	22	7
Egypt - 1st Generation	5	7
Egypt - 2nd Generation	25	3
Germany - 1st Generation	16	5
Germany - 2nd Generation	243	3

Children with no telephone in their homes (percent)	Children living in houses built before 1950 (percent)	Children in crowded homes (percent)
2	41	59
1	30	32
2	11	53
1	17	21
1	13	38
1	12	14
4	18	48
3	17	25
4	26	53
4	27	29
1	15	49
1	12	27
0	25	42
0	19	19
0	13	34
0	10	19
3	15	35
2	22	20
4	39	38
1	30	14
1	33	57
0	23	24
3	27	37
1	19	26
1	17	9
0	24	9
0	29	35
0	27	10
2	21	11
1	30	11
2	27	33
2	25	12
2	24	35
1	24	17
3	19	17
3	22	7

continued on next page

TABLE 2A-2b (Continued)

	Number of children (thousands)	Children in households with no car or truck (percent)
Greece - 1st Generation	3	7
Greece - 2nd Generation	65	3
Japan - 1st Generation	32	2
Japan - 2nd Generation	68	3
Barbados - 1st Generation	3	38
Barbados - 2nd Generation	11	26
Poland - 1st Generation	18	9
Poland - 2nd Generation	62	4
Turkey - 1st Generation	3	6
Turkey - 2nd Generation	12	4
Italy - 1st Generation	8	13
Italy - 2nd Generation	171	3
Portugal - 1st Generation	14	9
Portugal - 2nd Generation	64	3
United Kingdom - 1st Generation	31	5
United Kingdom - 2nd Generation	178	3
Canada - 1st Generation	33	3
Canada - 2nd Generation	230	2
South Africa - 1st Generation	5	2
South Africa - 2nd Generation	10	5
Netherlands - 1st Generation	2	7
Netherlands - 2nd Generation	36	1
India - 1st Generation	45	11
India - 2nd Generation	130	3
Philippines - 1st Generation	83	5
Philippines - 2nd Generation	316	2
Ireland - 1st Generation	4	7
Ireland - 2nd Generation	40	4

NOTE: Countries are listed from highest to lowest official poverty rate for first and second generations combined.

Children with no telephone in their homes (percent)	Children living in houses built before 1950 (percent)	Children in crowded homes (percent)
2	36	15
1	26	9
0	13	14
2	16	12
3	65	39
4	34	16
1	38	19
1	30	8
1	25	20
2	22	16
3	35	18
1	31	6
2	53	23
1	41	12
1	17	11
2	23	7
1	13	12
2	21	7
0	14	10
1	23	6
1	11	9
1	23	8
1	20	42
0	11	18
1	20	58
1	14	33
3	29	15
1	39	7

TABLE 2A-2c Parents' Labor Force Participation for First- and Second-Generation Children by Country of Origin for First and Second Generations Separately: 1990

	Number of children (thousands)	Children with fathers not in the labor force (percent)	Children with fathers not working full-time, year-round (percent)	Children with mothers not in the labor force (percent)
All First-Generation Children	2,084	12	41	45
All Second-Generation Children	6,288	6	28	41
Third and Later Generations by Race and Ethnicity:				
White, Non-Hispanic	40,201	4	19	34
Black, Non-Hispanic	8,031	11	34	33
Asian, Non-Hispanic	329	4	18	29
American Indian	562	14	46	40
Hispanic	3,489	8	30	43
First- and Second-Generation Children by Country of Origin:				
Laos - 1st Generation	49	51	68	64
Laos - 2nd Generation	64	46	68	67
Cambodia - 1st Generation	30	51	69	70
Cambodia - 2nd Generation	34	34	53	62
Dominican Republic - 1st Generation	48	12	40	45
Dominican Republic - 2nd Generation	131	10	38	54
USSR - 1st Generation	38	31	75	53
USSR - 2nd Generation	24	5	21	34
Mexico - 1st Generation	643	7	43	50
Mexico - 2nd Generation	1,975	7	37	50
Thailand - 1st Generation	36	58	73	74
Thailand - 2nd Generation	33	4	21	32
Vietnam - 1st Generation	99	30	57	52
Vietnam - 2nd Generation	33	11	33	42
Guatemala - 1st Generation	35	6	32	36
Guatemala - 2nd Generation	66	5	31	44
Honduras - 1st Generation	17	10	42	38
Honduras - 2nd Generation	35	8	35	43

TABLE 2A-2c (Continued)

	Number of children (thousands)	Children with fathers not in the labor force (percent)	Children with fathers not working full-time, year-round (percent)	Children with mothers not in the labor force (percent)
El Salvador - 1st Generation	77	3	35	30
El Salvador - 2nd Generation	126	5	31	36
Nicaragua - 1st Generation	39	6	38	25
Nicaragua - 2nd Generation	35	4	26	37
Haiti - 1st Generation	28	10	43	21
Haiti - 2nd Generation	77	7	33	22
Jordan - 1st Generation	2	26	60	65
Jordan - 2nd Generation	17	9	27	68
Belize - 1st Generation	3	11	44	29
Belize - 2nd Generation	12	8	30	32
Iraq - 1st Generation	4	21	43	59
Iraq - 2nd Generation	17	8	28	61
Ecuador - 1st Generation	12	6	40	31
Ecuador - 2nd Generation	52	4	28	41
Venezuela - 1st Generation	8	14	38	54
Venezuela - 2nd Generation	15	5	24	44
Israel - 1st Generation	13	13	34	55
Israel - 2nd Generation	46	5	24	54
Trinidad and Tobago - 1st Generation	12	13	49	24
Trinidad and Tobago - 2nd Generation	41	6	30	25
Colombia - 1st Generation	29	5	35	34
Colombia - 2nd Generation	88	4	26	40
Pakistan - 1st Generation	11	9	35	63
Pakistan - 2nd Generation	28	3	23	59
Costa Rica - 1st Generation	4	15	43	47
Costa Rica - 2nd Generation	19	7	29	36
Panama - 1st Generation	6	8	32	34
Panama - 2nd Generation	33	6	26	28
Brazil - 1st Generation	9	8	36	46
Brazil - 2nd Generation	21	5	25	48
Romania - 1st Generation	11	12	33	45
Romania - 2nd Generation	15	6	22	47
Spain - 1st Generation	6	7	48	42
Spain - 2nd Generation	22	4	21	40

continued on next page

TABLE 2A-2c (Continued)

	Number of children (thousands)	Children with fathers not in the labor force (percent)	Children with fathers not working full-time, year-round (percent)	Children with mothers not in the labor force (percent)
Lebanon - 1st Generation	8	12	40	63
Lebanon - 2nd Generation	28	8	24	60
Jamaica - 1st Generation	40	5	32	12
Jamaica - 2nd Generation	92	6	28	19
Guyana - 1st Generation	18	4	30	24
Guyana - 2nd Generation	28	6	27	27
Nigeria - 1st Generation	5	7	51	30
Nigeria - 2nd Generation	29	6	36	25
China - 1st Generation	34	9	41	27
China - 2nd Generation	97	4	22	32
Indonesia - 1st Generation	4	34	63	59
Indonesia - 2nd Generation	13	4	20	35
Iran - 1st Generation	24	17	45	50
Iran - 2nd Generation	52	5	21	44
Cuba - 1st Generation	27	7	37	37
Cuba - 2nd Generation	184	4	20	34
Peru - 1st Generation	18	4	34	31
Peru - 2nd Generation	43	4	25	36
Korea - 1st Generation	67	9	38	37
Korea - 2nd Generation	163	5	22	39
Syria - 1st Generation	2	13	51	62
Syria - 2nd Generation	13	7	29	57
Taiwan - 1st Generation	32	13	36	43
Taiwan - 2nd Generation	65	4	18	39
Argentina - 1st Generation	10	6	28	41
Argentina - 2nd Generation	26	2	19	45
Yugoslavia - 1st Generation	5	4	32	42
Yugoslavia - 2nd Generation	39	6	26	42
Hong Kong - 1st Generation	17	13	41	33
Hong Kong - 2nd Generation	39	3	13	30
Chile - 1st Generation	5	4	28	42
Chile - 2nd Generation	17	3	16	36
Australia - 1st Generation	3	7	17	74
Australia - 2nd Generation	14	3	16	43
Austria - 1st Generation	1	11	32	64
Austria - 2nd Generation	20	4	18	33

TABLE 2A-2c (Continued)

	Number of children (thousands)	Children with fathers not in the labor force (percent)	Children with fathers not working full-time, year-round (percent)	Children with mothers not in the labor force (percent)
France - 1st Generation	7	4	18	57
France - 2nd Generation	34	3	20	40
Hungary - 1st Generation	3	5	26	46
Hungary - 2nd Generation	22	5	19	40
Egypt - 1st Generation	5	7	32	42
Egypt - 2nd Generation	25	3	22	43
Germany - 1st Generation	16	6	22	52
Germany - 2nd Generation	243	3	18	36
Greece - 1st Generation	3	7	35	51
Greece - 2nd Generation	65	6	26	46
Japan - 1st Generation	32	5	22	90
Japan - 2nd Generation	68	3	19	43
Barbados - 1st Generation	3	1	28	14
Barbados - 2nd Generation	11	6	22	22
Poland - 1st Generation	18	4	26	31
Poland - 2nd Generation	62	4	19	35
Turkey - 1st Generation	3	11	23	52
Turkey - 2nd Generation	12	2	20	47
Italy - 1st Generation	8	6	30	55
Italy - 2nd Generation	171	5	21	47
Portugal - 1st Generation	14	5	37	31
Portugal - 2nd Generation	64	6	25	28
United Kingdom - 1st Generation	31	3	15	51
United Kingdom - 2nd Generation	178	3	17	36
Canada - 1st Generation	33	4	19	46
Canada - 2nd Generation	230	3	18	37
South Africa - 1st Generation	5	6	19	50
South Africa - 2nd Generation	10	2	15	46
Netherlands - 1st Generation	2	3	16	48
Netherlands - 2nd Generation	36	2	14	39
India - 1st Generation	45	4	27	31
India - 2nd Generation	130	2	16	37

continued on next page

TABLE 2A-2c (Continued)

	Number of children (thousands)	Children with fathers not in the labor force (percent)	Children with fathers not working full-time, year-round (percent)	Children with mothers not in the labor force (percent)
Philippines - 1st Generation	83	7	29	18
Philippines - 2nd Generation	316	5	20	18
Ireland - 1st Generation	4	5	29	56
Ireland - 2nd Generation	40	4	17	41

NOTE: Countries are listed from highest to lowest official poverty rate for first and second generations combined.

TABLE 2A-2d Parents' Education for First- and Second-Generation Children by Country of Origin for First and Second Generations Separately: 1990

	Number of children (thousands)	Children with fathers who have 8 or fewer years of education (percent)	Children with mothers who have 8 or fewer years of education (percent)	Children whose fathers have four or more years of college education (percent)	Children whose mothers have four or more years of college education (percent)
All First-Generation Children	2,084	34	38	23	14
All Second-Generation Children	6,288	23	22	25	17
Third and Later Generations by Race and Ethnicity:					
White, Non-Hispanic	40,201	3	2	28	20
Black, Non-Hispanic	8,031	6	4	12	9
Asian, Non-Hispanic	329	1	1	40	31
American Indian	562	8	6	9	7
Hispanic	3,489	9	10	12	7
First- and Second-Generation Children by Country of Origin:					
Laos - 1st Generation	49	48	66	8	6
Laos - 2nd Generation	64	36	56	7	2
Cambodia - 1st Generation	30	51	68	3	2
Cambodia - 2nd Generation	34	35	53	9	2
Dominican Republic - 1st Generation	48	42	43	8	4
Dominican Republic - 2nd Generation	131	22	25	10	6
USSR - 1st Generation	38	11	8	36	32
USSR - 2nd Generation	24	4	3	49	41
Mexico - 1st Generation	643	67	69	3	2
Mexico - 2nd Generation	1,975	51	48	4	3
Thailand - 1st Generation	36	50	68	8	4
Thailand - 2nd Generation	33	2	21	39	21

continued on next page

TABLE 2A-2d (Continued)

	Number of children (thousands)	Children with fathers who have 8 or fewer years of education (percent)	Children with mothers who have 8 or fewer years of education (percent)	Children whose fathers have four or more years of college education (percent)	Children whose mothers have four or more years of college education (percent)
Vietnam - 1st Generation	99	32	44	11	5
Vietnam - 2nd Generation	33	14	23	22	9
Guatemala - 1st Generation	35	45	52	7	3
Guatemala - 2nd Generation	66	30	32	10	6
Honduras - 1st Generation	17	33	36	13	6
Honduras - 2nd Generation	35	19	19	13	8
El Salvador - 1st Generation	77	47	51	5	3
El Salvador - 2nd Generation	126	33	35	7	4
Nicaragua - 1st Generation	39	22	23	23	11
Nicaragua - 2nd Generation	35	11	12	19	11
Haiti - 1st Generation	28	19	23	7	4
Haiti - 2nd Generation	77	13	15	17	12
Jordan - 1st Generation	2	14	17	31	11
Jordan - 2nd Generation	17	11	11	29	11
Belize - 1st Generation	3	20	14	7	7
Belize - 2nd Generation	12	8	5	16	7
Iraq - 1st Generation	4	21	41	23	9
Iraq - 2nd Generation	17	12	17	25	17
Ecuador - 1st Generation	12	22	20	16	9
Ecuador - 2nd Generation	52	12	12	18	9
Venezuela - 1st Generation	8	11	11	45	25
Venezuela - 2nd Generation	15	4	3	45	30
Israel - 1st Generation	13	5	6	50	34
Israel - 2nd Generation	46	5	6	38	32
Trinidad and Tobago - 1st Generation	12	15	12	13	6
Trinidad and Tobago - 2nd Generation	41	5	4	19	13
Colombia - 1st Generation	29	15	19	20	12
Colombia - 2nd Generation	88	10	9	22	13
Pakistan - 1st Generation	11	2	12	57	38
Pakistan - 2nd Generation	28	3	7	68	41

TABLE 2A-2d (Continued)

	Number of children (thousands)	Children with fathers who have 8 or fewer years of education (percent)	Children with mothers who have 8 or fewer years of education (percent)	Children whose fathers have four or more years of college education (percent)	Children whose mothers have four or more years of college education (percent)
Costa Rica - 1st Generation	4	16	21	18	10
Costa Rica - 2nd Generation	19	10	10	20	13
Panama - 1st Generation	6	2	8	24	10
Panama - 2nd Generation	33	2	3	26	18
Brazil - 1st Generation	9	11	13	44	31
Brazil - 2nd Generation	21	9	9	38	28
Romania - 1st Generation	11	13	18	34	28
Romania - 2nd Generation	15	7	5	42	34
Spain - 1st Generation	6	30	28	28	15
Spain - 2nd Generation	22	8	8	30	19
Lebanon - 1st Generation	8	28	23	18	11
Lebanon - 2nd Generation	28	10	9	40	24
Jamaica - 1st Generation	40	12	8	14	9
Jamaica - 2nd Generation	92	7	4	21	18
Guyana - 1st Generation	18	12	13	14	4
Guyana - 2nd Generation	28	3	5	27	16
Nigeria - 1st Generation	5	0	4	77	41
Nigeria - 2nd Generation	29	0	1	80	46
China - 1st Generation	34	30	35	28	17
China - 2nd Generation	97	13	15	43	32
Indonesia - 1st Generation	4	9	16	56	27
Indonesia - 2nd Generation	13	1	1	53	36
Iran - 1st Generation	24	4	7	60	29
Iran - 2nd Generation	52	1	1	71	43
Cuba - 1st Generation	27	30	29	11	9
Cuba - 2nd Generation	184	10	7	26	17
Peru - 1st Generation	18	6	8	26	14
Peru - 2nd Generation	43	5	5	30	19
Korea - 1st Generation	67	5	8	46	31
Korea - 2nd Generation	163	1	7	42	27
Syria - 1st Generation	2	16	21	27	14
Syria - 2nd Generation	13	9	9	44	20

continued on next page

TABLE 2A-2d (Continued)

	Number of children (thousands)	Children with fathers who have 8 or fewer years of education (percent)	Children with mothers who have 8 or fewer years of education (percent)	Children whose fathers have four or more years of college education (percent)	Children whose mothers have four or more years of college education (percent)
Taiwan - 1st Generation	32	7	7	62	35
Taiwan - 2nd Generation	65	1	3	77	60
Argentina - 1st Generation	10	14	15	31	26
Argentina - 2nd Generation	26	7	4	35	24
Yugoslavia - 1st Generation	5	14	20	28	17
Yugoslavia - 2nd Generation	39	19	19	17	14
Hong Kong - 1st Generation	17	28	31	15	7
Hong Kong - 2nd Generation	39	7	8	53	39
Chile - 1st Generation	5	9	10	28	17
Chile - 2nd Generation	17	4	4	35	23
Australia - 1st Generation	3	1	2	63	32
Australia - 2nd Generation	14	3	0	48	33
Austria - 1st Generation	1	12	3	47	38
Austria - 2nd Generation	20	1	1	45	37
France - 1st Generation	7	7	8	65	45
France - 2nd Generation	34	3	1	45	34
Hungary - 1st Generation	3	5	6	51	32
Hungary - 2nd Generation	22	6	2	38	29
Egypt - 1st Generation	5	2	5	75	59
Egypt - 2nd Generation	25	1	2	66	41
Germany - 1st Generation	16	2	5	47	27
Germany - 2nd Generation	243	2	1	34	22
Greece - 1st Generation	3	24	26	24	12
Greece - 2nd Generation	65	23	18	21	17
Japan - 1st Generation	32	2	2	78	45
Japan - 2nd Generation	68	2	2	44	26
Barbados - 1st Generation	3	10	13	19	12
Barbados - 2nd Generation	11	8	2	18	14
Poland - 1st Generation	18	7	6	32	27
Poland - 2nd Generation	62	6	5	30	22
Turkey - 1st Generation	3	13	17	46	34
Turkey - 2nd Generation	12	9	7	40	32

TABLE 2A-2d (Continued)

	Number of children (thousands)	Children with fathers who have 8 or fewer years of education (percent)	Children with mothers who have 8 or fewer years of education (percent)	Children whose fathers have four or more years of college education (percent)	Children whose mothers have four or more years of college education (percent)
Italy - 1st Generation	8	33	34	24	16
Italy - 2nd Generation	171	19	15	19	14
Portugal - 1st Generation	14	68	65	3	3
Portugal - 2nd Generation	64	38	34	8	5
United Kingdom - 1st Generation	31	1	3	56	27
United Kingdom - 2nd Generation	178	1	1	41	26
Canada - 1st Generation	33	4	3	58	31
Canada - 2nd Generation	230	3	2	38	26
South Africa - 1st Generation	5	1	1	63	35
South Africa - 2nd Generation	10	0	1	70	42
Netherlands - 1st Generation	2	0	3	60	34
Netherlands - 2nd Generation	36	2	1	40	26
India - 1st Generation	45	4	9	62	46
India - 2nd Generation	130	1	2	80	63
Philippines - 1st Generation	83	7	9	46	52
Philippines - 2nd Generation	316	3	6	37	45
Ireland - 1st Generation	4	12	7	36	13
Ireland - 2nd Generation	40	4	2	31	20

NOTE: Countries are listed from highest to lowest official poverty rate for first and second generations combined.

TABLE 2A-2e Language Use and Citizenship for First- and Second-Generation Children by Country of Origin for First and Second Generations Separately: 1990

	Number of children (thousands)	Children who do not speak English at home (percent)
All First-Generation Children	2,084	87
All Second-Generation Children	6,288	58
Third and Later Generations by Race and Ethnicity:		
White, Non-Hispanic	40,201	1
Black, Non-Hispanic	8,031	1
Asian, Non-Hispanic	329	3
American Indian	562	7
Hispanic	3,489	15
First- and Second-Generation Children by Country of Origin:		
Laos - 1st Generation	49	97
Laos - 2nd Generation	64	95
Cambodia - 1st Generation	30	97
Cambodia - 2nd Generation	34	87
Dominican Republic - 1st Generation	48	97
Dominican Republic - 2nd Generation	131	91
USSR - 1st Generation	38	96
USSR - 2nd Generation	24	57
Mexico - 1st Generation	643	97
Mexico - 2nd Generation	1,975	88
Thailand - 1st Generation	36	95
Thailand - 2nd Generation	33	32
Vietnam - 1st Generation	99	97
Vietnam - 2nd Generation	33	76
Guatemala - 1st Generation	35	98
Guatemala - 2nd Generation	66	83
Honduras - 1st Generation	17	93
Honduras - 2nd Generation	35	69
El Salvador - 1st Generation	77	98
El Salvador - 2nd Generation	126	90
Nicaragua - 1st Generation	39	97
Nicaragua - 2nd Generation	35	75

Children who do not speak English exclusively or very well (percent)	Children who are not U.S. citizens (percent)	Children who are not U.S. citizens, or who have at least 1 parent in the home who is not a citizen (percent)
45	84	87
19	N/A	59
N/A		N/A
N/A		N/A
N/A		N/A
N/A		N/A
N/A		N/A
57	89	91
65	N/A	88
62	89	92
54	N/A	80
55	85	89
31	N/A	68
61	83	84
12	N/A	29
59	86	89
32	N/A	74
65	93	94
9	N/A	56
52	78	81
34	N/A	51
56	89	91
26	N/A	76
48	88	92
18	N/A	64
53	89	91
35	N/A	79
58	96	97
22	N/A	69

continued on next page

TABLE 2A-2e (Continued)

	Number of children (thousands)	Children who do not speak English at home (percent)
Haiti - 1st Generation	28	91
Haiti - 2nd Generation	77	67
Jordan - 1st Generation	2	98
Jordan - 2nd Generation	17	55
Belize - 1st Generation	3	28
Belize - 2nd Generation	12	14
Iraq - 1st Generation	4	90
Iraq - 2nd Generation	17	62
Ecuador - 1st Generation	12	98
Ecuador - 2nd Generation	52	80
Venezuela - 1st Generation	8	95
Venezuela - 2nd Generation	15	49
Israel - 1st Generation	13	91
Israel - 2nd Generation	46	54
Trinidad and Tobago - 1st Generation	12	7
Trinidad and Tobago - 2nd Generation	41	5
Colombia - 1st Generation	29	96
Colombia - 2nd Generation	88	78
Pakistan - 1st Generation	11	94
Pakistan - 2nd Generation	28	60
Costa Rica - 1st Generation	4	94
Costa Rica - 2nd Generation	19	61
Panama - 1st Generation	6	86
Panama - 2nd Generation	33	32
Brazil - 1st Generation	9	93
Brazil - 2nd Generation	21	50
Romania - 1st Generation	11	91
Romania - 2nd Generation	15	54
Spain - 1st Generation	6	91
Spain - 2nd Generation	22	56
Lebanon - 1st Generation	8	92
Lebanon - 2nd Generation	28	62
Jamaica - 1st Generation	40	7
Jamaica - 2nd Generation	92	6
Guyana - 1st Generation	18	8
Guyana - 2nd Generation	28	7

Children who do not speak English exclusively or very well (percent)	Children who are not U.S. citizens (percent)	Children who are not U.S. citizens, or who have at least 1 parent in the home who is not a citizen (percent)
47	84	90
21	N/A	71
28	72	79
8	N/A	33
10	72	80
3	N/A	70
13	72	78
10	N/A	37
38	87	90
20	N/A	73
36	90	92
12	N/A	68
28	74	75
15	N/A	31
4	84	86
1	N/A	68
38	87	90
17	N/A	64
29	74	80
14	N/A	46
38	88	91
13	N/A	63
31	77	79
9	N/A	43
47	91	96
11	N/A	68
33	77	79
14	N/A	25
26	83	85
12	N/A	60
26	69	71
12	N/A	32
2	81	85
2	N/A	59
2	80	81
2	N/A	51

continued on next page

TABLE 2A-2e (Continued)

	Number of children (thousands)	Children who do not speak English at home (percent)
Nigeria - 1st Generation	5	59
Nigeria - 2nd Generation	29	15
China - 1st Generation	34	97
China - 2nd Generation	97	74
Indonesia - 1st Generation	4	88
Indonesia - 2nd Generation	13	20
Iran - 1st Generation	24	93
Iran - 2nd Generation	52	49
Cuba - 1st Generation	27	98
Cuba - 2nd Generation	184	77
Peru - 1st Generation	18	98
Peru - 2nd Generation	43	69
Korea - 1st Generation	67	92
Korea - 2nd Generation	163	50
Syria - 1st Generation	2	93
Syria - 2nd Generation	13	52
Taiwan - 1st Generation	32	96
Taiwan - 2nd Generation	65	68
Argentina - 1st Generation	10	96
Argentina - 2nd Generation	26	55
Yugoslavia - 1st Generation	5	94
Yugoslavia - 2nd Generation	39	57
Hong Kong - 1st Generation	17	97
Hong Kong - 2nd Generation	39	66
Chile - 1st Generation	5	94
Chile - 2nd Generation	17	66
Australia - 1st Generation	3	27
Australia - 2nd Generation	14	8
Austria - 1st Generation	1	84
Austria - 2nd Generation	20	22
France - 1st Generation	7	91
France - 2nd Generation	34	35
Hungary - 1st Generation	3	99
Hungary - 2nd Generation	22	35
Egypt - 1st Generation	5	88
Egypt - 2nd Generation	25	48

Children who do not speak English exclusively or very well (percent)	Children who are not U.S. citizens (percent)	Children who are not U.S. citizens, or who have at least 1 parent in the home who is not a citizen (percent)
27	89	89
3	N/A	81
63	83	85
23	N/A	32
43	89	92
6	N/A	37
34	89	90
10	N/A	57
36	84	89
15	N/A	42
42	88	89
16	N/A	59
38	81	85
14	N/A	43
35	77	77
10	N/A	37
41	80	81
16	N/A	39
26	89	91
12	N/A	50
22	77	86
8	N/A	39
54	77	78
22	N/A	23
32	87	90
12	N/A	57
3	93	95
3	N/A	71
32	68	71
7	N/A	26
30	90	91
5	N/A	49
28	75	81
11	N/A	20
27	65	67
10	N/A	28

continued on next page

TABLE 2A-2e (Continued)

	Number of children (thousands)	Children who do not speak English at home (percent)
Germany - 1st Generation	16	69
Germany - 2nd Generation	243	14
Greece - 1st Generation	3	87
Greece - 2nd Generation	65	69
Japan - 1st Generation	32	94
Japan - 2nd Generation	68	34
Barbados - 1st Generation	3	7
Barbados - 2nd Generation	11	2
Poland - 1st Generation	18	96
Poland - 2nd Generation	62	55
Turkey - 1st Generation	3	87
Turkey - 2nd Generation	12	45
Italy - 1st Generation	8	85
Italy - 2nd Generation	171	35
Portugal - 1st Generation	14	96
Portugal - 2nd Generation	64	69
United Kingdom - 1st Generation	31	19
United Kingdom - 2nd Generation	178	5
Canada - 1st Generation	33	30
Canada - 2nd Generation	230	7
South Africa - 1st Generation	5	18
South Africa - 2nd Generation	10	7
Netherlands - 1st Generation	2	77
Netherlands - 2nd Generation	36	9
India - 1st Generation	45	84
India - 2nd Generation	130	53
Philippines - 1st Generation	83	75
Philippines - 2nd Generation	316	21
Ireland - 1st Generation	4	17
Ireland - 2nd Generation	40	4

NOTE: Countries are listed from highest to lowest official poverty rate for first and second generations combined.

Children who do not speak English exclusively or very well (percent)	Children who are not U.S. citizens (percent)	Children who are not U.S. citizens, or who have at least 1 parent in the home who is not a citizen (percent)
15	78	84
4	N/A	34
27	58	69
10	N/A	34
66	96	97
10	N/A	62
2	72	76
1	N/A	53
31	80	86
9	N/A	45
18	79	84
5	N/A	44
21	60	71
7	N/A	37
28	80	85
12	N/A	58
3	90	92
1	N/A	59
5	91	92
2	N/A	57
4	84	84
2	N/A	43
10	89	88
3	N/A	41
24	84	90
10	N/A	60
27	72	76
5	N/A	36
5	87	90
0	N/A	44

TABLE 2A-3a Social and Economic Risk Factors for Third- and Later-Generation Children for Selected Race and Ethnic Groups: 1990

	Number of children (thousands)	Children in official poverty (percent)
Black, Non-Hispanic	8,031	40
Dominican Republic	12	40
American Indian	562	38
Hispanic	3,489	31
Mexico	2,203	28
Cuba	32	24
Guatemala	4	17
El Salvador	7	17
Ecuador	4	15
Peru	4	15
Honduras	4	14
Nicaragua	4	14
Columbia	13	13
White, Non-Hispanic	40,201	11
Panama	4	11
Asian, Non-Hispanic	329	10
Philippines	41	10
China	35	5
Japan	80	3
Korea	64	3

Children in relative poverty (percent)	Children in middle-class comfort (percent)	Children very well-off financially (percent)
51	25	9
50	24	8
51	24	7
42	31	11
39	32	11
31	35	21
23	31	26
24	36	29
21	38	25
21	41	31
23	36	29
16	42	25
18	33	40
17	42	26
16	45	17
14	38	37
16	45	24
7	34	52
6	37	51
5	40	47

continued on next page

TABLE 2A-3a (Continued)

	Children in one-parent families (percent)	Children whose fathers have less than a high school education (percent)
Black, Non-Hispanic	62	26
Dominican Republic	70	28
American Indian	40	28
Hispanic	42	30
Mexico	38	30
Cuba	47	17
Guatemala	41	16
El Salvador	49	23
Ecuador	50	8
Peru	46	15
Honduras	50	8
Nicaragua	41	14
Columbia	35	9
White, Non-Hispanic	18	12
Panama	52	5
Asian, Non-Hispanic	25	7
Philippines	37	11
China	20	4
Japan	17	3
Korea	11	2

NOTE: Groups are listed from highest to lowest official poverty rate.

Children whose mothers have less than a high school education (percent)	Children with 5 or more siblings (percent)	Children who live in linguistically isolated households (percent)
29	10	0
46	4	15
29	10	4
35	8	9
34	6	6
19	3	3
17	4	3
17	4	6
12	1	4
11	0	4
13	2	5
16	4	5
10	4	3
12	4	0
13	3	0
9	6	1
16	3	1
4	4	2
2	1	0
2	4	0

TABLE 2A-3b Household and Housing Risk Factors for Third- and Later-Generation Children for Selected Race and Ethnic Groups: 1990

	Number of children (thousands)	Children in households with no car or truck (percent)
Black, Non-Hispanic	8,031	30
Dominican Republic	12	50
American Indian	562	14
Hispanic	3,489	17
Mexico	2,203	9
Cuba	32	14
Guatemala	4	10
El Salvador	7	7
Ecuador	4	23
Peru	4	4
Honduras	4	8
Nicaragua	4	7
Columbia	13	7
White, Non-Hispanic	40,201	3
Panama	4	8
Asian, Non-Hispanic	329	4
Philippines	41	4
China	35	3
Japan	80	1
Korea	64	1

NOTE: Groups are listed from highest to lowest official poverty rate.

Children with no telephone in their homes (percent)	Children living in houses built before 1950 (percent)	Children in crowded homes (percent)
18	27	26
20	45	40
32	17	34
15	25	30
14	19	31
8	25	15
1	30	21
5	26	22
6	34	14
3	24	10
3	26	10
2	25	21
6	27	12
5	23	7
3	23	25
3	18	21
3	17	29
2	20	13
1	13	13
1	24	4

TABLE 2A-3c Parents' Labor Force Participation for Third- and Later-Generation Children for Selected Race and Ethnic Groups: 1990

	Number of children (thousands)	Children with fathers not in the labor force (percent)	Children with fathers not working full time, year-round (percent)	Children with mothers not in the labor force (percent)
Black, Non-Hispanic	8,031	11	34	33
Dominican Republic	12	17	43	48
American Indian	562	14	46	40
Hispanic	3,489	8	30	43
Mexico	2,203	7	29	40
Cuba	32	7	22	36
Guatemala	4	4	27	39
El Salvador	7	9	22	30
Ecuador	4	2	17	24
Peru	4	4	15	40
Honduras	4	5	24	32
Nicaragua	4	3	13	31
Columbia	13	1	17	33
White, Non-Hispanic	40,201	4	19	34
Panama	4	5	13	27
Asian, Non-Hispanic	329	4	18	29
Philippines	41	4	22	29
China	35	3	16	24
Japan	80	2	13	23
Korea	64	2	13	31

NOTE: Groups are listed from highest to lowest official poverty rate.

TABLE 2A-3d Children's Language Use for Third- and Later-Generation Children for Selected Race and Ethnic Groups: 1990

	Number of children (thousands)	Children who do not speak English at home (percent)	Children who do not speak English exclusively or very well (percent)
Black, Non-Hispanic	8,031	1	N/A
Dominican Republic	12	61	32
American Indian	562	7	N/A
Hispanic	3,489	15	N/A
Mexico	2,203	36	13
Cuba	32	29	8
Guatemala	4	32	10
El Salvador	7	24	7
Ecuador	4	24	6
Peru	4	28	8
Honduras	4	24	10
Nicaragua	4	25	8
Columbia	13	21	9
White, Non-Hispanic	40,201	1	N/A
Panama	4	23	7
Asian, Non-Hispanic	329	3	N/A
Philippines	41	7	3
China	35	12	5
Japan	80	4	1
Korea	64	2	1

NOTE: Groups are listed from highest to lowest official poverty rate.

TABLE 2A-3e Parents' Education for Third- and Later-Generation Children for Selected Race and Ethnic Groups: 1990

	Number of children (thousands)	Children with fathers who have 8 or fewer years of education (percent)
Black, Non-Hispanic	8,031	6
Dominican Republic	12	14
American Indian	562	8
Hispanic	3,489	9
Mexico	2,203	8
Cuba	32	3
Guatemala	4	5
El Salvador	7	7
Ecuador	4	2
Peru	4	3
Honduras	4	5
Nicaragua	4	0
Columbia	13	3
White, Non-Hispanic	40,201	3
Panama	4	0
Asian, Non-Hispanic	329	1
Philippines	41	1
China	35	1
Japan	80	0
Korea	64	1

NOTE: Groups are listed from highest to lowest official poverty rate.

Children with mothers who have 8 or fewer years of education (percent)	Children whose fathers have four or more years of college education (percent)	Children whose mothers have four or more years of college education (percent)
4	12	9
12	17	8
6	9	7
10	12	7
9	11	6
3	24	17
4	37	31
3	41	31
4	44	30
3	39	29
4	48	42
2	29	13
3	52	34
2	28	20
0	35	23
1	40	31
2	21	15
1	59	49
0	47	41
0	56	45

CHAPTER 3

Access to Health Insurance and Health Care for Children in Immigrant Families[1]

E. Richard Brown, Roberta Wyn, Hongjian Yu, Abel Valenzuela, and Liane Dong

An ongoing concern in immigration research is the extent to which poor access to social and economic opportunities creates structural barriers to immigrants' assimilation into the U.S. economy and society (Bean et al., 1994; Lee and Edmonston, 1994). Access to health insurance and health care is an important indicator of socioeconomic opportunity. Access to health care services, particularly for children, is important to ensure that acute and chronic conditions are diagnosed and treated in a timely manner, that health and development are adequately monitored, and that preventive services are provided as recommended (American Academy of Pediatrics, 1995). Without good access to primary medical care, acute conditions, such as middle-ear infections or streptococcus infections, can lead to chronic, often disabling, conditions. Without appropriate medical management, chronic conditions, such as asthma or diabetes, may lead to life-threatening medical emergencies and may impose economic and social burdens on families and society. Without adequate access to preventive care, such as immunizations and well-baby/child checkups, both chronic and acute conditions are more likely to occur, and developmental problems may go undiagnosed and

[1]The research on which this paper is based was supported by a grant from the Robert Wood Johnson Foundation.

untreated. All of these consequences may create additional barriers to successful adjustment by immigrants to their new society.

Health insurance provides an important degree of financial access to health care services. Numerous studies have demonstrated that children who have neither private health insurance or Medicaid or any other public coverage receive fewer physician visits overall, fewer visits for the care of chronic conditions, and fewer preventive health care services compared to insured children (Newacheck et al., 1996; Stoddard et al., 1994; Wood et al., 1990; Brown, 1989).

Other factors also influence access. Having a regular provider of care provides a connection to the health care system, facilitating both access to services and continuity of care. Having a regular provider has consistently been found to increase a person's use of health care services (Berk et al., 1995; Andersen and Davidson, 1996). Whether health care services are geographically available to children also has been found to affect their use of ambulatory care services and rates of avoidable hospitalizations (Andersen and Davidson, 1996; Valdez and Dallek, 1991). Cultural factors, including language barriers and customs, affect access for immigrant and other ethnic and racial minority population groups (Aday et al., 1993; Board on Children and Families, 1995).

Despite these benefits, the provision of publicly funded health care services to noncitizens in the United States has become a highly charged policy and political issue. The dispute has focused on both legal immigrants' entitlement to federal health and welfare programs and undocumented, or illegal, immigrants' use of government-funded health and educational services (Fix and Passel, 1994; U.S. General Accounting Office, 1995; Clark et al., 1994). Although recent major changes in federal law will affect legal and undocumented immigrants' entitlement to health care services and other programs, few studies have examined immigrants' access to health insurance coverage and health care services (Thamer et al., 1997; Edmonston, 1996).

The research and theoretical literature on access to health care has focused considerable attention on disparities by ethnicity and race. Latinos have very high uninsured rates, followed by Asians, African Americans, and non-Latino whites (Mendoza, 1994;

Valdez et al., 1993; Wyn et al., 1993). Latinos, African Americans, and Asians also have fewer physician visits than non-Latino whites, for general medical care, acute and chronic conditions, and preventive services (Aday et al., 1993; Wyn et al., 1993; Mendoza, 1994; Lieu et al., 1993; Vega and Amaro, 1994). However, few studies have examined the effects of immigration and citizenship status on health insurance coverage and access to health care, despite its central importance in understanding ethnicity, particularly for Latinos and Asians.

FOCUS AND IMPORTANCE OF THIS STUDY

This paper examines health insurance coverage and access to health care services among first-generation immigrant children and U.S. citizen or nonimmigrant children in immigrant families, compared to children in nonimmigrant families. The effects of immigration and citizenship status and ethnicity on uninsurance and on access to physician visits are examined. The extent to which immigrant children and U.S. citizen children in immigrant families have higher uninsured rates and/or less access to health care services has important policy and research implications.

Recent public policy changes may substantially reduce access for immigrant children and U.S. citizen children with noncitizen parents. In 1996 Congress dramatically reduced the entitlement of noncitizen immigrants to a broad range of federal public assistance programs, including Medicaid. Much of the debate has centered on undocumented and legal immigrant adults, with little attention to the potential impact of sweeping reforms on children—despite the fact that many of the changes taking place disproportionately affect children, particularly immigrant children, and may reduce their access to health care services. These policy changes have increased the importance of understanding factors that affect health insurance coverage and access to health care services among children in immigrant families.

METHODS

In this study two population-based surveys, the March 1996 Current Population Survey (CPS) and the 1994 National Health

Interview Survey (NHIS), were analyzed to assess the effects of immigration and citizenship status, ethnicity, and other factors on health insurance coverage and access to health care services. The CPS is a national, in-person and telephone, cross-sectional survey conducted by the U.S. Bureau of the Census to obtain information on employment, unemployment, and demographic status of the noninstitutionalized U.S. civilian population. The March 1996 CPS contains extensive information on household relationships, sources of income, ethnicity, citizenship, immigration status, nativity, and health insurance coverage of each household member. The CPS includes information on approximately 35,600 children from birth to age 17, usually reported by an adult family member.

The NHIS, which is administered by the National Center for Health Statistics, is a national in-person survey of the noninstitutionalized population and includes demographic, health status, and utilization information in the core survey. Special supplements were administered in 1994 to provide additional information on health insurance coverage, reported reasons for lack of coverage, and access to health care services. The 1994 NHIS includes information on approximately 32,000 children from birth to age 17, as reported by an adult family member. The NHIS does not contain information on citizenship status, and it contains only limited information on national origin.

Logistic regressions were used to examine the independent effects of immigration status, citizenship, and ethnicity on health insurance coverage and the effects of immigration status, ethnicity, and health insurance coverage on health care access.

UNINSURANCE, IMMIGRATION, AND CITIZENSHIP

Are children who are noncitizen immigrants at higher risk of being uninsured than citizen children in native-born families? Are U.S. citizen children in immigrant families at higher risk of being uninsured than those whose parents were born in this country? To answer these questions, we compared the health insurance status of children who are immigrant noncitizens, U.S. citizen children in families with one or more immigrant parents, and U.S. citizen children with U.S.-born parents. We used data on children and their families from the March 1996 CPS to examine health insurance coverage.

Variables Used in Analysis of Health Insurance Coverage

Our analytical approach is based on the premise that family characteristics strongly influence children's health insurance coverage. Most of the independent variables were structured to reflect this focus on the family by including, where relevant, information that characterizes the family as well as the child.

Health Insurance Status

A child's health insurance coverage is for the previous calendar year. The March 1996 CPS asked respondents about health insurance coverage for each family member during the previous calendar year. Children insured by any source at any time during 1995 were counted as insured, and those with no reported coverage of any kind during the year were categorized as uninsured.

Immigration and Citizenship Status

We classified children into three immigration and citizenship categories: (1) noncitizen immigrant child—that is, a child who was not born in the United States and is not a U.S. citizen; (2) U.S. citizen child in an immigrant family—that is, a child who is a citizen (U.S. born or naturalized) and has one or more parents who are foreign born, regardless of whether they are U.S. citizens; and (3) U.S. citizen child with both parents born in the United States (or, in a single-parent family, the one parent being U.S. born). Children who were born outside the United States to U.S.-born parents are counted as U.S. born. Noncitizen immigrant children and U.S. citizen children in immigrant families were further classified by the year in which the parent who is the primary worker immigrated to the United States.

Potential differences were examined among noncitizen children, citizen children in immigrant families, and children in non-immigrant families in their access to public or private health insurance coverage. First, we hypothesized that a child's citizenship status would be an important influence on whether he or she received private health insurance or Medicaid coverage. Although legal immigrants, regardless of citizenship status, were entitled to Medicaid in 1995, we anticipated that noncitizen children may have less access to these benefits. The CPS does not distinguish between legal and undocumented immigrants; noncitizens as defined in this paper include both groups. (The CPS also does not identify respondents as refugees or asylees.)

Second, we hypothesized that even among U.S. citizen children their parents' immigration status would affect the children's access to coverage. We expected that U.S. citizen children with U.S.-born parents were likely to have the best access to health insurance through employment or private purchase and, in the absence of private coverage, through Medicaid and other public programs. Families were classified as immigrant if either parent was foreign born and as U.S. born if both parents (or the one parent in a single-parent family) were born in the United States. We compared immigrant children's uninsurance rates with those of U.S.-born children, a relative standard.

Ethnicity

We classified children into four ethnic groups: Latinos, non-Latino whites, non-Latino blacks, and non-Latino Asians; for brevity and simplicity we use the terms "white," "black," and "Asian" to refer to persons in these non-Latino ethnic/racial groups. Sample size limitations did not permit analyses of other racial/ethnic groupings.

Family Income Related to Poverty

We classified children into one of four family income groups in relation to the poverty level, a standard set annually by the federal government and based on total family income from all sources and the number of persons in the family. In 1995, the year reflected in the CPS questions on health insurance coverage, the poverty level was set at $15,569 for a family of four.

Family Structure

We expected that single-parent families would, on average, provide fewer opportunities than two-parent families for children to receive health insurance coverage through the employment of a parent. On the other hand, children in low-income single-parent families would be more likely to qualify for Medicaid.

Family Work Status

We wanted to examine the effects of labor force participation and employment characteristics on children's health insurance coverage. We classified a family's working status on the basis of the adult (parent) whose labor force participation provided the best opportunity for family members to receive health insurance coverage (we sometimes call this person the "primary worker" or "primary breadwinner"). A family was classified as a "full-time, full-year employee family" if at least one of the parents reported working for an employer at least 35 hours per week for 50 to 52 weeks in 1995; a "full-time, part-year employee family" if a parent worked for an employer full time for less than 50 weeks; a "part-time employee family" if no parent worked as a full-time employee but one worked for an employer less than 35 hours a week; a "self-employed family" if a parent was self-employed; or a "nonworking family" if no parent worked during 1995. We tied several other variables to the parent identified as the primary worker.

Parent's Education Status

The educational attainment of the parent who is the primary worker was used to categorize the family's education status.

Country of Origin

We examined differences in health insurance coverage by the nativity of the child if the child is an immigrant or the parent who is the primary worker if the child is U.S. born.

State of Residence

We examined the influence of a child's state of residence on differences in health insurance coverage.

Health Status

The child's general health status is based on the parent's report of the child as being in excellent, very good, good, fair, or poor health. Perceived general health status is a widely used measure in health services research; no other measures of health status are available in the CPS. Because the great majority of children are reported to be in excellent or very good health, we dichotomized this variable for children into excellent/very good and good/fair/poor.

Uninsurance, Ethnicity, and Immigration and Citizenship Status

Noncitizen children and citizen children in immigrant families are more likely to lack health insurance coverage than children whose parents were born in the United States (see Figure 3-1). This disparity in coverage rates by immigration and citizenship status varies by ethnicity. Asian citizen children with U.S.-born parents have the lowest uninsured rate of any group (6 percent), but Asian children in immigrant families have an uninsured rate that is more than two times that (14 percent) for children in native-born families.[2] (The rate for Asian noncitizen children is not statistically different from the rate for citizen children with U.S.-born parents.) A much larger proportion of noncitizen black children are uninsured (37 percent), compared to black citizen children in immigrant families and those with U.S.-born parents (12 and 15 percent, respectively). Latino children are clearly the most disadvantaged, with the highest uninsured rates in each immigration and citizenship category, ranging from 16 percent for citizen children with U.S.-born parents to 53 percent for noncitizen

[2]All references in the text to differences in proportions between groups are statistically significant ($p < .05$) unless otherwise stated.

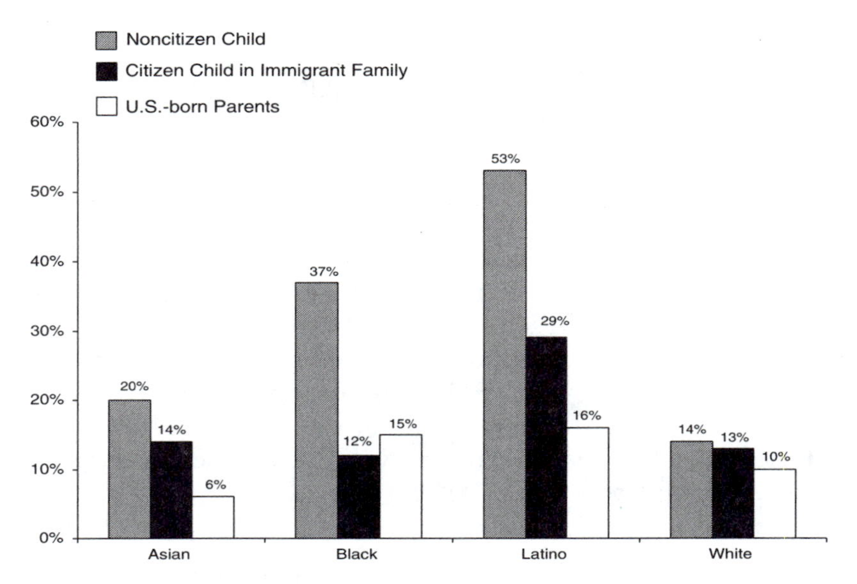

FIGURE 3-1 Percentage uninsured by ethnicity and immigration and citizenship status, ages 0 to 17, United States, 1995. SOURCE: March 1996 Current Population Survey.

children. White children have among the lowest uninsured rates, particularly low for white noncitizen children compared to noncitizen children in the other ethnic groups.

For most children, health insurance coverage is obtained through their parents' employment. In 1995, 66 percent of citizen children with U.S.-born parents were covered by one of their parent's employment-based insurance (see Table 3-1). But job-based insurance coverage varies considerably by ethnicity and immigration and citizenship status—ranging from a low of 22 percent for Latino noncitizen children to 74 percent for white U.S. citizen children with U.S.-born parents. It is striking that about two-thirds of Asian, black, and white citizen children in immigrant families have job-based health insurance, but only 35 percent of Latino children in such families do. It is also noteworthy that black and Latino citizen children with U.S.-born parents have especially low employment-based health insurance coverage rates.

The low rates of employment-based health insurance for some groups may be offset by higher rates of Medicaid coverage. Both black and Latino citizen children with U.S.-born parents would have even higher uninsured rates in the absence of Medicaid (Table 3-1). Within each ethnic group, much smaller percentages of noncitizen children are covered by either employment-based health insurance or Medicaid, leaving more of them uninsured. Asian and non-Latino white children have somewhat higher rates of "other" coverage, primarily privately purchased insurance. These higher rates are associated with higher family incomes and, in the case of Asian immigrant families, larger proportions engaged in self-employment, which provides fewer opportunities for employment-based health insurance coverage.

Uninsured rates among children vary by social and economic factors, in addition to the large differences by ethnicity and immigration and citizenship status. Within each ethnic and immigration and citizenship status group, uninsured rates are generally higher for children whose parents had less education (see Table 3-2). Low family income is also clearly associated with higher uninsured rates, although for most groups the near poor (those with family incomes between 100 and 199 percent of poverty) have higher uninsured rates than those with incomes below poverty, reflecting the greater protection that Medicaid offers to poor children compared to those above the poverty level. Children in self-employed families clearly have the highest uninsured rates in each ethnic and immigration and citizenship status group.

Ethnicity, Immigration and Citizenship Status, and Uninsurance

The wide differences in uninsured rates between children in immigrant and nonimmigrant families may be due, in part, to differences between these groups in factors such as educational attainment, family work status, and family income. To better understand these relationships, we used multivariate analysis to examine the independent effects of immigration and citizenship status on the probability of being uninsured.

Figure 3-2 illustrates the effects of ethnicity and immigration and citizenship status on the probability of being uninsured,

TABLE 3-1 Health Insurance Coverage of Children by Ethnicity and Immigration and Citizenship Status, Ages 0 to 17, United States, 1995

	Uninsured (%)	Employment-Based Insurance (%)	Medicaid (%)	Other [c] (%)	Total
All Children[a]					
Citizen child with U.S.-born parents	11	66	17	6	100 (N = 58,300,000)
Citizen child in Immigrant family	21	52	23	5	100 (N = 9,622,000)
Noncitizen child	36	35	23	6	100 (N = 2,341,000)
Asian[b]					
Citizen child with U.S.-born parents	6	69	12	12	100 (N = 474,000)
Citizen child in Immigrant family	14	66	13	7	100 (N = 1,774,000)
Noncitizen child	20	45	26	9	100 (N = 607,000)
Black[b]					
Citizen child with U.S.-born parents	15	42	40	4	100 (N = 10, 180,000)

Citizen child in immigrant family	12	69	17	3	100 (N = 709,000)
Noncitizen child	37	40	17	6	100 (N = 181,000)
Latino[b]					
Citizen child with U.S.-born parents	16	45	36	3	100 (N = 3,704,000)
Citizen child in immigrant family	29	35	34	2	100 (N = 4,638,000)
Noncitizen child	53	22	22	3	100 (N = 1,149,000)
White[b]					
Citizen child with U.S.-born parents	10	74	10	7	100 (N = 43,210,000)
Citizen child in immigrant family	13	68	12	7	100 (N = 2,465,000)
Noncitizen child	14	53	23	10	100 (N = 400,000)

[a]Includes individuals with "other race/ethnicity."
[b]"Latino" includes all Hispanic persons from the Americas. "Asian," "black," and "white" do not include any persons of Latino heritage.
[c]"Other" includes privately purchased health insurance, Medicare, and other public programs.

SOURCE: March 1996 Current Population Survey.

TABLE 3-2 Percentage of Children Uninsured by Sociodemographic Characteristics, Ethnicity, and Immigration and Citizenship Status, Ages 0 to 17, United States, 1995

	Latino (any race)		
	Noncitizen Child	Citizen Child in Immigrant Family	Citizen Child in U.S.-Born Family
All Children in Group	53 (47.8,58.0)	29 (27.6,31.1)	16 (11.2,19.3)
Age			
0-2	50 (24.1,76.2)	25 (20.8,29.7)	15 (10.6,19.6)
3-5	50 (32.0,68.2)	28 (23.4,33.0)	12 (7.9,16.7)
6-11	52 (43.4,59.7)	30 (25.6,34.1)	15 (11.4,18.5)
12-17	54 (46.9,61.5)	32 (26.7,36.7)	20 (15.5,24.0)
Family Structure			
Married couple with children	53 (47.3,59.1)	31 (27.8,33.2)	16 (13.4,19.4)
Single adult with children	51 (40.7,61.3)	23 (18.7,27.5)	15 (12.4,18.2)
Family Income			
Below poverty	59 (52.1,66.2)	27 (22.9,30.3)	17 (13.9,20.7)
100-199% of poverty level	47 (39.0,55.7)	37 (33.0,41.0)	21 (16.6,25.8)
200-299% of poverty level	53 (35.6,71.4)	23 (17.4,28.7)	17 (11.1,21.9)
300%+ of poverty level	16 (0,35.7)	13 (7.4,18.4)	5 (2.2,7.9)

Asian (non-Latino)		
Noncitizen Child	Citizen Child in Immigrant Family	Citizen Child in U.S.-Born Family
20 (18.1,23.0)	14 (10.2,19.1)	6 (2.4,10.8)
35 (2.8,67.6)	19 (11.8,25.3)	[a]
17 (1.3,32.6)	13 (7.0,18.2)	9 (0.,21.1)
17 (7.8,25.3)	11 (6.7,16.1)	8 (0.4,16.3)
22 (14.1,30.0)	13 (7.8,18.5)	6 (0,12.5)
17 (11.3,22.4)	14 (10.6,16.5)	4 (0.1,7.4)
41 (22.9,59.4)	15 (6.6,22.8)	11 (2.5,19.0)
17 (7.5,27.4)	17 (9.4,24.4)	11 (0,22.8)
29 (18.0,41.0)	26 (18.1,34.0)	5 (0,14.0)
30 (13.3,46.6)	17 (9.6,23.5)	15 (0,32.7)
8 (1.1,15.2)	6 (3.1,8.7)	3 (0,7.0)

continued on next page

TABLE 3-2 Continued

	Latino (any race)		
	Noncitizen Child	Citizen Child in Immigrant Family	Citizen Child in U.S.-Born Family
Family Work Status			
Full-time, full-year employee	55 (48.3,61.4)	31 (27.6,33.6)	15 (12.1,17.7)
Full-time, part-year employee	46 (34.1,57.2)	28 (22.2,33.2)	25 (17.1,31.9)
Part-time employee	64 (44.8,83.8)	23 (13.9,32.6)	20 (12.0,27.5)
Self-employed	79 (54.8,102.9)	55 (42.7,66.7)	60 (37.0,82.4)
Nonworking family	39 (24.0,54.3)	13 (7.9,18.1)	10 (6.8,13.6)
Education Status of Parent			
Less than 12 years	56 (50.2,61.9)	32 (29.4,35.5)	17 (13.4,20.7)
High school graduate	48 (34.6,61.8)	24 (19.2,28.9)	19 (15.3,22.9)
At least some college	34 (18.7,49.0)	22 (17.1,26.8)	11 (7.8,14.2)
Duration of Residence in U.S. of Parent[b]			
Pre-1970-1979	47 (36.3,63.0)	27 (23.0,30.3)	N.A.
1980-1983	52 (40.5,67.6)	30 (25.7,38.1)	N.A.
1984-1989	51 (38.1,56.1)	34 (28.0,40.0)	N.A.
1990-1996	57 (46.4,67.6)	28 (12.0,31.2)	N.A.

Asian (non-Latino)		
Noncitizen Child	Citizen Child in Immigrant Family	Citizen Child in U.S.-Born Family
22 (14.2,30.1)	11 (8.0,13.8)	5 (1.1,9.6)
20 (5.2,35.7)	27 (10.5,43.2)	7 (0,20.9)
20 (1.9,39.1)	26 (10.7,40.6)	10 (0,22.6)
40 (0,80.3)	43 (25.0,61.7)	10 (0,33.6)
13 (3.8,22.9)	8 (1.0,14.3)	4 (0,15.7)
12 (3.8,19.2)	13 (6.9,19.6)	[a]
38 (17.8,57.9)	23 (15.2,30.1)	6 (0,12.4)
22 (14.1,29.2)	11 (7.6,14.0)	7 (2.0,11.8)
23 (0,58.5)	10 (4.5,13.3)	N.A.
14 (0,28.3)	18 (11.0,31.4)	N.A.
20 (8.6,30.9)	16 (7.4,24.4)	N.A.
22 (13.0,31.0)	18 (0,26.4)	N.A.

continued on next page

TABLE 3-2 Continued

	Latino (any race)		
	Noncitizen Child	Citizen Child in Immigrant Family	Citizen Child in U.S.-Born Family
State of Residence in the U.S.[b]			
California	51 (44.0,56.7)	28 (25.2,30.5)	14 (10.3,17.2)
Florida	40 (25.8,53.0)	28 (21.1,34.8)	17 (8.9,24.5)
Illinois	45 (18.1,70.3)	25 (15.1,35.1)	13 (4.6,20.6)
New Jersey	57 (30.3,83.5)	17 (6.8,26.9)	14 (5.8,21.6)
New York	46 (29.6,61.4)	21 (12.9,29.5)	10 (5.7,14.6)
Texas	58 (47.8,67.5)	38 (32.0,42.8)	26 (22.5,29.7)
Other 44 states and District of Columbia	60 (50.6,70.3)	31 (25.1,37.2)	18 (14.1,20.8)

Asian (non-Latino)		
Noncitizen Child	Citizen Child in Immigrant Family	Citizen Child in U.S.-Born Family
15 (8.2,21.0)	13 (8.9,16.5)	9 (0,17.3)
28 (0.7,54.9)	4 (0,11.7)	*a*
a	9 (0,20.5)	*a*
23 (0,49.3)	5 (0,16.0)	7 (0,16.5)
39 (20.4,57.2)	19 (7.1,29.5)	18 (3.8,32.1)
27 (0,59.0)	25 (11.6,37.6)	15 (2.2,27.2)
28 (17.1,37.4)	13 (7.1,19.1)	10 (4.7,13.8)

continued on next page

TABLE 3-2 Continued

	African American (non-Latino)		
	Noncitizen Child	Citizen Child in Immigrant Family	Citizen Child in U.S.-Born Family
All Children in Group	37 (19.5,49.3)	12 (9.4,15.4)	15 (13.9,17.0)
Age			
0-2	35 (0,80.9)	19 (7.1,30.6)	15 (11.9,17.9)
3-5	29 (0,65.3)	10 (1.7,19.1)	13 (10.2,15.7)
6-11	43 (19.3,67.1)	9 (2.9,16.0)	15 (12.6,16.9)
12-17	35 (18.2,51.8)	10 (2.5,17.8)	16 (13.5,18.0)
Family Structure			
Married couple with children	34 (17.4,49.6)	6 (2.5,10.4)	15 (12.8,17.1)
Single adult with children	41 (21.7,60.5)	22 (12.4,30.8)	15 (13.2,16.2)
Family Income			
Below poverty	38 (17.3,59.6)	19 (9.2,28.7)	14 (11.7,15.4)
100-199% of poverty level	49 (26.3,71.5)	22 (10.3,33.1)	20 (17.5,22.9)
200-299% of poverty level	32 (2.1,61.7)	4 (0,8.9)	13 (10.3,16.5)
300%+ of poverty level	13 (0,35.0)	3 (0,6.9)	10 (7.8,13.0)

White (non-Latino)		
Noncitizen Child	Citizen Child in Immigrant Family	Citizen Child in U.S.-Born Family
14 (8.2,19.9)	13 (10.9,15.5)	10 (9.7,10.7)
14 (0,41.3)	13 (7.7,18.0)	11 (9.6,12.2)
2 (0,7.0)	15 (8.9,20.4)	10 (8.6,11.0)
15 (4.7,25.7)	14 (9.7,17.5)	10 (9.3,11.0)
18 (8.2,27.6)	12 (7.7,16.2)	10 (9.3,11.0)
13 (6.6,19.0)	11 (8.9,13.5)	9 (8.2,9.2)
21 (3.4,37.7)	27 (18.5,35.4)	16 (14.3,16.8)
25 (11.5,38.2)	18 (11.1,24.2)	23 (21.0,25.2)
14 (1.5,25.5)	31 (23.8,38.9)	18 (16.8,19.6)
6 (0,15.1)	12 (6.3,16.9)	9 (8.2,10.2)
8 (0,17.6)	6 (3.6,8.1)	4 (3.9,4.8)

continued on next page

TABLE 3-2 Continued

	African American (non-Latino)		
	Noncitizen Child	Citizen Child in Immigrant Family	Citizen Child in U.S.-Born Family
Family Work Status			
Full-time, full-year employee	39 (22.6,56.1)	9 (4.5,14.0)	14 (12.6,16.0)
Full-time, part-year employee	12 (0,32.8)	14 (1.8,26.0)	18 (14.0,21.3)
Part-time employee	32 (0,95.8)	25 (3.0,46.7)	18 (13.7,22.2)
Self-employed	[a]	44 (0,100)	55 (37.3,72.6)
Nonworking family	59 (29.9,88.2)	2 (1.2,22.5)	12 (9.5,13.8)
Education Status of Parent			
Less than 12 years	37 (16.7,56.9)	24 (10.9,37.5)	17 (14.5,19.5)
High school graduate	51 (26.8,75.1)	20 (9.7,31.1)	16 (14.1,18.3)
At least some college	24 (5.2,43.7)	4 (0.8,7.6)	12 (9.8,13.5)
Duration of Residence in U.S. of Parent [b]			
Pre-1970-1979	18 (0,39.9)	14 (9.6,23.2)	N.A.
1980-1983	17 (0,37.3)	31 (11.1,50.1)	N.A.
1984-1989	23 (3.1,45.3)	21 (11.9,35.8)	N.A.
1990-1996	33 (3.1,45.3)	14 (11.9,42.4)	N.A.

White (non-Latino)		
Noncitizen Child	Citizen Child in Immigrant Family	Citizen Child in U.S.-Born Family
12 (5.0,18.4)	11 (8.9,14.0)	7 (6.9,7.9)
18 (0,37.1)	11 (4.0,18.0)	16 (14.2,18.2)
7 (0,34.8)	14 (3.4,24.6)	19 (16.0,21.3)
17 (0,52.4)	40 (26.6,53.2)	30 (26.0,33.1)
21 (3.9,38.1)	9 (1.4,17.6)	16 (13.0,18.4)
24 (8.0,39.5)	22 (14.7,28.5)	23 (21.0,25.4)
13 (0,26.8)	15 (9.8,19.9)	13 (11.8,13.7)
11 (4.4,17.9)	10 (7.6,13.0)	6 (5.9,7.0)
17 (4.9,28.6)	12 (9.3,15.1)	N.A.
14 (1.4,26.5)	18 (6.8,21.9)	N.A.
21 (9.1,32.3)	17 (7.6,28.8)	N.A.
14 (11.9,18.6)	15 (5.5,19.8)	N.A.

continued on next page

TABLE 3-2 Continued

	African American (non-Latino)		
	Noncitizen Child	Citizen Child in Immigrant Family	Citizen Child in U.S.-Born Family
State of Residence in the U.S. [b]			
California	[a]	8 (0,21.5)	13 (8.8,16.2)
Florida	46 (24.5,67.3)	14 (5.9,23.0)	16 (11.4,19.6)
Illinois	[a]	54 (46.6,61.1)	14 (10.1,17.7)
New Jersey	33 (0,72.4)	12 (0,25.1)	8 (2.4,12.4)
New York	24 (7.4,40.1)	23 (15.4,31.0)	13 (8.9,16.7)
Texas	12 (10.2,14.3)	28 (18.8,36.7)	22 (17.1,26.2)
Other 44 states and District of Columbia	24 (9.3,38.7)	5 (0.9,8.5)	16 (14.2,16.7)

NOTE: Numbers in parentheses are 95% confidence intervals.

[a] Insufficient sample data to make population estimate.

[b] Estimates for these variables are an average of 1995 and 1996 CPS data.

SOURCE: March 1996 Current Population Survey.

White (non-Latino)		
Noncitizen Child	Citizen Child in Immigrant Family	Citizen Child in U.S.-Born Family
19 (9.6,28.1)	14 (9.6,18.1)	11 (9.4,12.6)
21 (2.4,40.1)	17 (8.1,25.7)	12 (10.1,14.3)
7 (0,15.5)	5 (0.4,9.1)	7 (5.1,8.3)
17 (0,35.1)	11 (4.7,17.6)	10 (6.9,11.7)
18 (5.9,28.5)	17 (11.9,21.8)	9 (6.6,9.7)
23 (0,51.0)	9 (2.4,14.7)	15 (12.7,16.8)
14 (7.5,21.1)	11 (8.4,13.6)	10 (9.7,10.6)

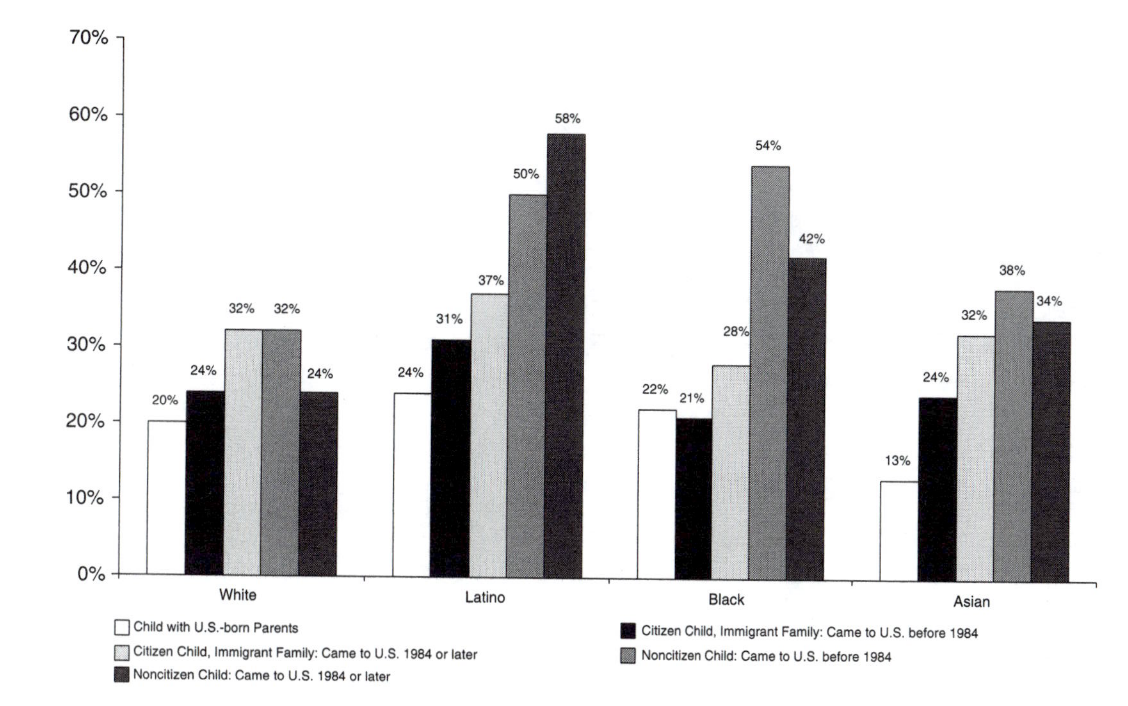

FIGURE 3-2 Predicted probabilities of uninsurance by ethnicity and immigration and citizenship status, ages 3 to 5, United States, 1995. Predicted probabilities are for a female child, 3 to 5 years old, in good to excellent health, living in a two-parent family with at least one parent employed full time for the full year, a family income of 100 to 199 percent of the federal poverty level, and one parent who is a primary worker and has not graduated from high school. SOURCE: March 1996 Current Population Survey.

based on our multivariate analysis. The figure shows how each combination of ethnicity and immigration and citizenship status affects the probability that a child with specific characteristics would be uninsured, holding constant factors other than ethnicity and immigration and citizenship status. We chose to illustrate the effect with a child who is female, 3 to 5 years old, in good to excellent health, living in a two-parent family in which at least one parent is employed full time for the full year, where the family income is between 100 and 199 percent of the federal poverty level, and where the parent who is the primary worker has not graduated from high school. The probabilities depicted in Figure 3-2 and discussed below are specific to this defined set of characteristics, but another set of characteristics would likely demonstrate similar relationships of ethnicity and immigration and citizenship status to the probability of uninsurance.

Immigration and citizenship status and ethnicity affect children's access to health insurance coverage. However, immigration and citizenship status affects the risk of uninsurance differently for different ethnic groups. Among Latinos with the defined characteristics, the probability of uninsurance is lowest for those with both parents born in the United States (24 percent; Figure 3-2 and Table 3-3). It is substantially greater among those children who are citizens but have at least one parent who is an immigrant and greater among those in this group whose parents immigrated to the United States in 1984 or later (37 percent) than for those whose families came earlier (32 percent). The probability of uninsurance is considerably greater still for noncitizen children, particularly those whose parents arrived in the United States in 1984 or later (58 percent). It is worth emphasizing that all of the children in this profile, including those whose probability of being uninsured reaches or exceeds 50 percent, are in families headed by a full-time full-year employee.

Among Asian children with the defined characteristics, the probability of uninsurance is similarly greater among those who are citizens in immigrant families than among children with U.S.-born parents, and it is greater still for noncitizen children. Citizen children with immigrant parents who arrived before 1984 have a lower probability of uninsurance than those who arrived more recently, but the relationship is reversed among noncitizen Asian

TABLE 3-3 Predicted Probabilities of Uninsurance by Ethnicity and Immigration and Citizenship Status, Ages 3 to 5, United States, 1995[a]

	White (%)	Latino (%)	Black (%)	Asian (%)
Child with U.S.-born parents	20	24	22	13
Citizen child, immigrant family				
Came to U.S. before 1984	25	32	21	24
Came to U.S. in 1984 or later	32	37	28	32
Noncitizen child				
Came to U.S. before 1984	32	50	54	38
Came to U.S. in 1984 or later	24	58	42	34

[a]Predicted probabilities are for a female child, 3 to 5 years old, in good to excellent health, living in a two-parent family, with at least one parent employed full time for the full year, a family income of 100 to 199 percent of the federal poverty level, and one parent who is a primary worker and has not graduated from high school.

SOURCE: March 1996 Current Population Survey.

children, with more recent arrivals having a lower probability of uninsurance.

For black children the effect of immigration and citizenship status on uninsurance seems more complex. Citizen children with U.S.-born parents and those with immigrant parents all seem to cluster with probabilities of being uninsured ranging from 21 to 28 percent. Noncitizen children, on the other hand, have a very high probability of uninsurance, particularly if their families came to the United States before 1984 (54 percent). Non-Latino white children with the defined characteristics follow a pattern similar to that of black children, although noncitizen white children fare better than similar children in any other ethnic group.

It is noteworthy that, even among children whose parents are U.S. born, Latino children have a greater probability of being uninsured than do non-Latino white children. Thus, even controlling for parents' educational attainment, family work status, and poverty level, Latino children in U.S.-born families are disadvantaged relative to other comparable children in other ethnic groups. Asian children of U.S.-born parents, on the other hand, have the lowest probability of being uninsured of any ethnic/immigration group.

State of Residence and Uninsurance

The state in which a child resides has a substantial effect on his or her probability of being uninsured. To illustrate how state of residence affects these probabilities, we have chosen to compare the probability of uninsurance for an Asian child and a Latino child with the same characteristics described above. In this illustration the child is a female, 3 to 5 years old, in good to excellent health, living in a two-parent family in which at least one parent is a full-time full-year employee, whose family income is 100 to 199 percent of the poverty level, and where the primary breadwinning parent has not graduated from high school.

Within each ethnic group, citizen children in immigrant families in Texas have the highest probability of being uninsured among the states examined, followed by similar children in Florida and New Jersey (see Figure 3-3 for Latinos and Asians and Table 3-4 for all ethnic groups). Children in California and New York fare somewhat better, while those in Illinois have the lowest probability of uninsurance. In each state Latino citizen children with immigrant parents have higher probabilities of being uninsured than do similar children in other ethnic groups.

Many factors contribute to these differences among the states in the probability of being uninsured. Differences among the states in their Medicaid eligibility policies may account for part of the differences in the probability of uninsurance. The federal Medicaid program mandates states to cover all pregnant women and children under age 6 up to 133 percent of the federal poverty level, reducing disparities in Medicaid income eligibility by state. However, some states, such as California, have established state-funded Medicaid eligibility for pregnant women and infants up to 200 percent of the poverty level. Some states, including California and Texas, have not yet eliminated financial asset tests for Medicaid; these asset tests exclude some very low-income persons whose assets may exceed restrictive allowable levels. In addition, states with very low income eligibility levels for Aid to Families with Dependent Children (AFDC), such as Texas and

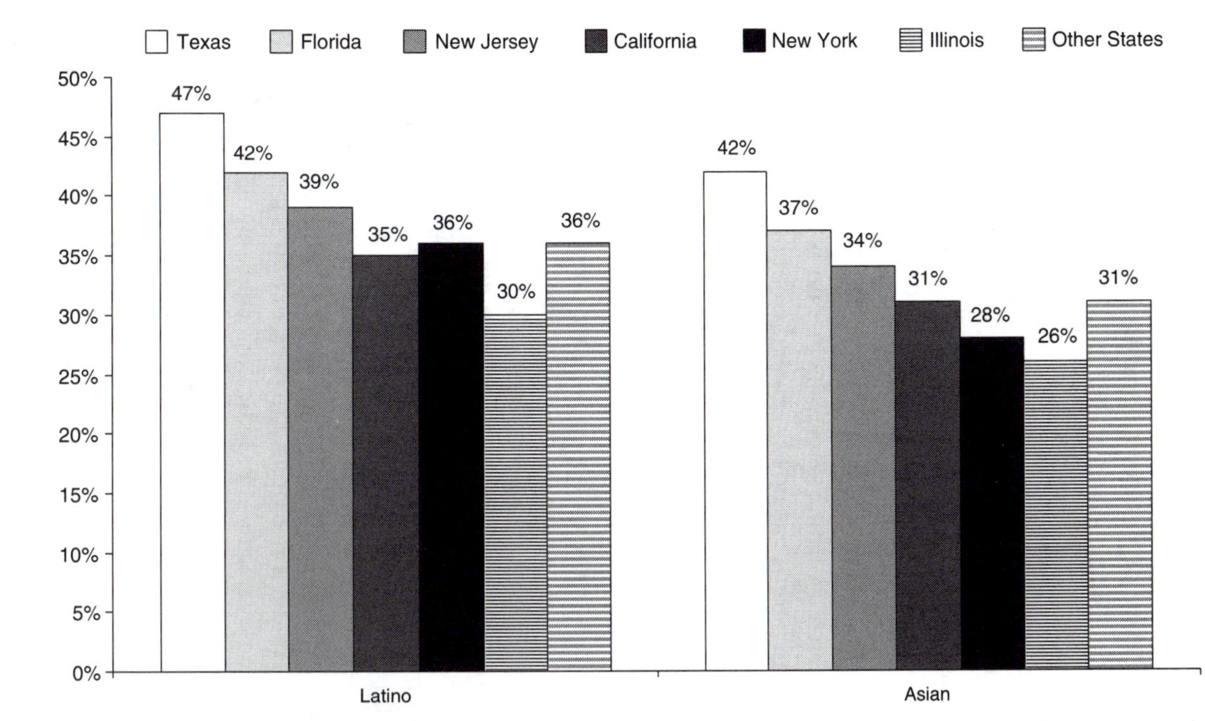

FIGURE 3-3 Predicted probabilities of uninsurance among citizen children with immigrant parents who immigrated to the United States in 1984 or later by ethnicity and state of residence, ages 3 to 5, 1995. Predicted probabilities are for a female child, 3 to 5 years old, in good to excellent health, living in a two-parent family with at least one parent employed full time for the full year, a family income of 100 to 199 percent of the federal poverty level, and one parent who is a primary worker and has not graduated from high school. SOURCE: March 1996 Current Population Survey.

TABLE 3-4 Predicted Probabilities of Uninsurance Among Citizen Children with Immigrant Parents Who Came to the United States in 1984 or Later by Ethnicity and State of Residence, Ages 3 to 5, United States, 1995[a]

State of Residence	White (%)	Latino (%)	Black (%)	Asian (%)
California	32	35	28	31
Florida	38	42	33	37
Illinois	26	30	23	26
New Jersey	35	39	31	34
New York	32	36	25	28
Texas	43	47	38	42
Rest of the U.S.	32	36	28	31

[a] Predicted probabilities for a female child, 3 to 5 years old, in good to excellent health, living in a two-parent family, with at least one parent employed full time for the full year, a family income of 100 to 199 percent of the federal poverty level, and one parent who is a primary worker and has not graduated from high school.

SOURCE: March 1996 Current Population Survey.

Florida, indirectly reduce Medicaid eligibility because AFDC conveys automatic Medicaid enrollment, which provides coverage to many children who otherwise would not be enrolled. Finally, some states, including Illinois, New York, and Texas, have short Medicaid application forms, reducing the burden on parents associated with the more typical long-form applications (Donna C. Ross, Center on Budget and Policy Priorities, personal communication, 1997). These are provisions that affect all children in a state—those in immigrant families as well as those with native-born parents—but each state may include a combination of policies that tend to increase Medicaid coverage and others that tend to reduce it. And they appear to result in differential proportions of low-income children covered by Medicaid. The proportion of all children below 150 percent of poverty who were covered by Medicaid varied from 75 percent in Illinois to 71 percent in New York to 65 percent in New Jersey and California to 58 percent in Texas and 59 percent in Florida (Kaiser Family Foundation, 1997).

Immigrant children may be particularly affected by two other policies that vary from state to state. Fear of being labeled a "public charge" may discourage immigrant parents from enrolling their children in Medicaid, fearing that this stigma may be used against them in any future immigration proceedings. Federal implementation of the prohibition against noncitizens being a "public charge" varies from one jurisdiction to another, including from state to state. A state policy that may facilitate extending coverage to children in immigrant families, as well as other children, is the establishment of state-funded non-Medicaid children's health insurance programs. New York and Florida have substantial non-Medicaid programs that provide health insurance to children, covering immigrant children who are not eligible for Medicaid as well as those who are eligible.

In addition to differences in Medicaid eligibility and enrollment, states differ in other factors that may contribute to differences in uninsured rates. These factors include the percentages of the working-age population who are unemployed, underemployed, or working in sectors of the economy that typically provide health benefits to relatively few workers (e.g., retail, service, agriculture, construction) and the percentage of the population with family incomes below the poverty line or who are near poor. Unemployment, for example, varied considerably among the states, with California having the highest annual rate (7.8 percent) in 1995; New York, New Jersey, and Texas had intermediate rates (ranging from 6.0 to 6.4 percent); and Florida and Illinois had the lowest rates (5.5 and 5.0 percent, respectively; see U.S. Bureau of Labor Statistics, 1997). The rankings of states by unemployment rate are not consistent with the rankings by probability of uninsurance, suggesting that a state's unemployment rate may have only a weak relationship with its probability of uninsurance.

All of these factors may contribute to differences among the states in the probability of uninsurance in ways that are not specifically measured in this study. Although we cannot quantify the effects of each policy, we believe that the combination of state-level Medicaid and other policies contributes to differences among the states in rates of uninsured children.

Country of Origin and Uninsurance

The differences in risk of uninsurance vary considerably by the country or region from which a child and/or immigrant parents emigrated (see Table 3-5). Approximately half of noncitizen children who were born in Cuba, Mexico, or Central America are uninsured, compared to substantially lower rates for those from other countries, perhaps reflecting the generally low educational attainment of their parents, which tends to restrict employment to jobs without health benefits. Noncitizen children from Hong Kong, Japan, Singapore, Taiwan, Europe, China, the Philippines, Malaysia, and Indonesia all rank lower in their rates of uninsurance than those from Latin American countries; for most of the children in more advantaged families, their lower uninsurance rates reflect higher rates of employment-based health insurance, which typically accrues to workers with higher levels of educational attainment. Noncitizen children from Cambodia, Laos, and Vietnam rank lowest in uninsured rates (9 percent), reflecting very high rates of Medicaid coverage (64 percent), rather than employment-based health insurance (24 percent).

Among citizen children in immigrant families, rates of uninsurance do not reach the same levels as among noncitizen children. Citizen children whose primary working parent was born in Mexico, Central America, India, Afghanistan, Bangladesh, or Pakistan have elevated rates of uninsurance (ranging from 25 to 32 percent), but those whose parents are from Korea have the highest uninsurance rate (42 percent). Controlling for immigration and citizenship status and year in which the primary working parent immigrated to the United States, as well as other predictors of insurance coverage, children whose families are from Korea are substantially more likely to be uninsured than are those with U.S.-born parents (see Table 3-6). Central American-origin children also fare more poorly compared with children with U.S.-born parents.

However, children whose families are from Cambodia, Laos, or Vietnam have a much lower risk of being uninsured than do children with U.S.-born parents. These children have a low risk of uninsurance despite the low educational attainment of their

TABLE 3-5 Percentage of Children Uninsured Among Noncitizen Children and Citizen Children in Immigrant Families by Country or Region of Origin, Ages 0 to 17, United States, 1994 and 1995 (average)

Country or Region of Origin[a]	Noncitizen Children		Citizen Children in Immigrant Families	
	% Uninsured	Total Number of Children in Population Group[b]	% Uninsured	Total Number of Children in Population Group[b]
Central America	55	153,000	32	682,000
Cuba	51	30,000	17	186,000
Mexico	48	843,000	29	3,194,000
South America	39	100,000	17	372,000
Caribbean	30	139,000	18	434,000
Africa	30	50,000	2	184,000
Cambodia, Laos, and Vietnam	9	232,000	13	473,000
China	27	53,000	16	216,000
Hong Kong, Japan, Singapore, and Taiwan	16	56,000	9	123,000
India, Afghanistan, Bangladesh, and Pakistan	39	106,000	25	327,000
Korea	38	50,000	42	135,000
Philippines, Malaysia, and Indonesia	25	78,000	7	382,000
Thailand and Burma	[c]	6,000	[c]	6,000
Canada	[c]	14,000	8	170,000
Europe	20	225,000	14	676,000

[a] Nativity of child for noncitizen children and nativity of primary working parent for citizen children in immigrant families.

[b] Total population sizes from the March 1996 Current Population Survey.

[c] Indicates sample size insufficient to make reliable estimates.

SOURCE: March 1995 and 1996 Current Population Surveys.

TABLE 3-6 Effect of Socioeconomic Factors, Immigration and Citizenship Status, Ethnicity, and Country of Origin on Uninsurance for Children, Ages 0 to 17, United States, 1995

Country or Region of Origin	Odds Ratio	95% Confidence Interval for Odds Ratio
Central America	1.69	1.11,2.59
Cuba	1.12	0.61,2.06
Mexico	1.19	0.81,1.76
South America	.98	0.61,1.59
Caribbean	1.50	0.79,2.88
Africa	.57	0.24,1.38
Cambodia, Laos, and Vietnam	0.27	0.14,0.52
China	1.02	0.50,2.08
Hong Kong, Singapore, Taiwan, and Japan	0.44	0.18,1.08
India, Afghanistan, Bangladesh, and Pakistan	1.28	0.71,2.31
Korea	3.40	1.65,6.98
Philippines, Malaysia, and Indonesia	.65	0.33,1.30
Thailand and Burma	2.21	0.45,10.85
Canada	1.33	0.76,2.34
Europe	0.79	0.52,1.18

NOTE: Model controls for age, gender, health status, family structure, family work status, family income, educational attainment of primary working parent, ethnicity, immigration and citizenship status, and year immigrated to the United States.

SOURCE: March 1996 Current Population Survey.

working parents (53 percent of whom have less than a high school education), low participation in the labor force (40 percent are in nonworking families), and high rates of poverty (48 percent have family incomes below the poverty line). Medicaid protects these children because federal law provides generous eligibility provisions for very low-income refugee and asylee families, although refugees and asylees who immigrated after enactment of the 1996 welfare reform legislation will be eligible for Medicaid only during their first five years in the United States.

Summary

Clearly, being a noncitizen or having immigrant parents increases a child's risk of being uninsured. Immigration and citizenship status of both the child and the primary breadwinning parent (i.e., the parent whose main activity determines the family's work status) have a substantial independent effect on children's risk of uninsurance, even controlling for the parent's educational attainment and even if the parent has resided in the United States for longer than 10 years, as well as core determinants of uninsurance (such as family work status and family income).

In general, noncitizen children have the greatest risk of being uninsured. Noncitizen Latino and Asian children, regardless of when their families immigrated to the United States, have a greater probability of being uninsured compared with similar children who were born in the United States and compared with white children with U.S.-born parents. Black and white noncitizen children's excess risk appears to be related to when their families immigrated, with those who immigrated before 1984 faring worse than those whose families immigrated later.

U.S. citizen children with immigrant parents also tend to be at greater risk of uninsurance compared to those with U.S.-born parents. Moreover, citizen children in immigrant families have a greater risk of being uninsured if their families immigrated to the United States in 1984 or later than if they immigrated earlier than 1984. Even after controlling for immigration and citizenship status, year in which parents immigrated, and important predictors of health insurance coverage, Korean- and Central American-origin children are more likely to be uninsured, for reasons that are not immediately clear.

Medicaid can offer protection to immigrant families, thereby reducing the risks of uninsurance. Southeast Asian immigrant children and their families have very low rates of uninsurance despite their very low socioeconomic status because their refugee and asylee status opens the door to relatively generous Medicaid eligibility provisions. The importance of Medicaid eligibility policies and other state health insurance policies is also suggested by the differences among the U.S. states of residence, although quantifying the effects of specific policies is beyond the scope of this paper. Public policy can play an important role in protecting children from being uninsured.

EFFECTS OF IMMIGRATION STATUS ON ACCESS TO CARE

Are children who are immigrants disadvantaged in their access to health care services compared to U.S.-born children in native-born families? Are U.S.-born children in immigrant families disadvantaged compared to those whose parents were born in the United States? To answer these questions, we compared the health care access and use of physician services of children who are immigrants, nonimmigrant children in families with one or more immigrant parents, and nonimmigrant children with U.S.-born parents. We used data on children and their families from the 1994 NHIS.

Variables Used in Analysis of Reasons for Uninsurance, Health Care Access, and Use of Health Care Services

The NHIS includes information that is not available in the CPS, including measures of health status, reasons for uninsurance, usual source of care, and use of health care services. In addition, some variables in the CPS are not available in the NHIS. As with the analyses of health insurance coverage, we structured several independent variables to characterize the families as well as the children.

Outcome Variables

Physician Visits. The number of physician visits during the past 12 months was obtained for all children. We examined the probability of at least one physician visit during the past year for all children, newborn through age 17. The American Academy of Pediatrics recommends annual visits for children and adolescents ages 24 months through age 17 (except for children ages 7 and 9) and more frequent visits for children under 24 months of age (American Academy of Pediatrics, 1995). Thus, our criterion of at least one physician visit during the past year provides a reasonable measure of the academy's recommendation for children over the age of 24 months and is a conservative estimate for children under this age.

Usual Person or Source of Care. Information was obtained on whether or not the child has a usual person or place for medical care. Having a usual source of care has been demonstrated to be a robust measure of access to health care services. We thus used usual source of care as an outcome variable in descriptive analyses but also as a predictor in all analyses of use of physician services.

Independent Variables

Immigrant Status. We classified children into three immigrant groups based on the immigrant status of the child and for U.S.-born children the immigrant status of the parents: (1) immigrant child—that is, a child not born in the United States; (2) U.S.-born child of immigrant parents—that is, a child born in the United States who has at least one immigrant parent; and (3) nonimmigrant child—that is, a U.S.-born child with U.S.-born parents (or, in a single-parent family, a parent who is U.S. born). Children not born in the United States to U.S.-born parents were classified as nonimmigrant children. The NHIS does not include any questions about citizenship status.

Educational Status. The educational attainment of the mother was used to characterize a family's educational status because a mother's educational attainment has been shown to be related to health care use. In single-father families the father's educational level was used.

Health Status. Two measures of health status were used to measure the health of the child. General health status was defined as "good to excellent health" or "fair or poor health." Children were also classified as having any limitation (unable to perform a major activity, limited in kind/amount of activity, limited in other activity) or as not having any limitations.

Reason for Lack of Coverage. We included information on why an uninsured child has no health insurance coverage.

Main Reasons for Lack of Coverage Among Children

The main reason reported (by adult respondents) for children's lack of coverage is the same regardless of immigrant status: health insurance coverage is unaffordable (see Table 3-7). Within each ethnic group, lack of affordability was the dominant reason for lack of coverage. The dominant role that affordability plays in limiting coverage highlights the need for improving the affordability of coverage through contributions from employers and/or public programs. The second most frequently cited reason for lack of coverage is related to employers not offering coverage—that is, the employer does not offer coverage at all, does not offer family coverage, or does not offer coverage to part-time employees. Job layoff or unemployment of the parent accounted for an additional, yet small, percentage of the reason for lack of coverage.

Beliefs about coverage—that it is not needed, dissatisfaction with coverage, or lack of belief in health insurance—account for an additional 5 percent of children overall, with some differences by ethnicity and immigrant status. The availability of free services or other options to obtain care explains only a small portion of uninsured children's lack of coverage. Thus, a perceived lack of need for coverage—either because of beliefs or other options for care—is not an important reason for lack of coverage for any of the immigrant groups.

Usual Person/Place of Care

Children not born in the United States are more likely to lack a usual person or place for health care (28 percent) than either U.S.-born children with immigrant parents (8 percent) or nonimmigrant children (5 percent; see Table 3-8). This large proportion of foreign-born children who lack a usual source of care is seen in each ethnic group. Latino immigrants in particular have high rates, with over one-third (36 percent) lacking a usual source of care.

TABLE 3-7 Main Reasons for Lack of Coverage Among Uninsured Children by Immigration and Ethnicity, Ages 0 to 17, United States, 1994

	Latino		
	Immigrant Child (%)	Child U.S.-Born, Immigrant Parents (%)	Child and Parents U.S. Born (%)
Too expensive	72	71	79
Employer does not offer or worker not eligible	13	12	9
Beliefs about coverage	3	5	1
Other options	4	3	1
Job layoff or unemployed	1	3	3
Other reasons	7	6	7
	Black		
Too expensive	[a]	[a]	71
Employer does not offer or worker not eligible	[a]	[a]	9
Beliefs about coverage	[a]	[a]	3
Other options	[a]	[a]	4
Job layoff or unemployed	[a]	[a]	4
Other reasons	[a]	[a]	9

[a] Sample size too small to make a reliable estimate.

SOURCE: 1994 National Health Interview Survey.

Asian		
Immigrant Child (%)	Child U.S.-Born, Immigrant Parents (%)	Child and Parents U.S. Born (%)
64	75	[a]
13	5	[a]
7	<1	[a]
< 1	<1	[a]
9	3	[a]
7	17	[a]
White		
68	74	76
10	9	5
12	11	5
1	3	<1
<1	2	4
9	<1	9

TABLE 3-8 Percentage of Children with No Usual Person or Place for Medical Care and Percentage Who Did Not Have a Physician Visit During the Past Year, by Immigration Status and Ethnicity, Ages 0 to 17, United States, 1994

	All Children		
Main Reason for Lack of Health Insurance Coverage	Immigrant Child (%)	Child U.S.-Born, Immigrant Parents (%)	Child and Parents U.S. Born (%)
No Usual Source of Care	28 (25,32)	8 (6,9)	5 (5,6)
Did Not Have a Physician Visit During Past Year			
All ages (0-17)	32 (28,36)	18 (16,19)	18 (17,19)
Ages 0-2	8 (0,19)	6 (4,8)	5 (4,6)
Ages 3-5	16 (7,24)	10 (8,13)	10 (9,12)
Ages 6-17	35 (31,40)	26 (123,28)	23 (23,24)

Immigrant children are less likely to have a usual source of care than nonimmigrant children regardless of their health insurance status—whether uninsured, on Medicaid, or with private/other coverage (data not shown). However, uninsured immigrant children are less likely to have a connection to the health care system (51 percent lack a usual source of care) than those with Medicaid or private/other coverage. Uninsurance increases the risk of not having a usual person/place for medical care for U.S.-born children of immigrant parents and for nonimmigrant as well as immigrant children.

The two main reasons identified for being without a usual source of care were the same for each ethnic group: lack of per-

Latino			Asian		
Immigrant Child (%)	Child U.S.-Born, Immigrant Parents (%)	Child and Parents U.S. Born (%)	Immigrant Child (%)	Child U.S.-Born, Immigrant Parents (%)	Child and Parents U.S. Born (%)
36 (30,42)	12 (10,14)	7 (6,9)	26 (19,33)	6 (3,8)	[a]
39 (33,45)	20 (17,23)	17 (15,20)	34 (26,43)	20 (16,24)	17 (8,26)
[a]	7 (4,11)	3 (1,6)	[a]	5 (0,11)	[a]
19 (4,34)	11 (6,15)	9 (5,13)	8 (0,43)	13 (6,21)	[a]
42 (35,49)	30 (26,34)	25 (22,29)	39 (130,48)	28 (22,34)	25 (12,38)

continued on next page

ceived need for or trust in doctors and lack of affordable care, including being uninsured. Relocation or lack of availability of a previous doctor and difficulty finding care also were identified but by a smaller proportion of respondents (see Table 3-9). The relative importance of these factors did vary, however, by immigrant group. Cost barriers were more important for children not born in the United States and U.S.-born children of immigrants than for nonimmigrant children. In contrast, the relocation of a previous physician was more important for nonimmigrant children.

Among children with a usual source of care, the physician

TABLE 3-8 Continued

Main Reason for Lack of Health Insurance Coverage	Black		
	Immigrant Child (%)	Child U.S.-Born, Immigrant Parents (%)	Child and Parents U.S. Born (%)
No Usual Source of Care	19 (8,31)	5 (2,9)	7 (6,8)
Did Not Have a Physician Visit During Past Year			
All ages (0-17)	19 (8,30)	14 (8,19)	23 (21,24)
Ages 0-2	*a*	9 (0,18)	8 (5,11)
Ages 3-5	*a*	10 (0,20)	12 (9,15)
Ages 6 -17	21 (9,33)	18 (10,27)	29 (27,32)

[a]Sample size too small to make a reliable estimate.

SOURCE: 1994 National Health Interview Survey.

office or private clinic is the most frequently reported site of care across immigrant groups (see Table 3-10). It is, however, more common for nonimmigrant children to use private offices than it is for immigrant children and U.S.-born children with immigrant parents. For children, having access to a health care provider is critical for reasons beyond acute care needs. Children need a regular connection for well-baby/child checkups, preventive care, and developmental assessments.

White		
Immigrant Child (%)	Child U.S.-Born, Immigrant Parents (%)	Child and Parents U.S. Born (%)
23 (17, 29)	5 (3, 6)	5 (4, 5)
27 (21,33)	16 (13,18)	17 (16, 18)
7 (0,25)	4 (1,8)	4 (3,5)
19 (4,34)	9 (5,13)	10 (9,12)
29 (22,36)	22 (19,26)	22 (21, 23)

Use of Health Care Services

Immigrant children are less likely than either children of immigrants or children with U.S.-born parents to have had a doctor visit during the past year (see Table 3-8). One-third (32 percent) of immigrant children did not have a doctor visit during the past 12 months. These lower rates for immigrant children are seen for Latinos, Asians, and whites but not for blacks. Comparisons by age show that children 6 to 17 years old across all immigrant groups are less likely than younger children to have had a physi-

TABLE 3-9 Reasons for No Usual Source of Care by Immigration Status Among Children with No Usual Source of Care, Ages 0 to 17, United States, 1994

	Immigrant Child (%)	Child of Immigrant Parents (%)	Nonimmigrant Child (%)
Don't need or like doctors	45	39	40
Can't afford, no insurance	40	40	24
Previous doctor not available/moved	4	8	17
Hard to find care	2	2	6
Speaks different language	< 1	< 1	< 1
Other	9	10	12

SOURCE: 1994 National Health Interview Survey.

TABLE 3-10 Type of Usual Source of Care by Immigration Status Among Children with a Usual Source of Care, Ages 0 to 17, United States, 1994

	Immigrant Child	Child of Immigrant Parents	Nonimmigrant Child
Doctor's office/private clinic	63	68	84
County/public clinic	9	7	4
Community/migrant clinic	6	3	3
Health maintenance organization/prepaid group	10	8	5
Emergency room	< 1	< 1	< 1
Other	11	13	5

SOURCE: 1994 National Health Interview Survey.

cian visit during the past year. These lower rates are more pronounced for immigrant children. The large proportion of children, especially immigrant children, who lack adequate contact with the health care system is a cause for concern, given the age-specific needs for well-child checkups and immunizations.

Uninsured children are less likely to have had a doctor visit during the past year than children with coverage. Among immigrant children, 43 percent of those without coverage did not have a recent doctor visit, compared to 28 percent of those with private/other coverage and 16 percent of their counterparts with Medicaid (data not shown in table). The comparative advantage of children with private/other coverage over uninsured children demonstrates the financial access that insurance coverage provides. The relative disadvantage of children with private/other coverage compared to Medicaid may be due to the financial barriers imposed on low-income populations by deductibles and copayments—prevalent with private insurance and absent or minimal with Medicaid. U.S.-born children of immigrants and nonimmigrant children also are disadvantaged by lack of coverage; those without coverage are twice as likely as those with Medicaid or private/other coverage to have not had a doctor visit during the past year.

Immigration, Ethnicity, Usual Source of Care, and Doctor Visits

To understand the factors that influence access to physician use, we conducted multivariate regression analyses. The models were tested for interactions among key analysis variables by examining the independent effects of these variables on children receiving at least one physician visit. When an interaction was suspected, based on observed changes in the direction of the coefficient, the presence of an interaction was tested. The models for physician visits account for the interactions found between poverty and immigration status and education and immigration status. We illustrate the effects of insurance status and having a usual source of care on receipt of physician visits by children with the following characteristics, held constant across different ethnic groups: U.S.-born child with at least one immigrant parent; child is female, 3 to 5 years old, in good to excellent health, with no activity limitations; living in a family of four with family income between 100 and 199 percent of poverty; and whose mother did not graduate from high school.

The presence or absence of health insurance and a usual source of care have a consistent and strong effect on the probability of having a doctor visit. Across all ethnic groups, children with the defined characteristics who have Medicaid coverage and a usual source of care have a higher probability of receiving a doctor visit compared with similar children who have Medicaid coverage but no usual source of care, those who are uninsured but have a usual source of care, and particularly those who are both uninsured and have no usual source of care (see Table 3-11 and Figure 3-4).

The difference between the conditions with the highest and lowest probabilities of physician visits within each ethnic group are dramatic. Among U.S.-born Asian children in immigrant families—the ethnic group that is most disadvantaged in access

TABLE 3-11 Predicted Probabilities of at Least One Physician Visit During Past Year Among U.S.-Born Children with Immigrant Parents by Ethnicity, Ages 3 to 5, United States,1994[a]

	Uninsured		Medicaid	
	No Usual Source of Care (%)	Has Usual Source of Care (%)	No Usual Source of Care (%)	Has Usual Source of Care (%)
Latino	63	83	81	92
Asian	51	76	72	88
Black	75	90	88	96
White	78	91	89	96

[a]U.S.-born child with at least one immigrant parent; child is female, 3 to 5 years old, in good to excellent health with no activity limitations, living in a family of four with family income of 100 to 199 percent of poverty level, and whose mother did not graduate from high school.

SOURCE: 1994 National Health Interview Survey.

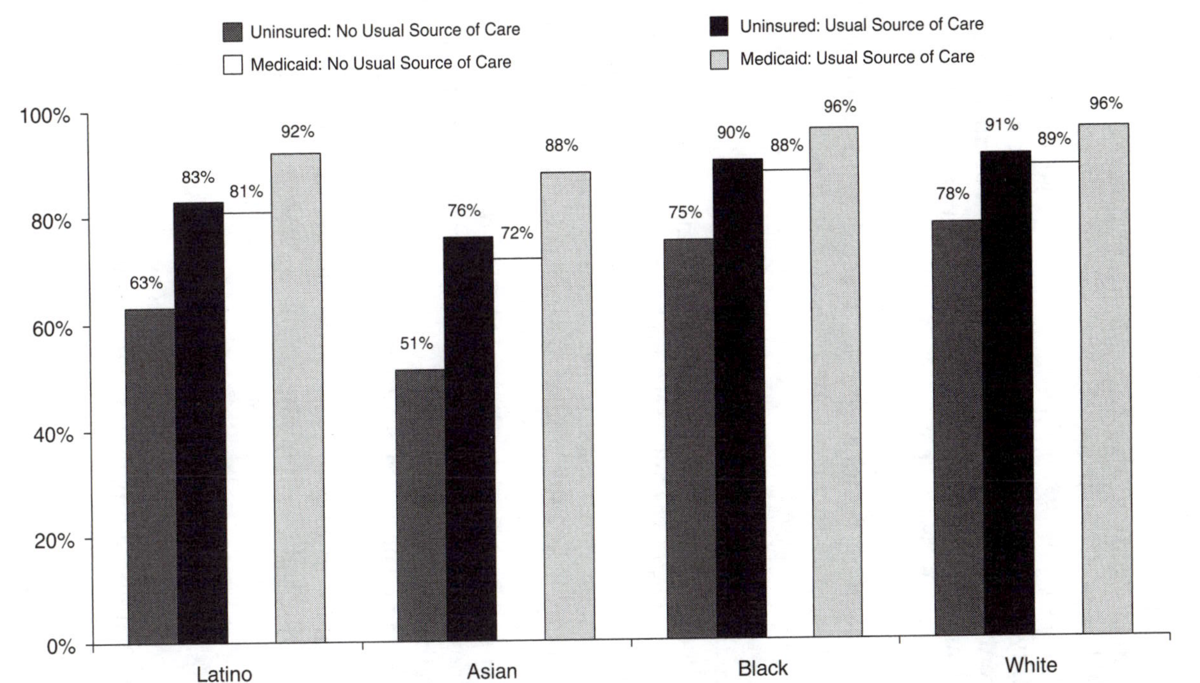

FIGURE 3-4 Predicted probabilities of having at least one physician visit during the past year among U.S.-born children with immigrant parents by ethnicity and other selected characteristics, ages 3 to 5, 1994. Predicted probabilities are for a female child, 3 to 5 years old, in good to excellent health, living in a two-parent family with at least one parent employed full time for the full year, a family income of 100 to 199 percent of the federal poverty level, and one parent who has not graduated from high school.
SOURCE: March 1994 National Health Interview Survey.

to doctor visits—those who are both uninsured and have no usual source of care have a 51 percent probability of receiving at least one physician visit in a year, compared with an 88 percent probability for similar children who have Medicaid coverage and a usual source of care. Uninsured U.S.-born Latino children in immigrant families who have no usual source of care have a 63 percent probability of at least one physician visit annually, compared with 92 percent for those who have Medicaid and a usual source of care. Black and white U.S.-born children in immigrant families demonstrate similar benefits of having both Medicaid and a regular source of care. The strong effect of usual source of care on the probability of having a doctor visit is unaffected by the type of source a child has—whether a private physician's office, a school or community clinic, a county hospital or clinic, or even a hospital emergency room (data not shown in table).

These predicted probabilities underscore the importance of having both health insurance coverage and a regular connection to the health care system. Children who have a usual source of care have even higher probabilities of receiving at least one physician visit, even if they are uninsured. Uninsured children with a usual source of care have rates similar to Medicaid children without a usual source. The combination of both Medicaid coverage and having a regular source of care provides the best opportunities for children to meet the recommended minimum number of contacts with the health care system.

We also examined access to health care for U.S.-born children in immigrant families in the six states with the largest immigrant populations (California, Texas, New York, Florida, Illinois, and New Jersey. To illustrate this relationship at the state level and to demonstrate the differences across states, we developed predicted probabilities of at least one physician visit for a U.S.-born child with at least one immigrant parent with the specified characteristics: Latino, female, 3 to 5 years old, good to excellent health and no activity limitations, family of four, family income between 100 and 199 percent of poverty, and mother who did not graduate from high school.

Within each of these six states, children were less likely to have received at least one physician visit if they were uninsured and lacked a usual source of care (see Figure 3-5). Moreover, dif-

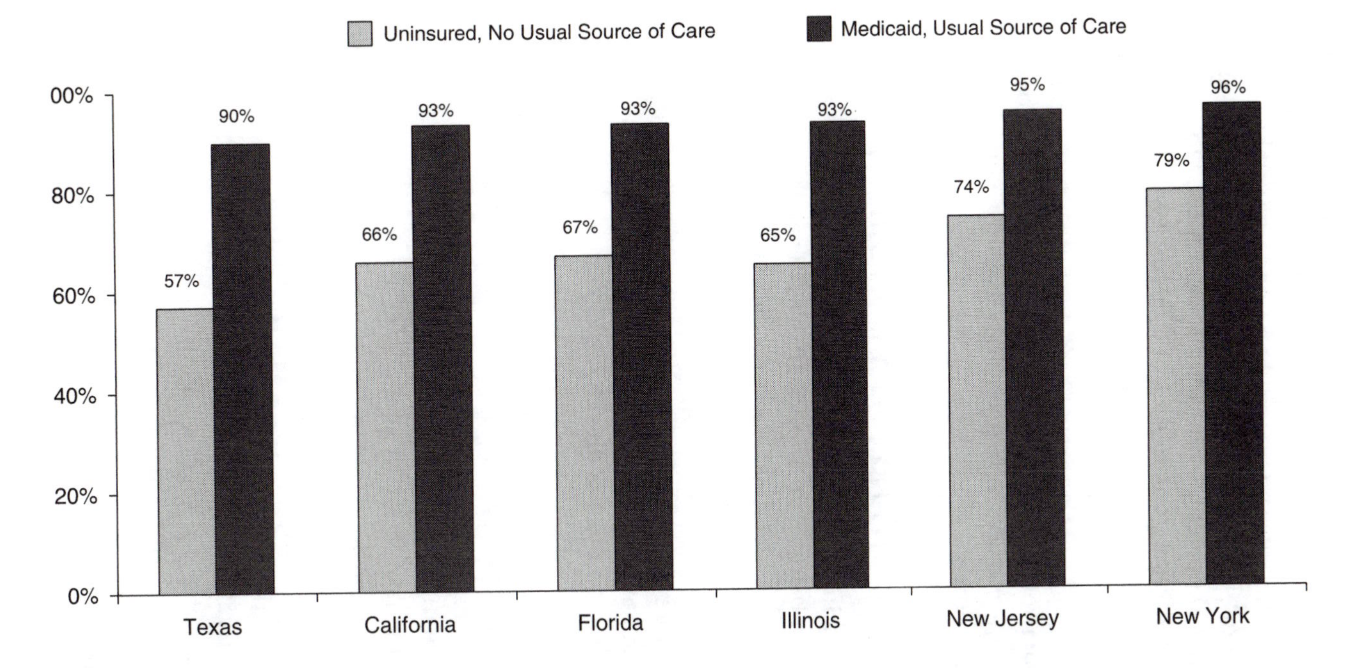

FIGURE 3-5 Predicted probabilities of having at least one physician visit during the past year among U.S.-born Latino children with immigrant parents by state of residence and other selected characteristics, ages 3 to 5, selected states, 1994. Predicted probabilities are for a female child, 3 to 5 years old, in good to excellent health, living in a two-parent family with at least one parent employed full time for the full year, a family income of 100 to 199 percent of the federal poverty level, and mother who has not graduated from high school. SOURCE: 1994 National Health Interview Survey.

ferences were found among the states. U.S.-born Latino children with immigrant parents in Texas had a much lower probability of a doctor visit if they were uninsured and had no usual source of care (57 percent) than if they had both Medicaid and a usual source of care (90 percent). Children in California, Florida, and Illinois all had similar probabilities of a doctor visit if they were uninsured and without a regular source (65 to 67 percent) and if they were covered by Medicaid and had a regular source (93 percent). Children in New Jersey and New York fared better still: 74 and 79 percent probability, respectively, if uninsured and no regular source of care and a 95 to 96 percent probability if on Medicaid with a regular source.

DISCUSSION AND POLICY IMPLICATIONS

Being a noncitizen or having immigrant parents puts a child at greater risk of being uninsured than are citizen children in native-born families. This risk is substantial even controlling for parents' education and the duration of parents' residence in the United States, as well as core determinants of uninsurance. The risk is greatest for noncitizen children, regardless of ethnicity. U.S. citizen children with immigrant parents also bear a greater risk of uninsurance than do those with U.S.-born parents.

If the primary working parent has lived in the United States for more than 10 years, the probability of uninsurance appears to be reduced, lending some support to arguments that the longer immigrants reside here the more similar they become to the native-born population. But having parents who have resided in this country for more than 10 years does not appear to protect noncitizen white, black, or Asian children. This suggests either that they face barriers to obtaining health insurance beyond those experienced by the native-born population or those who have become citizens, or that public policy or other factors intervene for more recent arrivals to decrease their risks of uninsurance.

Uninsured rates are higher among children in immigrant families from Korea and Central America than for those from other regions. Policies that extend Medicaid to refugees seem to protect children in immigrant families from Southeast Asia (specifically Vietnam, Cambodia, and Laos) from even the native-born population's risk of uninsurance. State Medicaid policies also seem to have a substantial effect on uninsurance among children across all ethnic, immigration, and citizenship groups.

Irrespective of ethnicity or immigration status, the unaffordability of health insurance coverage is the main reason for being uninsured. The combination of unaffordability and job-related reasons for uninsurance (e.g., employer does not offer it, job layoff, unemployment) underscores the weaknesses in this country's voluntary patchwork system of financing health insurance coverage. These problems particularly affect immigrants who come to the United States without the educational attainment needed to obtain jobs that could enable them and their families to live well above the poverty line. Children in immigrant families from Central America or some Asian countries experience greater risks of lack of insurance coverage. These risks seem not to be explained by educational attainment or living longer in the United States, suggesting that other barriers play an important role. It is noteworthy that Latino children, regardless of their own or their family's immigration and citizenship status, are at greater risk of uninsurance, even controlling for educational attainment, family work status, and family income. We should underscore the findings of this study that, even when immigrant parents work full time for the full year as employees, their children are more likely to be uninsured than are children in nonimmigrant families—and for some groups these increased risks are substantial.

Immigrant children and, to a lesser extent, U.S.-born children with immigrant parents are more likely to experience problems accessing health care services than are nonimmigrant children. Immigrant children are less likely to have a usual provider or source of care than are nonimmigrant children. This was seen for each ethnic group examined—Asian, black, Latino, and white. Also, U.S.-born Latino children with immigrant parents are less likely to have a usual provider or source of care. A usual provider or source of care is an important link to the health care system and is especially critical for children because they require ongoing preventive care and monitoring of their growth and emotional and social development. Even though health insurance coverage is an important determinant of having a usual source of care, it alone does not provide this important link. Other factors, such as culturally and geographically accessible services, are required.

Immigrant children overall are less likely than nonimmigrant children to have had even one physician visit in the past year. Asian children in immigrant families experience the lowest probability of a physician visit of any ethnic group, followed by Latino children in immigrant families. Having a usual source of care and health insurance coverage greatly reduces the disadvantage, but Asian children remain less likely to have had the recommended number of physician visits even after accounting for these factors.

Thus, even controlling for educational attainment and duration of residence in the United States, as well as for age, gender, family work status, and family income, substantial disparities in uninsurance remain between noncitizen immigrant children and citizen children with native-born parents. Citizen children with immigrant parents experience less risk, particularly if their primary working parent has lived in this country for at least 10 years. Citizenship appears to reduce but not eliminate children's risk of being uninsured. Similar disparities are found between immigrant and nonimmigrant children in access to health care services, although we could not include any measures of citizenship in our analysis because none are available in the NHIS. (The absence of adequate information on countries of origin and any information on citizenship status in the NHIS is a severe limitation for policy research on immigration.)

The findings of this study underscore the importance of policies that extend health insurance coverage and improve the availability and accessibility of health care services to immigrant and nonimmigrant populations—policies that reduce the obstacles to immigrant children obtaining health care. Simply living longer in the United States or getting more education will not, by themselves, remove disparities in health insurance coverage or access to services.

A variety of public policies have been established to reduce barriers to health insurance coverage and health care services. Legal immigrants were entitled to Medicaid when these surveys were conducted, and two states—New York and Florida—operated state-funded non-Medicaid health insurance programs for children. In addition, federal, state, and local governments have helped to support community and migrant health centers to meet the needs of low-income communities, including those with large concentrations of immigrants. These efforts to improve access were adopted because of widespread beliefs that good access to health care promotes educational achievement and economic opportunity for children and their families. Our study demonstrates the importance of programs and policies for assuring health insurance coverage and access to health care services for immigrant children. It will be important to study the relative effectiveness of Medicaid compared with state-funded non-Medicaid programs to assure health insurance coverage for children in immigrant families and to study the contributions of a variety of programs designed to enhance access to health care services.

Recent policy changes, however, are likely to weaken these existing public policies that ameliorate structural barriers to access in the health care system. The Personal Responsibility and Work Opportunity Reconciliation Act of 1996 terminated Medicaid eligibility for most new legal immigrants and, at state option, for legal immigrants who resided in the United States when the legislation was enacted on August 22, 1996. U.S. citizen children in immigrant families will continue to be eligible for Medicaid, and children who are noncitizen legal immigrants already residing in this country when the legislation was enacted will not lose their Medicaid entitlement if their states opt to continue to cover them. But children who immigrate legally to the United States after August 22, 1996, will not be eligible for nonemergency Medicaid unless their families are refugees or asylees (and then for only five years).

These policy changes thus may increase uninsurance among immigrant children. The effects of these policies may be at least partially offset by the State Children's Health Insurance Program, created by the federal Balanced Budget Act of 1997, if states make noncitizen children eligible for these programs. Uninsured low-income immigrant children and nonimmigrant children in immigrant families may experience further reductions in their access to health care services if funds are reduced for community health centers and other programs that finance services for low-income persons. These changes are likely to have a cumulative adverse effect on the health of immigrant children and even U.S. citizen children in immigrant families.

REFERENCES

Aday, L.A., C.E. Begley, D.R. Lairson, and C.H. Slater
1993 *Evaluating the Health Care System: Effectiveness, Efficiency and Equity*. Ann Arbor, Mich: Health Administration Press.

American Academy of Pediatrics
1995 Recommendations for preventive pediatric health care. *Pediatrics* 96(2):712.

Andersen, R.M., and P.L. Davidson
1996 Measuring access and trends. Pp. 13-40 in *Changing the U.S. Health Care System*. San Francisco: Jossey-Bass.

Bean, F.D., J. Chapa, R.R. Berg, and K.A. Sowards
1994 Educational and sociodemographic incorporation among Hispanic immigrants to the United States. Pp. 73-100 in *Immigration and Ethnicity: The Integration of America's Newest Arrivals*, B. Edmonston and J. Passel, eds. Washington, D.C.: The Urban Institute Press.

Berk, M.L., C.L. Schur, and J.C. Cantor
1995 Ability to obtain health care: Recent estimates from the Robert Wood Johnson Foundation National Access to Care Survey. *Health Affairs* 14(3):139-146.

Board on Children and Families
1995 Immigrant children and their families: Issues for research and policy. *The Future of Children: Critical Issues for Children and Youth* 5(2):72-89.

Brown, E.R.
1989 Access to health insurance in the United States. *Medical Care Review* 46(4):349-385.

Center on Budget and Policy Priorities
1997 *Medicaid Income Eligibility Guidelines for Children*. Washington, D.C.: Center on Budget and Policy Priorities.

Clark, R.L., J.S. Passel, W.N. Zimmerman, and M.E. Fix
1994 *Fiscal Impacts of Undocumented Aliens: Selected Estimates for Seven States*.Washington, D.C.: The Urban Institute.

Edmonston, B., ed.
1996 *Statistics on U.S. Immigration: An Assessment of Data Needs for Future Research*. Committee on National Statistics. Washington, D.C.: National Academy Press.

Fix, M., and J. Passel
1994 *Immigration and Immigrants: Setting the Record Straight*. Washington, D.C.: The Urban Institute Press.

Kaiser Family Foundation
1997 http://www.kff.org/state_health, accessed 9/14/97.

Lee, S.M., and B. Edmonston
1994 The socioeconomic status and integration of Asian immigrants. Pp. 101-138 in *Immigration and Ethnicity: The Integration of America's Newest Arrivals,* B. Edmonston and J. Passel, eds. Washington, D.C.: The Urban Institute Press.

Lieu, T.A., P.W. Newacheck, and M.A. McManus
1993 Race, ethnicity, and access to ambulatory care among U.S. adolescents. *American Journal of Public Health* 83(7):960-965.

Mendoza, F.S.
1994 The health of Latino children in the United States. *The Future of Children: Critical Issues for Children and Youth* 4(3):43-72.

Newacheck, P.W., D.C. Hughes, and J.J. Stoddard
1996 Children's access to primary care: Differences by race, income, and insurance status. *Pediatrics* 7(1):26-32.

Stoddard, J., R. St. Peter, and P. Newacheck
1994 Health insurance status and ambulatory care in children. *New England Journal of Medicine* 330:1421-1425.

Thamer, M., C. Richard, A.W. Casebeer, and N.F. Ray
1997 Health insurance coverage among foreign-born U.S. residents: The impact of race, ethnicity, and length of residence. *American Journal of Public Health* 87(1):96-102.

U.S. Bureau of Labor Statistics
1997 Website: ftp://stats.bls.gov/pub/news.release/srgune.txt, accessed 8/12/97.

U.S. General Accounting Office
1995 *Illegal Aliens: National Net Cost Estimates Vary Widely.* GAO/HEHS-95-133. Washington, D.C.: U.S. General Accounting Office.

Valdez, R.B., H. Morgenstern, E.R. Brown, R. Wyn, C. Wang, and W. Cumberland
1993 Insuring Latinos against the costs of illness. *Journal of the American Medical Association* 269:889-894.

Vega, W.A., and H. Amaro
1994 Latino outlook: Good health, uncertain prognosis. *Annual Review of Public Health* 15:39-67.

Valdez, R.B., and G. Dallek
1991 *Does the Health System Serve Black and Latino Communities in Los Angeles County*? Claremont, Calif.: Tomas Rivera Center.

Wood, D.L., R.A. Hayward, C.R. Corey, H.E. Freeman, and M.F. Shapiro
1990 Access to medical care for children and adolescents in the United States. *Pediatrics* 86(5):666-673.

Wyn, R., E.R. Brown, R.B. Valdez, H. Yu, W. Cumberland, H. Morgenstern, C. Hafner-Eaton, and C. Wang
1993 *Health Insurance Coverage of California's Latino Population and Their Use of Health Services.* Berkeley: California Policy Seminar, University of California.

APPENDIX 3A: VARIABLES USED IN ANALYSIS OF HEALTH INSURANCE COVERAGE

We used data on children and their families from the March 1996 Current Population Survey (CPS) to examine health insurance coverage.

Outcome Variable

Health Insurance Status

The child's health insurance coverage was the outcome variable in this portion of the study. The March CPS asks respondents about health insurance coverage for each family member during the previous calendar year. Children insured by any source at any time during 1995 were counted as insured. Because a person may have multiple sources of coverage reported for 1995, a single hierarchical variable was created to reflect rank ordering of reported health insurance coverage. We counted persons who reported having coverage through their own or a family member's employment at any time during 1995 as covered by employment-based health insurance. Children who did not have any private coverage but who had Medicaid coverage at any time during the year were counted as having coverage through that federal-state program. Persons who had other public coverage or privately purchased health insurance (i.e., not obtained through employment) were counted as "other coverage." Those with no reported coverage of any kind during the year were categorized as "uninsured."

Independent Variables

Immigration and Citizenship Status

We classified children into three immigration and citizenship categories: (1) noncitizen immigrant child—that is, a child who was not born in the United States and is not a U.S. citizen; (2) U.S. citizen child in an immigrant family—that is, a child who is a citizen (U.S. born or naturalized) and has one or more parents who are foreign born, regardless of whether they are U.S. citizens; and (3) U.S. citizen child with both parents born in the United States (or, in a single-parent family, one U.S.-born parent). Children who were born outside the United States to U.S.-born parents are counted as U.S. born. We classified families as immigrant if either parent was foreign born and as U.S. born if both parents (or the one parent in a single-parent family) were born in the United States. We further classified groups 1 and 2 above by the duration of residence in the United States, measured by the year in which the parent who is the primary worker immigrated to this country.

Ethnicity

We classified a child's ethnicity based on parent-reported race and ethnic information for the child. Children were categorized into four ethnic groups: Latinos are individuals of any race who identify themselves as Hispanics of American origin (Mexican, Puerto Rican, Cuban, Central or South American). Non-Latino whites, non-Latino blacks, and non-Latino Asians were categorized according to parent-identified race. Sample size limitations did not permit analyses of other racial/ethnic groupings.

Family Income Related to Poverty

Children were classified into one of four poverty-level groups based on family income measured in relation to the federal poverty level. The groupings used to classify children were below poverty (i.e., less than 100 percent of the federal poverty level), 100 to 199 percent of poverty, 200 to 299 percent of poverty, and 300+ percent of poverty. In 1995, the year reflected in the CPS questions on health insurance coverage, the poverty level was set at $15,569 for a family of four.

Family Structure

We categorized a child as living in a two-parent or a single-parent family.

Family Work Status

A family was classified as a "full-time, full-year employee family" if at least one of the parents reported working for an employer at least 35 hours per week for 50 to 52 weeks in 1995, as a "full-time, part-year employee family" if a parent worked for an employer full time for less than 50 weeks, as a "part-time employee family" if no parent worked as a full-time employee but one worked for an employer less than 35 hours a week, as "self-employed" if a parent was self-employed, or as "nonworking" if no parent worked during 1995. In the regression models we combined "full-time, part-year" and "part-time" employee families into "other employee."

Parent's Education Status

The educational attainment of the parent whose employment characterizes the family's work status (the primary worker) was used to categorize the family's education status.

Country of Origin

We categorized children by the nativity of the child if the child is an immigrant or the parent who is the primary worker if the child is U.S. born.

State of Residence

The child's state of residence is the residence at the time of the interview.

Variables Used in Analysis of Reasons for Uninsurance, Health Care Access, and Use of Health Care Services

We used data from the 1994 National Health Interview Survey (NHIS) to study reasons for uninsurance among uninsured children, whether a child has a usual source of care, and a child's use of health care services. Variables in the NHIS that are similar to those available in the CPS require no further definition, but we describe those that differ from the CPS variables discussed earlier.

Outcome Variables

Physician Visits

Information on physician visits was obtained using the following NHIS question: "During the past 12 months, about how many times did (child's name) see or talk to a medical doctor or assistant?" For infants and toddlers ages 0 through 24 months we examined the probability of no use versus three or more visits per year, and for children and adolescents over 24 months through age 17 we examined no use during the past year compared with at least one visit. These criteria follow the visit schedule recommended by the American Academy of Pediatrics for preventive care and immunizations.

Usual Person or Source of Care

Information on whether or not a child has a usual person or place for medical care was based on the NHIS question: "Is there a particular person or place that (child's name) usually goes to when sick or needs advice about health?" This includes those with one or more usual sources of care and a small number who use a hospital emergency room as a usual source of care. Having a usual source of care has been demonstrated to be a robust measure of access to health care services. We therefore used usual source of care as an outcome variable but also as a predictor of use of physicians' services.

Independent Variables

Immigrant Status

We classified children into three immigrant groups based on the immigrant status of the child and for U.S.-born children the immigrant status of the parents: (1) immigrant child—that is, a child not born in the United States; (2) U.S.-born child of immigrant parents—that is, a child born in the United States who has at least one immigrant parent; and (3) nonimmigrant child—that is, a U.S.-born child with U.S.-born parents (or in a single-parent family one U.S.-born parent). The NHIS does not include any questions about citizenship status.

Educational Status

The educational attainment of the mother was used to characterize the family's educational status. In single-father families the father's educational level was used.

Health Status

Two measures of health status based on parents' reports were used to measure children's health. General health status was measured as excellent, very good, good, fair, and poor and was recorded as good to excellent health and poor or fair. Activity limitations were measured as being unable to perform major activity, limited in kind/amount of activity, limited in other activity, or not limited and were recorded to reflect children with any limitation and those with no limitations.

Reason for Lack of Coverage

This information was based on two questions in the NHIS. The first asks respondents which of a series of statements describes why their child is not covered by any health insurance coverage. The second question asks what the main reason is for lack of coverage.

CHAPTER 4

The Health and Nutritional Status of Immigrant Hispanic Children: Analyses of the Hispanic Health and Nutrition Examination Survey

Fernando S. Mendoza and
Lori Beth Dixon

The Hispanic population will soon be the largest ethnic minority group in the United States. Its growth is being fueled by both a high fertility rate and immigration (Lewit et al., 1994). Indeed, over the past decade half of the increase in its population has been from immigration. As a result, federal and state public policies have focused more intently on immigrant Hispanics and their children. Although there has always been a flow of Hispanic immigrants to the United States, the recent upsurge in immigration has led to a debate about the use of public resources by immigrants, particularly their children, and concerns about the strain they cause on programs for other needy children. In reaction, federal and state governments have begun to enact changes in immigration and social welfare policies aimed at limiting public resources to immigrants, including children (e.g., congressional reform of immigration policy, Proposition 187 in California). However, two questions arise: What do we know about the nutritional and health status of immigrant Hispanic children? Are they disproportionately in need of nutrition-related and health care services? At present there is limited knowledge about their actual health and nutritional needs. If informed public policy is to be developed to deal with immigrant Hispanic children in the United States, accurate information about their health and nutritional needs is required.

Currently, about 60 percent of immigrant children are from Latin America, primarily Mexico, Cuba, and Central America (Bureau of the Census, 1994). Although immigrant children come from other countries too, such as those in Asia and Eastern Europe, for the most part Hispanics are now and will continue to be the major ethnic group of immigrant children in the United States. Furthermore, the problematic issues of poverty, low parental education, and difficulty in accessing health care encountered by many immigrant families and their children are common to Hispanics. Therefore, immigrant Hispanic children can be seen as instructive examples of immigrant children in general in the United States.

To evaluate the nutritional and health status of immigrant versus nonimmigrant Hispanic children, we examined the Hispanic Health and Nutrition Examination Survey, a health survey conducted by the National Center for Health Statistics (NCHS) in 1984 on the three major Hispanic subgroups in the United States (NCHS, 1985). This paper presents data on the growth patterns, dietary intakes, and prevalences of chronic medical conditions and the perceived health status of Mexican American, Puerto Rican, and Cuban American children and adolescents. We differentiate these findings by the birthplaces of the children and adolescents. Thus, this study provides one of the first large-scale nutritional and health status comparisons of immigrant and nonimmigrant Hispanic children in the United States.

METHODS

Sample

The study subjects were children, ages 6 months to 18 years, who participated in the Hispanic Health and Nutrition Examination Survey (HHANES) in 1984 (National Center for Health Statistics, 1985). This survey sampled Mexican American children from the five Southwestern states (California, Arizona, Colorado, New Mexico, and Texas), mainland Puerto Rican children from the New York City area, and Cuban American children from Dade County, Florida. These geographic regions contain the majority of children from these three Hispanic subgroups. Therefore, although not encompassing all children in the United States who are in these Hispanic subgroups, HHANES surveyed 73 percent of Mexican Americans, 53 percent of mainland Puerto Ricans, and 55 percent of Cuban Americans living in the United States at the time of the survey. Among those children and adolescents who were missed by the HHANES sampling were the homeless; those who were migrants; and, in general, those more difficult to contact, usually the poor. The survey obtained health and nutritional data from subjects through questionnaires, biochemical tests, and physical examinations. Unlike most other national health surveys, HHANES contains information from physicians' examinations of surveyed subjects. Therefore, this survey differentiates itself from other household health surveys by utilizing more than questionnaire data to determine health and nutritional status. The survey also contains information about children's birthplaces and for adolescents assesses generational status by determining their birthplace and their parents' birthplaces. No other documentation was available to determine citizenship status of a family or its child. As a result, for this study Mexican American children and adolescents were identified as being born either in Mexico or the United States; similarly, Cuban Americans were identified as being born in Cuba or the United States. Puerto Rican children were classified as being born either on the mainland or on the island of Puerto Rico.

Variables

All subjects had assessed demographic data, including age, sex, poverty status as measured by a poverty index,[1] parental education, and birthplace (United States, Mexico, Cuba, or Puerto Rico). Adolescent subjects also had generational status determined.[2] Subjects were assessed for their nutritional health by

---

[1]The poverty index is a proportion determined by the family's income divided by the cost of food and shelter for a family of similar size. A poverty index of 1.0 is the poverty line, while a poverty index of 2.0 is a family income of 200 percent of poverty.

[2]Generation status was determined as follows: first, foreign-born adolescent; second, U.S.-born adolescent with one or both parents foreign born; and third or greater, U.S.-born adolescent with both parents U.S. born.

using measures of anthropometry (height, weight, body mass index (weight/height^2)); daily dietary intake (as assessed by a food frequency questionnaire); and for children under age 12 a parental report of anemia. The physical health of children and adolescents was assessed by the presence of chronic medical conditions and parental reports of specific conditions. The assessment of chronic medical conditions was done by survey physicians through questionnaires and a standardized physical examination. A chronic medical condition was any medical condition that impaired the child's or adolescent's function for at least the three previous months. For children under age 12 a medical condition questionnaire was administered to parents that assessed whether the children had any of several listed medical conditions. Lastly, an overall subjective assessment of health status was determined for each subject by the survey physician. Survey physicians were asked to assess each adolescent's health as excellent, very good, good, fair, or poor. A rating of fair or poor was labeled as reporting poor health, while those reporting excellent, very good, or good health were labeled as reporting good health. In addition to physicians, adolescent subjects were asked to assess their health status using the same categories. If an adolescent was unable to answer, a parent (usually the mother) responded to the question.

Analyses

The HHANES is a complex, multistage, stratified, clustered survey that requires the use of sample weights and a complex sample design effect for population estimates and comparisons. Our analyses used sample weights for population estimates (i.e., percentages, means, and medians) and an average sample design effect of 1.5 as recommended by Delgaldo et al. (1990). Chi-square analyses had critical values divided by 1.5 to account for the design effect. Regression analysis utilized sample weight and a complex sample design effect of 1.0 since regression parameters included age, sex, and measures of socioeconomic status (SES). Accurate prevalence estimates require samples of 45 or greater. Those estimates with smaller samples are not reliable as population estimates but instead reflect values for only the sampled population.

Nutritional Status Assessment

The medians for weight and height of sampled children and adolescents were assessed by age, sex, ethnic group, and birthplace. Age was determined by prior birthday. For example, all children in the age 2 category ranged from 2.00 to 2.99 years old. The HHANES data on height and weight were compared to the NCHS midyear-age 50th percentile standard for 1983 for height and weight (i.e., all children age 2 were compared to NCHS median values of 2.5 years). Calculated body mass index (BMI) values for surveyed children and adolescents were compared to standardized values of BMI from the NHANES I (1971-1974) developed by Hammer et al. (1991). To compare HHANES groups with NCHS and BMI standards, children from two-year age groups (e.g., 2 to 2.9 years plus 3 to 3.9 years) were combined because of the small immigrant sample sizes in each individual age group. Regression analyses of anthropometric measures were done by age cohort (2 to 5 years, preschoolers; 6 to 11 years, school age; 12 to 18 years, adolescents), with age, sex, poverty, parental education, and whether the child or adolescent was foreign born as independent variables. The latter variable for Mexican American adolescents includes three groupings: foreign born, U.S. born with one or both parents foreign born, and U.S. born with U.S.-born parents.

The diets of children and adolescents were assessed by determining daily intakes of the four basic food groups. This was done by utilizing the same methodology developed by Murphy et al. (1990) to analyze food frequency data from the HHANES. This method estimates the completeness of the diet with respect to the four basic food groups by comparing the daily servings of each food compared to the recommendations for age by the U.S. Department of Agriculture's (USDA) Daily Food Guide. Maximum servings ranged from 12.5 to 14 per day of the four food groups. Statistical differences in dietary intake scores between U.S.- and foreign-born children were assessed by *t* test. A maternal report of anemia in a child, either current or past (ever having been treated for anemia), was examined for U.S.- and foreign-born children by chi-square analyses.

Health Status Assessment

The prevalence of chronic medical conditions was assessed for U.S.- and foreign-born children in each of the Hispanic subgroups and compared by chi-square analyses. Parental reports of selected medical conditions were compared by chi-square analyses for U.S.- and foreign-born children age 6 months to 11 years. The prevalence of perceived poor health status among adolescents as assessed by survey physicians and adolescents was compared by chi-square analyses for differences between U.S.- and foreign-born subjects.

RESULTS

The size and characteristics of each sample are presented in Table 4-1. For children 6 months to 11 years old, the three Hispanic groups differed demographically among themselves and within groups by birthplace. Compared to U.S.-born Mexican American children, foreign-born ones tended to have families that were poorer, less educated, predominantly Spanish speaking, and less likely to have a female-headed household. Puerto Rican chil-

TABLE 4-1 Demographics Profile of U.S. and Foreign-Born Hispanic Children and Adolescents

	Mexican American	
	U.S.	Mexico
6 mos.-11 yrs. sample (*N*)	2,493	272
% with female head of household	18	10
% in poverty	34	60
% parental education less than grade 9	36	77
% Spanish-speaking only	28	78
12-18 yrs. sample (*N*)	1,088	259
% female head of household	26	17
% in poverty	36	50
% parental education less than grade 9	41	81
% Spanish-speaking only	6	20
(*N*) Second generation	374	
(*N*) Third generation	705	

dren more frequently lived in female-headed households and in poverty than Mexican Americans or Cuban Americans. Puerto Rican children born on the island were similar to those born in the United States, except they were more likely to speak only Spanish. Cuban children born outside the United States were poorer and less well educated than U.S.-born Cuban children. The characteristics of the adolescent samples were similar to those of the younger age group. However, fewer foreign-born adolescents spoke only Spanish. Although the generational status of adolescents was available, only Mexican Americans had a significant number of subjects who were third-generation children or higher. In general, foreign-born children came from families that were poorer and less well educated than their U.S. counterparts.

The data for height and weight medians by age, sex, and birthplace for Mexican American, Puerto Rican, and Cuban American children are shown in Appendix 4A, Tables 4A-1 through 4A-6. The medians for U.S.- and foreign-born subjects (Puerto Ricans were divided into mainland and island born) were examined against the NCHS 50th percentile for age. Figures 4-1 through 4-4 plot the median values for height and weight of Mexican Ameri-

Puerto Rican		Cuban American	
U.S.	Puerto Rico	U.S.	Cuba
723	171	227	53
50	51	16	17
58	60	25	44
24	32	28	48
27	61	53	61
455	163	105	114
58	63	19	22
57	70	20	45
33	43	34	53
5	12	2	9
405		105	
44		0	

can males and females compared to the NCHS median or 50th percentile for age and sex. Values below the zero line indicate medians lower than the NCHS median, while values above the line are above the median. Because data were unstable owing to small sample sizes by age and sex, two-year averages are presented.

Compared to the NCHS height standard for 1983, foreign-born Mexican American males had median heights that were greater than the 50th percentile for ages 2 to 3 but were generally less than the 50th percentile for ages 4 to 17 years (Figure 4-1). The differences between the median heights of foreign-born Mexican American males and the NCHS age-appropriate median were as much as –4cm during childhood and early adolescence and then increased to about –8 cm in late adolescence. This suggests mild-to-moderate stunting of foreign-born males. Accordingly, the median heights of foreign-born Mexican American males in

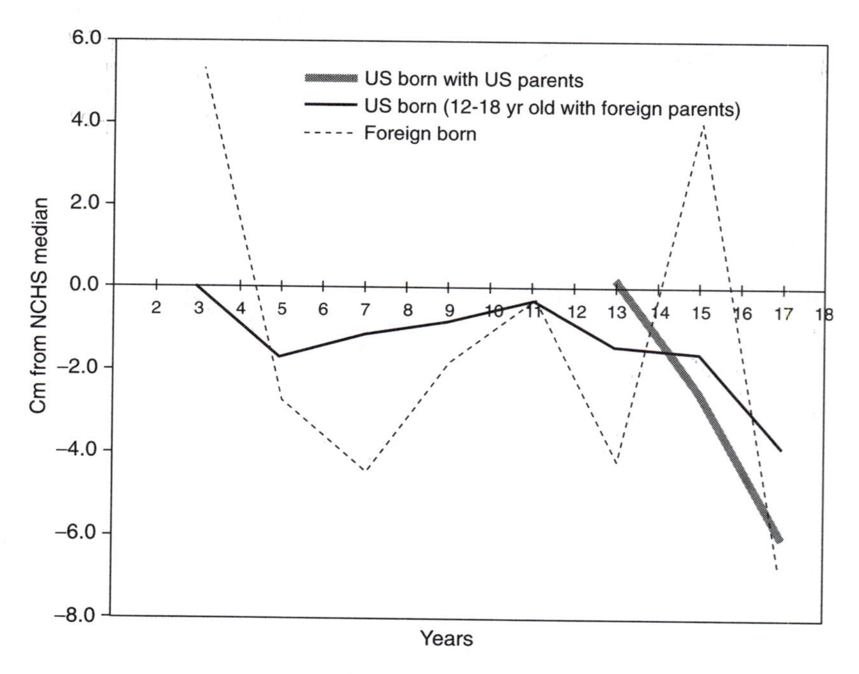

FIGURE 4-1 Median heights of Mexican American males by two-year intervals.

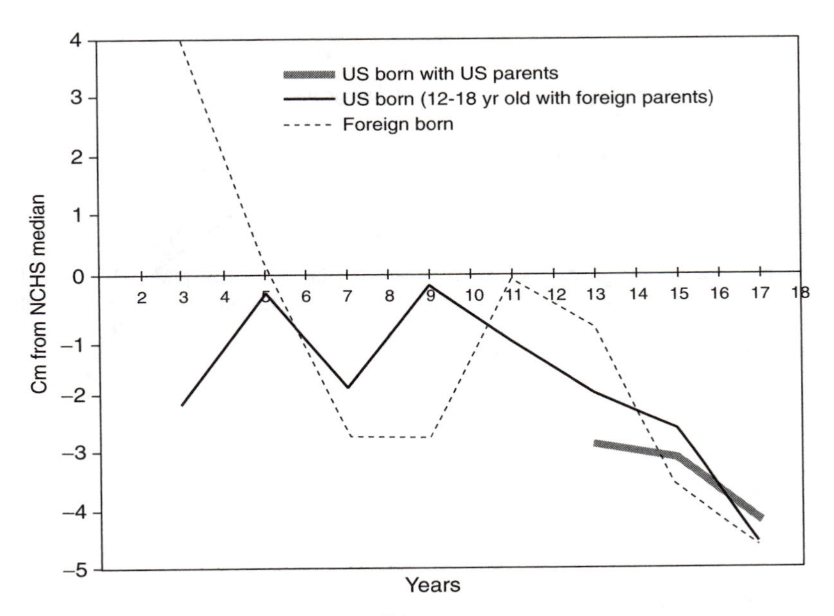

FIGURE 4-2 Median heights of Mexican American females by two-year intervals.

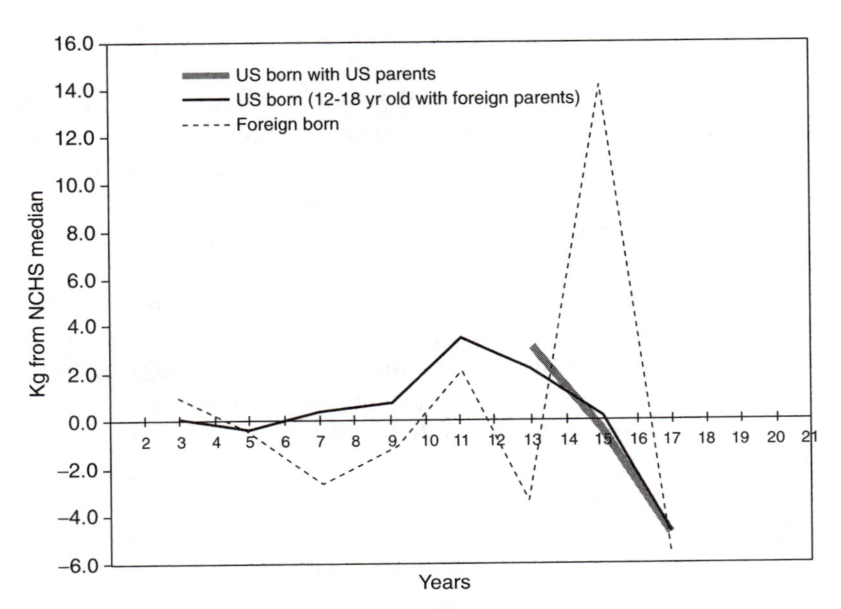

FIGURE 4-3 Median weights of Mexican American males by two-year intervals.

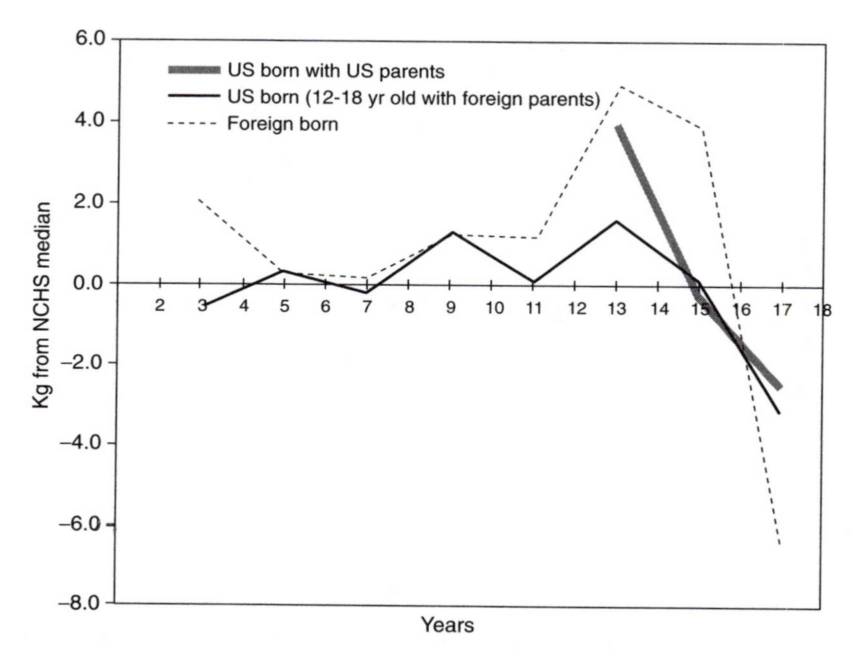

FIGURE 4-4 Median weights of Mexican American females by two-year intervals.

late adolescence were between the NCHS 5th and 10th percentiles for age. Although U.S.-born Mexican American males under age 12 were taller than their foreign-born counterparts, this decreased during adolescence, with medians averaging 5.7 cm below the 50th percentile or between the NCHS 10th and 25th percentiles at ages 16 to 18. Similarly, foreign-born Mexican American females had average median heights greater than the NCHS 50th percentile from ages 2 to 4 but then were generally below the 50th percentile from ages 5 to 17 (Figure 4-2). Specifically, the median heights of foreign-born Mexican American females were 1 to 2 cm less than their age-appropriate NCHS standard during childhood and early adolescence and then averaged 7 cm below the NCHS 50th percentile in late adolescence. In late adolescence the median heights of foreign-born females ranged between the NCHS 5th and 25th percentiles, indicating stunting among girls as well. Median heights for U.S.-born Mexican

American females compared to foreign-born females were improved, but like males they had less of a height advantage at the end of adolescence, with median heights ranging from the NCHS 10th to 25th percentiles.

Linear regressions were conducted on the heights of Mexican American children by age cohorts: 2 to 5 years, 6 to 11 years, and 12 to 18 years. Table 4-2 shows results from linear regressions on height with betas for variable levels compared to control levels (e.g., for children ages 2 to 5, male is a control variable with a beta of 0.0, while female is the variable of interest with a beta of –0.88). For children ages 2 to 5, main predictors were age, sex, and parental education (R^2 = .739). Those who were older and male and whose parents were more educated are taller. For school-age children, age and parental education were the main determinants (R^2 = .724). A stepwise regression indicated that the poverty score rather than parental education was a major determinant of height for school-age children. Adolescents were taller if they were older and male, had higher parental education, and were wealthier (R^2 = .358). (Stepwise regression selected the poverty index as a better predictor variable than parental education.) None of the regression analyses showed being foreign born as a significant determinant of height. However, in all three age groups a measure of SES predicted height.

The median weights of Mexican American children were less variant than their heights from the NCHS median or 50th percentile. Foreign-born boys through age 12 showed median weights that varied around the NCHS 50th percentile, from +1.3 kg above the 50th percentile to –2.9 kg below (Figure 4-3). During early adolescence, foreign-born boys' median weights were above the NCHS median and then fell below it after age 15, resulting in median weights around the NCHS 25th percentile. U.S.-born boys tended to be slightly heavier (–0.5 to +2.7 kg from the NCHS median) but likewise showed median weights below the NCHS 50th percentile after age 15. Their weight percentiles were also at the 25th percentile. Foreign and U.S.-born girls ages 2 to 15 had median weights above the NCHS median, with foreign-born girls usually heavier than U.S.-born girls (Figure 4-4). After age 15 both groups weighed below the NCHS median for age, with foreign-born adolescent girls having lower weights (NCHS 25th per-

TABLE 4-2 Regression Analyses for Height by Ethnic and Age Groupings

Age (years)	Model	
2-5	Overall R^2	
	df	
	Variable	*Level*
	Age	2 yrs.
		3 yrs.
		4 yrs.
		5 yrs.
	Gender	Female
		Male
	Birthplace	Other country
		U.S.
	Poverty score	
	Parental education	< Grade 9
		≥ Grade 9
6-11	Overall R^2	
	df	
	Variable	*Level*
	Age	6 yrs.
		7 yrs.
		8 yrs.
		9 yrs.
		10 yrs.
		11 yrs.
	Gender	Female
		Male
	Birthplace	Other country
		U.S.

Mexican American	Puerto Rican	Cuban
0.739	0.780	0.760
778	222	53
−21.14*	−24.09*	−22.78*
−13.87*	−15.77*	−12.32*
−6.67*	−7.25*	−3.95
0.00	0.00	0.00
−0.88**	−1.24***	−1.15
0.00	0.00	0.00
0.69	−1.93***	−2.41
0.00	0.00	0.00
0.002	0.001	−0.004
−0.96***	0.45	0.43
0.00	0.00	0.00
0.726	0.714	0.683
1117	364	110
−28.84*	−28.29*	−28.63*
−23.81*	−24.11*	−21.95*
−18.21*	−16.78*	−16.01*
−11.64*	−11.69*	−12.09*
−6.00*	−5.09*	−7.33**
0.00*	0.00	0.00
0.28	1.58***	−1.13
0.00	0.00	0.00
−1.14	−2.09***	−3.28***
0.00	0.00	0.00

continued on next page

TABLE 4-2 Continued

Age (years)	Model	
	Poverty score	
	Parental education	< Grade 9
		≥ Grade 9
12-18	Overall R^2	
	df	
	Variable	*Level*
	Age	12 yrs.
		13 yrs.
		14 yrs.
		15 yrs.
		16 yrs.
		17 yrs.
		18 yrs.
	Gender	Female
		Male
	Generation	First
		Second
		Third
	Poverty score	
	Parental education	< Grade 9
		≥ Grade 9

$^{*}p < .001$; $^{**}p < .01$; $^{***}p < .05$.

NOTE: For 12- to 18-year-old Mexican Americans, the generation variable has three levels (first, foreign born; second, U.S. born with foreign-born parents; third, U.S. born with U.S.-born parents). For 12- to 18-year-old Puerto Ricans and Cubans, the generation variable only has two levels (first, foreign born; second, U.S. born with U.S.-born parents).

Mexican American	Puerto Rican	Cuban
0.01	0.02*	0.003
–0.50*	–1.87***	0.69
0.00	0.00	0.00
0.413	0.391	0.478
986	466	155
–12.00*	–11.39*	–14.06*
–6.16*	–7.54*	–12.29*
–3.45*	–5.45*	–7.23***
–0.51	–2.33	–2.06
–0.82	–1.24	–3.70
0.61	–0.79	–1.24
0.00	0.00	0.00
–7.64*	–7.93*	–6.21*
0.00	0.00	0.00
–1.59	–0.82	0.45
0.64	0.00	0.00
0.00	—	—
0.005***	0.005	0.01
1.05***	–0.62	0.32
0.00	0.00	0.00

centile) than U.S.-born adolescents (25th to 50th percentiles). Regression analyses of weight (see Table 4-3) showed that for children ages 2 to 5, age, sex, and parental education were predictors of weight (R^2 = .488). Older males with higher parental education were heavier. For school-age children, being older and having higher income were associated with a higher weight (R^2 = .446). Among adolescents, only age and sex predicted weight (R^2 = 0.198). Neither socioeconomic factor—poverty index or parental education—predicted weight for adolescents, and, as with height, being foreign born was not predictive of weight among Mexican American children or adolescents.

Figures 4-5 and 4-6 show the proportion of Mexican American children and adolescents with BMI values above the 90th percentile. More than 10 percent of school-age and adolescent boys were above the 90th percentile, indicating greater obesity among these groups (Appendix 4A, Table 4A-7). Among adolescent boys, there appeared to be higher BMI values among U.S.-born adolescents, particularly those with U.S.-born parents. Foreign-born school-age girls had a higher proportion than U.S.-born girls who were above the 90th percentile. Among adolescent girls, U.S.-born adolescent girls with U.S.-born parents exceeded their counterparts. Regression analyses showed that for all age groups only age and gender were predictive variables (see Table 4-4).

Examination of the growth patterns of mainland- and island-born Puerto Rican children (under age 12) in HHANES showed that mainland-born children's median heights were similar to or greater than the NCHS 50th percentile (Appendix 4A, Tables 4A-3 and 4A-4). In contrast, island-born children showed heights below the NCHS 50th percentile, suggesting that stunting was present in this group. Both mainland- and island-born adolescents after age 12 had median heights that were consistently below average (from 1 to 7 cm), centering between the NCHS 10th and 25th percentiles for age. Similar to the Mexican American sample, both mainland- and island-born Puerto Rican children's and adolescents' weights averaged at or above the 50th percentile. Only in older adolescent island-born males did median weights fall below the NCHS average to the 25th percentile. For both mainland-born sexes and island-born females, median weights at the end of adolescence were either similar to or above the NCHS 50th percentile.

Regression analyses of height and weight for the Puerto Rican sample by age cohort are shown in Tables 4-2 and 4-3. For children ages 2 to 5, significant variables for height were age, gender, and birthplace. Children born in Puerto Rico were 2 cm shorter than their mainland counterparts. Among school-age children, in addition to age, gender, and birthplace, both the poverty score and parental education were significant variables for predicting height. Adolescents' height was best predicted by age and gender. Birthplace was not significant for adolescents, although it had a negative coefficient, consistent with the younger age groups. Regression analyses of weight showed that for children ages 2 to 5 only age was significant. Among school-age children, poverty score also was a significant variable. Adolescents' weights were best predicted by age, gender, and poverty score. As with the Mexican American sample, those in the Puerto Rican sample had a higher-than-expected proportion of school-age children and adolescents who were above the 90th percentile for BMI, approximately 15 percent (Appendix 4A, Table 4A-8). Regression analyses for BMI among all ages were nonpredictive.

The anthropometric analyses on Cuban American children and adolescents were limited because of the small sample sizes (Appendix 4A, Table 4A-5 and 4A-6). However, in general, they followed patterns similar to Puerto Rican children and adolescents. Foreign-born Cuban American children and adolescents were shorter and somewhat lower in weight than U.S.-born Cuban American children. Regression analyses (Tables 4-2 through 4-4) showed that height was primarily influenced by age. Only among school-age children was height significantly affected by birthplace, with foreign-born children about 3 cm shorter. Weight followed a similar pattern, with foreign-born school-age children being lighter than U.S.-born children. Like Puerto Ricans, data on BMI values for Cuban American children and adolescents showed a greater proportion of children above the 90th percentile, particularly children 6 to 11 years old (Appendix 4A, Table 4A-9). Regressions for BMI by age group showed age as the only consistent predictor; however, among school-age children, being foreign born was associated with a lower BMI.

TABLE 4-3 Regression Analyses for Weight by Ethnic and Age Groupings

Age (years)	Model	
2-5	Overall R^2	
	df	
	Variable	*Level*
	Age	2 yrs.
		3 yrs.
		4 yrs.
		5 yrs.
	Gender	Female
		Male
	Birthplace	Other country
		U.S.
	Poverty score	
	Parental education	< Grade 9
		≥ Grade 9
6-11	Overall R^2	
	df	
	Variable	*Level*
	Age	6 yrs.
		7 yrs.
		8 yrs.
		9 yrs.
		10 yrs.
		11 yrs.
	Gender	Female
		Male
	Birthplace	Other country
		U.S.
	Poverty score	
	Parental education	< Grade 9
		≥ Grade 9

Mexican American	Puerto Rican	Cuban
0.488	0.400	0.251
779	222	53
−6.45*	−8.83*	−6.19**
−4.48*	−6.71*	−1.37
−2.58*	−3.46*	−1.03
0.00	0.00	0.00
−0.51**	−0.65	1.15
0.00	0.00	0.00
0.04	−0.93	−1.23
0.00	0.00	0.00
0.001	0.005	0.002
−0.46***	−0.16	−2.35
0.00	0.00	0.00
0.446	0.412	0.456
1120	364	110
−19.81*	−16.34*	−23.06*
−16.75*	−15.40*	−19.40*
−13.82*	−10.51*	−13.58*
−8.68*	−7.86*	−11.50*
−4.60*	−1.13	−11.51*
0.00	0.00	0.00
−0.07	0.80	−1.39
0.00	0.00	0.00
−0.50	−1.77	−4.59***
0.00	0.00	0.00
0.005***	0.02*	0.0001
−0.44	−1.56	0.84
0.00	0.00	0.00

continued on next page

TABLE 4-3 Continued

Age (years)	Model	
12-18	Overall R^2	
	df	
	Variable	*Level*
	Age	12 yrs.
		13 yrs.
		14 yrs.
		15 yrs.
		16 yrs.
		17 yrs.
		18 yrs.
	Gender	Female
		Male
	Generation	First
		Second
		Third
	Poverty score	
	Parental education	< Grade 9
		≥ Grade 9

$^*p < .001$; $^{**}p < .01$; $^{***}p < .05$.

NOTE: For 12- to 18-year-old Mexican Americans, the generation variable has three levels (first, foreign born; second, U.S. born with foreign-born parents; third, U.S. born with U.S.-born parents). For 12- to 18-year-old Puerto Ricans and Cubans, the generation variable only has two levels (first, foreign born; second, U.S. born with U.S.-born parents).

Table 4-5 shows the daily intakes of the four basic food groups, both as a summary of total servings and as servings of individual food groups, according to the USDA Daily Food Guide. Small sample sizes limited the evaluations of foreign-born children under age 2. For children ages 2 to 5 there were no differences in daily intakes between foreign- or island-born children and those born in the United States in any of the Hispanic subgroups. However, in the 6- to 11-year age group, foreign-born Mexican American children consumed significantly higher amounts of bread, vegetables, and fruits and fewer servings of added fat than U.S.-born Mexican American children. No differ-

Mexican American	Puerto Rican	Cuban
0.198	0.182	0.283
985	468	156
−16.38*	−16.52*	−13.09*
−11.04*	−13.01*	−16.23*
−7.24*	−9.62*	−9.00***
−5.48*	−8.45*	−4.84
−2.89***	−1.81	−6.23
−3.16***	−3.09	0.91
0.00	0.00	0.00
−4.36*	−4.22*	−4.00***
0.00	0.00	0.00
−2.80	0.51	1.29
0.11	0.00	0.00
0.00	—	—
0.004	0.01***	0.01
−0.06	−0.28	0.64
0.00	0.00	0.00

ences were seen among mainland- or island-born Puerto Rican school-age children or between U.S.- and non-U.S.-born Cuban American children. Overall, for children ages 2 to 11, the total daily intake was 67 percent of recommended USDA amounts for foreign-born Mexican American children and 64 percent for U.S.-born Mexican Americans. Daily intakes for both mainland- and island-born Puerto Rican children were similar: 62 percent of recommended amounts. Cuban American foreign-born children scored lower compared to those who were U.S. born, 57 versus 62 percent of recommended amounts.

In the adolescent age group, although there were no signifi-

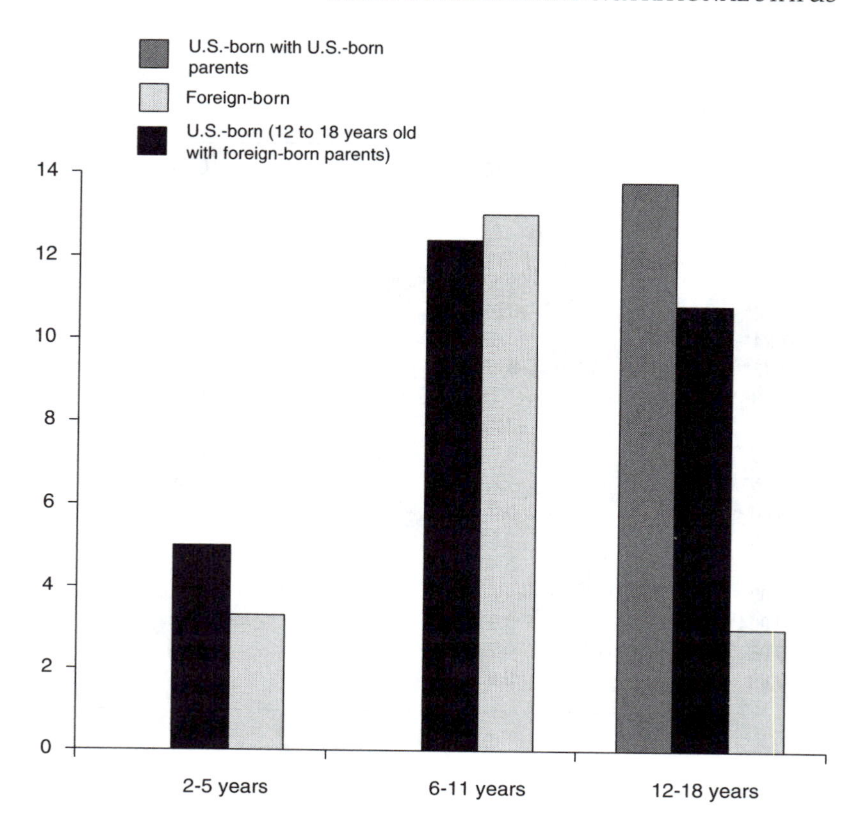

FIGURE 4-5 Percentage of Mexican American males with BMIs above 90th percentile.

cant differences in daily intakes of the four food groups between foreign- and U.S.-born groups, Mexican American and Puerto Rican adolescents reported better intakes than Cuban American adolescents (54 and 52 percent, respectively, versus 47 percent of the recommended intakes). Some significant individual food group differences were observed. Mexican American teens who were foreign born demonstrated greater intakes of breads, vegetables, and fruits with less added fat compared to their U.S. counterparts. Mainland-born Puerto Rican adolescents consumed greater amounts of milk and added fat compared to island-born Puerto Rican adolescents. Cuban American adolescents who

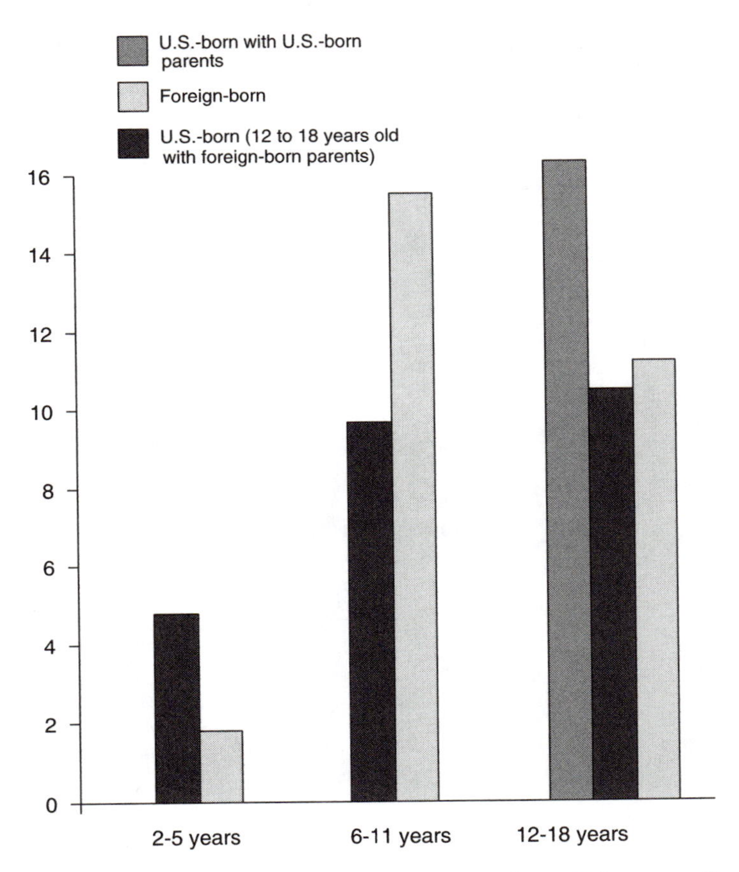

FIGURE 4-6 Mexican American females with BMIs above 90th percentile.

were foreign born ate more vegetables and fruits. In general, Hispanic adolescents showed mean dietary intakes ranging from 45 to 55 percent of the recommended daily intakes of the four basic food groups. Although not statistically significant, foreign-born Mexican American teens did slightly better in their mean dietary scores than U.S.-born teens, but this relationship was reversed for Puerto Rican and Cuban American adolescents. Milk and meat were eaten by Hispanic adolescents in the recommended amounts, but bread, vegetables, and fruits were consumed at 25 to 50 percent of the recommended levels.

The assessment of the health status of these three Hispanic

TABLE 4-4 Regression Analyses for BMI by Ethnic and Age Groupings

Age (years)	Model	
2-5	Overall R^2	
	df	
	Variable	*Level*
	Age	2 yrs.
		3 yrs.
		4 yrs.
		5 yrs.
	Gender	Female
		Male
	Birthplace	Other country
		U.S.
	Poverty score	
	Parental education	< Grade 9
		≥ Grade 9
6-11	Overall R^2	
	df	
	Variable	*Level*
	Age	6 yrs.
		7 yrs.
		8 yrs.
		9 yrs.
		10 yrs.
		11 yrs.
	Gender	Female
		Male
	Birthplace	Other country
		U.S.
	Poverty score	
	Parental education	< Grade 9
		≥ Grade 9

Mexican American	Puerto Rican	Cuban
0.038	0.022	0.190
777	222	53
0.52*	–0.31	1.18
0.22	–0.86	2.74
–0.22	–0.58	0.35
0.00	0.00	0.00
–0.25***	–0.11	1.53
0.00	0.00	0.00
–0.08	–0.24	–0.46
0.00	0.00	0.00
0.004	0.003	0.004
–0.17	–0.14	–2.58
0.00	0.00	0.00
0.134	0.097	0.200
1117	364	110
–3.41*	–1.57***	–4.69*
–2.75*	–2.14*	–4.10*
–2.37*	–1.09	–2.52***
–1.20*	–0.95	–2.54***
–0.66***	0.74	–3.69**
0.00	0.00	0.00
–0.12	0.06	–0.53
0.00	0.00	0.00
–0.0004	–0.28	–1.65***
0.00	0.00	0.00
0.001	0.005***	–0.001
–0.07	–0.21	0.28
0.00	0.00	0.00

continued on next page

TABLE 4-4 Continued

Age (years)	Model	
12-18	Overall R^2	
	df	
	Variable	*Level*
	Age	12 yrs.
		13 yrs.
		14 yrs.
		15 yrs.
		16 yrs.
		17 yrs.
		18 yrs.
	Gender	Female
		Male
	Generation	First
		Second
		Third
	Poverty score	
	Parental education	< Grade 9
		≥ Grade 9

$^*p < .001$; $^{**}p < .01$; $^{***}p < .050$.

NOTE: For 12- to 18-year-old Mexican Americans, the generation variable has three levels (first, foreign born; second, U.S. born with foreign parents; third, U.S. born with U.S.-born parents). For 12- to 18-year-old Puerto Ricans and Cubans, the generation variable has only two levels (first, foreign-born; second, U.S. born with U.S.-born parents).

subgroups showed some variability based on birthplace. The prevalence of chronic medical conditions for each subgroup is shown in Table 4-6. Both mainland- and island-born Puerto Rican children had the highest prevalences of chronic medical conditions and were the only Hispanic subgroup with a significant difference in prevalence between U.S.- and nonmainland-born children. Unfortunately, the small sample size of island-born Puerto Rican children did not allow for a population comparison and instead resulted in the statistical difference applying only to surveyed subjects. Small sample sizes also did not allow for comparison of Puerto Rican adolescents, but they too appeared to have a similar trend, with higher rates among island-born chil-

Mexican American	Puerto Rican	Cuban
0.069	0.087	0.108
985	466	155
−3.28*	−3.28*	−1.15
−2.56*	−2.75*	−2.97**
−1.79*	−1.88***	−1.38
−1.88*	−2.30**	−1.17
−0.92***	−0.17	−1.30
−1.31**	−0.95	0.60
0.00	0.00	0.00
0.50***	0.73	0.39
0.00	0.00	0.00
−0.62	0.41	0.30
−0.10	0.00	0.00
0.00	—	—
0.0001	0.003	0.001
−0.24	0.05	0.33
0.00	0.00	0.00

dren. The prevalence of chronic medical conditions among U.S.- and foreign-born Mexican Americans was basically equivalent, about 3.5 percent for children and 4.6 percent for adolescents. The Cuban American sample with chronic medical conditions was very small, and therefore statistical testing was not possible.

Specific medical conditions for children 6 months to 11 years old as reported by parents showed few differences based on birthplace; in general, few parents reported any such conditions (see Table 4-7). Puerto Rican children reported rates of asthma twice those of other U.S. children; children born in Puerto Rico had a higher prevalence, though nonstatistical, compared to mainland-born Puerto Ricans. Foreign-born Cuban American children had

TABLE 4-5 Mean Intakes of Food Groups by Latino Children According to Country of Birth

		Recommended	Mexican American	
Age (years)	Food Group[a]	Number of Servings[c]	U.S. Mean (n)[d]	Foreign Mean (n)
< 2	Four basic[b]	12.5 maximum	7.1 (308)	5.1 (3)
	Milk	2-3	2.0 (310)	0.9 (4)
	Meat	2-3	1.8 (318)	1.8 (3)
	Bread	4-6	2.5 (318)	2.3 (4)
	Vegetables and fruits	4-5	0.9 (319)	0.7 (4)
	Added sugar		1.4 (318)	0.8 (4)
	Added fat		0.8 (312)	0.1 (3)
2-5	Four basic	12.5 maximum	7.9 (783)	8.0 (44)
	Milk	2-3	2.2 (795)	2.2 (46)
	Meat	2-3	1.9 (825)	1.9 (59)
	Bread	4-6	2.8 (828)	3.0 (59)
	Vegetables and fruits	4-5	1.0 (831)	0.9 (60)
	Added sugar		1.9 (827)	2.1 (58)
	Added fat		1.2 (811)	1.1 (53)
6-11	Four basic	12.5 maximum	8.2 (1043)***	8.9 (176)***
	Milk	2-3	2.6 (1051)	2.7 (181)
	Meat	2-3	1.9 (1078)	1.9 (187)
	Bread	4-6	2.7 (1077)***	3.2 (191)***
	Vegetables and fruits	4-5	0.9 (1078)**	1.0 (190)**
	Added sugar		2.0 (1074)	1.9 (189)
	Added fat		1.3 (1053)*	1.1 (176)*
12-18	Four basic	14 maximum	7.4 (900)	7.7 (205)
	Milk	2-3	2.3 (910)	2.2 (209)
	Meat	2-3	1.8 (935)	1.8 (232)
	Bread	4-6	2.5 (937)*	2.8 (233)*
	Vegetables and fruits	4-5	0.8 (931)***	1.0 (234)***
	Added sugar		2.2 (937)	2.3 (231)
	Added fat		1.2 (910)*	1.0 (221)*

[a]Foods were counted according to the food grouping scheme developed by Murphy et al. (1990).

[b]Four basic refers to a dietary quality score that summed intakes from the four food groups (milk, meat, bread, vegetables and fruits) truncated at the recommended level for each age group according to the USDA Daily Food Guide.

[c]Recommended ranges of servings are based on the USDA Daily Food Guide, which was released in 1979; HHANES was conducted in 1982. The current Food Guide Pyramid recommends the following ranges of servings: 2-3 servings of dairy, 2-3 servings of meat or meat substitutes, 6-11 servings of breads, 5-9 servings of fruits and vegetables, and fat and

Puerto Rican		Cuban	
U.S. Mainland Mean (*n*)	Puerto Rico Mean (*n*)	U.S. Mean (*n*)	Foreign Mean (*n*)
7.1 (86)	6.7 (12)	7.1 (26)	0
1.9 (90)	1.8 (13)	2.1 (26)	0
1.7 (88)	1.7 (13)	1.7 (26)	0
2.5 (90)	2.4 (13)	2.3 (26)	0
1.0 (90)	0.7 (12)	1.0 (26)	0
1.6 (90)	1.2 (13)	2.8 (26)	0
0.6 (88)	0.7 (13)	0.5 (26)	0
7.4 (207)	7.5 (53)	7.7 (54)	6.6 (7)
2.4 (211)	2.4 (53)	2.3 (56)	2.5 (7)
1.9 (209)	1.9 (54)	1.8 (56)	1.7 (7)
2.2 (209)	2.3 (54)	2.5 (56)	1.6 (7)
1.0 (209)	1.0 (54)	1.0 (56)	0.8 (7)
2.4 (208)	1.9 (54)	2.9 (56)	4.0 (7)
1.0 (211)	0.8 (54)	1.0 (55)	1.2 (7)
7.9 (307)	8.0 (86)	7.9 (82)	7.7 (33)
2.7 (322)	2.7 (86)	2.7 (86)	2.7 (34)
1.9 (312)	1.9 (87)	1.9 (83)	1.8 (34)
2.3 (318)	2.5 (87)	2.4 (85)	2.3 (34)
1.0 (322)	0.9 (87)	0.9 (84)	0.9 (33)
2.5 (316)	2.3 (85)	2.4 (85)	3.2 (34)
1.2 (315)	1.2 (87)	1.3 (81)	1.1 (32)
7.5 (374)	7.1 (139)	6.7 (81)	6.4 (83)
2.9 (383)**	1.8 (140)**	2.6 (84)	2.1 (85)
1.8 (382)	1.8 (144)	1.7 (83)	1.7 (87)
1.9 (384)	2.1 (145)	1.8 (84)	1.7 (87)
0.9 (386)	0.8 (144)	0.7 (85)**	0.9 (88)**
3.0 (386)	3.0 (144)	3.2 (84)	2.9 (86)
1.2 (378)*	0.9 (142)*	1.1 (82)	1.1 (83)

sugars in moderation. The two guidelines are similar regarding where to place foods, with the significant exception that dessert foods such as cakes, pies, and cookies belong in the added fats group according to the USDA Daily Food Guide and are counted as breads in the Food Guide Pyramid (hence the notable increase in the recommended number of servings).

[d]All means are weighted according to the weight assigned to HHANES participants. Sample sizes below 45 are not large enough for robust statistical analyses; however, they are included here for descriptive purposes. For comparisons between U.S.-born and foreign-born children involving groups larger than 45, statistical significances are as follows: $^{*}p < .05$, $^{**}p < .01$, $^{***}p < .001$.

TABLE 4-6 Chronic Medical Conditions Among U.S.- and Foreign-Born Mexican American, Mainland Puerto Rican, and Cuban American Children

	Mexican American	
% with Chronic Medical Condition (*N*)[a]	U.S.-Born	Foreign-Born
0-11 year olds	3.4 (77)	3.5 (9)
12-18 year olds	4.7 (42)	4.6 (11)

[a]Samples less than $N = 45$ are not reliable population estimates.

[b]Significant difference at $p < .01$ between U.S.- and foreign-born Puerto Rican children. Samples less than 45 are significant only for surveyed subjects and not for overall population.

TABLE 4-7 Selected Parental Reported Medical Conditions for U.S.- and Foreign-Born Mexican American, Mainland Puerto Rican, and Cuban American Children (ages 6 mos. to 12 yrs.; percents (sample size[a])

	Mexican American	
Reported Condition[a]	U.S.-Born ($N = 2{,}493$)	Foreign-Born ($N = 272$)
Anemia now (1-2%)	1.3 (36)	.4 (1)
Ever treated for anemia	6.9 (171)	3.9 (110)
Asthma (5-10%)	4.7 (111)	4.0 (10)
Other lung diseases	3.7 (96)	6.4 (17)
Heart condition	3.5 (84)	3.3 (9)
Urinary tract infection (2.5%)	4.8 (117)	6.3 (17)
Seizures (5%)	3.1 (75)	2.1 (6)
Speech problems (2-5%)	3.3 (83)	4.6 (11)
Psychological problems	1.2 (31)	1.6 (4)
Mental retardation (3%)	0.4 (9)	0 (0)
Poisons	0.9 (22)	2.8 (6)

[a]Samples less than 45 are not reliable population estimates.

[b]Where possible estimation of reported prevalence for all children is noted (from *Nelson Textbook of Pediatrics*, 14th ed., Behrman and Vaughan, Philadelphia, 1992).

[c]Significant difference between U.S.- and foreign-born samples at $p < .05$. Samples less than 45 are significant only for surveyed subjects and not population difference.

Puerto Rican		Cuban American	
U.S.-Born	Foreign-Born	U.S.-Born	Foreign-Born
5.3 (31)	15.1[b] (23)	4.4 (7)	0 (0)
4.8 (17)	6.6 (10)	1.1 (1)	1.1 (1)

Puerto Rican		Cuban American	
Mainland-Born (N = 723)	Island-Born (N = 171)	U.S.-Born (N = 227)	Foreign-Born (N = 53)
3.8 (32)	2.7 (5)	2.0 (5)	0 (0)
14.5 (116)	19.6 (34)	13.8 (32)	12.1 (8)
18.8 (156)	26.9 (41)	6.7 (19)	22.6[c] (12)
2.4 (20)	3.1 (5)	7.0 (19)	3.8 (2)
6.2 (45)	2.3 (4)	5.2 (10)	1.8 (1)
2.8 (25)	1.3 (4)	5.5 (12)	2.7 (1)
4.3 (35)	5.0 (10)	2.5 (5)	4.3 (2)
5.4 (41)	7.3 (10)	3.6 (7)	2.4 (1)
3.4 (27)	6.6 (9)	1.7 (3)	4.5 (2)
1.8 (14)	2.3 (3)	0.5 (1)	0 (0)
2.0 (14)	1.6 (3)	2.0 (4)	1.9 (1)

a significantly higher prevalence of asthma than U.S.-born Cuban Americans, who had a prevalence similar to other U.S. children. However, because of small sample sizes these were considered only trends. Mexican Americans showed no significant difference between U.S.- and foreign-born children and overall reported a lower rate of asthma, 4 to 5 percent. Reports of children having anemia at the time of the survey ranged from 1 to 4 percent, compared to 1 to 2 percent for all U.S. children. Mainland-born Puerto Rican children had the highest prevalence (3.8 percent) and foreign-born Mexican Americans the lowest (0.4 percent). Likewise, reports of ever having received treatment for anemia were highest among Puerto Ricans and lowest among foreign-born Mexican Americans. For other conditions for which overall U.S. prevalence can be determined, only urinary tract infections appeared to be higher and mostly among Mexican American children.

Assessments of perceived health status demonstrated that only 1 percent of all Hispanic children and adolescents were rated in poor health by the survey physicians (see Table 4-8). However, among adolescents the prevalence of perceived poor health was substantially higher. Among all Hispanic subgroups, more adolescents perceived their health as poor than were perceived by survey physicians. Moreover, both foreign-born Mexican American and island-born Puerto Rican adolescents had prevalences that were almost twice those of U.S.-born adolescents.

DISCUSSION

This analysis provides one of the first overviews of the health and nutritional status of immigrant Hispanic children and adolescents, utilizing data from the Hispanic Health and Nutritional Examination Survey (HHANES) conducted in 1982-1984. Although now more than a decade old, the HHANES is, nonetheless, the only large-scale health and nutritional survey currently available on Hispanic children and adolescents. As such, it provides one of the few opportunities to examine immigrant Hispanic children in a comprehensive manner. Unfortunately, the HHANES cannot provide longitudinal information about nutrition and health because of its cross-sectional design and because

TABLE 4-8 Percentage of Adolescents with Poor Health as Assessed by Physicians and Adolescents

Age Group	Rater	Born in Other Country % (Total N)[a]	Born in U.S. % (Total N)
Mexican Americans			
2-11 year olds	Physician	1.4 (257)	1.2 (2206)
12-18 year olds	Physician	0.0 (234)	0.6 (917)
	Adolescent	32.0 (235)	16.5 (917)
Puerto Ricans			
2-11 year olds	Physician	0.0 (148)	0.3 (601)
12-18 year olds	Physician	0.7 (144)	0.7 (384)
	Adolescent	33.7 (144)	13.7 (385)
Cubans			
2-11 year olds	Physician	0.0 (41)	0.0 (164)
12-18 year olds	Physician	1.2 (90)	0.0 (85)
	Adolescent	8.3 (90)	7.2 (85)

[a]Total *N* refers to the unweighted sample size; percentages were calculated by using the sample weights provided in HHANES.

it did not determine age of entry or length of time in the United States for sample subjects. Thus, changes in the nutritional or health status of subjects since immigrating to the United States were not captured in these data. Despite these limitations, this study provides first-time comparisons of health and nutrition parameters for immigrant and nonimmigrant children and adolescents. More importantly, it examines the relationships of these parameters to the demographic variables of age, sex, poverty status, and parental education, thereby providing insights into why differences exist.

This paper focuses on the Mexican American population because of its large sample size in HHANES and because this population contains the greatest number of immigrant children in the United States. Accordingly, this is one of the first studies to differentiate foreign-born from U.S.-born Mexican American children and adolescents. Puerto Rican children are not immigrants but U.S. citizens whether born on the island of Puerto Rico or the U.S. mainland. This group was included because it is the second-largest Hispanic subgroup in the United States and has many of the same demographic characteristics as Mexican Americans, especially a high rate of poverty. The Cuban American sample, while having immigrant subjects, was small, thereby limiting analyses. Nonetheless, their data do provide a partial profile of the nutritional and health status of immigrant Cuban American children and adolescents.

The data from HHANES show that the nutritional status of immigrant Mexican American children and adolescents is variable compared to their U.S.-born Mexican American counterparts. Using the nutritional assessments of height, weight, body mass index, dietary intakes, and anemia, differences between foreign- and U.S.-born Mexican American children and adolescents were shown to exist but were mixed. For example, one of the primary anthropometric findings of the HHANES data showed that both immigrant and nonimmigrant Mexican American subjects were shorter than the NCHS median, the average for the United States. Although U.S.-born Mexican Americans were somewhat taller than those born in Mexico, low SES (as measured by the poverty index or parental education) and not birthplace was the best predictor of height. Given that the genetic potential for height of both immigrant and nonimmigrant Mexican Americans is most likely the same, differences between U.S.- and foreign-born subjects should be mostly environmental. Indeed, it is clear from this study that the heights of all three age cohorts were affected by factors assessing SES, either the poverty score or parental education. Moreover, since foreign-born Mexican American children and adolescents in HHANES had significantly higher poverty rates than their U.S.-born counterparts, it is interesting that greater differences did not exist in height (usually differences were less than 2 cm).

Other studies also have shown that poverty has a significant impact on Mexican Americans' stature (Martorell et al., 1987, 1988a, 1988b, 1989). In fact, height can be used as a measure of prolonged poverty because it reflects continued exposure to a detrimental environment for children's and adolescents' growth

(Martorell et al., 1988a, 1988b; Keller, 1991). Waterlow (1972) introduced the term "stunted" for children in developing countries with very low height for age and the term "wasted" for those with low weight for height. Subsequently, the term "stunting" has been used to imply that children in a defined population have not achieved their presumed potential in height because of negative environmental conditions, such as malnutrition, recurrent infections, or other disease processes. Martorell et al. (1989) have shown that, given middle-class economic conditions, almost all children around the world grow in ways similar to the NCHS standards, suggesting that much of what is seen in height differences between populations of children is due to poverty. Therefore, from the HHANES data it appears that, as populations, both immigrant and U.S.-born Mexican American children are mildly stunted compared to the U.S. standard, principally because of SES conditions. Of interest is that the stunting becomes greater in adolescence. While the lower height in the Mexican American adolescent population may indicate a genetically determined lower final adult height, this conclusion needs to be verified further. With one-third of the U.S.-born sample and half of the foreign-born sample living in poverty, it would be reasonable to assume that poverty's effect is significant for both. It is known that Mexican Americans in the HHANES were taller than the previous generation and like other populations experienced a secular trend of increasing height (Martorell et al., 1989). This suggests that environmental conditions improved for this population of children. Consequently, if they continue to improve, future surveys might reveal improved heights and elimination of the mild stunting presently seen in both immigrant and nonimmigrant Mexican American adolescents.

Even though Mexican American children and adolescents were found to be stunted, they did not appear to be wasted or clinically malnourished as a population. This is not to say that there are not subgroups of Mexican American children who suffer from hunger or malnutrition. Clearly, the level of poverty in the Mexican American sample, particularly in the foreign-born subsample, suggests that obtaining adequate food could have been problematic. Indeed, a survey done in Central California found that one in eight children were hungry, and most of these were poor migrant Mexican Americans (Mendoza, 1994). Nevertheless, the data on weight and BMI (weight/height^2), dietary intake, and anemia suggest that immigrant Mexican American children sampled in HHANES were not significantly wasted or clinically malnourished compared to either U.S.-born Mexican Americans or other U.S. children.

The weight profiles of immigrant Mexican Americans showed that during childhood their weights reasonably matched U.S. standards for age and sex. In fact, females were commonly heavier. The regression analyses for ages 2 to 5 and 6 to 11 indicate that birthplace was not a differentiating factor. Instead, socioeconomic factors were better predictors of weight. But the differential based on SES appeared to be small, about 0.5 kg as predicted by the regression's parameters. Overall, with all Mexican American children's weights more closely approximating the NCHS median than their heights, their weight to height proportions were above the median. Furthermore, it appeared from the BMI data, at least for school-age children, that obesity was a problem with a greater than expected proportion of children above the 90th percentile. This has been previously documented utilizing the anthropometric data, including skin-fold data, from the HHANES for all Mexican American children and youth (Kaplowitz et al., 1989). Unfortunately, this previous analysis did not differentiate foreign-born from U.S.-born children. The present study expands this conclusion to school-age immigrant Mexican American children as well.

Further support for adequate nutrition of immigrant Mexican American children can be derived from the dietary intake data which showed that immigrant school-age children consumed more from the four basic food groups than did U.S.-born Mexican Americans. While food frequency data in general have methodological issues of validity and reliability, applied to both immigrants and nonimmigrants, the data were useful in comparing these two groups. Our analysis showed that immigrant school-age children appeared to have a better-balanced diet, although the amounts per serving and thereby the actual caloric or nutrient intakes of these children could not be inferred from the data. Nonetheless, at a minimum it can be assumed that immigrant children did not have worse diets than U.S.-born Mexican American children, and certainly the weight data supported this conclusion. Unfortunately, at present there are no similarly calculated data for U.S. children overall that would allow for comparisons.

However, Munoz et al. (1997) recently analyzed the USDA's 1989-1991 Continuing Surveys of Food Intakes by Individuals. Their analysis examined the mean number of servings of food groups, and the percentage of individuals meeting national recommendations of dietary intakes. A lower percentage of Hispanic individuals ate the recommended dairy and grain servings and also had lower amounts of food energy than non-Hispanic whites. However, they did not differ in their intakes of fruits, vegetables, and meats. Overall, all children and adolescents were taking in fewer than the recommended servings of foods. Unfortunately, the Munoz study used a different methodology than the current study and also did not differentiate Hispanics by birthplace, subgroup, or poverty status. Thus, further research is needed to detail any specific deficiency in the diets of immigrant Hispanic children or adolescents. Lastly, the reported prevalence of anemia, both present and treated by physicians, is basically equal for both immigrants and nonimmigrants. (Since these data are by parental report, access to health care is an important bias that must be considered in the validity of these data.) Actual analysis of hemoglobin levels of the full sample of Mexican Americans confirmed that the prevalence of anemia among these children was similar to other U.S. children, less than 2 percent, thereby indicating a similar intake of iron, an essential nutrient (Castillo et al., 1990).

Nutritionally, the most disparate findings are for Mexican American adolescents. As noted above, the data indicate a substantial height deviation from the NCHS median. However, it must be remembered that the HHANES data are cross-sectional data and not longitudinal and therefore are not continuous from childhood to adolescence. Thus, what may be observed in these data for Mexican American adolescents is perhaps a cohort effect. That is, these adolescents might have been children during a time or place when environmental conditions were less favorable for growth, thereby affecting their linear growth spurt during early childhood, which has an important effect on final adult height (Proos, 1993). The adolescents in HHANES were born between

1964 and 1970. If nutritional support and health programs were less readily available to Mexican American children in general and for the poor in particular, this could have led to a greater degree of relative malnutrition and poor linear growth. If so, improved height would be expected for children born later, as a result of improved nutritional and health programs for the poor since that time. In fact, as also noted above, the HHANES sample of children are taller than previous samples of Mexican Americans, indicating a secular trend toward increasing height. Yet one argument against the cohort effect is that all three generational levels, first through third, seem to be affected similarly in their height. One would expect that later generations would have better growth in stature as a result of living in a developed country, but this does not seem to be the case. However, it is important to recall that, even among the second and third generations of Mexican Americans, poverty is still more prevalent than among non-Hispanic white children.

Thus, all three generations are impacted by poverty, and most likely this is the common denominator for the stunting seen among Mexican American adolescents. The weights and BMIs seen in both immigrant and nonimmigrant adolescents suggest that caloric intake is currently adequate, and hence at least this part of their nutritional status is adequate. Unfortunately, their intakes of the four basic food groups were less than adequate, suggesting that, although their total caloric intake may be more than adequate, their intake of essential nutrients may be wanting. With the high levels of poverty among all three generations probably limiting the diversity of their diets, this hypothesis is not unreasonable. It may be the lack of adequate nutrients in the diets of Mexican American immigrant and nonimmigrant adolescents that plays a role in their poor linear growth. Munoz et al. (1997) also found that teens were not taking in the recommended daily foods. Further research is needed to examine the question of dietary adequacy for Mexican American adolescents, both immigrants and nonimmigrants.

The growth patterns of Puerto Ricans were similar to Mexican Americans. However, there was a clearer distinction in height between mainland- and island-born Puerto Rican children ages 2 to 11 than between foreign- and U.S.-born Mexican American children. Both mainland- and island-born Puerto Rican adolescents also showed similar stunting in height as Mexican Americans. Likewise, as with Mexican Americans, Puerto Rican children and adolescents, whether born on the mainland or the island, showed weights that matched the NCHS median. This resulted in a greater percentage of children above the 90th percentile for BMI. Therefore, like Mexican Americans, obesity is a problem for this group of children and adolescents. Unlike Mexican Americans, however, there were few reported differences in food group intakes between mainland- and island-born Puerto Rican children. Finally, the rate of anemia was higher for Puerto Ricans compared to the other two Hispanic groups. It was not possible to determine whether this was due to a higher prevalence among Puerto Rican children or just better detection. However, since the sample of Puerto Rican children was drawn from a primarily inner-city population (New York City area), anemia secondary to lead toxicity needs to be considered as a possible cause for the higher prevalence. Cuban American children had very limited sample sizes, and therefore their findings must be considered only descriptive of the sample without generalizability.

Health status was assessed by three measures: prevalence of chronic medical conditions, reported medical conditions, and perceived health status. Among Mexican American immigrants, the prevalence of chronic medical conditions did not differ from U.S.-born Mexican Americans, nor did either group appear to have a higher prevalence than reported among U.S. children in general (about 5 percent). However, the very small sample sizes for foreign-born Mexican Americans make these estimates unreliable as a population estimate. A previous report of chronic medical conditions among all Mexican American children and adolescents also demonstrated no increased prevalence of any one specific chronic illness (Mendoza et al., 1991; Mendoza, 1994). Reported medical conditions by parents also had small sample sizes, and therefore it is difficult to make any definitive statement about the health status of immigrant Mexican American children from these data. Moreover, reporting is based on parents having knowledge of these conditions in their children. If their children had limited health care access, there may be a significant underreporting bias. Given these caveats, it appears that foreign-born Mexican American children are similar to U.S.-born ones and for the most part have similar rates of reported disease as other U.S. children. Only urinary tract infections were reported at a higher rate than the U.S. average. With the association of urinary tract infections being higher in uncircumcised males, this is an interesting finding since Mexican Americans have a low rate of circumcision.

The health parameter that seemed to differentiate foreign-born from U.S.-born Mexican Americans the most was the measure of perceived health status. In general, physicians identified a very small percentage of children and adolescents as being in poor health, approximately 1 percent. In contrast, both U.S.- and foreign-born Mexican American adolescents who responded to the question of perceived health status were much more likely to rate their own health as poor. Moreover, those who were foreign born were almost twice as likely to rate their health as poor than were U.S.-born adolescents. Not all respondents to this question were the adolescents themselves: in some cases their mothers responded. However, mothers also reported similar high percentages of their adolescents as being in poor health. This significant difference between U.S.- and foreign-born adolescents and physicians suggests that either physicians did not identify illness in this population, and indeed that immigrant adolescents have significant levels of untreated disease, or that physicians' concept of health differs from that of Mexican American adolescents. Clearly, a one-time assessment of health status by a physician can, at best, determine only major disease processes. It cannot assess levels of poor functioning as a result of recurrent illnesses, stress, or other factors that affect well-being. Moreover, it is not difficult to imagine that culture can play a significant role in determining an individual's perception of health. Given that physicians make their assessments on medical grounds while subjects usually use a broader range of factors to determine their health status, including their cultural perspective of health, it is not unexpected that there would be differences between physicians and subjects. Nevertheless, the fact that such a high percentage of adolescents reported this level of poor health is alarming, particularly if one considers the demands of adolescence and the importance of achieving functional independence during this period. Research is needed to explore the factors that contribute to these adolescents' sense of poor health.

Puerto Rican children and adolescents differed from Mexican Americans by their higher rate of chronic medical conditions. A previous analysis showed that almost half of these medical conditions were respiratory, principally asthma (Mendoza et al., 1991). This finding is reinforced by the reported high level of asthma among Puerto Rican children in this study. Although not statistically significant, the island population's reported rate of asthma was higher than that of Puerto Rican children born on the U.S. mainland. Gergen et al. (1988) reported a national prevalence of asthma to be 7.6 percent utilizing similar questionnaire data from the NHANES II (1976-1978). This would suggest that the rate of asthma is significantly higher than among other U.S. children. Other medical conditions reported by mothers did not appear to differ by birthplace nor were they higher than the national levels, although most had small sample sizes, thereby limiting their reliability. But as with Mexican Americans, Puerto Rican adolescents similarly demonstrated levels of perceived poor health that were both higher than physician ratings and higher among island-born adolescents. As noted above, multiple factors probably contribute to this disparity.

The data on Cuban Americans were insufficient to make any conclusions. However, it is interesting to note that the reported level of asthma was higher than in Mexican Americans but lower than in Puerto Ricans. Cuban American adolescents reported poor health perception levels similar to non-Hispanic white adolescents, about 5 to 10 percent.

In summary, immigrant Hispanic children and adolescents in HHANES, principally Mexican Americans, were found to be similar in nutritional status to U.S.-born Mexican Americans except for being somewhat shorter. However, the one caution is that the HHANES did not sample some groups of Hispanic children who were at high risk of health care problems because of their mobile residential status and among them were poor new immigrants. Given that exception, Mexican American immigrant children appeared to do well nutritionally, if they were not living in poverty. Poverty was the main determinant of differences in growth between immigrants and nonimmigrants. Thus, as economic conditions improve for Hispanic families and children living in poverty, we would expect them to have better nutritional parameters. Unfortunately, the opposite will also hold true. The cross-sectional nature of the data does not allow for analyses of how growth patterns might change over time; however, previous reports suggest that a secular trend of increasing height is occurring among Mexican Americans, presumably because of improved nutrition and health conditions as a result of better access to health and nutritional services. With regard to health status, the health parameters measured in HHANES were similar between foreign- and U.S.-born Mexican Americans. Only in the perception of health was there a significant difference, suggesting that perhaps factors less well measured by a physician's examination may be influencing what is considered good and poor health.

It is clear that these data are dated and that changes have occurred both in the type and number of Hispanic immigrants and in the numbers living in poverty. It is also clear that the response to these immigrants by the health and social welfare systems in this country is changing. It is not unreasonable to assume that the findings reported here may have worsened from a combination of these factors. Consequently, it is important to further research the differences found in this study and also to monitor changes in parameters that were better than expected in the face of high levels of poverty. NHANES III was released for public evaluation in December 1997 by the National Center for Health Statistics. This survey, which unfortunately was not available at the time the present paper was written, oversampled Mexican Americans and will be a valuable tool in further researching immigrant Mexican American children. However, the dynamics of immigration, particularly for Mexican Americans who travel to and from Mexico, require a more responsive system to monitor the health and nutritional status of these high-risk children. Collaborative efforts between the research community and public health and social welfare agencies to collect and evaluate data in a timely fashion would be of immense value in this endeavor.

REFERENCES

Bureau of the Census
1994 The Foreign-Born Population 1994. Current Population Survey, March 1994, Series P20-486. Washington, D.C.: U.S. Department of Commerce.

Castillo, R.O., M. Garcia, I.G. Pawson, R. Martorell, and F. Mendoza
1990 Iron status of U.S. Hispanic children. *Western Society for Pediatric Research* 38(1):189A.

Delgado, J., C. Johnson, I. Roy, and F. Trevino
1990 Hispanic health and nutrition examination survey: Methodological considerations. *American Journal of Public Health* 80:6-10.

Gergen, P., D. Mullally, and R. Evans
1988 National survey of prevalence of asthma among children in the United States, 1976-1980. *Pediatrics* 81(1):1-17.

Hammer, L., H. Kraemer, D. Wilson, P. Ritter, and S. Dornbusch
1991 Standardized percentile curves of body-mass index for children and adolescents. *American Journal of Diseases of Children* 145:259-263.

Kaplowitz, K., R. Martorell, and F. Mendoza
1989 Fatness and fat distribution in Mexican American children and youths from the Hispanic Health and Nutrition Examination Survey. *American Journal of Human Biology* 1:631-648.

Keller, W.
1991 Stature and weight as indicators of undernutrition. Pp. 113-122 in *Anthropometric Assessment of Nutritional Status*, J. Hines, ed. New York: Wiley-Liss.

Lewit, E.M., and L.G. Baker
1994 Race and ethnicity—changes for children. *The Future of Children, Critical Health Issues for Children and Youth* R:134-144.

Martorell, R., F.S. Mendoza, R.O. Castillo, I.G. Pawson, and C.C. Budge
1987 Short and plump physique of Mexican American children. *American Journal of Physical Anthropology* 73:475-487.

Martorell, R., R. Malina, R. Castillo, F. Mendoza, and I. Pawson
1988a Proportions in three ethnic groups: Children and youths 2-17 years in NHANES II and HHANES. *Human Biology* 60(2):205-222.

Martorell, R., F. Mendoza, and R. Castillo
1988b Poverty and stature in children. In *Linear Growth Retardation in Less Developed Countries*, J.C. Waterlow, ed. New York: Raven Press.

Martorell, R., F. Mendoza, and R. Castillo
1989 Genetic and environmental determinants of growth in Mexican Americans. *Pediatrics* 84(5):864-871.

Mendoza, F.
1994 The health of Latino children in the United States: Critical issues for children and youth. *The Future of Children* 4(3):43-72.

Mendoza, F., S.J. Ventura, R.B. Valdez, R. Castillo, L.E. Saldivar, K. Daisden, and R. Martorell

1991 Selected measures of health status of Mexican American, mainland Puerto Rican, and Cuban American children. *JAMA* 265(2):227-232.

Munoz, K., S. Krebs-Smith, R. Ballard-Barbash, and L. Cleveland

1997 Food intakes of US children and adolescents compared with recommendations. *Pediatrics* 100(3):323-329.

Murphy, S., R. Castillo, R. Martorell, and F. Mendoza

1990 An evaluation of food group intakes by Mexican American children. *Journal of the American Dietetic Association* 90(3):388-393.

National Center for Health Statistics

1985 *Plan and Operation of the Hispanic Health and Nutrition Examination Survey 1982-1984*. Vital and Health Statistics, Series 1, No. 19. DHHS Publication No. (PHS) 85-1321. Hyattsville, Md.: U.S. Department of Health and Human Services.

Proos, L.

1993 Anthropometry in adolescence—secular trends, adoption, ethnic and environmental differences. *Hormonal Research* 39(Suppl. 3):18-24.

Waterlow, J.C.

1972 Classification and definition of protein-calorie malnutrition. *British Journal of Medicine* 3:566-569.

APPENDIX 4A

TABLE 4A-1 Median Heights and Weights for Mexican American Children, Ages 2-11

	Median Heights (cm)		
Age	NCHS	U.S.-Born	Foreign-Born
Mexican American males, ages 2-11			
2	90.4	91.6	93.7
3	99.1	98.4	101.0
4	106.6	104.4	103.5
5	113.1	111.0	110.7
6	119.0	118.8	113.8
7	124.4	123.9	120.7
8	129.6	128.3	126.1
9	134.8	133.2	134.2
10	140.3	138.6	141.1
11	146.4	145.5	145.0
Mexican American females, ages 2-11			
2	90.0	89.2	91.2
3	97.9	96.8	99.5
4	105.0	104.6	107.1
5	111.6	110.8	108.9
6	117.6	117.2	116.8
7	123.5	121.6	122.2
8	129.3	128.0	127.9
9	135.2	136.2	135.2
10	141.5	139.7	143.2
11	148.2	146.6	145.9

Median Weights (kg)		
NCHS	U.S.-Born	Foreign-Born
13.5	14.1	14.2
15.7	15.3	17.0
17.7	17.2	15.9
19.7	19.4	19.2
21.7	21.6	19.3
24.0	24.4	22.7
26.7	27.4	26.4
29.7	30.0	28.5
33.3	33.9	34.6
37.5	40.2	40.4
13.0	12.8	13.6
15.1	14.8	16.4
16.8	16.6	17.8
18.6	18.8	18.2
20.6	20.7	21.5
23.3	23.8	25.7
26.6	27.2	25.5
30.4	32.4	36.4
34.7	35.5	37.7
39.2	39.4	38.4

TABLE 4A-2 Median Heights and Weights for Mexican American Adolescents

	Median Heights (cm)			
Age	NCHS	USB&USP[a]	USB&FBP	Foreign-Born
Mexican American males, ages 12-18				
12	153.0	151.3	150.6	154.8
13	159.9	161.1	159.7	151.3
14	166.2	163.7	167.4	174.4
15	171.5	169.7	167.1	163.4
16	175.2	171.1	170.4	171.7
17	176.7	169.0	175.4	167.5
18		169.8	167.8	165.1
Mexican American females, ages 12-18				
12	154.6	152.7	153.2	155.5
13	159.0	157.3	157.4	157.1
14	161.2	156.4	157.9	154.8
15	162.1	159.8	161.0	159.6
16	162.7	159.0	156.0	158.4
17	163.4	158.9	159.4	157.1
18		158.4	158.8	152.4

[a]First-generation children are all subjects who are foreign born; second-generation children are U.S. born and have one or both parents who are foreign born (USB&FBP); third-generation children are U.S. born and have parents who are both U.S. born (USB&USP).

Median Weights (kg)			
NCHS	USB&USP	USB&FBP	Foreign-Born
42.3	44.6	42.8	46.0
47.8	53.2	49.2	41.2
53.8	54.2	57.5	64.5
59.5	57.6	56.9	74.1
64.4	63.2	61.2	61.4
67.8	60.6	63.2	60.4
68.9	65.8	67.3	68.1
43.8	46.0	47.3	52.0
48.3	51.8	50.5	50.0
52.1	52.4	53.1	57.4
55.0	54.3	55.3	58.0
56.4	53.6	53.4	51.3
56.7	54.2	54.4	49.8
56.6	56.3	59.3	53.7

TABLE 4A-3 Median Heights and Weights for Puerto Rican Males, Ages 2-18

	Median Heights (cm)		
Age	NCHS	U.S.-Born	Foreign-Born
2	90.4	92.3	90.8
3	99.1	99.2	97.4
4	106.6	107.3	104.6
5	113.1	112.5	112.6
6	119.0	118.6	115.6
7	124.4	124.5	123.0
8	129.6	130.2	128.2
9	134.8	135.9	137.3
10	140.3	140.9	138.7
11	146.4	146.5	146.6
12	153.0	155.6	154.7
13	159.9	159.2	158.4
14	166.2	165.0	163.0
15	171.5	169.7	167.2
16	175.2	170.8	168.8
17	176.7	173.0	169.3
18	176.8	172.0	172.7

TABLE 4A-4 Median Heights and Weights for Puerto Rican Females, Ages 2-18

	Median Heights (cm)		
Age	NCHS	U.S.-Born	Foreign-Born
2	90.0	87.9	89.5
3	97.9	97.2	97.4
4	105.0	105.6	105.4
5	111.6	114.1	111.4
6	117.6	119.5	119.3
7	123.5	123.7	117.6
8	129.3	132.7	127.2
9	135.2	136.7	130.6
10	141.5	143.5	140.7
11	148.2	151.7	146.6
12	154.6	155.6	153.4
13	159.0	157.8	158.0
14	161.2	157.0	156.9
15	162.1	157.8	159.6
16	162.7	160.8	162.1
17	163.4	159.9	160.4
18	163.7	160.6	157.8

Median Weights (kg)		
NCHS	U.S.-Born	Foreign-Born
13.5	14.2	14.0
15.7	15.5	16.2
17.7	18.3	16.0
19.7	19.9	19.8
21.7	22.4	21.7
24.0	24.2	23.3
26.7	27.3	25.2
29.7	31.4	31.5
33.3	33.4	33.0
37.5	40.7	35.1
42.3	50.9	41.6
47.8	48.4	45.8
53.8	55.8	57.3
59.5	57.1	59.2
64.4	65.4	64.2
67.8	66.8	59.8
68.9	67.3	67.8

Median Weights (kg)		
NCHS	U.S.-Born	Foreign-Born
13.0	12.7	12.9
15.1	16.0	14.8
16.8	16.8	18.4
18.6	21.8	20.0
20.6	23.0	29.7
23.3	23.4	25.3
26.6	30.5	25.6
30.4	32.4	25.4
34.7	37.4	40.0
39.2	40.1	38.1
43.8	47.4	45.5
48.3	51.4	49.4
52.1	51.4	52.6
55.0	52.7	58.3
56.4	56.9	61.4
56.7	55.8	57.4
56.6	56.4	56.1

TABLE 4A-5 Median Heights and Weights for Cuban Males, Ages 2-18

Age	Median Heights (cm)		
	NCHS	U.S.-Born	Foreign-Born
2	90.4	91.4	
3	99.1	101.4	97.6
4	106.6	108.6	107.2
5	113.1	113.0	112.5
6	119.0	124.1	116.0
7	124.4	127.2	129.3
8	129.6	134.2	134.0
9	134.8	134.9	140.7
10	140.3	143.4	130.7
11	146.4	147.1	144.2
12	153.0	149.8	153.7
13	159.9	162.8	152.8
14	166.2	165.6	162.8
15	171.5	172.8	171.2
16	175.2	174.2	174.7
17	176.7	175.7	170.3
18	176.8	184.5	171.7

TABLE 4A-6 Median Heights and Weights for Cuban Females, Ages 2-18

Age	Median Heights (cm)		
	NCHS	U.S.-Born	Foreign-Born
2	90.0	89.9	
3	97.9	98.7	
4	105.0	106.2	109.1
5	111.6	114.1	111.7
6	117.6	120.8	117.6
7	123.5	127.2	126.7
8	129.3	131.1	123.7
9	135.2	139.4	129.0
10	141.5	142.8	131.3
11	148.2	147.0	148.5
12	154.6	157.6	153.5
13	159.0	155.8	157.8
14	161.2	163.3	155.3
15	162.1	158.6	164.2
16	162.7	155.5	159.1
17	163.4	160.8	160.5
18	163.7	160.5	158.5

Median Weights (kg)		
NCHS	U.S.-Born	Foreign-Born
13.5	13.7	
15.7	16.6	16.3
17.7	19.5	17.2
19.7	20.0	23.3
21.7	27.6	18.7
24.0	28.2	31.8
26.7	35.8	33.0
29.7	32.2	40.1
33.3	41.2	29.3
37.5	52.8	40.6
42.3	39.5	35.8
47.8	51.4	47.6
53.8	52.6	52.4
59.5	58.6	65.4
64.4	58.3	65.4
67.8	65.6	65.3
68.9	84.2	64.4

Median Weights (kg)		
NCHS	U.S.-Born	Foreign-Born
13.0	12.4	
15.1	16.5	
16.8	17.6	20.6
18.6	20.6	16.2
20.6	26.3	22.1
23.3	25.4	25.2
26.6	34.4	24.4
30.4	36.2	28.6
34.7	41.0	27.0
39.2	45.6	38.5
43.8	49.4	49.9
48.3	44.4	42.6
52.1	55.6	49.3
55.0	55.2	56.6
56.4	49.9	48.7
56.7	51.0	54.8
56.6	52.1	57.8

TABLE 4A-7 Body Mass Index and Percentage of BMI Above the 90th Percentile for Mexican American Children and Adolescents

		U.S Born with U.S.-Born Parents	
Age (years)	BMI Reference Average Median	Median BMI (*N*)	% > Reference 90th Percentile
Mexican American males			
2-5	16	—	—
6-11	16.1	—	—
12-18	19.8	20.2 (320)	13.9
Mexican American females			
2-5	15.6	—	—
6-11	16.4	—	—
12-18	19.8	21.3 (336)	16.2

U.S Born with Foreign-Born Parents		Foreign-Born	
Median BMI (*N*)	% > Reference 90th Percentile	Median BMI (*N*)	% > Reference 90th Percentile
15.9 (428)	5.1	16.0(39)	3.4
16.7 (539)	12.4	16.8(85)	13.1
20.4 (215)	11.0	20.8(32)	3.1
15.7 (384)	4.9	15.8 (22)	1.6
16.7 (541)	9.5	17.2 (108)	15.5
21.2 (227)	10.4	21.8 (27)	11.1

TABLE 4A-8 Median Body Mass Index and Percentage of BMI Above 90th Percentile for Puerto Rican Children and Adolescents

Age (years)	BMI Reference Average Median
Puerto Rican Males	
2-5	16
6-11	16.1
12-18	19.8
Puerto Rican Females	
2-5	15.6
6-11	16.4
12-18	19.8

TABLE 4A-9 Median Body Mass Index and Percentage of BMI Above the 90th Percentile for Cuban Children and Adolescents

Age (years)	BMI Reference Average Median
Cuban Males	
2-5	16
6-11	16.1
12-18	19.8
Cuban Females	
2-5	15.6
6-11	16.4
12-18	19.8

U.S. Mainland Born		Puerto Rico Born	
Median BMI (*N*)	% > Reference 90th Percentile	Median BMI (*N*)	% > Reference 90th Percentile
16.0 (110)	6.1	16.0(20)	7.1
16.8 (153)	15.1	16.3(51)	16.7
20.8 (191)	18.3	20.8(72)	17.3
16.1 (94)	5.7	15.8(32)	8.1
16.8 (171)	15.4	17.0(35)	8.9
21.1 (195)	19.8	22.2(74)	16.4

U.S. Born		Foreign Born	
Median BMI (N)	% > Reference 90th Percentile	Median BMI (N)	% > Reference 90th Percentile
16.2(27)	6.9	16.0 (5)	3.4
18.4(42)	28.3	18.4(19)	27.5
20.1(39)	16.4	21.0(55)	8.1
15.9(26)	10.1	15.2 (2)	0
18.9(44)	25.5	16.4(15)	11.8
20.6(45)	7.5	20.6(35)	7.2

CHAPTER 5

Immigration and Infant Health: Birth Outcomes of Immigrant and Native-Born Women

Nancy S. Landale, R.S. Oropesa, and Bridget K. Gorman

In recent years a number of studies have documented an epidemiological paradox. As initially framed (Guendelman, 1988; Markides and Coreil, 1986; Williams et al., 1986), the paradox was that rates of low birthweight and infant mortality are comparable for Mexican-origin and white infants, despite the much poorer socioeconomic profile of the former group. Subsequent studies (e.g., Guendelman et al., 1990; Scribner and Dwyer, 1989) have revealed another puzzling pattern within the Mexican-origin population, namely that the health outcomes of infants of foreign-born mothers are superior to those of infants of native-born mothers. Both sets of findings are contrary to expectations based on the risk factors emphasized in traditional biomedical models of public health (Scribner, 1996). They are also inconsistent with the classic assimilation model of immigrant adjustment (Park, 1950), which posits that the outcomes of immigrant groups improve the longer they reside in the United States.

In the current era of high rates of immigration and renewed interest in understanding both the current situations and the long-term trajectories of immigrant groups, this epidemiological paradox has generated widespread attention. Yet despite the diversity of post-1965 immigrants to the United States (Portes and Rumbaut, 1996), studies of immigrants' reproductive outcomes have focused primarily on the Mexican-origin population. Studies have not systematically assessed the health outcomes of infants of immigrant women from other national origins (see Cabral et al., 1990; Rumbaut and Weeks, 1989, 1996; and Singh and Yu, 1996, for exceptions). Thus, the extent to which the epidemiological paradox is characteristic of most or only a few immigrant groups has not been established.

The present study addresses this issue using data from the 1989, 1990, and 1991 Linked Birth/Infant Death Datasets (U.S. Department of Health and Human Services, 1995). The relationship between maternal nativity (U.S. versus foreign birthplace) and infant health is examined in a number of Latino and Asian groups, including Mexicans, Cubans, Puerto Ricans,[1] Central/South Americans, Chinese, Filipinos, Japanese, and other Asian/Pacific Islanders.

BACKGROUND

Over the past several decades, both the number and the diversity of U.S. immigrants have increased sharply (Portes and Rumbaut, 1996). Since the mid-1980s, about 1 million legal immigrants have been admitted to the United States each year (U.S. Immigration and Naturalization Service, 1996). These new immigrants have come primarily from countries in Asia and Latin America. In 1993, for example, about 40 percent were from Asia and 37 percent were from Latin America and the Caribbean. The major Asian source countries are mainland China, the Philippines, Vietnam, India, and Korea. Major origin countries in Latin America and the Caribbean include Mexico, the Dominican Republic, and El Salvador.

The recency of immigration from Asia and Latin America is evident in the high proportion of U.S.-born infants who have foreign-born mothers. Although 18 percent of all U.S. births are to foreign-born women, 62 percent of Latino births and 85 per-

[1]Puerto Ricans are not an immigrant group per se because of the commonwealth status of the island of Puerto Rico. Nonetheless, because they are one of the largest Hispanic groups in the United States, we include them in the analysis for comparative purposes. For Puerto Ricans the "foreign born" are those born in Puerto Rico.

cent of Asian/Pacific Islander births are to women who were themselves born outside this country (Ventura et al., 1995). These figures attest to the importance of understanding how immigrant status and the assimilation process among immigrants affect the health of infants and children.

Immigration, Assimilation, and Infant Health

Understanding the health outcomes observed among the offspring of immigrants requires attention to several interrelated aspects of the immigration and settlement process. First, given the well-documented relationship between socioeconomic position and health (Williams and Collins, 1995), the implications of the sources of immigration for the socioeconomic status of the immigrant population must be considered. There are striking differences in the educational attainment and skill levels of immigrants from various origin countries *at the time of their arrival in the United States.* The upper stratum of foreign-born groups tends to have higher educational and occupational attainment than the average for the native-born U.S. population. This category is comprised of Asian immigrants from India, Taiwan, Iran, Hong Kong, the Philippines, Japan, Korea, and China (Rumbaut, 1994). In the lower stratum are immigrants from Latin American and Caribbean countries, such as Mexico, El Salvador, Guatemala, and the Dominican Republic, who have low levels of educational attainment and tend to work in low-wage unskilled jobs. These divergent profiles stem from differences across origin countries in economic development and population composition. The type of immigrant flow (e.g., unskilled labor migration versus "brain drain" migration) also affects the socioeconomic composition of immigrants from various source countries.

In addition to their characteristics at time of arrival in this country, the way in which immigrants adapt to U.S. society affects the health and well-being of their children. The adaptation of immigrants traditionally has been studied within an assimilation framework which posits that immigrants will become increasingly similar to the native population as they spend more time in this country (Park, 1950; Gordon, 1964). Eventually, often after several generations, immigrants lose their socioeconomic and cultural distinctiveness. Because immigrants occupy the lower rungs of the socioeconomic ladder more often than not, the assimilation framework implies that immigrants (and their children) will initially experience a health disadvantage, which will decline with duration of residence (for the foreign born) and generation in the United States.

For a number of reasons (see Massey, 1995; Zhou, 1997), the patterns observed among recent immigrants are sometimes inconsistent with expectations based on the assimilation framework. One reason is the socioeconomic diversity of post-1965 immigrants. A significant number of immigrants are highly educated and skilled and thus attain high-status positions and middle-class lifestyles quickly upon arrival in the United States (Zhou, 1997). Although such immigrants experience social and cultural adjustments, the barriers they encounter are very different from those faced by immigrants who arrive with little human or financial capital. Thus, the nature of the assimilation process may differ substantially according to the resources immigrants possess at the time of immigration.

A related reason for departures from the classic assimilation pattern is that recent immigrants arrived in this country during a period of restricted economic growth and rising income inequality (Massey, 1995). In particular, opportunities for upward mobility are limited for those with little education and few skills. Thus, immigrants with low skill levels, like U.S.-born minority groups, face structural barriers to achievement. Their assimilation into the middle-class mainstream is also impeded by settlement in impoverished neighborhoods that lack resources and have extensive social problems.

The assimilation framework has also been challenged with respect to its assumptions about the role of origin cultures. The traditional theory presumed that forsaking the home culture was a necessary part of the process of Americanization, which ultimately improved the situation of immigrant groups. However, recent research shows that immigrant cultures often have protective features that contribute to the well-being of the foreign born and their offspring (Guendelman, 1988; Guendelman et al., 1990; Guendelman and Abrams, 1995; Rumbaut and Weeks, 1996; Rumbaut 1997; Scribner and Dwyer, 1989; Scribner, 1996). Furthermore, opportunities for biculturalism have increased for some immigrant groups (e.g., Mexicans) with the growth of ethnic communities in areas that receive an ongoing stream of new immigrants (Massey, 1995).

The epidemiological paradox is part of a growing set of research results that are contrary to the classic assimilation framework. In the following section we discuss possible explanations of the finding that the infants of foreign-born mothers are healthier at birth than the infants of native-born mothers.

Explanations of the Epidemiological Paradox

A number of factors potentially contribute to variations in infants' health by mothers' nativity status. An obvious first candidate is differences in the socioeconomic status (SES) of native- and foreign-born mothers (Williams and Collins, 1995). Previous studies documented that differences in the birth outcomes of native- and foreign-born Mexican-origin women are contrary to a socioeconomic model—that is, outcomes are better for foreign-born women, who generally have lower education and income than the native born. In addition, the pattern of superior birth outcomes among the foreign born holds in models in which SES is controlled.

The other explanatory factor emphasized in studies of racial/ethnic disparities in health is medical care. However, in studies of Mexicans the findings for prenatal care parallel those for SES: rates of low birthweight and infant mortality are lower for the foreign born, despite the fact that they receive less adequate prenatal care. Thus, research on birth outcomes in the largest immigrant group calls into question the prevailing public health model that focuses on the importance of SES and medical care.

Alternative explanations of the health advantage of foreign-born infants include the selective migration of healthier mothers to the United States and the protective influence of origin cultures (Guendelman, 1988). Although the former explanation has received little empirical study because of data limitations, the latter has been the focus of considerable research attention (Cobas et al., 1996; Collins and Shay, 1994; Guendelman, 1988; Guendelman et al., 1990; Guendelman and Abrams, 1995;

Rumbaut and Weeks, 1996; Scribner and Dwyer, 1989; Scribner, 1996). In particular, scholars have attempted to identify the behavioral mechanisms through which immigrant cultures (especially the Mexican culture) affect infant health. Included among the explanations offered are better nutrition, less smoking and drinking, and greater social support. As cultural norms erode with time in the United States, the beneficial health practices of immigrants apparently weaken.

How these various determinants of infant health operate for immigrant groups other than Mexican Americans is not well known. In the following sections we summarize our analyses of the effect of maternal nativity on low birthweight and infant mortality among non-Latino whites, non-Latino blacks, Mexicans, Cubans, Puerto Ricans, Central/South Americans, Chinese, Filipinos, Japanese, and other Asian/Pacific Islanders.

FINDINGS

Although the majority of infants born in the United States have non-Latino white or non-Latino black mothers, a growing share of U.S. births are to Latino or Asian women. During the period from 1989 through 1991, 14.2 percent of all U.S. births were to Latino women, with Mexicans constituting 9.1 percent. About 3.5 percent of newborns had Asian mothers. Given the recency of immigration from many Latin American and Asian countries, it is not surprising that a substantial share of the Latino and Asian women giving birth were foreign born. For non-Latino white and non-Latino black infants, the percentages with foreign-born mothers are relatively low—4.0 and 6.4, respectively.[2] But with the exception of Puerto Rican and Japanese infants, foreign-born mothers predominate in the Latino and Asian groups considered in our study. Among Latinos the share of births to foreign-born mothers was 62 percent among Mexicans, 79 percent among Cubans, and 96 percent among Central/South Americans. Among

[2]These numbers and those presented in all subsequent tables and figures are based on data from the 1989-1991 Linked Birth/Infant Death Datasets. The analysis is restricted to singleton births. See Appendix 5A for a full description of the datasets, sample, and variables.

Asian infants, about 86 percent of Filipinos, 89 percent of Chinese, and 94 percent of other Asian/Pacific Islanders had mothers born outside the United States.

The high proportion of births to foreign-born women in these groups illustrates the growing importance of understanding the impact of immigration on children born in the United States, who are U.S. citizens at birth regardless of their parents' citizenship status. A critical aspect of children's well-being at birth is their physical health, which is commonly measured for infants by rates of low birthweight and infant mortality.[3] In Figure 5-1 the percentage low birthweight is shown for infants of native-born and foreign-born women from each racial/ethnic group. With the exception of Japanese and other Asian/Pacific Islanders, the pattern is consistent with the epidemiological paradox in that the offspring of foreign-born mothers have more favorable birthweights than the offspring of native-born mothers.[4] Although the magnitude of the nativity difference in low birthweight is small for some groups (e.g., Puerto Ricans, Cubans, Central/South Americans), in others it is more substantial. For example, among Mexican-origin infants, the percentage of low-birthweight infants for those with foreign-born mothers is 4.1, compared to 5.4 for infants with native-born mothers. The figures for the offspring of foreign- and native-born Chinese mothers are 3.8 and 4.8, respec-

[3]Low birthweight is defined as a weight at birth of less than 2,500 grams. Infant mortality is defined as death during the first year of life.

[4]The other Asian/Pacific Islander group is heterogeneous with respect to national origins. It includes such diverse groups as Asian Indians, Koreans, Samoans, Vietnamese, and Guamanians. The 1989-1991 Linked Birth/Infant Death Datasets do not include information with which to distinguish these various national-origin groups, but such information is available for a subset of reporting states in the 1992-1994 National Center for Health Statistics (NCHS) Natality Files. Based on the 1992-1994 data, rates of low birthweight for singleton infants of foreign-born mothers for subgoups within the other Asian/Pacific Islander category are 9.33 for Asian Indians, 3.85 for Koreans, 4.22 for Samoans, 5.23 for Vietnamese, and 6.90 for Guamanians. Rates of low birthweight for infants of native-born mothers could not be calculated for these groups because of an insufficient number of cases. Because the 1992-1994 NCHS Natality Files are restricted to birth certificate data, rates of infant mortality also cannot be calculated for these Asian groups.

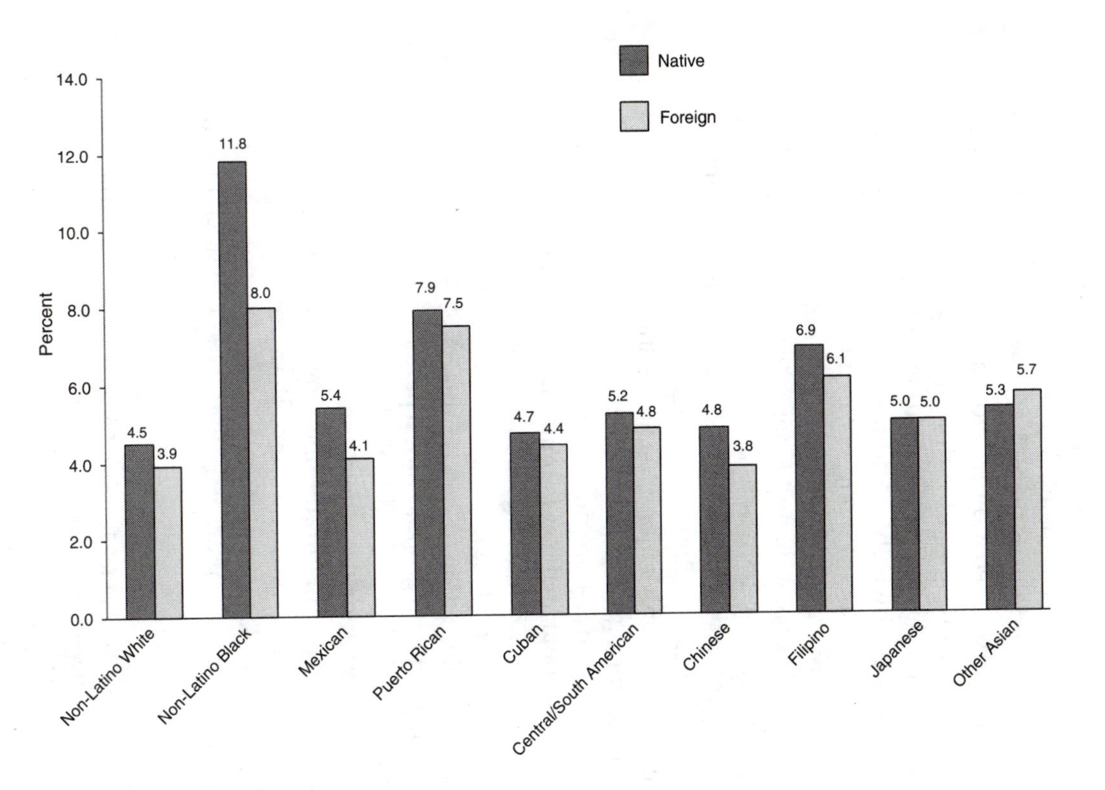

FIGURE 5-1 Nativity differences in low birthweight by ethnicity.

tively. Although data for blacks are presented largely for comparative purposes, the maternal nativity differential in low birthweight for blacks (8.0 versus 11.8) is striking.

Also evident in Figure 5-1 are large ethnic differentials in low birthweight. Indeed, the ethnic differentials are of considerably greater magnitude than the differences by maternal nativity. Of the groups considered, non-Latino blacks have a markedly higher percentage of low-weight births than all other groups. Puerto Ricans and Filipinos also stand out for their higher-than-average rates of low birthweight. Additionally, despite the slight health advantage of infants of foreign-born mothers compared to infants of native-born mothers within most ethnic groups, offspring of foreign-born women have higher rates of low birthweight than offspring of native-born non-Latino white women in the majority of ethnic groups (i.e., non-Latino blacks, Puerto Ricans, Central/South Americans, Filipinos, Japanese, and other Asian/Pacific Islanders). It is only among Mexicans and the Chinese that immigrants' offspring have lower rates of low birthweight than the offspring of native-born non-Latino whites.[5]

In additional analyses (summarized in Table 5A-2) we decomposed low birthweight into its two component parts: prematurity (< 2,500 grams and less than 37 weeks' gestation) and intrauterine growth retardation (< 2,500 grams and ≥ 37 weeks' gestation).[6] For prematurity all groups show a pattern consistent with the epidemiological paradox: the rate of prematurity is higher for infants of native-born mothers than for infants of foreign-born mothers. The rate of intrauterine growth retardation is higher for infants of native-born mothers than for non-Latino whites, non-Latino blacks, and all Latino groups. For Asians the role of maternal nativity is more variable. Low birthweight caused by

---

[5]The rate for infants of foreign-born Cuban women is essentially the same as that for native non-Latino women (4.4 versus 4.5).

[6]Intrauterine growth retardation has been defined in a number of different ways in the literature. Our purpose here is to distinguish low birthweight due to inadequate gestation from that caused by other causes. However, some definitions of intrauterine growth retardation (e.g., less than the tenth percentile for gestational age) classify a nontrivial share of infants weighing 2,500 grams or more as growth retarded.

intrauterine growth retardation is more common among infants of native-born mothers than infants of foreign-born mothers among the Chinese and Filipinos; however, the magnitude of the maternal nativity differential is much smaller than that for prematurity for both groups. Among the Japanese and other Asian/Pacific Islanders, infants of foreign-born mothers have higher rates of intrauterine growth retardation than infants of native-born mothers.

Figure 5-2 shows rates of infant mortality (deaths per 1,000 live births) by maternal nativity for each racial/ethnic group. For all groups except the Japanese the infant mortality rate is lower for children of immigrants than for children of the native born, although it is only slightly lower in some ethnic groups (e.g., Central/South Americans, Chinese). Among Latinos and Asians the largest differences are evident for Mexicans (5.3 versus 6.6 per 1,000) and Filipinos (4.8 versus 6.8 per 1,000). The infant mortality rate is also much lower for the offspring of black immigrants than for the offspring of black natives (10.5 versus 12.9 per 1,000). In contrast to the pattern for birthweight, infants of foreign-born mothers in almost all ethnic groups have lower rates of infant mortality than infants of native non-Latino white mothers. Blacks and Puerto Ricans are the only groups for which the infant mortality rate for children of foreign-born mothers is higher than that of children for native non-Latino white mothers.

Separate analyses (summarized in Table 5A-2) of neonatal mortality (death under 28 days of age) and postneonatal mortality (death between 28 days and one year of age) revealed a less consistent pattern. While the rate of neonatal mortality is lower for infants of foreign-born mothers than infants of native-born mothers for some groups (non-Latino whites, non-Latino blacks, Mexicans, Cubans, and Filipinos), for others (Central/South Americans, Chinese, Japanese, other Asian/Pacific Islanders) it is higher. In contrast, the postneonatal mortality rate is lower for immigrants' children than for natives' children for all groups except Cubans. Neonatal mortality is affected more by factors outside a mother's control (e.g., preexisting biological conditions of the mother, access to high-quality medical care) than is postneonatal mortality. Postneonatal death is generally affected more

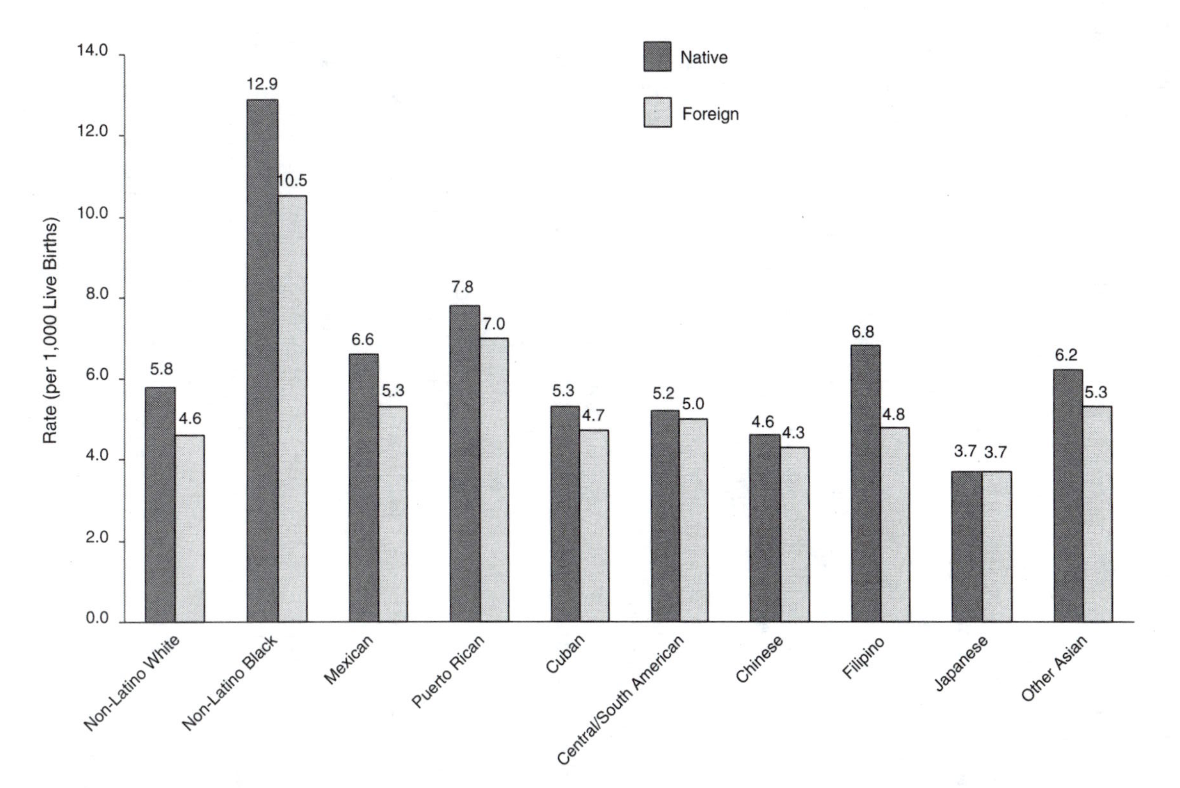

FIGURE 5-2 Nativity differences in infant mortality by ethnicity.

by socioeconomic and environmental factors that may vary more regularly with the mother's nativity status (Samuels, 1986).

Antecedent and Mediating Variables

How can the better reproductive outcomes of foreign-born women compared to native-born women be explained? To answer this question it is necessary to understand the causes of low birthweight and infant mortality and to determine how immigrant and native women differ with respect to important risk factors. Despite extensive research, the determinants of low birthweight are poorly understood (Shiono and Behrman, 1995). Nonetheless, there is widespread agreement that low birthweight owing to intrauterine growth retardation has somewhat different causes than low birthweight owing to preterm birth. There appear to be three major risk factors for low birthweight due to poor intrauterine growth: smoking during pregnancy, low maternal weight gain during pregnancy, and low prepregnancy weight (Kramer, 1987). Other factors (e.g., maternal age, maternal education, parity, infant sex, prior low-birthweight birth) have important direct and indirect influences on intrauterine growth but play a smaller role in accounting for variations. Less is known about the risk factors for preterm delivery. Factors with well-established causal effects are prepregnancy weight, prior history of prematurity or spontaneous abortion, in utero exposure to diethylstilbestrol, and smoking during pregnancy (Kramer, 1987).

Low birthweight is both a pregnancy outcome and a determinant of other pregnancy outcomes, such as infant death. In fact, low birthweight is the major determinant of neonatal mortality, accounting for two-thirds of neonatal deaths (Samuels, 1986). Thus, the risk factors for low birthweight have an indirect causal impact on neonatal mortality. Although low birthweight is also associated with postneonatal death, the relationship is weaker than in the neonatal period. Congenital anomalies, maternal demographic and socioeconomic characteristics (e.g., age, parity, education), and access to health care are especially important risk factors for postneonatal death.

The multiple risk factors for low birthweight and infant mortality are perhaps best understood in terms of a conceptual framework that distinguishes between antecedent and intervening variables. Antecedent variables are characteristics of the mother that influence her lifestyle and the medical care she receives during pregnancy, which in turn affect pregnancy outcomes. Antecedent factors available in the Linked Birth/Infant Death Datasets and considered in our analysis include maternal race/ethnicity, nativity, age, marital status, and education. Intervening variables are maternal behaviors that more directly affect reproductive outcomes, including smoking, drinking, nutritional intake (measured by weight gain during pregnancy),[7] and use of prenatal care. Also included in our analyses as control variables are the gender and birth order of the infant. A complete list of the variables and coding procedures is provided in Appendix 5A.

The most consistent differences in antecedent factors between native and foreign-born mothers pertain to age and marital status (see Table 5A-2). In most of the racial/ethnic groups, native-born mothers are more likely to be young (less than 20) and single than are foreign-born mothers. Nativity differences in education (the only indicator of socioeconomic status in our data) are more variable across ethnic groups. The pattern for Central/South Americans, the Chinese, and other Asian/Pacific Islanders is consistent with that revealed here and elsewhere for Mexicans: the foreign born have lower levels of educational attainment than the native born.[8] In contrast, among non-Latino whites, non-Latino blacks, Puerto Ricans, Cubans, and Filipinos, foreign-born mothers have more education than native-born mothers.[9] Thus, in the latter groups the more favorable birth outcomes of the foreign born are not at odds with a socioeconomic model.

Figure 5-3 presents information on the intervening variables. The data for smoking show that native-born mothers are substan-

[7]Ideally, the mother's prepregnancy weight would be controlled in models estimating the effect of weight gain during pregnancy on low birthweight. Unfortunately, there is no measure of prepregnancy weight in the 1989-1991 Linked Birth/Infant Death Datasets.

[8]Foreign-born Japanese mothers also have slightly lower levels of educational attainment that native-born Japanese mothers.

[9]The nativity difference in maternal education is small, however, for Puerto Ricans and Cubans.

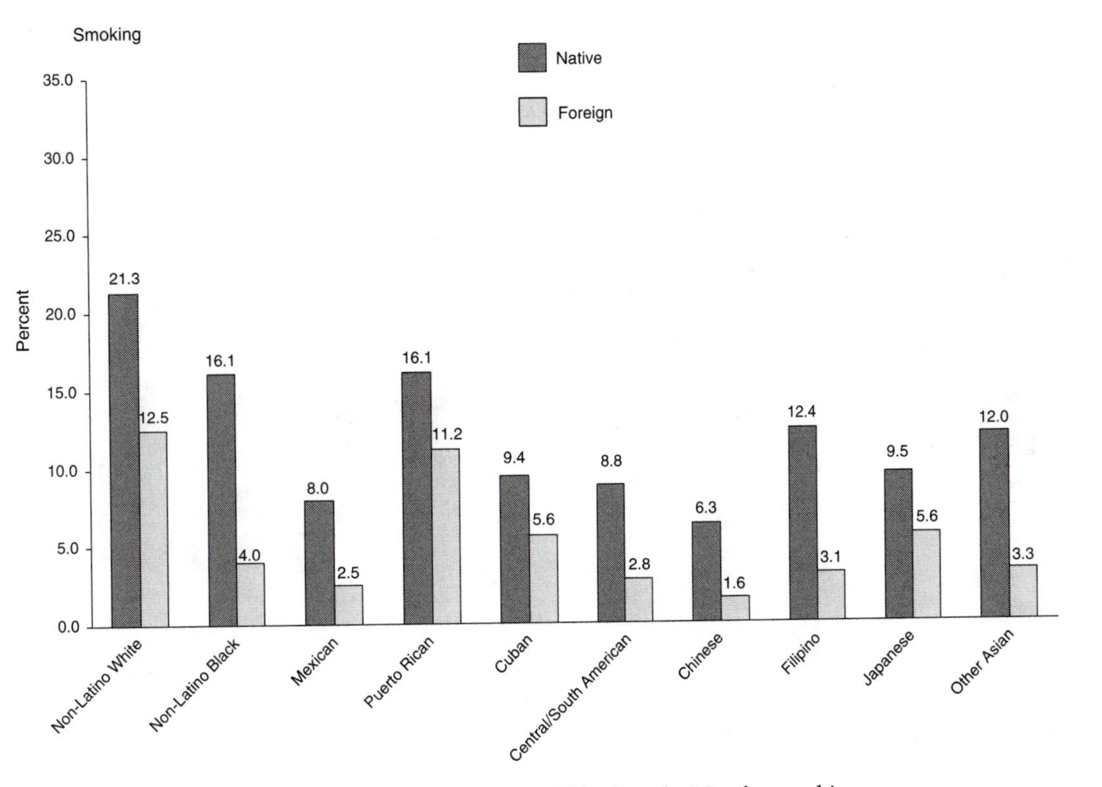

FIGURE 5-3 Nativity differences in intevening variables by ethnicity for smoking.

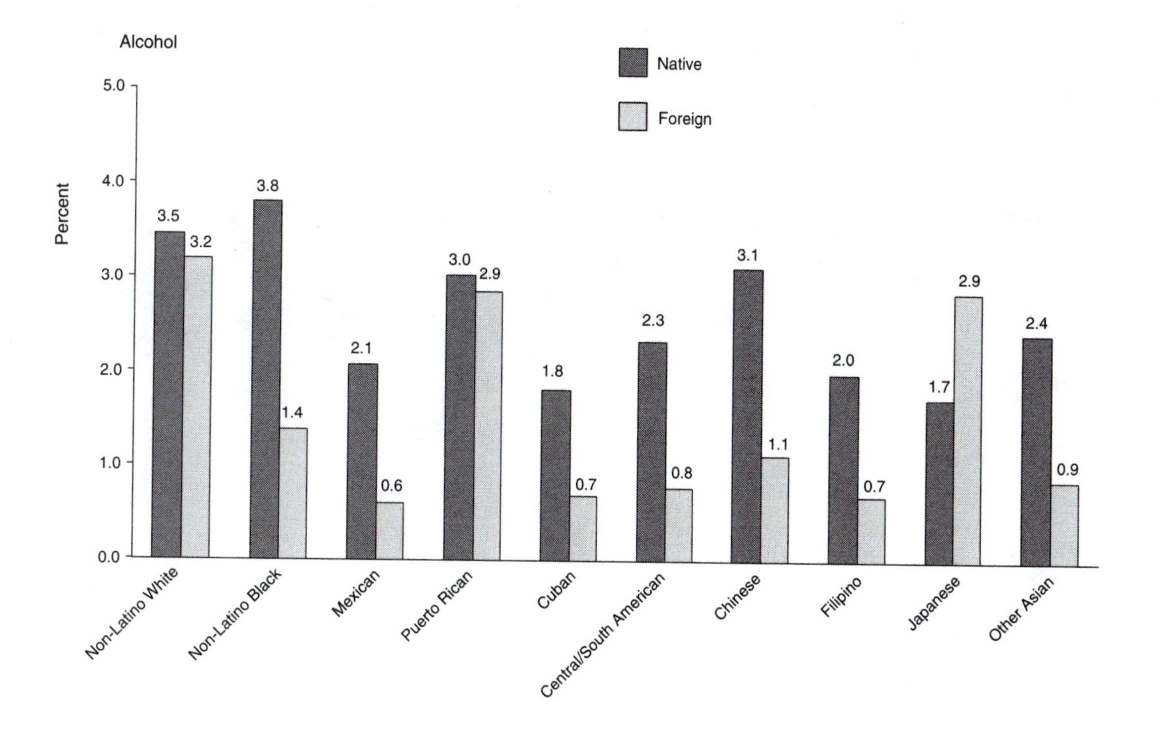

FIGURE 5-3 Continued. Alcohol.

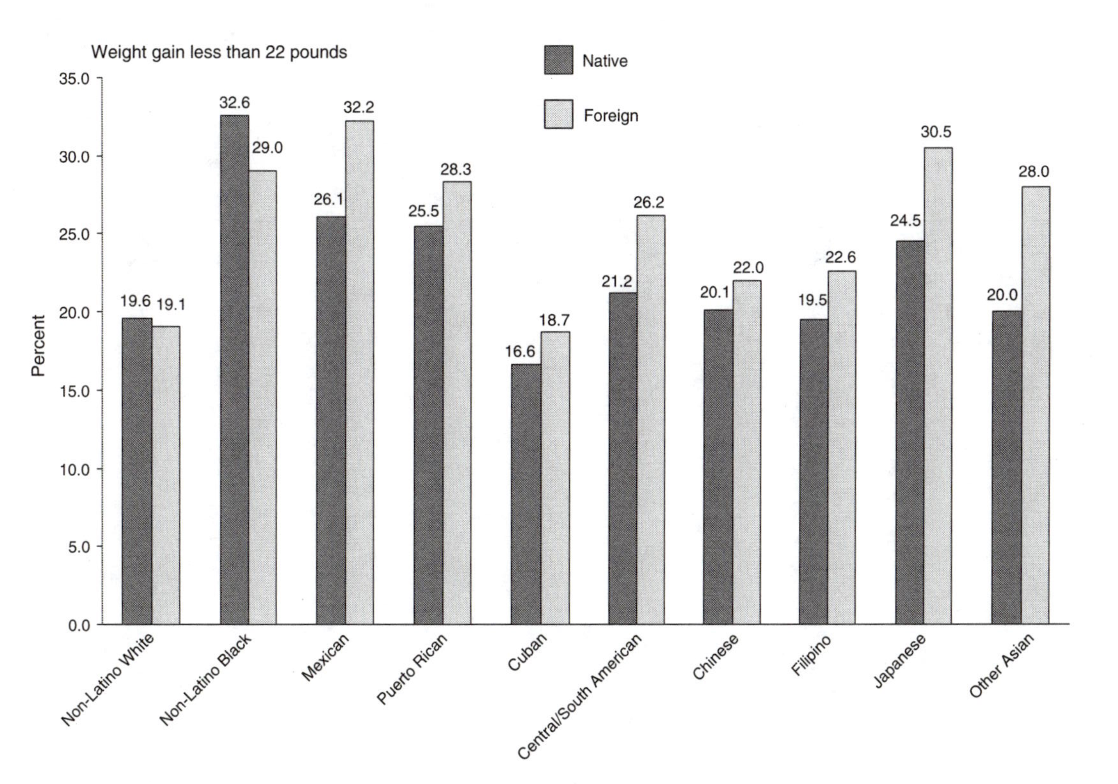

FIGURE 5-3 Continued. Weight gain less than 22 pounds.

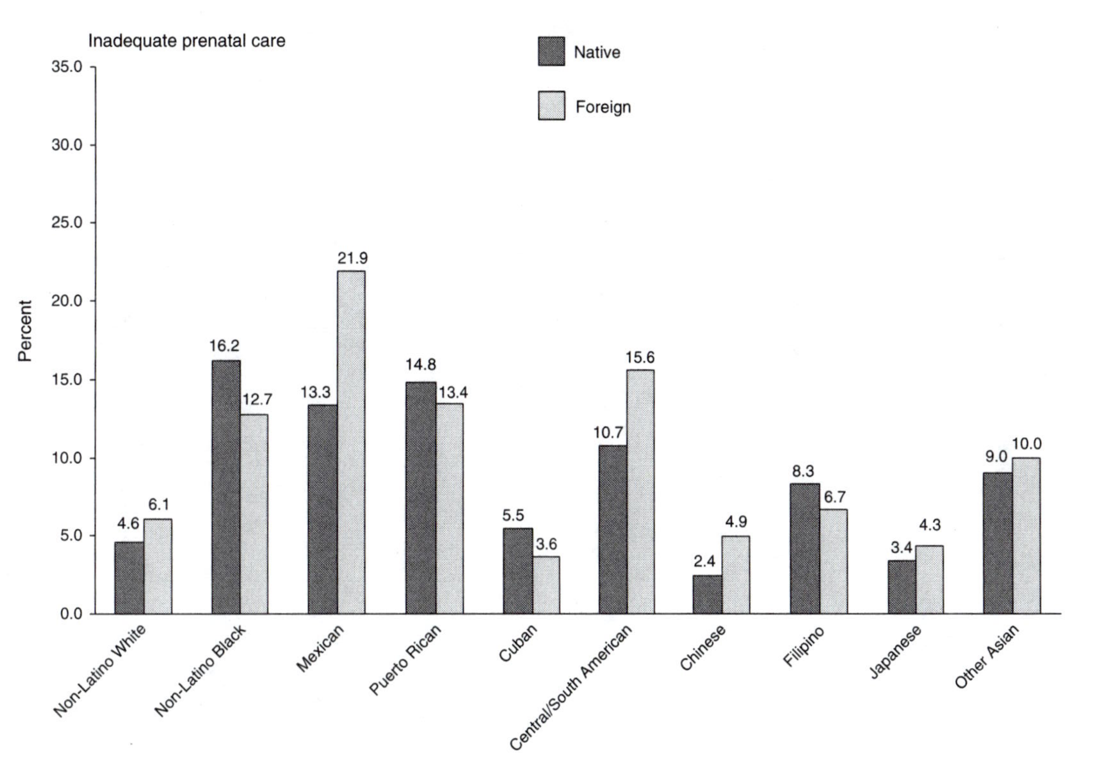

FIGURE 5-3 Continued. Inadequate prenatal care.

tially more likely to have smoked during pregnancy than are foreign-born mothers. For example, 8.0 percent of native-born Mexican mothers smoked while pregnant, compared to 2.5 percent of foreign-born Mexican mothers. The percentages for native and foreign-born Chinese mothers are 6.3 and 1.6, respectively. Given that smoking is one of the most important risk factors for low birthweight, this pattern undoubtedly contributes to the higher rate of low birthweight among infants of the native born compared to infants of the foreign born. Although the pattern for drinking is generally in the same direction (with the exception of the Japanese), the nativity differences are more moderate. Additionally, prior studies have demonstrated that drinking is a weaker predictor of infant birthweight than is smoking (Chomitz et al., 1995).

Nativity differences in maternal weight gain and prenatal care also are shown in Figure 5-3. Insufficient weight gain during pregnancy (less than 22 pounds) is an indicator of inadequate nutritional intake, which may affect intrauterine growth. Surprisingly, foreign-born women are generally more likely than native-born women to not gain sufficient weight during pregnancy. This is the case for all Latino and Asian groups, although in some cases the nativity difference is small. The pattern for prenatal care is highly inconsistent across racial/ethnic groups. Native-born blacks, Puerto Ricans, Cubans, and Filipinos are more likely to receive inadequate prenatal care (as measured by the Kessner Index) than their foreign-born counterparts. For all remaining groups the opposite pattern holds. However, Mexicans and Central/South Americans are the only groups in which the foreign born are substantially more likely to receive inadequate prenatal care than the native born (21.9 versus 13.3 percent for Mexicans; 15.6 versus 10.7 percent for Central/South Americans).

Multivariate Models

Low Birthweight

Can differences between immigrants and natives in infant birthweights be explained in terms of the risk factors identified above? To address this question we estimated multivariate models in which all antecedent and intervening variables were controlled (see Table 5A-3).[10] For most ethnic groups the predictors are related to infant birthweight in the expected direction. Nonetheless, net of all predictors, infants of foreign-born mothers continue to have a lower risk of low birthweight than infants of native-born mothers for all groups except Cubans, Japanese, and other Asian/Pacific Islanders. The risk factors that exhibit the most consistent relationships with low birthweight across ethnic groups are advanced maternal age (35+), single motherhood, first-birth status, maternal smoking, low maternal weight gain, and inadequate prenatal care. Maternal education is generally related to birthweight in the expected negative direction, but education appears to have weaker and less consistent effects than the other predictors in the multivariate models.

Figure 5-4 shows predicted rates of low birthweight calculated from the models in Table 5A-3. Both a best-case scenario and a worst-case scenario are shown for each racial/ethnic group. The best-case scenario shows predicted rates for female infants with the most favorable characteristics (i.e., second, third, or fourth children of 20- to 34-year-old married mothers with some college who received adequate prenatal care, did not smoke or drink, and gained at least 22 pounds during pregnancy). The worst-case scenario presents predicted rates for female infants with the least favorable characteristics (i.e., first children of single mothers less than 20 years of age who did not complete high school and who received inadequate prenatal care, smoked, drank, and gained less than 22 pounds during pregnancy).[11]

Under the best-case scenario, nativity differences in the percentages of low-birthweight infants are generally small. The largest nativity difference is for non-Latino blacks, for whom the

---

[10]Alcohol consumption was included in the equations for all groups except the Chinese and Japanese because there were too few cases in which the women drank alcohol during pregnancy to include drinking as a variable.

[11]Although women ages 35 and over exhibit poorer birth outcomes in our multivariate models of low birthweight than women under age 20, we use the latter group in calculating the predicted probabilities because first births to women age 35+ are very uncommon in the groups examined.

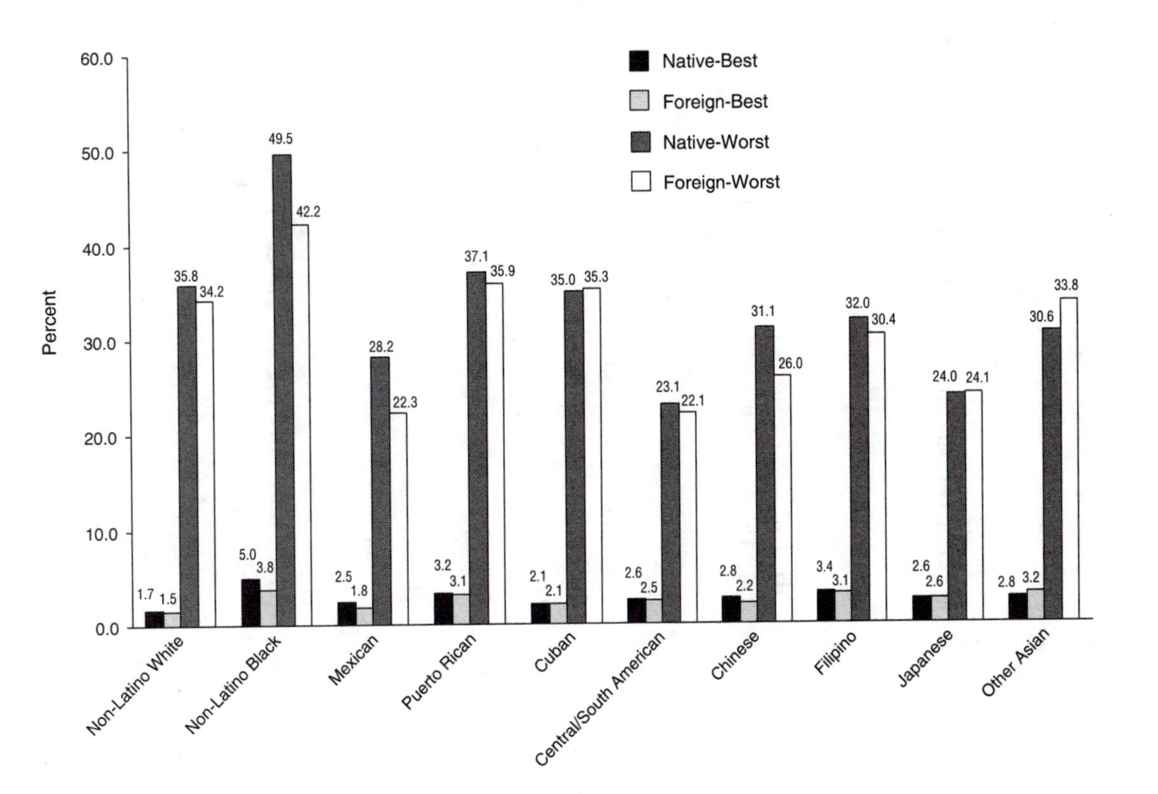

FIGURE 5-4 Predicted percentage of low-birthweight infants: best- and worse-case scenarios.

rates of low birthweight for infants with native- and foreign-born mothers are 5.0 and 3.8, respectively. Under the worst-case scenario, nativity differences are much greater for some ethnic groups, especially non-Latino blacks, Mexicans, and the Chinese. For example, the percentage of low-birthweight babies among high-risk Mexican infants of native-born mothers is 28.2, compared to 22.3 for comparable Mexican infants with foreign-born mothers. Nonetheless, Figure 5-4 makes clear that under the worst-case scenario racial/ethnic differences in low birthweight are greater than differences by maternal nativity.

Infant Mortality

Controlling for the full set of antecedent and intervening variables (see Table 5A-4), infants of foreign-born mothers continue to have a low risk of death compared to infants of native-born mothers (with the exception of the Chinese and Japanese). As was the case for low birthweight, single motherhood, smoking, low maternal weight gain during pregnancy, and inadequate prenatal care increase the risk of infant mortality. Maternal age and birth order have less consistent effects on infant mortality than on birthweight, and male infants are at higher risk of death than female infants even though they have a more favorable birthweight distribution. For most groups, education is negatively related to the risk of infant death, but the relationship is generally not strong.

Figure 5-5 illustrates the magnitude of the nativity differentials in low birthweight, controlling for the full set of covariates. Predicted rates of infant mortality are calculated from the equations in Table 5A-4, with best- and worst-case scenarios identical to those discussed previously for birthweight. Under the best-case scenario, rates of infant mortality are very low and nativity differentials are slight (although generally in the expected direction). Under the worst-case scenario, nativity differentials are more substantial. For example, among non-Latino whites, the infant mortality rates for infants of native- and foreign-born mothers, respectively, are 30.6 and 25.9 per 1,000. For Mexicans and Filipinos, comparable figures are 20.2 versus 15.7 and 74.7 versus 70.5. Nonetheless, it is apparent once again that the nativity dif-

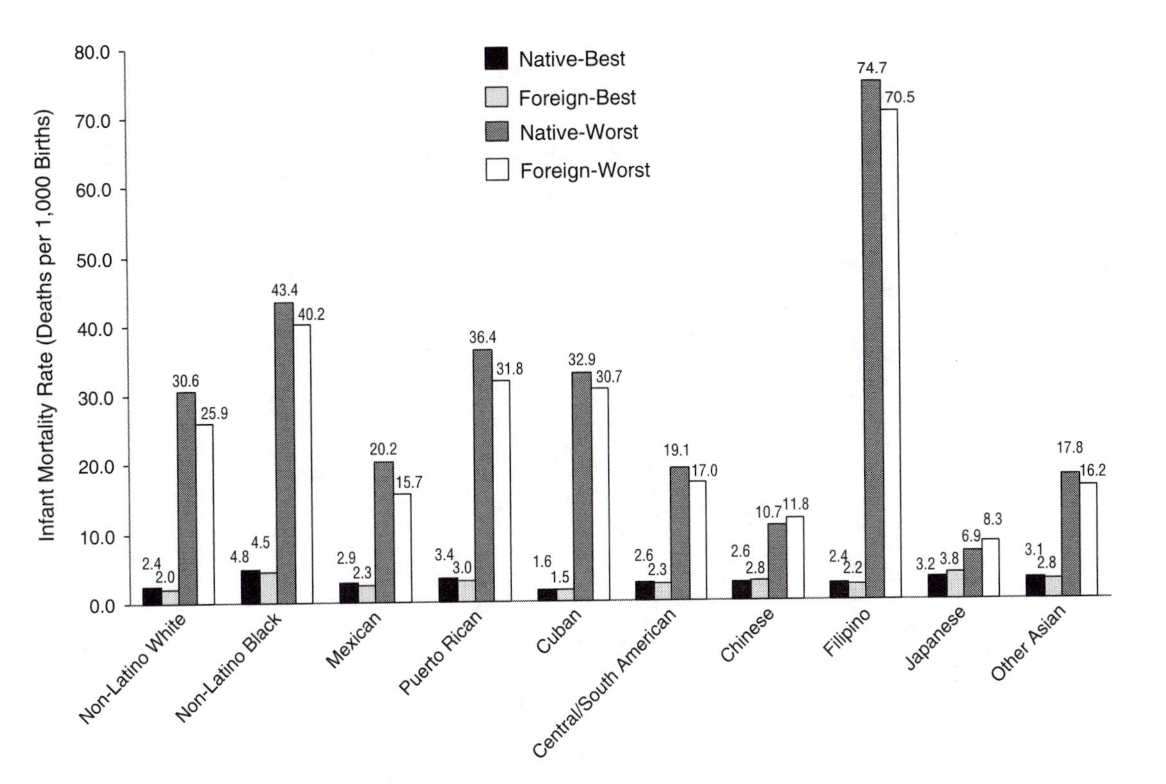

FIGURE 5-5 Predicted infant mortality rate: best- and worse-case scenarios.

ferences in infant mortality are small relative to the differences by race/ethnicity.[12]

IMPLICATIONS FOR FUTURE RESEARCH

Investigations of the impact of immigration on reproductive health face several challenges, the most notable of which are due to limitations of existing data. There are few representative national datasets on reproductive health with sufficient cases in specific national-origin groups to permit investigation. Moreover, the largest national datasets (NCHS Natality Files and the Linked Birth/Infant Death Datasets) are based on birth and death certificates, which contain limited information. While the analysis presented here advances our understanding of the effects of maternal nativity on infant health, only a subset of the potentially important explanatory variables was considered because of the limitations of the Linked Birth/Infant Death Datasets. For example, although we were able to include a measure of maternal education as a control for socioeconomic status, family income was not available in the data file. With incomplete information on socioeconomic status, socioeconomic differences between native- and foreign-born women cannot be ruled out as an explanation of the nativity differentials remaining in our multivariate models.

The Linked Birth/Infant Death Datasets, like many national datasets, include information on mothers' birthplaces but not information with which to ascertain the generational status of native-born mothers—that is, we cannot distinguish the native born of foreign parentage from the native born of native parentage. Furthermore, duration of residence in the United States cannot be determined for the foreign born. Our understanding of how immigration and settlement in the United States affect reproductive health would be greatly enhanced if the outcomes of the foreign born, the native born of foreign parentage, and the native born of native parentage could be compared. In addition,

[12]Table 5A-5 provides additional models of infant mortality in which low birthweight owing to prematurity and intrauterine growth retardation are controlled.

the effects of exposure to the U.S. social context on the health beliefs and behaviors of immigrants could be better understood if newly arrived immigrants could be distinguished from those with greater duration of residence in the United States.

Additionally, studies would benefit from the collection of detailed data on acculturation, social support, health beliefs, and health practices. Such data would allow researchers to examine the effects of immigration on health within the broader context of immigrant women's lives and to examine more fully the relationship between acculturation and the loss of protective behaviors. In short, much richer data are needed on a variety of U.S. immigrant groups in order to fully understand the epidemiological paradox. Collection of such data should be a higher priority than further analysis of the incomplete datasets available at the present time.

CONCLUSIONS

Our study adds further support to a growing literature documenting superior reproductive health outcomes among immigrants compared to native-born women. In almost all of the ethnic groups we examined, the rates of low birthweight and infant mortality were lower for the offspring of immigrants than for the offspring of the native born. At the same time, the magnitude of the nativity differential was in many cases quite small. In fact, Mexicans, the group that has been the focus of most studies of the epidemiological paradox, exhibit larger nativity differentials than most other ethnic groups. Thus, although foreign-born women have better reproductive health outcomes than native-born women, the differences are in many cases so small that they should not be given undue attention.

The generational composition of the native-born population of an ethnic group depends in large part on the recency of immigration from the origin country. For more recent immigrant groups, such as Central/South Americans, the native-born population is largely composed of the offspring of immigrants, who are still undergoing the assimilation process. For groups with a longer history in the United States, such as Mexicans, the native born are more heavily weighted toward the native born of native parentage. Without information on the generational composition of the native born, the extent to which ethnic differences in the magnitude of the nativity differentials in infant health are due to this factor cannot be determined.

Native-born mothers are more likely to be young and single than are foreign-born mothers, and both of these characteristics are related to poor infant health. These high-risk attributes are counterbalanced in some groups by higher educational attainment among native-born mothers. However, the effect of education on birthweight and infant mortality is fairly weak and varies across ethnic groups, although it is generally in the expected direction. Prenatal care utilization also fails to provide an explanation of the health advantage of the infants of immigrants: in some groups, immigrants have better reproductive health outcomes despite less adequate prenatal care, while in others there is little difference in the use of prenatal care between immigrants and natives.

Our analysis, like others (Cobas et al., 1996; Guendelman et al., 1990; Guendelman and Abrams, 1995; Rumbaut and Weeks, 1996), suggests that lifestyle factors play a major role in immigrant-native differentials in infant health. In particular, there are striking differences in smoking by maternal nativity, and smoking is one of the strongest predictors of low birthweight. Similarly, alcohol consumption is higher for the native born, and several studies show that drug use and consumption of unhealthy foods increase with each generation in the United States (Cabral et al., 1990; Guendelman and Abrams, 1995). Precisely why the native born are more likely to adopt unhealthy habits is an issue in need of further study.

Finally, although we have focused on nativity differences in infant health within ethnic groups, it should be noted that ethnic differences in birthweight and infant mortality are large and persist in multivariate analyses (i.e., models based on pooled data from all ethnic groups that include dummy variables for each ethnic group). Ethnicity remains an elusive "black box," and ethnic differences that remain in multivariate models are often explained in terms of vague concepts such as "culture." Further attention to the complex set of characteristics, beliefs, and health practices underlying ethnic differences in infant health would contribute to our understanding of the effects of immigration on children's well-being.

REFERENCES

Cabral, H., L.E. Fried, S. Levensen, H. Amaro, and B. Zuckerman

1990 Foreign-born and U.S.-born black women: Differences in health behaviors and birth outcomes. *American Journal of Public Health* 80:70-72.

Chomitz, V.R., L.W.Y. Cheung, and E. Lieberman

1995 The role of lifestyle in preventing low birth weight. *The Future of Children* 5:121-138.

Cobas, J.A., H. Balcazar, M.B. Benin, V. Keith, and Y. Chong

1996 Acculturation and low-birthweight infants among Latino women: A reanalysis of HHANES data with structural equation models. *American Journal of Public Health* 86:394-396.

Collins, J.W., and D.K. Shay

1994 Prevalence of low birth weight among Hispanic infants with United States-born and foreign-born mothers: The effect of urban poverty. *American Journal of Epidemiology* 139:184-192.

Gordon, M.M.

1964 *Assimilation in American Life.* New York: Oxford University Press.

Guendelman, S.

1988 Sociocultural factors in Hispanic pregnancy outcomes. In *Developing Public Health Social Work Programs to Prevent Low Birthweight and Infant Mortality: High Risk Populations and Outreach,* C.J. Morton and R.G. Hirsch, eds. Berkeley: University of California Press.

Guendelman, S., and B. Abrams

1995 Dietary intake among Mexican-American women: Generational differences and a comparison with white non-Hispanic women. *American Journal of Public Health* 85:20-25.

Guendelman, S., J.B. Gould, M. Hudes, and B. Eskenazi

1990 Generational differences in perinatal health among the Mexican American population: Findings from the HHANES 1982-1984. *American Journal of Public Health* 80(Suppl.):61-65.

Kessner, D.M., J. Singer, E.C. Kalk, and E.R. Schlesinger

1973 Methodology: New York City Analysis. In *Infant Death: An Analysis by Maternal Risk and Health Care.* Washington, D.C.: National Academy of Sciences.

Kramer, M.S.

1987 Determinants of low birthweight: Methodological assessment and meta-analysis. *Bulletin of the World Health Organization* 65:663-737.

Markides, K.S., and J. Coreil
1986 The health of Hispanics in the southwestern United States: An epidemiological paradox. *Public Health Reports* 101:253-265.

Massey, D.S.
1995 The new immigration and ethnicity in the United States. *Population and Development Review* 21:631-652.

Park, R.E.
1950 *Race and Culture.* Glencoe, Ill.: Free Press.

Portes, A., and R.G. Rumbaut
1996 *Immigrant America: A Portrait,* 2nd ed. Berkeley: University of California Press.

Rumbaut, R.G.
1997 Paradoxes (and orthodoxies) of assimilation. *Sociological Perspectives* 40(3):483-511.
1994 Origins and destinies: Immigration to the United States since World War II. *Sociological Forum* 9(4):583-621.

Rumbaut, R.G., and J.R. Weeks
1989 Infant health among Indochinese refugees: Patterns of infant mortality, birthweight, and prenatal care in comparative perspective. *Research in the Sociology of Health Care* 8:137-196.
1996 Unraveling a public health enigma: Why do immigrants experience superior perinatal outcomes? *Research in the Sociology of Health Care* 13B:337-391.

Samuels, B.
1986 Infant mortality and low birth weight among minority groups in the United States: A review of the literature. In *Report of the Secretary's Task Force on Black and Minority Health,* vol. VI. Bethesda, Md.: National Institutes of Health.

Scribner, R.
1996 Editorial: Paradox as paradigm—the health outcomes of Mexican Americans. *American Journal of Public Health* 86:303-305.

Scribner, R., and J.H. Dwyer
1989 Acculturation and low birthweight among Latinos in the Hispanic HANES. *American Journal of Public Health* 79:1263-1267.

Shiono, P.H., and R.E. Behrman
1995 Low birth weight: Analysis and recommendations. *The Future of Children* 5:4-18.

Singh, G.K., and S.M. Yu
1996 Adverse pregnancy outcomes: Differences between US- and foreign-born women in major racial and ethnic groups. *American Journal of Public Health* 86:837-843.

U.S. Department of Health and Human Services
1995 *Public Use Data File Documentation. Linked Birth/Infant Death Data Set: 1990 Birth Cohort.* Hyattsville, Md.: Centers for Disease Control and Prevention, National Center for Health Statistics.

U.S. Immigration and Naturalization Service
1996 *1994 Statistical Yearbook of the Immigration and Naturalization Service.* Washington, D.C.: U.S. Government Printing Office.

Ventura, S.J., J.A. Martin, S.M. Taffel, T.J. Matthews, and S.C. Clarke
1995 Advance report of final natality statistics, 1993. *Monthly Vital Statistics Report* 44(3).

Williams, D.R., and C. Collins
1995 US socioeconomic and racial differences in health: Patterns and explanations. *Annual Review of Sociology* 21:349-386.

Williams, R.L., N.J. Binkin, and E.J. Clingman
1986 Pregnancy outcomes among Spanish-surname women in California. *American Journal of Public Health* 76:387-391.

Zhou, M.
1997 Growing up American: The challenge confronting immigrant children and children of immigrants. *Annual Review of Sociology* 23:63-95.

APPENDIX 5A: DESCRIPTION OF SAMPLE AND DATA

The 1989-1991 Linked Birth/Infant Death Datasets, created by the National Center for Health Statistics, consist of birth certificate data for the birth cohorts of 1989, 1990, and 1991 and death certificate data for infants in those birth cohorts who died before their first birthdays. All births and infant deaths that occurred in the United States to U.S. residents and U.S. nonresidents are included. The file does not include (1) U.S.-born infants who died outside the United States, (2) deaths to foreign-born infants that occurred in the United States, and (3) births and deaths that occurred outside the United States to U.S. residents. In the 1989 file, infants born that year who died before their first birthdays in 1989 or 1990 are included as infant deaths. Similarly, infants born in 1990 who died before their first birthdays in 1990 or 1991 are included as infant deaths in the 1990 file. Infant deaths are defined in a comparable manner for the 1991 birth cohort.

The separate Linked Birth/Infant Death Datasets for the 1989, 1990, and 1991 birth cohorts were pooled for our analysis in order to obtain sufficient cases in each ethnic group. The pooled file includes a 10 percent random sample of non-Latino white and non-Latino black births and all births in other racial/ethnic groups. In addition, several restrictions were imposed on the pooled file prior to its use for our analysis. First, consistent with most studies of low birthweight and infant mortality, we include only singleton births. Second, based on maternal ethnicity, only infants of non-Latino white, non-Latino black, Mexican, Cuban, Puerto Rican, Central/South American, Chinese, Filipino, Japanese, and other Asian/Pacific Islander origins are included. Third, because comparisons of infants of native and foreign-born mothers are of primary interest in our study, we restricted our analytic sample to infants whose mothers were either born in the United States or born outside the United States and its territories. The only exception is Puerto Ricans, who are included and defined as foreign born if their mother was born in Puerto Rico. Because infant mortality is likely to be underestimated for births to nonresidents of the United States (who may return home after giving birth), births to nonresident mothers are excluded. Finally, cases with missing data on any of the independent variables considered in our analysis were excluded, with the following exception: for variables with more than 5 percent of cases with missing data (smoking, drinking, and weight gain during pregnancy), cases with missing data were included and a missing data indicator was entered into all multivariate models. Table 5A-1 lists the variables included in our analysis and provides information on coding.

TABLE 5A-1 Coding Scheme for Variables Included in Analyses of Low Birthweight and Infant Mortality

Variable	Codes
Low birthweight	2,500+ grams (reference)
	< 2,500 grams
Infant mortality	Survived until first birthday (reference)
	Died before first birthday
Race/ethnicity	Non-Hispanic white
	Non-Hispanic black
	Mexican
	Puerto Rican
	Cuban
	Central/South American
	Chinese
	Japanese
	Filipino
	Other Asian/Pacific Islander
Maternal birthplace	Native born (reference)
	Foreign born (for Puerto Ricans, born in Puerto Rico)
Maternal age	< 20
	20-34 (reference)
	35+
Maternal marital status	Married (reference)
	Single

continued on next page

TABLE 5A-1 Continued

Variable	Codes
Maternal education	Less than high school High school graduate (reference) Some college
Birth order of infant	1 2-4 (reference) 5+
Gender of infant	Female (reference) Male
Prenatal care (Kessner Index[a])	Adequate (reference) Intermediate Inadequate
Mother smoked during pregnancy	No (reference) Yes
Mother drank alcohol during pregnancy	No (reference) Yes
Weight gain during pregnancy	22+ lb. (reference) < 22 lb.

[a]The Kessner Index is based on information on the month that prenatal care began and the number of prenatal care visits (adjusting for length of gestation). The Kessner Index rates prenatal care as adequate, intermediate, or inadequate. To be classified as adequate, prenatal care must begin in the first trimester of pregnancy and consist of at least nine prenatal care visits for a normal-length pregnancy (36 or more weeks; Kessner et al., 1994).

TABLE 5A-2

TABLE 5A-2 Maternal and Infant Characteristics by Nativity and Race/Ethnicity: 1989-1991 Linked Birth/Infant Death Datasets

	Non-Latino White		Non-Latino Black	
	NB	FB	NB	FB
Outcomes				
Low birthweight	4.47	3.87	11.85	8.05
Preterm	2.57	2.18	7.41	5.36
Intrauterine growth retarded	1.90	1.70	4.44	2.69
Infant mortality	5.8	4.6	12.9	10.5
Neonatal	3.2	2.5	7.3	6.5
Postneonatal	2.6	2.1	5.6	4.0
Maternal Characteristics				
Age (years)				
< 20	9.99	4.14	24.74	7.53
20-34	80.68	81.57	69.75	79.03
35+	9.33	14.29	5.51	13.44
Education				
< High school	15.15	12.57	30.50	21.08
High school	39.6	33.63	43.34	38.89
Some college	45.24	53.8	26.16	40.03
Single 16.92	9.89	68.25	42.86	34.55
Infant Characteristics				
Birth order				
1	42.95	42.91	37.93	40.45
2-4	54.47	53.48	55.71	53.88
5+	2.58	3.61	6.36	5.68
Male	51.28	51.37	50.80	50.78
Health Behaviors				
Smoked	21.31	12.51	16.09	3.98
Drank	3.5	3.28	3.80	1.49
Weight gain <22 lb.	19.59	19.06	32.57	29.04
Prenatal Care				
Adequate	77.23	74.71	50.94	53.75
Intermediate	18.22	19.23	32.82	33.51
Inadequate	4.55	6.06	16.23	12.74
No. of cases	654,108	27,187	158,117	10,782

Mexican		Puerto Rican		Cuban	
NB	FB	NB	FB	NB	FB
5.38	4.14	7.91	7.46	4.71	4.4
3.13	2.32	4.6	4.30	2.89	2.74
2.25	1.82	3.31	3.16	1.81	1.66
6.6	5.3	7.8	7.0	5.3	4.7
3.5	3.1	4.3	4.5	3.8	3.1
3.1	2.1	3.4	2.5	1.5	1.5
24.08	13.74	26.08	16.63	18.14	4.39
70.43	78.49	70.58	75.11	78.49	83.88
5.50	7.77	3.34	8.27	3.37	11.73
41.34	73.59	41.85	42.18	22.18	16.03
39.46	17.94	36.35	33.37	32.69	34.60
19.20	8.47	21.8	24.45	45.13	49.37
33.07	56.73	53.4	25.21	16.05	
39.06	35.96	44.45	35.06	54.09	39.81
55.27	55.39	52.03	57.82	44.45	58.15
5.67	8.65	3.52	7.11	1.46	2.04
51.11	51.03	50.85	50.89	51.79	51.44
8.03	2.48	16.09	11.24	9.44	5.57
2.06	.57	2.99	2.89	1.76	.69
26.11	32.21	25.52	28.28	16.64	18.67
55.54	39.76	50.68	53.42	73.15	77.80
31.18	38.38	34.51	33.17	21.39	18.58
13.28	21.86	14.81	13.41	5.47	3.63
381,168	618,290	80,045	57,580	6,565	24,261

continued on next page

TABLE 5A-2 Continued

	Central/S. American		Chinese	
	NB	FB	NB	FB
Outcomes				
Low birthweight	5.17	4.78	4.81	3.8
Preterm	3.07	2.76	2.82	1.89
Intrauterine growth retarded	2.09	2.02	1.99	1.91
Infant mortality	5.2	5.0	4.6	4.3
Neonatal	2.6	3.0	1.4	2.1
Postneonatal	2.5	2.1	3.2	2.3
Maternal Characteristics				
Age (years)				
< 20	26.14	8.31	2.69	.67
20-34	70.16	80.8	71.68	80.79
35+	3.70	10.88	25.63	18.54
Education				
< High school	26.72	44.80	3.85	16.04
High school	35.09	33.06	11.67	29.55
Some college	38.19	22.14	84.49	54.41
Single	40.10	41.01	9.54	3.26
Infant Characteristics				
Birth order				
1	59.07	38.52	49.94	52.61
2-4	39.17	56.60	48.88	46.47
5+	1.75	4.88	1.19	.91
Male	50.21	51.16	51.12	52.12
Health Behaviors				
Smoked	8.79	2.80	6.26	1.60
Drank	2.33	.84	3.06	1.11
Weight gain <22 lb.	21.20	26.17	20.13	22.01
Prenatal Care				
Adequate	59.48	48.33	82.92	72.49
Intermediate	29.79	36.07	14.70	22.65
Inadequate	10.73	15.60	2.39	4.86
No. of cases	9,075	200,172	6,240	52,837

NOTE: NB, native born; FB, foreign born.

Filipino		Japanese		Other Asian/ Pacific Islander	
NB	FB	NB	FB	NB	FB
6.89	6.10	5.01	4.96	5.30	5.73
3.88	3.24	2.54	2.21	3.09	2.82
3.00	2.86	2.47	2.75	2.21	2.91
6.8	4.8	3.7	3.7	6.2	5.3
3.2	2.9	1.6	1.8	2.6	2.9
3.6	2.0	2.1	1.9	3.6	2.5
18.39	3.49	3.82	.86	12.33	5.79
74.84	76.80	74.33	79.11	75.9	81.36
6.78	19.71	21.85	20.03	11.77	12.85
15.05	8.94	3.05	2.49	13.01	26.36
42.64	22.15	22.53	25.71	30.96	28.81
42.31	68.91	74.42	71.80	56.03	44.83
32.04	12.34	12.46	5.09	22.69	11.06
48.16	43.66	48.76	49.79	50.33	41.71
49.12	54.19	50.22	49.26	46.92	50.27
2.72	2.16	1.02	.95	2.75	8.01
50.92	52.02	51.26	51.38	51.44	51.39
12.40	3.07	9.52	5.79	12.01	3.25
2.02	.75	1.70	2.92	2.38	.90
19.49	22.61	24.54	30.46	20.0	27.97
63.39	67.99	79.77	78.15	68.59	61.93
28.34	25.31	16.83	17.57	22.39	28.07
8.27	6.70	3.39	4.29	9.02	10.00
9,426	59,079	12,029	10,941	10,748	177,374

TABLE 5A-3 Odds Ratios from Logistic Regression Models of Low Birthweight, by Race/Ethnicity: 1989-1991 Linked Birth/Infant Death Datasets

	Non-Latino White	Non-Latino Black	Mexican	Puerto Rican
Maternal Characteristics				
Foreign born	.929	.743	.733	.950
Age (years)				
< 20	.907	.890	1.049	.975
20-34	—	—	—	—
5+	1.456	1.273	1.518	1.411
Education				
< High school	1.209	1.094	1.025	1.096
High school	—	—	—	—
Some college	.834	.952	.942	.952
Single	1.193	1.203	1.206	1.289
Infant Characteristics				
Birth order				
1	1.729	1.300	1.538	1.344
2-4	—	—	—	—
5+	.896	1.072	.973	1.278
Male	.850	.802	.932	.885
Health Behaviors				
Smoked	1.986	1.758	1.773	1.623
Drank	1.123	1.496	1.112	1.328
Weight gain < 22 lb.	2.985	2.606	2.423	2.592
Prenatal care				
Adequate	—	—	—	—
Intermediate	1.330	1.151	1.137	1.044
Inadequate	1.830	1.690	1.530	1.617
No. of cases	681,295	168,899	999,458	137,625

NOTE: NB, native born; FB, foreign born.

Cuban	Central/ South American	Chinese	Filipino	Japanese	Other Asian/ Pacific Islander
1.011	.946	.778	.927	1.009	1.157
.874	1.127	1.130	1.189	.871	1.249
—	—	—	—	—	—
1.376	1.539	1.363	1.529	1.124	1.375
1.160	1.003	1.072	.976	.801	1.029
—	—	—	—	—	—
.901	.993	.868	1.028	1.010	.956
1.376	1.230	1.332	1.195	1.208	1.196
1.487	1.498	1.446	1.579	1.553	1.596
—	—	—	—	—	—
1.121	.917	.843	.928	.770	.716
.896	.891	.878	.899	.838	.857
1.987	1.537	2.120	1.498	2.608	1.459
.946	1.015	.754	1.001	.923	1.309
2.995	2.498	2.351	2.567	2.641	2.351
—	—	—	—	—	—
1.089	1.031	1.143	1.297	1.215	1.131
1.914	1.378	1.573	1.648	1.442	1.335
30,826	209,247	59,077	68,505	22,970	188,122

TABLE 5A-4 Odds Ratios from Logistic Regression Models of Infant Mortality by Race/Ethnicity, 1989-1991 Linked Birth/Infant Death Datasets

	Non-Latino White	Non-Latino Black	Mexican	Puerto Rican
Maternal Characteristics				
Foreign born	.841	.924	.976	.871
Age (years)				
< 20	1.103	.920	1.160	1.292
20-34	—	—	—	—
35+	.998	.998	1.257	1.437
Education				
< High school	1.265	1.108	1.068	1.132
High school	—	—	—	—
Some college	.880	.997	.933	1.077
Single	1.411	1.185	1.585	1.108
Infant Characteristics				
Birth order				
1	.975	1.197	.899	1.001
2-4	—	—	—	—
5+	1.052	1.145	1.145	1.427
Male	1.305	1.132	1.283	1.183
Health Behaviors				
Smoked	1.308	1.299	1.575	1.227
Drank	.868	1.166	.940	1.366
Weight gain < 22 lb.	2.813	2.699	2.086	2.690
Prenatal Care				
Adequate	—	—	—	—
Intermediate	1.345	1.073	0.967	0.980
Inadequate	1.859	1.574	1.192	1.608
No. of cases	681,295	168,899	999,458	137,625

Cuban	Central/ South American	Chinese	Filipino	Japanese	Other Asian/ Pacific Islander
.929	.890	1.106	.939	1.205	.909
.897	1.104	1.226	1.602	.993	1.100
—	—	—	—	—	—
1.150	1.515	1.138	1.203	1.368	1.386
.795	1.087	1.040	.988	1.897	.785
—	—	—	—	—	—
.671	.955	.913	.895	1.241	.766
1.942	1.388	4.361	1.935	2.863	1.730
1.239	1.069	.795	.861	.698	.930
—	—	—	—	—	—
1.863	1.045	1.881	1.429	.827	1.085
1.202	1.246	1.247	1.154	1.066	1.150
1.130	.595	.402	1.443	1.315	1.418
1.316	2.547	—	1.790	—	.963
4.607	2.119	1.978	2.551	1.013	1.966
—	—	—	—	—	—
0.965	0.858	1.101	1.360	1.216	1.093
1.240	1.258	1.100	1.766	.690	1.215
30,826	209,247	59,077	68,505	22,970	188,122

TABLE 5A-5 Odds Ratios from Logistic Regression Models of Infant Mortality by Race/Ethnicity, 1989-1991 Linked Birth/Infant Death Datasets

	Non-Latino White	Non-Latino Black	Mexican	Puerto Rican
Maternal Characteristics				
Foreign born	.877	1.042	.907	.908
Age (years)				
< 20	1.101	.935	1.110	1.295
20-34	—	—	—	—
35+	.861	.876	1.026	1.205
Education				
< High school	1.195	1.076	1.061	1.077
High school	—	—	—	—
Some college	.916	.994	.942	1.083
Single	1.292	1.094	1.459	.949
Infant Characteristics				
Birth order				
1	.789	1.086	.760	.878
2-4	—	—	—	—
5+	1.123	1.083	1.159	1.258
Male	1.331	1.209	1.277	1.218
Low birthweight				
Preterm	25.446	18.157	29.937	24.257
Intrauterine growth retarded	6.205	3.423	8.118	5.579
Health Behaviors				
Smoked	1.049	1.027	1.251	1.009
Drank	.780	.931	.870	1.112
Weight gain < 22 lb.	1.691	1.607	1.335	1.624
Prenatal Care				
Adequate	—	—	—	—
Intermediate	1.209	1.019	.928	1.011
Inadequate	1.403	1.190	.990	1.298
No. of cases	681,295	168,899	999,458	137,625

Cuban	Central/ South American	Chinese	Filipino	Japanese	Other Asian/ Pacific Islander
.941	.949	1.193	.984	1.197	.884
.928	1.042	1.092	1.427	.788	.978
—	—	—	—	—	—
.917	1.202	1.019	.978	1.301	1.195
.738	1.092	1.018	.982	2.046	.790
—	—	—	—	—	—
.715	.956	.941	.882	1.255	.767
1.674	1.255	3.730	1.756	2.656	1.586
1.093	.897	.726	.733	.636	.781
—	—	—	—	—	—
1.771	1.073	1.785	1.469	.881	1.213
1.229	1.263	1.237	1.178	1.072	1.186
43.143	33.312	24.281	22.416	20.668	22.246
5.005	6.563	7.397	6.935	3.643	7.708
.855	.492	.295	1.214	.910	1.133
1.40	2.474	—	1.483	—	.866
2.359	1.274	1.301	1.570	.713	1.320
—	—	—	—	—	—
.979	.866	1.059	1.255	1.160	1.044
.733	1.10	.868	1.371	.518	1.075
30,826	209,247	59,077	68,505	22,970	188,122

CHAPTER 6

The Health Status and Risk Behaviors of Adolescents in Immigrant Families

Kathleen Mullan Harris

Immigrant children and the children of immigrants are an increasing focus of social and economic concerns in America. Language barriers, low economic status and poverty, and alien social and cultural practices stigmatize and isolate immigrant youth from mainstream youth cultures and slow the process by which immigrant youth assimilate into American society. At a time when state and federal policies seek to restrict health care services and benefits to the immigrant population, immigrant families face increasing rates of poverty and limited access to health care (Wolfe, 1994). As a result, the health status of immigrant youth and families is thought to be especially precarious (Klerman, 1993). This chapter examines the physical and emotional health status and health risk behaviors of immigrant adolescents and native-born adolescents with immigrant parents relative to adolescent health in native-born families. Generational differences are assessed by country of origin and ethnic group background, and the extent to which family and neighborhood context explains the within and across ethnic group differences in health outcomes is analyzed.

BACKGROUND

The process of immigrant assimilation and adaptation to American culture and the extent to which immigrant youth achieve equally with children from nonimmigrant families has occupied much of the recent research and political discourse over immigration (Portes, 1996; Rumbaut, 1995). The standard model of immigrant progress is conceptualized as an intergenerational process (Gordon, 1964; Lieberson, 1980). The first generation of immigrants, those who were not born in the United States, are rarely expected to achieve socioeconomic parity with the native population. Learning a new language, adjusting to a different educational system, and experiencing native prejudice and hostility toward those with a foreign accent and culture are major obstacles for immigrants.

The second generation, U.S.-born children of immigrants, are socialized in American schools and neighborhoods, receive a mainstream education, and obtain the skills needed to participate in the American occupational structure. Their progress is evidenced by the narrowing of the gap in various educational and socioeconomic outcomes between the second generation and the native population (Hirschman, 1996). The third generation of immigrants, native-born children with native-born parents but immigrant grandparents, are thought to differ little from the fourth or higher generations because any ethnic influence of grandparents is thought to be relatively minor in a home in which parents do not speak a foreign language and were educated and socialized in American schools and neighborhoods.

This "straight-line" model of immigrant adaptation or "Americanization" can also be applied to an intragenerational process of assimilation. The classical hypothesis argues that longer residence in the United States leads to socioeconomic progress and the narrowing of differentials with the native-born population. There is evidence of this process in the reduction of income differentials (Jasso and Rosenzweig, 1990). More specific to immigrant youth, the age at which children arrive in the United States may affect their process of adaptation. Children who arrive in their preschool years can more easily adapt to the American educational system, learn the English language, and be less stigmatized without a noticeable accent than children who arrive in this country during their adolescence.

Despite the popularity and longevity of the classical model of immigrant adaptation, scholars have recently begun to question this hypothesis of Americanization. Revisionist theses of immigrant adaptation have evolved from the study of "new immigrants," who since the 1960s have largely come from Asia and Latin America (Gans, 1992; Reimers, 1992; Rumbaut, 1996). One revisionist perspective focuses primarily on the changing U.S. economy and the labor market in which immigrants work. Because employment opportunities for unskilled workers contracted appreciably during the 1980s as a result of the industrial restructuring of the U.S. economy (Wilson, 1987) and the early 1980s recession (Blackburn et al., 1990; Freeman and Holzer, 1991), the recent generation of immigrants is expected to experience declining economic and social prospects, relative to previous generations. Similar to other less educated or low-income segments of the U.S. population, low- and unskilled immigrants must find work in the service sector, which provides only jobs that are low paying and lack security or avenues for advancement that previous generations of immigrants enjoyed in blue-collar work and union-supported jobs.

A revisionist thesis to the classical model is the segmented assimilation thesis (Portes and Zhou, 1993). This perspective argues that the new generation of immigrants may experience different adaptation processes according to the social and economic context of the "segment" of the U.S. population in which they assimilate. As a result, greater exposure to American culture may be associated with mixed prospects for socioeconomic attainment. For instance, the classical hypothesis would argue that adolescents who arrived in the United States at a younger age and who have spent more time here will assimilate into society more readily than immigrant adolescents who arrived more recently. If, however, greater exposure to American society has primarily been in inner-city environments, where many new immigrants settle and where the social environment and economic opportunities have been declining, immigrant children with longer U.S. residence (and a younger age at arrival) may not be doing better than recent arrivals.

Revisionist theories developed from renewed scholarly interest in the social and economic mobility of immigrants when the "new immigration" waves were documented in the 1990 census. Almost 20 million immigrants were counted in the 1990 census, representing a smaller percentage of the total population than that recorded in the peak years of immigration in the early twentieth century but the highest absolute number of immigrants ever recorded (Farley, 1996). The most dramatic change in the contemporary waves of immigration, however, was a shift in the composition of immigrants away from Europe toward far greater representation from Asia and Latin America. Among the Asian immigrants counted in the 1990 census, more than half had arrived since 1980, and 50 percent of Latin American immigrants arrived in those 10 years as well. Among European immigrants, only 20 percent had entered the United States in the past 10 years. Moreover, the country-of-origin composition of immigrants to the United States between 1980 and 1990 shows that 90 percent of immigrants were from Asia, Latin America, and Africa.

This chapter examines the health status and health risk behaviors of a population of adolescents who represent this "new immigration." Using data from a nationally representative study of adolescents in American schools in grades 7 through 12, the study includes immigrant youth who arrived in the United States between 1975 and 1994 and native-born youth of immigrant parents. Health outcomes and behaviors among foreign-born youth and native-born youth with foreign-born parents are contrasted with adolescents in native-born families (native-born youth with native-born parents).

Adolescent Health, Development, and Assimilation

As a minority group becomes more highly assimilated into mainstream American values and customs, changes in health-related attitudes and behaviors also may occur. Acceptance of the predominant values may make such a group more amenable to the prevailing social norms of health behaviors. The pattern of diseases characterizing the group may also shift toward that experienced by the majority group (Mendoza et al., 1990).

However, behavioral changes may yield unwanted outcomes. For example, low levels of assimilation are associated with lower rates of completed suicide among Mexican Americans (Earls et al., 1990). An increasingly cited finding is that foreign-born Mexican Americans experience lower rates of infant mortality and low birthweight than other groups (Bautista-Hayes, 1990; Landale et al., this volume). Subsequent generations of Mexican Americans appear to lose this advantage, which may be a consequence of adopting the lifestyle and habits of the dominant culture.

How do assimilation theories apply to adolescents? Adolescence is often characterized as a period of turmoil and rebellion from traditional constraints associated with family, adult supervision, and institutional expectations. While much has been written about the developmental period of adolescence, how is this process of human development from a child into an adult compounded by being an immigrant or having immigrant parents? In a period where being different or "standing out" takes on crucial social significance to being accepted into peer networks and school culture, peer acceptance and blending into the current society may be even more important for immigrant adolescents, who are already different in their appearance, dress, or speech.

The main socializing agents during adolescence include the family, peers, school, community, and the larger society, which all contribute uniquely to the socialization process (Dornbusch, 1989; Perry et al., 1993). Among immigrant youth, family influence can have especially poignant effects, either coddling youth within the boundaries of their ethnic culture and traditional behaviors or turning them away from their own ethnic culture and family traditions that define their difference within American society. As youth increasingly value peer friendships and peer relationships, concurrent distancing from the family origin constitutes a central task of adolescence (Perry et al., 1993). This normal developmental process of waning family involvement and increasing peer influence during adolescence may be especially alien to the cultural practices and models of respect in immigrant families and may create family tensions and divided loyalties for immigrant adolescents.

For adolescents in immigrant families, development and socialization overlap with assimilation into American society, such that the sometimes rocky road of adolescence may be especially rocky for immigrant children who begin the developmental process as "more different" than adolescents in native-born families. Thus, there is an inherent tension in the adjustment process of immigrant adolescents as they strive to be accepted by the majority population and at the same time cope with socializing agents in their families and neighborhoods who either wish to deter the assimilation process, which is compounded by adolescent rebellion and acting out, or facilitate it through the neighborhood influence of peers. How this tension plays out in the lives of immigrant adolescents will furthermore vary by ethnic background.

ANALYSIS STRATEGY

This analysis examines how ethnic background and immigrant status influence physical and emotional health status and health risk behaviors and whether family and neighborhood context explains any of the observed differences in health outcomes. Data are from the National Longitudinal Study of Adolescent Health (Add Health), a nationally representative study of over 20,000 adolescents in grades 7 through 12 in the United States in 1995 (see Appendix 6A for a more detailed description of the data and sample).

This study focuses on three dimensions of health: physical health, emotional health, and health risk behaviors. Physical health outcomes are measured as dichotomous variables and include (1) fair or poor general health, (2) whether the adolescent ever missed school in the past month for a health or emotional problem, (3) learning difficulties, (4) obesity, and (5) asthma. A physical health problems index based on these five outcomes also is presented. Emotional health outcomes include two continuous indexes measuring psychological distress and positive well-being.

Health risk behaviors are self-reported by the adolescent and include (1) ever having had sexual intercourse, (2) age at first intercourse, (3) use of birth control at first intercourse, (4) delinquency, (5) violence, and (6) use of controlled substances. Delinquency, violence, and use of controlled substances are measured as continuous indexes in multivariate models only, while dichotomous measures indicating high-risk involvement in these behaviors are used in descriptive analysis. A risky behaviors index based on sexual behavior, delinquency, violence, and use of controlled substances is presented as well. A detailed description of the construction of these measures is contained in Appendix 6A, and sample means for health outcomes are shown in the last column of Table 6A-1.

The analysis will proceed in three stages. The first stage examines differences in physical and emotional health and health risk behaviors by immigrant status. Foreign-born adolescents with foreign-born parents are those children who were not born in the United States or were born U.S. citizens abroad and thus migrated to this country as children (in most cases with their immigrant parents). Native-born adolescents with foreign-born parents are children born in the United States (and thus are U.S. citizens) but who have at least one parent who is foreign born. Adolescents in native-born families are children who were born in the United States to native-born parents. Children in native-born families may have grandparents or great-grandparents who were immigrants, but because the immigration experience is much farther removed from the social context of their childhood and adolescent development, this category is considered the native population and the fundamental comparison group for immigrant children and the children of immigrants.

This stage of analysis also explores the extent to which bivariate health differentials by immigrant status are due to differences in the demographic composition of the three immigrant groups by controlling for children's age and gender. Finally, the assimilation process for immigrant children is examined by contrasting health outcomes by age at entry into the United States and length of time here.

Stage two of the analysis explores whether differences in health status and risky behaviors by immigrant status persist within country of origin and ethnic background. Ethnic background is controlled by contrasting health outcomes within the country of origin for immigrant children and the children of immigrants and the parallel ethnic group identified for youth in native-born families. Ethnic group backgrounds matched to country-of-origin classifications result in the following range of ethnic groups specific to countries or regions: Mexico, Cuba, Central and South America, Puerto Rico, Africa and the Afro Caribbean, China, the Philippines, Japan, Vietnam, other Asian and Pacific

Islands, and Europe and Canada (see Appendix 6A for a more detailed description of classification strategies).

Stage three of the analysis employs multivariate regression methods to assess the relative effects of immigrant status by ethnic group categories on the various health outcomes compared to the baseline effect for non-Hispanic white adolescents in native-born families. Subsequent regression models then explore the extent to which these effects operate through differences in family context and neighborhood context, which vary by immigrant status and ethnic group background. Family context is defined by measures of family income, family structure, mother's education, and parental supervision in the home when the adolescent goes to school, comes home from school, during evening meals, and when the adolescent goes to bed. Aspects of the neighborhood context include region and urbanicity of residence, youth's familiarity and association with neighbors, and the cohesiveness and safety of the neighborhood. For greater description of these variables and the regression methods used, see Appendix 6A.

RESULTS

Health Differentials by Immigrant Status

If we accept the view that native-born children of immigrants have adopted the values and culture of American society more so than immigrant youth, we can observe health differentials across immigrant status as representing an assimilation process. This perspective is based on the argument that the children of immigrants represent the first members of their community to be educated and socialized in American institutions, whereas immigrant adolescents may carry with them the socialization and educational experience they received in their country of origin, depending on the age at which they entered the United States.

This perspective is addressed in Table 6A-1, which examines physical health status, emotional health, and health risk behaviors of immigrant adolescents and native-born adolescents with immigrant parents in comparison to adolescents in native-born families, who are further subgrouped into native populations of non-Hispanic whites, non-Hispanic blacks, non-Hispanic other races, and Hispanics. If we view generation as representing the degree of assimilation, the results indicate a pattern of increasing adoption of the mainstream behaviors of adolescents in native-born families with increasing assimilation into American culture. For nearly all of the outcomes examined, native-born youth with immigrant parents have poorer physical health and a greater propensity to engage in risky behaviors than foreign-born youth. The children of immigrants are more likely than immigrant youth to have fair or poor health (10.7 versus 9.2 percent), to have missed school because of a health or emotional problem in the past month (36.5 versus 33.5 percent), to experience learning difficulties (12.5 versus 9.3 percent), to be obese (26.7 versus 17.0 percent), to have asthma (8.1 versus 4.8 percent), to have ever had sex (33.9 versus 31.3 percent) and at a younger age (14.9 versus 15.1 percent), to engage in four or more delinquent acts (25.0 versus 15.8 percent), to be involved in three or more violent acts (21.3 versus 14.6 percent), and to use three or more controlled substances (17.4 versus 8.3 percent). Differences in the likelihood of using birth control at first intercourse and in symptoms of psychological distress or feelings of positive well-being are negligible between the two immigrant generations.

Reflecting the heterogeneity of the native-born families, health outcomes vary considerably across racial and ethnic groups in the native population. In general, non-Hispanic whites have more favorable health outcomes than the other native ethnic groups. For instance, non-Hispanic whites report the lowest levels of fair or poor general health, the highest use of birth control at first intercourse, and the fewest symptoms of psychological distress across both immigrant generations and all native populations. Certain health outcomes advantage or disadvantage particular native ethnic groups. For instance, non-Hispanic blacks are the most sexually active (55 percent), with the youngest average age at first sexual intercourse (13.8), but they are the least likely among the native groups to use three or more controlled substances (8.6 percent).

The native subpopulations of youth of non-Hispanic other races and Hispanic youth stand out, however, with the poorest physical health and the highest levels of risky behaviors. Moreover, knowing that the ethnic composition of immigrant children and the children of immigrants largely represents the "new immigration" from Latin America and Asia, the native subpopulations represented by non-Hispanic other adolescents (largely Asian Americans) and Hispanic adolescents are most similar in their ethnic background and may represent the "segment" of the U.S. native population to which immigrant youth assimilate. If we contrast the health status and risky behaviors of foreign-born youth and native-born youth with foreign-born parents with the native populations of non-Hispanic Asian and American Indian and Hispanic adolescents, a fairly linear pattern is observed. Non-Hispanic Asian and American Indian and Hispanic native youth are more likely to report fair or poor health (14.5 and 13.1 percent, respectively) than native-born youth with foreign-born parents (10.7 percent) and foreign-born youth (9.2 percent). Similarly, non-Hispanic Asian and American Indian and Hispanic native youth are more likely to miss school because of a health or emotional problem, to have learning difficulties, to be obese, and to have asthma than native-born youth with foreign-born parents, who have the second-highest levels of health problems, and foreign-born youth, who have the lowest levels of health problems. This pattern is further reflected in the health problems index, showing that health problems increase as the immigrant experience becomes more distant by generation.

A consistent linear pattern is also found for health risk behaviors. Non-Hispanic Asian and American Indian and Hispanic youth in native families are more likely to have ever had sex (39.2 and 45.3 percent, respectively) than native-born youth with foreign-born parents (33.9 percent) and foreign-born youth (31.3 percent) and to have had first intercourse at a younger age (14.4 and 14.2 years old, respectively) than native-born youth with foreign-born parents (14.9 years) and foreign-born youth (15.1 years). Similarly, non-Hispanic Asian and American Indian and Hispanic youth in native-born families are more likely to engage in delinquency, violence, and controlled substance use than native-born youth with foreign-born parents, who report the second-highest involvement in health risk behaviors, and foreign-born youth, who report the lowest involvement in risky behaviors. The risky behaviors index displays this linear pattern as well.

In sum, the most striking finding from Table 6A-1 is the pattern of assimilation displayed by the increasing health problems and increasing propensity to engage in health risk behaviors across immigrant generations of youth, especially comparing immigrant children and the children of immigrants to the native populations of non-Hispanic Asian and American Indian and Hispanic youth. Perhaps the most consistent finding, however, is that foreign-born adolescents have better physical health and engage in fewer risky behaviors, with the exception of the use of birth control at first intercourse. Foreign-born youth experience fewer physical health problems, have less experience with sex, are less likely to engage in delinquent and violent behavior, and are less likely to use controlled substances than native-born youth. Note that all of the differences reported in Table 6A-1 are statistically significant at the 0.01 level, with the exception of psychological distress and positive well-being.

The findings on health status and health risk behavior are summarized in Figures 6-1 and 6-2, which show the percentage distributions on the physical health problems index (Figure 6-1) and the risky behaviors index (Figure 6-2) for foreign-born youth, native-born youth of foreign-born parents, and the native populations of non-Hispanic whites, non-Hispanic blacks, non-Hispanic other races (Asian and American Indian), and Hispanic youth. Figure 6-1 illustrates the linear relationship in physical health problems by immigrant status and the health advantage of foreign-born adolescents. The physical health problems index counts the number of health problems out of the five measured (Table 6A-1), and Figure 6-1 displays the percentage distribution with zero, one, and two or more health problems by immigrant status. Focusing on the bottom level of bars showing the percentage with no health problems, foreign-born youth have the fewest health problems, and native-born youth with foreign-born parents have the second- fewest health problems, equal with the native population of non-Hispanic whites. Non-Hispanic blacks have the next-largest percentage of youth with no health problems, followed by non-Hispanic Asian and American Indian youth; Hispanic youth have the fewest with no health problems. This same pattern is seen at the second level of bars in the percentage of youth with zero or one health problem. Conversely, the percentage with two or more health problems grows as one

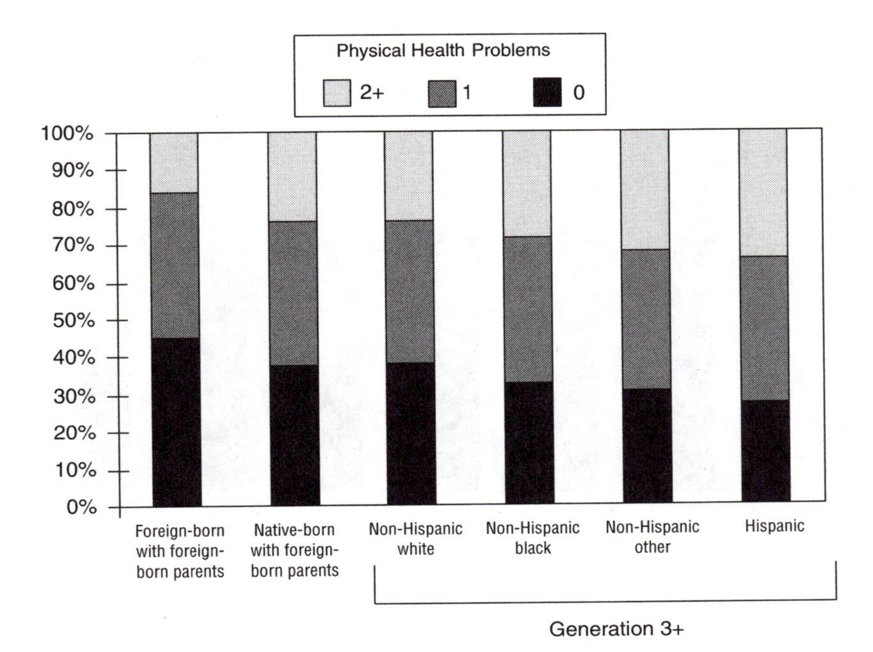

FIGURE 6-1 Physical health problems by generation.

moves across immigrant generations to the native populations that are most similar to the ethnic backgrounds of the majority of youth in immigrant families.

Figure 6-2 displays a similar pattern for the risky behaviors index, showing the percentage distribution of involvement in zero, one, and two or more risky behaviors by immigrant status. The linear pattern is less striking than in Figure 6-1 but is still evident in the percentage of youth involved in zero or one risky behavior (the second level of bars). Again, moving across immigrant generation and native ethnic groups, the percentage engaged in zero or one risky behavior decreases, while the top shaded portions of the bars, the percentages engaged in two or more risky behaviors, increase. Less engagement in risky behaviors is again evident for immigrant children, and while the children of immigrants are less involved in risky behaviors than are youth in native-born families with a similar ethnic background,

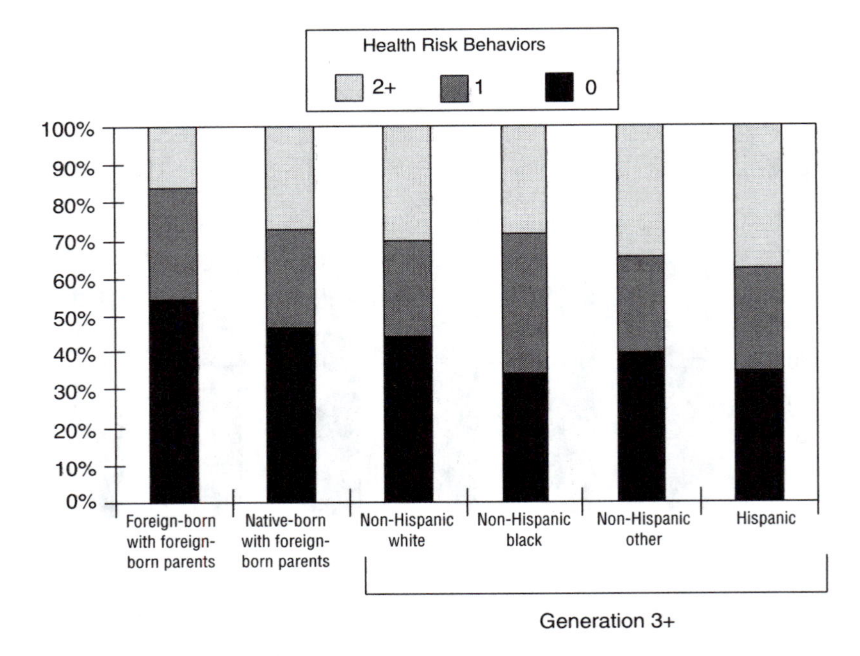

FIGURE 6-2 Risky behaviors index by generation.

the advantage is slightly less than it was for physical health status.

Demographic Composition of Immigrant Families

The health differentials documented in Table 6A-1 and Figures 6-1 and 6-2 are dramatic and fairly consistent but may be a consequence of differences in the demographic characteristics of immigrant families. Immigrant children as a group are older on average than the children of immigrant or native-born parents. Nearly 75 percent of foreign-born adolescents are 16 to 21 years old, whereas about 60 percent of native-born adolescents with foreign-born parents and 52 percent of youth in native-born families are among the older adolescents in this age group. The sex composition of immigrant and native-born adolescent groups is similar with even representation of female and male adolescents.

To explore the possibility that differences in the age composition of immigrant and native-born adolescent groups may explain some of the differences in health outcomes, physical health status and health risk behaviors were examined among younger (11 to 15 years old) and older (16 to 21 years old) adolescents in immigrant and native-born families. Health differentials were somewhat attenuated among the younger adolescents, but the results (not shown) were consistent with those in Table 6A-1 and the majority of differences were statistically significant.

Health Differentials Among Immigrant Youth

To further test the assimilation model from an intragenerational perspective, health outcomes by time in the United States for immigrant youth are examined. The results are dramatically consistent: the longer the time since arrival in the United States, the poorer are the physical health outcomes and the greater the likelihood of engaging in health risk behaviors.[1] Age at arrival is correlated with time in the United States, and the same results emerge when health differentials by age at arrival in the United States are examined.

Figure 6-3 summarizes these results by presenting means on the physical health problems index (top panel) and the risky behaviors index (bottom panel) by years in the United States for foreign-born youth. A remarkably linear and statistically significant pattern is evident, indicating that with more years of exposure and assimilation into American culture, physical health problems increase, as do risky behaviors.

Health Differentials by Immigrant Status and Ethnic Background

The aggregate differences by immigrant status documented thus far mask likely variations in the relationships between immigrant status and health by country of origin and ethnic background. Differences in the ethnic composition of foreign-born youth and native-born youth with foreign-born parents and in

[1]Similar to Table 6A-1, there is no significant relationship between time in the United States and psychological distress or feelings of positive well-being.

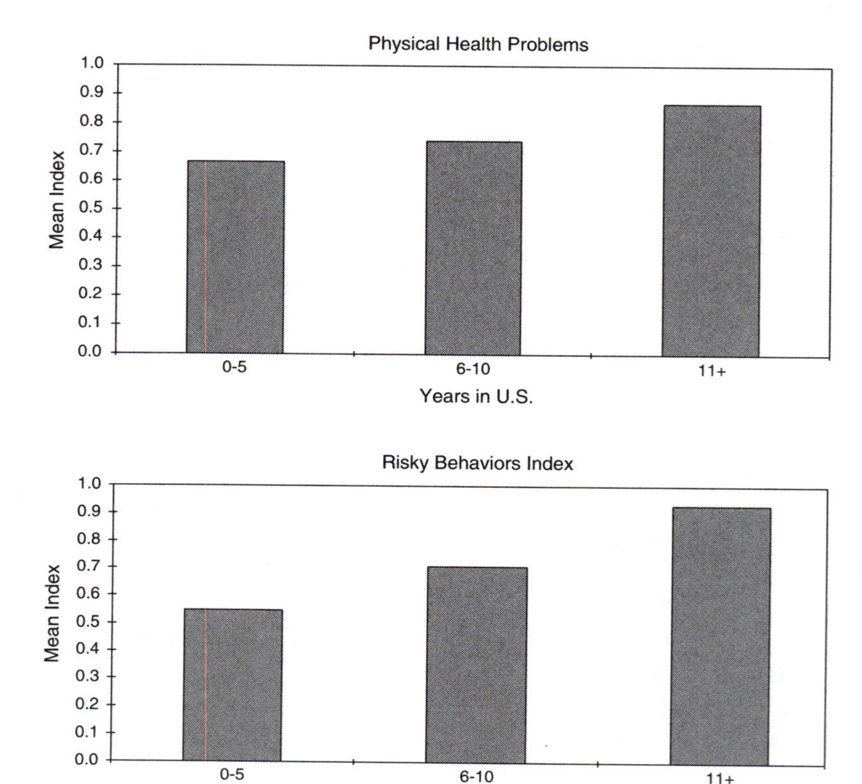

FIGURE 6-3 Mean index scores of foreign-born youth with foreign-born parents by time in the United States.

the relationship between ethnic background and health may partially explain the aggregate patterns found in Table 6A-1. The next stage of analysis therefore controls for ethnic background and examines differences in health outcomes by immigrant status within ethnic groups. Table 6A-2 presents these results.

Ethnic background is defined for 11 countries or regions of origin that permit comparisons by immigrant status: Mexico, Cuba, Central and South America, Puerto Rico, China, the Philippines, Japan, Vietnam, other Asia, Africa and the Afro Caribbean, and Europe and Canada. Ethnic background classifications are based on the adolescent's birthplace and the immigrant parent's birthplace for foreign-born youth and native-born youth with foreign-born parents, respectively. Adolescents in native-born families who indicated they were of Hispanic or Asian background were classified according to the specific ethnic group they identified in the survey (see Appendix 6A-1 for further details about this classification). Immigrant status is indicated by FB (foreign-born), NB/FB (native-born to foreign-born parents), and NB (youth in native-born families). Youth of Puerto Rican background were classified according to whether they were island-born (IB), mainland-born to island-born parents (MB/IB), or mainland-born to mainland-born parents (MB).

The generational comparisons of youth of African and Afro Caribbean background and European and Canadian background deserve a word of caution. African and Afro Caribbean background cannot be specifically determined for youth in native-born families; however, the native population of non-Hispanic blacks probably represents prior immigration from these regions. Therefore, foreign-born youth and native-born youth with foreign-born parents from Africa and the Afro Caribbean who also indicated they were non-Hispanic and of the black race are compared with the native population of non-Hispanic blacks.[2] In a similar manner, foreign-born youth and native-born youth with foreign-born parents from Europe and Canada who are non-Hispanic and white are compared with non-Hispanic white adolescents in native-born families. Because the native populations of non-Hispanic blacks and non-Hispanic whites represent a more heterogeneous ethnic composition than the immigrant populations of youth with African and Afro Caribbean ancestry and European and Canadian ancestry, respectively, these comparisons are loose and may not reflect a parallel ethnic group similarity across immigrant status to the same degree as in the other ethnic group comparisons.

Data in Table 6A-2 are complex and not all findings are sig-

[2]Because youth from Africa and the Afro Caribbean are black immigrants and treated as blacks by American society, their small numbers are combined in all analyses.

nificant, but the general pattern confirms the aggregate findings: foreign-born youth experience better physical health and engage in fewer risky behaviors than native-born youth with foreign-born parents. Focusing only on significant effects, the most consistent results are shown for learning difficulties, obesity, and asthma among the physical health outcomes and for all risky behaviors for nearly all of the ethnic groups. The strongest and most consistent results are found for Mexican, Central and South American, Filipino, and other Asian youth. Foreign-born Mexican youth are less likely to have missed school for a health or emotional problem in the past month and are less likely to have learning difficulties, to be obese, or to have asthma than native-born youth with foreign-born Mexican parents. Similarly, foreign-born Mexican youth are less likely than native-born youth of Mexican parents to have ever had sex, to engage in multiple delinquent or violent acts, and to use three or more controlled substances, though they are equally likely to experience psychological distress.

Exceptions to this pattern appear for the African and Afro Caribbean ethnic group. Although the physical health of foreign-born youth from Africa and the Afro Caribbean is better than that of native-born youth with parents of African or Afro Caribbean descent, foreign-born youth are more likely to have ever had sex than native-born adolescents. Another exception to the health advantage associated with foreign birth occurs for asthma and sexual behavior among youth from Europe and Canada. Foreign-born youth have higher rates of asthma and sexual behavior than native-born youth with European or Canadian parents, though the differences are small. Finally, minor differences between Chinese immigrant children and the children of Chinese immigrants also operate in the opposite direction for the general health and "missed school due to a health problem" outcomes.

Nevertheless, even for these exceptions, immigrant children and the children of immigrants experience fewer health problems and engage in fewer risky behaviors than youth in native families across all ethnic groups. For instance, even though foreign-born African and Afro Caribbean youth have higher rates of sexual activity than native-born youth with African or Afro Caribbean parents, they are still less likely to have ever had sex than the native population of non-Hispanic blacks. Similarly, native non-Hispanic whites have higher rates of asthma than immigrant children or the children of immigrants from Europe and Canada. Moreover, comparing across immigrant groups to the native population within ethnic background tells a story of increasing health problems and increasing risky behaviors for the majority of significant relationships. This finding is most consistent for youth of Mexican, Central and South American, Chinese, Filipino, and other Asian background.

Consistent with findings presented in Table 6A-1, use of birth control at first intercourse and emotional health outcomes do not follow this pattern. In general, there is no significant variation in the use of birth control or emotional health by immigrant status and ethnic group background. The only exception is the one significant relationship for use of birth control among youth of Mexican background. Use of birth control is more prevalent among sexually active adolescents in the native Mexican population (56.5 percent), followed by youth with immigrant parents (52.5 percent), and is least prevalent among sexually active immigrant youth from Mexico (42.5 percent).

Immigrant status does not influence symptoms of psychological distress or feelings of positive well-being among youth across the various ethnic backgrounds in these descriptive data. Previous research has produced mixed results regarding the relationship between depressive symptoms and immigrant status. Some research suggests that immigrant children experience acculturative stress as they adjust to a foreign culture, learn a new language, and try to fit into mainstream youth society (Kao, this volume; Rumbaut, 1994), while other studies find immigrants to experience fewer depressive symptoms than the native population such that becoming "Americanized" increases levels of distress among youth (Rumbaut, 1997a, 1997b).

On certain outcomes and for certain ethnic groups, the children of immigrants experience the most risk in their physical health and health risk behaviors. For instance, native-born youth with Mexican immigrant parents are more likely to miss school because of a health or emotional problem and to be obese than both the native population (differences are slight) and immigrant children from Mexico. Native-born youth with Cuban immigrant parents are more likely to engage in multiple acts of delinquency than either immigrant or native Cuban youth. Finally, mainland-born Puerto Rican youth of island-born parents are much more likely to be obese than island-born youth and mainland-born youth of mainland-born Puerto Rican parents.

Nevertheless, the dominant finding in Table 6A-2 is the prevalence of a health advantage associated with immigrant status among the major ethnic groups in America. As the immigrant experience becomes more distant across generations, youth become more similar to the native population in their health status and health risk behaviors. To the extent that immigrant adjustment and assimilation involve the adoption of health status and behavioral norms in the native ethnic subgroup with which immigrants are identifying, a segmented assimilation process is furthermore evident in these data.

Multivariate Analysis

The final stage of analysis entails testing for the significant and independent effects of immigrant status and ethnic background categories displayed in Table 6A-2 and exploring possible explanations of significant differences that are associated with variations in the family and neighborhood context of different ethnic group generations. Multivariate regression analysis is used to model each of the health outcomes as a function of immigrant status and ethnic group category (essentially an interaction effect) relative to the baseline effect (reference category) of native non-Hispanic whites, the majority native ethnic group of youth in America.

Table 6A-3 displays the results of the multivariate analysis of the five physical health outcomes, the psychological distress outcome, the four health risk behavior outcomes, the physical health problems index, and the risky behaviors index. For each outcome, three models are estimated. The first model estimates the effects of immigrant status and ethnic group categories relative to the baseline effect for native non-Hispanic whites, controlling for the age and sex of the adolescent. Model 2 controls for family context effects, and model 3 explores the influence of neighborhood differences.

There are important structural differences in family context by immigrant status and ethnic background that might explain the health differentials found in the descriptive analysis. For instance, native-born youth of foreign-born parents are more likely to live with their biological parents (67 percent) and less likely to live in a step- or other family form (16 percent). Youth in native-born families are the least likely to live with both of their biological parents (47 percent) and the most likely to live with a single parent (27 percent). Foreign-born adolescents lie between these extremes with 55 percent living with two biological parents, 24 percent living in a stepfamily or other family form, and 21 percent living with a single parent. Nevertheless, immigrant children experience the highest poverty rates. More than a third of immigrant youth live in poverty (38 percent), compared to 22 percent of youth with immigrant parents and 20 percent of youth in native-born families. Average family income further reflects this differential in economic status, with mean family income ranging from $33,976, $44,185, and $47,090 for foreign-born youth, native-born youth with foreign-born parents, and youth in native-born families, respectively.

The main sources of neighborhood context differences are geographic location and neighborhood familiarity and cohesiveness. Increasing familiarity and association with people in the neighborhood occurs with native birth, with the least neighborhood familiarity evident among Asian ethnic groups and the most familiarity among African and Afro Caribbean ethnic groups. Neighborhood cohesiveness and safety seem to characterize the neighborhoods of native youth and are greater among Asian ethnic groups than Hispanic ethnic groups. Note that the estimated effects of family and neighborhood context on health outcomes are not of central interest in this analysis; rather the interest is the extent to which health differentials by immigrant status and ethnic group are due to the family and neighborhood contexts of the different immigrant and ethnic groups.

Table 6A-3 contains a massive amount of data analysis, and here only the most important and general results are highlighted. The main findings are summarized in Figures 6-4 and 6-5 and discussed below. First, there are consistently beneficial and significant effects (shown in bold) of foreign birth on health prob-

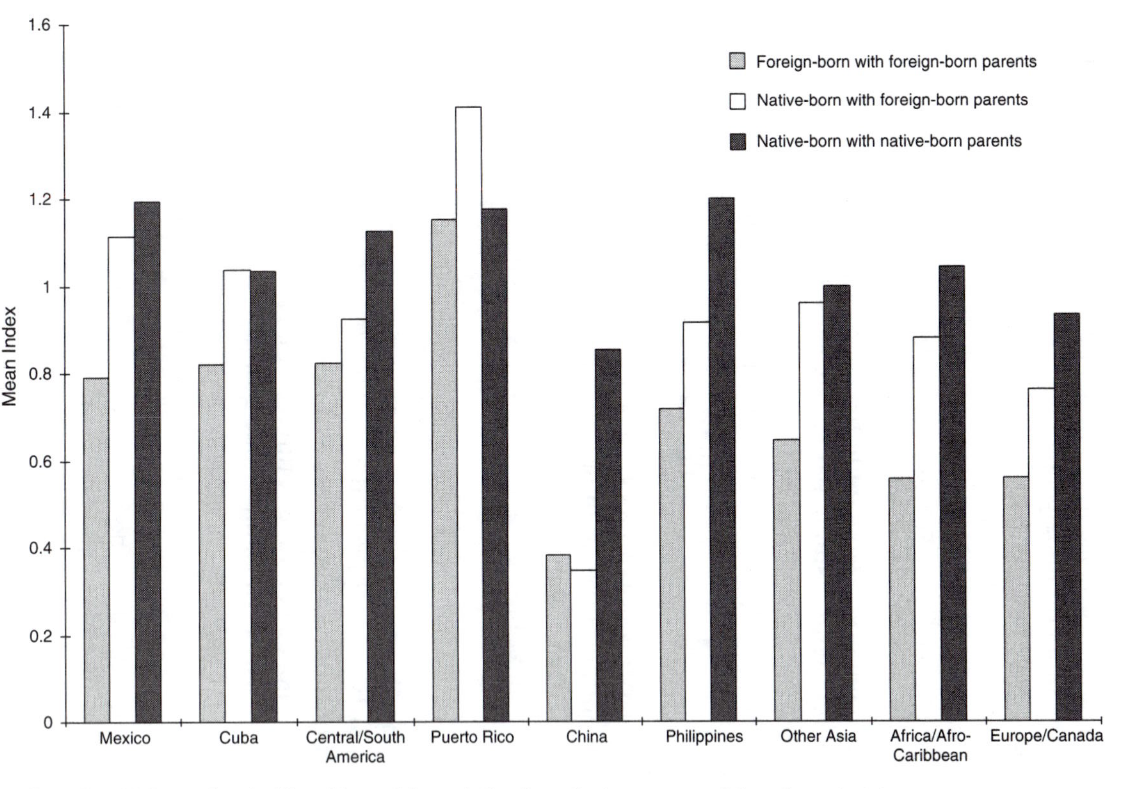

FIGURE 6-4 Mean physical health problems index by ethnic group and immigrant status.

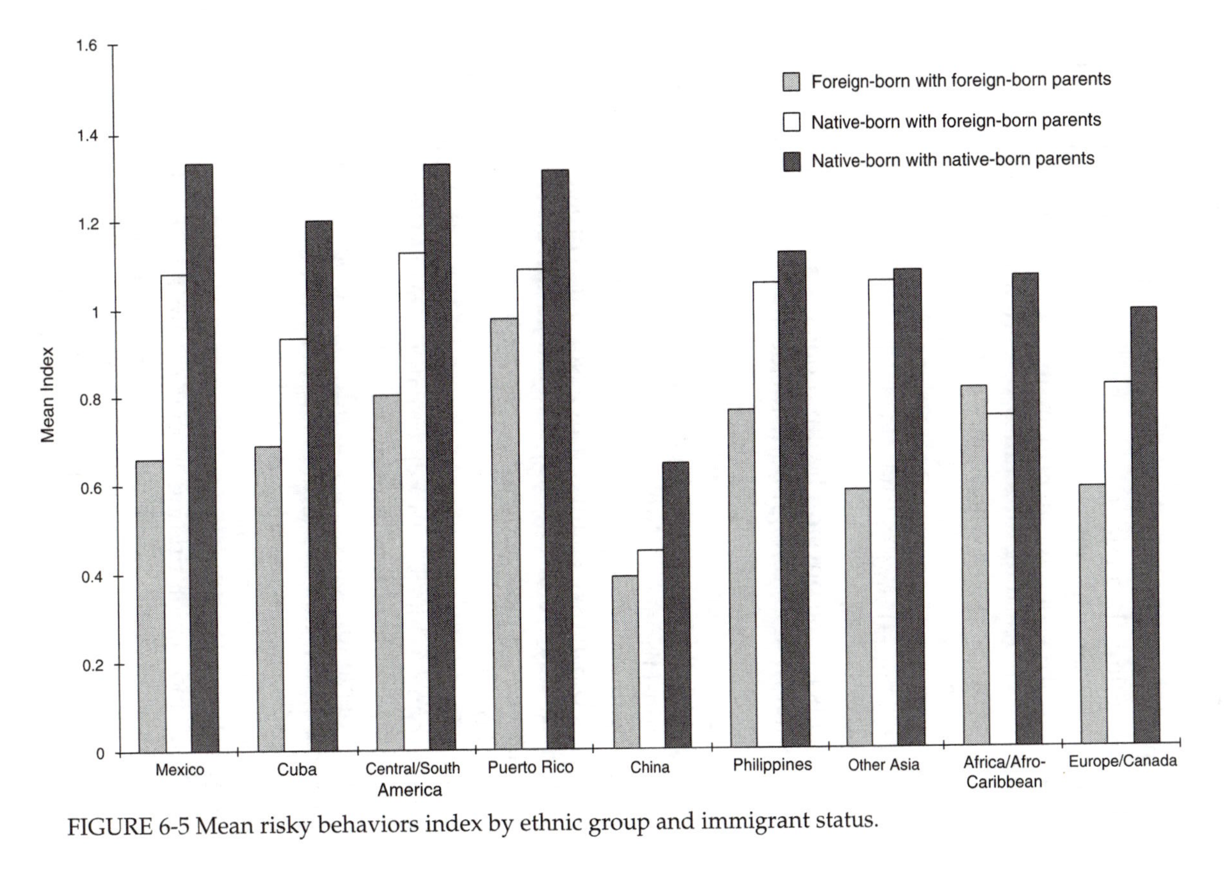

FIGURE 6-5 Mean risky behaviors index by ethnic group and immigrant status.

lems and health risk behaviors for all ethnic groups, controlling for demographic composition and family and neighborhood context (i.e., in model 3). Because the negative coefficients indicate that immigrant children experience *fewer* health problems and risky behaviors than native-born non-Hispanic white youth, foreign birth is a health advantage. Health outcomes for which the beneficial effects of foreign birth are most prevalent across all ethnic groups are learning difficulties, obesity, asthma, and the risky behaviors of sexual activity, delinquency, violence, and use of controlled substances. Across all measures of health outcomes, the most consistent beneficial effects of foreign birth are found for Mexican, Central and South American, Chinese, Filipino, and other Asian youth.

Results for the physical health problems and risky behaviors indexes show that foreign-born Mexican, Cuban, Central and South American, Chinese, Filipino, other Asian, African and Afro Caribbean, and European and Canadian youth have significantly fewer health problems and engage in fewer risky behaviors than native non-Hispanic white youth. Island-born Puerto Rican youth do not enjoy these beneficial effects, suggesting a commonality with U.S. native youth culture. Nor is this protective quality conferred to native-born youth with immigrant parents, with the exception of Chinese and African and Afro Caribbean ethnicity. Native-born Chinese youth with immigrant parents have better physical health and engage in fewer risky behaviors than native non-Hispanic white youth, while native-born African and Afro Caribbean youth with immigrant parents are less likely to engage in risky behaviors only. Apparently, native-born youth in Chinese immigrant families and, to a lesser extent, those in African and Afro Caribbean immigrant families are deterred from the assimilation process into mainstream U.S. youth culture that we observed for other ethnic groups.

A second major finding is that controlling for family and neighborhood context does not diminish the beneficial effects on physical health and risky behavior outcomes for foreign-born youth. Thus, the protective quality of immigrant status for adolescents is not related to family and neighborhood context. Rather, controlling for family and neighborhood context increases the beneficial effects of foreign birth on physical health problems for Mexican, Cuban, Central and South American, Filipino, and African and Afro Caribbean youth and on risky behaviors for African and Afro Caribbean youth. This suggests that differences in family and neighborhood contexts operate to increase health risks for immigrant youth from these regions, and when these factors are controlled, the beneficial influence of foreign birth increases. Here poverty status plays an important role in increasing health risks for immigrant youth and, once its effect is held constant, immigrant status becomes even more important in reducing health problems and risky behaviors.

Third, family and neighborhood context matter most for native minority youth, who experience greater health problems and risky behaviors than native non-Hispanic white youth. Among Mexican, Central and South American, Puerto Rican, Filipino, and African and Afro Caribbean youth in native-born families, when family and neighborhood contexts are controlled, the adverse effects of native birth and ethnic group on health status and risky behaviors diminish or become insignificant. This result indicates that family and neighborhood factors, particularly family poverty status, among these ethnic groups in the native population explain their poorer health outcomes and greater risky behaviors relative to non-Hispanic whites.

Fourth, although descriptive analysis did not indicate significant variations in emotional health by immigrant status and ethnic group background, multivariate results show a general pattern of greater distress levels among native-born ethnic minority youth and less emotional distress among foreign-born adolescents relative to non-Hispanic white youth in native-born families.[3] Greater psychological distress is found among native-born Mexican youth and mainland-born Puerto Rican youth regardless of whether their parents were immigrants and among Chinese and African and Afro Caribbean youth in native-born families. Foreign birth apparently protects youth from psychological distress as well. Foreign-born youth from Cuba, Europe, and Canada en-

[3]Similar results (though opposite in sign) were obtained for the regression analysis of positive well-being. They are not presented here because of space limitations but are available from the author.

joy better emotional health than non-Hispanic white youth in native-born families. The one exception is that foreign-born youth and native-born youth of immigrant parents from the Philippines—the most Americanized of immigrant groups with a common language and exposure to America—experience more depressive symptoms than native non-Hispanic white youth.

Figures 6-4 and 6-5 summarize the multivariate results of the effects of immigrant status and ethnic group categories on health. Figure 6-4 presents the predicted mean physical health problems index by immigrant status and ethnic background, adjusted for demographic characteristics, family context, and neighborhood context of the youth (i.e., based on model 3). The graph shows that, for all ethnic groups except Cuba, Puerto Rico, and China, there is a consistent relationship between immigrant status and physical health problems: physical health problems increase with greater exposure to American society across native birth of generations. Note further the varying levels of physical health problems by ethnic group. Chinese youth have the lowest levels of physical health problems, followed by youth of European or Canadian and other Asian backgrounds. Puerto Rican youth have the highest level of physical health problems, with nearly as high levels among Mexican, Cuban, and Central and South American youth.

Figure 6-5 presents the adjusted mean risky behaviors index by immigrant status and ethnic background (predicted from the equation for model 3). Again, with the exception of Africa and the Afro Caribbean, the relationship between immigrant status and risky behaviors is remarkably consistent for all ethnic groups: engagement in risky behaviors increases with greater exposure and socialization in American society, as represented by native birth of generations. For certain ethnic groups (Cuba, Central and South America, Europe, and Canada) the relationship is linear. For other groups (Mexico, other Asia) the main difference is between foreign-born youth and native-born youth regardless of whether their parents were immigrants. Finally, among Puerto Rican, Chinese, and African and Afro Caribbean youth, both immigrant children and the children of immigrants display much lower involvement in risky behaviors than youth in native-born families.

The extent to which certain ethnic groups experience segmented assimilation can be clearly seen in Figure 6-5, where the risky behaviors of native-born children of immigrant parents have surpassed those of the mainstream youth population of non-Hispanic whites and approach those of their native-born ethnic group. In particular, native-born Mexican, Central and South American, Filipino, and other Asian youth with immigrant parents and mainland-born Puerto Rican youth with island-born parents are more involved in risky behaviors than non-Hispanic youth in native-born families.

Note finally that Chinese youth stand out as the ethnic group least engaged in risky behaviors. Because of intense familial and ethnic pressure to maintain the family reputation and focus only on achievement goals in American society, it is possible that Chinese youth may have under-reported their engagement in risky behaviors in this survey; however, this potential bias cannot be explored with the data at hand. Youth of Hispanic origin, on the other hand, display the greatest involvement in risky behaviors, followed by Asian youth, where native-born Filipino and other Asian youth with foreign-born parents are especially involved in risky behaviors.

CONCLUSION

This research has provided evidence to support both classical and revisionist theories about the assimilation process of immigrant youth. With greater time and socialization in U.S. institutions, neighborhoods, and youth culture, immigrant children increasingly adopt behavioral norms regarding health status and health risk. Studying a broad array of health outcomes, both the intergenerational (Figures 6-1 and 6-2) and intragenerational (Figure 6-3) perspectives revealed a classical assimilation model of health behaviors. When health differentials were examined within ethnic groups, support for "segmented" assimilation was evident in that immigrant youth over the generations tend to adopt the health behaviors and norms of their native ethnic group in the U.S. population more so that any other segment of the U.S. population. Moreover, the segmentation of immigrant assimilation seems to be along the lines of ethnicity rather than neighborhood context.

The greatest degree of assimilation was displayed by youth from Mexico, Central and South America, the Philippines, and other Asian countries (Table 6A-2 and Figures 6-4 and 6-5). With each successive generation of exposure and socialization in American culture, physical health problems and risky behaviors of youth in immigrant families approached the levels manifest in the respective native ethnic population of youth. Other ethnic groups displayed a different pattern of adjustment. For instance, the largest differences in health outcomes among youth from Cuba and Vietnam were between immigrant and native-born youth, regardless of whether their parents were immigrants. Whereas among youth from China, Africa and Afro Caribbean, and Europe and Canada, those in immigrant families, both foreign- and native-born youth with foreign-born parents, were distinctly different with lower levels of physical health problems and risky behaviors than youth in native-born families.

A clear and consistent finding in this research was the protective nature of immigrant status. Foreign-born youth experienced more favorable physical and emotional health and less involvement in risky behaviors than native-born youth of foreign-born parents and native-born youth of native-born parents, and this effect held across country of origin and ethnic background. Analysis showed that this protective quality was not related to the family or neighborhood context of immigrant children. Rather for some ethnic groups, family and neighborhood factors such as poverty, single-parent households, and unsafe or isolating neighborhoods reduced the health advantage associated with immigrant status. These findings for a broad range of health outcomes can be added to the small set of studies showing that immigrant status confers a health advantage for birth outcomes (see Landale et al., this volume).

Future research on immigrant children should attempt to uncover the mechanisms behind the health protection of foreign birth. This study explored structural features of the family and neighborhood context, but other data are needed to address the potential roles of parenting behaviors, extended kin relationships and exchange of social resources, and community control and social capital. Moreover, the loss of health protection and the increase in psychological distress as ethnic minorities assimilate into American youth culture warrant further research. Data on peer networks, social supports, school involvement and context, and parent-adolescent conflict and relationships during adolescence would provide a place to start to explore the sources of distress in the lives of ethnic minority youth who are part of the native population.

REFERENCES

Bautista-Hayes, D.E.
1990 Latino Health Indicators and the Underclass Model: From Paradox to New Policy Models. Chicano Studies Research Center, UCLA, unpublished manuscript.

Bearman, P.S., J. Jones, and J.R. Udry
1997 The National Longitudinal Study of Adolescent Health: Research Design. URL: http://www.cpc.unc.edu/projects/addhealth/design.html.

Beck, A.T.
1978 *Depression Inventory*. Philadelphia: Center for Cognitive Therapy.

Blackburn, M.L., D.E. Bloom, and R.B. Freeman
1990 *Why Has the Economic Position of Less-Skilled Workers Deteriorated in the United States?* In *A Future of Lousy Jobs*, G. Burtless, ed. Washington, D.C.: Brookings Institution.

Dornbusch, S.M.
1989 The sociology of adolescence. Pp. 223-259 in *Annual Review of Sociology*, W.R. Scott and J. Blake, eds. Palo Alto, Calif.: Annual Reviews.

Earls, F., J.I. Escobar, and S.M. Manson
1990 Suicide in minority groups: Epidemiological and cultural perspectives. Pp. 571-598 in *Suicide over the Life Cycle*, S.J. Blumenthal and D.J. Kupfer, eds. Washington, D.C.: American Psychiatric Association Press.

Farley, R.
1996 *The New American Reality: Who We Are, How We Got Here, Where We Are Going*. New York: Russell Sage Foundation.

Freeman, R.B., and H. Holzer
1991 *The Deterioration of Employment and Earnings Opportunities for Less Educated Young Americans: A Review of the Evidence*. Department of Economics, Harvard University. Mimeo.

Gans, H.J.
1992 Second generation decline: Scenarios for the economic and ethnic futures of post-1965 American immigrants. *Ethnic and Racial Studies* 15:173-192.

Gordon, M.M.
1964 *Assimilation in American Life: The Role of Race, Religion, and National Origin*. New York: Oxford University Press.

Hirschman, C.
1996 Studying immigrant adaptation from the 1990 population census: From generational comparisons to the process of "becoming American." Pp. 54-81 in *The New Second Generation*, A. Portes, ed. New York: Russell Sage Foundation.

Jasso, G., and M.R. Rosenzweig
1990 *The New Chosen People: Immigrants to the United States*. New York: Russell Sage Foundation.

Klerman, L.V.
1993 The influence of economic factors on health-related behaviors in adolescents. Pp. 38-57 in *Promoting the Health of Adolescents: New Directions of the Twenty-first Century*, S.G. Millstein, A.C. Petersen, and E.O. Nightingale, eds. New York: Oxford University Press.

Lieberson, S.
1980 *A Piece of the Pie: Black and White Immigrants Since 1880*. Berkeley: University of California Press.

Mendoza, F.S., S.J. Ventura, B. Valdez, R. Castillo, L.E. Saldivar, K. Baisden, and R. Martorelli
1990 Selected measures of health status for Mexican-American, mainland Puerto Rican, and Cuban-American children. *Journal of the American Medical Association* 265:227-232.

Perry, C.L., S.H. Kelder, and K.A. Komro
1993 The social world of adolescents: Family, peers, schools, and the community. Pp. 73-96 in *Promoting the Health of Adolescents: New Directions of the Twenty-first Century*, S.G. Millstein, A.C. Petersen, and E.O. Nightingale, eds. New York: Oxford University Press.

Portes, A., ed.
1996 *The New Second Generation*. New York: Russell Sage Foundation.

Portes, A., and M. Zhou
1993 The new second generation: Segmented assimilation and its variants. *Annals of the American Academy of Political and Social Sciences* 530:74-96.

Radloff, L.S.
1977 The CES-D scale: A self-report depression scale for research in the general public. *Applied Psychology Measurement* 1:385-401.

Reimers, D.M.
1992 *Still the Golden Door: The Third World Comes to America*, 2nd ed. New York: Columbia University Press.

Rumbaut, R.G.
1994 The crucible within: Ethnic identity, self-esteem, and segmented assimilation among children of immigrants. *International Migration Review* 28:748-794.
1995 The new Californians: Comparative research findings on the educational progress of immigrant children. Pp. 17-69 in *California's*

Immigrant Children: Theory, Research and Implications for Educational Policy, R.G. Rumbaut and W.A. Cornelius, eds. La Jolla: Center for U.S.-Mexican Studies, University of California, San Diego.

1996 Origins and destinies: Immigration, race, and ethnicity in contemporary America. Pp. 21-42 in *Origins and Destinies: Immigration, Race, and Ethnicity in America,* S. Pedraza and R.G. Rumbaut, eds. Belmont, Calif.: Wadsworth Publishing Co.

1997a Paradoxes (and orthodoxies) of assimilation. *Sociological Perspectives.*

1997b Ties that bind: Immigration and immigrant families in the United States. Pp. 3-46 in *Immigration and the Family: Research and Policy on U.S. Immigrants,* A. Booth, A.C. Crouter, and N.S. Landale, eds. Hillsdale, N.J.: Lawrence Erlbaum Associates.

Wilson, W.J.

1987 *The Truly Disadvantaged: The Inner-City, the Underclass, and Public Policy.* Chicago: University of Chicago Press.

Wolfe, B.L.

1994 Reform of health care for the nonelderly poor. Pp. 253-288 in *Confronting Poverty: Prescriptions for Change,* S.H. Danziger, G.D. Sandefur, and D.H. Weinberg, eds. New York: Russell Sage Foundation.

World Health Organization

1995 *Physical Status: The Use and Interpretation of Anthropometry.* WHO Technical Report Series 854. Geneva: World Health Organization.

APPENDIX 6A: DESCRIPTION OF DATA AND SAMPLE

The National Longitudinal Study of Adolescent Health (Add Health) is a nationally representative study of adolescents in grades 7 through 12 in the United States in 1995. Add Health was designed to help explain the causes of adolescent health and health risk behaviors with special emphasis on the effects of multiple contexts of adolescent life. The study used a school-based design to sample high schools and their feeder middle or junior high schools.[4] From the school sample (using school rosters), a random subsample of around 20,000 adolescents was selected with whom in-home interviews were conducted with the adolescent and a parent, usually the mother.

Minority populations are represented in proportion to their size in the general population, yielding sufficient samples for separate analyses of major ethnic groups nationwide. A number of special samples were also selected from the in-school sample. The study included an oversample of several ethnic samples—including Puerto Rican, Cuban, and Chinese adolescents. The special ethnic samples, large sample size, and national representation make this an ideal dataset with which to study immigrant youth and families.

The initial in-home sample contained 20,745 adolescents ages 11 to 21. Parental interviews were completed for 17,394 adolescents, so outcomes based on parental reports and multivariate analysis are based on this sample size (see Bearman et al., 1997, for a detailed description of the Add Health study).

Health Outcome Measures

Physical health outcomes are measured as dichotomous variables and include (1) fair or poor general health, (2) whether the adolescent ever missed school for a health or emotional problem, (3) learning difficulties, (4) obesity, and (5) asthma. A physical health problems index was then constructed using these five physical health outcomes for graphical illustration of results. (See Table 6A-1, *Total* column, for overall sample mean.)

---

[4]Dropouts, the highest-risk adolescents, are therefore not part of the sample.

Both the adolescent and his or her parent were asked to rate the adolescent's general health. If the adolescent or the parent indicated that the adolescent's health was fair or poor, this outcome was coded one (9.7 percent), whereas if both the parent and the adolescent rated the adolescent's health as good, very good, or excellent, the outcome was coded 0. Adolescents were asked how often they missed school in the past month because of a health or emotional problem. The majority indicated that they never missed school for these reasons (65 percent) and only a small minority missed school once a week or every day. Therefore, those who ever missed school in the past month for health or emotional reasons were coded 1 (35.3 percent).

Learning difficulties were coded 1 if the parent reported that the adolescent had a specific learning disability (i.e., difficulties with attention, dyslexia) or received any type of special education service in the past 12 months (15.4 percent). Obesity is measured by computing the body mass index (BMI or weight in kilograms divided by height in meters squared), using the adolescent's self-reported weight and height. Using age- and sex-specific standard distributions for BMI based on data from the NHANES I (National Health and Examination Survey; WHO, 1995), adolescents who fell above the standard BMI for the 85th percentile were considered extremely overweight and obese (25.3 percent).

Finally, whether the adolescent had asthma was reported by the parent, resulting in a sample mean of nearly 12 percent of adolescents with asthma. The physical health problems index was constructed by summing the incidence of each of the five physical health outcomes and ranges from 0 for adolescents who have none of these physical health problems to 5 for adolescents who have all of the physical health problems indicated by each of the outcome measures. The sample average index is 0.97 physical health problems.

Emotional health is measured by constructing two indexes based on items from the CES-D Scale (Radloff, 1977) and some from the Beck Inventory (Beck, 1978). Psychological distress includes 15 items that measure depressive symptoms such as feeling depressed, bothered by things, fearful, and sad. Responses range from 1 (never) to 4 (all the time), and the index represents the mean item score across the 15 items with a reliability (Cronbach's alpha) of 0.86. The positive well-being index includes four items that measure positive feelings such as feeling hopeful about the future, feeling happy, and enjoying life. Items also range from 1 to 4, and the index again represents the mean item score with a reliability of 0.71. Sample means are 1.49 for psychological distress and 2.99 for positive well-being.

Health risk behaviors are self-reported by the adolescent and include the following: (1) ever having had sexual intercourse, (2) age at first intercourse, (3) use of birth control at first intercourse, (4) delinquency, (5) violent behavior, and (6) use of controlled substances. A risky behaviors index based on sexual activity, delinquency, violence, and use of controlled substances also is presented. For the entire sample of adolescents ages 11 to 21, 40 percent reported ever having had sexual intercourse (see Table 6A-1 for sample means). Among those who have had sex, the average age at first intercourse was 14.5, and 64 percent used birth control at first intercourse.

Delinquency is measured by constructing an index of 11 delinquent or illegal behaviors in which the youth engaged such as painting graffiti, damaging property, shoplifting, running away from home, stealing a car, selling drugs, and burglary. In descriptive analysis a dichotomous measure indicating whether the youth engaged in four or more delinquent acts is used (21.6 percent), and in multivariate analysis the count of delinquent acts expressed as a proportion of all possible and nonmissing responses is used. The reliability (Cronbach's alpha) of the index is 0.80.

Violence is measured as an index based on nine items in which the youth reports violent behavior and use of weapons, including such items as fighting, having pulled a knife or gun on someone, having shot or stabbed someone, and having used a weapon in a fight. The dichotomous measure used in descriptive analysis identifies youth who engaged in three or more acts of violence (21.9 percent), and the multivariate analysis uses the proportionate measure with a reliability of 0.80.

Controlled substance use is measured by an index containing five items that indicate ever having used any of the following controlled substances: cigarettes, alcohol, chewing tobacco, marijuana, and hard drugs (inhalants, cocaine, other illegal drugs, or injected illegal drugs).[5] Descriptive analysis identifies youth who used three or more substances (19.4 percent), and multivariate analysis uses the proportionate measure (Cronbach's alpha = 0.68).

The risky behaviors index sums the dichotomous indicators of ever having had sex, having engaged in four or more delinquent acts, having engaged in three or more acts of violence, and having used three or more controlled substances and ranges from 0 for having been involved in no risky behaviors to 4 for having been involved in all four risky behaviors. The sample index average is 1.03 risky behaviors.

Youth Characteristics and Ethnic Background

Demographic characteristics include the youth's age and gender and serve as control variables in multivariate models. The gender distribution is even, and the average age of the sample is 15.5. Parallel country-of-origin classifications are used for immigrant children and for the children of immigrants (if both parents are immigrants, the country of origin of the father was chosen unless it was missing; if so, the mother's country of origin was selected).[6] Race/ethnicity is defined for all adolescents, but the measure is used to classify youth in native-born families in aggregate comparisons to youth in immigrant families. Four racial/ethnic categories are formed: non-Hispanic whites, non-Hispanic black, non-Hispanic other (American Indian, Asian, or other race), and Hispanic.

Add Health provides data on the ethnic background of youth in native-born families for adolescents of Hispanic or Asian background. Moreover, adolescents are permitted to check multiple ethnic group backgrounds. A small minority (7 to 8 percent) re-

[5] The controlled substance use index was developed by Karl Bauman, a collaborator on the Add Health study who is with the Department of Health Behavior and Health Education, University of North Carolina.

[6] When both parents are immigrants, the large majority are conationals; only 9 percent of native-born youth with two immigrant parents have mixed origins.

ported multiple ethnic group backgrounds. While there is substantive significance potentially related to the identity of multiple ethnic backgrounds among youth (see Rumbaut, 1994), these cases are too few to explore in any meaningful way within the analytical framework of this chapter. Therefore, a randomization procedure was used to assign youth with multiple ethnic backgrounds to one ethnic group within Hispanic and Asian ethnic backgrounds. Some youth (N = 34) indicated both Hispanic and Asian backgrounds. Because a randomization procedure did not seem appropriate for the Asian Hispanic biethnic youth and to capture the potential influence of both of the ethnic group backgrounds these youth indicated, these cases were doublecounted in the analysis.[7]

Family Context

Family context represents both the structural and the supportive features of the family environment as indicated by family income, family structure, mother's education, and parental supervision in the home. Family income is measured as a set of dummy variables: (1) less than $16,000, or below poverty for a family of four in 1995; (2) $16,000 to $29,999; (3) $30,000 to $49,999; (4) $50,000 or more (reference); and (5) a dummy variable for missing income data. Family structure is measured as a five-category variable, operationalized as a set of dummy variables that identify youth who live with (1) two biological parents (reference); (2) stepparents (step, adopted, or foster); (3) mother only; (4) father only; and (5) other family forms (with grandparents, aunts, uncles, or other relatives or in group homes). Mother's education is measured as four dummy variables: (1) less than high school (reference), (2) high school diploma or GED, (3) some college, and (4) college or postgraduate schooling.

Parental supervision is a count variable ranging from 0 to 4 indicating whether a parent is present in the home most or all of

---

[7]I acknowledge the advice of Mary Waters in helping me develop strategies to deal with multiple ethnic backgrounds.

the time the adolescent (1) goes to school in the morning, (2) comes home from school in the afternoon, (3) eats the evening meal (five to seven dinners a week), and (4) goes to bed at night. The sample mean is 3.0.

Neighborhood Context

Geographical context includes the region (West, South, Northeast, and the reference Midwest) and urbanicity of residence (urban, suburban, and reference rural) because immigrant groups are concentrated in a handful of states in the United States and are overrepresented in metropolitan areas (Farley, 1996). Youth's familiarity and association with neighbors are measured by two items. Neighborhood familiarity is coded 1 if the youth knows most of the people in the neighborhood *and* has stopped on the street to talk with someone who lives in the neighborhood and is coded 0 otherwise. Neighborhood cohesiveness is coded 1 if the adolescent reports that people in his or her neighborhood look out for each other and is coded 0 otherwise. Finally, neighborhood safety is coded 1 if the adolescent reports usually feeling safe in his or her neighborhood.

Analytic Methods

Descriptive analyses present the mean scores of emotional health indexes and the dichotomous measures of physical health and risky behavior outcomes (percentage with a particular physical health problem or engaging in a risky behavior) by immigrant status and ethnic group background. Multivariate analyses rely on three forms of regression: (1) logit models to estimate the dichotomous physical health outcomes; (2) a hazard model to estimate the risk of first sexual intercourse, accounting for exposure time (i.e., age); (3) and ordinary least squares models to estimate the linear proportionate indexes of risky behaviors.

TABLE 6A-1 Health Outcomes by Immigrant Status and Race/Ethnicity of Adolescents in Native-Born Families (means)

	Foreign-Born	Native-Born/ Foreign-Born Parents
Physical Health		
General health is fair or poor	9.2	10.7
Missed school due to a health or emotional problem	33.5	36.5
Learning difficulties	9.3	12.5
Obesity	17.0	26.7
Asthma	4.8	8.1
Health Problems	.74	.94
Emotional Health		
Psychological distress	1.54	1.52
Positive well-being	2.85	2.87
Health Risk Behaviors		
Ever had sex	31.3	33.9
Age at first intercourse[a]	15.1	14.9
Birth control used at first intercourse[a]	56.2	57.3
Four or more delinquent acts	15.8	25.0
Three or more acts of violence	14.6	21.3
Use of three or more controlled substances	8.3	17.4
Risky behaviors index	.70	.98
N	1,651	2,526

[a]These outcomes are based on the sample of adolescents who reported ever having had sex ($N = 8,226$).

Native-Born with Native-Born Parents				
Non-Hispanic White	Non-Hispanic Black	Non-Hispanic Other	Hispanic	Total
8.1	11.5	14.3	13.1	9.7
33.6	37.1	40.2	41.1	35.4
16.9	14.3	15.6	18.3	15.4
23.4	29.9	31.5	31.0	25.3
12.2	13.5	14.9	15.7	11.8
.93	1.05	1.17	1.20	.97
1.45	1.52	1.54	1.54	1.49
3.06	2.99	2.89	2.89	2.99
36.7	54.8	39.2	45.3	40.4
14.8	13.8	14.4	14.2	14.5
67.1	64.2	60.5	58.3	63.8
21.9	18.0	26.3	29.6	21.6
19.4	27.2	26.4	31.5	21.9
25.1	8.6	24.3	25.3	19.4
1.03	1.09	1.17	1.32	1.03
10,248	4,312	456	1,429	20,622

NOTE: With the exception of age at first intercourse and emotional health, all differences are statistically significant at the 0.001 level.

TABLE 6A-2 Health Outcomes of Adolescents by Immigrant Status and Ethnic Background

	Mexico		
	FB[a]	NB/FB	NB
Physical Health			
General health is fair or poor	13.0	15.5	13.4
Missed school due to a health or emotional problem	33.3**	43.2**	41.3**
Learning difficulties	6.9**	12.9**	18.4**
Obesity	25.7*	33.6*	32.8*
Asthma	1.0**	5.5**	13.1**
Health Problems	.80**	1.13**	1.20**
Emotional Health			
Psychological distress	1.54	1.58	1.54
Positive well-being	2.67	2.71	2.89
Health Risk Behaviors			
Ever had sex	35.1**	38.7**	45.9**
Age at first intercourse[b]	15.1**	15.1**	14.3**
Birth control used at first intercourse[b]	42.5*	52.5*	56.5*
Four or more delinquent acts	14.0**	25.3**	30.6**
Three or more acts of violence	16.6**	24.9**	32.9**
Use of three or more controlled substances	8.5**	19.7**	29.5**
Risky behaviors index	.75**	1.09**	1.39**
N	317	741	686

Cuba			Central/South America			Puerto Rico		
FB	NB/FB	NB	FB	NB/FB	NB	IB	MB/IB	MB
7.6	9.1	5.6	12.2	11.2	10.5	11.8	16.9	12.9
35.7	39.0	36.1	35.5**	26.2**	41.0**	38.0	46.4	40.2
10.8	17.9	9.4	11.1*	15.8*	20.7*	19.1	18.9	17.5
22.9	30.5	33.3	21.9	27.1	20.8	24.0*	39.3*	29.7*
8.0	9.5	12.5	3.7**	10.8**	20.1**	16.7	16.7	17.9
.85*	1.04*	.97	.84**	.92	1.12**	1.12	1.42	1.18
1.46	1.49	1.47	1.52	1.50	1.51	1.57	1.53	1.56
2.97	2.90	2.91	2.91	2.93	3.00	3.01	2.84	2.84
40.6	39.3	44.4	38.5	37.0	46.5	35.3	39.7	48.1
15.2*	14.7*	14.3*	14.8*	14.2*	13.9*	14.1	14.3	14.3
62.1	57.7	62.5	57.4	64.7	58.1	47.1	58.2	62.6
13.2*	23.0*	22.2*	13.6**	31.2**	34.2**	17.7	25.5	29.8
11.9**	21.9**	22.2**	16.9**	25.3**	30.4**	25.5	28.2	32.4
4.0**	15.5**	36.1**	8.6**	18.2**	29.6**	15.7	15.5	19.6
.70**	1.00**	1.25**	.78**	1.13**	1.42**	.94	1.09	1.29
224	265	36	278	187	162	51	142	342

continued on next page

TABLE 6A-2 Continued

	China		
	FB	NB/FB	NB
Physical Health			
General health is fair or poor	3.7*	3.5*	10.9*
Missed school due to a health or emotional problem	16.8*	15.4*	31.3*
Learning difficulties	3.8	1.2	7.8
Obesity	10.4	10.0	19.1
Asthma	3.9**	4.7**	17.7**
Health Problems	.37**	.35	.90**
Emotional Health			
Psychological distress	1.53	1.45	1.53
Positive well-being	2.90	2.99	2.91
Health Risk Behaviors			
Ever had sex	9.5*	12.6*	22.2*
Age at first intercourse[a]	17.2*	15.2*	14.7*
Birth control used at first intercourse[b]	75.0	64.7	64.3
Four or more delinquent acts	12.2	17.5	22.2
Three or more acts of violence	8.4	8.4	11.1
Use of three or more controlled substances	4.7	10.5	12.5
Risky behaviors index	.35*	.49	.68*
N	107	143	64

Philippines			Japan			Vietnam		
FB	NB/FB	NB	FB	NB/FB	NB	FB	NB/FB	NB
7.8**	11.3**	22.5**	—[c]	0.0	10.3	3.3	9.7	—
44.3	39.8	51.7	—	42.4	43.1	18.0	16.1	—
5.9	7.2	13.9	—	20.7	7.6	8.3	10.5	—
11.4**	20.5**	26.7**	—	18.2	22.4	5.2	19.4	—
6.3**	10.5**	22.2**	—	3.5	17.3	8.3	15.8	—
.73*	.92*	1.29*	—	.79	.98	.43*	.89*	—
1.64	1.61	1.49	—	1.40	1.48	1.48	1.48	—
2.78	2.77	2.85	—	3.08	2.80	2.73	3.05	—
30.8**	38.3**	51.1**	—	36.4	22.8	11.7	29.0	—
15.6**	15.1**	14.8**	—	15.3	15.6	15.8	13.8	—
53.3	46.6	46.7	—	58.3	84.6	42.9	44.4	—
22.2	29.0	23.6	—	24.2	24.6	8.3	19.4	—
15.0	20.6	23.6	—	27.3	15.8	10.0	22.6	—
12.0**	20.0**	25.8**	—	24.2	12.1	4.9	6.5	—
.80**	1.09**	1.25**	—	1.12	.75	.35	.77	—
309	275	89	2	33	58	61	31	4

continued on next page

TABLE 6A-2 Continued

	Other Asia		
	FB	NB/FB	NB
Physical Health			
General health is fair or poor	11.2	14.9	17.1
Missed school due to a health or emotional problem	29.8	40.1	42.5
Learning difficulties	16.1	6.8	12.1
Obesity	9.5**	37.1**	39.5**
Asthma	2.3*	9.3*	13.8*
Health Problems	.68*	.99*	1.16*
Emotional Health			
Psychological distress	1.55	1.56	1.59
Positive well-being	2.83	2.86	2.83
Health Risk Behaviors			
Ever had sex	14.2**	27.5**	48.8**
Age at first intercourse[b]	14.7	14.2	14.2
Birth control at first intercourse[b]	61.9	47.4	42.5
Four or more delinquent acts	20.3*	34.0*	29.3*
Three or more acts of violence	17.6**	25.7**	36.6**
Use of three or more controlled substances	7.2**	17.3**	35.4**
Risky behaviors index	.59**	1.02**	1.50**
N	152	208	82

[a]FB, foreign-born youth; NB/FB, native-born youth with foreign-born parents; NB, youth in native-born families; IB, island-born youth; MB/IB, mainland-born youth with island-born parents; MB, mainland-born youth with mainland-born parents.

Africa/Afro-Caribbean			Europe/Canada		
FB	NB/FB	NB	FB	NB/FB	NB
1.4**	6.3**	11.5**	8.2	4.9	8.1
31.5	35.1	37.1	26.5	33.4	33.6
11.5	17.6	14.3	13.5	14.5	16.9
17.4	27.2	29.8	4.3**	18.6**	23.4**
3.9*	6.6*	13.5*	10.5*	7.5*	12.2*
.57**	.89	1.05**	.54**	.76	.93**
1.49	1.46	1.52	1.37	1.43	1.45
3.07	3.08	2.99	3.18	3.09	3.06
49.3**	34.2**	54.8**	29.2**	28.2**	36.7**
14.3*	14.6*	13.8*	15.5**	15.5**	14.8**
69.4	81.6	64.3	92.3	71.7	67.1
9.6	14.3	18.0	10.2	20.6	21.8
17.8	22.3	27.2	8.2*	16.0*	19.3*
6.9	4.5	8.5	18.4	20.3	25.1
.84*	.76	1.09*	.67*	.85	1.03*
73	112	4,302	49	326	10,218

[b]These outcomes are based on the sample of adolescents who ever had sex ($N = 8,226$).

[c]Cell size < 30.

*Differences are statistically significant at the 0.05 level.

**Differences are statistically significant at the 0.01 level.

TABLE 6A-3 Parameter Estimates of Ethnic Group and Generation on Adolescents' Physical Health and Health Behavior Outcomes

	Substance Use		
	1	2	3
Constant	**–0.33**	**–0.16**	**–0.13**
	(0.02)	**(0.02)**	**(0.02)**
MALE	**0.03**	**0.03**	**0.03**
	(0.00)	**(0.00)**	**(0.00)**
AGE	**0.04**	**0.03**	**0.03**
	(0.00)	**(0.00)**	**(0.00)**
MEX-FB	**–0.15**	**–0.14**	**–0.13**
	(0.02)	**(0.02)**	**(0.02)**
MEX-NB/FB	**–0.04**	**–0.03**	–0.02
	(0.01)	**(0.01)**	(0.01)
MEX-NB	**0.03**	**0.02**	**0.03**
	(0.01)	**(0.01)**	**(0.01)**
CUB-FB	**–0.20**	**–0.20**	**–0.16**
	(0.02)	**(0.02)**	**(0.02)**
CUB-NB/FB	**–0.08**	**–0.08**	**–0.05**
	(0.02)	**(0.02)**	**(0.02)**
CUB-NB	0.06	0.05	0.06
	(0.05)	(0.05)	(0.05)
CSA-FB	**–0.16**	**–0.17**	**–0.15**
	(0.02)	**(0.02)**	**(0.02)**
CSA-NB/FB	**–0.05**	**–0.06**	**–0.05**
	(0.02)	**(0.02)**	**(0.02)**
CSA-NB	0.01	0.00	0.00
	(0.02)	(0.02)	(0.02)
PR-IB	–0.05	–0.05	–0.04
	(0.04)	(0.04)	(0.04)
PR-MB/IB	–0.04	**–0.05**	0.04
	(0.02)	**(0.02)**	(0.02)
PR-MB	–0.02	**–0.03**	**–0.03**
	(0.02)	**(0.02)**	**(0.02)**
CHIN-FB	**–0.21**	**–0.21**	**–0.19**
	(0.04)	**(0.03)**	**(0.03)**
CHIN-NB/FB	**–0.14**	**–0.12**	**–0.11**
	(0.03)	**(0.03)**	**(0.03)**
CHIN-NB	**–0.08**	**–0.07**	–0.06
	(0.04)	**(0.03)**	(0.03)

Psychological Distress			Health Problems Index			Risky Behaviors Index		
1	2	3	1	2	3	1	2	3
1.08	**1.32**	**1.52**	**0.98**	**1.07**	**1.20**	**–1.28**	**–0.53**	**–0.41**
(0.03)	**(0.03)**	**(0.04)**	**(0.07)**	**(0.08)**	**(0.09)**	**(0.08)**	**(0.09)**	**(0.10)**
–0.11	**–0.10**	**–0.10**	**0.04**	**0.04**	**0.04**	**0.31**	**0.32**	**0.31**
(0.01)	**(0.01)**	**(0.01)**	**(0.01)**	**(0.01)**	**(0.01)**	**(0.02)**	**(0.02)**	**(0.02)**
0.03	**0.02**	**0.02**	0.00	–0.01	–0.01	**0.14**	**0.12**	**0.12**
(0.00)	**(0.00)**	**(0.00)**	(0.00)	(0.00)	(0.00)	**(0.01)**	**(0.00)**	**(0.00)**
0.09	0.04	0.00	–0.13	**–0.30**	**–0.38**	**–0.42**	**–0.45**	**–0.44**
(0.03)	(0.03)	(0.03)	(0.07)	**(0.07)**	**(0.08)**	**(0.08)**	**(0.08)**	**(0.08)**
0.12	**0.08**	**0.07**	**0.18**	0.07	–0.01	0.02	0.01	0.01
(0.02)	**(0.02)**	**(0.02)**	**(0.04)**	(0.04)	(0.05)	(0.05)	(0.05)	(0.05)
0.08	**0.05**	**0.03**	**0.26**	**0.18**	**0.12**	**0.33**	**0.26**	**0.26**
(0.02)	**(0.02)**	**(0.02)**	**(0.04)**	**(0.04)**	**(0.04)**	**(0.05)**	**(0.05)**	**(0.05)**
–0.03	**–0.07**	**–0.08**	–0.11	**–0.26**	**–0.23**	**–0.44**	**–0.50**	**–0.41**
(0.03)	**(0.03)**	**(0.03)**	(0.07)	**(0.07)**	**(0.07)**	**(0.08)**	**(0.08)**	**(0.08)**
0.01	–0.02	–0.02	0.11	0.01	0.04	–0.11	**–0.18**	–0.09
(0.03)	(0.03)	(0.03)	(0.06)	(0.06)	(0.07)	(0.07)	**(0.07)**	(0.07)
0.04	0.02	0.03	0.10	0.07	0.08	0.17	0.10	0.14
(0.07)	(0.07)	(0.07)	(0.17)	(0.17)	(0.17)	(0.20)	(0.20)	(0.19)
0.04	0.00	–0.02	–0.10	**–0.23**	**–0.26**	**–0.30**	**–0.38**	**–0.34**
(0.03)	(0.03)	(0.03)	(0.07)	**(0.07)**	**(0.07)**	**(0.08)**	**(0.08)**	**(0.08)**
0.03	0.00	0.00	0.00	–0.08	–0.12	0.14	0.05	0.05
(0.03)	(0.03)	(0.03)	(0.08)	(0.08)	(0.08)	(0.09)	(0.09)	(0.09)
0.04	0.02	0.00	**0.19**	0.14	0.08	**0.35**	**0.29**	**0.25**
(0.03)	(0.03)	(0.03)	**(0.08)**	(0.08)	(0.08)	**(0.10)**	**(0.09)**	**(0.09)**
0.13	0.12	0.11	0.22	0.14	0.12	0.02	–0.02	–0.01
(0.06)	(0.06)	(0.06)	(0.15)	(0.15)	(0.15)	(0.18)	(0.17)	(0.17)
0.11	**0.08**	**0.08**	**0.48**	**0.38**	**0.33**	0.09	0.03	0.00
(0.04)	**(0.03)**	**(0.03)**	**(0.09)**	**(0.09)**	**(0.09)**	(0.10)	(0.10)	(0.10)
0.12	**0.08**	**0.07**	**0.24**	**0.15**	**0.11**	**0.32**	**0.22**	**0.18**
(0.02)	**(0.02)**	**(0.02)**	**(0.06)**	**(0.06)**	**(0.06)**	**(0.07)**	**(0.06)**	**(0.07)**
0.06	0.05	0.03	**–0.54**	**–0.55**	**–0.57**	**–0.68**	**–0.68**	**–0.62**
(0.05)	(0.05)	(0.05)	**(0.13)**	**(0.13)**	**(0.13)**	**(0.15)**	**(0.15)**	**(0.15)**
0.02	0.06	0.05	**–0.59**	**–0.50**	**–0.53**	**–0.56**	**–0.42**	**–0.39**
(0.04)	(0.04)	(0.04)	**(0.10)**	**(0.10)**	**(0.10)**	**(0.12)**	**(0.12)**	**(0.12)**
0.14	**0.16**	**0.14**	–0.09	–0.04	–0.12	–0.21	–0.15	–0.15
(0.05)	**(0.05)**	**(0.05)**	(0.14)	(0.14)	(0.14)	(0.15)	(0.15)	(0.15)

continued on next page

TABLE 6A-3 Continued

	Substance Use		
	1	2	3
PHIL-FB	**–0.14**	**–0.13**	**–0.13**
	(0.02)	**(0.02)**	**(0.02)**
PHIL-NB/FB	**–0.06**	**–0.05**	**–0.05**
	(0.02)	**(0.02)**	**(0.02)**
PHIL-NB	–0.01	–0.03	–0.03
	(0.03)	(0.03)	(0.03)
OTAS-FB	**–0.16**	**–0.16**	**–0.15**
	(0.02)	**(0.02)**	**(0.02)**
OTAS-NB/FB	**–0.04**	**–0.04**	–0.03
	(0.02)	**(0.02)**	(0.02)
OTAS-NB	0.02	0.02	0.02
	(0.02)	(0.02)	(0.02)
AFR-FB	**–0.18**	**–0.19**	**–0.19**
	(0.04)	**(0.04)**	**(0.04)**
AFR-NB/FB	**–0.18**	**–0.18**	**–0.18**
	(0.03)	**(0.03)**	**(0.03)**
AFR-NB	**–0.11**	**–0.13**	**–0.12**
	(0.01)	**(0.01)**	**(0.01)**
EUR-FB	–0.04	–0.03	–0.03
	(0.04)	(0.04)	(0.04)
EUR-NB/FB	–0.02	–0.01	–0.01
	(0.02)	(0.02)	(0.02)
INC16		0.00	0.00
		(0.01)	(0.01)
INC30		–0.01	–0.01
		(0.01)	(0.01)
INC50		**–0.01**	**–0.01**
		(0.01)	**(0.01)**
INCMISS		**–0.02**	**–0.02**
		(0.01)	**(0.01)**
STEP		**0.05**	**0.05**
		(0.01)	**(0.01)**
MOTHONLY		**0.03**	**0.03**
		(0.01)	**(0.01)**
FATHONLY		**0.06**	**0.05**
		(0.01)	**(0.01)**
OTHER		**0.07**	**0.06**
		(0.01)	**(0.01)**

Psychological Distress			Health Problems Index			Risky Behaviors Index		
1	2	3	1	2	3	1	2	3
0.14	**0.15**	**0.11**	**−0.21**	**−0.18**	**−0.30**	**−0.36**	**−0.31**	**−0.34**
(0.03)	**(0.03)**	**(0.03)**	**(0.07)**	**(0.07)**	**(0.07)**	**(0.08)**	**(0.08)**	**(0.08)**
0.17	**0.19**	**0.15**	−0.02	0.04	−0.06	−0.02	0.04	0.03
(0.03)	**(0.03)**	**(0.03)**	(0.07)	(0.07)	(0.07)	(0.08)	(0.08)	(0.08)
0.02	−0.01	−0.04	**0.26**	**0.23**	0.13	0.10	0.01	−0.02
(0.05)	(0.05)	(0.05)	**(0.12)**	**(0.12)**	(0.12)	(0.14)	(0.14)	(0.14)
0.07	0.06	0.06	**−0.29**	**−0.31**	**−0.34**	**−0.46**	**−0.45**	**−0.42**
(0.04)	(0.04)	(0.04)	**(0.09)**	**(0.09)**	**(0.09)**	**(0.11)**	**(0.11)**	**(0.11)**
0.06	**0.07**	0.05	0.02	0.04	−0.01	0.03	0.07	0.08
(0.03)	**(0.03)**	(0.03)	(0.07)	(0.07)	(0.07)	(0.08)	(0.08)	(0.08)
0.06	0.06	0.03	0.06	0.07	−0.01	0.12	0.11	0.09
(0.04)	(0.04)	(0.04)	(0.09)	(0.09)	(0.09)	(0.10)	(0.10)	(0.10)
0.00	−0.04	−0.04	**−0.37**	**−0.44**	**−0.46**	**−0.42**	**−0.51**	**−0.50**
(0.06)	(0.06)	(0.05)	**(0.14)**	**(0.14)**	**(0.14)**	**(0.16)**	**(0.16)**	**(0.15)**
0.03	0.02	0.02	−0.07	−0.06	−0.08	**−0.25**	**−0.26**	**−0.28**
(0.04)	(0.04)	(0.04)	(0.11)	(0.11)	(0.11)	**(0.12)**	**(0.12)**	**(0.12)**
0.07	**0.03**	**0.02**	**0.11**	0.02	0.02	**0.09**	−0.02	−0.02
(0.01)	**(0.01)**	**(0.01)**	**(0.02)**	(0.02)	(0.02)	**(0.02)**	(0.02)	(0.02)
−0.13	−0.12	**−0.14**	**−0.39**	**−0.38**	**−0.42**	**−0.44**	**−0.41**	**−0.40**
(0.07)	(0.07)	**(0.07)**	**(0.17)**	**(0.17)**	**(0.17)**	**(0.19)**	**(0.19)**	**(0.19)**
−0.01	0.00	0.00	**−0.17**	**−0.13**	**−0.16**	**−0.14**	−0.08	−0.10
(0.02)	(0.02)	(0.02)	**(0.06)**	**(0.06)**	**(0.06)**	**(0.07)**	(0.06)	(0.06)
	0.06	**0.05**		**0.20**	**0.20**		**0.12**	**0.10**
	(0.01)	**(0.01)**		**(0.03)**	**(0.03)**		**(0.03)**	**(0.03)**
	0.02	0.01		**0.14**	**0.14**		0.05	0.04
	(0.01)	(0.01)		**(0.02)**	**(0.02)**		(0.03)	(0.03)
	0.00	0.00		**0.05**	**0.06**		0.00	0.00
	(0.01)	(0.01)		**(0.02)**	**(0.02)**		(0.02)	(0.02)
	0.01	0.00		0.02	0.02		**−0.08**	**−0.09**
	(0.01)	(0.01)		(0.03)	(0.03)		**(0.03)**	**(0.03)**
	0.07	**0.06**		**0.08**	**0.07**		**0.27**	**0.27**
	(0.01)	**(0.01)**		**(0.02)**	**(0.02)**		**(0.02)**	**(0.02)**
	0.04	**0.03**		**0.13**	**0.12**		**0.17**	**0.17**
	(0.01)	**(0.01)**		**(0.02)**	**(0.02)**		**(0.02)**	**(0.02)**
	0.09	**0.08**		**0.13**	**0.12**		**0.26**	**0.25**
	(0.02)	**(0.02)**		**(0.05)**	**(0.05)**		**(0.05)**	**(0.05)**
	0.09	**0.09**		**0.16**	**0.14**		**0.35**	**0.34**
	(0.02)	**(0.02)**		**(0.04)**	**(0.04)**		**(0.05)**	**(0.05)**

continued on next page

TABLE 6A-3 Continued

	Substance Use		
	1	2	3
HS		0.00	0.00
		(0.01)	(0.01)
SOMECOLL		0.00	0.00
		(0.01)	(0.01)
COLLPLUS		**–0.02**	**–0.01**
		(0.01)	**(0.01)**
PPRESIND		**–0.04**	**–0.04**
		(0.00)	**(0.00)**
URBAN			**–0.04**
			(0.01)
SUBURBAN			**–0.01**
			(0.01)
WEST			–0.01
			(0.01)
NRTHEAST			0.00
			(0.01)
SOUTH			**–0.03**
			(0.01)
NFAM			**0.04**
			(0.00)
LOOKOUT			**–0.04**
			(0.00)
NSAFE			–0.01
			(0.01)
N			16893
-2 LOG L			
Adjusted R^2			0.14
prob			0.0001

Psychological Distress			Health Problems Index			Risky Behaviors Index		
1	2	3	1	2	3	1	2	3
	–0.05	**–0.05**		**–0.12**	**–0.12**		**–0.07**	**–0.07**
	(0.01)	**(0.01)**		**(0.02)**	**(0.02)**		**(0.03)**	**(0.03)**
	–0.07	**–0.07**		**–0.12**	**–0.13**		**–0.08**	**–0.07**
	(0.01)	**(0.01)**		**(0.02)**	**(0.02)**		**(0.03)**	**(0.03)**
	–0.09	**–0.09**		**–0.23**	**–0.23**		**–0.20**	**–0.18**
	(0.01)	**(0.01)**		**(0.03)**	**(0.03)**		**(0.03)**	**(0.03)**
	–0.05	**–0.04**		0.00	0.00		**–0.16**	**–0.16**
	(0.00)	**(0.00)**		(0.01)	(0.01)		**(0.01)**	**(0.01)**
		–0.04			–0.03			**–0.06**
		(0.01)			(0.02)			**(0.03)**
		–0.01			–0.01			0.00
		(0.01)			(0.02)			(0.02)
		0.03			**0.14**			0.01
		(0.01)			**(0.02)**			(0.03)
		0.01			**0.07**			0.02
		(0.01)			**(0.02)**			(0.03)
		0.01			–0.01			**–0.08**
		(0.01)			(0.02)			**(0.02)**
		0.00			**0.05**			**0.23**
		(0.01)			**(0.02)**			**(0.02)**
		–0.05			**–0.06**			**–0.18**
		(0.01)			**(0.02)**			**(0.02)**
		–0.16			**–0.17**			**–0.16**
		(0.01)			**(0.02)**			**(0.03)**
		16894			16099			16708
		0.1			0.05			0.13
		0.0001			0.0001			0.0001

continued on next page

TABLE 6A-3 Continued

	Asthma			Ever Had Sex		
	1	2	3	1	2	3
Constant	**−1.27**	**−1.56**	**−1.58**	**−8.31**	**−7.73**	**−7.71**
	(0.21)	**(0.26)**	**(0.29)**	**(0.14)**	**(0.16)**	**(0.17)**
MALE	**0.10**	**0.10**	**0.11**	**0.07**	**0.09**	**0.08**
	(0.05)	**(0.05)**	**(0.05)**	**(0.03)**	**(0.03)**	**(0.03)**
AGE	**−0.05**	**−0.04**	**−0.04**	**0.28**	**0.27**	**0.27**
	(0.01)	**(0.01)**	**(0.01)**	**(0.01)**	**(0.01)**	**(0.01)**
MEX–FB	**−2.62**	**−2.49**	**−2.63**	**−0.37**	**−0.44**	**−0.33**
	(0.71)	**(0.71)**	**(0.72)**	**(0.13)**	**(0.15)**	**(0.15)**
MEX–NB/FB	**−0.85**	**−0.83**	**−1.01**	−0.08	−0.07	0.02
	(0.18)	**(0.19)**	**(0.20)**	(0.07)	(0.08)	(0.08)
MEX–NB	0.08	0.12	−0.07	**0.25**	**0.14**	**0.19**
	(0.13)	(0.13)	(0.14)	**(0.07)**	**(0.07)**	**(0.08)**
CUB–FB	−0.40	−0.39	−0.24	−0.17	−0.24	−0.17
	(0.27)	(0.27)	(0.28)	(0.13)	(0.13)	(0.14)
CUB–NB/FB	−0.26	−0.25	−0.11	0.00	−0.08	−0.03
	(0.23)	(0.23)	(0.23)	(0.11)	(0.12)	(0.12)
CUB–NB	0.05	0.08	0.11	0.10	0.06	0.13
	(0.54)	(0.54)	(0.54)	(0.28)	(0.29)	(0.29)
CSA–FB	**−1.25**	**−1.18**	**−1.17**	**−0.26**	**−0.29**	−0.20
	(0.36)	**(0.36)**	**(0.37)**	**(0.12)**	**(0.13)**	(0.13)
CSA–NB/FB	−0.15	−0.21	−0.26	0.08	−0.02	0.04
	(0.26)	(0.27)	(0.27)	(0.14)	(0.14)	(0.14)
CSA–NB	**0.60**	**0.58**	**0.49**	0.21	0.19	0.21
	(0.21)	**(0.22)**	**(0.22)**	(0.14)	(0.14)	(0.14)
PR–IB	0.35	0.31	0.34	−0.02	−0.10	−0.04
	(0.42)	(0.42)	(0.42)	(0.31)	(0.31)	(0.32)
PR–MB/IB	0.38	0.40	0.30	0.20	0.10	0.17
	(0.24)	(0.24)	(0.25)	(0.14)	(0.15)	(0.15)
PR–MB	**0.45**	**0.43**	0.32	**0.31**	**0.21**	**0.28**
	(0.16)	**(0.16)**	(0.17)	**(0.09)**	**(0.10)**	**(0.10)**
CHIN–FB	−1.22	−1.17	−1.19	**−2.42**	**−2.39**	**−2.26**
	(0.72)	(0.72)	(0.72)	**(0.71)**	**(0.71)**	**(0.71)**
CHIN–NB/FB	**−1.06**	**−1.02**	**−1.07**	**−1.01**	**−0.82**	**−0.82**
	(0.51)	**(0.51)**	**(0.51)**	**(0.32)**	**(0.32)**	**(0.34)**
CHIN–NB	0.39	0.44	0.28	−0.36	−0.34	−0.29
	(0.37)	(0.37)	(0.37)	(0.34)	(0.36)	(0.36)

Delinquency			Violence		
1	2	3	1	2	3
0.14	**0.26**	**0.29**	**0.15**	**0.23**	**0.24**
(0.01)	**(0.02)**	**(0.02)**	**(0.01)**	**(0.02)**	**(0.02)**
0.04	**0.04**	**0.04**	**0.10**	**0.10**	**0.10**
(0.00)	**(0.00)**	**(0.00)**	**(0.00)**	**(0.00)**	**(0.00)**
0.00	0.00	0.00	**0.00**	**–0.01**	**–0.01**
(0.00)	(0.00)	(0.00)	**(0.00)**	**(0.00)**	**(0.00)**
–0.05	**–0.03**	**–0.05**	0.00	–0.02	**–0.03**
(0.01)	**(0.01)**	**(0.01)**	(0.01)	(0.01)	**(0.01)**
0.02	**0.03**	**0.02**	**0.04**	**0.03**	**0.02**
(0.01)	**(0.01)**	**(0.01)**	**(0.01)**	**(0.01)**	**(0.01)**
0.04	**0.04**	**0.03**	**0.08**	**0.07**	**0.06**
(0.01)	**(0.01)**	**(0.01)**	**(0.01)**	**(0.01)**	**(0.01)**
–0.06	**–0.05**	**–0.04**	**–0.03**	**–0.05**	**–0.05**
(0.01)	**(0.01)**	**(0.01)**	**(0.01)**	**(0.01)**	**(0.02)**
0.00	0.00	0.02	0.01	0.00	0.00
(0.01)	(0.01)	(0.01)	(0.01)	(0.01)	(0.01)
0.01	0.00	0.00	0.02	0.01	0.01
(0.04)	(0.03)	(0.03)	(0.04)	(0.03)	(0.03)
–0.03	**–0.03**	**–0.03**	–0.01	–0.03	**–0.03**
(0.01)	**(0.01)**	**(0.01)**	(0.01)	(0.01)	**(0.01)**
0.02	0.02	0.01	**0.04**	0.03	0.02
(0.02)	(0.02)	(0.02)	**(0.02)**	(0.02)	(0.02)
0.07	**0.07**	**0.05**	**0.06**	**0.05**	**0.04**
(0.02)	**(0.02)**	**(0.02)**	**(0.02)**	**(0.02)**	**(0.02)**
0.00	0.00	0.00	0.04	0.03	0.02
(0.03)	(0.03)	(0.03)	(0.03)	(0.03)	(0.03)
0.03	**0.03**	0.02	**0.08**	**0.06**	**0.05**
(0.02)	**(0.02)**	(0.02)	**(0.02)**	**(0.02)**	**(0.02)**
0.04	**0.04**	**0.02**	**0.10**	**0.08**	**0.07**
(0.01)	**(0.01)**	**(0.01)**	**(0.01)**	**(0.01)**	**(0.01)**
–0.03	–0.03	–0.03	–0.03	–0.03	–0.03
(0.03)	(0.03)	(0.03)	(0.03)	(0.03)	(0.03)
–0.04	–0.03	**–0.03**	**–0.07**	**–0.05**	**–0.04**
(0.02)	(0.02)	**(0.02)**	**(0.02)**	**(0.02)**	**(0.02)**
0.01	0.01	0.00	–0.05	–0.04	–0.04
(0.03)	(0.03)	(0.03)	(0.03)	(0.03)	(0.03)

continued on next page

TABLE 6A-3 Continued

	Asthma			Ever Had Sex		
	1	2	3	1	2	3
PHIL–FB	**–0.67**	**–0.61**	**–0.80**	**–0.58**	**–0.46**	**–0.37**
	(0.29)	**(0.29)**	**(0.29)**	**(0.14)**	**(0.14)**	**(0.15)**
PHIL–NB/FB	–0.16	–0.15	–0.39	–0.16	–0.06	0.01
	(0.23)	(0.23)	(0.24)	(0.12)	(0.13)	(0.13)
PHIL–NB	**0.72**	0.57	0.45	0.33	0.22	0.27
	(0.29)	(0.31)	(0.32)	(0.18)	(0.19)	(0.20)
OTAS–FB	**–1.30**	**–1.22**	**–1.28**	**–1.21**	**–1.19**	**–1.19**
	(0.51)	**(0.51)**	**(0.51)**	**(0.28)**	**(0.29)**	**(0.30)**
OTAS–NB/FB	–0.33	–0.31	–0.39	–0.12	–0.07	–0.01
	(0.25)	(0.25)	(0.25)	(0.13)	(0.13)	(0.14)
OTAS–NB	0.22	0.15	–0.07	0.16	0.17	0.19
	(0.27)	(0.27)	(0.28)	(0.16)	(0.16)	(0.17)
AFR–FB	–1.18	–1.09	–1.12	–0.30	–0.33	–0.32
	(0.72)	(0.72)	(0.73)	(0.25)	(0.25)	(0.26)
AFR–NB/FB	–0.66	–0.67	–0.81	–0.28	–0.31	–0.22
	(0.42)	(0.42)	(0.46)	(0.19)	(0.19)	(0.20)
AFR–NB	**0.12**	0.09	0.12	**0.50**	**0.38**	**0.36**
	(0.06)	(0.06)	(0.07)	**(0.03)**	**(0.03)**	**(0.04)**
EUR–FB	–0.13	–0.06	–0.07	–0.19	–0.24	–0.31
	(0.53)	(0.53)	(0.54)	(0.32)	(0.36)	(0.38)
EUR–NB/FB	**–0.55**	**–0.52**	**–0.56**	–0.23	–0.13	–0.12
	(0.23)	**(0.23)**	**(0.23)**	(0.12)	(0.12)	(0.12)
INC16		0.10	0.14		**0.10**	0.07
		(0.09)	(0.09)		**(0.05)**	(0.05)
INC30		0.04	0.07		0.06	0.03
		(0.08)	(0.08)		(0.04)	(0.04)
INC50		–0.01	0.01		0.02	0.00
		(0.07)	(0.07)		(0.04)	(0.04)
INCMISS		–0.07	–0.06		–0.05	–0.08
		(0.08)	(0.09)		(0.05)	(0.05)
STEP		0.03	0.02		**0.33**	**0.34**
		(0.06)	(0.07)		**(0.04)**	**(0.04)**
MOTHONLY		**0.14**	0.12		**0.23**	**0.25**
		(0.07)	(0.07)		**(0.04)**	**(0.04)**
FATHONLY		–0.06	–0.07		**0.24**	**0.25**
		(0.16)	(0.16)		**(0.08)**	**(0.08)**
OTHER		–0.01	–0.02		**0.42**	**0.41**
		(0.14)	(0.14)		**(0.07)**	**(0.07)**

Delinquency			Violence		
1	2	3	1	2	3
0.01	0.01	–0.01	–0.01	–0.01	–0.01
(0.01)	(0.01)	(0.01)	(0.01)	(0.01)	(0.01)
0.06	**0.06**	**0.04**	0.01	0.02	0.02
(0.01)	**(0.01)**	**(0.01)**	(0.01)	(0.01)	(0.01)
0.00	–0.01	–0.03	0.00	–0.01	–0.01
(0.02)	(0.02)	(0.02)	(0.02)	(0.02)	(0.02)
–0.01	0.00	–0.01	–0.01	–0.01	–0.01
(0.02)	(0.02)	(0.02)	(0.02)	(0.02)	(0.02)
0.04	**0.04**	**0.03**	**0.04**	**0.04**	**0.04**
(0.01)	**(0.01)**	**(0.01)**	**(0.01)**	**(0.01)**	**(0.01)**
0.03	0.02	0.01	0.02	0.02	0.01
(0.02)	(0.02)	(0.02)	(0.02)	(0.02)	(0.02)
–0.08	**–0.09**	**–0.10**	0.00	–0.02	–0.02
(0.03)	**(0.03)**	**(0.03)**	(0.03)	(0.03)	(0.03)
–0.03	–0.03	**–0.04**	0.03	0.02	0.02
(0.02)	(0.02)	**(0.02)**	(0.02)	(0.02)	(0.02)
–0.02	**–0.03**	**–0.02**	**0.06**	**0.04**	**0.04**
(0.00)	**(0.00)**	**(0.00)**	**(0.00)**	**(0.00)**	**(0.00)**
–0.06	–0.06	**–0.07**	–0.05	–0.05	–0.05
(0.03)	(0.03)	**(0.03)**	(0.03)	(0.03)	(0.03)
0.00	0.00	0.00	–0.02	–0.01	–0.02
(0.01)	(0.01)	(0.01)	(0.01)	(0.01)	(0.01)
	0.00	0.00		**0.04**	**0.04**
	(0.01)	(0.01)		**(0.01)**	**(0.01)**
	–0.01	–0.01		**0.02**	**0.02**
	(0.00)	(0.00)		**(0.00)**	**(0.00)**
	–0.01	**–0.01**		**0.01**	**0.01**
	(0.00)	**(0.00)**		**(0.00)**	**(0.00)**
	–0.03	**–0.03**		0.00	0.00
	(0.01)	**(0.00)**		(0.01)	(0.01)
	0.02	**0.02**		**0.03**	**0.03**
	(0.00)	**(0.00)**		**(0.00)**	**(0.00)**
	0.02	**0.01**		**0.02**	**0.02**
	(0.00)	**(0.00)**		**(0.00)**	**(0.00)**
	0.03	**0.03**		**0.04**	**0.04**
	(0.01)	**(0.01)**		**(0.01)**	**(0.01)**
	0.03	**0.03**		**0.04**	**0.04**
	(0.01)	**(0.01)**		**(0.01)**	**(0.01)**

continued on next page

TABLE 6A-3 Continued

	Asthma			Ever Had Sex		
	1	2	3	1	2	3
HS		0.00	–0.03		–0.04	–0.04
		(0.08)	(0.08)		(0.04)	(0.04)
SOMECOLL		**0.20**	**0.16**		**–0.12**	**–0.10**
		(0.08)	**(0.08)**		**(0.04)**	**(0.04)**
COLLPLUS		0.06	0.05		**–0.28**	**–0.25**
		(0.09)	(0.09)		**(0.05)**	**(0.05)**
PPRESIND		0.03	0.04		**–0.14**	**–0.14**
		(0.03)	(0.03)		**(0.01)**	**(0.01)**
URBAN			–0.04			**–0.13**
			(0.08)			(0.04)
SUBURBAN			–0.05			–0.02
			(0.07)			(0.04)
WEST			**0.26**			–0.07
			(0.07)			(0.04)
NRTHEAST			**0.16**			–0.06
			(0.08)			(0.05)
SOUTH			**–0.13**			0.03
			(0.07)			(0.04)
NFAM			0.07			**0.20**
			(0.06)			**(0.03)**
LOOKOUT			0.03			**–0.10**
			(0.06)			**(0.03)**
NSAFE			–0.14			**–0.07**
			(0.08)			(0.04)
N			16751			16891
–2 LOG L			11977			52918
Adjusted R						
prob			0.0001			0.0001

Delinquency			Violence		
1	2	3	1	2	3
	–0.01	–0.01		**–0.02**	**–0.02**
	(0.00)	(0.00)		**(0.00)**	**(0.00)**
	0.01	0.01		**–0.02**	**–0.02**
	(0.00)	(0.00)		**(0.00)**	**(0.00)**
	0.00	0.00		**–0.04**	**–0.03**
	(0.01)	(0.01)		**(0.01)**	**(0.01)**
	–0.03	**–0.03**		**–0.02**	**–0.02**
	(0.00)	**(0.00)**		**(0.00)**	**(0.00)**
		0.01			**0.01**
		(0.00)			**(0.00)**
		0.01			0.01
		(0.00)			(0.00)
		0.01			0.01
		(0.00)			(0.00)
		0.01			0.01
		(0.00)			(0.00)
		–0.03			–0.01
		(0.00)			(0.00)
		0.03			**0.04**
		(0.00)			**(0.00)**
		–0.03			**–0.02**
		(0.00)			**(0.00)**
		–0.03			**–0.05**
		(0.00)			**(0.00)**
		16815			16821
		0.06			0.12
		0.0001			0.0001

continued on next page

TABLE 6A–3 Continued

	General Health Fair/Poor			Missed School		
	1	2	3	1	2	3
Constant	**–3.27**	**–2.62**	**–2.04**	**–0.71**	**–0.51**	**–0.41**
	(0.24)	**(0.29)**	**(0.31)**	**(0.15)**	**(0.18)**	**(0.20)**
MALE	**–0.33**	**–0.31**	**–0.31**	**–0.37**	**–0.36**	**–0.37**
	(0.05)	**(0.05)**	**(0.05)**	**(0.03)**	**(0.03)**	**(0.03)**
AGE	**0.07**	**0.05**	**0.04**	0.01	0.01	0.01
	(0.02)	**(0.02)**	**(0.02)**	(0.01)	(0.01)	(0.01)
MEX–FB	**0.61**	0.24	0.16	–0.06	–0.18	**–0.39**
	(0.20)	(0.21)	(0.22)	(0.15)	(0.16)	**(0.16)**
MEX–NB/FB	**0.82**	**0.49**	**0.43**	**0.39**	**0.28**	0.09
	(0.12)	**(0.12)**	**(0.14)**	**(0.09)**	**(0.09)**	(0.10)
MEX–NB	**0.61**	**0.42**	**0.34**	**0.32**	**0.24**	0.11
	(0.13)	**(0.13)**	**(0.14)**	**(0.09)**	**(0.09)**	(0.10)
CUB–FB	–0.03	–0.46	–0.49	0.08	–0.10	–0.09
	(0.26)	(0.28)	(0.29)	(0.15)	(0.16)	(0.17)
CUB–NB/FB	0.13	–0.22	–0.19	0.18	0.10	0.14
	(0.23)	(0.24)	(0.25)	(0.14)	(0.14)	(0.15)
CUB–NB	–0.33	–0.26	–0.23	0.14	0.20	0.22
	(0.73)	(0.74)	(0.74)	(0.37)	(0.38)	(0.38)
CSA–FB	**0.45**	0.03	0.02	0.06	–0.05	–0.12
	(0.21)	(0.23)	(0.23)	(0.14)	(0.15)	(0.16)
CSA–NB/FB	0.35	0.13	0.17	**–0.35**	**–0.46**	**–0.50**
	(0.25)	(0.26)	(0.26)	**(0.18)**	**(0.18)**	**(0.18)**
CSA–NB	0.38	0.28	0.21	**0.34**	0.23	0.10
	(0.26)	(0.27)	(0.27)	**(0.17)**	(0.18)	(0.18)
PR–IB	0.43	0.29	0.13	0.08	0.04	0.09
	(0.48)	(0.49)	(0.54)	(0.32)	(0.33)	(0.34)
PR–MB/IB	**0.88**	**0.66**	**0.66**	**0.57**	**0.48**	**0.41**
	(0.23)	**(0.24)**	**(0.25)**	**(0.18)**	**(0.18)**	**(0.19)**
PR–MB	**0.56**	0.32	0.27	**0.35**	**0.24**	0.17
	(0.17)	(0.18)	(0.19)	**(0.12)**	**(0.12)**	(0.13)
CHIN–FB	–0.43	–0.45	–0.49	**–1.08**	**–1.05**	**–1.07**
	(0.60)	(0.60)	(0.60)	**(0.39)**	**(0.39)**	**(0.39)**
CHIN–NB/FB	–0.86	–0.57	–0.56	**–0.85**	**–0.72**	**–0.78**
	(0.59)	(0.59)	(0.59)	**(0.29)**	**(0.29)**	**(0.29)**
CHIN–NB	0.58	0.58	0.52	–0.08	–0.15	–0.34
	(0.41)	(0.44)	(0.45)	(0.30)	(0.31)	(0.31)

Learning Difficulties			Obesity		
1	2	3	1	2	3
−2.29	**−2.51**	**−2.55**	**−0.36**	−0.31	−0.18
(0.20)	**(0.24)**	**(0.26)**	**(0.16)**	(0.20)	(0.22)
0.65	**0.67**	**0.68**	**0.31**	**0.33**	**0.32**
(0.04)	**(0.04)**	**(0.05)**	**(0.04)**	**(0.04)**	**(0.04)**
0.02	0.02	**0.03**	**−0.06**	**−0.07**	**−0.06**
(0.01)	(0.01)	**(0.01)**	**(0.01)**	**(0.01)**	**(0.01)**
−1.02	**−1.27**	**−1.45**	0.03	−0.27	−0.20
(0.28)	**(0.28)**	**(0.29)**	(0.18)	(0.19)	(0.20)
−0.32	**−0.55**	**−0.69**	**0.57**	**0.37**	**0.41**
(0.13)	**(0.13)**	**(0.14)**	**(0.09)**	**(0.10)**	**(0.11)**
0.11	−0.02	−0.17	**0.53**	**0.43**	**0.45**
(0.11)	(0.12)	(0.12)	**(0.09)**	**(0.10)**	**(0.10)**
−0.52	**−0.93**	**−1.03**	−0.05	−0.25	−0.20
(0.24)	**(0.25)**	**(0.27)**	(0.18)	(0.19)	(0.19)
0.06	−0.10	−0.12	**0.31**	0.16	0.23
(0.17)	(0.18)	(0.18)	**(0.15)**	(0.15)	(0.16)
−0.69	−0.70	−0.76	0.44	0.54	0.57
(0.61)	(0.62)	(0.62)	(0.38)	(0.39)	(0.39)
−0.52	**−0.86**	**−0.97**	−0.09	−0.25	−0.19
(0.22)	**(0.24)**	**(0.24)**	(0.17)	(0.18)	(0.18)
−0.09	−0.24	−0.41	0.17	0.08	0.16
(0.22)	(0.22)	(0.23)	(0.18)	(0.19)	(0.19)
0.29	0.16	0.01	−0.15	−0.13	−0.11
(0.21)	(0.22)	(0.22)	(0.21)	(0.21)	(0.21)
0.15	−0.14	−0.26	0.29	0.21	0.33
(0.40)	(0.42)	(0.43)	(0.35)	(0.35)	(0.35)
0.15	−0.06	−0.48	**0.81**	**0.69**	**0.79**
(0.23)	(0.23)	(0.25)	**(0.18)**	**(0.18)**	**(0.19)**
0.04	−0.13	**−0.42**	**0.36**	**0.28**	**0.34**
(0.16)	(0.16)	**(0.17)**	**(0.13)**	**(0.13)**	**(0.14)**
−1.68	**−1.59**	**−1.68**	**−1.03**	**−1.05**	**−1.00**
(0.72)	**(0.72)**	**(0.73)**	**(0.47)**	**(0.47)**	**(0.47)**
−2.93	**−2.73**	**−2.77**	**−1.26**	**−1.20**	**−1.31**
(1.01)	**(1.01)**	**(1.01)**	**(0.40)**	**(0.40)**	**(0.43)**
−0.85	−0.73	−0.85	−0.30	−0.31	−0.26
(0.52)	(0.53)	(0.53)	(0.35)	(0.37)	(0.37)

continued on next page

TABLE 6A–3 Continued

	General Health Fair/Poor			Missed School		
	1	2	3	1	2	3
PHIL–FB	–0.14	0.08	–0.18	**0.42**	**0.44**	0.17
	(0.26)	(0.27)	(0.28)	**(0.14)**	**(0.15)**	(0.15)
PHIL–NB/FB	0.38	**0.63**	**0.49**	0.26	**0.32**	0.12
	(0.22)	**(0.22)**	**(0.23)**	(0.14)	**(0.15)**	(0.15)
PHIL–NB	**1.26**	**1.05**	**0.88**	**0.58**	**0.52**	0.33
	(0.28)	**(0.31)**	**(0.32)**	**(0.24)**	**(0.25)**	(0.26)
OTAS–FB	–0.18	–0.31	–0.48	–0.22	–0.14	–0.19
	(0.37)	(0.40)	(0.43)	(0.21)	(0.21)	(0.21)
OTAS–NB/FB	0.39	**0.44**	0.38	0.08	0.10	–0.02
	(0.23)	**(0.23)**	(0.23)	(0.15)	(0.15)	(0.15)
OTAS–NB	0.46	0.49	0.34	0.31	0.30	0.07
	(0.29)	(0.29)	(0.31)	(0.19)	(0.19)	(0.20)
AFR–FB	–1.62	–1.79	–1.78	0.16	0.03	0.06
	(1.01)	(1.02)	(1.02)	(0.29)	(0.30)	(0.30)
AFR–NB/FB	–0.14	–0.18	–0.07	–0.06	–0.07	–0.13
	(0.40)	(0.40)	(0.41)	(0.22)	(0.22)	(0.24)
AFR–NB	**0.42**	**0.18**	**0.18**	**0.14**	0.02	0.01
	(0.06)	**(0.07)**	**(0.07)**	**(0.04)**	(0.04)	(0.05)
EUR–FB	–0.45	–0.33	–0.40	–0.62	–0.67	**–0.90**
	(0.73)	(0.74)	(0.74)	(0.40)	(0.43)	**(0.46)**
EUR–NB/FB	**–0.62**	–0.49	–0.50	–0.09	–0.03	–0.05
	(0.29)	(0.29)	(0.29)	(0.13)	(0.13)	(0.13)
INC16		**0.52**	**0.50**		**0.21**	**0.22**
		(0.09)	**(0.10)**		**(0.06)**	**(0.06)**
INC30		**0.42**	**0.41**		**0.15**	**0.16**
		(0.09)	**(0.09)**		**(0.05)**	**(0.05)**
INC50		0.09	0.09		**0.10**	**0.10**
		(0.08)	(0.08)		(0.05)	(0.05)
INCMISS		**0.23**	**0.22**		0.06	0.07
		(0.09)	**(0.09)**		(0.06)	(0.06)
STEP		**0.19**	**0.20**		**0.11**	**0.10**
		(0.07)	**(0.07)**		**(0.04)**	**(0.04)**
MOTHONLY		**0.27**	**0.25**		**0.19**	**0.17**
		(0.07)	**(0.07)**		**(0.05)**	**(0.05)**
FATHONLY		**0.44**	**0.42**		0.18	0.16
		(0.15)	**(0.15)**		(0.10)	(0.10)

Learning Difficulties			Obesity		
1	2	3	1	2	3
–1.21	**–1.27**	**–1.43**	**–0.76**	**–0.67**	**–0.71**
(0.30)	**(0.33)**	**(0.33)**	**(0.22)**	**(0.22)**	**(0.23)**
–1.02	**–0.91**	**–1.06**	–0.06	0.02	0.02
(0.27)	**(0.28)**	**(0.29)**	(0.17)	(0.17)	(0.18)
–0.28	–0.31	–0.51	0.14	0.06	–0.04
(0.34)	(0.36)	(0.39)	(0.28)	(0.29)	(0.31)
–0.21	–0.25	–0.36	**–1.18**	**–1.28**	**–1.22**
(0.27)	(0.28)	(0.29)	**(0.35)**	**(0.37)**	**(0.37)**
–0.74	**–0.66**	**–0.76**	0.32	**0.30**	**0.35**
(0.25)	**(0.25)**	**(0.25)**	(0.16)	**(0.16)**	**(0.16)**
–0.66	**–0.63**	**–0.69**	0.09	0.14	0.07
(0.32)	**(0.32)**	**(0.32)**	(0.22)	(0.22)	(0.23)
–0.51	–0.80	**–0.93**	–0.52	–0.66	–0.83
(0.44)	(0.48)	**(0.48)**	(0.41)	(0.44)	(0.48)
0.02	–0.07	–0.10	0.18	0.20	0.19
(0.29)	(0.30)	(0.30)	(0.25)	(0.25)	(0.26)
–0.18	**–0.38**	**–0.40**	**0.34**	**0.26**	**0.26**
(0.06)	**(0.06)**	**(0.06)**	**(0.04)**	**(0.05)**	**(0.05)**
–0.30	–0.25	–0.32	**–2.35**	**–2.27**	**–2.22**
(0.48)	(0.49)	(0.50)	**(1.02)**	**(1.02)**	**(1.02)**
–0.16	–0.04	–0.12	**–0.38**	**–0.37**	**–0.35**
(0.17)	(0.17)	(0.18)	**(0.16)**	**(0.16)**	**(0.16)**
	0.35	**0.38**		**0.23**	**0.21**
	(0.08)	**(0.08)**		**(0.07)**	**(0.07)**
	0.27	**0.30**		**0.20**	**0.17**
	(0.07)	**(0.07)**		**(0.06)**	**(0.06)**
	–0.01	0.01		**0.16**	**0.15**
	(0.06)	(0.06)		**(0.05)**	**(0.05)**
	0.02	0.03		0.01	0.00
	(0.08)	(0.08)		(0.06)	(0.06)
	0.45	**0.45**		**–0.15**	**–0.15**
	(0.06)	**(0.06)**		**(0.05)**	**(0.05)**
	0.40	**0.36**		0.05	0.05
	(0.06)	**(0.06)**		(0.05)	(0.05)
	0.30	**0.30**		–0.02	–0.02
	(0.13)	**(0.13)**		(0.11)	(0.12)

continued on next page

TABLE 6A–3 Continued

	General Health Fair/Poor			Missed School		
	1	2	3	1	2	3
OTHER		**0.27**	0.23		**0.29**	**0.26**
		(0.13)	(0.14)		**(0.09)**	**(0.09)**
HS		**–0.31**	**–0.31**		**–0.10**	**–0.11**
		(0.07)	**(0.07)**		**(0.05)**	**(0.05)**
SOMECOLL		**–0.45**	**–0.47**		**–0.11**	**–0.14**
		(0.08)	**(0.08)**		**(0.05)**	**(0.05)**
COLLPLUS		**–0.83**	**–0.82**		**–0.27**	**–0.28**
		(0.10)	**(0.10)**		**(0.06)**	**(0.06)**
PPRESIND		**–0.09**	**–0.09**		**–0.04**	**–0.04**
		(0.03)	**(0.03)**		**(0.02)**	**(0.02)**
URBAN			**–0.29**			**0.11**
			(0.09)			**(0.05)**
SUBURBAN			–0.13			**0.06**
			(0.08)			**(0.05)**
WEST			**0.22**			**0.24**
			(0.09)			**(0.05)**
NRTHEAST			0.17			–0.01
			(0.09)			(0.06)
SOUTH			0.10			**–0.12**
			(0.08)			**(0.04)**
NFAM			–0.09			**0.15**
			(0.06)			**(0.04)**
LOOKOUT			**–0.20**			**–0.16**
			(0.06)			**(0.04)**
NSAFE			**–0.33**			**–0.16**
			(0.07)			**(0.05)**
N			16892			16847
–2 LOG L			10255			21477
Adjusted R^2						
prob			0.0001			0.0001

NOTE: Bolded coefficients statistically significant at the .05 level or less.

Learning Difficulties			Obesity		
1	2	3	1	2	3
	0.32	**0.24**		0.12	0.15
	(0.12)	**(0.13)**		(0.10)	(0.10)
	–0.31	**–0.30**		**–0.12**	–0.11
	(0.07)	**(0.07)**		**(0.06)**	(0.06)
	–0.29	**–0.29**		**–0.19**	**–0.17**
	(0.07)	**(0.07)**		**(0.06)**	**(0.06)**
	–0.43	**–0.42**		**–0.33**	**–0.31**
	(0.08)	**(0.08)**		**(0.06)**	**(0.07)**
	0.07	**0.08**		0.02	0.02
	(0.02)	**(0.02)**		(0.02)	(0.02)
		0.21			**–0.25**
		(0.07)			**(0.06)**
		0.15			**–0.13**
		(0.06)			**(0.05)**
		0.20			0.07
		(0.07)			(0.06)
		0.31			0.08
		(0.07)			(0.06)
		–0.03			**0.12**
		(0.06)			**(0.05)**
		0.06			–0.01
		(0.05)			(0.04)
		0.04			–0.06
		(0.05)			(0.04)
		–0.45			–0.07
		(0.07)			(0.06)
		16684			16470
		13553			18109
		0.0001			0.0001

CHAPTER 7

Educational Profile of 3- to 8-Year-Old Children of Immigrants[1]

Christine Winquist Nord and
James A. Griffin

This chapter provides a broad overview of the educational experiences of young children of immigrants and contrasts their experiences with those of children of native-born parents using data from a 1996 national survey, the National Household Education Survey, sponsored by the U.S. Department of Education (Nolin et al., 1997). The profile is restricted to children 3 to 8 years old who live with at least one biological, adoptive, step-, or foster parent. As in other chapters of this volume, children are classified as children of immigrants if they have at least one parent who was not born in the United States or in a territory of the United States. Children of immigrants who were foreign born are referred to as foreign-born or immigrant children. Children of immigrants who were born in the United States or one of its territories are referred to as native-born children of immigrants.

Children of immigrants are expected to account for more than half the growth in the school-aged population between 1990 and 2010 (Passel and Fix, 1995). Despite their growing numbers, relatively little is known about their educational experiences (Portes

[1]This paper is intended to promote the exchange of ideas among researchers and policy makers. The views expressed in it are part of ongoing research and analysis and do not necessarily reflect the position of the U.S. Department of Education.

and MacLeod, 1996). Information about young children of immigrants is particularly scarce (Board on Children and Families, 1995). Yet the early childhood years are critical for children's cognitive and social development. It is during these years that children begin to develop and expand their ability to communicate effectively with others and begin to acquire reading and math skills that lay the foundation for their future school success and ultimately their success in the work force. The years before children enter formal schooling are especially important in preparing them for school, as is recognized in Goal One of the National Education Goals, which states that "by the year 2000, all children in America will start school ready to learn" (National Education Goals Panel, 1996). This goal reminds us that how children do in school is determined in part by things that have happened before they ever set foot in a classroom. Learning more about the family circumstances and educational experiences of children of immigrants during these important early years will enable educators and policy makers to develop better ways of serving these children and their families.

Researchers have consistently found that certain family characteristics, such as family composition (e.g., number and type of parents, number of siblings), economic well-being, and parental education, exert a strong influence on children's school success (Zill, 1996; Portes and MacLeod, 1996; McLanahan and Sandefur, 1994; Featherman and Hauser, 1978; Blau and Duncan, 1967). Family involvement in children's lives, both at home and at school, also is important for children's school success (Nord et al., forthcoming; U.S. Department of Education, 1994; Henderson and Berla, 1994). A useful way of thinking about these and other family influences on children's development is to think of them as resources that parents offer their children. These resources can be grouped into three distinct types of capital: human, financial, and social (Lee, 1993; Muller, 1993; Coleman, 1991; Becker, 1981). Human capital is usually measured as parental education, though it encompasses other skills and specialized knowledge that parents have acquired. Financial capital is measured by the income and economic security of a family, which influences the quality of the environment that children are raised in; the types of schools they attend; and the types of educational materials that parents can purchase for them such as books, extracurricular classes, or computers. Social capital taps both the direct interactions between parents and children and the indirect influences on children of parents' relationships with others in the family, with the children's schools, and with other persons and institutions that influence children. Parental involvement at home and at school falls within this domain. Some family characteristics, such as family composition, span all three types of family resources. For example, the presence of two parents versus one influences family income as well as the number of adults present to interact with children. Moreover, many single-parent families are maintained by mothers with relatively low levels of education (Rawlings, 1994; Zill and Nord, 1994).

The three types of family resources described above influence children from birth throughout their school careers. Young children not only learn from their parents and other family members at home but also benefit from exposure to early childhood programs prior to first grade (Boocock, 1995; Howes, 1988). Early childhood programs (e.g., Head Start) are especially beneficial for children from disadvantaged backgrounds (Boocock, 1995; Hofferth et al., 1994). Such programs help prepare children to be "ready to learn" when they enter formal schooling (Zill and Wolpow, 1991). Once children enter formal schooling, schools also exert a strong influence on children's cognitive and social development (Alexander and Entwisle, 1996; Coleman et al., 1982; Rutter et al., 1979).

This chapter provides information on family resources that children of immigrants have that may influence their later school success. It also provides information on the extent to which they attend early childhood programs, characteristics of the schools they attend, and their experiences at school. Detailed tables on these topics are contained in the appendix. The tables provide information on whether the children were native or foreign born and on the children's races and ethnicities.[2] Due to sample size

[2]Throughout this chapter Hispanic children are designated as such and are not included in other racial or ethnic categories. Thus, white children are white non-Hispanic children, black children are black non-Hispanic children, and Asian children are Asian non-Hispanic children.

constraints, not all categories of race and ethnicity could be used for both children of immigrants and children of native-born parents. Information is shown for Hispanic, Asian, and white children of immigrants.[3] There were too few black children in immigrant families to show separately. Information is shown for white, black, and Hispanic children of native-born parents. There were too few children of native-born parents who were Asian to show separately. In the discussion below, selected information from the appendix tables is highlighted; refer to the tables for additional information.

THE NATIONAL HOUSEHOLD EDUCATION SURVEY

The data presented in this chapter were collected as part of the 1996 National Household Education Survey (NHES:96) sponsored by the National Center for Education Statistics (Collins et al., 1997). The NHES is a random digit dial telephone survey that uses computer-assisted telephone interviewing technology to collect data on high-priority topics that could not be addressed adequately through school- or institution-based surveys. NHES:96 was conducted from January to April 1996 and included interviews with parents of 20,792 children 3 years old through grade 12. This chapter focuses on the 7,717 children who were 3 to 8 years old and their parents. More details on NHES:96 are provided in Appendix 7A.

According to data from NHES:96, there are nearly 23 million children ages 3 to 8 who live with at least one biological, adoptive, step-, or foster parent. Of these, over 3 million or 14 percent

[3]It was not possible to determine the countries of origin of any of the children of immigrants in the survey. In 1996 immigrants from Mexico accounted for over a quarter of the foreign-born population in the United States (Hansen and Faber, 1997). Twelve percent of the foreign-born population in 1996 was from Central or South America. Approximately 25 percent of the foreign-born population was from Asia, which includes persons from the Philippines, China, India, Vietnam, Korea, and other Asian countries. Just over 10 percent of the foreign-born population was from one of the Caribbean islands, including Cuba, the Dominican Republic, and Jamaica. Seventeen percent of the foreign-born population was from Europe. Some of the foreign-born population immigrated recently, while others have lived in the United States for many years.

live with at least one parent who is not a native of the United States (see Table 7A-1). Most young children of immigrants are native born (2.8 million or 87 percent), although approximately 430,000 are foreign born. Immigrant children tend to be somewhat older than native-born children of immigrants. Only 21 percent of immigrant children are 3 or 4 years old compared to 38 percent of native-born children of immigrants and 33 percent of children of native-born parents. The majority of immigrants' children 3 to 8 years old are Hispanic (54 percent). Twenty-six percent are white, 9 percent are black, 7 percent are Asian,[4] and 4 percent are some other race or ethnicity. In contrast, 72 percent of children of native-born parents are white, 17 percent are black, 8 percent are Hispanic, less than 1 percent are Asian, and 3 percent are some other race or ethnicity.

Family Resources

Children of immigrants and children of native-born parents often have very different family backgrounds. However, the differences are not always to the advantage of the children of native-born parents.

Family Composition

Number of Parents. Children who grow up with two biological parents fare better in a wide variety of domains, including school,

[4]The Asian children of immigrants interviewed in the NHES may not be representative of all Asian children of immigrants. Bilingual interviewers were available for Spanish-speaking households but not for households that spoke other foreign languages. Thus, Asian households in which no adult spoke English would not have been interviewed. For this reason the Asian sample may be biased toward families that have at least one English speaker. Such families may tend to have higher incomes. As shown later, however, approximately one-third of Asian children of immigrants are in households with incomes below the poverty threshold. According to data from the Current Population Survey, in 1993 about 12 percent of Asian and Pacific Islander families had incomes below the poverty threshold (Bureau of the Census, 1994). Typically, families with children are more apt to be poor. Thus, the Asian sample in the NHES:96 does not appear to be unduly biased toward high-income families.

compared to children who live apart from one or both of their parents (McLanahan and Sandefur, 1994; Rumbaut, this volume). In this respect, children of immigrants have an advantage over children of native-born parents because they are more likely to live with both their biological parents: 77 percent of children of immigrants live with both their biological parents compared to 63 percent of children of native-born parents. Among children of immigrants, whether the children were native or foreign born makes no difference in the likelihood that they live with both their biological parents. However, Asian and white children of immigrants are more likely than Hispanic children of immigrants to live with both their biological parents (88 percent each versus 72 percent). The proportion of Hispanic children of immigrants, however, who live with both their biological parents is virtually the same as that of white children of native-born parents (72 versus 73 percent), much higher than the 49 percent of Hispanic children of native-born parents who live with both biological parents.

Presence of Siblings. Children from smaller families tend to go further and do better in school than children from larger families (Blake, 1989). Children of immigrants are somewhat less likely than children of native-born parents to have no siblings in their households and are more likely to have three or more siblings in their households. Hispanic children of immigrants are particularly likely to have three or more siblings. Twenty-six percent of Hispanic children of immigrants have three or more siblings. In contrast, 15 percent of Hispanic children of native-born parents, 11 percent of Asian, and 9 percent of white children of immigrants, and 13 and 17 percent, respectively, of white and black children of native-born parents have that many siblings.

Human and Financial Capital

Parental Education. The diversity of the immigrant population is reflected in the education levels of children's parents (see Figure 7-1). Children of immigrants are more likely than children of native-born parents to live in a household in which the most highly educated parent has less than a high school education (23 versus 7 percent). On the other hand, children of immigrants are as likely

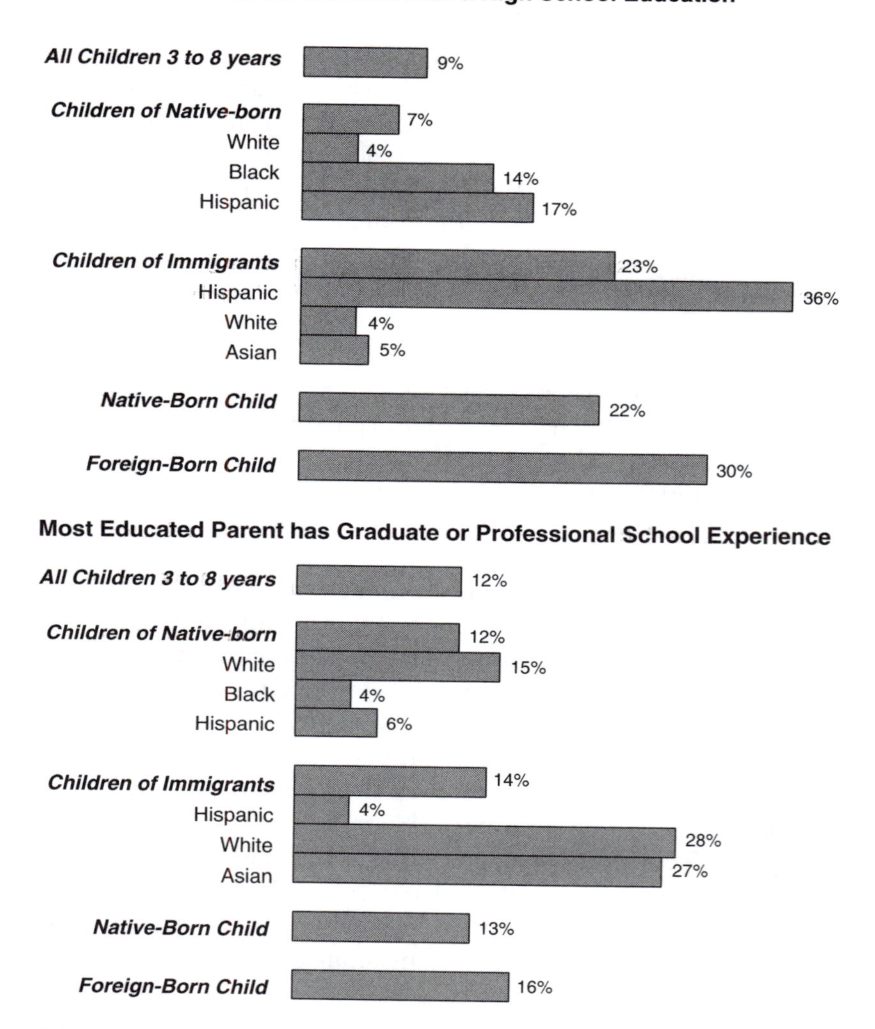

FIGURE 7-1 Percentage of children ages 3 to 8 years by selected levels of parental education. NOTE: Hispanic children are designated as such and are not included in any other racial or ethnic categories. SOURCE: U.S. Department of Education, National Center for Education Statistics, 1996 National Household Education Survey.

as children of native-born parents to have a parent with graduate or professional school experience (14 and 12 percent, respectively). Hispanic children of immigrants are substantially more likely than other children of immigrants or children of native-born parents to live in households in which the most educated parent has less than a high school education. Thirty-six percent of Hispanic children of immigrants live in such households, compared to 17 percent of Hispanic children of native-born parents and 4 percent each of white children of native-born parents and Asian children of immigrants. Asian and white children of immigrants, on the other hand, are substantially more likely than Hispanic children of immigrants or children of native-born parents to live in households in which a parent has graduate or professional school experience. Twenty-eight percent of Asian and 27 percent of white children of immigrants live in such households compared to 15 percent of white children of native-born parents, 6 percent of Hispanic children of native-born parents, and 4 percent each of Hispanic children of immigrants and black children of native-born parents.

Language Spoken at Home. Language acquisition is one of the most notable accomplishments of young children. How well they learn to speak English may affect how well they adapt to school. A study of eighth graders found that students who mostly or always spoke a language other than English at home scored lower on standardized math and reading tests than students who spoke English at home (Kao, this volume). Moreover, the students tended to feel more alienated from their peers and had a lower sense of self-esteem and locus of control than students who spoke English at home. Children learn to speak through listening to and interacting with their parents and others around them. Many young children of immigrants have parents who do not usually speak English at home (49 percent). Hispanic and Asian children are particularly likely to live with parents who do not usually speak English at home (71 and 68 percent, respectively), while only 12 percent of white children of immigrants have parents who usually speak some other language at home. In contrast, 99 percent of children of native-born parents have parents who usually speak English at home. However, 10 percent of Hispanic children of native-born parents have parents who do not usually speak English at home. The differences between children of native-born parents and children of immigrants in the languages that they hear at home means that upon entering school children of immigrants may not know English as well as their peers do.

Poverty Status. Poverty is associated with poor educational outcomes for children, including low achievement test scores, grade repetition, problem behaviors that result in suspension or expulsion, and dropping out of school (Zill et al., 1995b; McLanahan and Sandefur, 1994). Although children of immigrants are more likely than children of native-born parents to live in poverty (36 versus 24 percent), the majority do not. There are differences in the likelihood of living in poverty by children's races and ethnicities. Fifty-three percent of Hispanic children of immigrants live in poverty compared to 32 percent of Asian and 11 percent of white children of immigrants. Hispanic children of immigrants are more likely to live in poverty than Hispanic children of native-born parents (53 versus 36 percent) and are as likely as black children of native-born parents to live in poverty (53 versus 52 percent). In contrast, only 15 percent of white children of native-born parents live in poverty.

Social Capital

In recognition of the importance of parents to young children's learning, one objective of Goal One of the National Education Goals states that parents should be their children's first teachers, devoting time each day to helping their preschool children learn (National Education Goals Panel, 1996; see Table 7A-2). Although this goal focuses on preschool children, parental involvement in children's education is known to be important for older children as well. This section examines the extent to which immigrant and native-born families are involved with their children's learning at home and at school.[5]

[5]The information presented here is based on parent reports. It is possible that parents have a tendency to give the "socially desirable" response and thus overstate the extent to which they engage in different activities with their children or

Parent Involvement at Home. Among the things that parents can do that help their children's later school success are teaching their young children letters and numbers; reading to them; working on projects with them; taking them to museums, zoos, and other educational outings; and sharing day-to-day activities with them (Bredekamp, 1987). The NHES:96 data show that most parents of young children are serving as their children's first teachers: 93 percent of children 3 years old through kindergarten have parents or other family members who taught them letters, words, or numbers in the past week. Children of immigrants and children of native-born parents are essentially the same in this regard.[6] Ninety-four percent of native-born children have parents or other family members who taught them letters, words, or numbers in the past week, compared to 92 percent of children of immigrants. There are some differences when children of immigrants are examined by their races and ethnicities. Asian children of immigrants are more likely than Hispanic children of immigrants to have been taught letters, numbers, or words by family members in the past week. Ninety-seven percent of Asian children of immigrants not yet enrolled in grade 1 or higher were taught letters, words, or numbers by their parents or other family members in the previous week compared to 90 percent of Hispanic children of immigrants.

Most young children ages 3 to 8, regardless of whether they are children of immigrants or native-born parents, were told a story in the past week by someone in their family. Seventy-six percent of children of immigrants and 77 percent of children of native-born parents had been told a story in the past week. Asian

---

are involved in their children's schools. However, even if there is a tendency for parents to be overly positive about their involvement in their children's lives, group differences probably reflect true differences because there is no a priori reason to believe that one group of parents is more likely than another to give the socially desirable response.

[6]The NHES:96 did not ask what language the parents or other family members used when they taught their children words, letters, or numbers or what language they used when they told their children stories or read to them. Some immigrant family members may have been using their native tongues when teaching and reading to their children.

and white children of immigrants are more likely than Hispanic children of immigrants to have been told a story in the previous week (83 and 84 percent, respectively, versus 71 percent). Among native-born children, 79 percent of Hispanic children, 78 percent of white children, and 73 percent of black children had been told a story by a family member in the past week.

Most young children were also read to in the previous week: 89 percent of children of immigrants ages 3 through third grade were read to by someone in their family at least once in the past week, as were 93 percent of children of native-born parents. A much smaller, though not insubstantial, proportion were read to every day (see Figure 7-2). Children of immigrants were less likely than children of native-born parents to be read to every day (37 versus 45 percent). There are also differences by children's races and ethnicities. Asian and white children of immigrants

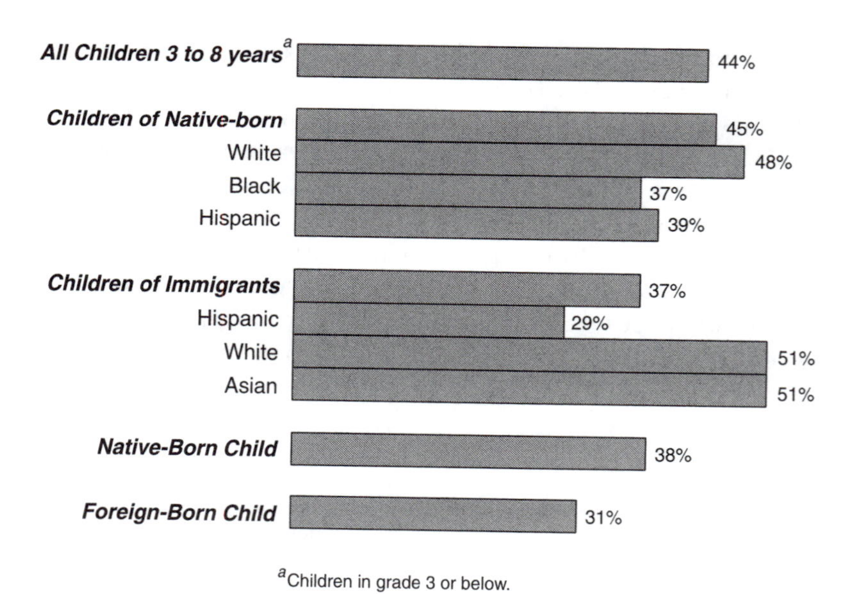

FIGURE 7-2 Percentage of children, ages 3 to 8 years, who were read to every day in the past week by a family member. NOTE: Hispanic children are designated as such and are not included in any other racial or ethnic categories. SOURCE: U.S. Department of Education, National Center for Education Statistics, 1996 National Household Education Survey.

were more likely to be read to every day than were Hispanic children of immigrants (51 percent each versus 29 percent). Among children of native-born parents, 48 percent of white, 37 percent of black, and 39 percent of Hispanic children were read to every day in the past week by someone in their families.

Children are less likely to go on educational outings with their parents than they are to share activities at home with them. Even so, a sizable minority of children had visited a library; gone to a play, concert, or other live show; visited an art gallery, museum, or historical site; or visited a zoo or aquarium with a family member in the past month. Children of native-born parents are more likely than children of immigrants to have visited a library and to have gone to a play, concert, or live show with a family member in the past month. Forty-five percent of children of native-born parents and 38 percent of children of immigrants visited the library with a family member in the past month. Similarly, 30 percent of children of native-born parents attended a play, concert, or live show with their parents compared to 26 percent of children of immigrants. It is possible that lack of fluency in English is a barrier to these activities for some immigrant parents. There are also differences among children of immigrants by children's races and ethnicities. Over half of Asian and white children of immigrants (54 and 51 percent, respectively) visited the library and a third (34 and 33 percent, respectively) went to some type of live show in the past month with a family member compared to 27 percent of Hispanic children of immigrants who visited a library and 21 percent who went to a live show with a family member. Children of immigrants, however, are more likely than children of native-born parents to have visited a zoo or aquarium in the past month with a family member (23 versus 16 percent).

Parental Involvement at School. Another way in which parents encourage their children's school success is to become involved in their children's schools. Such involvement, among other things, demonstrates to the children that they value education. However, parents who do not speak English well or who are not familiar with the school system may not feel comfortable getting involved in schools. Or, perhaps, schools are not very welcoming of non-English-speaking parents, which could discourage the parents from becoming involved. Alternatively, some immigrant groups may believe that they should not interfere with what they consider school responsibilities. Such parents, however, may be very involved at home.

The NHES:96 asked parents whether any adult in the household had participated in four types of school activities since the beginning of the school year: attending a general school meeting, attending a regularly scheduled parent-teacher conference with the child's teacher, attending a school or class event, or volunteering at school. Parents (or other adults) who participated in at least three of these four activities are be said to be highly involved in their children's schools. Those who participated in only two activities are said to be moderately involved. And those who participated in none or only one activity are said to have low involvement in their children's schools. Only 15 percent of children of native-born parents and 17 percent of children of immigrants have parents with low levels of involvement in their schools. Native-born parents are more likely than immigrant parents to show high levels of involvement in their children's schools (see Figure 7-3). Sixty-five percent of children of native-born parents have parents who are highly involved in their schools, compared to 57 percent of children of immigrants. Hispanic and Asian children of immigrants are less likely than white children of native-born parents to have parents with high levels of involvement in their schools (49 and 57 percent, respectively, versus 68 percent). Hispanic children of immigrants are also less likely than Hispanic children of native-born parents to have parents with high levels of involvement in their schools (49 versus 59 percent).

Immigrant parents are much less likely than native-born parents to volunteer at their children's schools. Fifty-three percent of children of native-born parents have parents who volunteered at their school, compared to 38 percent of children of immigrants. Foreign-born children of immigrants are less likely than native-born children of immigrants to have parents who volunteered at their schools (24 versus 41 percent). Hispanic and Asian children of immigrants are less likely than white children of immigrants or white children of native-born parents to have parents who volunteered at their schools. Twenty-nine percent of Hispanic and 36 percent of Asian children of immigrants have parents who volun-

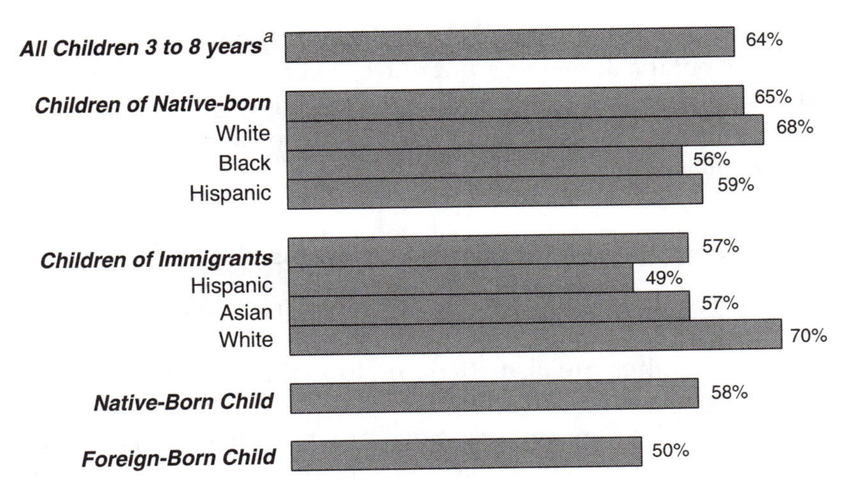

FIGURE 7-3 Percentage of children, ages 3 to 8 years, whose parents are highly involved in their schools. NOTE: Hispanic children are designated as such and are not included in any other racial or ethnic categories. SOURCE: U.S. Department of Education, National Center for Education Statistics, 1996 National Household Education Survey.

teered at their schools, compared to 54 percent of white children of immigrants and 56 percent of white children of native-born parents. It is likely that lack of fluency in English makes volunteering more difficult for some Asian and Hispanic immigrant parents.

Immigrant parents, however, are as likely as native-born parents to attend regularly scheduled parent-teacher conferences (82 versus 79 percent). Similarly, foreign-born children of immigrants are as likely as native-born children of immigrants to have parents who attended parent-teacher conferences (84 versus 81 percent). And Hispanic children of immigrants are as likely as Hispanic children of native-born parents to have parents who attended a parent-teacher conference (83 versus 78 percent). Moreover, white and Asian children of immigrants are more likely than white children of native-born parents to have parents who attended parent-teacher conferences (86 percent each versus 79 percent).

What is most important about the above school involvement data are not the differences but rather that most parents of young children, immigrant and nonimmigrant alike, are interested in their children's learning and show their interest by participating in school activities.

Attendance at Early Childhood Programs

Almost all U.S. children attend kindergarten before beginning first grade (Zill et al., 1995a; see Table 7A-3). More and more younger children are also attending formal programs in school-like settings such as preschool, nursery school, Head Start programs, and day care centers. Such programs help prepare children for regular school. Policy makers are concerned, however, that not all children have equal access to good early childhood education programs. This concern is articulated in one of the objectives of the first National Education Goal that all children start school ready to learn. The objective states that all disadvantaged and disabled children will have access to high-quality, developmentally appropriate programs (National Education Goals Panel, 1996). Research finds though that this objective has not yet been met (Hofferth et al., 1994).

Attendance at Early Childhood Programs. The NHES:96 indicates that, among children who are not yet enrolled in kindergarten or elementary school, 55 percent are enrolled in some type of early childhood program (see Figure 7-4). Children of native-born parents are more likely than children of immigrants to attend such programs (58 versus 41 percent). Among children of immigrants, Hispanic and Asian children are less likely than white children to attend early childhood programs (31 and 35 percent, respectively, versus 57 percent). Hispanic children of immigrants are also substantially less likely than Hispanic children of native-born parents to be enrolled in early childhood programs (31 versus 47 percent).

Participation in Head Start Programs. Head Start is primarily intended to serve children from low-income families. Among poor children not yet enrolled in kindergarten, about 38 percent attend

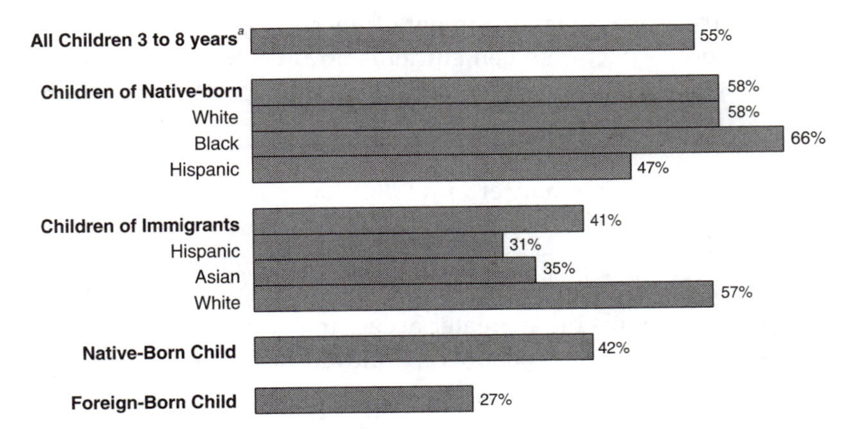

FIGURE 7-4 Percentage of children attending early childhood programs by immigrant status and race/ethnicity. NOTE: Hispanic children are designated as such and are not included in any other racial or ethnic categories. SOURCE: U.S. Department of Education, National Center for Education Statistics, 1996 National Household Education Survey.

Head Start.[7] Poor children of immigrants, however, are less likely than poor children of native-born parents to attend Head Start (25 versus 46 percent). Poor Hispanic and Asian children of immigrants are about equally likely to attend Head Start programs (25 versus 22 percent). However, poor Hispanic children of immigrants are less likely than poor Hispanic children of native-born parents to attend Head Start (25 versus 33 percent).

School Characteristics

Children are influenced not only by their parents but also by their schools. Characteristics of schools that may be important include structural aspects (e.g., public versus private, the size of a

[7] This estimate accords well with other sources. Stewart (1993) estimated that about 40 percent of eligible 4 year olds were enrolled in Head Start. A smaller proportion of eligible 3 year olds was enrolled in Head Start.

school), the learning environment of the schools (e.g., school discipline and respect between students and teachers), and the extent to which schools involve parents in their children's learning (e.g., school practices).

Type of School. Coleman et al. (1982) have argued that private schools, particularly religiously affiliated ones, instill a greater sense of community among students, teachers, and parents. The greater sense of community, in turn, means that students attending private schools have greater access to social capital than students attending public schools. Children of immigrants are no more or less likely than children of native-born parents to attend private schools. Most children enrolled in elementary school attend the public schools assigned to them. Seventy percent of children of immigrants and 71 percent of children of native-born parents attend the public schools assigned to them. Sixteen percent of children of immigrants and 17 percent of children of native-born parents attend public elementary schools of their parents' choice. Ten percent of children of immigrants and 10 percent of children of native-born parents attend private religiously affiliated schools. And 5 percent of children of immigrants and 3 percent of children of native-born parents attend private schools with no religious affiliation.

School Size. School size, like school type, may be associated with differences in the sense of community within schools. It is more difficult to establish ties among parents, students, and teachers in larger schools than it is in smaller ones. The NHES:96 data reveal that children of immigrants are more likely than children of native-born parents to attend very large schools. Thirteen percent of young children of immigrants attend schools with 1,000 or more students compared to 8 percent of children of native-born parents. Among children of immigrants, foreign-born children are more likely than native-born children to attend very large elementary schools (23 versus 11 percent). They are also less likely than native-born children of immigrants to attend small elementary schools—that is, schools of under 300 students (14 versus 23 percent). Hispanic children of immigrants are particularly unlikely to attend small elementary schools. Sixteen percent of Hispanic children of immigrants attend elementary schools of less than 300 students compared to 42 percent of Asian and 31 percent of white children of immigrants and 28 percent of white children of native-born parents.

School Environment. Children are better able to learn if the schools they attend are well disciplined and there is a sense of community (Rutter et al., 1979). The NHES:96 asked parents of children in grades 1 and above the extent to which they agreed that teachers maintain good discipline in the classroom, that the principal and assistant principal maintain good discipline at school, and that most students and teachers at the school respect each other. Children of immigrants are less likely than children of native-born parents to have parents who strongly agree that teachers maintain good discipline in the classroom and that students and teachers respect each other. Forty-six percent of children of immigrants have parents who strongly agree that teachers maintain good discipline in the classrooms compared to 53 percent of children of native-born parents. Thirty-eight percent of children of immigrants have parents who strongly agree that most students and teachers respect each other compared to 46 percent of children of native-born parents. It is possible that differences in the use of language qualifiers may be a factor in these results. For example, immigrant parents may be less comfortable using the qualifier "strongly" in their responses. There are, however, no significant differences between children of immigrants and children of native-born parents in the proportion whose parents strongly agree that the principal and assistant principal maintain good discipline in their schools (48 versus 51 percent).

Hispanic children of immigrants are less likely than white children of immigrants and white children of native-born parents to have parents who strongly agree with each of the above statements. For example, 36 percent of Hispanic children of immigrants have parents who strongly agree that teachers maintain good discipline in their classrooms, compared to 62 percent of white children of immigrants and 55 percent of white children of native-born parents. Similarly, 30 percent of Hispanic children of immigrants have parents who strongly agree that teachers and students respect each other, compared to 52 percent of white children of immigrants and 48 percent of white children of native-born parents.

School Practices. Parental involvement is strongly linked to children's school success. Existing research suggests that school practices to involve parents are important influences on parental involvement (Vaden-Kiernan, 1996; Dauber and Epstein, 1989). For example, parents are more likely to become involved in their children's schools if the schools communicate with them about school programs and activities and encourage their involvement. The importance of schools in fostering parental involvement is reflected in the eighth National Education Goal, which calls for every school to promote partnerships that will increase parental involvement (National Education Goals Panel, 1996).

Parents were asked whether they strongly agreed, agreed, disagreed, or strongly disagreed with the following statements: "My child's school welcomes my family's involvement with the school" and "My child's school makes it easy to be involved there." Children of native-born parents are more likely than children of immigrants to have parents who strongly agree with each of these statements. Sixty-five percent of children of native-born parents have parents who strongly agree that their children's schools welcome their involvement, compared to 53 percent of children of immigrants. Similarly, 57 percent of children of native-born parents have parents who strongly agree that the schools make involvement easy compared to 45 percent of children of immigrants. Foreign-born children of immigrants are less likely than native-born children of immigrants to have parents who strongly agree with these statements. Forty percent of foreign-born children have parents who strongly agree that their schools welcome family involvement compared to 55 percent of native-born children of immigrants. Similarly, 38 percent of foreign-born children of immigrants have parents who strongly agree that schools make involvement easy compared to 47 percent of native-born children of immigrants.

Hispanic children of immigrants are less likely than white children of immigrants and white and Hispanic children of native-born parents to have parents who strongly agree that their schools welcome their family's involvement and make involvement easy. Thirty-nine percent of Hispanic children have parents who strongly agree that their schools welcome their family's involvement, compared to 70 percent of white children of immigrants, 67 percent of white children of native-born parents, and 58 percent of Hispanic children of native-born parents. Similarly, 38 percent of Hispanic children of immigrants have parents who strongly agree that their schools make involvement easy, compared to 58 percent of white children of immigrants and 60 percent of white children and 52 percent of Hispanic children of native-born parents.

Children's School Experiences

Parents were asked a series of questions about their children's experiences at school (see Table 7A-5). Parents of children in grades 1 and above were asked whether they strongly agreed, agreed, disagreed, or strongly disagreed that their children enjoyed school. They were also asked what grades their children received overall during the current school year and whether their children participated in any extracurricular activities either at school or elsewhere during the current school year. Parents of children in kindergarten and above were asked if their children had ever repeated a grade since entering kindergarten. Parents of all children were asked whether teachers at the school had contacted them since the beginning of the school year because of any problems the children were having. Parents of children in kindergarten and above were asked two questions: whether they had been contacted about behavior problems their children were having at school and whether they had been contacted about problems their children were having with schoolwork.

Get Mostly A's. One measure of children's academic success is how well they are doing in school. According to the parents' reports, children of immigrants are not significantly more likely than children of native-born parents to be getting mostly A's (46 versus 42 percent).[8] There are also no significant differences be-

[8]Parents may have a tendency to be overly positive about their children's academic achievement. It is likely that, if school records were used to obtain information on children's academic success, the proportion who received mostly A's would be lower.

tween foreign-born and native-born children of immigrants in the likelihood that they are getting mostly A's (47 versus 46 percent). Asian children of immigrants, however, are substantially more likely than Hispanic immigrant or white children of native-born parents to have parents who report that they get mostly A's. Sixty-three percent of Asian children of immigrants get mostly A's according to their parents, compared to 41 percent of Hispanic children of immigrants and 43 percent of white children of native-born parents.

Enjoy School. Children who enjoy school are more likely to perform better academically and to remain in school (Csikszentmihalyi, 1990). Most parents report that their children enjoy school. Children of immigrants and children of native-born parents are very similar in this regard. Forty-five percent of the children of immigrants had parents who strongly agreed that they enjoyed school, compared to 51 percent of the children of native-born parents. Hispanic children of immigrants are less likely than white children of immigrants and white children of native-born parents to enjoy school, according to their parents. Thirty-seven percent of Hispanic children of immigrants had parents who strongly agreed that they enjoyed school, compared to 56 percent of white children of immigrants and 52 percent of white children of native-born parents. There are no significant differences between Hispanic and Asian children of immigrants or between Hispanic children of immigrants and Hispanic children of native-born parents in the proportion who enjoy school.

Participation in Extracurricular Activities. Participation in extracurricular activities reduces risky behaviors in adolescence, such as dropping out of school, becoming a teen parent, using drugs, or engaging in delinquent conduct (Zill et al., 1995c). It also provides more opportunities to establish connections to other young people and adults and to develop new skills. Children of immigrants are significantly less likely than children of native-born parents to participate in extracurricular activities either inside or outside school. Approximately 76 percent of children of native-born parents participated in such activities compared to 63 percent of children of immigrants. There are differences in the likelihood of participating in extracurricular activities by children's races and ethnicities. Asian and white children of immigrants are substantially more likely than Hispanic children of immigrants to participate in extracurricular activities either inside or outside school (78 and 79 percent, respectively, versus 49 percent). Hispanic children of immigrants, however, are not significantly less likely than Hispanic children of native-born parents to participate in extracurricular activities (49 versus 57 percent).

Problems in School. Problems in school, if not attended to, can develop into larger problems that can eventually lead to school failure and to dropping out of school. Children of immigrants are no more or less likely than children of native-born parents to experience behavior or schoolwork-related problems that result in a teacher contacting their parents (25 versus 29 percent). There are no significant differences among children of immigrants in the likelihood that they experience school problems by whether they are native or foreign born or by their races and ethnicities. Hispanic children of immigrants are marginally more likely than Asian children of immigrants to experience problems in school, but the difference is only significant at the 0.10 level after using a Bonferonni adjustment to the t test for the number of comparisons being made. Asian children of immigrants, however, are less likely than white children of native-born parents to experience problems at school (17 versus 27 percent).

Grade Repetition. Grade repetition is a sign of academic difficulties. Children who have repeated a grade may also experience a lower sense of self-esteem and more difficulties getting along with their younger classmates. Children of immigrants are no more likely than children of native-born parents to have ever repeated a grade since entering kindergarten. Five percent of children were reported as having ever repeated a grade, regardless of whether they are children of immigrants or children of native-born parents. Six percent of foreign-born children of immigrants have ever repeated a grade.

Summary and Discussion

In the coming decades the American education system will face growing numbers of children of immigrants. The information presented in this chapter underscores what others have found: children of immigrants are not a homogeneous group. There are distinct differences among young children of immigrants by whether they themselves were native or foreign born and by their ethnicity. As a group, young children of immigrants face many challenges to their educational success. Among these are the relatively high proportion who are living in poverty and whose parents have low levels of education. This is particularly true of Hispanic children of immigrants, over half of whom have household incomes that are below the poverty threshold and more than a third of whom live in households in which the most educated parent has less than a high school education. Asian children of immigrants, however, are not immune to economic difficulties: approximately one-third of Asian children of immigrants also live in households with incomes below the poverty threshold. Foreign-born children of immigrants are more likely than native-born children of immigrants to live in poverty and to have parents with low levels of education.

Simple tabulations suggest that children of immigrants who are not yet enrolled in kindergarten or elementary school are less likely than native-born children to be enrolled in early childhood programs. Poor children of immigrants also appear less likely than poor children of native-born parents to be enrolled in Head Start. It might be worthwhile for Head Start programs and other early childhood programs to target children of immigrants in order to help them adapt more quickly to American culture and language so that they will be ready to learn upon entry into school.

Another potential challenge to the educational success of children of immigrants is the high proportion of Hispanic and Asian immigrants whose parents do not usually speak English at home. Although some of these parents may have a rudimentary or even better knowledge of English, to the extent that they are not comfortable speaking English it will be more difficult for them to communicate with their children's teachers and other school personnel. Moreover, their children will not be hearing English spoken regularly at home, which could impede their own acquisition of the language. Increasing the participation of young children of immigrants in Head Start and other early childhood programs would help the children learn English more quickly.

Children of immigrants, however, also have a number of strengths that should serve them well as they enter and progress through school. An important strength is the large proportion of children of immigrants who live with both biological parents. Another strength is the interest that their families show in their education. Many young children of immigrants not yet in elementary school have parents who are serving as their children's first teachers by teaching them letters, words, and numbers; by telling them stories; and by reading to them at least occasionally each week. Although some of the parents may be using their native languages rather than English in teaching and reading to their children, studies have suggested that literacy in their native non-English language can contribute to children's academic success (Bankston and Zhou, 1995). There are several mechanisms by which literacy in one's native language might affect school success. One possibility is that there is a transfer of information such that things learned in one language are transferred more easily to the second. A second possibility is that children who are bilingual have access to more social capital: that of their own ethnic communities and that of their schools and the larger American society (Bankston and Zhou, 1995).

The data presented in this chapter also reveal that the majority of parents of young children of immigrants are involved in their children's schools. Though the proportion of children of immigrants whose parents are highly involved is not as large as the proportion of native-born children whose parents are highly involved, only a small proportion have parents who show only low levels of involvement in their schools. Immigrant parents appear particularly interested in attending parent-teacher conferences: 80 percent or more of children of immigrants had parents who attended regularly scheduled parent-teacher conferences. The data also suggest, however, that immigrant parents are less likely than native-born parents to feel that their children's schools welcome their involvement and make involvement easy for them.

LIMITATIONS OF THE DATA

There are several limitations of the data that need to be recognized. First, the NHES:96 is a telephone survey of households. About one-quarter of children living in poverty live in households without telephones. Adjustments were made through the use of weights so that estimates apply to all households with and without telephones. It is not known, however, how well the adjustments did at reflecting specific characteristics or opinions of households without telephones.

Second, interviews were conducted only in English or Spanish. Households without an English or Spanish speaker were not interviewed. Language problems accounted for about 6 percent of all nonresponses to the parent survey (Montaquila and Brick, 1997). Most nonresponses were due to refusals to be interviewed (62 percent). It is possible that immigrant households were more reluctant to be interviewed than nonimmigrant households. Response rates across census regions, however, are quite similar. Given that a majority of immigrants live in the Western part of the country, the similarity of the response rates provides some evidence that nonresponse among immigrants is not a large problem.

Sample sizes for some groups (such as the Asian immigrant and foreign-born populations) are small. For that reason, estimates provided in this chapter should be interpreted cautiously. No estimate is provided if the denominator used to calculate a percentage consisted of 30 or fewer cases. Finally, the NHES:96 is a cross-sectional survey and as such provides only a snapshot of children of immigrants at a point in time. Longitudinal data, such as the Early Childhood Longitudinal Survey—Kindergarten Cohort, sponsored by the U.S. Department of Education, will allow researchers to examine the developmental trajectories of young children as they progress through school.

IMPLICATIONS FOR FUTURE RESEARCH

It was not possible with the NHES:96 data to examine the countries of origin of children of immigrants. Even with the rather crude ethnic categories available, however, differences among children of immigrants in their family resources and school experiences were noted. Other studies have shown that there are distinct differences depending on country of origin within both Hispanic and Asian immigrant populations. Future studies should examine differences in family resources and in the school experiences of children from different countries.

The data in this chapter also suggest that children of immigrants are less likely than children of native-born parents to attend early childhood programs. Children of immigrants and children of native-born families, however, differ in family background characteristics, such as parental education and economic well-being, which can influence their attendance at early childhood programs. An important question is whether differences in attendance at early childhood programs persist once these factors are taken into account.

Similarly, the data in this chapter suggest that poor children of immigrants are less likely to attend Head Start than poor children of native-born parents. Children of immigrants are making up an increasing proportion of the school-aged population. As shown, many children of immigrants face economic disadvantages. Head Start is the primary program aimed at helping disadvantaged children prepare for formal schooling. More information is needed on the extent to which children of immigrants have access to Head Start programs. Information is also needed on the extent to which immigrant parents who are eligible for Head Start do not enroll their children in a program and why.

REFERENCES

Alexander, K.L., and D.R. Entwisle
1996 Schools and children at risk. Pp. 67-88 in *Family-School Links: How Do They Affect Educational Outcomes?*, A. Booth and J.F. Dunn, eds. Mahwah, N.J.: Lawrence Erlbaum Associates.

Bankston, C.L., III, and M. Zhou
1995 Effects of minority-language literacy on the academic achievement of Vietnamese youth in New Orleans. *Sociology of Education* 68(1):1-17.

Becker, G.S.
1981 *A Treatise on the Family*. Cambridge, Mass.: Harvard University Press.

Blake, J.
1989 *Family Size and Achievement*. Berkeley: University of California Press.

Blau, P.M., and O.D. Duncan
1967 *The American Occupational Structure*. New York: The Free Press.

Board on Children, Youth, and Families, Commission on Behavioral and Social Sciences and Education, National Research Council and Institute of Medicine
1995 Children of immigrants and their families: Issues for research and policy. *The Future of Children* 5(2):72-89.

Boocock, S.S.
1995 Early childhood programs in other nations: Goals and outcomes. *The Future of Children* 5(3):94-114.

Bredekamp, S., ed.
1987 *Developmentally Appropriate Practice in Early Childhood Programs Serving Children from Birth Through Age 8*. Expanded edition. Washington, D.C.: National Association for the Education of Young Children.

Bureau of the Census
1994 *Statistical Abstract of the United States: 1994*, 114th ed. Washington, D.C.

Collins, M., J.M. Brick, M.J. Nolin, N. Vaden-Kiernan, S. Gilmore, K. Chandler, and C. Chapman
1997 *National Household Education Survey of 1996: Data File User's Manual, Volume 1*. NCES 97-425. U.S. Department of Education, National Center for Education Statistics.

Coleman, J.S.
1991 *Parental Involvement in Education*. Policy Perspectives. Washington, D.C.: U.S. Department of Education, Office of Educational Research and Improvement.

Coleman, J.S., T. Hoffer, and S. Kilgore
1982 *High School Achievement: Public, Catholic and Private Schools Compared*. New York: Basic Books.

Csikszentmihalyi, M.
1990 Literacy and intrinsic motivation. *Daedalus, Journal of the American Academy of Arts and Sciences* (Spring):115-140.

Dauber, S.L., and J.L. Epstein
1989 *Parent Attitudes and Practices of Parent Involvement in Inner-City Elementary and Middle Schools*. Report 33. Baltimore: The Johns Hopkins University Center for Social Organization of Schools.

Featherman, D.L., and R.M. Hauser
1978 *Opportunity and Change*. New York: Academic Press.

Hansen, K.A., and C.S. Faber
1997 The Foreign-Born Population: 1996. Current Population Reports, P20-494. Washington, D.C.: Bureau of the Census, U.S. Department of Commerce.

Henderson, A.T., and N. Berla
1994 *A New Generation of Evidence: The Family Is Critical to Student Achievement*. Washington, D.C.: National Committee for Citizens in Education.

Hofferth, S.L., J. West, R. Henke, and P. Kaufman
1994 *Access to Early Childhood Programs for Children at Risk.* NCES 93-372. Washington, D.C.: U.S. Department of Education, National Center for Education Statistics.

Howes, C.
1988 Relations between early child care and schooling. *Developmental Psychology* 24:53-57.

Lee, S.A.
1993 Family structure effects on student outcomes. Pp. 43-75 in *Parents, Their Children, and Schools,* B. Schneider and J.S. Coleman, eds. Boulder, Colo.: Westview Press.

McLanahan, S., and G. Sandefur
1994 *Growing Up with a Single Parent: What Hurts, What Helps.* Cambridge, Mass.: Harvard University Press.

Montaquila, J., and J.M. Brick
1997 *Unit and Item Response Rates, Weighting, and Imputation Procedures in the 1996 National Household Education Survey.* Working Paper. National Center for Education Statistics, U.S. Department of Education, Washington, D.C.

Muller, C.
1993 Parent involvement and academic achievement: An analysis of family resources available to the child. Pp. 77-113 in *Parents, Their Children, and Schools,* B. Schneider and J.S. Coleman, eds. Boulder, Colo.: Westview Press.

National Education Goals Panel
1996 *The National Education Goals Report: Building a Nation of Learners, 1996.* Washington, D.C.: U.S. Government Printing Office.

Nolin, M.J., M. Collins, J.M. Brick, and K. Chandler
1997 *An Overview of the National Household Education Survey: 1991, 1993, 1995, and 1996.* NCES 97-448. National Center for Education Statistics, U.S. Department of Education, Washington, D.C.

Nord, C.W., D. Brimhall, and J. West
1997 *Fathers' Involvement in Their Children's School.* NCES 98-092. Washington, DC: National Center for Education Statistics.

Passel, J.S., and M. Fix
1995 U.S. immigration in a global context: Past, present, and future. *Global Legal Studies Journal* (online) II(1). http://www.law.indiana.educ/glsj/vol2/passel.html#FN15.

Portes, A., and D. MacLeod
1996 Educational progress of children of immigrants: The roles of class, ethnicity, and school context. *Sociology of Education* 69(4):255-275.

Rawlings, S.W.
1994 Household and Family Characteristics: March 1993. Current Population Reports, P20-477. Washington, D.C.: Bureau of the Census, U.S. Department of Commerce.

Rutter, M., B. Maughan, P. Mortimore, and J. Ouston
1979 *Fifteen Thousand Hours*. Cambridge, Mass.: Harvard University Press.

Saluter, A.F.
1996 Marital Status and Living Arrangements: March 1995. Detailed tabulations from the Current Population Survey, PPL-52. Washington, D.C.: Bureau of the Census, U.S. Department of Commerce.

Stewart, A.
1993 *Head Start: A Fact Sheet*. Washington, D.C.: Congressional Research Service.

U.S. Department of Education
1994 *Strong Families, Strong Schools: Building Community Partnerships for Learning*. Washington, D.C.: U.S. Department of Education.

Vaden-Kiernan, N.
1996 Parents' reports of school practices to involve families. In *Statistics in Brief*. Washington, D.C.: National Center for Education Statistics, U.S. Department of Education.

Zill, N.
1996 Family change and student achievement: What we have learned; What it means for schools. Pp. 175-184 in *Family-School Links: How Do They Affect Educational Outcomes?*, A. Booth and J.F. Dunn, eds. Mahwah, N.J.: Lawrence Erlbaum Associates.

Zill, N., M. Collins, J. West, and E.G. Hausken
1995a *Approaching Kindergarten: A Look at Preschoolers in the United States*. Statistical Analysis Report, NCES 95-280. Washington, D.C.: U.S. Department of Education, National Center for Education Statistics.

Zill, N., K.A. Moore, E.W. Smith, T. Stief, and M.J. Coiro
1995b The life circumstances and development of children in welfare families: A profile based on national survey data. In *Escape from Poverty: What Makes a Difference for Poor Children?*, P.L. Chase-Lansdale and J. Brooks-Gunn, eds. New York: Cambridge University Press.

Zill, N., C.W. Nord, and L.S. Loomis
1995c *Adolescent Time Use, Risky Behavior, and Outcomes: An Analysis of National Data*. Report prepared for the Office of Human Services Policy, Office of the Assistant Secretary for Planning and Evaluation, U.S. Department of Health and Human Services, Washington, D.C.

Zill, N., and C.W. Nord
1994 *Running in Place: How American Families Are Faring in a Changing Economy and an Individualistic Society*. Washington, D.C.: Child Trends, Inc.

Zill, N., and E. Wolpow
1991 School readiness: Examining a national goal. *Principal* 70(5):14-18.

APPENDIX 7A: THE 1996 NATIONAL HOUSEHOLD EDUCATION SURVEY

The 1996 National Household Education Survey (NHES:96) is a telephone survey conducted for the U.S. Department of Education, National Center for Education Statistics, by Westat. Data collection took place from January through April 1996. The sample was selected using list-assisted, random digit dialing methods. Adjustments were made so that the totals were consistent with the total number of persons in all (telephone and nontelephone) households. The sample is thus nationally representative of all civilian noninstitutionalized persons in the 50 states and the District of Columbia. Data were collected using computer-assisted telephone interviewing technology.

The Parent and Family Involvement in Education (PFI) component of the NHES:96, which is the basis of this chapter, employed a sample of children ages 3 through grade 12. Up to three instruments were used to collect data on the school and family experiences of these children. A household screener, administered to an adult member of the household, was used to determine whether any children of the appropriate ages or grades lived in the household, to collect information on each household member, and to identify the appropriate parent/guardian respondent for the sampled child. For sampling purposes, children residing in the household were grouped into younger children (age 3 through grade 5) and older children (grades 6 through 12). One younger child and one older child from each household could have been sampled for the NHES:96. If the household contained more than one younger child or more than one older child, one from each category was randomly sampled as an interview subject. An interview was conducted with the parent/guardian most knowledgeable about the subject child regarding the care and education of the child. Following the interview and receipt of parental permission, another interview was conducted with youth in grades 6 through 12. Because the focus of this chapter is the educational experiences of children 3 to 8 years old, only information from the household screener and the parent/guardian interview was used.

Response Rates

The NHES:96 survey completed screeners with 55,838 households, of which 19,337 contained a child sampled for the PFI component. The response rate for the screener was 69.9 percent. The completion rate for the interview with parents of children ages 3 through grade 12 was 89.4 percent. Thus, the overall response rate for the interview with parents of students ages 3 through grade 12 was 62.5 percent (the product of the screener response rate and the parent interview completion rate). This chapter is based on a subset of the total PFI population: children 3 to 8 years old. The unweighted number of cases included in this analysis is 7,717. Of these, 1,178 are children of immigrants.

For the NHES:96, item nonresponse (the failure to complete some of the items in an otherwise completed interview) was very low. The item nonresponse rates for most variables used in this chapter were less than 2 percent. Items with missing responses (i.e., don't know, refused, or not ascertained) were imputed using a hot-deck[9] procedure. As a result, no missing values remain.

Description of Variables

A number of variables used in this chapter were derived by combining information from two or more questions in the NHES:96. The derivation of such variables is described in this section. The NHES:96 files contain a few composite variables (such as language usually spoken at home by parent(s) and education of most educated parent in the household). Composite variables included in the NHES:96 file are not described. See the NHES:96 *User's Manual* (Collins et al., 1997) for copies of the screener, survey instruments, and a description of the composite variables included in the file.

Immigrant Status

The screener to NHES:96 asked if everyone in the household was born in one of the 50 states or the District of Columbia. If the

[9]A hot-deck procedure involves matching on selected variables and randomly selecting a subset that comes close.

answer was *no*, the screener respondent was asked in what country each person was born. On the NHES:96 file this information was coded into three categories: (1) 50 states or the District of Columbia; (2) U.S. territories: Puerto Rico, Guam, American Samoa, U.S. Virgin Islands, Mariana Islands, or Solomon Islands; and (3) some other country. Linking the person numbers[10] of the child's parents to the person numbers of the household members, the birthplace of each parent was established. Parents were classified as native born if they were born in the United States or one of its territories. They were classified as foreign born if they were born elsewhere. A similar procedure was followed to determine whether the subject children were born in the United States or one of its territories or in another country.

Children were classified as being children of immigrants if at least one of their parents was born in a country other than the United States or one of its territories. No information was available on parents not living in the household. For children not living with both their biological parents, there could be some misassignment of children to nonimmigrant status. For example, if children had a foreign-born father and an American mother but the father was no longer in their household, the children would be misclassified as children of native-born parents.

Number of Parents

The NHES:96 asked respondents the relationship of each household member to the subject child. If a mother was identified, the respondent was asked whether the mother was the birth mother, adoptive mother, stepmother, or foster mother. A parallel question was asked about the father in the household. This information was used to classify children as living in two-parent families with both biological parents, living in other two-parent families, or living in single-parent families. Children not living with either parent were excluded from the analyses.

[10]The survey gave each person in a household a distinct number, which is used to distinguish easily between members of a household.

Number of Siblings and Other Relatives in Household

These indicators were created by examining the relationship of each household member to the subject child. Simple counters were created that increased by one each time the appropriate relationship (sibling, grandparent, other relative) was identified. The counter of the number of siblings present in the household was topcoded at three or more. The number of grandparents and the number of other relatives were recoded into dichotomous variables that took a value of zero if no such relative was present and a value of one otherwise.

Poverty Measure

The poverty measure presented in this chapter was developed by combining information about household composition and household income. In the NHES:96, household income was collected in increments of $5,000; however, exact income to the nearest $1,000 was also collected if the household's poverty status was ambiguous based on the increment reported. A household's size and income were compared to the poverty thresholds provided by the Bureau of the Census. A household is considered poor if:

- the number of household members is two and household income is $10,259 or less;
- the number of household members is three and household income is $12,158 or less;
- the number of household members is four and household income is $16,000 or less;
- the number of household members is five and household income is $18,408 or less;
- the number of household members is six and household income is $21,000 or less;
- the number of household members is seven and household income is $24,000 or less;
- the number of household members is eight and household income is $26,237 or less; or
- the number of household members is nine or more and household income is $31,280 or less.

This poverty measure results in 26 percent of children ages 3 to 8 years being classified as living in poverty in the NHES:96. This percentage is similar to traditional measures of poverty (Saluter, 1996).

Receipt of Federal Assistance

Respondents were asked: "In the past 12 months, has your family received funds or services from any of the following programs? . . . (a) Women, Infants, and Children, or WIC? (b) Food stamps? (c) AFDC or Aid to Families with Dependent Children?" Respondents who answered *yes* to any of the three sources of assistance were classified as having received federal assistance in the past 12 months.

Parental Involvement at School

The NHES:96 asked about four types of school activities that parents could participate in during the school year. The activities are typical of those available in most schools: attendance at a general school meeting, attendance at a regularly scheduled parent-teacher conference, attendance at a school or class event, and serving as a volunteer at school. Two question formats were used to ask respondents about attendance at a general school meeting. Half of the sample was asked a single question, while the other half was asked two questions about different types of school meetings. The single question asked about attendance at a general school meeting—for example, an open house, a back-to-school night, or a meeting of a parent-teacher organization. The two questions asked about attendance at an open house or back-to-school night and attendance at a meeting of a parent-teacher or parent-teacher-student organization. To create a single variable about attendance at a school meeting, the two items asked in the second set were combined.

The indicator of parental involvement was created by counting the number of school activities that an adult in the household had participated in. The indicator ranges from zero (parent or other adult in the household participated in none of the four activities) to four (a parent or other adult participated in all four activities). As noted in the text, parents were said to have low involvement in their children's schools if they had done none or only one of the four activities. They were categorized as having moderate involvement if they had done two of the activities. And they were categorized as having high involvement if they had participated in at least three of the four activities.

Child Gets Mostly A's

If parents reported that their children received mostly A's in school, this dichotomous variable was assigned a value of one. If parents reported that their children received mostly B's, C's, D's, or F's in school, the variable was assigned a value of zero. Some children attended schools that did not give letter grades. For these children, if parents reported that their children's work was *excellent*, the children were coded as receiving mostly A's; otherwise, the children received a value of zero on this variable.

Child Participates in Extracurricular Activities

Parents of children in kindergarten through grade 5 were asked whether their child had participated in any school activities such as team sports, band, chorus, or safety patrol. They were also asked whether during the school year the child had participated in any activities outside school, such as music lessons, church or temple youth group, scouting, or organized team sports, like soccer. If parents reported *yes* to either of these questions, the child was said to have participated in extracurricular activities; otherwise, the child was said not to have participated.

Problems in School

This variable was created by combining answers to three different questions. Parents of children attending early childhood programs were asked if a teacher or provider had contacted them because of any problems that the child was having there. Parents of children in kindergarten and above were asked two questions. The first was whether a teacher had contacted them this year about any behavioral problems the child was having. The second was whether a teacher had contacted them this year about any problems with schoolwork that the child was having. Children were said to have problems if their parents said *yes* to any of these questions. Otherwise, they were said to have not had any problems at school this year. Children not enrolled in school were not included in analyses of this variable.

Appendix Tables 7A-1 through 7A-5 follow

TABLE 7A-1 Percentage of Children with Selected Personal and Family Characteristics by Immigrant Status and Child's Race and Ethnicity: Children Ages 3 to 8, 1996

Characteristic	Total: Children Ages 3-8	Children of Immigrants	
		Total	Native-Born
Total (thousands)	22,959	3,213	2,782
Child's Characteristics			
Age			
3 to 4 years	34%	36%	38%
4 to 5 years	33	35	36
7 to 8 years	33	29	26
Sex			
Male	51	52	54
Female	49	48	46
Race/ethnicity			
White, non-Hispanic	65	26	27
Black, non-Hispanic	16	9	9
Hispanic	15	54	53
Asian	1	7	7
Other	3	4	4
Family Composition			
Number of parents			
Two biological parents	65	77	77
Other two-parent family	8	4	4
One-parent family	28	19	19
Number of siblings			
None	17	14	14
One	43	39	40
Two	26	27	27
Three or more	15	19	19
Presence of grandparents			
None	94	93	92
One or more	6	7	8
Presence of other relatives			
None	94	91	91
One or more	6	9	9

Foreign-Born	Hispanic	Asian	White
430	1,734	239	837
21%	37%	41%	30%
34	36	31	38
45	27	28	31
40	55	43	49
60	45	57	51
22	0	0	100
5	0	0	0
60	100	0	0
10	0	100	0
3	0	0	0
77	72	88	88
6	4	3	4
17	24	9	8
15	11	26	16
35	33	36	51
33	31	28	24
17	26	11	9
98	94	82	95
2	6	18	5
89	90	90%	95
11	10	10	5

continued on next page

TABLE 7A-1 Continued

Characteristic	Total: Children Ages 3-8	Children of Immigrants	
		Total	Native-Born
Human and Financial Capital			
Education of most educated parent in household			
Less than high school	9%	23%	22%
High school graduate or equivalent	31	27	28
Vocational/technical school or some college	31	21	21
College graduate	16	16	16
Graduate or professional school	12	14	13
Language parents usually speak at home			
Both/only English	91	43	45
One English/one non-English	2	9	9
Both/only non-English	8	49	45
Language child speaks at home			
English	92	50	52
Spanish	5	33	32
Spanish/English equally	2	9	8
Other language	1	8	7
Household income			
< $15,000	24	32	31
$15,000-$25,000	16	22	21
$25,000-$35,000	14	11	11
$35,000-$50,000	18	13	14
$50,000-$75,000	15	11	11
< $75,000	12	11	11
Household income below poverty threshold	26	36	35
Received federal assistance (WIC, food stamps, or AFDC) in past 12 months	28	37	38
Received WIC in past 12 months	16	24	25

Foreign-Born	Hispanic	Asian	White
30%	36%	4%	5%
23	34	22	19
15	18	19	24
16	7	27	26
16	4	28	27
25	18	26	80
6	11	6	8
69	71	68	12
35	23	45	88
37	59	0	2
15	17	1	1
13	1	54	9
35	45	30	11
31	29	12	13
10	11	7	13
9	8	19	18
9	4	15	21
6	3	18	24
45	53	32	11
30	52	26	13
18	35	17	5

continued on next page

TABLE 7A-1 Continued

Characteristic	Total: Children Ages 3-8	Children of Immigrants	
		Total	Native-Born
Received food stamps in past 12 months	21	25	26
Received AFDC in past 12 months	13	11	12
Home ownership			
Own home	57	45	49
Rent home	38	50	46
Other Arrangement	5	5	5

TABLE 7A-1 Continued: Children of Native-Born

Characteristic	Children of Native-Born			
	Total	White	Black	Hispanic
Total (thousands)	19,746	14,166	3,326	1,652
Child's Characteristics				
Age				
3 to 4 years	33%	32%	35%	39%
4 to 5 years	33	33	33	32
7 to 8 years	34	35	32	30
Sex				
Male	51	51	48	54
Female	49	49	52	46
Race/ethnicity				
White, non-Hispanic	72	100	0	0
Black, non-Hispanic	17	0	100	0
Hispanic	8	0	0	100
Asian	<1	0	0	0
Other	3	0	0	0
Family Composition				
Number of parents				
Two biological parents	63	73	29	49
Other two-parent family	8	9	6	10
One-parent family	29	19	65	42

Foreign-Born	Hispanic	Asian	White
17	37	17	7
7	16	6	4
22	35	50	67
77	58	49	30
1	7	1	3

TABLE 7A-1 Continued: Children of Native-Born

	Children of Native-Born			
Characteristic	Total	White	Black	Hispanic
Number of siblings				
None	17	16	21	16
One	43	45	36	39
Two	26	26	25	29
Three or more	14	13	17	15
Presence of grandparents				
None	94	96	88	91
One or more	6	4	12	9
Presence of other relatives				
None	95	97	85	91
One or more	5	3	15	9
Human and Financial Capital				
Education of most educated parent in household				
Less than high school	7	4	14	17
High school graduate or equivalent	32	29	41	34

continued on next page

TABLE 7A-1 Continued: Children of Native-Born

Characteristic	Children of Native-Born			
	Total	White	Black	Hispanic
Vocational/technical school or some college	33%	33%	33%	34%
College graduate	16	19	8	10
Graduate or professional school	12	15	4	6
Language parents usually speak at home				
Both/only English	99	100	100	87
One English/ one non-English	0	0	0	3
Both/only non-English	1	0	0	10
Language child speaks at home				
English	99	100	100	89
Spanish	1	0	0	6
Spanish/English equally	1	0	0	5
Other language	0	0	0	0
Household income				
< $15,000	23	15	52	36
$15,000-$25,000	16	15	16	20
$25,000-$35,000	15	16	11	14
$35,000-$50,000	19	21	12	15
$50,000-$75,000	16	19	5	10
< $75,000	12	15	3	7
Household income below poverty threshold	24	15	52	36

TABLE 7A-1 Continued: Children of Native-Born

Characteristic	Children of Native-Born			
	Total	White	Black	Hispanic
Received federal assistance (WIC, food stamps, or AFDC) in past 12 months	27%	18%	55%	42%
Received WIC in past 12 months	14	10	26	21
Received food stamps in past 12 months	20	12	48	35
Received AFDC in past 12 months	14	8	34	22
Home ownership				
Own home	59	70	26	39
Rent home	36	26	67	55
Other arrangement	5	4	8	6

NOTE: Hispanic children are designated as such and are not included in any of the other racial or ethnic categories. The *Total* columns include children of other races and ethnicities not shown. Because of rounding, percentages may not sum to 100.

SOURCE: U.S. Department of Education, National Center for Education Statistics, 1996 National Household Education Survey.

TABLE 7A-2 Percentage of Children with Selected Types of Social Capital by Immigrant Status: Children Ages 3 to 8, 1996

Characteristic	Total: Children 3-8 Years	Children of Immigrants	
		Total	Native-Born
Total (thousands)	22,959	3,213	2,782
Family Involvement at Home			
In the past week, someone in family:			
Taught child letters, words, or numbers[a]	93%	92%	93%
Taught child songs or music[a]	76	73	73
Took child along while doing errands[a]	95	91	90
Number of times read to child[b]:			
Not at all	7	11	11
Once or twice	20	26	25
Three or more times	28	25	26
Every day	44	37	38
Told child a story	77	76	77
Worked on arts and crafts project with child	72	65	66
Played a game, sport, or exercised with child	92	86	87
Involved child in household chores	95	86	86
Worked on a project with child like building, making, or fixing something[c]	67	56	58
In the past month, someone in the family:			
Visited the library with child	44	38	38
Went to a play, concert, or other live show with the child	30	26	27
Visited an art gallery, museum, or historical attraction with child	20	20	20
Visited a zoo or aquarium with child	17	23	23
Talked with child about family history or ethnic heritage	52	55	54
Attended an event with child sponsored by a community, ethnic, or religious group	50	41	41
Attended an athletic or sporting event in which child was not a player	33	22	24

Foreign-Born	Hispanic	Asian	White
430	1,734	239	837
86%	90%	97%	94%
68	70	72	78
97	88	79	99
13	14	6	7
34	32	18	17
23	25	25	24
31	29	51	51
74	71	83	84
59	59	74	74
82	81	92	94
83	84	74	90
51	47	59	69
32	27	54	51
21	21	34	33
17	15	24	27
21	20	32	26
60	52	50	61
39	35	38	51
12	18	19	30

continued on next page

TABLE 7A-2 Continued

Characteristic	Total: Children 3-8 Years	Children of Immigrants	
		Total	Native-Born
Family Involvement at School			
Parents' involvement in school[d]			
Low	15%	17%	17%
Moderate	21	26	25
High	64	57	58
Parent attended a general school meeting	83	82	83
Parent attended class or school event	67	61	61
Parent volunteered at school	51	38	41
Parent attended parent-teacher conference	79	82	81

TABLE 7A-2 Continued: Children of Native-Born

Characteristic	Children of Native-Born			
	Total	White	Black	Hispanic
Total (thousands)	19,746	14,166	3,326	1,652
Family Involvement at Home				
In the past week, someone in family:				
Taught child letters, words, or numbers[a]	94%	93%	96%	91%
Taught child songs or music[a]	76	76	83	69
Took child along while doing errands[a]	95	96	94	94
Number of times read to child[b]:				
Not at all	7	6	8	8
Once or twice	19	17	25	24
Three or more times	29	28	30	29
Every day	45	48	37	39
Told child a story	77	78	73	79

Foreign-Born	Hispanic	Asian	White
17%	21%	13%	10%
33	30	30	20
50	49	57	70
78	79	81	87
60	54	56	73
24	29	36	54
84	83	88	86

TABLE 7A-2 Continued: Children of Native-Born

	Children of Native-Born			
Characteristic	Total	White	Black	Hispanic
Worked on arts and crafts project with child	73%	75%	66%	72%
Played a game, sport, or exercised with child	93	94	92	87
Involved child in household chores	96	97	95	92
Worked on a project with child like building, making, or fixing something[c]	68	70	63	67
In the past month, someone in the family:				
Visited the library with child	45	47	40	39

continued on next page

TABLE 7A-2 Continued: Children of Native-Born

	Children of Native-Born			
Characteristic	Total	White	Black	Hispanic
Went to a play, concert, or other live show with the child	30%	29%	36%	27%
Visited an art gallery, museum, or historical attraction with child	20	19	22	20
Visited a zoo or aquarium with child	16	14	23	21
Talked with child about family history or ethnic heritage	51	47	65	54
Attended an event with child sponsored by a community, ethnic, or religious group	51	52	52	43
Attended an athletic or sporting event in which child was not a player	35	36	33	27
Family Involvement at School				
Parents' involvement in school[d]				
Low	15	13	21	17
Moderate	20	19	23	24
High	65	68	56	59
Parent attended a general school meeting	84	84	81	82
Parent attended class or school event	68	71	57	64
Parent volunteered at school	53	56	42	46
Parent attended parent-teacher conference	79	79	76	78

[a]Applies only to children not yet in first grade.
[b]Applies to children age 3 through grade 3.
[c]Applies to children in grades 1 and above.
[d]Applies to children enrolled in preschool programs or regular school.

NOTE: Hispanic children are designated as such and are not included in any of the other racial or ethnic categories. The *Total* columns include children of other races and ethnicities. Because of rounding, percentages may not sum to 100.

SOURCE: U.S. Department of Education, National Center for Education Statistics, 1996 National Household Education Survey.

TABLE 7A-3 FOLLOWS

TABLE 7A-3 Percentage of Children Enrolled in School and Selected Characteristics of Their Schools by Immigrant Status and Child's Race and Ethnicity: Children Ages 3 to 8, 1996

Characteristic	Total: Children Ages 3-8	Children of Immigrants	
		Total	Native-Born
Total (thousands)	22,959	3,213	2,782
Attends an early childhood program[a]	55%	41%	42%
Attends government-sponsored early childhood program[b]	33	45	44
Proportion of eligible children attending Head Start[a,c]	38	25	26
School Characteristics[d]			
Public school			
Assigned	70	69	69
Chosen	17	16	16
Private school:			
Religious affiliation	10	10	10
No religious affiliation	3	5	5
Size of school			
<300 students	25	22	23
300-599	47	46	46
600-999	19	20	19
>1,000	9	13	11

Foreign-Born	Hispanic	Asian	White
430	1,734	239	837
27%	31%	35%	57%
e	76	*e*	19
20	25	22	18
72	80	64	59
17	15	16	13
7	4	13	16
4	1	7	13
14	16	42	31
43	47	34	47
20	20	16	17
23	17	8	5

continued on next page

TABLE 7A-3 Continued

	Children of Native-Born			
Characteristic	Total	White	Black	Hispanic
Total (thousands)	19,746	14,166	3,326	1,652
Attends an early childhood program[a]	58%	58%	66%	47%
Attends government-sponsored early childhood program[b]	32	23	58	46
Proportion of eligible children attending Head Start[a,c]	46	33	62	33
School Characteristics[d]				
Public school				
Assigned	71	72	67	68
Chosen	17	14	25	22
Private school				
Religious affiliation	10	11	6	10
No religious affiliation	3	3	3	<1
Size of school				
<300 students	26	28	22	19
300-599	47	47	48	47
600-999	19	18	20	22
>1,000	8	8	10	12

[a]Restricted to children not enrolled in kindergarten or higher grade.

[b]Restricted to children enrolled in an early childhood program.

[c]Estimate obtained by dividing the proportion of children enrolled in Head Start by the proportion of children whose household incomes were below the poverty threshold.

[d]Restricted to children enrolled in kindergarten or higher grade.

[e]Too few cases to reliably estimate.

NOTE: Hispanic children are designated as such and are not included in any of the other racial or ethnic categories. The *Total* columns include children of other races and ethnicities not shown. Because of rounding, percentages may not sum to 100.

SOURCE: U.S. Department of Education, National Center for Education Statistics, 1996 National Household Education Survey.

TABLE 7A-4 FOLLOWS

TABLE 7A-4 Percentage of Children by Their School Environments, Practices of Schools to Involve Their Parents, and by Immigrant Status and Child's Race and Ethnicity: Children Ages 3 to 8, 1996

Characteristic	Total: Children Ages 3-8	Children of Immigrants	
		Total	Native-Born
Total (thousands)	22,959	3,213	2,782
School Environment[a]			
Strongly agree that:			
Teachers maintain discipline in classroom	52%	47%	48%
Principal maintains discipline in school	51	48	50
Teachers and students respect each other	45	38	40
School Practices			
Strongly agree that:			
School welcomes family's involvement	63	53	55
School makes involvement easy[a]	56	45	47
School is understanding of needs of families who don't speak English[a,b] (Yes)	95	95	94
How often school provides newsletters, memos, or notices to all parents			
0 times	5	8	8
1-2 times	8	9	9
3 or more times	87	82	82
How well school has been doing at:			
Letting parent know how child is doing in school/program			
Very well	68	71	70
Could do better	23	21	21
Doesn't do well	9	8	9
Helping parent understand developmental stages of children			
Very well	53	57	56
Could do better	30	28	29
Doesn't do	17	15	15
Letting parent know of volunteer opportunities at school			
Very well	73	67	67
Could do better	19	23	23
Doesn't do	8	10	10

Foreign-Born	Hispanic	Asian	White
430	1,734	239	837
40%	36%	48%	62%
42	39	57	64
33	30	37	52
40	39	60	70
38	38	40	58
99	97	95	*c*
7	10	12	6
10	10	10	7
83	80	77	88
76	73	61	68
20	19	32	22
4	7	7	9
64	64	53	49
23	24	39	34
13	12	8	17
72	64	60	74
21	25	35	17
7	11	5	9

continued on next page

TABLE 7A-4 Continued

Characteristic	Total: Children Ages 3-8	Children of Immigrants	
		Total	Native-Born
Providing information about how to help child with homework[a]			
Very well	54%	65%	63%
Could do better	29	25	26
Doesn't do	17	11	11
Providing information about why child is placed in particular groups or classes[a]			
Very well	48	53	52
Could do better	24	21	21
Doesn't do	28	26	27

TABLE 7A-4 Continued: Children of Native-Born

Characteristic	Children of Native-Born			
	Total	White	Black	Hispanic
Total (thousands)	19,746	14,166	3,326	1,652
School Environment[a]				
Strongly agree that:				
Teachers maintain discipline in classroom	53%	55%	43%	49%
Principal maintains discipline in school	51	54	44	45
Teachers and students respect each other	46	48	36	44
School Practices				
Strongly agree that:				
School welcomes family's involvement	65	67	56	58
School makes involvement easy[a]	57	60	49	52

Foreign-Born	Hispanic	Asian	White
73%	73%	58%	51%
19	21	29	28
8	6	13	17
61	57	43	51
17	18	38	23
21	24	20	26

TABLE 7A-4 Continued: Children of Native-Born

Characteristic	Children of Native-Born Total	White	Black	Hispanic
School is understanding of needs of families who don't speak English[a,b] (Yes)	c	c	c	c
How often school provides newsletters, memos, or notices to all parents				
0 times	4%	4%	6%	7%
1-2 times	8	6	11	12
3 or more times	88	90	83	81
How well school has been doing at:				
Letting parent know how child is doing in school/program				
Very well	68	66	72	72
Could do better	23	24	21	20
Doesn't do well	9	9	7	8

continued on next page

TABLE 7A-4 Continued

Characteristic	Children of Native-Born			
	Total	White	Black	Hispanic
Helping parent understand developmental stages of children				
Very well	52%	50%	58%	52%
Could do better	31	32	25	32
Doesn't do	17	18	17	16
Letting parent know of volunteer opportunities at school				
Very well	74	75	72	74
Could do better	18	18	20	16
Doesn't do	8	8	9	10
Providing information about how to help child with homework[a]				
Very well	53	50	59	57
Could do better	30	33	22	24
Doesn't do	17	17	19	19
Providing information about why child is placed in particular groups or classes[a]				
Very well	47	45	51	58
Could do better	25	27	19	20
Doesn't do	28	28	31	22

[a]Applies only to children in grade 1 and above.
[b]Only asked if household respondent spoke a language other than English.
[c]Too few cases to reliably estimate.

NOTE: Hispanic children are designated as such and are not included in any of the other racial or ethnic categories. The *Total* columns include children of other races and ethnicities not shown. Because of rounding, percentages may not add to 100.

SOURCE: U.S. Department of Education, National Center for Education Statistics, 1996 National Household Education Survey.

TABLE 7A-5 FOLLOWS

TABLE 7A-5 Percentage of Children with Selected Student Outcomes by Immigrant Status and Children's Race and Ethnicity: Children Ages 3 to 8, 1996

Characteristic	Total: Children Ages 3-8	Children of Immigrants	
		Total	Native-Born
Total (thousands)	22,959	3,213	2,782
Student Outcome			
Child gets mostly A's[a]	58%	54%	54%
Child enjoys school[a]	50	45	46
Child participates in extracurricular activities[b]	74	63	65
Child experienced problems at school[b]	29	25	26
Child ever repeated a grade[b]	5	5	5

TABLE 7A-5 Continued: Children of Native-Born

Characteristic	Children of Native-Born			
	Total	White	Black	Hispanic
Total (thousands)	19,746	14,166	3,326	1,652
Student Outcome				
Child gets mostly A's[a]	58%	43%	38%	40%
Child enjoys school[a]	51	52	47	48
Child participates in extracurricular activities[b]	76	79	71	57
Child experienced problems at school[b]	29	27	39	31
Child ever repeated a grade[b]	5	4	6	7

NOTE: Hispanic children are designated as such and are not included in any of the other racial or ethnic categories. The *Total* columns include children of other races and ethnicities not shown. Because of rounding, percentages may not sum to 100.

[a]Applies to children in grades 1 and above.
[b]Applies to children in kindergarten and higher grades.

SOURCE: U.S. Department of Education, National Center for Education Statistics, 1996 National Household Education Survey.

Foreign-Born	Hispanic	Asian	White
430	1,734	239	837
53%	41%	63%	51%
37	37	51	56
56	49	78	79
24	30	17	22
6	8	3	3

CHAPTER 8

Psychological Well-Being and Educational Achievement Among Immigrant Youth[1]

Grace Kao

Since enactment of the Immigration and Naturalization Act of 1965, the United States has witnessed a large influx of immigrants who are diverse in their ethnic and social backgrounds. The 1965 act eliminated severe restrictions on Asia and Africa by placing identical numerical limits on migrants from all countries, including those of the Western Hemisphere. Unlike earlier waves of immigrants who were predominantly European, most post-1965 immigrants to the United States have come from Asia and Latin America.

The new immigrants have generated much research about their experiences, but most of the studies have focused on the *socioeconomic* attainment of adult migrants. As a result, researchers know little about the *social-psychological* costs to those who migrate. In addition, research on adult migrants is more comprehensive than that on children. Children of adult migrants may suffer more than their native peers in managing two conflicting worlds—their parents and their peers. Moreover, the increased diversity in metropolitan-area schools is largely driven by the growing numbers of Hispanic and Asian children. For instance, the Population Reference Bureau (1989) has estimated that over

[1]An earlier draft of this paper was presented at the annual meeting of the Population Association of America, Washington, D.C., March 1997.

half of all students from 49 of the 100 largest school districts are black, Hispanic, or Asian.

INTRODUCTION

This chapter focuses on immigrant and ethnic differences in social-psychological well-being and educational achievement of adolescent youth. The focus is on the following questions: How do immigrant (first-generation) children and native-born children of immigrants (second-generation children) differ from native-born (third-generation and beyond) whites of native-born parents in their psychological well-being? Second, to what extent can generational differences in psychological well-being be attributed to difficulty with English, prior educational experiences, and enrollment in specialized programs? Third, how are generational differences in psychological well-being associated with educational performance?

This chapter is organized as follows. First, I review previous research that implies three social-psychological dimensions on which immigrant children may differ from native-born children. I then review racial, ethnic, and generational patterns of educational achievement and explore why there is an apparent anomaly as immigrant children may have lower self-perceptions yet still manage to do well in school, despite the well-documented link between mental health and educational performance among adolescents (Covington, 1984; March, 1986; Rosenberg, 1989; Rosenberg et al., 1989). Then I describe the data, from the National Education Longitudinal Study (NELS) of 1988, used for the analyses. Next, descriptive and empirical analyses are explained, focusing on the relationship between immigrant status and psychological well-being, as well as the link between psychological well-being and educational performance.

Psychological Stress of Immigration on Adults and Children

While historic and ethnographic research on the adaptation processes of immigrant adults clearly documents the immense stress and burden on self-esteem that accompanies settlement in a foreign locale, it is less clear whether children suffer comparable stress. Anecdotal evidence suggests that children may adapt to American society more quickly, since they learn English faster than their adult counterparts. In addition, children may be less committed to or knowledgeable about cultural practices of their parents' country of origin; therefore, their acculturation process may be less strained.

Immigrant children and children of immigrants may, however, experience additional sources of anxiety. Children of immigrant parents must maneuver through the world of their parents and that of mainstream America. Moreover, norms of parent-child relationships in middle-class America may be at odds with norms of parental authority in the country of origin (Dornbusch et al., 1987). Increased reliance on children further threatens traditional parental authority when children serve as translators, since they may be the only members of their families who speak and write English well enough to communicate with others. They are more likely than children of native-born parents to assume adult-like roles at an early age, since they become their family's only means of communicating with English-speaking society. While these experiences may extend a sense of empowerment to children in immigrant families, more likely such children may be embarrassed by their parents' inability to function in an English-speaking adult world. Moreover, they may resent their parents for subjecting them to adult responsibilities in contrast to the American notion of a childhood free of such chores.

Psychological Well-Being of Immigrant Youth

Because immigrant minority youth experience greater psychological strains in their adaptation process than native-born whites, I explore the aspects of psychological well-being that are most likely to differentiate immigrant adolescents from their native-born counterparts. Since the migration experience has been documented to produce significant psychological distress, "even among the best prepared and most motivated and even under the most receptive of circumstances" (Portes and Rumbaut, 1990:144), it is worthwhile to examine how immigrant youth and native-born youth of immigrant parents differ in psychological well-being from native-born youth of native-born parents.

First, youth from immigrant families may feel greater alienation among their school peers (Padilla and Durán, 1995). The extent to which recent arrivals to the United States are isolated at school can be devastating, since they are not only visibly foreign to native white youth but also to their native-born ethnic counterparts. Feelings of alienation among immigrant adolescents stem not only from visual cues such as dress but also their lack of fluency in English. In fact, recent immigrants are sometimes referred to as being "fresh off the boat" by their ethnic counterparts. Native-born ethnics may be extremely motivated to differentiate themselves (who only look nonwhite) from same ethnics (who not only look nonwhite but have "foreign" customs and beliefs) in order to make themselves seem more American. Because minority immigrant youth face additional difficulties stemming from their minority and "foreigner" status, one might expect them to report higher rates of alienation from school peers.

Moreover, they may suffer in terms of their self-esteem and feelings of self-efficacy (Padilla and Durán, 1995). Immigrant youth may have diminished feelings of self-efficacy because adapting to life in the United States can promote feelings of helplessness (Portes and Rumbaut, 1990). Refugee groups such as the Indochinese or Cubans as well as more recent arrivals may be especially vulnerable to feelings of low self-efficacy since they are more likely to attribute their circumstances to influences beyond their control. Self-efficacy is an especially vital dimension of adolescent well-being because it signals the extent to which teenagers believe they can influence their future outcomes. Youth who believe they have much control over the direction of their lives are more likely to take responsibility for their actions and are more motivated to work toward their ambitions (Bandura, 1993, 1995). Therefore, self-efficacy fosters motivation, thus promoting engagement in learning activities that lead to increased proficiency in educational skills (Bandura, 1995; Zimmerman, 1995). Hence, self-efficacy is associated with elevated aspirations and achievement.

Immigrant and minority youth may also be prone to low self-esteem as they come to terms with issues of self-identification (Rumbaut, 1994). Some researchers have argued that because immigrant adolescents are more likely to encounter stressful events, they may be at greater risk of low self-esteem (Padilla and Durán, 1995). For instance, Padilla and Durán concluded from their study of immigrant youth that "immigrant students have very low self-images in general and low appraisals of their intellectual, physical, or social attributes" (Padilla and Durán, 1995:139). However, while Padilla and Durán documented the source of stress in the lives of immigrant Mexican students, they did not provide comparable data for native-born whites. Thus, it is unclear whether immigrant youth suffer in their overall mental health relative to white native-born youth.

Ethnic and Immigrant Patterns in Educational Achievement

Researchers agree that there is a positive relationship between self-esteem and grades (and self-efficacy and grades), although the causal order between psychological well-being and grade performance is unclear (Rosenberg et al., 1995). For instance, Covington (1984) argues that the lower academic performance of some minority youth stems from their lower self-esteem. Thus, in order to improve their academic performance, school intervention programs must focus on raising the self-esteem of minority students. Other researchers (Rosenberg et al., 1989) argue that grades have a stronger effect on self-esteem than self-esteem has on grades. They posit that, while there is some reciprocal influence between performance and self-esteem, the primary causal mechanism is that performance leads to changes in self-esteem. Since I am primarily concerned with how the relationship between these characteristics may differ for immigrant youth and because the data I use are cross-sectional, I cannot evaluate the debate regarding the correct causal order between grades and psychological well-being.

Despite myriad reasons to be concerned with the psychological well-being of immigrant children and the well-known association between social-psychological status and educational achievement, recent studies suggest that immigrant youth and native-born youth of immigrant parents perform well in school (Rumbaut, 1990; Caplan et al., 1991; Kao and Tienda, 1995). Since positive self-perceptions are associated with higher scholastic achievement, one may expect immigrant children to earn lower grades than their native-born counterparts (Covington, 1984). However, immigrant children, on average, earn similar or higher grades than their same-race third-generation counterparts (Kao and Tienda, 1995). Despite the additional stresses experienced by immigrant children, they manage to excel at school. In fact, much of the literature on Asian American youth focuses on their educational successes (Sue and Okazaki, 1990; Kao, 1995). Many recent studies of the schooling experiences of immigrant children comment on the propensity of teachers to prefer recent immigrants to their more "Americanized" counterparts because they are often more responsive to the authority of teachers (Rumbaut, 1995). However, there is no concrete evidence that teachers favor immigrant youth in their evaluation of students' schoolwork.

DATA AND DEFINITION OF VARIABLES

To explore our research questions, I used the 1988 NELS. This national survey utilized a two-stage probability sampling design that first selected a nationally representative sample of 1,052 schools, from which 24,599 eighth graders were surveyed. The study then followed them at two-year intervals through 1994, when most of the sample members were about 20 years old. It is unique not only because it began before the transition to high school, thus capturing a psychologically tumultuous period, but also because it oversampled Hispanics and Asians. In addition, NELS also surveyed school administrators, parents, and teachers (National Center for Education Statistics, 1990). Because NELS oversampled Hispanics and Asians and because it interviewed parents and students, immigrant differences in psychological well-being and educational achievement can be examined. Because the base-year survey included more recent immigrants and larger samples of minority students, for these analyses I relied solely on the 1988 base-year survey.

DESCRIPTIVE TABULATIONS

Overall, immigrant Asian, Hispanic, and black youth tend to have lower psychological well-being scores. Figure 8-1 presents race and generational differences in locus of control or feelings of

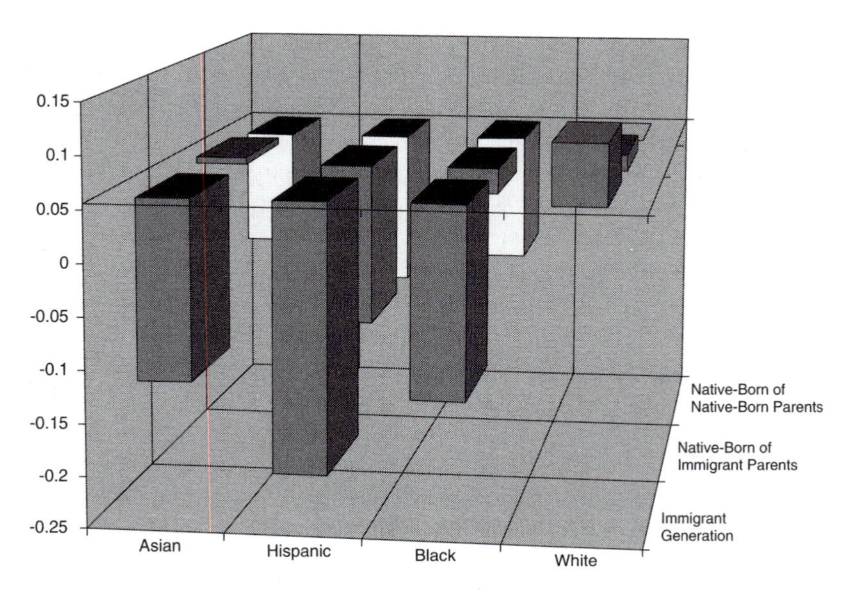

FIGURE 8-1 Locus of control by race and generational status. The baseline is the score of white third-generation youth (native-born children of native-born parents).

self-efficacy in graphic form. (These are the same numbers that appear in Table 8-1 under "Locus of control"). Locus of control was constructed by NCES from a battery of six questions. The average scores of all nonmissing items were taken and then standardized such that the mean score is zero and the standard deviation is one. Simply put, the higher the score, the more a youth feels in control of his or her life (for more detailed information about how these variables were constructed, see Table 8-2). The floor or baseline of this graph (as well as subsequent figures) is set at the level of white native-born youth of native-born parents. This group (white native-born youth of native-born parents) is the logical comparison group because they are the majority both in terms of race and immigrant status. The colors of the bar correspond with their immigrant status, such that light gray columns correspond to immigrant youth, dark gray bars represent native-born youth with one immigrant parent, and white columns depict native-born youth with native-born parents. Immigrant youth who are Asian, Hispanic, or black all suffer from a depressed sense of control over their lives. In addition, Hispanic youth of any generational status feel less self-efficacy than native-born whites with native-born parents. The graph clearly shows the influence of minority status on self-efficacy for blacks, Hispanics, and Asians; in addition, immigrant minority youth clearly suffer in their feelings of control over their lives compared to native-born whites with native-born parents. The patterns in this figure are consistent with findings on adult immigrants; immigrant status coupled with minority status negatively influences feelings of self-efficacy.

I also examined racial and generational differences in self-concept (or self-esteem). Overall, I did not find a consistent pattern among the racial/generational groups in self-esteem, except that black youth tend to have extremely positive self-conceptions.[2] Numerous researchers have found this apparent anomaly and explain it by stressing the importance of family and friends in determining the self-esteem of black youth and the relative lack of influence of others' views of them. For instance, Hughes and Demo (1989) argue that blacks' belief that racial discrimination limits their socioeconomic opportunities becomes reflected in their relatively low self-efficacy but not their self-esteem. Self-esteem is determined primarily by significant others such as friends and family rather than the society (or school) at large, while self-efficacy has more to do with feelings of control over one's life chances.

Next, I examined the extent to which immigrant minority youth feel alienated from their school peers (see Figure 8-2). To do this, I constructed a measure of alienation or "being unpopular," using an item that asked students to evaluate whether their peers see them as "very popular," "somewhat popular," or "not at all popular." Those who answered "not at all popular" received a score of one for being unpopular and zero otherwise. Thus, groups with higher scores feel more alienated or think that they do not fit in with their school peers. To a great extent this mea-

[2]Due to space limitations, I have not included these patterns in graphic form; see Table 8-1 for tabulations.

TABLE 8-1 Descriptive Characteristics of Eighth- and Tenth-Grade Youth, by Race and Generational Status

	Asians		
	Immigrant Generation	Native-Born of Foreign-Born Parents	Native-Born of Native-Born Parents
Psychological Well-Being—Grade 8			
Locus of control	−0.117*** (0.605)	0.062 (0.583)	−0.063** (0.656)
Self-concept	−0.029 (0.643)	0.080** (0.664)	−0.135* (0.622)
Unpopular	0.248*** (0.432)	0.186 (0.389)	0.184 (0.388)
Middle school GPA	3.323*** (0.652)	3.357*** (0.679)	2.905 (0.832)
Math test scores	54.626*** (9.857)	58.409*** (9.986)	51.850 (11.267)
Reading test scores	50.856*** (9.616)	56.034*** (9.310)	49.936** (10.108)
Proportion female	0.499 (0.500)	0.481 (0.500)	0.487 (0.501)
Parent's education	14.651 (2.705)	16.199*** (2.841)	14.995* (2.409)
Family income (in $10,000)	3.815*** (3.816)	6.415*** (4.967)	5.150 (4.010)
Home Language Use			
Non-English language only	0.150*** (0.357)	0.126*** (0.333)	0.021* (0.144)

Hispanics			Whites
Immigrant Generation	Native-Born of Foreign-Born Parents	Native-Born of Native-Born Parents	Native-Born of Native-Born Parents
−0.202***	−0.105***	−0.102***	0.056
(0.628)	(0.641)	(0.648)	(0.605)
−0.066	−0.058	−0.009	−0.016
(0.638)	(0.668)	(0.660)	(0.662)
0.252***	0.231***	0.163	0.170
(0.435)	(0.421)	(0.370)	(0.376)
2.759***	2.779***	2.757***	2.959
(0.738)	(0.718)	(0.735)	0.751)
45.882***	46.676***	46.282***	52.547
(9.100)	(8.758)	(8.990)	(9.837)
45.065***	46.722***	47.399***	52.355
(9.187)	(9.154)	(9.322)	(9.717)
0.504	0.536*	0.511	0.498
(0.501)	(0.499)	(0.500)	(0.500)
12.049***	12.595***	13.280***	14.546
(2.630)	(2.623)	(2.166)	(2.433)
2.240***	2.779***	2.857***	4.648
(2.522)	(2.890)	(2.275)	(3.900)
0.238***	0.180***	0.101***	0.007
(0.426)	(0.384)	(0.301)	(0.085)

continued on next page

TABLE 8-1 Continued

	Asians		
	Immigrant Generation	Native-Born of Foreign-Born Parents	Native-Born of Native-Born Parents
Mostly non-English language	0.530*** (0.500)	0.323*** (0.468)	0.058*** (0.234)
Mostly English	0.216*** (0.412)	0.420*** (0.494)	0.105*** (0.307)
English only	0.104*** (0.306)	0.131*** 0.338)	0.817*** (0.388)
Ever repeated a grade	0.126 (0.332)	0.049*** (0.217)	0.132 (0.340)
Ever skipped a grade	0.108*** (0.311)	0.043*** (0.203)	0.021 (0.144)
Currently enrolled in a bilingual program	0.109*** (0.312)	0.033 (0.180)	0.079** (0.270)
Currently enrolled in gifted classes	0.322*** (0.468)	0.377*** (0.485)	0.302*** (0.460)
N	659	440	187

Hispanics			Whites
Immigrant Generation	Native-Born of Foreign-Born Parents	Native-Born of Native-Born Parents	Native-Born of Native-Born Parents
0.604*** (0.490)	0.475*** (0.500)	0.208*** (0.406)	0.006 (0.077)
0.087*** (0.283)	0.242*** (0.428)	0.344*** (0.475)	0.039 (0.194)
0.071*** (0.257)	0.103*** (0.305)	0.347*** (0.476)	0.948 (0.223)
0.248*** (0.433)	0.209*** (0.407)	0.215*** (0.411)	0.148 (0.355)
0.074*** (0.262)	0.042*** (0.201)	0.028*** (0.165)	0.012 (0.108)
0.130*** (0.337)	0.062*** (0.242)	0.062*** (0.241)	0.034 (0.182)
0.178 (0.383)	0.172 (0.377)	0.178 (0.383)	0.187 (0.390)
360	880	1,259	13,952

continued on next page

TABLE 8-1 Continued

	Blacks		
	Immigrant Generation	Native-Born of Foreign-Born Parents	Native-Born of Native-Born Parents
Psychological Well-Being—Grade 8			
Locus of control	–0.128** (0.657)	0.030 (0.613)	–0.075*** (0.622)
Self-concept	0.058 (0.682)	0.211*** (0.654)	0.190*** (0.606)
Unpopular	0.256* (0.439)	0.183 (0.388)	0.128*** (0.334)
Middle school GPA	2.990 (0.699)	2.852 (0.710)	2.723*** (0.692)
Math test scores	47.902*** (9.201)	46.623*** (9.948)	44.122*** (8.333)
Reading test scores	48.185*** (10.541)	48.441*** (10.284)	45.027*** (9.005)
Proportion female	0.471 (0.502)	0.516 (0.502)	0.512 (0.500)
Parent's education	14.116 (2.681)	14.678 (2.537)	13.351*** (2.113)
Family income (in $10,000)	2.838*** (2.725)	3.627** (3.259)	2.303*** (2.246)

Whites		
Immigrant Generation	Native-Born of Foreign-Born Parents	Native-Born of Native-Born Parents
0.115	0.072	0.056
(0.594)	(0.605)	(0.605)
0.043	0.044*	–0.016
(0.686)	(0.674)	(0.662)
0.218	0.144	0.170
(0.414)	(0.352)	(0.376)
3.138**	3.061***	2.959
(0.721)	(0.712)	(0.751)
55.119***	53.973***	52.547
(10.338)	(9.976)	(9.837)
54.133*	53.500**	52.355
(9.712)	(9.522)	(9.717)
0.497	0.501	0.498
(0.501)	(0.500)	(0.500)
15.803***	15.052***	14.546
(2.891)	(2.632)	(2.433)
5.764***	5.743***	4.648
(4.948)	(4.531)	(3.900)

continued on next page

TABLE 8-1 Continued

	Blacks		
	Immigrant Generation	Native-Born of Foreign-Born Parents	Native-Born of Native-Born Parents
Home Language Use			
Non-English language only	0.046*** (0.211)	0.082*** (0.275)	0.009 (0.092)
Mostly non-English language	0.161*** (0.370)	0.082*** (0.275)	0.008 (0.090)
Mostly English	0.126*** (0.334)	0.139*** (0.348)	0.029* (0.167)
English only	0.667*** (0.474)	0.697*** (0.462)	0.955 (0.209)
Ever repeated a grade	0.205 (0.406)	0.185 (0.390)	0.252*** (0.434)
Ever skipped a grade	0.084*** (0.280)	0.033* (0.179)	0.028*** (0.165)
Currently enrolled in a bilingual program	0.065 (0.248)	0.047 (0.213)	0.089*** (0.285)
Currently enrolled in gifted classes	0.205 (0.406)	0.216 (0.414)	0.225*** (0.418)
N	87	122	2,292

***$p < .001$; **$p < .01$; *$p < .05$.

SOURCE: National Education Longitudinal Study, 1988.

Whites		
Immigrant Generation	Native-Born of Foreign-Born Parents	Native-Born of Native-Born Parents
0.083*** (0.276)	0.058*** (0.235)	0.007 (0.085)
0.249*** (0.433)	0.109*** (0.312)	0.006 (0.077)
0.223*** (0.417)	0.270*** (0.444)	0.039 (0.194)
0.446*** (0.498)	0.563*** (0.496)	0.948 (0.223)
0.144 (0.352)	0.129 (0.335)	0.148 (0.355)
0.073*** (0.261)	0.031*** (0.174)	0.012 (0.108)
0.050 (0.219)	0.029 (0.167)	0.034 (0.182)
0.262** (0.441)	0.202 (0.401)	0.187 (0.390)
192	769	13,952

TABLE 8-2 Definition of Variables

Psychological Well-Being

1. *Locus of control* is the composite of the items listed below. BYS44K is a reverse scoring item, so the values were reversed before performing computations. Each of these six items was standardized separately to a mean of zero and a standard deviation of one. All nonmissing components were averaged.

BYS44B I don't have enough control over the direction of my life.
BYS44C In my life, good luck is more important than hard work.
BYS44F When I try to get ahead, somebody or something stops me.
BYS44G My plans hardly ever work out; planning makes me unhappy.
BYS44K I am almost certain I can make my plans works.
BYS44M Chance and luck are very important in my life.

2. *Self-concept* is the composite of the items listed below. BYS44A, BYS44D, BYS44E, and BYS44H are reverse scoring items, so the values were reversed before performing computations. Each of the above seven items was standardized separately to a mean of zero and a standard deviation of one. All nonmissing items were averaged.

BYS44A I feel good about myself.
BYS44D I feel I am a person of worth, the equal of other people.
BYS44E I am able to do things as well as most other people.
BYS44H On the whole, I am satisfied with myself.
BYS44I I feel useless at times.
BYS44J At times I think I am no good at all
BYS44L I feel I do not have much to be proud of.

3. *Unpopular* (alienation) (= 1 when BYS56A = 3).
Exact wording:
BYS56A "How do you think other students in your classes see you? As popular? Answer categories: I = Very, 2 = Somewhat, 3 = Not at all."

School Achievement Outcomes

1. GPA is an average of the self-reports for grades in the four subject areas (English, mathematics, science, social studies). It was computed by converting the response categories to a five-point scale (mostly A's = 4, B's = 3, C's = 2, D's = 1, mostly below D = .5) and taking the mean of all nonmissing values of these four variables equally weighted. The mean was rounded to one decimal place. The range for BYGRADS is 0.5 to 4.0.

Exact wording: BYS81 "For each of the school subjects listed below, mark the statement that best describes your grades from sixth grade up till now."
(answer categories: "Mostly A's (a numerical average of 90 to 100); mostly B's (80 to 89);

TABLE 8-2 Continued

mostly C's (70 to 79); mostly D's (60 to 69); mostly below D (below 60); does not apply to me—my classes are not graded.)"

2. Math Standardized Test Score
"*Mathematics* (40 questions, 30 minutes). Test items included word problems, graphs, equations, quantitative comparisons, and geometric figures. Some questions could be answered by simple application of skills or knowledge; others required the student to demonstrate a more advanced level of comprehension and/or problem solving."

3. Reading Standardized Test Score
"*Reading Comprehension* (21 questions, 21 minutes). This subtest contained five short reading passages, with three to six questions about the content of each. Questions encompassed understanding the meaning of words in context, identifying figures of speech, interpreting the author's perspective, and evaluating the passage as a whole."

Family Background Characteristics

1. Family Income: Exact wording BYP80: "What was your total family income from all sources in 1987? (If you are not sure about the amount, please estimate.)"

   1 = none; 2 = less than $1,000; 3 = $1,000-$2,999; 4 = $3,000-$4,999; 5 = $5,000-$7,999; 6 = $7,500-$9,999; 7 = $10,000-$14,999; 8 = $15,000-$19,999; 9 = $20,000-$24,999; 10 = $25,000-$34,999; 11 = $35,000-$49,999; 12 = $50,000-$74,999; 13 = $75,000-$99,999; 14 = $100,000-$199,999; 15 = $200,000 or more

   All categories recoded to midpoint value to ease interpretation of *t*-test results.

2. Parent's Education
Parent's education characterizes the level of education attained by either of the parents of the student. It was constructed by NCES using parent questionnaire data (BYP30 and BYP31). Student data (BYS34A and BYS34B) were used whenever parent data were either missing or not available.

School Experiences

1. Ever Repeated (BYS74). Exact wording: "Were you ever held back (made to repeat) a grade in school? (Yes or No)."

2. Ever Skipped (BYP41). Exact wording: "Was your eighth grader ever skipped a grade in school? (Yes or No)."

continued on next page

TABLE 8-2 Continued

Home Language Use

- Non-English only
- Non-English dominant
- English dominant
- English only

Variable constructed by NCES. Taken from student questionnaire; when student item was missing, parent questionnaire information was used.

Program Participation

1. Bilingual Education
2. Gifted Classes

Exact wording BYS68: "Are you enrolled in any of the following special programs/services? (A) Classes for gifted or talented students. (B) Special instruction for those whose first language is not English—for example, bilingual education or English as a second language (not regular English classes)."

SOURCE: National Center for Education Statistics (1990).

sure captures the relative comfort level of students at school. Again, immigrant youth of all racial and ethnic backgrounds feel more alienated from their school peers than native-born whites of native-born parents. These patterns are consistent with the difficulty of adaptation and acceptance of immigrant youth. They may be ostracized from both nonimmigrant white and minority children for being different. In contrast, native-born minority youth of native-born parents are relatively well integrated in school compared to their immigrant counterparts. Native-born African Americans of native-born parents are most likely to feel accepted by their relevant school peers.

The relationship between psychological well-being and academic performance among youth is well established; hence, since minority immigrant youth are susceptible to low self-efficacy and feelings of alienation, one might expect their precarious psychological well-being to negatively influence their academic achievement (Rosenberg et al., 1989, 1995). In fact, Figure 8-3 clearly shows that immigrant youth tend to earn higher grades than their

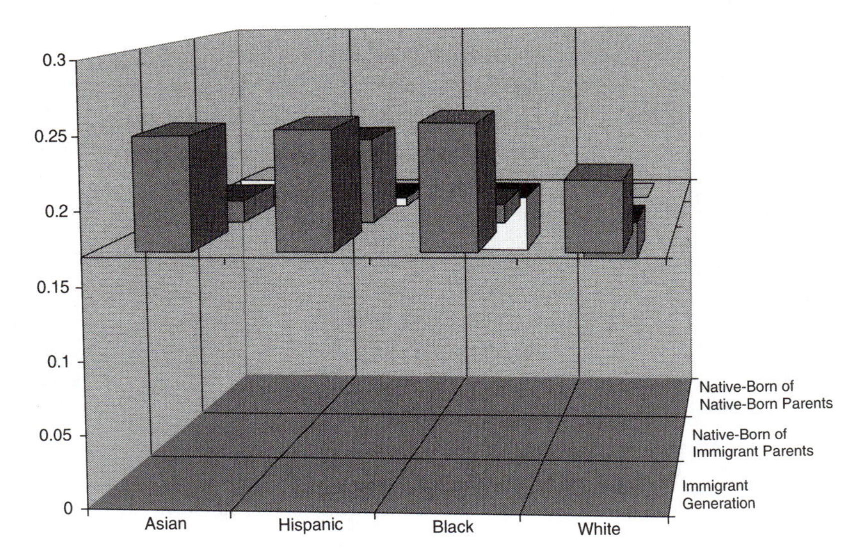

FIGURE 8-2 Alienation at school by race and generational status. The baseline is the score of white third-generation youth (native-born children of native-born parents).

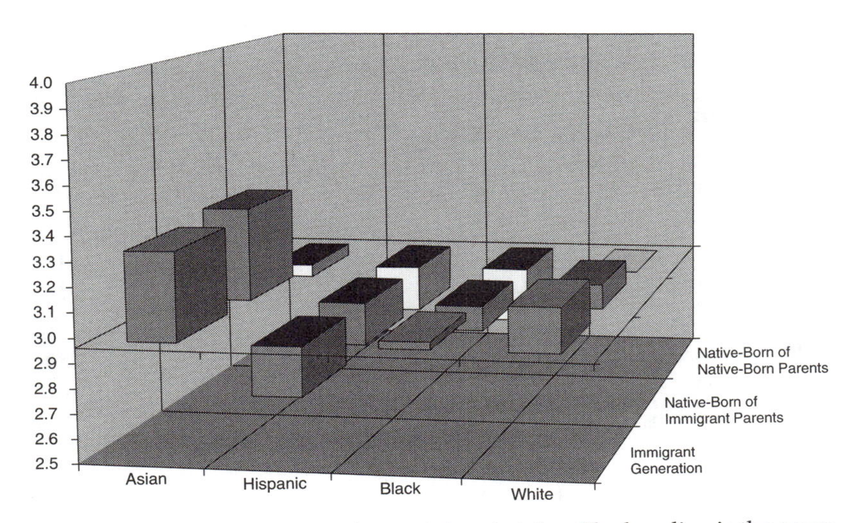

FIGURE 8-3 GPA by race and generational status. The baseline is the score of white third-generation youth (native-born children of native-born parents).

native-born counterparts. This pattern of immigrants' success in school is not consistent among Hispanics because this figure does not take into account differences in socioeconomic status. Subsequent figures present estimates of the influence of race and generational status after taking into account variations in socioeconomic background.

Table 8-1 presents descriptive tabulations of major psychological well-being and academic achievement outcome measures as well as background characteristics of each racial/generation group. The asterisks indicate the significance levels of *t*-test results comparing each racial/generation group to native-born white youth with U.S.-born parents.

As the graphs indicated, immigrant minority youth especially suffer from low feelings of self-efficacy (or locus of control) and are more likely to feel "unpopular" or alienated at school. However, they do not differ from native white youth in self-esteem. Native-born Asian and Hispanic youth with immigrant parents also are more prone to feelings of alienation from their peers. Hispanic youth have the worst feelings about themselves, with little difference between foreign-born and native-born youth of foreign-born parents; however, their poor well-being scores may stem from the low socioeconomic status of their families. The upcoming empirical analyses will allow us to differentiate the influence of immigrant status and ethnicity from that of social class.

Generational differences in academic outcomes are substantial among Asian youth. Asians with immigrant parents (regardless of whether they are immigrant or native-born) tend to have higher grades and perform better on standardized math and reading tests. Native-born Asians with immigrant parents have especially high achievement test scores since they benefit from having English-language skills compared to their foreign-born counterparts. Part of the striking difference by generational status among Asians may be due to ethnic differences in the composition of immigrant youth, native-born youth of foreign-born parents, and native-born youth of native-born parents. Native-born Asians of native-born parents have greater shares of Filipinos and Pacific Islanders, who tend to have lower achievement outcomes, while first- and second-generation youth include greater numbers of Chinese, Southeast Asians, and South Asians, all of whom have higher performance measures. Because of the small sample sizes that result after dividing the Asian sample by ethnicity and generational status, I can only examine how generational status influences outcomes for the two largest Asian ethnic groups: Chinese and Filipinos. I also examine Mexicans and other Hispanics in subsequent tabulations. In addition, severely LEP (limited English proficient) students were inadvertently excluded from the sampling frame of the base-year survey of NELS since their lack of English skills makes it difficult for them to fill out a questionnaire. Hence, the negative influence of having no or little English-language skills is underestimated in all of the models.

In contrast, for Hispanic youth, generational status seems to have little effect on academic performance. However, note that Hispanic immigrants tend to be less educated and have lower incomes than their native-born counterparts. Hence, one would expect Hispanic children of immigrants to have poorer educational outcomes. In fact, elsewhere we found that after controlling for parental socioeconomic status, Hispanic children of immigrant parents (both foreign-born and native-born youth) had slightly higher educational outcomes (Kao and Tienda, 1995). Similar to Asians, black youth with immigrant parents (both foreign- and native-born youth) tend to have better scholastic performance than blacks with native-born parents. Unlike Asians, however, immigrant blacks tend to perform at slightly higher levels than native-born blacks of immigrant parents. These patterns provide some evidence of Portes's (1995) segmented assimilation thesis, which argues that some minority groups assimilate downward since their native-born same-ethnic counterparts occupy somewhat lower status than immigrants. Specifically, because of the unique position of blacks in American society, and the tendency to identify blacks as members of the underclass, black immigrants are faced with prospects of assimilation that may downgrade their odds of socioeconomic mobility.

One reason that black immigrant youth tend to be more successful in school can be attributed to their parents' higher levels of education and family income compared to native-born parents of native-born blacks. Again, these descriptive tabulations support the notion of segmented assimilation, thus motivating immigrant black parents to emphasize their immigrant and ethnic identification as distinct from black Americans (Waters, 1994). A similar argument can be made for Hispanic immigrants (see Matute-Bianchi, 1986).

Note that native-born Asian youth with immigrant parents, on average, have at least one parent with a college degree (mean = 16.202 years of school), which is the highest of any racial/immigrant group. They also have a mean family income of more than $60,000, compared to $46,000 for white native youth. This is in stark contrast to their immigrant counterparts, whose parents have, on average, more than a high school education (mean = 14.639 years of school) and whose family income is in the mid-$30,000 range. In contrast to the vast generational differences between Asian families, there is little generational differentiation in the material resources available to Hispanic households. The typical Hispanic youth has at least one parent with only a high school education (mean ranges from 12.197 to 13.370 years of school) and family incomes in the $20,000 range. Again, while Hispanic families who have lived in the United States longer tend to have more education and income, differences between the generations are modest.

Hispanic families are also distinct in their extensive use of Spanish at home. About 83 percent of immigrant Hispanic youth use their native language primarily or exclusively at home, while the comparable figure for immigrant Asians is 68 percent. Among native-born youth of foreign-born parents, 58 percent still use Spanish primarily at home, while the figure is about 43 percent for native-born Asians with immigrant parents. Almost 82 percent of Asian native-born youth of native-born parents speak only English at home, while only 39 percent of their Hispanic counterparts do so. Hispanic immigrant youth are more likely than their white or Asian native-born peers to be enrolled in a bilingual program. These patterns suggest that Hispanic families are more likely to retain their native language than are their Asian counterparts, which may make it more difficult for their children to gain acceptance from non-Hispanic peers at school. Moreover, participation in bilingual programs can physically isolate participants from the rest of the student body. Again, recall that these figures somewhat underestimate the numbers of families who do not speak English at home since severely LEP youth were excluded from the base-year sample of the NELS. However, since severely LEP youth were excluded on an individual basis, there is no reason to suspect that their exclusion disproportionately affects certain racial and ethnic groups.

Previous school experiences of being held back or skipping a grade can have significant consequences on students' academic orientations (Pallas, 1989). Researchers have most often argued that grade retention does more harm than good because the experience can lower self-esteem, increase the odds of premature school withdrawal, and disrupt peer groups. An exception to the pervasive scholarly position on grade retention is a recent book on grade retention in primary school by Alexander et al. (1994). They found that grade retention improved children's test scores relative to their low-achieving peers who were not held back. Moreover, while low-achieving first graders had low self-esteem prior to being held back a grade, after retention their self-esteem rose, presumably because their grades and test scores were much better during their second time in first grade. However, their self-esteem was considerably lower than either the poor-performing nonretainees and other nonretainees by the time they reached eighth grade. In other words, the experience of repeating first grade had negative impacts on self-esteem seven years later.

With respect to previous and current educational experiences, native-born Asians of immigrant parents are less likely to have ever repeated a grade and Hispanic youth of all generational statuses are more likely to have ever repeated a class. In addition, only black native-born youth of native-born parents are more likely than whites to have ever repeated a class. While these descriptive tabulations show a distinct ethnic difference in patterns of grade retention, they do not clearly show generational differences in the likelihood of repeating a grade except among blacks.

In contrast, Asian youth of all generational statuses as well as black native-born youth of native-born parents are more likely to be currently enrolled in a gifted or honors class than their white counterparts. While Asians' higher participation in gifted classes is consistent with their higher test scores and grade point averages (GPAs), it is unclear why blacks, who have lower test scores and GPAs, are more likely to be enrolled in honors classes compared to whites.

Overall, I found immigrant minority youth to feel less in control of their lives and more alienated from school peers than whites of native-born parents. Immigrant youth also tend to have parents who earn less money and are less well educated than their minority counterparts of native-born parents. However, despite immigrant minorities' relatively disadvantaged backgrounds and additional difficulties in gaining acceptance by school peers, they do as well or better academically than their third-generation minority counterparts. Moreover, immigrant youth do not suffer from low self-esteem relative to native-born whites of native-born parents. These tabulations show immigrant youth to be relatively resilient in their academic performance despite feelings of limited control over their lives and their difficult social adaptation at school.

Table 8-3 presents tabulations that show how generational status influences the outcomes of Chinese, Filipino, and Mexican youth. These are the only ethnic groups that are large enough to divide into the three generational groups. For Chinese youth, immigrant status has a noticeable negative influence on locus of control and is associated with increased feelings of alienation. However, Chinese youth of immigrant parents (both native-born and immigrant youth) tend to have better academic outcomes than native-born youth of native-born parents who are same ethnics or whites. Filipinos do not suffer in terms of psychological well-being, although youth with immigrant parents perform well compared to their counterparts with native-born parents.

The psychological profiles of Mexican children are worse than that of Hispanics overall. Immigrant Mexican youth have extremely low self-efficacy and self-concept and are more likely to feel alienated at school. However, because immigrant Mexican children come from relatively low socioeconomic status (SES) family backgrounds, I cannot differentiate the influences of immigrant status from class in these tabulations. It is clear that, despite their lower family SES, immigrant Mexican children have remarkable school outcomes—their grades and test scores are comparable to native-born Mexicans (either with immigrant or native-born parents) who have more privileged family backgrounds.

EMPIRICAL ANALYSES

To disentangle the influences of immigrant status and ethnicity from SES on psychological well-being, Table 8-4 presents ordinary least squares and logistic regression estimates of the effects of race and generational status on psychological well-being indicators: locus of control, self-concept, and alienation (feeling "unpopular"). Model 1 of each outcome measure includes only race, generational status variables, and gender in order to quickly document descriptive variations in psychological well-being. Model 2 adds parents' SES, as measured by their education and family income. Since adults from low SES backgrounds are more likely to exhibit signs of low self-esteem and because immigrant groups differ dramatically in their material well-being and educational backgrounds, I want to differentiate the potential effects of the migration experience from SES on the outcome measures. Finally, model 3 under each outcome variable adds other dimensions of student life that may account for discrepant psychological well-being outcomes of immigrant and nonimmigrant youth. First, I include measures of home language use since lack of English being spoken at home, especially among children with immigrant parents, may signal parents' relative inability to communicate in English. Hence, these youth may be more susceptible to low self-efficacy and increased feelings of alienation at school.[3] Previous school experiences, such as skipping or repeating a grade, may foster feelings of incompatibility with peers at school. Finally, enrollment in bilingual education programs may further isolate minority children from the rest of the school; hence, I expect enrollment in these programs to increase alienation among youth. On the other hand, enrollment in gifted classes should be associated with higher levels of self-esteem and achievement.

Some of the results of Table 8-4 are summarized in Figures 8-4 and 8-5. Figure 8-4 presents estimates of the influence of race and generational status on self-efficacy after controlling for variations

---

[3]However, our models are likely to underestimate the severity of the lack of English use at home on well-being, since the most severely LEP students were necessarily excluded from the NELS sample.

TABLE 8-3 Descriptive Characteristics of Eighth-Grade Youth, by Ethnicity and Generational Status

	Chinese		
	Immigrant Generation	Native-Born of Foreign-Born Parents	Native-Born of Native-Born Parents
Psychological Well-Being—Grade 8			
Locus of control	−0.241*** (0.591)	0.011 (0.567)	0.073 (0.757)
Self-concept	−0.115 (0.644)	−0.021 (0.709)	−0.058 (0.659)
Unpopular	0.349*** (0.479)	0.283** (0.453)	0.192 (0.402)
Middle school GPA	3.356*** (0.654)	3.447*** (0.568)	2.992 (0.957)
Math test scores	56.802*** (9.350)	61.363*** (8.531)	53.077 (13.564)
Reading test scores	49.480** (10.166)	58.204*** (7.887)	49.797 (10.538)
Proportion female	0.500 (0.502)	0.472 (0.502)	0.500 (0.510)
Parent's education	14.045* (2.758)	15.944*** (3.252)	14.923 (2.607)
Family income (in $10,000)	3.353*** (3.490)	6.160*** (4.481)	4.708 (4.247)
Home Language Use			
Non-English language only	0.201*** (0.403)	0.111*** (0.316)	0.038 (0.196)
Mostly non-English language	0.619*** (0.487)	0.454*** (0.500)	0.077*** (0.272)

Filipinos			Whites
Immigrant Generation	Native-Born of Foreign-Born Parents	Native-Born of Native-Born Parents	Native-Born of Native-Born Parents
–0.156 (0.631)	0.011 (0.553)	–0.006 (0.806)	0.056 (0.605)
–0.043 (0.578)	0.023 (0.641)	–0.330 (0.561)	–0.016 (0.662)
0.207 (0.407)	0.198 (0.400)	0.312 (0.479)	0.170 (0.376)
3.203** (0.687)	3.247*** (0.689)	3.013 (0.740)	2.959 (0.751)
50.736 (9.600)	56.085*** (9.888)	53.651 (11.786)	52.547 (9.837)
49.181** (9.219)	54.587* (9.239)	55.297 (9.983)	52.355 (9.717)
0.454 (0.500)	0.444 (0.499)	0.500 (0.516)	0.498 (0.500)
15.426*** (1.973)	15.896*** (2.214)	13.875 (1.147)	14.546 (2.433)
3.912 (3.044)	5.558* (4.165)	3.797 (1.382)	4.648 (3.900)
0.139*** (0.347)	0.217*** (0.414)	0.000 (0.000)	0.007 (0.085)
0.518*** (0.502)	0.278*** (0.450)	0.062** (0.250)	0.006 (0.077)

continued on next page

TABLE 8-3 Continued

	Chinese		
	Immigrant Generation	Native-Born of Foreign-Born Parents	Native-Born of Native-Born Parents
Mostly English	0.134*** (0.342)	0.333*** (0.474)	0.192*** (0.402)
English only	0.045*** (0.208)	0.102*** (0.304)	0.692*** (0.471)
School Experiences			
Ever repeated a grade	0.121 (0.327)	0.029** (0.167)	0.208 (0.415)
Ever skipped a grade	0.143*** (0.351)	0.111*** (0.316)	0.077** (0.272)
Currently enrolled in a bilingual program	0.144*** (0.353)	0.037 (0.191)	0.043 (0.209)
Currently enrolled in gifted classes	0.317*** (0.467)	0.402*** (0.493)	0.400** (0.500)
N	134	107	25

Filipinos			Whites
Immigrant Generation	Native-Born of Foreign-Born Parents	Native-Born of Native-Born Parents	Native-Born of Native-Born Parents
0.269*** (0.445)	0.417*** (0.495)	0.000 (0.000)	0.039 (0.194)
0.074*** (0.263)	0.087*** (0.283)	0.938 (0.250)	0.948 (0.223)
0.119 (0.325)	0.027*** (0.164)	0.200 (0.414)	0.148 (0.355)
0.131*** (0.339)	0.009 (0.093)	0.000 (0.000)	0.012 (0.108)
0.091** (0.289)	0.009 (0.096)	0.000 (0.000)	0.034 (0.182)
0.216 (0.413)	0.291** (0.456)	0.333 (0.488)	0.187 (0.390)
108	114	16	13,952

continued on next page

TABLE 8-3 Continued

	Mexicans		
	Immigrant Generation	Native-Born of Foreign-Born Parents	Native-Born of Native-Born Parents
Psychological Well-Being—Grade 8			
Locus of control	−0.282***	−0.151***	−0.113***
	(0.619)	(0.626)	(0.633)
Self-concept	−0.148**	−0.098**	−0.025
	(0.620)	(0.649)	(0.663)
Unpopular	0.288***	0.263***	0.140*
	(0.454)	(0.441)	(0.348)
Middle school GPA	2.707***	2.760***	2.743***
	(0.734)	(0.700)	(0.743)
Math test scores	45.393***	45.639***	46.383***
	(8.721)	(7.891)	(8.903)
Reading test scores	43.420***	45.772***	47.671***
	(8.590)	(8.575)	(9.193)
Proportion female	0.500	0.545*	0.521
	(0.501)	(0.498)	(0.500)
Parent's education	11.200***	11.887***	13.066***
	(2.071)	(2.165)	(1.997)
Family income (in $10,000)	1.796***	2.239***	2.773***
	(1.869)	(2.037)	(2.103)
Home Language Use			
Non-English language only	0.251***	0.169***	0.112***
	(0.435)	(0.375)	(0.315)
Mostly non-English language	0.612***	0.515***	0.191***
	(0.488)	(0.500)	(0.393)

Other Hispanics			Whites
Immigrant Generation	Native-Born of Foreign-Born Parents	Native-Born of Native-Born Parents	Native-Born of Native-Born Parents
–0.086** (0.620)	–0.049* (0.684)	–0.068** (0.685)	0.056 (0.605)
0.012 (0.656)	0.003 (0.642)	–0.025 (0.683)	–0.016 (0.662)
0.219 (0.416)	0.166 (0.373)	0.206 (0.405)	0.170 (0.376)
2.853 (0.746)	2.796** (0.681)	2.803** (0.747)	2.959 (0.751)
46.970*** (10.121)	48.547*** (9.844)	46.674*** (9.103)	52.547 (9.837)
47.662*** (9.732)	48.484*** (9.591)	47.613*** (9.658)	52.355 (9.717)
0.496 (0.502)	0.487 (0.501)	0.541 (0.499)	0.498 (0.500)
13.512*** (2.968)	14.000** (2.984)	14.033** (2.400)	14.546 (2.433)
2.990*** (3.324)	3.783** (4.008)	3.290*** (2.446)	4.648 (3.900)
0.187*** (0.391)	0.218*** (0.414)	0.045*** (0.208)	0.007 (0.085)
0.610*** (0.490)	0.366*** (0.483)	0.082*** (0.275)	0.006** (0.077)

continued on next page

TABLE 8-3 Continued

	Mexicans		
	Immigrant Generation	Native-Born of Foreign-Born Parents	Native-Born of Native-Born Parents
Mostly English	0.087*** (0.282)	0.227*** (0.419)	0.396*** (0.489)
English only	0.050*** (0.219)	0.089*** (0.285)	0.302*** (0.460)
School Experiences			
Ever repeated a grade	0.273*** (0.447)	0.214*** (0.410)	0.214*** (0.410)
Ever skipped a grade	0.081*** (0.274)	0.042*** (0.200)	0.025** (0.157)
Currently enrolled in a bilingual program	0.141*** (0.349)	0.067*** (0.250)	0.047 (0.212)
Currently Enrolled in gifted classes	0.186 (0.390)	0.149* (0.356)	0.162 (0.369)
N	215	578	763

***$p < .001$; **$p < .01$; *$p < .05$.

SOURCE: National Education Longitudinal Study, 1988.

in SES background. These columns correspond exactly to the regression coefficients in model 2 under "Locus of Control" in Table 8-4. Overall, minority immigrant youth are most susceptible to low self-efficacy. Moreover, native-born minority youth of native-born parents also have lower self-efficacy than their native-born counterparts with immigrant parents. This pattern indirectly suggests the changing nature of the minority experience in this country. As immigrants, minority youth must struggle with the acculturation process and learn to understand how things

Other Hispanics			Whites
Immigrant Generation	Native-Born of Foreign-Born Parents	Native-Born of Native-Born Parents	Native-Born of Native-Born Parents
0.106*** (0.309)	0.269*** (0.445)	0.238*** (0.427)	0.039 (0.194)
0.098*** (0.298)	0.147*** (0.355)	0.635*** (0.482)	0.948 (0.223)
0.184 (0.390)	0.180 (0.386)	0.212** (0.409)	0.148 (0.355)
0.050*** (0.219)	0.052*** (0.222)	0.029* (0.169)	0.012 (0.108)
0.147*** (0.356)	0.062* (0.242)	0.069** (0.254)	0.034 (0.182)
0.200 (0.402)	0.222 (0.416)	0.198 (0.400)	0.187 (0.390)
121	195	242	13,952

work in the United States. Native-born youth of immigrant parents are more Americanized than their immigrant counterparts and suffer less in feelings of self-efficacy. However, native-born minority youth of native-born parents may become increasingly frustrated with their more limited path to upward mobility, as some researchers have argued in explaining the relatively low self-efficacy of blacks. Thus, it is likely that native-born children of immigrant parents have the highest sense of self-efficacy, while immigrant youth suffer primarily from their immigrant status and

TABLE 8-4 Effects of Race and Immigrant Status on Psychological Well-Being of Eighth Graders

	Locus of Control		
	Model 1	Model 2	Model 3
Constant	0.066*** (0.007)	–0.478*** (0.028)	–0.845*** (0.031)
Asian immigrant	–0.169*** (0.024)	–0.159*** (0.025)	–0.197*** (0.029)
Asian native of foreign-born	0.010 (0.030)	–0.063* (0.030)	–0.093** (0.032)
Asian native of native-born	–0.114* (0.045)	–0.135** (0.045)	–0.077 (0.046)
Hispanic immigrant	–0.253*** (0.033)	–0.132*** (0.033)	–0.019 (0.039)
Hispanic native of foreign-born	–0.155*** (0.021)	–0.066** (0.022)	–0.009 (0.026)
Hispanic native of native-born	–0.153*** (0.018)	–0.087*** (0.018)	–0.020 (0.021)
Black immigrant	–0.180** (0.066)	–0.100 (0.066)	–0.105 (0.068)
Black native of foreign-born	–0.021 (0.056)	–0.015 (0.056)	0.051 (0.058)
Black native of native-born	–0.126*** (0.014)	–0.062*** (0.014)	–0.010 (0.015)
White immigrant	0.063 (0.045)	–0.006 (0.046)	0.011 (0.046)
White native of foreign-born	0.021 (0.023)	–0.009 (0.023)	–0.012 (0.023)

Self-Concept		
Model 1	Model 2	Model 3
0.100*** (0.007)	–0.259*** (0.030)	–0.603*** (0.034)
–0.012 (0.026)	–0.006 (0.026)	–0.096** (0.031)
0.092** (0.031)	0.039 (0.032)	–0.022 (0.034)
–0.120* (0.047)	–0.130** (0.048)	–0.088 (0.050)
–0.048 (0.034)	0.037 (0.036)	0.058 (0.043)
–0.032 (0.022)	0.028 (0.023)	0.033 (0.028)
0.011 (0.019)	0.050* (0.019)	0.068** (0.023)
0.068 (0.069)	0.142* (0.071)	0.109 (0.075)
0.232*** (0.059)	0.220*** (0.059)	0.257*** (0.064)
0.211*** (0.015)	0.259*** (0.015)	0.304*** (0.016)
0.058 (0.047)	0.018 (0.049)	0.010 (0.051)
0.061* (0.024)	0.045 (0.025)	0.026 (0.026)

continued on next page

TABLE 8-4 Continued

	Locus of Control		
	Model 1	Model 2	Model 3
Female	–0.029***	–0.026**	–0.079***
	(0.008)	(0.008)	(0.008)
Parent's education		0.033***	0.012***
		(0.002)	(0.002)
Family income (in $10,000)		0.013***	0.009***
		(0.001)	(0.001)
Middle school GPA			0.252***
			(0.006)
Home Language Use			
Non-English only			–0.094***
			(0.027)
Mostly non-English			–0.084***
			(0.022)
Mostly English			0.017
			(0.017)
English only			—
School Experiences			
Ever repeated a grade			–0.053***
			(0.012)
Ever skipped a grade			–0.007
			(0.029)
Currently enrolled in bilingual education program			–0.150***
			(0.021)
Currently enrolled in a gifted program		0.005	
Adjusted R^2	0.013	0.045	0.136

Self-Concept		
Model 1	Model 2	Model 3
–0.234***	–0.231***	–0.274***
(0.009)	(0.009)	(0.009)
	0.022***	0.003
	(0.002)	(0.002)
	0.009***	0.007***
	(0.001)	(0.001)
		0.219***
		(0.007)
		–0.062*
		(0.029)
		0.021
		(0.024)
		0.053**
		(0.019)
		—
		–0.004
		(0.013)
		0.056
		(0.032)
		–0.042
		(0.023)
	0.033**	
0.042	0.055	0.116

continued on next page

TABLE 8-4 Continued

	Unpopular (Alienation)[a]		
	Model 1	Model 2	Model 3
Constant	–1.633*** (0.032)	–0.959*** (0.132)	–0.605*** (0.147)
Asian immigrant	0.481*** (0.102)	0.445*** (0.103)	0.376** (0.124)
Asian native of foreign-born	0.124 (0.130)	0.261* (0.132)	0.235 (0.146)
Asian native of native-born	0.133 (0.208)	0.178 (0.209)	0.161 (0.210)
Hispanic immigrant	0.455** (0.146)	0.267 (0.147)	0.095 (0.167)
Hispanic native of foreign-born	0.380*** (0.092)	0.232* (0.093)	0.089 (0.114)
Hispanic native of native-born	–0.043 (0.088)	–0.164 (0.089)	–0.238* (0.100)
Black immigrant	0.275 (0.302)	0.174 (0.303)	0.129 (0.305)
Black native of foreign-born	0.072 (0.269)	0.027 (0.270)	–0.022 (0.272)
Black native of native-born	–0.339*** (0.076)	–0.489*** (0.077)	–0.485*** (0.078)
White immigrant	0.349 (0.196)	0.444* (0.198)	0.401* (0.204)
White native of foreign-born	–0.232* (0.116)	–0.161 (0.116)	–0.189 (0.120)
Female	0.093* (0.040)	0.079* (0.040)	0.099* (0.040)

TABLE 8-4 Continued

	Unpopular (Alienation) [a]		
	Model 1	Model 2	Model 3
Parent's education		−0.029** (0.010)	−0.011 (0.010)
Family income (in $10,000)		−0.055*** (0.007)	−0.050*** (0.007)
Middle school GPA			−0.207*** (0.027)
Home Language Use			
Non-English only			0.388*** (0.114)
Mostly non-English			0.188 (0.097)
Mostly English			−0.050 (0.083)
English only			—
School Experiences			
Ever repeated a grade			−0.030 (0.056)
Ever skipped a grade			0.396** (0.125)
Currently enrolled in bilingual education program			−0.191 (0.104)
Currently enrolled in a gifted program			−0.212***
Adjusted R^2	0.005	0013	0.020

***$p < .001$; **$p < .01$; *$p < .05$.

[a]Logistic regression model in which unpopular = 1; psuedo R^2 presented in place of adjusted R^2.

SOURCE: National Education Longitudinal Study, 1988: Base Year.

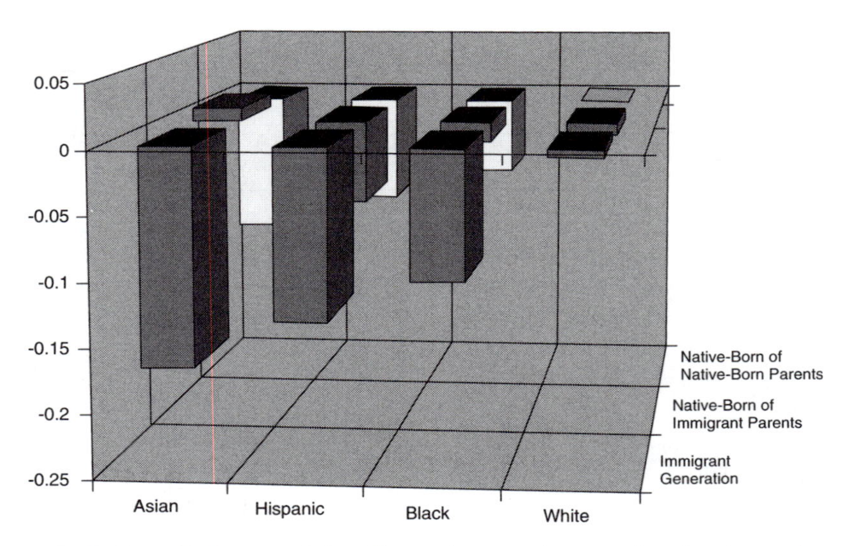

FIGURE 8-4 Estimates of the effects of race and generational status on locus of control: controlling for SES differences. The baseline is the score of white third-generation youth (native-born children of native-born parents).

third-generation youth (native-born youth of native-born parents) suffer from their minority status.

Figure 8-5 presents estimates of the effects of race and generational status on alienation at school, controlling for SES differences. These estimates are taken from model 2 of the "unpopular" models in Table 8-4. It is clear that immigrant youth of all ethnic backgrounds suffer from feelings of alienation from their school peers. Moreover, native-born Asians (both with immigrant and native-born parents) and native-born Hispanics of immigrant parents also experience feelings of discomfort compared to native-born whites with native-born parents. Only native-born Hispanics and African Americans of native-born parents feel accepted by their peers. This pattern of low acceptance of Asians of all generational status groups may be due to their small numbers, which makes it unlikely for Asian youth to attend schools with significant numbers of same ethnics.

Results of the full models are presented in Table 8-4. As expected, minority immigrant children are less likely to feel efficacious. Specifically, model 1 shows that Asian immigrants, all His-

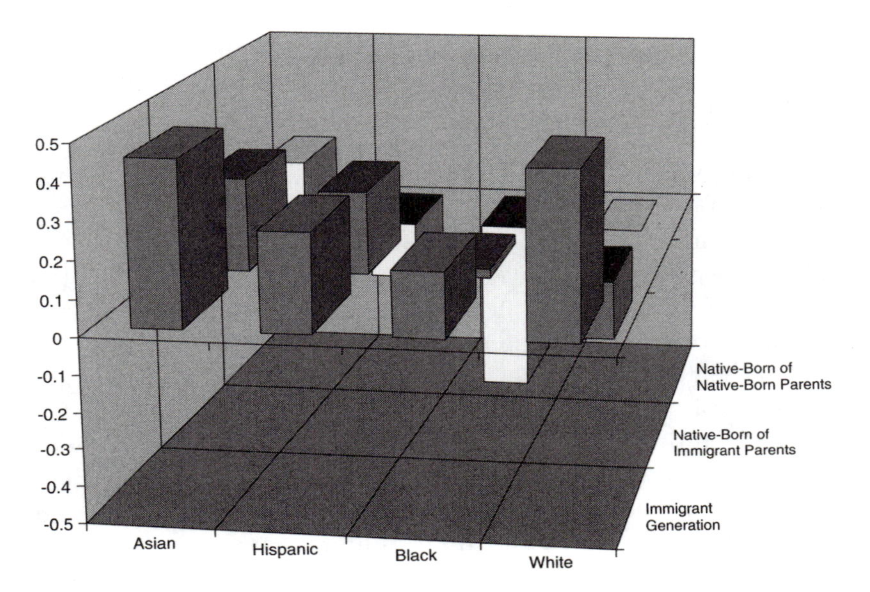

FIGURE 8-5 Estimates of the effects of race and generation status on alienation at school: controlling for SES differences. The baseline is the score of white third-generation youth (native-born children of native-born parents).

panic youth, and immigrant and native-born blacks feel less in control of their lives than do native-born whites of native-born parents. These effects persist even after adding measures of parental SES, which suggests that minority immigrant status negatively affects young people's feelings of self-efficacy.

To disentangle the influence of immigrant minority status on self-efficacy, I add measures of home language use, grades, and school experiences in model 3. Again, while there are certainly reciprocal effects between grades and psychological well-being, I am less interested in the causal order between the two than how the association between grades and psychological well-being may differ among immigrant youth. Overall, these characteristics account for all of the negative influences of minority generational status on self-esteem for all groups except Asian youth of immigrant parents. In other words, the lower self-efficacy of Hispanic and black youth is completely accounted for after including measures of home language use, grades, and school experiences in model 3. As expected, GPA is positively associated with feelings of efficacy, while having ever repeated a grade lowers feelings of self-efficacy.

The languages used at home and at school are also associated with self-efficacy. Again, I find that youth whose families primarily use a non-English language suffer in their self-efficacy. Presumably, immigrants who have difficulty communicating in English face greater hardships in their daily lives, which can lead to feelings of helplessness. Youth who are currently enrolled in a bilingual program are also more likely to feel that their lives are out of their control.

In contrast to the results on self-efficacy, I find little group differentiation in terms of self-concept, except that black second-generation and native-born youth tend to have extremely high levels of self-concept. Thus, I find no support for Padilla and Durán's (1995) expectation that immigrant youth suffer more from low self-esteem than do native-born youth. However, youth whose home language is not English have lower self-concept than those whose home language is exclusively English. Those children who speak mostly English tend to have higher self-esteem than their counterparts who speak only English at home. Presumably those who speak mostly English at home are families who have sufficient English skills and have maintained their language of origin.

Some immigrant minority youth, however, feel more alienated at school than their native white counterparts. Immigrant Asians and Hispanics are most likely to feel "unpopular" at school, while American blacks are least likely to feel alienated at school. Native-born Hispanics of immigrant parents also feel more alienated than white natives, while there is weak evidence that second-generation Asian youth also do not fit in as well as whites. Moreover, while SES and gender reduce almost one-half of the racial/generational effects for Hispanics, they have little bearing on the magnitude of the racial/generational effects among Asians.

Table 8-5 presents identical models as Table 8-4, except here I use more differentiated measures of ethnicity within the racial categories used earlier. The results generally parallel our findings for Table 8-4. Most noticeable are the ethnic group differences in feelings of acceptance. Chinese youth of immigrant parents (both foreign-born and native-born) feel alienated at school, and these effects cannot be accounted for by SES differences or school experiences. However, Filipino youth do not significantly differ from whites in feelings of alienation. Similarly, Mexican immigrant youth are also alienated from their school peers, but gender and SES account for one-half of the effect of being a foreign- or native-born child of foreign-born parents. However, adding SES and gender to the models actually increases the association between race and generational status among native-born Mexicans of native-born parents. Again, I can account for the remainder of the differences by including measures of home language use, grades, and school experiences for foreign- and native-born youth of foreign-born parents among Mexicans, but these characteristics do not explain the experiences of native-born Mexicans of native-born parents.

Table 8-6 presents the effects of race and immigrant status on academic performance, using a layout comparable to Table 8-4. Again, I summarize the findings for GPA outcomes controlling for SES (model 2) in Figure 8-6. Essentially, I found that Asians with immigrant parents have the highest grades. In model 1, Asian and white immigrant youth and children of immigrants tend to earn higher marks than their native-born counterparts of native-born parents. Asian children of immigrant parents (both foreign-born and native-born youth) also earn higher grades and math test scores, while Asian native-born youth of immigrant parents have higher reading test scores as well. Native-born Asians of native-born parents perform at comparable levels to white native-born youth of native-born parents except in reading scores. Asians are unique because native-born children of immigrant parents perform as well on grades and better than immigrant children on math and reading scores. Elsewhere I argued that children of immigrant parents, regardless of their own immigration histories, benefit from their parents' optimism and expectations, which drive them to achieve (Kao and Tienda, 1995).

After controlling for differences in socioeconomic background, Hispanic immigrant youth tend to have higher grades than their same-ethnic native-born counterparts of native-born parents. Note that while immigrant Hispanics in model 2 are statistically indistinguishable from whites in their grades, native-born Hispanics of native-born parents earn lower grades than

TABLE 8-5 Effects of Ethnicity and Immigrant Status on Psychological Well-Being: Chinese, Filipino, Mexican, and Other Hispanic Youths

	Locus of Control		
	Model 1	Model 2	Model 3
Constant	0.061*** (0.007)	–0.481*** (0.031)	–0.840*** (0.035)
Chinese immigrant	–0.286*** (0.053)	–0.234*** (0.053)	–0.279*** (0.058)
Chinese native of foreign-born	–0.035 (0.059)	–0.096 (0.059)	–0.136* (0.059)
Chinese native of native-born	0.028 (0.122)	–0.022 (0.123)	0.022 (0.126)
Filipino immigrant	–0.203*** (0.059)	–0.232*** (0.058)	–0.207*** (0.061)
Filipino native of foreign-born	–0.047 (0.057)	–0.111* (0.056)	–0.132* (0.057)
Filipino native of native-born	–0.051 (0.153)	–0.027 (0.150)	–0.104 (0.163)
Mexican immigrant	–0.327*** (0.042)	–0.177*** (0.043)	–0.073 (0.051)
Mexican native of foreign-born	–0.195*** (0.026)	–0.084** (0.027)	–0.030 (0.032)
Mexican native of native-born	–0.157*** (0.023)	–0.100*** (0.023)	–0.026 (0.026)
Other Hispanic immigrant	–0.131* (0.056)	–0.079 (0.055)	0.055 (0.061)
Other Hispanic native of foreign-born	–0.094* (0.044)	–0.066 (0.045)	0.026 (0.047)
Other Hispanic native of native-born	–0.112** (0.040)	–0.086* (0.040)	0.009 (0.042)

Self-Concept		
Model 1	Model 2	Model 3
0.108***	−0.263***	−0.619***
(0.007)	(0.034)	(0.039)
−0.096	−0.049	−0.128*
(0.056)	(0.058)	(0.065)
−0.011	−0.063	−0.150*
(0.063)	(0.064)	(0.065)
−0.039	−0.078	−0.062
(0.127)	(0.129)	(0.136
−0.035	−0.048	−0.083
(0.063)	(0.062)	(0.067)
0.030	−0.014	−0.075
(0.061)	(0.061)	(0.063)
−0.311	−0.288	−0.453*
(0.162)	(0.161)	(0.180)
−0.127**	−0.009	−0.021
(0.044)	(0.046)	(0.057)
−0.067*	0.016	0.017
(0.028)	(0.029)	(0.035)
0.000	0.042	0.066*
(0.024)	(0.025)	(0.028)
0.031	0.065	0.120
(0.059)	(0.060)	(0.067)
0.020	0.040	0.080
(0.047)	(0.048)	(0.052)
0.005	0.027	0.083
(0.042)	(0.043)	(0.046)

continued on next page

TABLE 8-5 Continued

	Locus of Control		
	Model 1	Model 2	Model 3
Female	–0.032*** (0.009)	–0.026** (0.009)	–0.079*** (0.009)
Parent's education		0.034*** (0.002)	0.011*** (0.002)
Family income (in $10,000)		0.011*** (0.001)	0.008*** (0.001)
Middle school grades			0.258*** (0.007)
Home Language Use			
Non-English only			–0.100** (0.032)
Mostly non-English			–0.086** (0.027)
Mostly English			–0.011 (0.020)
English only			—
School Experiences			
Ever repeated a grade			–0.052*** (0.014)
Ever skipped a grade			–0.001 (0.037)
Currently enrolled in a bilingual program			–0.155*** (0.025)
Currently enrolled in a gifted program			–0.001 (0.013)
Adjusted R^2	0.012	0.044	0.139

Self-Concept		
Model 1	Model 2	Model 3
–0.255*** (0.010)	–0.249*** (0.010)	–0.288*** (0.010)
	0.022*** (0.002)	0.002 (0.003)
	0.009*** (0.002)	0.006*** (0.002)
		0.228*** (0.008)
		–0.055 (0.035)
		0.017 (0.030)
		0.032 (0.022)
		—
		0.001 (0.015)
		0.033 (0.041)
		–0.049 (0.028)
		0.034* (0.014)
0.038	0.051	0.114

continued on next page

TABLE 8-5 Continued

	Unpopular (Alienation)[a]		
	Model 1	Model 2	Model 3
Constant	–1.615*** (0.033)	–0.837*** (0.148)	–0.485** (0.164)
Chinese immigrant	0.944*** (0.207)	0.873*** (0.209)	0.760** (0.232)
Chinese native of foreign-born	0.691** (0.222)	0.831*** (0.224)	0.779** (0.241)
Chinese native of native-born	0.421 (0.513)	0.421 (0.516)	0.422 (0.522)
Filipino immigrant	0.265 (0.253)	0.265 (0.254)	0.115 (0.270)
Filipino native of foreign-born	0.182 (0.245)	0.278 (0.247)	0.222 (0.259)
Filipino native of native-born	1.116 (0.571)	1.065 (0.572)	1.204* (0.581)
Mexican immigrant	0.622*** (0.185)	0.351 (0.188)	0.198 (0.212)
Mexican native of foreign-born	0.519*** (0.108)	0.300** (0.111)	0.157 (0.138)
Mexican native of native-born	–0.199 (0.116)	–0.346** (0.117)	–0.422** (0.130)
Other Hispanic immigrant	0.275 (0.253)	0.164 (0.255)	–0.008 (0.272)
Other Hispanic native of foreign-born	0.047 (0.210)	–0.020 (0.211)	–0.181 (0.225)
Other Hispanic native of native-born	0.271 (0.180)	0.193 (0.181)	0.156 (0.184)
Female	0.063 (0.044)	0.047 (0.044)	0.070 (0.045)

TABLE 8-5 Continued

	Unpopular (Alienation)[a]		
	Model 1	Model 2	Model 3
Parent's education		−0.035** (0.011)	−0.013 (0.011)
Family income (in $10,000)		−0.059*** (0.008)	−0.053*** (0.008)
Middle school grades			−0.228*** (0.031)
Home Language Use			
Non-English only			0.358** (0.138)
Mostly non-English			0.220 (0.120)
Mostly English			−0.078 (0.099)
English Only			—
School Experiences			
Ever repeated a grade			−0.001 (0.062)
Ever skipped a grade			0.511*** (0.152)
Currently enrolled in a bilingual program			−0.254* (0.126)
Currently enrolled in a gifted program			−0.227*** (0.065)
Adjusted R^2	0.005	0.015	0.023

***$p < .001$; **$p < .01$; *$p < .05$.

[a]Logistic regression model in which unpopular = 1; pseudo R^2 presented in place of adjusted R^2.

SOURCE: National Education Longitudinal Study, 1988: Base Year.

TABLE 8-6 Influence of Race and Immigrant Status on Academic Achievement: Asian, Hispanic, Black, and White Eighth Graders

	Grades		
	Model 1	Model 2	Model 3
Constant	2.879***	1.761***	2.209***
	(0.008)	(0.033)	(0.032)
Asian immigrant	0.371***	0.370***	0.321***
	(0.029)	(0.029)	(0.032)
Asian native of foreign-born	0.408***	0.263***	0.158***
	(0.036)	(0.035)	(0.035)
Asian native of native-born	–0.045	–0.081	–0.095
	(0.054)	(0.053)	(0.051)
Hispanic immigrant	–0.192***	0.031	0.020
	(0.039)	(0.039)	(0.044)
Hispanic native of foreign-born	–0.178***	–0.019	–0.034
	(0.026)	(0.025)	(0.029)
Hispanic native of native-born	–0.196***	–0.085***	–0.076**
	(0.022)	(0.021)	(0.023)
Black immigrant	0.041	0.113	0.112
	(0.079)	(0.078)	(0.077)
Black native of foreign-born	–0.103	–0.110	–0.141*
	(0.067)	(0.066)	(0.066)
Black native of native-born	–0.230***	–0.119***	–0.111***
	(0.017)	(0.017)	(0.017)
White immigrant	0.187***	0.072	0.040
	(0.054)	(0.054)	(0.052)
White native of foreign-born	0.109***	0.063*	0.051
	(0.027)	(0.027)	(0.026)
Female	0.144***	0.152***	0.150***
	(0.010)	(0.010)	(0.010)

Math Test Scores		
Model 1	Model 2	Model 3
52.667***	32.796***	38.054***
(0.105)	(0.412)	(0.417)
2.235***	2.355***	2.650***
(0.388)	(0.363)	(0.416)
6.008***	3.231***	2.546***
(0.470)	(0.437)	(0.454)
–0.542	–1.521*	–1.012
(0.709)	(0.658)	(0.663)
–6.498***	–2.456***	–0.730
(0.527)	(0.500)	(0.570)
–5.687***	–2.694***	–1.782***
(0.341)	(0.323)	(0.376)
–6.098***	–3.885***	–3.242***
(0.287)	(0.271)	(0.300)
–4.498***	–3.346***	–2.776**
(1.054)	(0.986)	(1.007)
–5.756***	–5.785***	–5.095***
(0.887)	(0.824)	(0.845)
–8.255***	–6.006***	–5.497***
(0.220)	(0.210)	(0.218)
2.734***	0.517	0.769
(0.709)	(0.675)	(0.679)
1.585***	0.469	0.723*
(0.362)	(0.341)	(0.338)
–0.561***	–0.371**	–0.942***
(0.133)	(0.125)	(0.125)

continued on next page

TABLE 8-6 Continued

	Grades		
	Model 1	Model 2	Model 3
Parent's education		0.073***	0.045***
	(0.002)	(0.002)	
Family income (in $10,000)		0.013***	0.006***
		(0.002)	(0.001)
Psychological Well-Being			
Locus of control			0.246***
			(0.009)
Self-concept			0.103***
			(0.009)
Unpopular			–0.043***
			(0.013)
Home Language Use			
Non-Engligh only			0.047
			(0.030)
Mostly non-English			0.040
			(0.024)
Mostly English			0.010
			(0.019)
English only			—
School Experiences			
Ever repeated a grade			–0.375***
			(0.013)
Ever skipped a grade			0.086**
			(0.033)
Currently enrolled in a bilingual program			–0.176***
			(0.024)
Currently enrolled in a gifted program			0.375***
			(0.012)
Adjusted R^2	0.040	0.114	0.276

Math Test Scores		
Model 1	Model 2	Model 3
	1.245***	0.931***
(0.030)	(0.030)	
	0.371***	0.282***
	(0.020)	(0.019)
		2.592***
		(0.123)
		–0.033
		(0.115)
		0.488**
		(0.165)
		–0.868*
		(0.386)
		–1.234***
		(0.315)
		0.031
		(0.247)
		—
		–4.675***
		(0.173)
		1.298**
		(0.423)
		–4.216***
		(0.306)
		5.403***
		(0.157)
0.106	0.252	0.362

continued on next page

TABLE 8-6 Continued

	Reading Test Scores		
	Model 1	Model 2	Model 3
Constant	51.270*** (0.105)	32.805*** (0.418)	38.168*** (0.425)
Asian immigrant	–1.326*** (0.385)	–1.281*** (0.368)	–0.088 (0.423)
Asian native of foreign-born	3.886*** (0.467)	1.458** (0.443)	1.305** (0.462)
Asian native of native-born	–2.233** (0.705)	–2.938*** (0.668)	–2.219** (0.674)
Hispanic immigrant	–7.148*** (0.522)	–3.560*** (0.505)	–1.110 (0.580)
Hispanic native of foreign-born	–5.547*** (0.338)	–2.833*** (0.327)	–1.590*** (0.383)
Hispanic native of native-born	–4.813*** (0.286)	–2.889*** (0.275)	–1.901*** (0.306)
Black immigrant	º3.963*** (1.060)	–2.772** (1.014)	–1.571 (1.035)
Black native of foreign-born	–3.768*** (0.885)	–3.728*** (0.839)	–3.314*** (0.861)
Black native of native-born	–7.199*** (0.219)	–5.276*** (0.213)	–4.524*** (0.222)
White immigrant	1.940** (0.703)	0.229 (0.683)	1.068 (0.690)
White native of foreign-born	1.309*** (0.359)	0.409 (0.346)	0.554 (0.344)
Female	1.847*** (0.132)	2.006*** (0.126)	1.486*** (0.127)
Parent's education		1.190*** (0.031)	0.883*** (0.031)

TABLE 8-6 Continued

	Reading Test Scores		
	Model 1	Model 2	Model 3
Family income (in $10,000)		0.242*** (0.020)	0.153*** (0.019)
Psychological Well-Being			
Locus of control			3.054*** (0.125)
Self-concept			–0.035 (0.117)
Unpopular			0.346* (0.168)
Home Language Use			
Non-Engligh only			-1.292** (0.394)
Mostly non-English			–1.815*** (0.320)
Mostly English			0.271 (0.252)
English only			—
School Experiences			
Ever repeated a grade			–4.192*** (0.176)
Ever skipped a grade			1.164** (0.430)
Currently enrolled in a bilingual program			–6.042*** (0.311)
Currently enrolled in a gifted program			3.875*** (0.160)
Adjusted R^2	0.085	0.202	0.303

***$p < .001$; **$p < .01$; *$p < .05$.
SOURCE: National Education Longitudinal Study, 1988: Base Year.

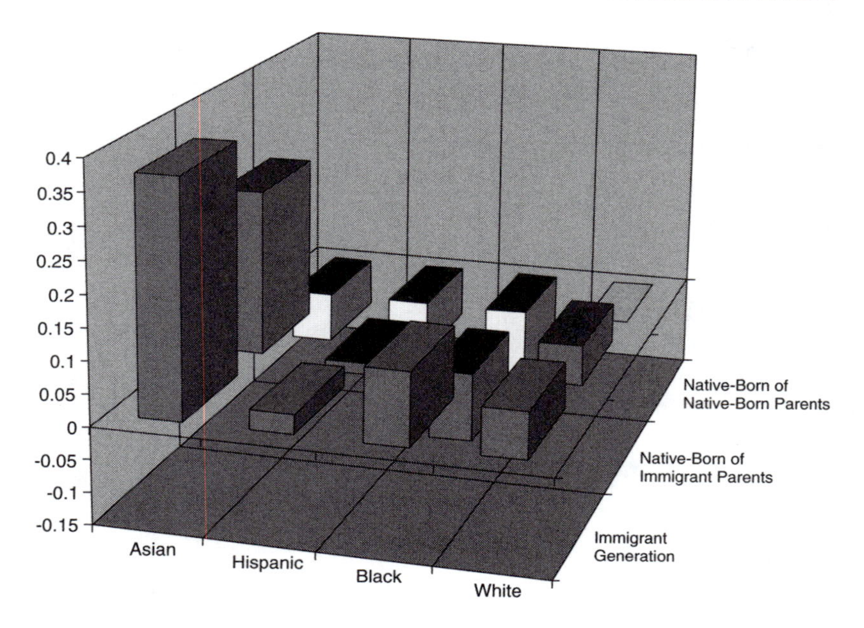

FIGURE 8-6 Estimates of the effects of race and generational status on GPA: controlling for SES differences. The baseline is the score of white third-generation youth (native-born children of native-born parents).

same-SES native-born whites of native-born parents. The inclusion of socioeconomic status accentuates the immigrant advantage for Hispanics. Hence, the gradual erosion of academic performance by generational status is clear and raises troubling questions regarding what it is about the prolonged effects of minority status that decreases educational outcomes.

However, Hispanic youth of all generational backgrounds earn lower grades and lower math and reading test scores than white youth. The difference in GPAs between foreign-born and native-born Hispanics of immigrant parents and whites is rendered insignificant after the inclusion of family background, while individual schooling experience variables make little difference to these effects. However, even with these control measures, Hispanic third-generation youth still earn lower grades. All Hispanics earn lower test scores than white native-born youth of native-born parents. Overall, Hispanic youth with immigrant parents earn higher grades and math test scores after controlling for SES, while they earn higher reading scores after including controls for SES and individual school experiences than their counterparts with native-born parents.

Among blacks, youth with immigrant parents earn comparable grades while American blacks earn lower grades and lower math and reading test scores than white native-born youth. The general pattern of higher academic performance among immigrant youth is apparent across all groups, although it is most stunning among blacks and Asians. It is clear that among blacks acculturation is linked to lower academic performance and test scores across each of the models.

Furthermore, these results suggest that psychological well-being and academic outcomes are positively associated. Note that locus of control is strongly associated with all three measures of school achievement, yet immigrant youth suffer from feelings of low self-efficacy. These results support Bandura's (1995) thesis that feelings of greater self-efficacy foster motivation and development of learning skills, although I cannot establish the causal order in these models. It is still unclear, however, how immigrant youth manage to succeed in school compared to their native-born counterparts (both same ethnics and whites) despite feelings of low self-efficacy. Youth from immigrant households may also be disadvantaged in their achievement test scores since households that mostly use a non-English language have youth with lower math and reading test scores.

Another facet of the experience of immigrant youth is their higher enrollment rates in bilingual programs in eighth grade, which is associated with lower grades and lower math and reading test scores. No doubt, immigrant youth are overrepresented in bilingual programs, yet some still manage to earn remarkably high scores, especially compared to their minority counterparts from native-born families. Having ever repeated a grade is associated with lower grades and lower achievement test scores, while the experience of having ever skipped a grade is linked to higher grades and math test scores.

To examine whether these stunning generational differences among Asians can be attributed to differences in the ethnic composition of racial groups, Table 8-7 examines the influence of ethnicity and generational status. Overall, the degeneration of

TABLE 8-7 Influence of Ethnicity and Immigrant Status on Academic Achievement: Chinese, Filipino, Mexican, and Other Hispanic Students

	Grades		
	Model 1	Model 2	Model 3
Constant	2.880*** (0.008)	1.685*** (0.037)	2.170*** (0.036)
Chinese immigrant	0.407*** (0.065)	0.443*** (0.064)	0.439*** (0.066)
Chinese native of foreign-born	0.501*** (0.072)	0.359*** (0.070)	0.244*** (0.066)
Chinese native of native-born	0.043 (0.146)	–0.031 (0.142)	–0.119 (0.140)
Filipino immigrant	0.259*** (0.073)	0.188** (0.069)	0.221** (0.068)
Filipino native of foreign-born	0.312*** (0.070)	0.180** (0.067)	0.125 (0.064)
Filipino native of native-born	0.060 (0.192)	0.114 (0.183)	0.086 (0.180)
Mexican immigrant	–0.241*** (0.051)	0.066 (0.052)	0.085 (0.058)
Mexican native of foreign-born	–0.196*** (0.032)	0.029 (0.031)	0.026 (0.036)
Mexican native of native-born	–0.209*** (0.028)	–0.080** (0.027)	–0.060* (0.029)
Other Hispanic immigrant	–0.095 (0.068)	–0.003 (0.066)	–0.005 (0.069)
Other Hispanic native of foreign-born	–0.152** (0.054)	–0.119* (0.053)	–0.131* (0.053)
Other Hispanic native of native-born	–0.153** (0.049)	–0.125** (0.048)	–0.109* (0.047)
Female	0.139*** (0.011)	0.149*** (0.011)	0.147*** (0.011)

Math Test Scores		
Model 1	Model 2	Model 3
52.609***	31.964***	37.638***
(0.112)	(0.467)	(0.471)
4.510***	5.590***	6.651***
(0.857)	(0.798)	(0.860)
9.055***	6.509***	5.809***
(0.952)	(0.875)	(0.854)
0.788	–0.334	0.329
(1.916)	(1.769)	(1.798)
–1.595	–2.642**	–1.471
(0.975)	(0.883)	(0.901)
3.886***	1.534	1.925*
(0.918)	(0.836)	(0.826)
1.362	2.333	0.829
(2.441)	(2.210)	(2.229)
–6.887***	–1.588*	0.394
(0.692)	(0.657)	(0.758)
–6.621***	–2.601***	–1.510**
(0.423)	(0.399)	(0.472)
–5.891***	–3.538***	–2.796***
(0.368)	(0.343)	(0.378)
–5.323***	–3.474***	–0.992
(0.906)	(0.832)	(0.899)
–3.754***	–3.030***	–1.794**
(0.707)	(0.660)	(0.689)
–5.590***	–4.827***	–4.323***
(0.642)	(0.601)	(0.610)
–0.639***	–0.448**	–1.005***
(0.151)	(0.141)	(0.141)

continued on next page

TABLE 8-7 Continued

	Grades		
	Model 1	Model 2	Model 3
Parent's education		0.079*** (0.003)	0.048*** (0.003)
Family income (in $10,000)		0.012*** (0.002)	0.005** (0.002)
Psychological Well-Being			
Locus of control			0.254*** (0.011)
Self-concept			0.105*** (0.010)
Unpopular			–0.055*** (0.014)
Home Language Use			
Non-English only			0.038 (0.036)
Mostly non-English			0.010 (0.031)
Mostly English			0.021 (0.023)
School Experiences			
Ever repeated a grade			–0.397*** (0.015)
Ever skipped a grade			0.089* (0.042)
Currently enrolled in a bilingual progrm			–0.186*** (0.029)
Currently enrolled in a gifted program			0.398*** (0.014)
Adjusted R^2	0.022	0.105	0.282

Math Test Scores		
Model 1	Model 2	Model 3
	1.318***	0.971***
	(0.034)	(0.034)
	0.341***	0.261***
	(0.022)	(0.021)
		2.531***
		(0.139)
		–0.050
		(0.129)
		0.500**
		(0.183)
		–1.211**
		(0.470)
		–1.769***
		(0.400)
		–0.098
		(0.297)
		–4.847***
		(0.199)
		1.224*
		(0.535)
		–4.361***
		(0.373)
		5.680***
		(0.180)
0.049	0.212	0.333

continued on next page

TABLE 8-7 Continued

	Reading Test Scores		
	Model 1	Model 2	Model 3
Constant	51.197***	32.356***	38.000***
	(0.110)	(0.473)	(0.480)
Chinese immigrant	–2.596**	–1.939*	0.200
	(0.847)	(0.808)	(0.876)
Chinese native of foreign-born	6.171***	3.988***	3.777***
	(0.941)	(0.886)	(0.870)
Chinese native of native-born	–2.286	–2.985	–3.212
	(1.895)	(1.791)	(1.832)
Filipino immigrant	–2.808**	–3.902***	–2.390**
	(0.955)	(0.886)	(0.909)
Filipino native of foreign-born	2.764**	0.647	0.933
	(0.908)	(0.846)	(0.842)
Filipino native of native-born	3.273	4.059	1.722
	(2.494)	(2.311)	(2.271)
Mexican immigrant	–8.689***	–4.084***	–1.906*
(0.681)	(0.662)	(0.769)	
Mexican native of foreign-born	–6.412***	–2.922***	–1.791***
	(0.417)	(0.403)	(0.480)
Mexican native of native-born	–4.448***	–2.462***	–1.617***
	(0.364)	(0.347)	(0.385)
Other Hispanic immigrant	–4.406***	–2.921***	0.035
	(0.892)	(0.839)	(0.916)
Other Hispanic native of foreign-born	–3.562***	–2.781***	–1.507*
	(0.698)	(0.666)	(0.700)
Other Hispanic native of native-born	–4.545***	–4.083***	–3.089***
	(0.634)	(0.607)	(0.620)
Female	1.772***	1.997***	1.512***
	(0.150)	(0.143)	(0.143)

TABLE 8-7 Continued

	Reading Test Scores		
	Model 1	Model 2	Model 3
Parent's education		1.234***	0.904***
		(0.035)	(0.035)
Family income (in $10,000)		0.213***	0.132***
		(0.023)	(0.022)
Psychological Well-Being			
Locus of control			3.050***
			(0.142)
Self-concept			–0.071
			(0.132)
Unpopular			0.293
			(0.187)
Home Language Use			
Non-English only			–1.208*
			(0.478)
Mostly non-English			–1.727***
			(0.407)
Mostly English			0.203
			(0.303)
School Experiences			
Ever repeated a grade			–4.333***
			(0.202)
Ever skipped a grade			1.023
			(0.545)
Currently enrolled in a bilingual progrm			–6.324***
			(0.379)
Currently enrolled in a gifted program			4.032***
			(0.183)
Adjusted R^2	0.045	0.172	0.280

***$p < .001$; **$p < .01$; *$p < .05$.

SOURCE: National Education Longitudinal Study, 1988: Base Year.

academic performance is clear for all ethnic groups. Native-born Chinese youth of native-born parents, for instance, earn lower grades and lower math and reading test scores than their immigrant counterparts in most models and than native-born Chinese of immigrant (second-generation) parents in all models. Among Filipinos, children of immigrant parents tend to earn higher grades than their counterparts with native-born parents. However, only native-born children of immigrant parents earn higher math and reading scores than their native-born counterparts with native-born parents, and this difference is rendered statistically insignificant after adding measures of socioeconomic background. Thus, the immigrant advantage is less prevalent among Filipino youth.

While the patterns for Mexicans are less consistent, Mexican youth of immigrant parents earn higher grades and higher math scores than youth with native-born parents. Native-born Mexicans of native-born parents earn the highest reading scores after inclusion of SES measures.

CONCLUSION

Overall, the difficulty of being a minority as well as an immigrant has profound detrimental effects on one's psychological well-being. Immigrant youth face rejection from both native-born whites and native-born members of their same ethnic groups, which makes them feel more alienated at school than their native-born counterparts. Moreover, immigrant minority status lowers perceptions of control over the direction of one's life. Nevertheless, immigrant minority children do extremely well in school. Indeed, minority immigrant youth exhibit signs of strong resilience. Despite the difficulty of transition to life in the United States, as evidenced in their lower sense of control over their lives and feeling "unpopular" at school, they manage to have better school outcomes than their minority counterparts from native-born families. Indeed, through their high academic outcomes, immigrant minority students not only add to the diversity of students in American schools but are a positive influence on their peers.

It is clear that immigrant parents promote the educational success of their children (Kao and Tienda, 1995). Immigrant families are especially optimistic about their children's odds of upward mobility and are very resilient to the difficulties of their immigrant status. However, if we are to take the current course of native-born minorities of native-born parents to be the future course of the offspring of children of immigrants, the United States must reflect on what it is about assimilation that lowers the educational trajectory of minority students. As Portes (1995) has argued, we must consider that for today's children of immigrant families assimilation may imply the process of becoming members of marginalized ethnic minority groups.

REFERENCES

Alexander, K., D. Entwisle, and S. Dauber

1994 *On the Success of Failure: A Reassessment of the Effects of Retention in the Primary Grades.* Cambridge: Cambridge University Press.

Bandura, A.

1993 Perceived self-efficacy in cognitive development and functioning. *Educational Psychologist* 28:117-148.

1995 Exercise of personal and collective efficacy in changing societies. In *Self-Efficacy in Changing Societies*, A. Bandura, ed. New York: Cambridge University Press.

Caplan, N., M.H. Choy, and J.K. Witmore

1991 *Children of the Boat People: A Study of Educational Success.* Ann Arbor: University of Michigan Press.

Covington, M.

1984 The motive for self-worth. In *Research on Motivation in Education*, vol. 1, *Student Motivation*, R. Ames and C. Ames, eds. New York: Academic Press.

Dornbush, S.M., P.L. Ritter, P.H. Leiderman, D.F. Roberts, and M.J. Fraleigh

1987 The relation of parenting style to adolescent school performance. *Child Development* 58:1244-1257.

Hughes, M., and D.H. Demo

1989 Self-perceptions of black-Americans: Self-esteem and personal efficacy. *American Journal of Sociology* 95:132-159.

Kao, G.

1995 Asian-Americans as model minorities? A look at their academic performance. *American Journal of Education* 103:121-159.

Kao, G., and M. Tienda

1995 Optimism and achievement: The educational performance of immigrant youth. *Social Science Quarterly* 76:1-19.

March, H.W.
1986 Global self-esteem: Its relation to specific facets of self-concept and their importance. *Journal of Personality and Social Psychology* 51:1224-1236.

Matute-Bianchi, M.E.
1986 Ethnic identities and patterns of school success and failure among Mexican-descent and Japanese-American students in a California high school: An ethnographic analysis. *American Journal of Education* 95:233-255.

National Center for Education Statistics
1990 *The National Education Longitudinal Study of 1988: User's Manual, Base Year: Student Component Data File User's Manual*. Washington, D.C.: U.S. Department of Education.

Padilla, A.M., and D. Durán
1995 The psychological dimension in understanding immigrant students. In *California's Immigrant Children: Theory, Research, and Implications for Educational Policy*. San Diego: Center for U.S.-Mexican Studies.

Pallas, A.M., G. Natriello, and E.L. McDill
1989 The changing nature of the disadvantaged population: Current dimensions and future trends. *Educational Researcher* 18:16-22.

Population Reference Bureau
1989 *America in the 21st Century: Human Resource Development*. Washington, D.C.: Population Reference Bureau.

Portes, A.
1995 Segmented assimilation among new immigrant youth: A conceptual framework. In *California's Immigrant Children: Theory, Research, and Implications for Educational Policy*, R. Rumbaut and W. Cornelius, eds. San Diego: Center for U.S.-Mexican Studies.

Portes, A., and R. Rumbaut
1990 *Immigrant America: A Portrait*. Berkeley: University of California Press.

Rosenberg, M.
1989 *Society and the Adolescent Self-Image*. Revised Edition. Middletown, Conn.: Wesleyan University Press.

Rosenberg, M., C. Schooler, and C. Schoenback
1989 Self-esteem and adolescent problems: Modeling reciprocal effects. *American Sociological Review* 54:1004-1018.

Rosenberg, M., C. Schooler, C. Schoenback, and F. Rosenberg
1995 Global self-esteem and specific self-esteem: Different concepts, different outcomes. *American Sociological Review* 60:141-156.

Rumbaut, R.G.
1990 *Immigrant Students in California Public Schools: A Summary of Current Knowledge*. Report No. 11. Baltimore: Center for Research on Effective Schooling for Disadvantaged Students, Johns Hopkins University.
1994 The crucible within: Ethnic identity, self-esteem, and segmented assimilation among children of immigrants. *International Migration Review* 28:748-794.

1995 The new Californians: Comparative research findings on the educational progress of immigrant children. In *California's Immigrant Children: Theory, Research, and Implications for Educational Policy*, R. Rumbaut and W. Cornelius, eds. San Diego: Center for U.S.-Mexican Studies.

Sue, S., and S. Okazaki

1990 Asian-American educational achievements: A phenomenon in search of an explanation. *American Psychologist* 45:913-920.

Waters, M.C.

1994 Ethnic and racial identities of second-generation black immigrants in New York City. *International Migration Review* 28:795-820.

Zimmerman, B.

1995 Self-efficacy and educational development. In *Self-Efficacy in Changing Societies*, A. Bandura, ed. New York: Cambridge University Press.

CHAPTER 9

Passages to Adulthood: The Adaptation of Children of Immigrants in Southern California

Rubén G. Rumbaut

While the rapid growth of international migration to the United States over the past few decades has led to a mushrooming research literature and an intensified public debate about the new immigrants and their impact on American society, less noticed has been the fact that all the while a new generation of Americans raised in immigrant families has been coming of age. In due course its members will decisively shape the character of their ethnic communities and their success or failure. Indeed, the long-term effects of contemporary immigration will hinge more on the trajectories of these youth than on the fate of their parents. The children of immigrants thus constitute the most consequential and lasting legacy of the new mass immigration to the United States (cf. Portes, 1996; Rumbaut, 1995; Zhou, 1997).

The size of this youthful population—including both immigrant children and U.S.-born children of immigrants—has already surpassed the prior record set by the offspring of European immigrants earlier in this century. Among children under 18 years of age, the 1990 census counted nearly 6 million U.S.-born children living with immigrant parents and another 2 million foreign-born children ages 0 to 17, combining to form a "new second generation" of some 8 million children as of that time (see Oropesa and Landale, 1997). By 1998 the immigrant population of the United

States increased even faster—from 20 million to 27 million—with the number of children of immigrants growing commensurately. Furthermore, while one-third of the immigrant population of the United States resided in California, over 40 percent of under-18 children of immigrants lived in California. Hence, the size and concentration of this emerging population, added to its diverse national and socioeconomic origins and forms of adaptation, make its present evolution extraordinarily important.

This chapter presents the latest results of a comprehensive longitudinal study of the educational performance and social, cultural, and psychological adaptation of children of immigrants, the new second generation now growing up in American cities. Since late 1991 the Children of Immigrants Longitudinal Study has followed the progress of a large sample of teenagers representing over 70 nationalities in two key areas of immigrant settlement in the United States: Southern California (San Diego) and South Florida (Miami and Fort Lauderdale). The original survey, conducted in spring 1992 (T1), interviewed over 5,200 students enrolled in the eighth and ninth grades in schools of the San Diego Unified School District (N = 2,420) and the Dade and Broward County Unified School Districts (N = 2,842). The sample was drawn in the junior high grades, a level at which dropout rates are still relatively rare, to avoid the potential bias of differential dropout rates between ethnic groups at the senior high school level. For purposes of the study, students were eligible to enter the sample if they were U.S. born but had at least one immigrant (foreign-born) parent or if they themselves were foreign born and had come to the United States at an early age, most before age 10. (For selected T1 results and further information on its research design, see Portes, 1995, 1996; Portes and Rumbaut, 1996; Portes and Schauffler, 1996; and Rumbaut 1994a, 1995, 1997a.)

Three years after the original survey, in 1995-1996 (T2), a second survey of the same group of children of immigrants was conducted—this time supplemented by in-depth interviews with a stratified sample of their parents as well—using survey questionnaires specially developed for longitudinal and comparative analyses. The purpose of this follow-up effort was to add a temporal dimension to the study and ascertain changes over time in the family situation, school achievement, educational and occupational aspirations, language use and preferences, ethnic identities, experiences and expectations of discrimination, and social and psychological adaptation of these youth. By this time the children, who were originally interviewed in junior high when most were 14 or 15 years old (the mean age at T1 was 14.2), had reached the final year of senior high school and were making their passages into adulthood, firming up plans for their future as well as their outlooks on the surrounding society. This chapter examines a wide range of findings from that latest survey, focusing on changes observed over time (from T1 to T2) among youth in the San Diego longitudinal sample and also on two key indices of psychological well-being: self-esteem and depression.

IMMIGRANTS AND THEIR TYPES: THE SAN DIEGO LONGITUDINAL SAMPLE

Reflecting patterns of recent immigration into Southern California, the principal nationalities represented in the San Diego sample are Mexican, Filipino, Vietnamese, Laotian, Cambodian, and smaller groups of other children of Asian immigrants (mostly Chinese, Japanese, Indian, Korean) and Latin American immigrants. These groups are representative of some of the principal types of immigrants in California today and in contemporary American society (cf. Portes and Rumbaut, 1996). Thus:

- Mexicans constitute by far the largest legal and illegal immigrant population in both California and the United States—indeed, they form part of the largest, longest, and most sustained labor migration in the contemporary world—and San Diego, situated along the Mexican border, has long been a major area of settlement. The 1990 census showed that among adults over 25 Mexican immigrants had the lowest education levels of any major U.S. ethnic group, native or foreign born (see Rumbaut, 1994b).
- Since the 1960s, Filipinos have formed the second-largest immigrant population in this country, and they are the largest Asian-origin immigrant group in California and the United States. Many have come as professionals (nurses most conspicuously) and through military connections (especially the U.S. Navy, making San Diego with its huge Navy base a primary area of settle-

ment). The 1990 census showed that Filipino immigrants as a whole have the lowest poverty rate of any sizable ethnic group in the United States.

- Since the end of the Indochina war in 1975, refugees from Vietnam, Cambodia, and Laos have formed the largest refugee population both in California and the United States. The 1990 census found the highest poverty and welfare dependency rates in the country among Laotians and Cambodians. Comparative research on the mental health of Indochinese refugees and other ethnic groups has also found the highest levels of depressive symptomatology and posttraumatic stress disorder among the adult survivors of the "killing fields" of Cambodia—raising questions about the psychological well-being of their children in the United States (see Rumbaut, 1991a, 1991b, 1996; Vega and Rumbaut, 1991).

Remarkably, although the 27 million immigrants in the United States in 1998 came from over 140 different countries, fully 35 percent came from only three: Mexico, the Philippines, and Vietnam. More remarkably still, these three nationalities accounted for the majority (55 percent) of the 8.1 million foreign-born people in California in 1996. And fully 90 percent of this study's San Diego sample consisted of children of parents from Mexico; the Philippines; and Vietnam, Laos, and Cambodia—representing distinct groups of immigrant laborers, professionals, and refugees with sharply contrasting migration histories and contexts of exit and reception.

The 1995-1996 survey in San Diego succeeded in reinterviewing 85.2 percent of the baseline sample of 2,420 students, for a total of 2,063 (see Table 9-1 for reinterview rates by national origin and gender). Students who had moved, transferred, or dropped out of school during the intervening years were followed throughout, and even the majority of dropouts were located and reinterviewed. It was because of the difficulty in tracking these harder-to-locate cases that the data collection period extended into 1996. With some exceptions (e.g., higher-status youth from intact families who owned their own homes in San Diego at T1 were better represented at T2), the sample is largely the same. In fact, Indochinese students from the poorest

TABLE 9-1 Reinterview Rates and Sociodemographic Characteristics of Children of Immigrants in San Diego, California, by National Origin of Their Parents and Gender of the Children

Characteristics[a]	Mexico	Philippines	Vietnam	Cambodia
N of sample, T1 (1992)	727	808	361	94
N of sample, T2 (1995-1996)	578	716	302	88
% Reinterviewed at T2	80.0	88.6	83.7	93.6
Nativity of Children				
% Foreign born	38.8	43.4	84.4	97.7
% U.S. born	61.2	56.6	15.6	2.3
Year of Birth				
% 1975-1976	18.1	17.0	23.5	22.7
% 1977	45.3	51.5	42.4	44.3
% 1978	36.6	31.5	34.1	33.0
Year of U.S. Arrival				
% Born in United States	61.2	56.6	15.6	2.3
% 1976-1979	10.2	10.3	20.9	11.4
% 1980-1984	10.2	15.1	35.8	62.5
% 1985-1990	18.3	18.0	27.8	23.9
U.S. Citizenship				
% Citizen at T1 (1992)	69.2	78.6	32.5	6.8
% Citizen at T2 (1995)	73.4	85.6	46.4	11.4
Nativity of Parents[b]				
Parents are conationals	73.7	79.5	89.7	80.7
One parent born in United States	17.8	16.9	2.3	0.0

[a] Data are from the longitudinal sample of 2,063 respondents surveyed in 1992 (T1) and again in 1995-1996 (T2). When originally interviewed in spring 1992, all respondents were enrolled in the eighth or ninth grades in the San Diego City Schools; eligible respondents had to have at least one parent who was foreign born.

Laos					
Lao	Hmong	Others[c]	Female	Male	Total
154	53	223	1,211	1,209	2,420
143	50	186	1,040	1,023	2,063
92.9	94.3	83.4	85.9	84.6	85.2
95.8	94.0	47.3	55.3	56.0	55.6
4.2	6.0	52.7	44.7	44.0	44.4
36.3	12.0	17.2	16.2	23.3	19.8
41.3	52.0	45.7	47.7	46.1	46.9
22.4	36.0	37.1	36.1	30.6	33.3
4.2	6.0	52.7	44.7	44.0	44.4
20.3	22.0	9.1	13.2	12.3	12.7
46.9	46.0	17.2	21.5	22.3	21.9
28.7	26.0	21.0	20.6	21.4	21.0
16.8	8.0	68.8	59.0	59.5	59.3
23.8	12.0	73.7	66.1	66.2	66.1
95.1	90.0	58.6	78.6	79.2	78.9
0.0	0.0	31.2	14.2	13.8	14.0

[b]When the parents were not conationals (i.e., not born in the same country), the mother's nationality determined the child's national origin classification, except where the mother was U.S. born. Over 50 different nationalities (countries of birth of fathers and mothers) were represented in the sample overall.

[c]Includes smaller immigrant groups from Asia (Chinese, Indian, Japanese, Korean, Thai), Latin America, and the Caribbean.

families in the survey (the smaller-sized Cambodian, Lao, and Hmong groups) had reinterview rates above 90 percent, as did the high socioeconomic status "other Asians" (Chinese, Japanese, Indian, Korean). No nationality had reinterview rates below 80 percent. The percentages of female and foreign-born youth were the same at both points in time. As during the baseline survey, this data collection effort for the most part took place during repeated visits to schools with the cooperation of the San Diego City Schools, including administrators, principals, teachers, and other staff.

CHILDREN OF IMMIGRANTS: A PORTRAIT

Basic demographic characteristics of the longitudinal sample of 2,063 (those youth interviewed in both surveys) are provided in Table 9-1, including their birthplace, year of birth, year of arrival in the United States, and U.S. citizenship status at T1 and T2, broken down by the national origin of their parents and gender. Some points merit highlighting. The sample is about evenly balanced between foreign-born and U.S.-born children of immigrants. However, most of the Mexicans (61 percent) and Filipinos (57 percent) were born in the United States, reflecting long-established migration histories, while the Indochinese groups, a legacy of U.S. involvement in the war in Vietnam and its spread into Cambodia and Laos, are all overwhelmingly foreign-born recent arrivals. The 16 percent of Vietnamese who were born in the United States comprise a salient and historically important exception, as will become clearer in what follows: they are largely the children of the comparatively elite "first wave" of South Vietnamese who were evacuated as Saigon fell in April 1975 (over 80 percent of the youth in the sample were born in 1977 or 1978, and none were born before 1975).

Too often analysts who rely on nativity and ethnicity data, such as those available through the decennial census, tend to conceive of ethnicity as a fixed quality or constant (e.g., "Mexican," "Vietnamese") and of nativity as a sort of continuous variable (i.e., a proxy for generation or time in the United States) and to assume that differences between foreign-born and U.S.-born co-ethnics reflect processes of change (typically of assimilation) over time or generation. But here the confounding of period and cohort effects can loom large, missing the importance of class and other differences between heterogeneous "waves" and "vintages" of immigrants from the same country in different historical contexts (as the example of the 1975 Vietnamese exiles illustrates). It can also miss the crucial importance of intermarriage among non-compatriots, as the data on parental nativity suggest (see the bottom panel of Table 9-1). In our sample, about three-fourths of the parents were conationals (the other fourth consisted of mothers and fathers who were not born in the same country—representing over 50 nationalities overall); and in 14 percent of the cases one parent was U.S. born (ranging from virtually none of the Indochinese to one-sixth of the Mexicans and Filipinos and nearly one-third of the "others"). Thus, far from being a fixed characteristic, the very assignment of national origin to the children in our sample became fluid and problematic in a substantial proportion of cases. In such cases where the parents were not conationals, the mother's nationality determined the child's national origin classification, except where the mother was U.S. born, in which case the father's nationality was determinative (for an elaboration of this methodological problem, see Rumbaut, 1994a).

Substantive results of the adaptive trajectories of these children of immigrants from approximately the beginning (T1) to the end (T2) of high school—as sketched in the tables of data that follow—cover their family's economic situation, school achievement and effort, educational and occupational aspirations, language proficiency and preference, ethnic self-identities, perceptions of discrimination, and global self-esteem and depressive symptoms. These findings are summarized below.

Family Socioeconomic Status and Neighborhood Contexts

The modest family origins of many of these children, the highly educated backgrounds of others, and the gradual improvement of their economic situation over time are described in Table 9-2. Only a tiny proportion of Mexican and Indochinese fathers and mothers (with the signal exception of the U.S.-born Vietnamese, who as noted are the children of the first wave of 1975 refugees) have college degrees, well below the 1990 U.S. norm of 20

TABLE 9-2 Family Socioeconomic Status and Neighborhood Characteristics of Children of Immigrants in San Diego, California, by Nativity of the Children and National Origin of Their Parents, in 1992 (T1) and 1995 (T2)

Characteristics by National Origin and Nativity[a]	Time	Mexico	
		FB[a]	US
Socioeconomic Status			
Father			
% College graduate	T1	7.1	6.5
% Less than high school	T1	76.3	59.9
% In the labor force	T1	79.9	81.4
% In the labor force	T2	74.1	78.2
Mother			
% College graduate	T1	2.7	4.5
% Less than high school	T1	82.6	66.9
% In the labor force	T1	58.0	55.4
% In the labor force	T2	63.4	66.1
Home			
% Family owns home	T1	18.3	44.1
% Family owns home	T2	27.5	52.8
% Moved to new home	T2	52.7	32.0
Family's Economic Situation (since 3 yrs. ago)			
% Better	T1	56.5	56.4
% Worse	T1	9.4	9.4
% Better	T2	44.8	42.3
% Worse	T2	14.8	14.8
Neighborhood Profile[c] (1990 census tract data)			
% Below poverty line	T1	55.5	47.4
% Foreign born	T1	34.0	31.3
% White	T1	39.3	42.7
% Speak English only	T1	48.0	51.3

Philippines		Vietnam		Cambodia[b]
FB	US	FB	US	FB
37.0	23.5	11.0	36.2	4.5
16.4	15.1	66.3	31.9	77.3
86.2	79.8	51.4	89.4	22.7
81.0	85.9	62.4	93.6	35.2
37.9	43.0	5.9	25.5	4.5
22.5	17.5	71.4	48.9	85.2
84.2	90.6	36.9	72.3	12.5
84.9	89.1	43.1	74.5	15.9
65.3	86.4	28.6	70.2	11.4
74.2	88.8	28.6	74.5	8.0
37.9	25.4	45.7	25.5	43.7
56.7	46.9	58.4	55.6	45.9
5.9	11.7	9.2	11.1	15.3
49.2	38.6	39.4	19.1	22.1
13.5	22.4	14.2	25.5	12.8
16.9	16.4	35.2	21.1	57.7
29.4	29.6	28.4	23.4	33.1
46.3	45.9	56.3	66.3	42.7
61.3	61.0	61.0	70.3	51.1

continued on next page

TABLE 9-2 Continued

Characteristics by National Origin and Nativity[a]	Time	Laos: Lao[b] FB	Laos: Hmong[b] FB
Socioeconomic Status			
Father			
% College graduate	T1	11.2	2.0
% Less than high school	T1	65.7	86.0
% In the labor force	T1	32.9	20.0
% In the labor force	T2	40.6	34.0
Mother			
% College graduate	T1	4.2	0
% Less than high school	T1	76.2	98.0
% In the labor force	T1	25.2	12.0
% In the labor force	T2	31.5	10.0
Home			
% Family owns home	T1	25.2	2.0
% Family owns home	T2	36.6	4.0
% Moved to new home	T2	44.4	50.0
Family's Economic Situation (since 3 yrs. ago):			
% Better	T1	56.6	54.0
% Worse	T1	7.0	2.0
% Better	T2	38.7	30.6
% Worse	T2	14.1	12.2
Neighborhood Profile:[c] (1990 census tract data)			
% Below poverty line	T1	51.2	44.4
% Foreign born	T1	34.0	34.7
% White	T1	34.3	50.2
% Speak English only	T1	48.8	51.5

[a]FB = foreign-born children; US = U.S.-born children.

[b]No separate columns for U.S.-born youths from Cambodia and Laos are included because there were only a handful of such cases in the sample.

[c]Social and economic characteristics of the neighborhood (census tract) where respondent lived at the time of the T1 (1992) survey; data are drawn from the 1990 census.

All Others		Total		
FB	US	FB	US	Total
35.2	39.8	18.1	19.3	18.7
31.8	12.2	53.7	33.6	44.8
76.1	83.7	62.3	81.1	70.6
79.5	91.8	74.5	83.8	73.0
25.0	24.5	14.7	24.9	19.2
35.2	18.4	60.5	38.8	50.9
64.8	76.3	51.5	74.0	61.5
68.2	85.7	55.0	79.0	65.6
44.3	80.6	34.8	68.0	49.5
54.0	81.6	41.1	72.7	55.1
47.7	20.4	44.9	27.8	37.3
52.3	56.1	55.8	52.1	54.1
11.6	14.3	8.4	11.0	9.6
45.5	30.6	41.8	38.2	40.2
19.3	15.3	14.3	18.8	16.3
29.8	22.8	37.7	29.6	34.0
21.1	21.8	30.5	29.1	29.9
65.7	67.7	47.1	48.1	47.5
70.3	71.4	56.7	58.8	57.6

percent for adults ages 25 and over. By contrast, 43 percent of Filipino mothers have college degrees, well above national norms. The contrast is made even sharper by looking at the proportion of parents with less than a high school education—that is, less than what their children have already achieved: most of the more recently arrived foreign-born children from Mexico, Vietnam, Laos, and Cambodia have fathers and mothers who never completed secondary-level schooling. Mexican fathers and mothers, however, have high rates of labor force participation (both above national norms), whereas the Indochinese refugees have very low rates, indicative of their eligibility for and use of public assistance (again with the notable exception of the U.S.-born children of the 1975 Vietnamese).

Home ownership is a telling indicator of socioeconomic advancement and spatial stability. About half of the total sample lived in families who owned their own homes in 1992 (T1); three years later (T2) that proportion had edged up to 55 percent. But there is a huge gap between groups by nativity and nationality (see Figure 9-1). At T1 only a third of foreign-born children (in more recently immigrated families) lived in homes owned by their parents, compared to two-thirds of native-born children (in longer-resident families, by definition); by T2 the respective figures were 41 versus 73 percent. By nationality the socioeconomic gap is far wider, ranging at T2 from a low of 4 percent among Hmong families from Laos and 8 percent among the Cambodians to 89 percent among native-born Filipinos. On the other hand, one indicator of life change that was appraised positively by most of the youth was moving to a new home: 45 percent of the foreign-born children had moved to another home after T1, compared to 28 percent of the native-born children.

These homes are located in neighborhoods that range from the poorest in San Diego (particularly for Mexican, Cambodian, and Laotian immigrant families) to upper-middle-class suburbs, as suggested by the 1990 census tract data in Table 9-2. Still, for the sample as a whole at T1, their neighborhoods were located in census tracts with a poverty rate of 34 percent on average, much higher than the 1990 rates for the city of San Diego (13.4 percent)

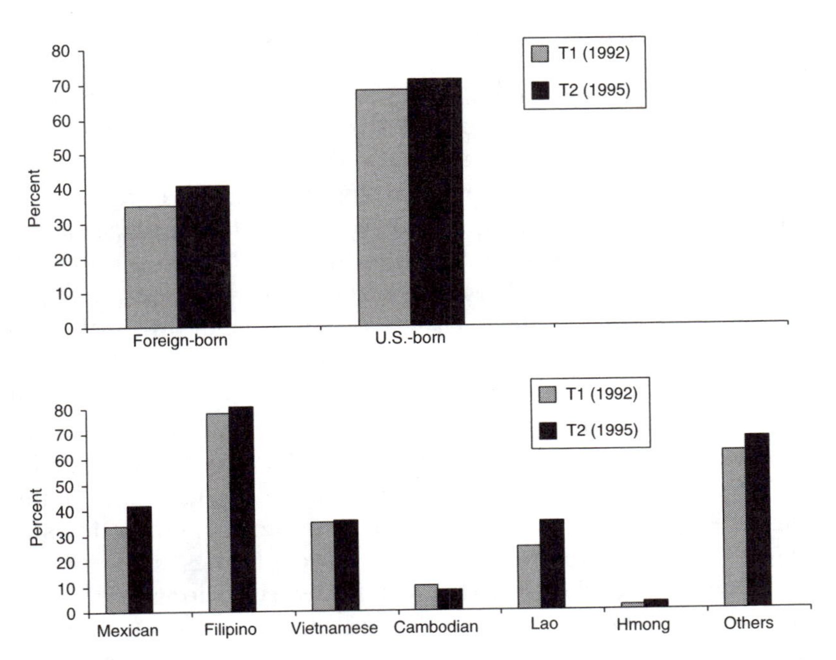

FIGURE 9-1 Homeownership, at T1 and T2, San Diego children of immigrants sample, by (top) nativity and (bottom) national origin (percentage).

and the United States (13.1 percent). They are also located in areas with above-average proportions of immigrants (30 percent are foreign born, versus 20 percent for the city overall) and with below-average proportions of white residents who speak English only.

The children, nonetheless, are quite optimistic about their families' economic progress. Asked in 1992 whether they believed their family's economic situation was better (or much better), the same, or worse (or much worse) than it had been three years before, 54 percent said it was better, compared to 10 percent who felt it had worsened. Asked the same question in 1995-1996, 40 percent believed it had improved, while 16 percent said it had worsened. Perceptions of downward mobility are significantly associated with depressive symptoms, as will be seen in a later section on psychological well-being outcomes.

Family Structure and the Quality of Family Relationships

Family and school are the central interpersonal contexts shaping the experiences of youth as they make their passages into adulthood. Table 9-3 presents data on the size and composition of family households and on a variety of indicators of the quality of parent-child relationships. At both T1 and T2, family structure emerged as a key determinant of educational performance outcomes—as well as of self-esteem and depressive symptoms. The presence of both natural parents at home is significantly and strongly associated with positive outcomes over time. Indeed, a vivid illustration of the effects of an intact family is the fact that it was a principal predictor of the probability that a student was reinterviewed at T2: while the overall reinterview rate was a solid 85.2 percent, the reinterview rate for students living in intact families at T1 was over 90 percent, compared to 75 percent for students living in stepfamilies or single-parent homes at T1.

Over time in the United States, for every nationality the size of their households decreases (as the economic need to pool resources with extended family members lessens). But there is also evidence, as Table 9-3 shows, that the proportion of intact families with both natural parents at home also decreases slightly, mainly as a result of marital separation or divorce. The sharpest declines were seen among the Hmong and the Cambodians (in the latter case involving a greater number of deaths of parents between T1 and T2 than for any other group). In general, the higher the socioeconomic status of these groups, the larger the proportion of intact families. The highest proportions (around 85 percent) of such stable family structures were noted among U.S.-born Vietnamese and Filipino children and the lowest (around 60 percent) for Mexican families, a figure matched in T2 by the Hmong and the Cambodians.

In addition to the importance of family structure is the question of the quality of familial relationships—that is, of the cohesiveness of families and of the degree of parent-child conflict—and of their effects, net of structural factors. Nearly three-fourths of the youth in the San Diego sample lived in intact families (74 percent at T1, 72 percent at T2), but within these families there is significant variance in the level of cohesiveness and conflict among family members. Indeed, growing up in immigrant families is often marked by wide linguistic and other acculturative gaps between parents and children that can exacerbate intergenerational conflicts, cause the children to feel embarrassed rather than proud of their parents as they try to fit in with native peers, and even lead to role reversals, as children assume adult roles prematurely by dint of circumstance. An indication of the importance of such relationships was suggested in an earlier multivariate analysis of cross-sectional results at T1 (Rumbaut, 1994a), which found that our measure of parent-child conflict emerged as the single strongest determinant—much more so than an intact family structure—of both self-esteem and depression. The same parent-child conflict index had a more significant and stronger (negative) effect on educational achievement (grade point average (GPA)) and aspirations than the weaker (positive) effect of an intact family structure (Rumbaut, 1997a). We will return to those analyses below.

Table 9-3 presents data on *family cohesion* (a three-item measure used at T2, scaled 1 to 5, as detailed in Appendix 9A); *familism* (a three-item scale, identified through factor analysis and used at T1 and T2, measuring a deeply ingrained sense of collective obligation to the family); *parent-child conflict* (a three-item scale also identified through factor analysis and used at T1 and T2); and the proportion of children who indicated *embarrassment* about their parents at both T1 and T2. The families of Mexico-born youth were the most cohesive and familistic and were characterized by relatively low and actually decreasing parent-child conflict over time, while those of U.S.-born Mexican youth have average scores in cohesion and conflict. Mexican-origin children, regardless of nativity, were significantly less likely to report embarrassment about their parents than any other nationality in the sample. By contrast, levels of parent-child conflict were otherwise significantly higher among foreign-born children than U.S.-born children generally, and by nationality such conflict was highest for the Filipino and Indochinese groups. The Hmong youth, who experience the greatest contextual dissonance between the world of their parents (the majority of whom are preliterate highlanders, with the Hmong language being but an oral tradition until missionaries in Laos developed a written notation for it in the

TABLE 9-3 Family Structure and Quality of Family Relationships of Children of Immigrants in San Diego, California, by Nativity of the Children and National Origin of Their Parents, in 1992 (T1) and 1995 (T2)

Characteristics by National Origin and Nativity[a]	Time	Mexico	
		FB[a]	US
Family-Household			
Family-household size	T1	5.1	4.5
	T2	4.5	4.1
% Intact family (both natural parents at home)	T1	62.1	65.5
	T2	58.0	60.7
% Stepfamily	T1	14.7	10.7
	T2	12.5	9.6
% Single parent, other	T1	23.2	23.7
	T2	29.5	29.7
% Grandparents at home	T1	6.7	8.5
	T2	3.6	6.8
% Uncles/aunts at home	T1	11.2	8.2
	T2	4.9	5.4
Family Relationships[b]			
Family cohesion (1-5)	T2	3.92	3.58
Familism scale (1-4)	T1	2.21	1.97
	T2	2.01	1.82
Parent-child conflict (1-4)	T1	1.67	1.69
	T2	1.57	1.66
% Embarrassed by parent	T1	6.7	8.2
	T2	10.3	6.2

1950s) and the Southern California megalopolitan world in which they are growing up, seemed caught in a quandary: they were the most apt to express embarrassment about and conflict with their parents at both T1 and T2, despite exhibiting high cohesion and familism scores at the same time. Familism scores were generally higher for foreign-born children than U.S.-born children in this sample and tended to decline over time in the United States, suggesting a growing acculturation to the individualistic values of American society.

Philippines		Vietnam		Cambodia[b]
FB	US	FB	US	FB
4.8	4.3	5.4	5.0	5.5
4.4	3.9	5.1	4.6	4.9
75.9	85.4	74.9	87.2	70.5
73.3	84.4	74.5	85.1	62.5
12.2	5.4	5.1	2.1	5.7
11.6	4.0	5.1	2.1	3.4
11.9	9.1	20.0	10.6	23.9
15.1	11.6	20.4	12.8	34.1
27.3	22.7	14.5	6.4	13.6
22.8	15.1	14.1	6.4	10.2
15.4	10.6	16.1	23.4	12.5
11.9	7.7	14.5	12.8	13.6
3.61	3.50	3.43	3.24	3.45
1.88	1.84	2.17	1.80	2.11
1.86	1.78	2.17	2.01	2.01
1.78	1.72	1.84	1.78	1.94
1.86	1.74	1.86	1.88	1.96
20.6	16.5	22.4	42.6	33.0
16.7	17.0	19.2	12.8	22.7

continued on next page

Patterns of Achievement: School Performance, Schoolwork, and School Contexts

An important reason for following this sample of students over time was to find out about their educational performance, their likelihood of dropping out of school before graduation, and the main determinants of these outcomes. One key question was whether the level of attainment exhibited by these children of immigrants matched, exceeded, or fell below the average for grades 9 through 12 for the San Diego school district overall (the nation's eighth largest). A fairly precise comparison of official GPAs and

TABLE 9-3 Continued

		Laos	
Characteristics by National Origin and Nativity[a]		Lao[b]	Hmong[b]
	Time	FB	FB
Family-Household			
Family-household size	T1	5.6	6.9
	T2	5.2	5.6
% Intact family (both natural parents at home)	T1	75.5	76.0
	T2	78.3	60.0
% Stepfamily	T1	5.6	4.0
	T2	6.3	4.0
% Single parent, other	T1	18.9	20.0
	T2	15.4	36.0
% Grandparents at home	T1	20.3	12.0
	T2	18.2	4.0
% Uncles/aunts at home	T1	10.5	8.0
	T2	9.1	2.0
Family Relationships[b]			
Family cohesion (1-5)	T2	3.55	3.79
Familism scale (1-4)	T1	2.17	2.16
	T2	2.22	2.13
Parent-child conflict (1-4)	T1	1.78	1.97
	T2	1.85	2.10
% Embarrassed by parent	T1	19.6	34.0
	T2	16.8	34.0

[a]FB = foreign-born children; US = U.S.-born children.

[b]See Appendix 9A for the composition and reliability of these scales. Family cohesion was measured by a three-item scale scored from 1 (never) to 5 (always). The three-item familism

dropout rates is possible, since the school system is the same source of information for both measures and both populations. Academic GPAs (the percentage of students with GPAs below 2.0 and above 3.0), broken down by grade level (9 through 12), for all schools districtwide in San Diego in 1993-1994, were compared against the GPAs earned in grades 9 through 12 in those schools by the entire original sample of 2,420 children of immigrants during 1992-1995. The results showed that at every grade level the children of immigrants outperformed the district norms, although

All Others		Total		
FB	US	FB	US	Total
3.8	3.3	5.2	4.3	4.8
3.4	3.1	4.7	3.9	4.4
61.4	71.4	71.3	76.4	73.5
64.8	73.5	69.3	73.9	71.3
11.4	12.2	9.5	8.0	8.8
8.0	9.2	8.4	6.8	7.7
27.3	16.3	19.3	15.6	17.6
27.3	17.3	22.4	19.3	21.0
14.8	11.2	17.1	15.0	16.1
10.2	8.2	13.9	10.6	12.5
9.1	4.1	13.1	9.7	11.6
1.1	3.1	9.8	6.4	8.3
3.71	3.48	3.63	3.51	3.58
2.04	1.65	2.08	1.87	1.99
1.96	1.63	2.04	1.80	1.93
1.70	1.59	1.78	1.70	1.75
1.73	1.57	1.81	1.70	1.76
26.1	26.5	20.2	15.6	18.2
20.5	15.3	17.2	12.8	15.3

scale is scored 1 (disagree a lot) to 4 (agree a lot). The parent-child conflict scale also consists of three items, scored 1 (not true at all) to 4 (very true). The data reported in the table are mean scores for these three scales.

the gap narrowed over time and grade level. For example, only 29 percent of all ninth graders in the district had GPAs above 3.0 (top students with A's and B's in their academic classes), compared to a much higher 44 percent of the ninth graders from immigrant families; and while 36 percent of ninth graders districtwide had low GPAs under 2.0 (less than a C on average), only half as many (18 percent) of the children of immigrants performed as poorly. Those differentials declined over time by grade level, so that the advantage by the twelfth grade is reduced to a few percentage points in favor of the children of immigrants.

The GPA gap narrows at least in part because a greater proportion of students districtwide drop out of school than do youth from immigrant families. The multiyear dropout rate for students in grades 9 through 12 in the San Diego schools in 1994 was 16.2 percent, nearly triple the rate of 5.7 percent for the entire original sample of children of immigrants—that is, of the 2,420 students who were originally interviewed in 1992 in the eighth and ninth grades, only 5.7 percent were officially determined to have dropped out of school at any point by 1996. That dropout rate is significantly lower than the dropout rates for preponderantly native non-Hispanic white (10.5 percent) and black (17.8 percent) high school students. Among students from immigrant families, the highest dropout rate (8.5 percent) was for Hispanic (mostly Mexican-origin) students, but even that rate was noticeably lower than the district norm and lower than the rate for non-Hispanic whites.

Table 9-4 describes the school performance of these youth over time and provides data on the level of effort they invested (comparing daily hours spent doing homework versus watching television) and on a range of characteristics of their school contexts. In terms of national origin there are major differences seen in all indicators of school performance. The highest GPAs were earned by Vietnamese and especially the "other Asian" (Chinese, Korean, Japanese, Indian) students, although the Vietnamese have average dropout rates relative to other nationalities in the sample as well as an above-average number of school suspensions (mostly for fighting and disruption/defiance). The lowest dropout rates were evidenced by the Lao and the Hmong—the two ethnic groups from Laos—while the Cambodians had the lowest number of school suspensions. Filipinos performed above average on all outcome measures. The Mexicans, on the other hand, evidenced significantly lower GPAs and higher rates of dropping out and of being suspended from school than any other group in the sample—although it bears recalling the above-mentioned finding that they still showed a lower multiyear dropout rate than that for the district as a whole and for mostly native non-Hispanic white and black students in the school system.

These results are remarkable enough in view of the relatively low socioeconomic status of a substantial proportion of the immigrant families. They become all the more remarkable in the context of other school data displayed in Table 9-4. At T1 over a quarter (28.7 percent) of the students were classified as LEP (limited English proficient) by their schools, ranging from virtually none of the native-born Filipinos to around two-thirds of the foreign-born Mexican, Cambodian, and Hmong students. That classification is supported by nationally standardized ASAT (Abbreviated Stanford Achievement Test) scores measuring English reading skills: the sample as a whole scored just below the fortieth percentile nationally, and the foreign-born groups with the highest proportion of LEP students scored in the bottom quartile nationally. That language handicap reflects their relatively recent arrival as nonnative English speakers; a language other than English is spoken in the homes of nearly all of these students (96 percent at T2), although, as will be shown below, their fluency in the parental language tends to atrophy over time, while their ability in and preference for English increase. On the other hand, as would be expected, all groups do better in math computation than English reading tests (for an earlier districtwide study, see Rumbaut and Ima, 1988). At T1 their ASAT math achievement test scores placed the sample as a whole at the fiftieth percentile nationally, with some students achieving extraordinarily high scores, notably the U.S.-born Vietnamese and "other Asian" students, placing most of them in the top quartile nationally. In fact, a disproportionate number of U.S.-born students were classified as *gifted* by the schools, as shown in Table 9-4.

One key reason for these students' above-average GPAs, despite significant socioeconomic and linguistic handicaps, is shown in the middle panel of Table 9-4. *They work for it*. At both T1 and T2 these students reported spending an average of over two hours per day on homework, with the foreign-born students compensating for language and other handicaps by significantly outworking their U.S.-born peers. From the end of junior high at T1 to the end of senior high at T2, the level of effort put into schoolwork increased across all nationalities. The sole exception in this regard were the Hmong, who at T1 posted the highest average number of daily homework hours (2.9) but decreased to 2.6 hours at

TABLE 9-4 School Performance, Schoolwork, and School Contexts of Children of Immigrants in San Diego, California, by Nativity of the Children and National Origin of Their Parents, in 1992 (T1) and 1995 (T2)

Characteristics by National Origin and Nativity[a]	Time	Mexico	
		FB[a]	US
School Performance			
Academic GPA[b]	T1	2.37	2.25
	T2	2.32	2.31
Reading: national percentile[c]	T1	22.3	29.0
Math: national percentile[d]	T1	28.5	33.5
% Classified as LEP[e]	T1	62.5	26.8
% Classified as gifted[f]	T1	4.9	6.5
% Dropped out since T1[g]	T2	5.4	6.5
% Suspended since T1[h]	T2	22.8	24.3
Homework and TV			
Homework hours daily	T1	1.73	1.66
	T2	2.05	1.88
TV-watching hours daily	T1	2.80	3.02
	T2	2.20	2.39
School Contexts			
School Safety (% agree)	T2		
% Many gangs in school		36.9	38.7
% Frequent ethnic fights		44.1	44.3
% Disruptions by others		45.9	45.7
% Don't feel safe there		24.9	26.3
School Events (this year)	T2		
% Had property stolen		36.8	37.4
% Was offered drugs		20.3	33.4
% Was threatened		18.1	13.4
% Got in physical fight		20.3	16.1
School Teaching (agree)	T2		
% Teaching is good		90.1	85.5
% Teachers are interested		86.4	80.7
% Grading is fair		74.4	72.8
% Discipline is fair		76.8	73.2

Philippines		Vietnam		Cambodia[b]
FB	US	FB	US	FB
3.02	2.98	3.05	3.21	2.75
2.86	2.95	3.05	3.14	2.58
50.2	54.0	33.3	63.4	14.0
57.9	62.3	57.4	70.6	35.8
13.8	0.5	45.1	4.3	70.1
19.3	24.4	11.8	38.3	1.1
2.3	2.7	3.1	2.1	3.4
11.9	12.1	21.2	10.6	17.0
2.57	2.33	2.55	2.58	2.27
2.79	2.61	2.89	2.89	2.44
3.21	3.09	2.64	2.41	2.72
2.51	2.37	2.18	2.20	2.26
56.6	53.1	51.0	46.8	60.2
46.6	44.0	54.9	66.0	67.0
55.3	54.3	58.8	46.8	54.0
23.8	22.5	21.7	25.5	25.0
48.2	41.7	45.1	55.3	42.0
24.4	31.3	13.3	36.2	10.2
21.6	17.6	16.1	23.4	21.6
15.8	9.7	17.6	10.9	17.0
85.9	88.6	85.4	85.1	86.4
83.0	82.5	77.4	78.7	85.2
74.9	72.5	70.6	66.0	71.6
78.1	73.3	72.3	74.5	70.1

continued on next page

TABLE 9-4 Continued

Characteristics by National Origin and Nativity[a]	Time	Laos: Lao[b] FB	Laos: Hmong[b] FB
School Performance			
Academic GPA[b]	T1	2.89	2.92
	T2	2.89	2.63
Reading: national percentile[c]	T1	22.6	15.8
Math: national percentile[d]	T1	42.6	30.6
% Classified as LEP[e]	T1	49.0	66.0
% Classified as gifted[f]	T1	5.6	0.0
% Dropped out since T1[g]	T2	2.8	4.0
% Suspended since T1[h]	T2	13.3	18.0
Homework and TV			
Homework hours daily	T1	2.36	2.86
	T2	2.47	2.58
TV-watching hours daily	T1	2.63	2.40
	T2	2.25	1.96
School Contexts			
School Safety (% agree)	T2		
% Many gangs in school		62.7	77.6
% Frequent ethnic fights		72.1	77.5
% Disruptions by others		64.1	67.3
% Don't feel safe there		30.8	46.9
School Events (this year)	T2		
% Had property stolen		49.0	38.0
% Was offered drugs		16.8	10.0
% Was threatened		19.6	22.0
% Got in physical fight		21.8	12.0
School Teaching (agree)	T2		
% Teaching is good		92.3	87.8
% Teachers are interested		81.7	64.6
% Grading is fair		76.9	65.3
% Discipline is fair		75.9	72.9

[a]FB = foreign-born children; US = U.S.-born children.

[b]Cumulative academic grade point average (A = 4, B = 3, C = 2, D = 1, F = 0), weighted for advanced placement and honors courses (for which A = 5, B = 4, C = 3).

[c]National percentile rank based on the English reading vocabulary and comprehension subtest of the Abbreviated Stanford Achievement Test (ASAT).

[d]National percentile rank based on the mathematics subtest of the ASAT.

[e]LEP: limited English proficient student, as officially classified by the school system, based partly on standardized English proficiency tests.

[f]Gifted: official school classification, based on standardized tests and other evaluations.

[g]A dropout, as officially defined by the California State Department of Education, is any student in grades 7 through 12 who left school before graduation or attainment of its legal equivalent (e.g., GED) and did not return to school or another educational program by mid-October of the

All Others		Total		
FB	US	FB	US	Total
3.06	3.11	2.87	2.72	2.80
3.16	3.24	2.80	2.73	2.77
44.2	69.9	33.4	46.3	39.5
56.9	69.2	47.5	51.9	49.6
34.1	1.0	42.5	11.4	28.7
21.6	45.9	11.2	20.2	15.2
3.4	2.0	3.4	4.0	3.7
18.2	12.2	17.2	16.9	17.1
2.33	2.32	2.36	2.08	2.23
2.85	2.65	2.61	2.34	2.49
2.53	2.60	2.81	2.98	2.88
2.39	1.80	2.29	2.31	2.30
36.0	41.2	51.9	46.0	49.3
45.9	36.1	53.8	44.8	49.8
57.5	43.3	55.8	49.7	53.1
26.7	18.6	25.5	24.0	24.8
50.6	35.1	44.5	40.3	42.6
21.8	28.9	18.3	32.1	24.4
14.9	16.5	18.9	16.3	17.7
11.6	10.3	17.2	12.7	15.2
83.9	80.4	87.4	86.3	86.9
79.1	79.4	81.7	80.8	81.3
79.1	74.2	73.9	72.3	73.2
75.9	74.2	75.5	73.2	74.5

following year, as evidenced by a transcript request or other reliable documentation. The rates indicated are the percentage of students who dropped out at any time between spring 1992 and spring 1996.

[h]Percentage suspended from school for any reason at least once between 1991 and 1995. Suspending a student from school for one or more days is, except for expulsion, the most severe official reaction to student disciplinary infractions. Most (nearly 80%) of the suspensions in the San Diego school district are meted out for physical injury (fights, threats, attempts) and disruption/defiance; others include property damage, tobacco/alcohol/drugs, and weapons infractions. Suspensions rise sharply in grade 7, peaking in grade 8, and dropping steadily until grade 12, and male students are suspended far more often than females (districtwide the male-to-female suspension ratio was 3:1 in 1993-1994, a 10-year low). The average suspension in grades 9 through 12 is approximately 2.5 days.

T2 (still above the sample average); not surprisingly, that drop in effort was matched by a drop in their GPAs from 2.92 at T1 to 2.63 at T2, the main drop in GPA among all groups in the sample. GPA, more so than achievement test scores, is a measure of school performance that reflects the level of effort made by the student and rewarded by the teacher. Overall, the children of immigrants generally maintained their level of GPA attainment from T1 (2.80) to T2 (2.77).

In multivariate analyses at T1 the number of daily homework hours emerged as the strongest single predictor of higher GPAs, while the number of hours spent watching television daily was significantly associated with lower GPAs (see Rumbaut, 1995, 1997b). By T2 the data show that students who had dedicated more hours to schoolwork in junior high did significantly better in terms of educational achievement three years later. Conversely, students who spent a large number of hours in front of the television by age 14 were more prone to perform poorly in subsequent years. The negative effect of television on children's academic performance is confirmed by these findings—although the effect, while still significantly negative, becomes weaker. Table 9-4 shows that for all groups without exception the average amount of time spent watching television declined from the early to midadolescent years at T1 to the end of high school and adolescence at T2, as the students matured and got drivers' licenses and part-time jobs. Still, taken together, these results suggest that, even among students from low socioeconomic backgrounds, those with ambition and work discipline were more prone to get ahead educationally.

What other factors were found to be most predictive of children of immigrants' educational achievement and aspirations? A preliminary multivariate analysis (not shown for reasons of space) suggests that falling behind or getting ahead in school is largely determined by the same set of factors. Children who come from intact families with both natural parents present at home do much better—that is, they have higher GPAs, lower dropout rates and suspensions, and higher aspirations. This is even more pronounced in families (even intact families) with lower levels of conflict in parent-child interactions. The greater the stability of the family, both structurally *and* emotionally, the greater the educational achievement and aspirations—and, in addition, the higher the self-esteem and the lower the level of depressive symptoms. Overall, low-conflict intact families exhibit the best outcomes across the board, while high-conflict nonintact families fare the worst in high dropout and school suspension rates, although high-conflict families regardless of type of parental structure yield equally poor GPAs, self-esteem, and depression scores. The quality of familial relationships, even more than family structure, has very significant effects on school performance.

Similarly, youth who come from high-status families also have a distinct advantage. Those whose mothers and fathers have a college education perform much better in terms of achieving high GPAs and remaining in school without disciplinary action taken against them, than do those whose parents have lesser levels of education. These same patterns are evident for other indicators of socioeconomic status, such as homeownership and neighborhood poverty rates. Students who stay in school and earn higher grades with fewer suspensions tend to attend suburban schools in higher-status areas. It is scarcely surprising that more cohesive and resourceful home and school environments lead to higher educational achievement. In this respect, children of immigrants are no different than native-born children.

While gender makes only a slight difference in terms of remaining in school, it strongly affects grades and suspensions, with females exhibiting superior performance compared to male students as well as an edge in educational aspirations. For both males and females, however, hard work and a clear sense of future goals pay off handsomely. High occupational goals in early adolescence (which are detailed in the next section) are closely associated with remaining in school and with better educational performance. So is the influence of peers: the worst educational outcomes, by far, were associated with having close friends who themselves had dropped out of school or had no plans for college; conversely, the best outcomes were attained by students whose circle of friends largely consisted of college-bound peers.

The bottom panel in Table 9-4 now shifts the focus to specific events and circumstances in the school attended by the respondent. The items listed were factor analyzed and found to make up three factors (which were subsequently combined to produce three indices): (1) an index of perceived *school safety*—including the presence of gangs at school, the frequency of interracial or interethnic fights, appraisals of the level of disruptions by others experienced at school, and whether the respondent felt safe at school; (2) an index of *stressful school events* occurring to the respondent in the current year—including one or more instances of getting into a physical fight, being threatened, being offered drugs, or having personal property stolen while at school; and (3) a measure of *teaching quality and fairness*—appraisals of whether the teachers are interested and the teaching is good and of the fairness of grading and discipline. Despite very high reports of disruptions, gang presence and interethnic fights at school (about 50 percent reported these), not feeling safe at school (25 percent did not feel safe), and a high incidence of stressful events (from thefts to threats), almost nine-tenths (87 percent) gave high marks to their teachers, in part another way of underscoring the value they place on education. As will be detailed below, it turns out that these indices of contextual factors had significant effects in multivariate analyses of self-esteem and depressive symptoms at T2.

Patterns of Ambition: Educational and Occupational Aspirations and Values

Children of immigrants are ambitious and their goals—both their aspirations and their expectations— remain stable over time, as evidenced by the results shown in Table 9-5. At both T1 and T2 an identical 61 percent aspired to an advanced degree. Asked for a *realistic* assessment of their chances of fulfilling their aspirations, at T1, 35 percent "realistically" expected to obtain advanced degrees and another 39 percent would not be satisfied with less than a college degree. At T2, as the high school years came to a close, these proportions edged up slightly—37 percent now "realistically" expected to earn advanced degrees and another 41 percent expected to graduate from college—showing the resilience over time of these aspirations. The proportion of those who, based on a realistic assessment, believed that they would not reach as far as a college degree dropped from 26 percent at T1 to 22 percent at T2. Given the modest family origins and material resources of many of these children, their ambitions and even realistic expectations may be quite disproportionate with what many will be able to achieve in the end. In part, their optimism may be triggered by their appraisal of the economic progress of their families (as seen above in Table 9-2) and by their own efforts so far (as suggested by the results presented in Table 9-4).

Ambition matters. The research literature shows that high expectations are necessary for subsequent achievement. However, there are significant variations both among immigrant communities and in the social context that would make attainment of their expectations possible. While most of these youth aim high, the loftiest goals are found among the Filipinos, Vietnamese (most notably the children of the 1975 refugees), and "other Asians," with about half of them (whether foreign born or native born) believing that they would achieve a postgraduate degree—percentages that *increased* over time. The least ambitious expectations are seen among the Mexicans, Cambodians, and Laotians—who are also the groups whose expectations *decreased* over time. Thus, there are major differences in aspirations by family socioeconomic status, and this gap appears to widen over time. Children from better-off families have predictably higher and more secure plans for the future. The correlations between parental socioeconomic status variables and children's educational goals and expectations are positive and highly significant.

Indeed, even more ambitious than these children are their own parents. As Table 9-5 clearly shows, asked what their parents' expectations were for their educational futures, the students felt that their parents expected them to achieve at a much higher level than the students themselves aspired to. Indeed, for many immigrants that is precisely the purpose of bringing their children to the United States. For example, at T2, while 37 percent of the students expected to attain an advanced degree, 60 percent of their parents did so; and while 22 percent of the children expected to stop short of a college degree, only 9 percent of the parents held such a low expectation. Parental expectations are significantly correlated with students' school performance.

In sharp contrast to perceived parental pressures to achieve are the plans of the students' close friends—and here again the types of peer groups the students are embedded in vary in part

TABLE 9-5 Educational and Occupational Aspirations and Expectations of Children of Immigrants and of Their Parents and Peers by Nativity of the Children and National Origin of Their Parents, in 1992 (T1) and 1995 (T2)

Characteristics by National Origin and Nativity[a]	Time	Mexico	
		FB[a]	US
Educational Aspirations			
% Advanced degree	T1	53.8	48.4
	T2	48.7	47.5
% College degree	T1	22.0	28.9
	T2	26.3	31.6
% Less than college	T1	24.2	22.7
	T2	25.0	20.9
Educational Expectations[b]			
% Advanced degree	T1	33.0	28.0
	T2	25.9	23.2
% College degree	T1	30.4	35.6
	T2	31.3	44.4
% Less than college	T1	36.6	36.4
	T2	42.9	32.5
Parents' Aspirations[c]			
% Advanced degree	T2	57.1	47.2
% College degree	T2	27.2	36.7
% Less than college	T2	15.6	16.1
Occupational Aspirations			
% Upper-level	T1	61.2	63.6
white-collar job	T2	66.1	59.6
Plans of Most Friends[d]			
% Dropped out of school	T2	6.7	8.3
% No college plans	T2	11.4	11.6
% Get a job after high school	T2	33.5	32.2
% Go to 2-year college	T2	25.9	24.9
% Go to 4-year university	T2	26.2	26.7

Philippines		Vietnam		Cambodia[b]
FB	US	FB	US	FB
75.8	71.1	55.2	89.4	54.0
72.7	70.7	64.3	87.2	51.1
19.4	24.7	32.1	6.4	33.3
21.9	22.8	26.3	10.6	34.1
4.8	4.2	12.7	4.3	12.6
5.5	6.5	9.4	2.1	14.8
40.8	40.2	37.3	46.8	23.9
46.9	43.2	46.3	51.1	21.6
42.4	43.2	39.6	44.7	40.9
38.6	43.5	38.4	42.6	47.7
16.7	16.5	23.1	8.5	35.2
14.5	13.3	15.3	6.4	30.7
65.3	63.5	62.7	78.7	58.0
31.2	32.1	26.7	21.3	33.0
3.5	4.4	10.6	0.0	9.1
74.9	80.7	67.8	76.6	69.3
82.0	83.7	76.1	80.9	76.1
1.9	1.7	3.6	0.0	3.4
4.8	4.5	5.5	6.4	11.5
32.2	26.3	15.5	19.1	25.3
31.4	27.4	18.3	23.4	38.6
50.5	54.0	47.4	57.4	45.5

continued on next page

TABLE 9-5 Continued

Characteristics by National Origin and Nativity[a]	Time	Laos	
		Lao[b]	Hmong[b]
		FB	FB
Educational Aspirations			
% Advanced degree	T1	42.9	40.0
	T2	50.3	54.0
% College degree	T1	32.1	26.0
	T2	28.7	30.0
% Less than college	T1	25.0	34.0
	T2	21.0	16.0
Educational Expectations[b]			
% Advanced degree	T1	20.3	12.0
	T2	21.7	6.0
% College degree	T1	33.6	30.0
	T2	47.6	62.0
% Less than college	T1	46.2	58.0
	T2	30.8	32.0
Parents' Aspirations[c]			
% Advanced degree	T2	56.6	48.0
% College degree	T2	28.7	36.0
% Less than college	T2	14.7	16.0
Occupational Aspirations			
% Upper-level	T1	62.9	50.0
white-collar job	T2	73.4	58.0
Plans of Most Friends[d]			
% Dropped out of school	T2	3.5	4.0
% No college plans	T2	6.4	4.0
% Get a job after high school	T2	25.4	16.0
% Go to 2-year college	T2	24.6	30.0
% Go to 4-year university	T2	42.3	36.0

[a]FB = foreign-born children; US = U.S.-born children.

[b]Responses to the question, "And *realistically* speaking, what is the highest level of education you think you will get?"

[c]Responses to the question, "What is the highest level of education that your parents want you to get?"

[d]The question asked "How many of your friends have . . . ?" Data above show the applicable responses pertaining to "many or most friends" of the respondent.

All Others		Total		
FB	US	FB	US	Total
65.9	75.3	59.0	63.6	61.1
68.2	72.2	60.7	62.5	61.5
28.4	23.7	26.4	25.1	25.8
23.9	21.6	25.9	25.7	25.8
5.7	1.0	14.6	11.3	13.1
8.0	6.2	13.4	11.8	12.7
50.0	49.0	34.2	36.6	35.3
56.8	61.2	36.8	37.5	37.1
35.2	42.9	37.2	40.2	38.5
30.7	26.5	39.2	42.1	40.5
14.8	8.2	28.6	23.2	26.2
12.5	12.2	24.0	20.4	22.4
64.8	66.3	60.5	58.5	59.6
31.8	32.7	29.7	33.1	31.2
3.4	1.0	9.8	8.4	9.2
70.5	76.5	67.2	73.4	70.0
78.4	76.5	74.8	73.3	74.2
6.9	3.1	4.0	4.3	4.1
8.0	6.1	7.0	7.7	7.3
16.1	17.5	25.6	27.2	26.3
20.7	11.3	26.4	24.4	25.5
51.7	55.1	43.6	43.2	43.4

by family socioeconomic status. Children from higher-status families, growing up in neighborhoods where residents have low poverty rates and high levels of education, are also much less likely to have friends who have dropped out of high school, who have no college plans, or who plan to skip college and get a full-time job after high school. Conversely, most of the friends of these advantaged youth also intend to attend four-year colleges or universities. The sharpest contrast in these friendship networks is seen between the U.S.-born Vietnamese (57 percent of whom report that most of their friends plan to attend four-year colleges or universities, while virtually none have friends who dropped out of school) and Mexican students (only a quarter of whom have friends who plan to attend four-year colleges, a third have friends who plan to get a job after high school, and about 8 percent have close friends who had already dropped out of school). These social circles can exercise a powerful influence in either reinforcing or undercutting adolescents' high aspirations and confidence in reaching them.

Table 9-5 also reports results at T1 and T2 of the occupational aspirations of children of immigrants. The proportion aspiring to upper-level white-collar professions increased from 70 percent of the total sample at T1 to 74 percent at T2. Such goals increased for every group, by nativity and nationality, except for U.S.-born youth of Mexican parents, for whom a slight decline was registered (from 64 to 60 percent). For the overall sample the proportion of native-born children of immigrants who reported such aspirations remained identical (73 percent) from junior high to the end of senior high, while such aspirations increased for foreign-born youth from two-thirds of them at T1 to three-fourths at T2. In general, as in the case with educational aspirations, the stability and resilience of these occupational aspirations over time is underscored by these latest data. And as with educational goals, higher-status families encourage loftier occupational goals in their children. By and large, children of immigrants imitate their native peers in preferring careers perceived as the most prestigious and remunerative.

The professions of choice at T1 (not shown in Table 9-5) were physician (22 percent), engineer (14 percent), business executive/manager (10 percent), lawyer (8 percent), and computer programmer (7 percent). In the T2 survey three years later the top three choices were again physician (20 percent), engineer (15 percent), and business executive/manager (14 percent), followed now by nurse/physical therapist (13 percent) and professor/teacher (9 percent). By T2 the choice of law as a career fell to ninth place, below clerical/sales (5 percent), while computer programmer remained the choice of 7 percent of the sample. In the most popular career choices there were noticeable differences by nationality at both T1 and T2. By the latest survey, almost a third of the Vietnamese (30 percent) aspired to become physicians—up from 24 percent in 1992—and another 18 percent aspired to business management—up from 12 percent in the first survey. Among the Filipinos, the proportion planning to become doctors declined over this time from 28 to 23 percent, while the choice of a nursing career more than doubled from 9 to 22 percent (the career modeled by many of their mothers). Among the Mexicans and the other Indochinese groups, occupational plans became more realistic, with the proportions planning to become doctors and lawyers declining significantly by T2, while more modest professions increased in popularity. Still, notably, by T2 Mexicans ranked above all other groups in their aspiration to become lawyers.

Finally, as depicted in Figure 9-2, the children of immigrants in this sample almost universally value the importance of a good education. Out of a variety of choices given in the T2 survey, 90 percent ranked a good education as "very important" (more than any other value), and another 81 percent deemed becoming an expert in one's field "very important," while only half as many (45 percent) equally valued "having lots of money."

Language Shifts: English Proficiency and Preference

Language preference is a key index of cultural assimilation. Over 90 percent of these children of immigrants reported speaking a language other than English at home, mostly with their parents. But as seen in Table 9-6, at T1 two-thirds of the total sample (66 percent) already preferred to speak English instead of their parents' native tongue, including 56 percent of the foreign-born youth and 78 percent of the U.S.-born youth. Three years later the proportion had grown significantly to over four-fifths (82 per-

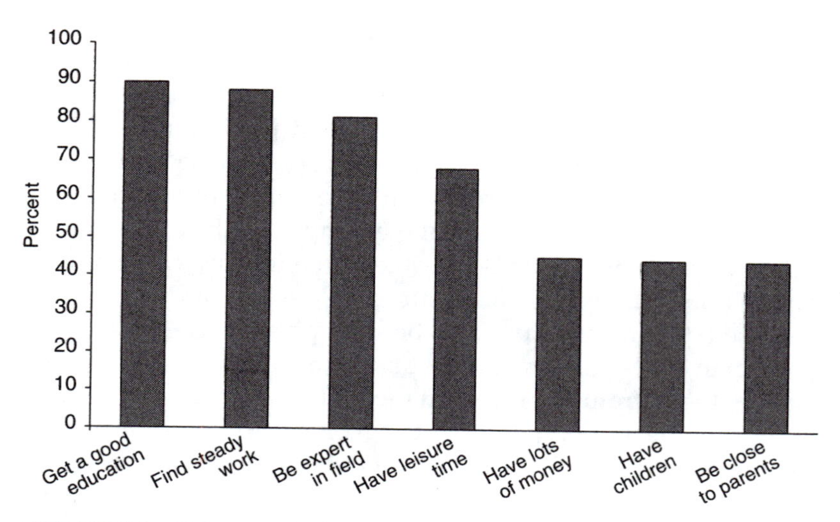

FIGURE 9-2 Values ranked "very important," T2 (1995), San Diego children of immigrants sample (percentage).

cent), including 72 percent of the foreign-born youth and over 90 percent of the U.S.-born youth. The most linguistically assimilated in this respect were the Filipinos, among whom 92 percent of those born in the Philippines (where English is an official language) and 98 percent of those born in the United States preferred English by T2. But even among the most mother-tongue-retentive group—the Mexican-origin youth living in a Spanish-named city on the Mexican border with a large Spanish-speaking immigrant population and a wide range of Spanish-language radio and television stations—the force of linguistic assimilation was incontrovertible: while at T1 only a third (32 percent) of the Mexico-born children preferred English, by T2 that preference had doubled to 61 percent; and while just over half (53 percent) of the U.S.-born youth preferred English at T1, that proportion had jumped to four-fifths (79 percent) three years later (see Figure 9-3).

A main reason for this rapid language shift in use and preference has to do with their increasing fluency in English (both spoken and written) relative to their level of fluency in their mother tongue. Respondents were asked to evaluate their ability to speak, understand, read, and write in both English and the non-English mother tongue; the response format (identical to the item used in the U.S. census) ranged from "not at all" and "not well" to "well" and "very well." Over two-thirds of the total sample reported speaking English "very well" (67 percent at T1, growing to 71 percent at T2), compared to only about a third who reported an equivalent level of spoken fluency in the non-English language. Naturally, these differentials are much more pronounced among U.S.-born youth, most of whom (87 percent) spoke English "very well," while only a fourth of them could speak their parental language "very well." But even among the foreign born, those who spoke English very well surpassed by 59 to 44 percent those who spoke the foreign language just as well.

The differences in reading fluency (not shown in the table for reasons of space) are much sharper still: those who can read English "very well" triple the proportion of those who can read a non-English language very well (68 to 23 percent). Only the Mexican-born youth maintained by T2 an edge in their reported knowledge of Spanish over English, and even they indicated a preference for English. The ability to maintain a sound level of literacy in a language—particularly in languages with entirely different alphabets and rules of syntax and grammar, such as many of the Asian languages brought by immigrants to California—is nearly impossible in the absence of schools that teach it and a community in which it can be regularly practiced.

As a consequence, the bilingualism of these children of immigrants becomes increasingly uneven and unstable. The data in Table 9-6 and Figure 9-3 vividly underscore the rapidity with which English triumphs and foreign languages atrophy in the United States—even in San Diego, with the busiest international border crossing in the world—as the second generation not only comes to speak, read, and write it fluently but prefers it overwhelmingly to their parents' native tongue.

This linear pattern of rapid linguistic assimilation is constant across nationalities and socioeconomic levels and suggests that, over time, the use of and fluency in foreign languages will inevitably decline—results that directly rebut nativist alarms about the perpetuation of foreign-language enclaves in immigrant commu-

TABLE 9-6 Language Preference and Proficiency and Ethnic Self-Identity Among Children of Immigrants in San Diego, California, by Nativity of the Children and National Origin of their Parents, in 1992 (T1) and 1995 (T2)

Characteristics by National Origin and Nativity[a]	Time	Mexico	
		FB[a]	US
English Language			
% Prefers English	T1	32.1	52.8
	T2	62.5	78.2
% Speaks it "very well"	T1	38.5	74.1
	T2	48.2	77.7
Non-English Language			
% Speaks it "very well"	T1	74.0	44.8
	T2	78.1	49.9
Ethnic Self-Identity[b]			
% "American"	T1	0.0	2.8
	T2	0.0	2.0
% Hyphenated American	T1	14.7	40.4
	T2	12.1	39.3
% National origin	T1	33.5	8.2
	T2	67.9	26.3
% Racial/pan-ethnic	T1	51.3	44.9
	T2	18.8	27.7
% Mixed ethnicity, other	T1	0.4	3.7
	T2	1.3	4.8
Ethnic Identity Salience[c]			
"How important is this identity to you?"	T2		
% Very important		73.2	65.5
% Somewhat important		18.8	25.1
% Not important		8.0	9.4

Philippines		Vietnam		Cambodia[b]
FB	US	FB	US	FB
81.4	95.8	43.9	91.5	67.0
92.6	98.0	69.0	91.5	85.2
75.2	94.3	45.9	95.7	48.9
83.3	93.6	47.8	89.4	50.0
23.2	2.0	41.3	10.6	33.3
23.0	3.6	38.7	4.3	33.3
0.3	5.2	2.4	8.5	2.3
1.0	2.0	0.0	2.1	0.0
50.8	66.2	43.9	70.2	46.6
21.9	48.4	28.2	51.1	30.7
41.8	21.5	45.9	19.1	40.9
72.7	42.5	56.1	36.2	48.9
3.5	1.2	0.4	0.0	1.1
0.6	2.0	14.5	8.5	20.5
3.5	5.9	7.5	2.1	9.1
3.9	5.2	1.2	2.1	0.0
75.5	65.2	58.9	61.7	57.5
21.0	26.2	26.1	29.8	29.9
3.5	8.6	15.0	8.5	12.6

continued on next page

TABLE 9-6 Continued

Characteristics by National Origin and Nativity[a]	Time	Laos: Lao[b] FB	Laos: Hmong[b] FB
English Language			
% Prefers English	T1	51.7	66.0
	T2	74.1	58.0
% Speaks it "very well"	T1	44.1	22.0
	T2	49.0	30.0
Non-English Language			
% Speaks it "very well"	T1	42.0	50.0
	T2	40.6	44.0
Ethnic Self-Identity[b]			
% "American"	T1	0.7	4.0
	T2	0.7	0.0
% Hyphenated American	T1	28.7	26.0
	T2	19.6	12.0
% National origin	T1	61.5	62.0
	T2	67.1	48.0
% Racial/pan-ethnic	T1	2.1	2.0
	T2	11.2	38.0
% Mixed ethnicity, other	T1	7.0	6.0
	T2	1.4	2.0
Ethnic Identity Salience[c]			
"How important is this identity to you?"	T2		
% Very important		58.2	78.0
% Somewhat important		30.5	11.3
% Not important		14.0	8.0

[a]FB = foreign-born children; US = U.S.-born children.

[b]Responses to the open-ended survey question: "How do you identify, that is, what do you call yourself?" "Hispanic," "Chicano," "Latino," "Black," and "Asian" are classified as racial or pan-ethnic identities; a "Hmong" ethnic identity is included under "national origin"; "Cuban-Mexican" or "Chinese-Thai" are under "mixed" identities.

All Others		Total		
FB	US	FB	US	Total
55.7	92.9	56.1	78.4	66.0
72.7	99.0	75.8	89.8	82.0
59.8	93.9	52.2	86.2	67.3
70.5	93.9	58.5	87.0	71.2
49.4	11.2	43.4	20.3	33.1
50.6	18.2	43.7	25.7	36.3
3.4	18.4	1.3	5.8	3.3
3.4	9.2	0.6	2.7	1.6
18.2	38.8	35.8	53.0	43.4
9.1	25.5	20.2	42.4	30.1
44.3	11.2	44.3	15.7	31.6
18.2	11.2	60.7	32.3	48.1
22.7	17.3	13.2	19.8	16.1
58.0	40.8	15.8	16.8	16.2
11.4	14.3	5.4	5.7	5.5
11.4	13.3	2.7	5.7	4.0
60.2	53.1	67.1	63.6	65.5
22.7	29.2	23.4	26.2	24.6
17.0	17.7	9.5	10.2	9.8

[c]A follow-up question asked "How important is this identity to you, that is, what you call yourself?" The highest salience scores were found among those identifying by national origin; the lowest were among those identifying as "American"; in between were the salience scores for hyphenated American and racial/pan-ethnic identities.

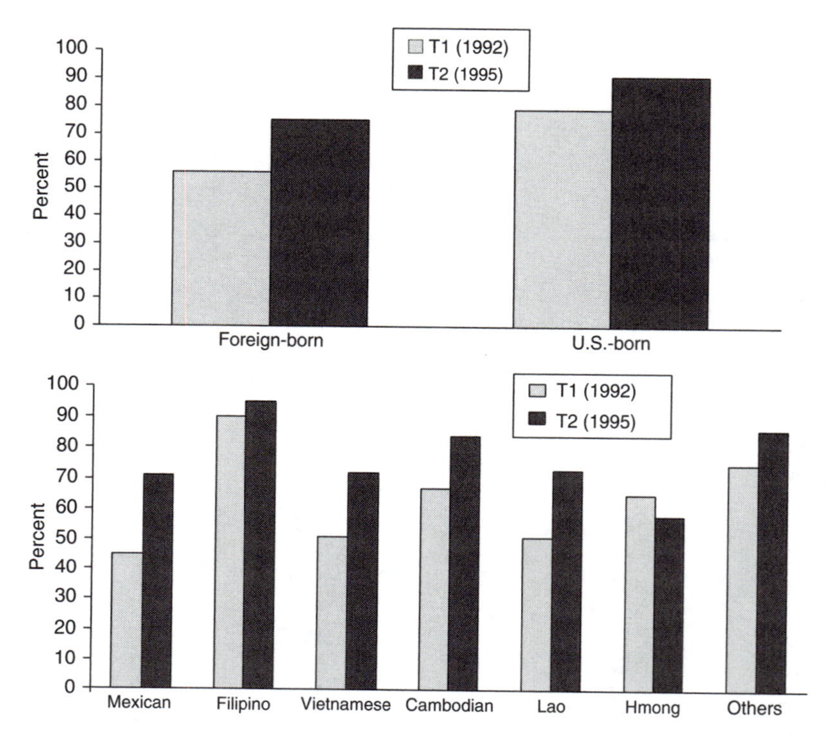

FIGURE 9-3 Percentages who preferred English, at T1 and T2, San Diego children of immigrants sample, by (top) nativity and (bottom) national origin.

nities. There is little reason to doubt, based on these findings, that the linguistic outcomes for the third generation—the grandchildren of the present wave of immigrants—will be any different than what has been the age-old pattern in American immigration history: the grandchildren may learn a few foreign words and phrases as a quaint vestige of their ancestry, but they will most likely grow up speaking English only.

Ethnic Identity Shifts and Perceptions of Discrimination

In both surveys an identical open-ended question was asked to ascertain each respondent's ethnic self-identity. The results (and the wording of the question) are presented in the middle panel of Table 9-6. Four main types of ethnic identities became apparent: (1) a plain "American" identity; (2) a hyphenated American identity; (3) a national origin identity (e.g., Mexican, Filipino, Vietnamese); and (4) a pan-ethnic minority identity (e.g., Hispanic, Latino, Chicano, Asian, black). The way adolescents see themselves is significant. Self-identities and ethnic loyalties can often influence patterns of behavior and outlook independent of the status of their families or the types of schools that children attend. That significance is confirmed by the students themselves: the overwhelming majority perceive their ethnic identity as "important" to themselves and over half deem it "very important." Ethnic self-identities vary significantly over time—yet not in a straight-line fashion, like an arrow, as was the case with the language shift to English, but in a reactive nonlinear dialectical fashion, rather more like a boomerang. The data in Table 9-6 illustrate that pattern compellingly.

In 1992 almost a third (32 percent) of the sample identified by national origin; the largest proportion (43 percent) chose a hyphenated American identification, a small fraction (3.3 percent) identified as plain "American," and 16 percent selected pan-ethnic minority identities. Whether a youth was born in the United States or elsewhere made a great deal of difference in the type of identity selected at T1: the foreign born were three times more likely to identify by national origins (44 percent) than were the U.S. born (16 percent); conversely, U.S.-born youth were much more likely to identify as "American" or hyphenated American than were the foreign born and somewhat more likely to identify in pan-ethnic terms. Those findings at T1 seemed suggestive of an assimilative trend from one generation to another. But by the T2 survey (conducted in the months after the passage, with 59 percent of the vote, of Proposition 187 in California in November 1994) the results were quite the opposite from what would have been predicted by a straight-line identificational assimilation perspective.

In 1995 the biggest gainer by far in terms of the self-image of these youth was the foreign nationality identity, increasing from 32 percent of the sample at T1 to nearly half (48 percent) now. This shift took place among both foreign-born and U.S.-born youth, as Table 9-6 shows. This occurred among most but not all national origin groups and was particularly sharp among youth of Mexican and Filipino descent. Overall, pan-ethnic identities remained at 16 percent at T2, but that figure conceals a notable decline among Mexican-origin youth in "Hispanic" and "Chicano" self-identities and an extremely sharp upswing in the proportion of youth now identifying pan-ethnically as "Asian" or "Asian American," especially among the smallest groups such as the "other Asians" (Chinese, Korean, Japanese, Thai) and the Hmong among the Indochinese. The simultaneous rapid decline of both the plain "American" (cut in half to a miniscule 1.6 percent) and hyphenated American (dropping from 43 to 30 percent) self-identities points to the rapid growth of a reactive ethnic consciousness. Furthermore, the measure of the salience or importance that the youth gave to their chosen identities (not shown in the table) showed that the strongest salience scores were reported for national origin identities and the weakest for plain "American" ones, with hyphenates scoring in between in salience.

Change over time, thus, has been not toward assimilative mainstream identities (with or without a hyphen) but rather a return to and a valorization of the immigrant identity for the largest groups and toward pan-ethnic identities among the smallest groups, as these youth become increasingly aware of the ethnic and racial categories in which they are classified by mainstream American society—and this among a sample of children of immigrants less than 2 percent of whom self-report racially as "white."

The process of growing ethnic awareness is also evident in the evolution of their perceptions, experiences, and expectations of racial and ethnic discrimination. These are detailed in the bottom panel of Table 9-6. Reported experiences of discrimination against themselves increased from 64 to 69 percent of the sample in the last survey (see Figure 9-4). Virtually every group reported more such experiences of rejection or unfair treatment as they grew older, with the Hmong registering the sharpest increase (to 82 percent), but about two-thirds of every other nationality in San Diego uniformly reported such experiences.

There is little doubt that racial and ethnic prejudice is the main factor driving such negative experiences. Among those suffering discrimination, their own race or nationality are the overwhelming forces perceived to account for that unfair treatment. Further-

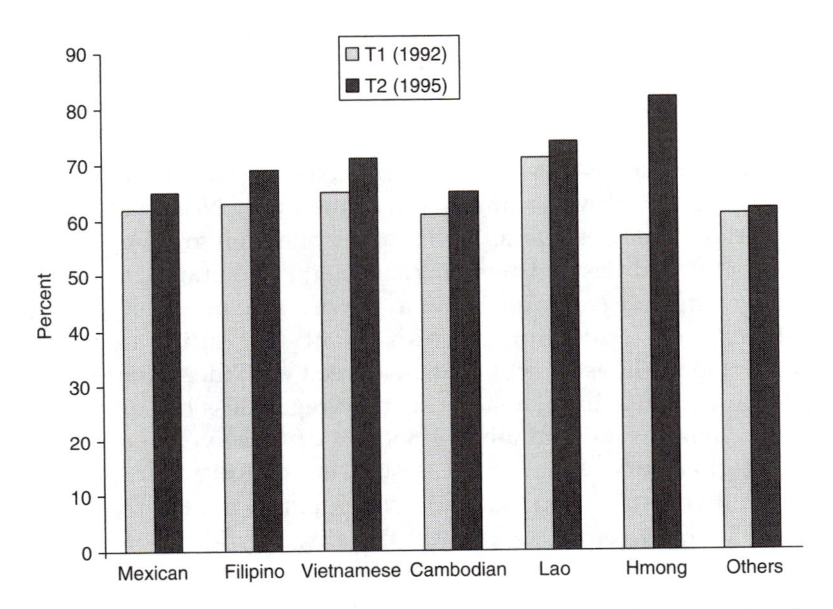

FIGURE 9-4 Percentages who experienced being discriminated against, by national origin, San Diego children of immigrants sample.

more, such experiences of discrimination tend to be associated over time with the development of a distinctly more pessimistic stance about their chances to reduce discriminatory treatment on meritocratic grounds through higher educational achievement. As Table 9-6 shows, in both surveys the students were asked to agree or disagree with the statement, "No matter how much education I get, people will still discriminate against me." In 1992, 37 percent of the total sample agreed with that gloomy assessment; by 1995-1996 the proportion had grown to 41 percent. Such expectations of external discrimination on ascribed rather than achieved grounds—and thus of perceived danger and threatening circumstances beyond one's control—were found in a multivariate analysis of the original survey data to be significant predictors of depressive symptomatology (see Rumbaut, 1994a). That finding, as will be shown in the following section, is now confirmed again three years later.

Perhaps because of their awareness of racial discrimination

and ethnic inequality, second-generation youth are not ready to endorse all aspects of American society. Asked how often they prefer "American ways," an identical minority of 41 percent in both surveys reported that they did so most of the time. Instead the majority of children of immigrants take a selective stance, preferring American ways only some of the time. Nonetheless, it is important to emphasize as well that despite their growing awareness of the realities of American racism and intolerance, most continue to affirm a sanguine belief in the promise of equal opportunity through educational achievement—including nearly 60 percent in the latest survey who disagreed with the statement that people will discriminate against them regardless of educational merit. Even more tellingly, 63 percent of these youth agreed in the original survey that "there is no better country to live in than the United States," and that endorsement grew to 71 percent three years later. Majorities of every nationality, regardless of whether they were foreign born or U.S. born, agreed with that appraisal, ranging from nearly 60 percent among the Mexicans and Cambodians to a high of 85 percent among U.S.-born children of the 1975 Vietnamese refugees, whose families generally experienced a supportive and welcoming context of reception through a historic resettlement program organized by the U.S. government.

Psychological Well-Being: Patterns and Predictors of Self-Esteem and Depression

This final section examines two key cognitive and affective dimensions of psychosocial adaptation and well-being: self-esteem and depression. The measure of global self-esteem used is the 10-item Rosenberg scale. Depressive symptoms are measured with the four-item Center for Epidemiological Studies-Depression (CES-D) subscale. Both are scored on a scale of 1 to 4 as the mean of the items composing the measure (the composition, scoring, and reliability of these widely used scales are specified in Appendix 9A). Self-esteem and depression are inversely related (the correlation between the two measures at T1 was –0.362, and at T2 it was –0.418), but they are determined by distinct sets of factors and thus are not simply two sides of the same psychological coin, as will be made clear by the results of multiple linear regressions.

Furthermore, the T1 score on each scale is significantly but only moderately correlated with the T2 score on the same scale three years later (0.411 for self-esteem, 0.297 for depression), suggesting that considerable change occurs over time in the psychological dimensions of well-being tapped by these measures, particularly with regard to depressive symptoms.

Table 9-7 sketches a detailed picture of self-esteem and depression scores at T1 and T2, broken down by gender for a wide range of hypothesized predictors: national origin, nativity, age at arrival, citizenship, socioeconomic status, family structure and parent-child conflict, English proficiency and preference, aspirations, ethnic self-identity, and experiences and expectations of discrimination. These bivariate results portray the differing social patterning of each of the measures of psychological well-being: some of the predictor variables (e.g., parent-child conflict) show clear and significant linear relationships with both well-being outcomes, while others are significantly associated with one but not the other (e.g., U.S. citizenship, parents' education, and English preference are significantly associated with self-esteem but not with depression, while being discriminated against is much more strongly linked with depression than with self-esteem). These data are presented separately by gender because of the very significant differences found between males and females on both measures: females report significantly lower self-esteem and higher levels of depressive symptomatology, a finding consistent with other studies of adolescents and adults among both immigrants and natives and majority and minority populations (see Vega and Rumbaut, 1991). However, as depicted in Table 9-7 and Figure 9-5, for both males and females in this sample there is a statistically significant if moderate increase in self-esteem from T1 to T2, while for both males and females their slightly higher scores in depressive symptoms by T2 are not significantly different.

A least squares multiple linear regression analysis of each of these two dependent variables—self-esteem and depression as of T2, when these youth were nearing the end of adolescence and secondary schooling—is presented in Table 9-8. Both equations examine the independent net effects of the same five sets of predictor variables hypothesized to influence self-esteem and depres-

TABLE 9-7 Self-Esteem and Depression Among Male and Female Children of Immigrants:[a] Patterns of Psychological Well-Being and Change Over Time, 1992 (T1) and 1995 (T2)

Correlates[b] of Psychological Well-Being	Male		Female		Total	
	T1	T2	T1	T2	T1[c]	T2[c]
SELF-ESTEEM						
Total	3.23	3.33	3.17	3.26	3.20	3.29
National Origin					***	***
Mexican	3.19	3.38	3.17	3.33	3.18	3.36
Filipino	3.33	3.37	3.20	3.27	3.26	3.32
Vietnamese	3.10	3.17	3.10	3.12	3.10	3.15
Cambodian	3.21	3.35	2.96	3.07	3.06	3.18
Lao	3.03	3.17	3.08	3.18	3.06	3.17
Hmong	3.01	3.24	2.97	3.09	2.99	3.17
Others	3.45	3.41	3.38	3.41	3.41	3.41
Nativity					***	***
Foreign born	3.16	3.29	3.11	3.21	3.13	3.25
U.S. born	3.33	3.38	3.24	3.33	3.28	3.35
Age at Arrival					***	***
All life in U.S.	3.33	3.38	3.24	3.33	3.28	3.35
0-5 years old	3.21	3.32	3.20	3.29	3.21	3.31
6-11 years old	3.19	3.27	3.08	3.14	3.13	3.20
12-15 years old	2.93	3.20	2.87	3.09	2.91	3.15
U.S. Citizenship					***	***
Citizen	3.33	3.37	3.24	3.31	3.28	3.34
Not a citizen	3.10	3.24	3.06	3.16	3.08	3.20
Mother's Education					***	***
College graduate	3.35	3.35	3.24	3.25	3.29	3.30
High school graduate	3.33	3.41	3.23	3.34	3.28	3.38
Less than high school	3.13	3.27	3.11	3.22	3.12	3.24
Father's Occupation					***	***
White collar	3.35	3.36	3.24	3.31	3.29	3.33
Blue collar	3.25	3.36	3.18	3.31	3.09	3.33
Not in labor force	3.10	3.24	3.09	3.15	3.09	3.19

TABLE 9-7 Continued

Correlates[b] of Psychological Well-Being	Male		Female		Total	
	T1	T2	T1	T2	T1[c]	T2[c]
SELF-ESTEEM						
Family Economic Status					NS	**
Better than 3 years ago	3.24	3.38	3.18	3.30	3.21	3.35
Same as 3 years ago	3.24	3.30	3.17	3.23	3.20	3.27
Worse than 3 years ago	3.17	3.25	3.11	3.25	3.14	3.25
Family Structure					***	**
Both natural parents	3.27	3.34	3.18	3.29	3.23	3.31
Two-parent stepfamily	3.19	3.38	3.21	3.23	3.20	3.31
Single-parent family	3.10	3.26	3.08	3.19	3.09	3.22
Parent-Child Conflict					***	***
Low conflict	3.36	3.45	3.28	3.39	3.32	3.42
Medium conflict	3.10	3.18	3.03	3.13	3.06	3.15
High conflict	2.70	2.91	2.80	2.84	2.75	2.87
Embarrassed of Parents					***	***
No	3.27	3.34	3.20	3.28	3.24	3.31
Yes	3.09	3.24	2.98	3.13	3.04	3.19
English Proficiency					***	***
Speaks it "very well"	3.36	3.41	3.26	3.35	3.31	3.38
Speaks it "well"	3.02	3.15	2.99	3.05	3.00	3.11
Speaks it "not well"	2.81	2.95	2.79	2.78	2.80	2.86
English Preference					***	***
Prefers English	3.30	3.37	3.20	3.28	3.25	3.32
Prefers other language	3.10	3.15	3.10	3.17	3.10	3.16
Educational Aspirations					***	***
Advanced degree	3.34	3.51	3.30	3.37	3.32	3.43
College degree	3.27	3.30	3.11	3.24	3.20	3.27
Less than college degree	3.08	3.14	3.00	3.05	3.05	3.11
Occupational Aspirations					*	*
High-status profession	3.29	3.35	3.19	3.28	3.23	3.31
Middle-status job	3.23	3.30	3.10	3.18	3.17	3.25
Low-status job	3.15	3.27	3.16	3.14	3.15	3.23

continued on next page

TABLE 9-7 Continued

Correlates[b] of Psychological Well-Being	Male		Female		Total	
	T1	T2	T1	T2	T1[c]	T2[c]
SELF-ESTEEM						
Ethnic Self-Identity					NS	NS
American	3.36	3.48	3.54	3.08	3.42	3.33
Hyphenated American	3.29	3.38	3.19	3.32	3.24	3.35
National origin	3.13	3.28	3.10	3.23	3.12	3.26
Racial/pan-ethnic	3.25	3.39	3.16	3.23	3.20	3.30
Mixed identity, other	3.26	3.23	3.23	3.40	3.24	3.32
Experienced Discrimination					***	NS
Has been discriminated against by others	3.22	3.31	3.12	3.25	3.17	3.28
Has *not* been . . .	3.27	3.36	3.25	3.27	3.26	3.31
Expected Discrimination					**	***
Will be discriminated against despite merit	3.19	3.27	3.13	3.20	3.16	3.24
Will *not* be . . .	3.26	3.38	3.19	3.29	3.22	3.33
DEPRESSIVE SYMPTOMS						
Total	1.54	1.57	1.75	1.79	1.65	1.68
National Origin					NS	*
Mexican	1.56	1.52	1.76	1.76	1.66	1.64
Filipino	1.52	1.59	1.81	1.86	1.66	1.72
Vietnamese	1.62	1.62	1.70	1.76	1.66	1.69
Cambodian	1.57	1.53	1.73	1.69	1.66	1.63
Lao	1.52	1.57	1.64	1.57	1.58	1.57
Hmong	1.56	1.61	1.80	1.94	1.66	1.76
Others	1.39	1.62	1.72	1.86	1.57	1.75
Nativity					NS	NS
Foreign born	1.56	1.59	1.76	1.79	1.66	1.69
U.S. born	1.51	1.55	1.75	1.79	1.63	1.67
Age at Arrival					*	NS
All life in U.S.	1.51	1.55	1.75	1.79	1.63	1.67
0-5 years old	1.53	1.58	1.72	1.77	1.63	1.68
6-11 years old	1.54	1.59	1.76	1.78	1.66	1.69
12-15 years old	1.69	1.61	1.88	1.93	1.77	1.75

TABLE 9-7 Continued

Correlates[b] of Psychological Well-Being	Male		Female		Total	
	T1	T2	T1	T2	T1[c]	T2[c]
DEPRESSIVE SYMPTOMS						
U.S. Citizenship					NS	NS
Citizen	1.52	1.56	1.74	1.78	1.63	1.67
Not a citizen	1.57	1.60	1.78	1.82	1.68	1.71
Mother's Education					NS	NS
College graduate	1.47	1.63	1.76	1.85	1.61	1.74
High school graduate	1.53	1.57	1.73	1.76	1.63	1.66
Less than high school	1.57	1.55	1.77	1.79	1.67	1.67
Father's Occupation					**	NS
White collar	1.51	1.59	1.62	1.77	1.59	1.68
Blue collar	1.50	1.54	1.78	1.76	1.64	1.65
Not in labor force	1.63	1.61	1.78	1.82	1.71	1.72
Family Economic Status					***	***
Better than 3 years ago	1.51	1.49	1.73	1.76	1.62	1.62
Same as 3 years ago	1.52	1.58	1.74	1.75	1.64	1.67
Worse than 3 years ago	1.83	1.81	1.85	1.94	1.84	1.88
Family Structure					***	***
Both natural parents	1.50	1.54	1.71	1.76	1.60	1.65
Two-parent stepfamily	1.67	1.54	1.90	1.83	1.78	1.68
Single-parent family	1.66	1.72	1.85	1.88	1.76	1.81
Parent-Child Conflict					***	***
Low conflict	1.43	1.43	1.61	1.64	1.52	1.53
Medium conflict	1.67	1.78	1.94	1.95	1.81	1.87
High conflict	2.03	2.03	2.30	2.21	2.16	2.13
Embarrassed of Parents					***	*
No	1.51	1.56	1.72	1.78	1.62	1.67
Yes	1.66	1.65	1.93	1.86	1.78	1.75

continued on next page

TABLE 9-7 Continued

Correlates[b] of Psychological Well-Being	Male		Female		Total	
	T1	T2	T1	T2	T1[c]	T2[c]
DEPRESSIVE SYMPTOMS						
English Proficiency					**	NS
Speaks it "very well"	1.51	1.57	1.73	1.80	1.62	1.69
Speaks it "well"	1.59	1.59	1.78	1.77	1.68	1.67
Speaks it "not well"	1.67	1.59	1.92	1.82	1.79	1.70
English Preference					NS	NS
Prefers English	1.52	1.55	1.74	1.80	1.63	1.68
Prefers other language	1.58	1.66	1.78	1.73	1.68	1.69
Educational Aspirations					**	NS
Advanced degree	1.48	1.50	1.68	1.77	1.60	1.66
College degree	1.51	1.57	1.79	1.80	1.64	1.68
Less than college degree	1.63	1.66	1.84	1.83	1.72	1.73
Occupational Aspirations					NS	NS
High-status profession	1.53	1.58	1.75	1.77	1.65	1.68
Middle-status job	1.52	1.52	1.70	1.89	1.60	1.68
Low-status job	1.57	1.57	2.00	1.90	1.66	1.68
Ethnic Self-Identity					***	*
American	1.48	1.50	1.57	2.08	1.51	1.72
Hyphenated American	1.52	1.56	1.76	1.75	1.64	1.66
National origin	1.59	1.58	1.76	1.80	1.68	1.69
Racial/pan-ethnic	1.51	1.52	1.74	1.76	1.63	1.66
Mixed identity, other	1.54	1.85	1.73	1.97	1.63	1.91
Experienced Discrimination					***	***
Has been discriminated against by others	1.59	1.63	1.84	1.83	1.72	1.73
Has *not* been . . .	1.45	1.44	1.60	1.72	1.52	1.59

TABLE 9-7 Continued

Correlates[b] of Psychological Well-Being	Male		Female		Total	
	T1	T2	T1	T2	T1[c]	T2[c]
DEPRESSIVE SYMPTOMS						
Expected Discrimination					***	***
Will be discriminated against despite merit	1.64	1.68	1.83	1.89	1.73	1.77
Will *not* be . . .	1.47	1.48	1.71	1.74	1.60	1.62

[a]Measured by the 10-item Rosenberg Self-Esteem Scale (1-4) and the four-item CES-D depression subscale (1-4). See Appendix 9A for the items composing the two scales and their scoring. The longitudinal sample of 2,063 is evenly split between males (1,023) and females (1,040).

[b]All variables as measured at T1 and T2, reflecting changes over time, except constants such as gender, national origin, generation, age at arrival, parents' education, and parents' ethnicity; that is, psychological well-being outcomes at T1 reported in this table are associated with predictor variables (such as family structure and English proficiency) measured at T1 and T2 outcomes with variables measured at T2.

[c]Statistical significance of differences in group mean scores: $^{*}p < .05$, $^{**}p < .01$, $^{***}p < .001$; NS = not significantly different.

sion: (1) gender, national origin, and age at arrival in the United States (a four-point scale, with 0 = born in the United States, 1 = 0 to 5 years of age at arrival, 2 = 6 to 10 years, and 3 = 11 to 15 years); (2) intrafamily contexts and stressors; (3) extrafamily contexts and stressors (including expected discrimination, the school indices previously discussed, friends' no-college plans, and the proportion of the neighborhood population that speaks English only, as an indicator of contextual dissonance); (4) achievement and aspiration variables; and (5) two items dealing with concerns over one's physical appearance and popularity with the opposite sex. Standardized regression coefficients and t ratios are shown for all significant effects, and the change in the square of the multiple correlation coefficient (ΔR^2) upon the entry of each set of predictor variables is noted as an indicator of the "explained" variance contributed by those predictors. The full model shown explains about 45 percent of the variance in self-esteem scores ($R^2 = 0.454$) and about half as much of the variance in depression

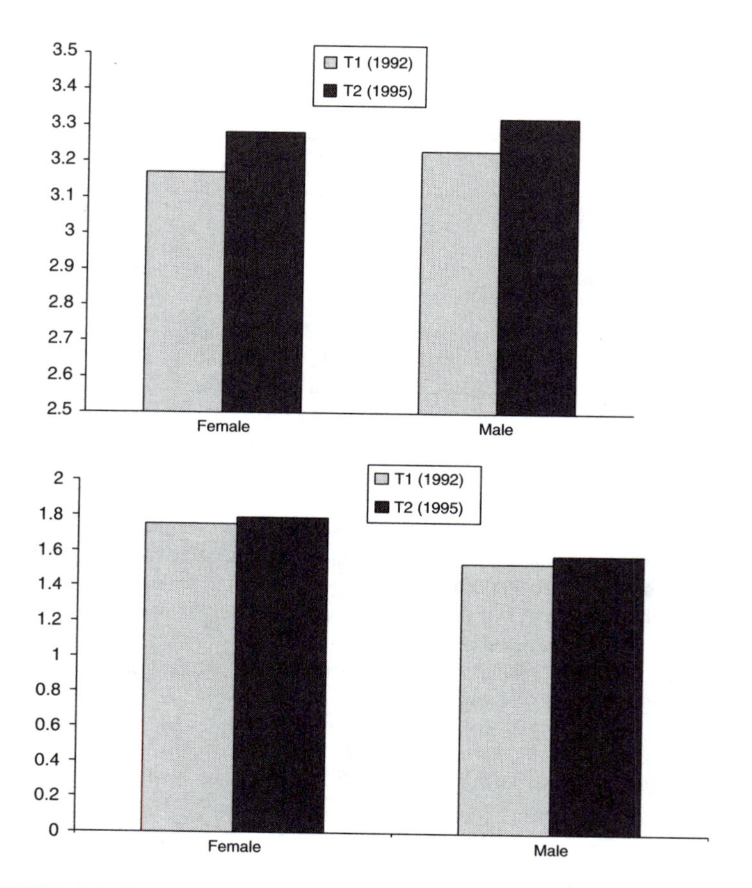

FIGURE 9-5 (Top) Global self-esteem score, at T1 and T2, San Diego children of immigrants sample, by gender and (bottom) CES-D depression score, at T1 and T2, by gender.

scores, 22 percent ($R^2 = 0.223$). Some of the most salient results of these analyses merit highlighting.

First, as had been found earlier in multiple regressions with the T1 data, gender remains one of the most significant predictors of both well-being measures even after controlling for a score of other variables. Significantly lower self-esteem and much higher levels of depressive symptoms are observed for females in this sample; and the effect for self-esteem is considerably reduced after the entry of the last set of variables (concern with physical looks and popularity with the opposite sex). Age at arrival washes out of the self-esteem equation but remains significantly associated with depression: the more recently arrived the immigrant (and the older age at time of arrival), the higher the depression score, net of other factors. That finding is consistent with T1 results as well and with the expectations of theories of acculturative stress among immigrants. The national origin dummy variables entered, however—Filipino and Vietnamese ethnicity—wash out of the depression equation but are significantly linked to lower self-esteem. This again confirms the T1 finding that among national origin groups only the Filipinos and Vietnamese reflect statistically significantly lower self-esteem scores, again raising questions about possible psychosocial vulnerabilities and dynamics among these two groups of children of immigrants, not captured by the data, that may be linked to a diminished sense of self-worth.

The findings are all the more intriguing in view of recent reports by the Centers for Disease Control, based on surveys in San Diego and elsewhere, that found Filipinos in San Diego schools as reporting the highest levels of suicidal ideation and attempts of any major ethnic group, despite the comparative socioeconomic advantages of that population (Kann et al., 1995). Similar findings have been supported in a separate study by Wolf (1997) of Filipino youth in two California sites. No other nationalities showed significant associations with either dependent variable in other models tested, a finding that is of particular interest in the case of the Cambodian youth, given the elevated levels of depression and posttraumatic stress symptoms found among adult Cambodian refugees, including Cambodian parents in San Diego (see Rumbaut, 1991a; Rumbaut and Ima, 1988).

Second, intrafamily factors have very significant effects on both dependent variables, particularly the measure of parent-child conflict, which, as in T1, emerges as one of the principal predictors of emotional well-being in these populations. By contrast, family structure washes out of the self-esteem equation and retains a weak though still significant protective effect against depressive symptoms. A stronger effect is seen for the measure of family cohesion. Perceptions of downward economic mobility in the family's situation are significantly associated with depression

TABLE 9-8 Predictors of Self-Esteem and Depressive Symptoms Among Children of Immigrants: Least-Squares Multiple Regressions for San Diego Sample, T2 (1995-96)[a]

	Self-Esteem (Mean = 3.298)			
Predictor Variables	Beta	*T* ratio	*p*	ΔR^2
Gender, Age at Arrival, Ethnicity				0.033***
Gender (0 = male, 1 = female)	–0.056	(–3.12)	**	
Age at arrival in the United States[b]			NS	
Filipino	–0.075	(–3.85)	***	
Vietnamese	–0.065	(–3.49)	***	
Intrafamily Contexts and Stressors				0.147***
Intact family			NS	
Parent-child conflict	–0.180	(–9.15)	***	
Family cohesion	0.091	(4.85)	***	
Family economic situation worse			NS	
Family moved to another home	0.068	(3.97)	***	
Seriously ill or disabled since T1	–0.056	(–3.34)	**	
Extra-Family Contexts and Stressors				0.026***
English-only in neighborhood	–0.046	(–2.57)	**	
School perceived as unsafe	–0.086	(–4.77)	***	
Teaching quality and fairness			NS	
School stress events experienced			NS	
Friends' no-college plans			NS	
Discrimination trumps education			NS	
Achievement and Aspirations				0.098***
Educational achievement (GPA)	0.069	(3.49)	***	
Educational aspirations	0.143	(7.21)	***	
English language proficiency	0.197	(9.30)	***	
LEP status at T1	–0.068	(–3.10)	**	
Looks and Opposite Sex				0.150***
Dissatisfied with physical looks	–0.343	(–19.58)	***	
Popular with opposite sex	0.169	(9.66)	***	
R^2				0.454
Adjusted R^2				0.448

[a]Standardized regression coefficients (betas), with *T* ratios in parentheses. ΔR^2 = change in the square of the multiple correlation coefficient. Significance levels $^*p < .05$, $^{**}p < .01$, $^{***}p < .0001$; NS = not significant. See Appendix 9A for details of measurement.

CES-D Depression (Mean = 1.681)			
Beta	*T* ratio	*p*	ΔR^2
			0.032***
0.165	(7.72)	***	
0.044	(1.93)	*	
		NS	
		NS	
			0.127***
–0.048	(–2.36)	*	
0.200	(8.52)	***	
–0.050	(–2.24)	*	
0.055	(2.70)	**	
		NS	
0.045	(2.21)	*	
			0.024***
0.067	(3.13)	**	
0.042	(1.97)	*	
–0.042	(–1.97)	*	
0.050	(2.18)	*	
0.058	(2.61)	**	
0.054	(2.58)	**	
			0.001 NS
		NS	
		NS	
		NS	
		NS	
			0.039***
0.185	(8.85)	***	
–0.069	(–3.33)	**	
		0.223	
		0.215	

[b]A four-point variable, where 0 = born in the United States, 1 = 0 to 5 years old at arrival, 2 = 6 to10 years old at arrival, and 3 = 11 to15 years old at arrival. It is an index of both length of residence in the United States and, if foreign born, age/developmental stage at arrival in the United States.

but not self-esteem. Family contexts clearly if varyingly shape psychological outcomes among these youth.

The third set of predictor variables begins to show more significant divergences among the determinants of the two well-being outcome variables. Four of the predictors in that set wash out of the self-esteem equation but retain significant net effects on depressive symptoms—notably expectations of discrimination (underscoring the point made earlier), as well as stressful school events experienced, and the decision of most close friends to not go to college (but instead to drop out or get a job). These variables appear generally to have in *common the experience of perceived danger and lack of control over threatening life events*—characteristics that have been specifically associated with depressive symptomatology. Interestingly, the proportion of English-only speakers in the neighborhood—an indicator of contextual dissonance—emerges as a significant predictor of both lower self-esteem and higher depression. The finding lends support to theoretical predictions, following Rosenberg (1979), that self-esteem should be lower in contexts where social dissimilarity is greater, along with exposure to negative stereotypes and reflected appraisals of one's group of origin.

The fourth set of predictors has to do with *competence in role performance*—variables that measure educational achievement and aspirations and achieving a command of English. All of these have strong and significant effects on self-esteem, but all of them wash out of the equation predicting depressive symptoms. The explained variance contributed by this set of predictors to the self-esteem equation is a robust 10 percent (0.098 added to the R^2) but virtually zero to the depression equation (adding a mere 0.001 to the R^2).

Finally, the last two items entered have significant net effects on both equations—although the added explained variance to the self-esteem model contributed by these two items is far greater than that for the depression model (0.150 to 0.039). Indeed, the item indicating dissatisfaction with one's physical looks had the largest beta coefficient in the final self-esteem model, and its entry into the model significantly reduced the direct effect of gender on self-esteem. It is worth noting here that females were about twice as likely as males (29 to 17 percent) to report dissatisfaction with their looks at T2. And among national origin groups, the most dissatisfied with their physical looks were the Vietnamese and Filipinos, with the Vietnamese also being the most likely to report not feeling popular with the opposite sex.

In all of these respects it becomes clear that self-esteem and depressive symptoms are measures of different cognitive and affective dimensions of psychological well-being, subject to a different set of determinants, which throw additional light on the adaptational challenges that children of immigrants confront in their passages to adulthood in American contexts. In some respects the patterns are quite similar to what one would expect to find with a sample of nonimmigrant nonminority youth. In others the findings frame what at first appears as an "achievement paradox": for example, recently arrived, lower socioeconomic status immigrant youth work harder and achieve better grades than their more assimilated native-born peers yet have a poorer psychological well-being profile, much as females too consistently outperform their male counterparts yet register lower self-esteem and higher depression. And in still other respects—particularly with regard to issues of nonnative language competency, contextual dissonance, recency of arrival, entry into a minority status, and experiences and expectations of ethnoracial discrimination—our results suggest that children of immigrants face distinct acculturative challenges and the potential for intergenerational conflict over these issues within their families that significantly add to the developmental challenges of adolescence.

Despite these added challenges—or perhaps because of them—the overall picture that emerges from this study is one of noteworthy achievement and resilient ambition in a situation of extraordinary diversity. Whether and to what extent these can be sustained as these youth make their entry into the world of work and careers, as they form new families of their own, and as they seek to carve out a meaningful place in the years ahead in the society of which they are the newest members—and whether and to what extent their already diverging trajectories will diverge further still as they become exposed to and absorbed by different segments of American society—are open empirical questions that will remain unanswered until the new century that beckons them ahead.

ACKNOWLEDGMENTS

This chapter is based on data collected in San Diego, California, by the Children of Immigrants Longitudinal Study. I gratefully acknowledge the support provided by research grants from the Andrew W. Mellon Foundation (1991-1996) and the Russell Sage Foundation (1994-1996). The study was conceived and conducted in collaboration with Alejandro Portes and carried out in conjunction with a parallel survey in South Florida directed by Professor Portes and funded by additional grants from the Spencer, Russell Sage, and National Science foundations. The project in the San Diego area, which I directed, was made possible by the generous cooperation of over 2,000 immigrant families and scores of administrators, principals, teachers, and other staff members of the San Diego City Schools; by the assistance extended by the sociology departments of San Diego State University and Michigan State University; by the work of a team of over two dozen interviewers fluent in Spanish, Tagalog, Vietnamese, Cambodian, Lao, Hmong, and other languages representative of the immigrant families that have made San Diego their home; and by the extraordinary commitment of my core research staff, especially Linda Borgen, Norm Borgen, Kevin Keogan, Laura Lagunas, and James Ainsworth. I am indebted to Charles F. Hohm, Leif Jensen, and Donald J. Hernandez for their careful comments on an earlier version of this chapter and to the National Research Council's Committee on the Health and Adjustment of Immigrant Children and Families, under whose auspices this chapter was prepared.

REFERENCES

Hansen, K.A., and C.S. Faber

1997 The foreign born population: 1996. Current Population Reports, P20-494. Washington, D.C.: Bureau of the Census, U.S. Department of Commerce.

Kann, L., et al.

1995 Youth risk behavior surveillance—United States, 1993. *Morbidity and Mortality Weekly Report* 44(SS-1):1-56.

Oropesa, R.S., and N.S. Landale

1997 In search of the new second generation: Alternative strategies for identifying second generation children and understanding their acquisition of English. *Sociological Perspectives* 40(3).

Portes, A.
1995 Children of immigrants: Segmented assimilation and its determinants. Pp. 248-279 in *The Economic Sociology of Immigration: Essays on Networks, Ethnicity, and Entrepreneurship*, A. Portes, ed. New York: Russell Sage Foundation.

Portes, A., ed.
1996 *The New Second Generation*. New York: Russell Sage Foundation.

Portes, A., and R.G. Rumbaut
1996 *Immigrant America: A Portrait*, 2nd ed. Berkeley: University of California Press.

Portes, A., and R. Schauffler
1996 Language acquisition and loss among children of immigrants. Pp. 432-443 in *Origins and Destinies: Immigration, Race, and Ethnicity in America*, S. Pedraza and R.G. Rumbaut, eds. Belmont, CA: Wadsworth.

Rosenberg, M.
1979 *Conceiving the Self*. New York: Basic Books.

Rumbaut, R.G.
1991a The agony of exile: A study of Indochinese refugee adults and children. Pp. 53-91 in *Refugee Children: Theory, Research, and Services*, F.L. Ahearn and J.L. Athey, eds. Baltimore: Johns Hopkins University Press.

1991b Migration, adaptation, and mental health: The experience of Southeast Asian refugees in the United States. Pp. 381-424 in *Refugee Policy: Canada and the United States*, H. Adelman, ed. Toronto: York Lanes Press.

1994a The crucible within: Ethnic identity, self-esteem, and segmented assimilation among children of immigrants. *International Migration Review* 28(4):748-794.

1994b Origins and destinies: Immigration to the United States since World War II. *Sociological Forum* 9(4):583-621.

1995 The new Californians: Comparative research findings on the educational progress of immigrant children. Pp. 17-70 in *California's Immigrant Children: Theory, Research, and Implications for Educational Policy*, R.G. Rumbaut and W. Cornelius, eds. La Jolla: Center for U.S.-Mexican Studies, University of California, San Diego.

1996 A legacy of war: Refugees from Vietnam, Laos, and Cambodia. Pp. 315-333 in *Origins and Destinies: Immigration, Race, and Ethnicity in America*, S. Pedraza and R.G. Rumbaut, eds. Belmont, CA: Wadsworth.

1997a Ties that bind: Immigration and immigrant families in the United States. Pp. 3-46 in *Immigration and the Family: Research and Policy on U.S. Immigrants*, A. Booth, A.C. Crouter, and N.S. Landale, eds. Mahwah, NJ: Lawrence Erlbaum Associates.

1997b Paradoxes (and orthodoxies) of assimilation. *Sociological Perspectives* 40(3):481-509.

Rumbaut, R.G., and K. Ima
1988 *The Adaptation of Southeast Asian Refugee Youth: A Comparative Study*. Washington, D.C.: U.S. Office of Refugee Resettlement.

Vega, W.A., and R.G. Rumbaut

1991 Ethnic minorities and mental health. *Annual Review of Sociology* 17:351-383.

Wolf, D.

1997 Family secrets: Transnational struggles among children of Filipino immigrants. *Sociological Perspectives* 40(3).

Zhou, M.

1997 Growing up American: The challenge confronting immigrant children and children of immigrants. *Annual Review of Sociology* 23:63-95.

APPENDIX 9A

TABLE 9A-1 Composition and Reliability of Selected Scales, and Scoring of Items, at TI and T2 (San Diego longitudinal sample, $N = 2{,}063$)

Scale and Scoring	Cronbach's Alpha	
	T1	T2
Rosenberg self-esteem (10 items: scored 1 to 4)	0.81	0.81
CES-D depression (four items: scored 1 to 4)	0.74	0.77
Familism scale (three items: scored 1 to 4)	0.60	0.62
Family cohesion scale (three items: scored 1 to 5)	—	0.84
Parent-child conflict (three items: scored 1 to 4)	0.58	0.63
(Fourth item added at T2)	—	0.72

Items and Measures
I feel I am a person of worth, at least on an equal basis with others. I feel I have a number of good qualities. I am able to do things as well as most other people. I take a positive attitude toward myself. On the whole, I am satisfied with myself. All in all, I am inclined to think I am a failure *[reverse score].* I feel I do not have much to be proud of *[reverse score].* I wish I could have more respect for myself *[reverse score].* I certainly feel useless at times *[reverse score].* At times I think I am no good at all *[reverse score].* 1 = Disagree a lot, 2 = Disagree, 3 = Agree, 4 = Agree a lot
[How often during the past week:] I did not feel like eating; my appetite was poor. I could not "get going." I felt depressed. I felt sad. 1 = Rarely, 2 = Some of the time (1 or 2 days a week), 3 = Occasionally (3 or 4 days), 4 = Most of the time (5 to 7 days)
One should find a job near his/her parents even if it means losing a better job somewhere else. When someone has a serious problem, only relatives can help. In helping a person get a job, it is always better to choose a relative rather than a friend. 1 = Disagree a lot, 2 = Disagree, 3 = Agree, 4 = Agree a lot
Family members like to spend free time with each other. Family members feel very close to each other. Family togetherness is very important. 1 = Never, 2 = Once in a while, 3 = Sometimes, 4 = Often, 5 = Always
In trouble with parents because of different way of doing things. My parents are usually not very interested in what I have to say. My parents do not like me very much. My parents and I often argue because we don't share the same goals. 1 = Not true at all, 2 = Not very true, 3 = Partly true, 4 = Very true

continued on next page

TABLE 9A-1 Continued

Scale and Scoring	Cronbach's Alpha	
	T1	T2
Educational aspirations (two items: scored 1 to 5)	0.80	0.83
English proficiency index (four items: scored 1 to 4)	0.94	0.93
Foreign language index (four items: scored 1 to 4)	0.96	0.92

Items and Measures
What is highest level of education you would like to achieve? And *realistically* speaking, what is the highest level of education you think you will get? 1 = Less than high school, 2 = High school, 3 = Some college, 4 = Finish college, 5 = Finish a graduate degree
How well do you (speak, understand, read, write) English? 1 = Not at all, 2 = Not well, 3 = Well, 4 = Very well
How well do you (speak, understand, read, write) *[foreign languages]*? 1 = Not at all, 2 = Not well, 3 = Well, 4 = Very well

CHAPTER 10

Receipt of Public Assistance by Mexican American and Cuban American Children in Native and Immigrant Families[1]

Sandra L. Hofferth

The public perception that immigrants are costly, particularly because they rely on public assistance more than natives do, contributed to provisions in the Parental Responsibility and Work Opportunity Reconciliation Act (PRWORA) of August 1996 restricting immigrants' access to public assistance. This new legislation denies some forms of public assistance (e.g., food stamps) to almost all immigrants until citizenship and denies other forms of public assistance (Aid to Families with Dependent Children (AFDC), Medicaid) to new immigrants for five years. It allows states to deny AFDC, Medicaid, and Title XX social services block grant funds to immigrants who came to the United States before August 1996, although almost all states have opted to continue this coverage. Thus, it is a surprise to many that, when demographic and economic differences between them are controlled, analyses of working-age populations have found immigrants to be significantly less likely to receive public assistance of various kinds than natives (Fix and Passel, 1994).

There are a variety of types and sources of public assistance, however, and there may be differences in immigrant receipt among them. Additionally, previous analyses have focused on

[1]An early version of this paper was presented at the annual meeting of the Population Association of America, March 26-30, 1997, in Washington, D.C.

working-age populations or on households; none has focused on children. The issue is whether immigrants' needs represent a disproportionate burden on federal funds relative to those of comparable natives. This chapter focuses on public assistance receipt by native and immigrant Mexican and Cuban American children and their families compared with children in white native families using data collected from 1990 to 1995 in a nationally representative survey that oversampled Mexican and Cuban American families.

INTRODUCTION

Eligibility of Immigrants for Public Assistance Benefits

Even prior to the passage of PRWORA, the context for the current study, many immigrants were, in fact, ineligible for public assistance benefits. Undocumented immigrants were eligible only for such things as emergency medical care and the Women, Infants, and Children supplemental program (WIC; Fix and Passel, 1994). Mexico, El Salvador, and Guatemala account for more than half of all illegal immigrants today and 80 percent of those legalized under the Immigration Reform and Control Act (IRCA) of 1986. Immigrants who legalized their status under IRCA were barred from receiving public assistance for five years. Additionally, if legal permanent residents applied for public assistance programs during their first three years in the United States, their sponsor's income was to be included in determining eligibility. As a result, many legal permanent residents were not eligible.

Because of the circumstances under which they arrived in the United States, usually with no money or provisions, refugees have had greater access to special assistance for their first five years here than nonrefugees. While refugees comprise only about 10 percent of immigrants in a given year, they constitute a substantial proportion of some immigrant groups, such as Cubans, Eastern Europeans, and Southeast Asians (Fix and Passel, 1994).

Limitations on public assistance make it likely that immigrants receive some types but not others. Refugees and elderly immigrants have high rates of participation in Medicaid and Supplemental Security Income (SSI), for example (Fix and Passel,

1994). It is important, therefore, to look separately at the different types of public assistance benefits offered and to consider the country of origin and refugee status of immigrants. Whether immigrants have access to benefits depends first and foremost on their economic status; a prime condition for eligibility for most public assistance programs is a low level of income, usually around the poverty threshold.

Eligibility may also depend on the head of household's age, health, marital status, and number and ages of the children. Younger heads and those with many or younger children may be more likely to receive AFDC and less likely to be eligible for SSI and other welfare. Married heads and those in good health will have less need for assistance. Since unemployment is higher and wages lower among those with low levels of schooling, lesser education may also be associated with greater program eligibility. There are also substantial differences in public assistance programs across states and regions of the country. Generally, benefits are lower in the South, while they are higher in the West and Northeast. Since residents are more likely to qualify for and receive benefits in a high- compared with a low-benefit state, regional differences should be taken into account. Finally, poor economic conditions in the local community, such as high unemployment rates, may make receipt of public assistance more likely.

Previous Research

Other studies have conducted in-depth comparisons of the public assistance receipt of immigrants compared with natives. Immigrant households are generally more likely to receive various forms of public assistance (Tienda and Jensen, 1986). Once socioeconomic and demographic differences between natives and immigrants were taken into account using the 1976 Survey of Income and Education, both Blau (1984) and Simon and Akbari (1996) found that immigrants were less likely to receive welfare payments (including AFDC, other welfare, and SSI) than the native born. Analyses based on the 1970 and 1980 censuses also found immigrant families to be generally less likely than natives to receive public assistance, all else being equal (Jensen, 1988; Tienda and Jensen, 1986).

A recent paper based on the Survey of Income and Program Participation reports that, while immigrant-native differences in the probability of receiving cash benefits were small, differences widened once noncash benefits were included, since immigrants generally tended to have higher receipt of noncash benefits (Borjas and Hilton, 1996). Households whose head was foreign born were found to receive cash benefits, Medicaid, and vouchers (food stamps, WIC, heating assistance) for a shorter proportion of time than natives, after controlling for a variety of demographic factors that differed between native and immigrant households. However, when housing subsidies and school breakfasts and lunches were added to the set, households with a foreign-born head received assistance for a significantly longer proportion of time than those with a native-born head. It is important to determine exactly which forms of public assistance immigrants are more likely to receive and whether this relationship is explained by other characteristics of the family, particularly demographic characteristics and poverty level.

Children Versus Adults

Although immigrant children represent a sizable component of the next generation, most research on immigrants to date has focused on adults (Edmonston, 1996). Because immigrant families tend to be larger in size, with more children, focusing on families may or may not represent how well children are doing. High rates of immigration have led to dramatic changes in the racial and ethnic composition of the student population in the United States over the past decade. Hispanic and Asian enrollment is rising steadily while white enrollment is declining and black enrollment remains largely constant (National Center for Education Statistics, 1993). Between 1979 and 1989, the number of persons age 5 and older in the United States who were reported to speak a language other than English at home increased by about 40 percent, from 9 to 12 percent. Between 1986 and 1991, the limited English proficient (LEP) student population grew by over 50 percent, while the total student population grew by only 4 percent

(Fix and Passel, 1994). This rapid growth in the number and share of non-English-speaking students has created problems and challenges for schools. The new students are increasingly likely to be poor and are not only culturally unlike previous student cohorts but unlike each other. In some schools, dozens of language groups are represented. Over half of all students from 49 of the largest 100 school districts are black, Hispanic, or Asian (Population Reference Bureau, 1989). This has led to considerable concern about how well their families are doing economically and how much of a burden they place on state and local government services.

What Is an Immigrant?

We usually think of an immigrant as someone born in another country who arrives in the United States some time after birth, while a native is a person born in the United States. Because of the special dependent circumstances of children, we are interested in children of foreign-born parents, whether or not the child was born in this country. Of course, whether or not a child was born in the United States is a critical piece of information, as it is a critical distinction for eligibility for public programs. All persons born in the United States are U.S. citizens and are entitled to all of the rights of citizenship, including public programs. Therefore, we would expect the families of U.S.-born children to have the highest likelihood of receipt of public assistance, compared with other groups. The important comparison would be between foreign-born children of foreign-born parents (first generation) and native-born children of foreign-born parents (second generation) or native-born parents (third generation). The latter should be more likely to receive public assistance purely because of increased eligibility.

Other Nativity Differences

Foreign birth also implies a shorter length of residence in the United States and a lesser degree of adjustment to U.S. life. It is expected that families may need substantial assistance after they first arrive here, their needs declining as they adjust to their new lives. This would lead us to expect higher receipt of public assistance in the first and second generations. Concerns have been raised about differences in the assimilation of immigrant children and children of immigrants. While adopting American language and ways has been a prerequisite for success in the past, recent research on the relationship between generational status and school performance contradicts this straight-line assimilation hypothesis (Kao and Tienda, 1995). Rather than school performance improving over generations as immigrants learn English and local customs, it appears to worsen.

One hypothesis is that immigration is likely to be selective of behaviors, values, and/or cultural groups that promote achievement. Many immigrant groups have very strong achievement orientations and values; after all, in many cases they made considerable sacrifices to come here (Duran and Weffer, 1992; Kao and Tienda, 1995). They have strong family networks that also help to maintain their values (Portes and Zhou, 1992). They expect to work hard in their new country, and they are self-sufficient. The longer immigrants have been here, and the more exposure to the values of native groups around them, the more they may lose the strong ties and values that maintain self-sufficiency and high performance (Kao and Tienda, 1995). As immigrants begin to face reality, they may lose some of this optimism and become disillusioned with their prospects for social mobility (Kao and Tienda, 1995). This would suggest highest receipt of public assistance by the third generation.

Evidence for this hypothesis is not very strong, however, as few studies have detailed the kinds of values, behaviors, and parenting practices of immigrant and native groups that are needed to test this hypothesis. The present study examines one's own nativity and parental nativity as a proxy for successive assimilation into American society. To test this hypothesis, receipt of public assistance by families of children with foreign-born parents (first- and second-generation children) is compared with families of native-born children with native-born parents (third-generation children).

Focus of This Chapter

This chapter focuses on the following programs: AFDC, SSI, other welfare, Medicaid, food stamps, heating assistance, and housing assistance (rent subsidies or public housing). Other welfare consists of general assistance and miscellaneous state assistance. In 1994 total federal expenditures for these seven programs amounted to more than $250 billion (Bureau of the Census, 1996). Medicaid was the largest program. AFDC, SSI, food stamps, and housing assistance were smaller but similar in expenditures to each other. General assistance and energy assistance (heating assistance) were small programs. In terms of benefits, however, food stamps reached almost as many recipients as did Medicaid, with AFDC reaching about half as many recipients. The interest here is in the following differences in receipt of public assistance: (1) generational differences between immigrant and native children of the same ethnic background, (2) racial/ethnic differences between children of the same immigrant generation, and (3) differences between Mexican and Cuban immigrant and native children of different generations and white native-born children.

RESULTS

Description of the Sample

The total sample consists of 11,691 children under age 18 who were participants in at least one year of the 1990 to 1992 waves of the Panel Study of Income Dynamics (see Appendix 10A for a description of the sample). The full analysis sample consists of 221 foreign-born Mexican American children (first generation); 1,116 native-born Mexican children of a foreign-born parent (second generation); 1,224 native-born Mexican children of native-born parents (third generation); and 238 Mexican children missing information on nativity.[2] The sample also includes 63

[2]Children missing nativity information are primarily those not living with a parent. Birthplace of the child, which determines whether the child is of the first generation, is known for almost all children. If the child is not of the first genera-

first-generation Cuban children, 243 second-generation Cuban children, 57 third-generation Cuban children, and 42 Cuban children missing nativity information. There are 786 Puerto Rican children; 178 other Hispanic children; 3,915 white children; 3,534 black children; and 74 children of other races/ethnicities—all U.S. born of U.S.-born parents.

To provide a descriptive picture of the children in this study, I selected the most recent year, 1992. Table 10-1 shows basic weighted distributions of child and family characteristics for the 9,872 individual children who were under age 18 in 1992 by ethnicity and nativity. (For variable definitions, see Appendix 10B.) On average, children were 8 years old, and the household head of the family in which they lived was age 37, married, in good health, had graduated from high school, and had 2.3 children, of which the youngest was 6 years old.

Number of Children

Children's family size varies with ethnicity and nativity. As expected, first-generation Mexican American children's families are the largest, with 3.8 children on average, compared with 3 children in families of second-generation children, and 2.6 in native children's families. Children in black, other Latino, and Puerto Rican families are in the next-largest-size families, with about 2.5 children each, and children in Cuban families are in the smallest families, with 1.9 in first-generation Cuban children's families, 2 children in second-generation children's families, and 1.6 children in third-generation children's families. White children's families averaged 2.2 children.

Education of Household Head

Education levels were lowest for Mexican children's families. Of foreign-born Mexican children, 84 percent were in a family

---

tion and no information is available about the parent, the parental birthplace cannot be determined. In this case I am unable to distinguish between those with a native-born or a foreign-born parent—that is, whether they are second- or third-generation children.

TABLE 10-1 Characteristics of U.S. Children and Their Families by Ethnicity and Nativity, 1992

	Age	Age of Household Head	Health	Marital Status of Head	Age of Youngest Child	Number of Children Under 18
Mexican1	13.10	40.12	0.18	0.77	6.03	3.83
Mexican2	7.42	37.79	0.31	0.84	4.54	3.02
Mexican3	7.88	35.09	0.61	0.60	5.34	2.60
Mexican4	8.73	44.42	0.24	0.49	5.31	2.55
Cuban1	14.49	42.60	0.45	0.93	10.17	1.87
Cuban2	7.12	42.00	0.41	0.74	5.57	2.06
Cuban3	4.97	31.20	0.68	0.88	4.33	1.59
Cuban4	9.70	54.93	0.11	0.74	9.70	1.00
Puerto Rican	8.00	36.40	0.34	0.48	5.58	2.52
Other Latino	8.44	36.44	0.63	0.69	6.24	2.50
White	8.56	37.98	0.69	0.85	6.70	2.23
Black	8.12	36.36	0.46	0.39	5.50	2.51
Other	5.67	36.41	0.75	0.74	4.33	1.74
Total	8.41	37.52	0.61	0.74	6.29	2.34

	Poverty Status	Less Than High School	High School Graduate	Some College	College Degree or Higher	Missing Education
Mexican1	0.62	0.84	0.12	0.01	0.01	0.01
Mexican2	0.31	0.66	0.18	0.07	0.04	0.05
Mexican3	0.31	0.44	0.29	0.19	0.05	0.03
Mexican4	0.35	0.65	0.15	0.13	0.02	0.06
Cuban1	0.13	0.30	0.34	0.24	0.13	0.00
Cuban2	0.23	0.23	0.34	0.21	0.11	0.10
Cuban3	0.08	0.23	0.42	0.06	0.27	0.01
Cuban4	0.16	0.66	0.19	0.00	0.16	0.00
Puerto Rican	0.45	0.57	0.27	0.07	0.04	0.05
Other Latino	0.21	0.17	0.49	0.17	0.10	0.08
White	0.08	0.16	0.33	0.21	0.29	0.01
Black	0.41	0.29	0.44	0.18	0.07	0.02
Other	0.15	0.22	0.25	0.15	0.34	0.04
Total	0.17	0.23	0.34	0.20	0.22	0.02

TABLE 10-1 Continued

	Northeast	North-Central	West	South	Missing Region	Unemployment Rate	N
Mexican1	0.03	0.06	0.83	0.08	0.00	6.84	154
Mexican2	0.01	0.09	0.72	0.16	0.01	7.68	946
Mexican3	0.00	0.27	0.44	0.27	0.02	6.78	1,057
Mexican4	0.03	0.20	0.54	0.23	0.00	7.74	189
Cuban1	0.16	0.00	0.04	0.75	0.00	8.56	40
Cuban2	0.10	0.06	0.05	0.79	0.01	8.64	213
Cuban3	0.19	0.00	0.21	0.60	0.00	8.08	50
Cuban4	0.72	0.00	0.00	0.28	0.00	8.58	27
Puerto Rican	0.64	0.11	0.10	0.15	0.07	7.83	606
Other Latino	0.13	0.34	0.19	0.34	0.01	6.94	149
White	0.23	0.32	0.17	0.28	0.01	6.69	3,410
Black	0.13	0.22	0.10	0.55	0.00	7.11	2,968
Other	0.29	0.03	0.36	0.27	0.05	6.83	63
Total	0.20	0.28	0.19	0.32	0.01	6.85	9,872

NOTE: 1 = first generation; 2 = second generation; 3 = third generation; 4 = missing generation.

whose head had less than a high school education. This dropped to 66 percent for native-born Mexican American children of a foreign-born parent and was 44 percent for native-born children of native-born parents. Puerto Rican children also were educationally disadvantaged. More than half of all Puerto Rican children lived in families in which the head had less than a high school education. Cuban parents were the best educated; fewer than one-third of first-generation Cuban children lived in a family whose head had less than a high school education. In fact, 37 percent lived in a family in which the head had some college. Only 23 percent of native-born Cuban children had a (native- or foreign-born) parent with less than a high school education. Twenty-nine percent of black and 17 percent of other Latino children lived in families in which the head had less than a high school education. In contrast, only 16 percent of white children lived in a family in which the head had less than a high school education; 50 percent lived in a family in which the head had completed at least some college.

Parents' Marital Status

More than three-quarters of first- and second-generation Mexican children and Cuban children lived with two married parents. About 85 percent of white children and 69 percent of other Latino children also were living with married parents. Black children were least likely to live with two married parents; in 1992 only 39 percent did so. Puerto Rican children were a close second, with 48 percent living with two married parents. One disturbing generational difference is that among Mexican Americans the proportion living with married parents was lower in the third generation (60 percent) than in the second generation. This was not true for Cuban families.

Poverty Status

Poverty rates are very high for all Mexican, Puerto Rican, and black children's families. Poverty rates for families of Cuban children are quite low; third-generation Cuban children's families are no more likely than white children's families to be poor.

Geographic Location

One major difference between Mexicans and Cubans is where they settle in the United States. As expected, Mexican children are concentrated in the western United States and Cuban children in the South (Florida). These groups also disperse over time, though they still maintain a significant concentration in their original area of settlement. While 83 percent of foreign-born Mexican children live in the West, 72 percent of native-born Mexican children of foreign-born parents do, compared with only 44 percent of native-born Mexican children of native-born parents. The concentration of Cuban children is a bit higher—75 percent of foreign-born children, 79 percent of native-born children of foreign-born parents, and 60 percent of Cuban children of native-born parents live in the South. In contrast, 17 percent of whites live in the West, 32 percent live in the North-Central United States, 28 percent live in the South, and 23 percent live in the Northeast. The pattern of other Latinos, who are long-time residents of the

United States, is similar to that of whites—only 19 percent reside in the West, 34 percent live in the North-Central United States, 34 percent live in the South, and 13 percent live in the Northeast.

Receipt of Public Assistance by Ethnicity and Nativity

Table 10-2 shows weighted means of the proportion of U.S. children under age 18 receiving public assistance in 1992 by the combination of ethnicity and nativity. Examining the cash, noncash, and total columns, it is seen that 6 percent of white children received cash assistance, 14 percent received noncash assistance, and 14 percent received either cash or noncash assistance.

Ethnic Differences

Compared with whites, all Latino groups showed higher probabilities of receipt of all forms of public assistance. This ranges from 60 to 61 percent of families of first-generation Mexican children and native Puerto Rican children to 40 percent of second-generation Cuban children and 29 percent of native other Latino children. However, blacks have high rates of receipt as well, with 60 percent receiving some form of assistance. Native-born families of Mexican American children and Cuban children have lower rates of receipt of public assistance than families of black children.

Nativity Differences

Looking at receipt of all forms of assistance, it can be seen that families of second- and third-generation Mexican American children have lower levels of receipt than do families of first-generation children. In contrast, differences in public assistance receipt between generations are small for Cuban American children.

Type of Assistance Differences

Differences by type of assistance are substantial. First- and second-generation Mexican children's families have rates of AFDC and SSI receipt that are lower than third-generation Mexi-

TABLE 10-2 Proportion of U.S. Children Receiving Public Assistance by Ethnicity and Nativity, 1992

	AFDC	SSI	Other Welfare	Food Stamps	Medicaid
Mexican1	0.03	0.00	0.07	0.47	0.38
Mexican2	0.05	0.03	0.04	0.26	0.24
Mexican3	0.18	0.05	0.03	0.30	0.26
Mexican4	0.15	0.09	0.12	0.37	0.49
Cuban1	0.04	0.06	0.00	0.22	0.25
Cuban2	0.04	0.08	0.05	0.25	0.37
Cuban3	0.07	0.20	0.00	0.10	0.31
Cuban4	0.06	0.06	0.00	0.06	0.06
PRican	0.11	0.07	0.17	0.37	0.44
Other Latino	0.23	0.03	0.05	0.24	0.27
White	0.04	0.02	0.01	0.08	0.08
Black	0.27	0.06	0.05	0.42	0.37
Other	0.05	0.03	0.03	0.14	0.18
Total	0.09	0.03	0.02	0.17	0.17

	Housing	Heating	Cash	Noncash	Total
Mexican1	0.17	0.25	0.10	0.59	0.61
Mexican2	0.07	0.10	0.11	0.37	0.38
Mexican3	0.11	0.18	0.23	0.44	0.45
Mexican4	0.04	0.11	0.31	0.58	0.61
Cuban1	0.04	0.02	0.07	0.32	0.32
Cuban2	0.06	0.01	0.16	0.40	0.40
Cuban3	0.05	0.00	0.27	0.35	0.35
Cuban4	0.26	0.00	0.06	0.33	0.33
PRican	0.30	0.21	0.31	0.60	0.60
Other Latino	0.11	0.17	0.23	0.29	0.29
White	0.02	0.05	0.06	0.14	0.14
Black	0.25	0.17	0.34	0.58	0.60
Other	0.07	0.00	0.11	0.24	0.27
Total	0.08	0.09	0.13	0.26	0.27

NOTE: 1 = first generation; 2 = second generation; 3 = third generation; 4 = missing generation.

can children's families, levels comparable to that of whites. First-generation Mexican American children, in contrast, live in families that are more likely to receive other welfare, food stamps, Medicaid, heating assistance, and housing assistance than second- and third-generation children. This table does not adjust for the large socioeconomic and demographic differences shown in Table 10-2 among the different ethnic and nativity groups. The next step is to adjust for these differences.

Multivariate Analysis of Receipt of Public Assistance

While wanting to compare the public assistance receipt of families of foreign-born children and native-born children of foreign-born parents with that of native children of native-born parents, we also want to adjust for the extent of disadvantage to see whether higher receipt of public assistance is due primarily to these socioeconomic differences, to recency of arrival in the United States, or to something else. This is done in three steps. The first step includes the combined ethnicity/nativity variable, study year (to adjust for trends in welfare over time), and region of residence (to adjust for regional differences in the generosity of public assistance programs; see Table 10-3). The second step includes whether a child's family is poor (to adjust for program eligibility; see Table 10-4). The third step adds a variety of controls for other differences between children's families that might explain differences in the receipt of public assistance (see Table 10-5). If differences in receipt by generation within ethnicity decline once other factors are controlled, we can conclude that it is not immigration per se but the socioeconomic and demographic characteristics of the families of immigrant children that make them appear to use public assistance at a higher rate than those with native-born parents.[3] Adding them in separate steps per-

[3]These results are presented in terms of odds ratios, comparing the odds of receiving a form of public assistance for children of a particular ethnic/nativity group with that of native-born white children of native-born parents. The percent difference in odds is calculated as (odds ratio-1)*100. This represents the percent difference in the adjusted odds of receiving assistance between the category of interest and the comparison category (here native-born white children of native-born parents).

TABLE 10-3 Odds Ratios from Regression of Public Assistance on Ethnicity and Nativity

	Receipt of Cash Assistance			
	AFDC	SSI	Other Welfare	One or More
Mexican				
First generation	0.88	3.01*	3.84*	1.92*
Second generation	2.13*	2.38*	3.14*	2.72*
Third generation	6.63*	5.02*	4.43*	6.71*
Missing	4.77*	6.22*	13.87*	7.20*
Cuban				
First generation	2.73*	5.54*	0.95	2.95*
Second generation	3.03*	6.88*	5.48*	5.05*
Third generation	5.74*	1.58	3.57*	5.09*
Missing	1.34	6.95*	6.75*	3.17*
Puerto Rican	8.98*	9.37*	12.96*	13.55*
Other Latino	5.29*	2.83*	5.14*	5.24*
White	Omitted	Omitted	Omitted	Omitted
Black	10.36*	6.97*	7.23*	10.91*
Missing ethnicity	5.00*	1.83	4.95*	5.54*
Year				
1990	Omitted	Omitted	Omitted	Omitted
1991	1.01	1.23*	1.03	1.02
1992	0.97	1.33*	1.25*	1.09*
Region				
South	Omitted	Omitted	Omitted	Omitted
Northeast	0.87	1.27*	6.28*	1.92*
North-Central	2.45*	1.37*	1.42*	2.09*
West	1.61*	0.83	1.37*	1.42*
Missing region	0.57	0.28	1.54	0.54*

+p < .10; *p < .05; **p < .01.

Receipt of Noncash Assistance					Cash or Noncash
Food Stamps	Medicaid	Housing	Heating	One or More	One or More
5.55*	5.19*	5.99*	2.97*	6.50*	6.23*
5.34*	4.80*	3.85*	2.72*	4.75*	4.58*
7.15*	6.18*	5.47*	4.92*	6.14*	6.08*
5.54*	10.43*	2.75*	3.31*	7.70*	8.10*
3.69*	4.68*	1.77	0.87	3.39*	3.27*
3.92*	6.96*	2.20*	1.12	4.15*	4.25*
3.36*	6.64*	3.90*	0.34	4.16*	4.00*
4.98*	3.92*	4.15*	—	4.99*	5.47*
11.71*	13.21*	14.99*	4.33*	13.37*	13.07*
4.01*	3.59*	6.49*	2.05*	3.37*	3.37*
Omitted	Omitted	Omitted	Omitted	Omitted	Omitted
7.22*	7.29*	11.56*	3.25*	7.71*	7.81*
5.06*	3.77*	10.94*	1.18	4.61*	5.19*
Omitted	Omitted	Omitted	Omitted	Omitted	Omitted
1.02	1.13*	1.00	1.10	1.04	1.06+
1.06	1.19*	1.05	1.07	1.11*	1.14*
Omitted	Omitted	Omitted	Omitted	Omitted	Omitted
1.12*	1.53*	2.32*	1.65*	1.36*	1.37*
1.17*	1.39*	0.76*	1.54*	1.14*	1.14*
0.60*	1.08	0.95	0.59*	0.81*	0.85*
0.19*	0.64*	1.38	—	0.77	0.74+

TABLE 10-4 Odds Ratios from Regression of Public Assistance on Ethnicity and Nativity

	Receipt of Cash Assistance			
	AFDC	SSI	Other Welfare	One or More
Mexican				
First generation	0.16*	1.82	1.81*	0.43*
Second generation	0.61*	1.65*	1.76*	0.93
Third generation	2.67*	3.57*	2.61*	3.17*
Missing	1.97*	4.51*	8.82*	3.82*
Cuban				
First generation	1.23	4.35*	0.70	1.56
Second generation	1.39	5.58*	3.95*	3.17*
Third generation	4.71*	1.36	3.25*	4.47*
Missing	0.63	5.99*	5.34*	2.07
Puerto Rican	2.57*	5.89*	6.00*	5.16*
Other Latino	2.94*	2.24*	3.85*	3.29*
White	Omitted	Omitted	Omitted	Omitted
Black	4.27*	4.84*	4.29*	5.58*
Missing Ethnicity	2.04*	1.36	3.53*	2.87*
Year				
1990	Omitted	Omitted	Omitted	Omitted
1991	0.99	1.23*	1.02	1.01
1992	0.90*	1.31*	1.24*	1.05
Region				
South	Omitted	Omitted	Omitted	Omitted
Northeast	0.80*	1.23	6.95*	2.31*
North-Central	2.73*	1.28*	1.30*	2.28*
West	2.44*	0.89	1.59*	2.02*
Missing region	0.35*	0.22*	1.13	0.29*
Characteristics of child's family in poverty	19.12*	2.62*	4.39*	14.26*

+ p <.10; *p < .05; **p < .01.

Receipt of Noncash Assistance					Cash or Noncash
Food Stamps	Medicaid	Housing	Heating	One or More	One or More
1.25	1.48*	2.43*	1.02	2.01*	1.92*
1.97*	2.08*	1.93*	1.18	2.19*	2.11*
3.64*	3.21*	3.01*	2.47*	3.68*	3.68*
2.59*	6.99*	1.49*	1.57*	5.41*	5.84*
1.99*	3.03*	1.14	0.47	2.18*	2.09*
2.57*	5.57*	1.47	0.64*	3.21*	3.35*
2.80*	6.53*	3.25*	0.23*	4.07*	3.89*
4.59*	3.14*	3.23*	—	4.99*	5.63*
4.56*	6.03*	7.05*	1.47*	7.15*	6.99*
2.24*	2.14*	4.46*	1.13	2.07*	2.10*
Omitted	Omitted	Omitted	Omitted	Omitted	Omitted
3.37*	3.70*	6.74*	1.43*	4.73*	4.87*
2.49*	1.88*	6.96*	0.57	2.64*	3.18*
Omitted	Omitted	Omitted	Omitted	Omitted	Omitted
1.00	1.15*	1.00	1.08	1.03	1.06
1.00	1.19*	1.02	1.02	1.07+	1.11*
Omitted	Omitted	Omitted	Omitted	Omitted	Omitted
1.13	1.69*	2.53*	1.76*	1.54*	1.54*
1.10	1.37*	0.65*	1.52*	1.12*	1.12*
0.64	1.41*	1.11	0.66*	0.97	1.04
0.06*	0.30*	1.04	—	0.32*	0.30*
22.47*	12.38*	5.55*	8.23*	18.56*	18.60*

TABLE 10-5 Odds Ratios from Regression of Public Assistance on Ethnicity and Nativity

	Receipt of Cash Assistance			
	AFDC	SSI	Other Welfare	One or More
Mexican				
First generation	0.08*	0.52*	0.87	0.14*
Second generation	0.30*	0.64*	0.89	0.36*
Third generation	1.27*	1.83*	1.37	1.41*
Missing	0.86	0.84	3.23*	1.06
Cuban				
First generation	1.66	3.10*	0.78	1.91*
Second generation	0.91	2.44*	2.14*	1.82*
Third generation	2.28*	0.75	1.55	2.09*
Missing	0.89	1.52	2.86	1.30
Puerto Rican	0.99	2.15*	2.53*	1.84*
Other Latino	1.84*	1.40	2.43*	2.03*
White	Omitted	Omitted	Omitted	Omitted
Black	2.03*	2.33*	2.21*	2.57*
Missing Ethnicity	1.37	0.79	1.91	1.70*
Year				
1990	Omitted	Omitted	Omitted	Omitted
1991	0.96	1.25*	1.00	0.96
1992	0.79*	1.23*	1.06	0.85*
Region				
South	Omitted	Omitted	Omitted	Omitted
Northeast	0.62*	1.31*	7.80*	2.19*
North-Central	2.38*	1.32*	1.23	2.13*
West	2.45*	1.00	1.73*	2.25*
Missing region	0.59	0.41	2.09	0.50*
Characteristics of Child's Family				
In poverty	8.99*	1.54*	2.32*	7.03*
Age of household head	0.99*	1.06*	1.03*	1.02*
Healthy	0.90*	0.61*	0.95	0.87*
Parents married	0.19*	0.47*	0.32*	0.19*
Head: < high school degree	1.95*	1.77*	1.39*	2.22*
Head: high school degree	Omitted	Omitted	Omitted	Omitted
Head: some college	1.12	0.96	0.62*	0.87*
Head: college degree	0.26*	0.15*	0.14*	0.17*

TABLE 10-5 Continued

	Receipt of Cash Assistance			
	AFDC	SSI	Other Welfare	One or More
Missing education	1.40*	1.56*	1.00	1.46*
Age of youngest child	0.95*	1.00	0.94*	0.94*
Number of children	1.14*	1.21*	1.12*	1.18*
Unemployment rate	1.10*	1.05*	1.09	1.12*

	Receipt of Noncash Assistance					Cash or Noncash
	Food Stamps	Medicaid	Housing	Heating	One or More	One or More
Mexican						
First generation	0.58*	0.66*	2.20*	0.63*	0.80+	0.74*
Second generation	0.96	0.89	1.65*	0.78*	0.94	0.88+
Third generation	1.87*	1.57*	2.22*	1.60*	1.88*	1.87*
Missing	1.12	2.17*	1.21	0.81	1.69*	1.72*
Cuban						
First generation	2.73*	4.03*	1.31	0.46	2.71*	2.54*
Second generation	1.93*	3.60*	1.40	0.43*	2.17*	2.21*
Third generation	1.69	3.57*	2.15*	0.16*	2.40*	2.24*
Missing	2.59*	1.78	2.07	—	1.92+	2.10*
Puerto Rican	2.18*	2.70*	4.81*	0.82*	3.48*	3.36*
Other Latino	1.54*	1.20	3.56*	0.82	1.30+	1.34*
White	Omitted	Omitted	Omitted	Omitted	Omitted	Omitted
Black	1.83*	1.98*	4.98*	0.88	2.63*	2.63*
Missing Ethnicity	1.88*	1.33	6.47*	0.46*	2.29*	2.55*
Year						
1990	Omitted	Omitted	Omitted	Omitted	Omitted	Omitted
1991	0.97	1.13*	1.00	1.10	1.01	1.04
1992	0.85*	1.06	1.00	0.98	0.99	1.02
Region						
South	Omitted	Omitted	Omitted	Omitted	Omitted	Omitted
Northeast	1.00	1.56*	2.35*	1.65*	1.41*	1.41*
North-Central	0.92	1.19*	0.55*	1.44*	0.98	0.99
West	0.60*	1.48*	1.05	0.64*	0.94	1.02
Missing region	0.08*	0.45*	1.31	—	0.45*	0.43*

TABLE 10-5 Continued

	Receipt of Noncash Assistance					Cash or Noncash
	Food Stamps	Medicaid	Housing	Heating	One or More	One or More
Characteristics of Child's Family						
In poverty	12.05*	6.52*	3.62*	4.98*	9.98*	10.14*
Age of household head	0.99*	1.02*	0.98*	1.01*	1.01*	1.02*
Healthy	0.77*	0.81*	0.98	0.71*	0.74*	0.74*
Parents married	0.32*	0.30*	0.47*	0.49*	0.29*	0.29*
Head: < high school degree	1.48*	1.81*	1.29*	1.23*	1.84*	1.87*
Head: high school degree	Omitted	Omitted	Omitted	Omitted	Omitted	Omitted
Head: some college	0.77*	0.78*	0.89	0.94	0.72*	0.74*
Head: college degree	0.19*	0.20*	0.66*	0.15*	0.29*	0.28*
Missing education	1.28*	1.50*	1.30*	0.91	1.64*	1.57*
Age of youngest child	0.95*	0.91*	0.98*	0.97*	0.92*	0.92*
Number of children	1.28*	1.14*	1.00	1.09*	1.21*	1.21*
Unemployment rate	1.13*	1.10*	1.03*	1.03*	1.07*	1.08*

+p < .10; *p < .05; **p < .01.

mits determination of whether poverty or other family characteristics explain the greater receipt among immigrant groups shown in Table 10-2. Ethnic differences reflect different historical circumstances of the various groups, cultures, and other unmeasured factors. See Appendix 10C for a description of the analysis sample.

Cash Assistance

The three components of cash assistance are AFDC, SSI, and other welfare programs. Six percent of white children in the study lived in families receiving cash assistance in a single year, on average, during the early 1990s.

AFDC. On average, 4 percent of white children lived in families receiving AFDC in a single year (Table 10-2). With only year and region controlled, first-generation Mexican children are neither more or less likely to be in families receiving AFDC, whereas second- and third-generation children are more likely to be in such families. Being poor is an important criterion for AFDC receipt, and poverty explains the greater receipt among second-generation but not first- and third-generation Mexican children. Once differences in year, region of residence, and poverty status are controlled, both first- and second-generation Mexican children are significantly less likely to be in families receiving AFDC, whereas third-generation children remain significantly more likely to be in families receiving AFDC than white children. Controlling for additional demographic factors increases the gap in public assistance receipt between first- and second-generation Mexican Americans and native whites but does not change the conclusions. With differences in socioeconomic status and other factors held constant, foreign-born Mexican American children are 92 percent less likely in terms of odds and native-born Mexican American children of foreign-born parents are 70 percent less likely to be in families receiving AFDC than native white children. Third-generation Mexican American children are 27 percent more likely than white children to live in families receiving public assistance. The predicted probabilities of AFDC receipt from this full model for a child in an average family, by ethnicity and generation, are shown in Figure 10-1.

Higher levels of poverty explain the greater public assistance receipt of first- and second-generation Cuban American children. Once differences in poverty are taken into account as well as year and region, first- and second-generation Cuban children are neither more or less likely to be in families receiving AFDC than white children, though, as for Mexicans, third-generation children remain more likely to live in families receiving AFDC. Adjusting for additional demographic factors does not change the results. While Cuban first-generation children appear to have a higher probability than white children of living in a family receiving AFDC (0.036 compared with 0.022 in Figure 10-1), this difference is not statistically significant.

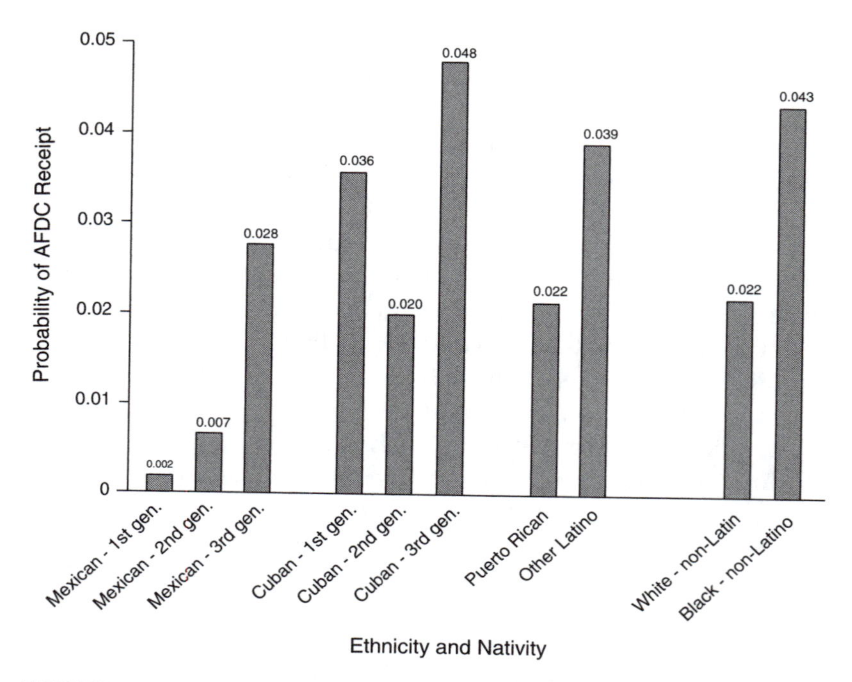

FIGURE 10-1 Predicted probability of AFDC receipt by ethnicity and nativity.

SSI. SSI receipt is more characteristic of older families; children in families with an older head are more likely to be receiving SSI than those with a younger head (see Table 10-5). On average, only 2 percent of white children spent time in families receiving SSI in any one year (Table 10-2). From a multivariate model with only year and region (Table 10-3), the receipt of SSI by families of minority children exceeds that of white children. Greater SSI use by minority Mexican American children can be explained by their demographic characteristics but not their economic status. Once poverty as well as region and year are controlled, first- and second-generation Mexican children remain more likely to receive SSI than white children, although only the coefficient for the second generation is statistically significant. The important factors explaining SSI use are the age, health status, and education of the household head. Once these additional demographic variables

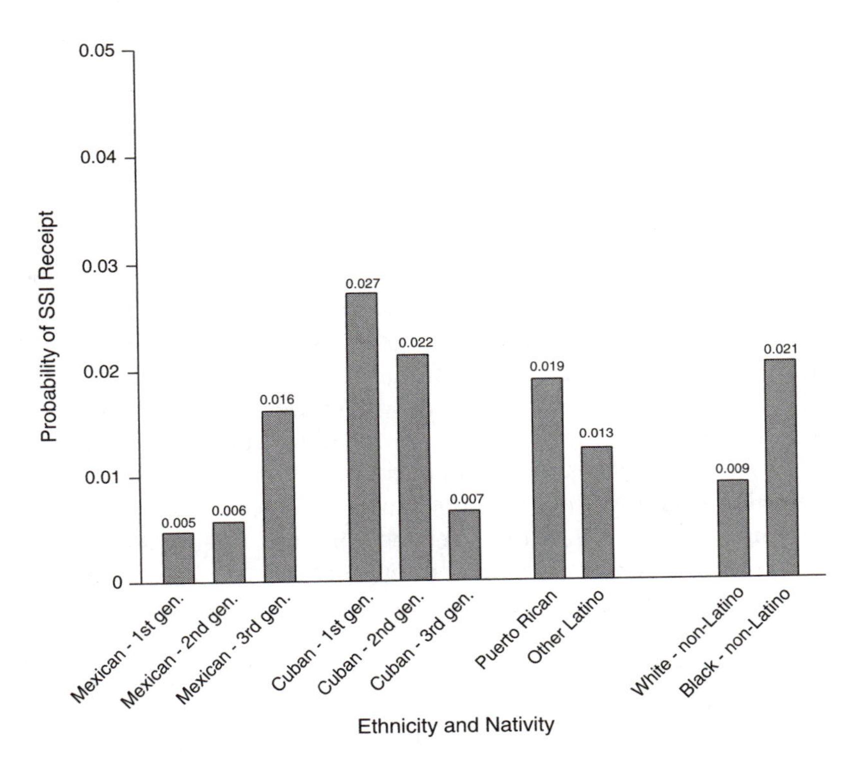

FIGURE 10-2 Predicted probability of SSI receipt by ethnicity and nativity.

are added, first-generation Mexican American children live in families that are 48 percent less likely and second-generation Mexican American children live in families that are 36 percent less likely in terms of odds than white children to be receiving SSI. Third-generation Mexican American families are 83 percent more likely to be receiving SSI. Predicted probabilities of SSI receipt are shown in Figure 10-2.

Adjusting for all socioeconomic and demographic variables, first- and second-generation Cuban children remain significantly more likely to be in families receiving SSI, but the third generation does not differ from white children in SSI receipt. Foreign-born Cuban children are three times as likely and native-born children of foreign-born parents are more than twice as likely, in terms of odds, than native white children to live in families receiving

SSI. Puerto Rican and black children are other ethnic groups more likely than whites to be in families receiving SSI. The predicted probability of receipt of SSI, holding the controls at their average, is shown in Figure 10-2.

Other Welfare. The results for other welfare programs differ little from those of AFDC and SSI. On average, only 1 percent of white children were in families receiving other welfare in the early 1990s (Table 10-2). While Hispanic and other minority groups all showed elevated probabilities of receiving other welfare, relative to whites, controlling for demographic differences explained the elevated rates only among Mexican American children. Poverty was not the reason for elevated receipt, since after including poverty status Mexicans were still substantially more likely to be in families receiving other welfare. However, once the demographic factors were controlled, first-, second-, and third-generation Mexican American children were neither more or less likely to receive other forms of welfare than native-born white children of native parents.

First-generation Cuban children were neither more or less likely to receive other forms of welfare than white children, and second-generation Cuban children were significantly more likely to receive other welfare, with or without adjusting for other factors. Third-generation Cuban children were significantly more likely to live in families receiving welfare until demographic factors were controlled; once controlled, the difference between them and native whites was still positive but no longer statistically significant.

Noncash Benefits

Noncash benefits are the most common form of public assistance, with 14 percent of white children living in families receiving food stamps, Medicaid, housing assistance, or heating assistance in a single year.

Food Stamps. On average, 8 percent of white children were in families receiving food stamps in one survey year (Table 10-2). Almost half of first-generation Mexican children were in families receiving food stamps, a higher proportion than for any other group. Not surprisingly, therefore, all Mexican children are significantly more likely than whites to receive food stamps after adjusting for region and year. When adjustment is made for poverty as well as region and year, the difference between the odds of first-generation Mexican children and white children receiving food stamps becomes insignificant, although second-generation Mexican children remain considerably (97 percent) more likely to be in such families. When adjustment is also made for differences in demographic characteristics, first-generation Mexican children become 42 percent less likely to be in families receiving food stamps than native-born white children, and second-generation children are neither more or less likely than white children to be in families receiving food stamps. Differences in receipt of food stamps reflect not just differences in income levels but also differences in demographic characteristics. Third-generation Mexican children continue to be more likely than white children to receive food stamps, with or without controls for other factors. The predicted probability of a child's family receiving food stamps is depicted in Figure 10-3, with control variables at their average values.

Among Cuban children, including a measure of poverty makes little difference to receipt of food stamps. The relationship remains positive and significant for all but the third generation. Adding in the demographic variables shows that among Cubans, in contrast to Mexicans, first- and second-generation children are the most likely to receive food stamps, with the third generation being the least likely as well as about as likely as white native children. Puerto Ricans, other Latinos, and blacks are also more likely than whites to live in families receiving food stamps (Figure 10-3).

Medicaid. On average, 8 percent of white children received Medicaid in one study year (Table 10-2). A high proportion of first-generation Mexican children were in families receiving Medicaid (38 percent). As with food stamps, controlling for poverty status of the household does not explain the high use of Medicaid. Rather, greater receipt is due to differences in demographic characteristics of the family. Once family characteristics are controlled,

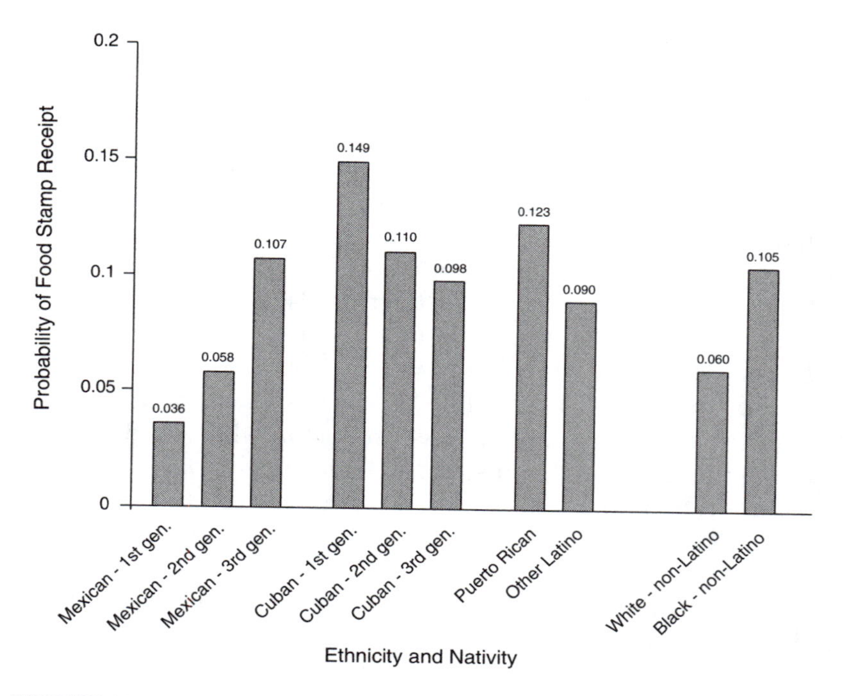

FIGURE 10-3 Predicted probability of food stamp receipt by ethnicity and nativity.

first-generation Mexican children were 34 percent less likely than white children to be in families receiving Medicaid. Second-generation Mexican children were as likely as whites to be in families receiving Medicaid; and third-generation Mexican children were more likely than whites to receive Medicaid.

Cuban children were highly likely to live in families receiving Medicaid. Even controlling for socioeconomic and demographic characteristics of their households, first-generation Cuban American children are four times as likely in terms of odds to be in families receiving Medicaid. Second- and third-generation Cuban children are also highly likely to be in such families. Puerto Rican and black children also are more likely than white children to be in families receiving Medicaid. The predicted probabilities of Medicaid receipt are shown in Figure 10-4.

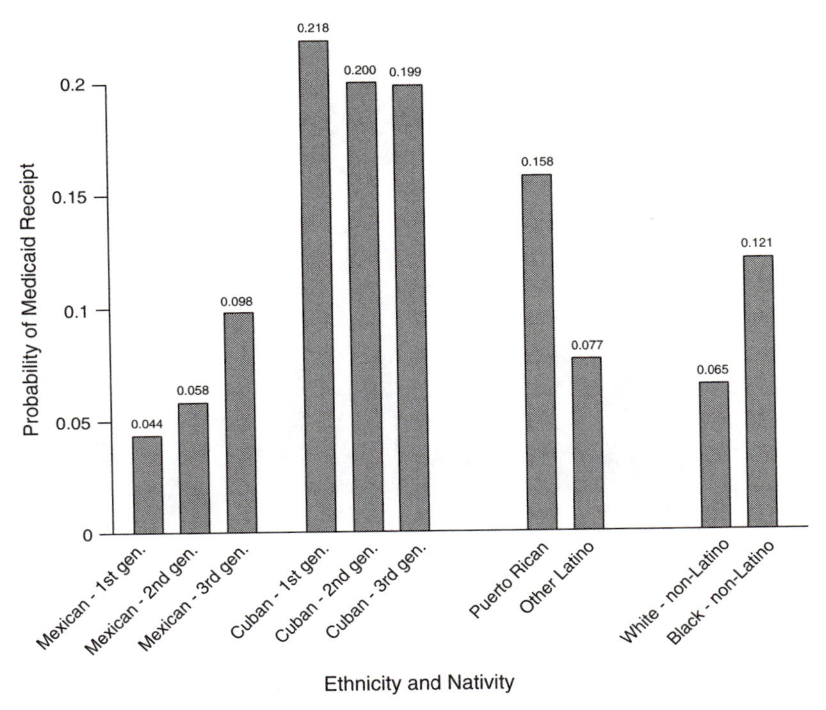

FIGURE 10-4 Predicted probability of Medicaid receipt by ethnicity and nativity.

Housing. Only 2 percent of white children lived in families that received subsidized housing in one study year (Table 10-2). Housing is the only form of assistance in which first-generation Mexican American children are as likely as third-generation children and more likely than white children to receive public assistance. This relationship persists even after controls are introduced for socioeconomic status and demographic characteristics. The survey questions ask about residence in public housing projects as well as about receipt of other forms of housing assistance, such as vouchers. Researchers have pointed out that survey respondents are unable to distinguish between private and public sources of assistance and substantially overreport both living in public housing and receiving housing assistance (Houser, 1997). Thus, it is possible that many recent immigrants are recipients of assistance

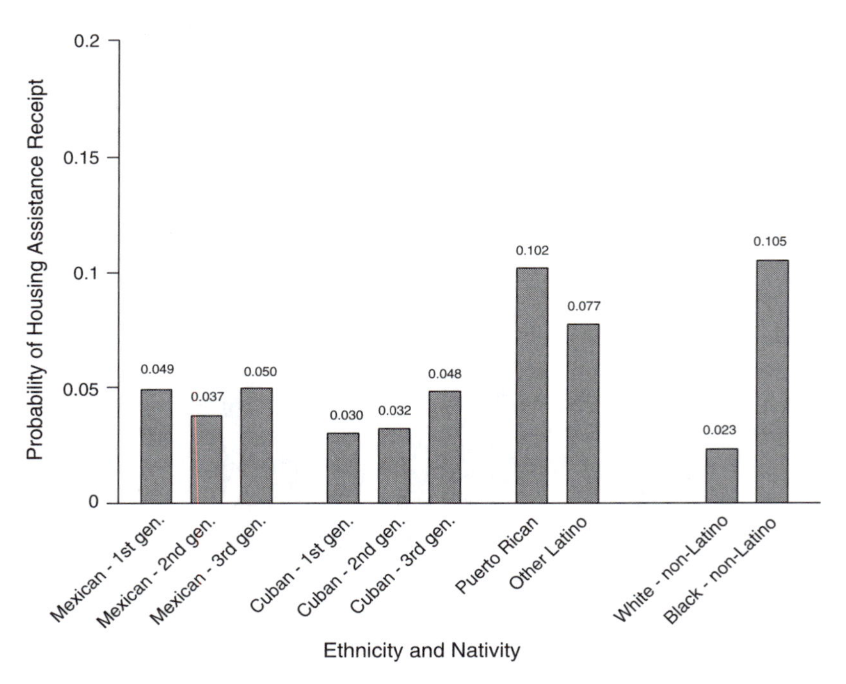

FIGURE 10-5 Predicted probability of housing assistance receipt by ethnicity and nativity.

from private local nonprofit or state agencies instead of federal sources.

Receipt of housing assistance by the families of first- and second-generation Cuban children does not differ significantly from that of whites, all else being equal. Their greater receipt before controls is due to differences in both poverty and demographic characteristics. Receipt of housing assistance by third-generation Cuban children's families remains higher than that of whites after controlling for economic and demographic characteristics. The predicted probabilities of housing assistance receipt for the various ethnicity/nativity groups are shown in Figure 10-5.

Heating Assistance. On average, 5 percent of white children were in families that received assistance in heating their homes. The differences between Mexican children and white children in the receipt of heating assistance are due to both economic and demographic factors. Adjusting for poverty reduces the difference between first- and second-generation Mexican children and white children to nonsignificance. Adjusting for differences in demographic factors also results in first- and second-generation Mexican American children being significantly less likely than white children to be in families that received heating assistance. In contrast, third-generation Mexican children are more likely than white children to be in families receiving heating assistance.

Controlling only for year and region, second- and third-generation Cuban children are neither more or less likely than white children to be in families receiving heating assistance. Once poverty status is controlled, Cuban children are less likely than white children to live in families receiving heating assistance. This could be due to differences in where these groups locate in the United States, with first- and second-generation Mexican Americans and Cubans residing in more temperate climates than Puerto Ricans. Black children and Puerto Rican children are significantly more likely than white children to be in families receiving heating assistance, and they are more likely to live in northern parts of the United States. While controls are in place for region of the country, these regions are sufficiently wide that there could be variations in the need for heat. For example, Washington, D.C., is included in the South and Seattle in the West. Third-generation Mexican children are more dispersed geographically than the first and second generations, which could explain the difference in heating assistance among Mexican Americans by generation.

Total. About 14 percent of white children were in families that received either cash or noncash assistance in one year between 1990 and 1995 (Table 10-2). All racial and ethnic minority children are more likely than white children to receive either cash or noncash assistance. This is not surprising, since they are more likely to be socioeconomically disadvantaged. Once these economic and demographic differences are controlled, the differences diminish, though they disappear only for first- and second-generation Mexican children. Net of all control variables, first- and second-generation Mexican immigrant children were 26 and 12 percent, respectively, less likely than third-generation native white children to receive either cash or noncash assistance. Third-generation Mexican children were significantly more likely to receive cash or noncash assistance. Net of socioeconomic and other factors, first-, second-, and third-generation Cuban children were twice as likely to be in families receiving public assistance as white children. This reflects their greater eligibility for and use of services as refugees. The major users of public assistance are those to whom that assistance is directed by public policy. Puerto Rican children were 3.4 times and black children 2.6 times as likely to be in families receiving public assistance as white children. Thus, it is not solely immigrants who place heavy demands on U.S. funds for public assistance. However, some negative long-term implications are suggested by the fact that native-born Mexican children of native-born parents are significantly more likely to receive public assistance than are comparable native-born white children.

SUMMARY AND CONCLUSIONS

The most important finding of this paper is that the higher level of receipt of some forms of public assistance by Mexican-born children and children of Mexican-born parents is due to their disadvantaged socioeconomic and demographic characteristics, not to their immigrant status per se. Higher levels of receipt of public assistance by Cuban American children are likely due to their particular circumstances upon entry into this country, such as the special refugee status of Cuban children's families.

The public perception is that minority groups are heavy users of public assistance programs, and it is the case that the chance of a minority child's family receiving public assistance is higher than that of a white family; however, this is not due to recent immigration. When socioeconomic and demographic factors are controlled, first-generation Mexican American children are less likely to receive AFDC, SSI, food stamps, Medicaid, and heating assistance than are whites; they are more likely to receive housing assistance. Second-generation Mexican American children are less likely to receive AFDC, SSI, and heating assistance; more likely to receive housing assistance; and about as likely as whites to receive food stamps and Medicaid. Third-generation Mexican American children are more likely to receive almost all forms of assistance. Thus, the "immigrant optimism" hypothesis is supported for Mexicans. The lesser receipt by first-generation Mexican children may be due to less legal eligibility, to fear of discovery among undocumented immigrants, or to a greater work ethic among recent arrivals. Greater receipt of housing assistance by Mexican children's families may result from private assistance being misreported as public assistance. Noncitizen Mexican Americans would be especially affected by budgetary cutbacks in food stamps and Medicaid.

In contrast, Cuban children are more likely than white children to receive all forms of public assistance, regardless of nativity, once other factors are controlled. First-generation Cuban American children live in families that are about as likely to receive AFDC, other welfare, housing assistance, and heating assistance as whites. Their pattern of receipt of SSI, food stamps, and Medicaid follows the more typical straight-line assimilation model, with greater use in the first and second generations than in the third generation. This is likely to be due to the fact that Cubans enter the United States as refugees, which makes them immediately eligible for a variety of public assistance programs. The 1996 federal welfare reform legislation will affect their eligibility for these forms of public assistance once they have been in this country for five years. Other Hispanic children, third generation or more, were also more likely to be receiving public assistance than white children.

Most striking, however, is the substantial receipt of public assistance by Puerto Rican and black children's families, which are much more likely than white children's families to receive every form of public assistance except AFDC (Puerto Ricans) and heating assistance (blacks), even after controlling for economic and demographic factors. Puerto Ricans and blacks are all U.S. citizens. Rather than recency of entry into the United States, it is disadvantaged socioeconomic and demographic status that contributes to the continued receipt of public assistance by Mexicans. Among Cubans it is probably their special status as refugees. Greater receipt by Puerto Rican and black children's families was not explained by the variables included in this study.

Since children of Hispanic origin generally (including other Latinos) were found to be more likely to receive all forms of public assistance compared with native whites, I suspect that people perceive Hispanic children to be receiving public assistance and to presume they are immigrants. In fact, half of Hispanic Americans were born in the United States (Fix and Passel, 1994). While Cubans have high rates of public assistance in the first two generations, they are integrated by the third generation, perhaps at least partly because of the assistance they received. In contrast, the analyses I conducted showed that for several forms of public assistance it is third-generation Mexican American children (not those of the first or second generation) who are more likely than whites to receive public assistance. Other Latinos also have higher rates of receipt of many forms of public assistance. If these Hispanic groups are not incorporated more rapidly into mainstream American society but are marginalized, the third generation will continue to need temporary assistance, a challenge to welfare reformers. Furthermore, the fact that black and Puerto Rican children continue to be very significantly higher recipients of public assistance suggests that, rather than recency of entry into the United States, it is the failure of minority racial/ethnic groups to be fully integrated into mainstream American society that is the problem.

REFERENCES

Blau, F.

1984 The use of transfer payments by immigrants. *Industrial and Labor Relations Review* 37(2):222-239.

Borjas, G., and L. Hilton

1996 Immigration and the welfare state: Immigrant participation in means-tested entitlement programs. *Quarterly Journal of Economics* CVXI:575-604.

Bureau of the Census

1996 How we're changing. Current Population Reports P23(191):1-4. Washington, D.C.: U.S. Department of Commerce.

Duran, B., and R. Weffer

1992 Immigrants' aspirations, high school process, and academic outcomes. *American Educational Research Journal* 29(1):163-181.

Edmonston, B. (ed.)

1996 *Statistics on U.S. Immigration: An Assessment of Data Needs for Future Research.* Committee on National Statistics, National Reseach Council. Washington, D.C.: National Academy Press.

Fix, M., and J. Passel
1994 *Immigration and Immigrants*. Washington, D.C.: The Urban Institute.

Houser, S.
1997 The Effects of Tenant-Based and Project-Based Housing Assistance on Employment. Paper presented at the annual meeting of the Western Economic Association, Seattle, July 10-12.

Jensen, L.
1988 Patterns of immigration and public assistance utilization, 1970-1980. *International Migration Review* XXII(1):51-83.

Kao, G., and M. Tienda
1995 Optimism and achievement: The educational performance of immigrant youth. *Social Science Quarterly* 76(1):1-19.

National Center for Education Statistics
1993 *The Condition of Education 1993*. Washington, D.C.: U.S. Department of Education.

Population Reference Bureau
1989 *America in the 21st Century: Human Resource Development*. Washington, D.C.: Population Reference Bureau.

Portes, A., and M. Zhou
1992 Gaining the upper hand: Economic mobility among immigrant and domestic minorities. *Ethnic and Racial Studies* 15(4):491-522.

Simon, J., and A. Akbari
1996 Determinants of welfare payment use by immigrants and natives in the United States and Canada. Pp. 79-100 in *Immigrants and Immigration Policy: Individual Skills, Family Ties, and Group Identities*, H. Duleep and W. Phanindra, eds. Greenwich, Conn.: JAI Press.

Tienda, M., and L. Jensen
1986 Immigration and public assistance participation: Dispelling the myth of dependency. *Social Science Research* 15:372-400.

APPENDIX 10A: DATA AND MEASURES

Now in its thirtieth year of data collection, the Panel Study of Income Dynamics (PSID) is a longitudinal survey of a representative sample of U.S. men, women, children, and the families in which they reside. Data on employment, income, wealth, housing, food expenditures, transfer income, and marital and fertility behavior have been collected annually since 1968. Between 1990 and 1995, a sample of 2,043 Latino households was added to the existing PSID sample of 7,300 households. This sample was drawn from a 1989 study of political affiliation and participation directed by Rodolfo de la Garza (University of Texas) and was conducted by the Institute for Survey Research at Temple University. The original sample was drawn from a sample of 40 out of 382 U.S. counties with the highest concentrations of Latino individuals. These counties provide coverage of slightly more than 90 percent of the three most prevalent Latino groups in the United States: Puerto Rican, Cuban, and Mexican American. Cuban and Puerto Rican households were selected at substantially higher rates to obtain larger samples of the two groups so that analysts could make more precise statements about them. The PSID obtained permission from the investigators to reinterview the respondents, obtained contact information from Temple University, and attempted interviews with a subsample of the Latino National Political Survey (LNPS) respondents. The response rate to the PSID was 74.8 percent. Forty percent of the living 1990 Latino nonresponse was successfully interviewed in a special recontact effort in 1992. Therefore, the number of Latinos increased to 2,258 by 1992, despite attrition. The response rate is close to 92 percent from year to year, which is good but lower than the 97 percent for the core.

APPENDIX 10B: MEASURES

Public Assistance. Similar to Borjas and Hilton (1996), the measures of public assistance receipt of a child's family include AFDC, SSI, other welfare, Medicaid, food stamps, heating assistance, and housing assistance (rent subsidy or public housing). Other welfare consists of general assistance and miscellaneous state assistance.

Nativity and Ethnicity. The 1990 early-release dataset included a set of questions from the 1989 LNPS, such as immigrant status, birthplace, and parents' birthplaces as well as the core PSID questions. These data were used in conjunction with special questions asked in 1990 and 1992 to identify the birthplaces of child and parent. A first-generation child was born outside the United States. A second-generation child was born in the United States to at least one foreign-born parent. A third- or later-generation child was born in the United States to a native-born parent. All blacks, whites, and other Latinos were assigned to the third generations, as their families had been in the study since 1968. In addition, a set of questions identified both race and Hispanic origin and, for the LNPS respondents, whether they were Cuban, Mexican, or Puerto Rican in origin. Many of the original 1968 Latinos could also be coded as Mexican, Puerto Rican, or Cuban in background. "Other Latinos" therefore are from the original 1968 PSID but tend to be from places other than Mexico, Cuba, and Puerto Rico.

Health. The health measure for a household's head comes from a question on general health: "Would you say your health in general is excellent, very good, good, fair, or poor?" "Excellent" and "very good" were coded 1; "good," "fair," and "poor" were coded 0.

Age of Household Head, Number of Children Under 18 in the Household, Age of Youngest Child, Marital Status of Household Head. All are obtained in the household composition section of the PSID survey and are edited to be consistent from year to year.

Education of Household Head. This comes from a series of questions about schooling that are updated each year only for new heads.

Unemployment Rate. This is the unemployment rate in the county of residence.

Region of Residence. Individual addresses are coded by the region of the country in which they fall—Northeast, North-Central, South, West, and "missing" region.

APPENDIX 10C: ANALYSIS PLAN

Because final measures of income were not available in the 1993 through 1995 data, the data file analyzed here includes data from 1990 through 1992 only. Weights were drawn from the 1992 data. All children who were under age 18 in at least one year between 1990 and 1992 were selected, and a file with one record for each year that each child was in the PSID and under age 18, the child-year file, was created. Because children can be in the study for up to three years between 1990 and 1992, that greatly expands the number of analysis years. Once separate child-year records are created and years in which the child was 18 years of age or older are deleted, we observe 28,834 child-years, comprised of 489 first-generation Mexican person-years; 2,716 second-generation child-years; 2,914 third-generation child-years; and 415 child-years in which generation was missing. For Cuban children there are 156 first-generation child-years, 623 second-generation child-years, and 125 third-generation child-years, with 61 missing child-years. We observed 1,727 Puerto Rican child-years. There are 431 other Hispanic children child-years; 10,124 white child-years; 8,882 black child-years; and 171 other ethnicity child-years.

Data Caution. The results from a child-based analysis cannot be expected to be identical to those from a family-based analysis. If immigrant families have more children than native families, their behavior will be more accurately represented more frequently in a child-based analysis than in a family-based analysis. If immigrant families are only slightly less likely to receive public assistance, the effects are likely to be stronger when children or child/person-years become the unit of analysis.

CHAPTER 11

Receipt of Public Assistance by Immigrant Children and Their Families:
Evidence from the Survey of Income and Program Participation

Peter David Brandon

National debate over immigration policy is not new in the United States. The immigration debate in the United States dates back to the colonies, which argued over who was ultimately responsible for destitute newcomers. In recent times, though, the debate has focused mainly on immigrants' adjustment to American society and their alleged displacement of native-born workers in the job market.

With passage of the Personal Responsibility and Work Opportunity Reconciliation Act of 1996, which greatly affects safety net provisions for immigrants, it is clear that the relationship between immigration and social policy is again a critical part of the national debate over immigration policy. The 1996 legislation reflects a public perception[1] that immigrants should pay their own way and that it is wrong for immigrants to depend on welfare.[2]

There is evidence that immigrant households have higher rates of welfare receipt and that the rates have increased over time (Borjas and Hilton, 1996). Yet because the U.S. welfare system contains such a patchwork of programs addressing so many dif-

[1]See Primus (1996).

[2]Refugees are treated differently from other immigrants because of the circumstances under which they arrived in this country. In the early 1990s refugees comprised only about 10 percent of all immigrants, however.

ferent needs and populations, much more research is needed to explore immigrants' utilization of public assistance programs. And although immigrant children comprise a large part of the immigrant population as well as representing a sizable fraction of the welfare caseload, no previous analyses apart from Hofferth (this volume) and Currie (1997) have focused on needy immigrant children. Using data from the Survey of Income and Program Participation, this chapter begins to fill this gap in our knowledge by providing a more complete picture of immigrant children and their families' participation in means-tested entitlement programs. In essence, the real picture differs from the one framed in the public's eye.

CONTEXT AND BACKGROUND STUDIES

Until the new welfare legislation became law in August 1996, legal immigrants could receive benefits from federal public assistance programs. If immigrants were needy or unemployed, they faced the same eligibility rules as citizens. Basically, administrative rules for public assistance drew no real distinctions between legal permanent residents and citizens. Even undocumented immigrants were eligible for some emergency relief, such as medical care.[3]

In the context of the old welfare system, several important national-level studies compared public assistance receipt between immigrant and native groups. Blau (1984, 1986), Simon (1981), and Simon and Akbari (1996) used the 1976 Survey of Income and Education (SIE) to conclude that immigrant families received substantially less in annual transfer payments than native families. Tienda and Jensen (1986) updated Blau's 1984 analysis by using 1980 census data rather than the 1976 SIE. They demonstrated that rates of welfare use in 1979 were higher for natives than for immigrants when other factors such as age, education, and marital status were taken into account.

[3]Title IV of the Personal Responsibility and Work Opportunity Reconciliation Act of 1996 changed who gets welfare and how they get it. The crucial point is that the new provisions affect legal and illegal immigrants. For more background, see U.S. House of Representatives (1996).

Five years later Borjas and Trejo (1991) reexamined issues that Blau (1984) and Tienda and Jensen (1986) had raised about immigrant participation in the American welfare system. Using both the 1970 and 1980 censuses, their work distinguished itself from previous works by investigating intracohort changes in welfare participation over time. The important findings from their study were that among households headed by males the gap in welfare receipt between natives and immigrants grew larger over the decade, but immigrant households headed by females were converging with native households headed by females.

Borjas and Hilton (1996) have suggested that studies should include all noncash benefits when attempting to understand welfare receipt by immigrants. Although these researchers found that immigrant-native differences in the receipt of cash benefits were small, those differences grew significantly after noncash benefits were included.

The studies cited above have helped us understand the propensity of immigrants to participate in the U.S. welfare system. To varying degrees, each study has implied that future researchers must recognize the differences in demographic profiles among immigrant groups; some researchers may even argue that there is no typical immigrant profile for welfare utilization. In any case, these studies indicated the need for more research (1) to identify differences in welfare use among immigrants according to the ethnic group to which they belong and (2) to learn about differences in welfare use according to the degree of assimilation immigrants have undergone. As the present study shows, successive generations of immigrants have different propensities to enter the U.S. welfare system. Indeed, Kao and Tienda (1995) have suggested that as new cohorts of immigrant children assimilate they do worse in the U.S. mainstream with respect to school performance, not better.

Moreover, past studies—like those cited above—have focused on welfare receipt among immigrant adults or households. Equally imperative, however, is learning about the lives and economic conditions of immigrant children. Despite large numbers of immigrant children comprising the next generation (Edmonston, 1996), only a scant amount of research documents their economic well-being, performance in school, health, and, as this study highlights, their exposure to the U.S. welfare system. But as Hofferth (this volume) states, a better understanding of how well immigrant children are faring in U.S. society is vital, particularly as schools become more racially and ethnically diverse, as the number of non-English-speaking children grows, and as the costs of supporting needy minority children rise.

DATA DESCRIPTION AND EMPIRICAL APPROACH

This study used data from the 1986, 1987, 1988, 1990, and 1991 panels of the Survey of Income and Program Participation (SIPP). The SIPP is a longitudinal survey of a random sample of the U.S. population. The five SIPP panels spanned the period from October 1985 through March 1992. Each wave of the survey was conducted every four months, so each participant was interviewed three times a year about his or her economic experiences over the past four months, including benefits received from many different means-tested entitlement programs. As the households were reinterviewed at four-month intervals for six, seven, or eight waves, depending on the particular panel, the survey provided 24, 28, or 32 consecutive months of data for each household.[4] Besides providing monthly details about the use of cash and non-cash transfer programs, it also collected monthly data on household composition, employment, and sources of private income.[5]

The SIPP was well suited to the present study because it also reports the race and ethnicity of each respondent; where each respondent was born; and, if born abroad, the year of arrival in the United States.[6] With this information, persons were classified

[4]Rotation group 1 of the 1986 panel was followed for only 24 months instead of 28 months.

[5]The empirical approach developed in this study parallels Hofferth's (this volume) study of Mexican, Puerto Rican, and Cuban immigrants. It distinguishes itself from her study by capitalizing on the larger sample size and scope of the SIPP to study all immigrants, including immigrants from specific places such as Asia, Eastern Europe, and Western Europe.

[6]The SIPP does not report if a household entered the United States with a refugee visa, but it does identify some countries that send refugees: Cuba, Czechoslovakia, Hungry, Poland, the former Soviet Union, and Vietnam.

according to whether they were natives or immigrants and according to their race and ethnicity. Immigrants in the sample were those who were born abroad and who were not naturalized citizens of the United States or persons who were born abroad to citizens of the United States.

Possessing year of arrival as well as having birthdates of children permitted determination of whether children came to the United States with their parents or were born after their parents arrived here. If children were born before their parents immigrated to the United States, they were classified as foreign-born children; if they were born after at least one of their parents arrived here, they were classified as native born. Children born to native-born parents were classified as native born. In one set of analyses where the focus was the impact of immigrant generation on whether a child resided in a family that received public assistance, the latter group was the comparison group. To summarize, children were classified as (1) foreign-born children, (2) native-born children with at least one foreign-born parent, and (3) native-born children with native-born parents.

The SIPP collected data on all persons over age 15 in each household as well as data on all other persons, including children, who lived with or moved into any given household. A person in each household was called the "household reference person." This person is the one who either owns or rents the house. Analyses were restricted to the sample of persons who were household reference persons, who were at least 15 years old, and who reported that they were the parents (or guardians) of children under age 18.[7]

Once it had been established which children under the age of 18 lived in households that were and were not receiving some form of public assistance, a research file was generated in which the child became the unit of analysis while maintaining pertinent household information and data about program participation. Since the sample of children remained in the SIPP for about two

[7]The SIPP does not identify children under age 15 who lived independently, although the number undercounted would probably be small and leave results unchanged.

years on average (see Table 11A-1), this feature of the survey was exploited to create a person-year file. In other words, a file was created wherein one record represented a year for each year that a child was in the SIPP and remained under age 18. The empirical models therefore calculated the probability that a child under age 18 was in a family that received some form of public assistance in a single year. Thus, the results presented in this study were based on the child person-year as the unit of analysis.[8]

Key demographic information on household heads was appended to each child in the sample as well as indicators of immigrant generation, race, and ethnicity. These factors were affixed because age of household heads, citizenship, marital status, education levels, health, family size, and ages of youngest dependents were expected to influence whether children were in a family that received some sort of public assistance in a single year of childhood. Finally, to control for trends in recipiency over time, several binary variables were created, representing the year in which each child was in the survey.

Table 11-1 lists the welfare programs studied and the benefits that each program provides. The programs were Aid to Families with Dependent Children (AFDC); Supplemental Security Income (SSI); other welfare; Medicaid; food stamps; heating assistance; housing assistance (rent subsidies or public housing); Women, Infants, and Children (WIC); general assistance (GA); and school lunches. Table 11-2 provides definitions of the variables representing the characteristics of families, and Table 11-3 presents the incidence of types of public assistance use for the child person-year sample. Other tables contained in Appendix 11A display summary statistics of the sample (Table 11A-1) and results of regressing participation in each public assistance program on ethnicity, recency of arrival, and poverty status, controlling for the demographic variables and the year in which program participation occurred (Tables 11A-2 through 11A-5).

---

[8]Results that are based on the child, or the child person-year, may differ from those in which the family is the unit of analysis. For instance, immigrants have larger families, making children in these families underrepresented in family-based analyses.

TABLE 11-1 Description and Costs of Means-Tested Programs, 1991

Program Description	Annual Costs (billions of $)
Cash Programs	
Aid to Families with Dependent Children (AFDC): Provides means-tested cash benefits to low-income single-parent households.	21.0
Supplemental Security Income (SSI): Provides means-tested cash benefits to needy aged, blind, and disabled persons.	18.5
General assistance[a]: Provides means-tested cash benefits to needy persons who do not quality for one of the federally assisted programs.	3.2
Other welfare: Unspecified in the SIPP.	N.A.
Noncash programs	
Medicaid: Provides medical assistance to low-income persons who are aged, blind, disabled, members of families with dependent children, certain other pregnant women and children, and other qualified medically needy persons.	94.5
Food stamps: Vouchers are distributed to increase the food-purchasing power of eligible low-income households.	21.0
Special Supplemental Food Program for Women, Infants, and Children (WIC): Provides food, food vouchers, and nutritional supplements to low-income pregnant and postpartum women and their infants and children up to age 5.	2.3
Low-income energy assistance: Helps low-income households meet energy-related expenses.	1.6
Housing assistance: Participating households can live in low-rent housing built by the federal government (i.e., public housing) or in private housing and receive government subsidies for their rent.	16.9
School lunch program: Distributes free or reduced-priced lunches to low-income children enrolled in school.	4.8[b]

NOTE: N.A. = not available from sources cited.

[a]Combined with other welfare here.

[b]Also includes school breakfast program.

SOURCES: U.S. House of Representatives (1993) and Bureau of the Census (1991, 1993). Costs of each of the programs include expenditures incurred at all levels of government (federal, state, and local). The costs of general assistance are for the 1990 fiscal year.

TABLE 11-2 Definitions of Variables

Variable	Definition
Citizen	1 if head of household is native-born or naturalized citizen; 0 otherwise.
Gen1	1 if child is foreign born with foreign-born parents; 0 otherwise.
Gen2	1 if child is native born with foreign-born parents; 0 otherwise.
Mexican	1 if from Mexico; 0 otherwise.
Puerto Rican	1 if from Puerto Rico; 0 otherwise.
Cuban	1 if from Cuba; 0 otherwise.
Other Latino	1 if from other Latino origin; 0 otherwise.
Black	1 if black; 0 otherwise.
Asian	1 if from Asian country[a]; 0 otherwise.
Eastern European	1 if from Eastern European country[b]; 0 otherwise.
Western European	1 if from Western European country[c]; 0 otherwise.
Other	1 if from other country; 0 otherwise.
Year1	1 if first year of panel; 0 otherwise.
Year2	1 if second year of panel; 0 otherwise.
Year3	1 if third year of panel; 0 otherwise.
Year4	1 if fourth year of panel; 0 otherwise.
Agehd	Age of household head.
Health	1 if head of household is unable to work due to health problems; 0 otherwise.
Married	1 if head of household is married; 0 otherwise.
Lths	1 if head of household has less than high school education; 0 otherwise.
Smec	1 if head of household has some college education; 0 otherwise.
Colp	1 if head of household has beyond college education; 0 otherwise.
Ynage	Age of youngest child in household.
Nkids	Number of children in household.
South	1 if living in the South; 0 otherwise.
Western	1 if living in the West; 0 otherwise.
North	1 if living in the Northeast; 0 otherwise.
Belowpov	1 if annual family income is below the poverty line; 0 otherwise.
Cash	If ever received either AFDC, GA, SSI, or other welfare; 0 otherwise.
Noncash	If ever received either Medicaid, food stamps, WIC, heating or housing assistance; 0 otherwise.
Total	If ever received any form of cash or noncash assistance; 0 otherwise.

[a]Included but not exclusive of China, Japan, Korea, Philippines, and Vietnam.

[b]Included but not exclusive of the former Soviet Union, Poland, Hungary, and Czechoslovakia.

[c]Included but not exclusive of the United Kingdom, Sweden, Norway, Portugal, Italy, Ireland, Greece, Germany, and Austria.

TABLE 11-3 Annual Probability of Children Receiving Public Assistance in Children's Years in the Survey of Income and Program Participation

Generation Within Ethnicity	AFDC	SSI	Other Welfare	Food Stamps	Medicaid
Mexican1	0.17	0.04	0.02	0.36	0.24
Mexican2	0.12	0.08	0.01	0.36	0.22
Mexican3	0.24	0.06	0.02	0.40	0.29
Puerto Rican	0.42	0.12	0.02	0.52	0.52
Cuban	0.03	0.08	0.00	0.22	0.13
Asian1	0.27	0.20	0.0	0.31	0.31
Asian2	0.14	0.10	0.0	0.17	0.14
Asian3	0.18	0.06	0.03	0.23	0.07
WestEuro1	0.04	0.00	0.00	0.26	0.10
WestEuro2	0.07	0.04	0.00	0.13	0.10
WestEuro3	0.07	0.03	0.01	0.13	0.09
EastEuro1	0.04	0.00	0.00	0.15	0.05
EastEuro2	0.03	0.00	0.00	0.05	0.14
EastEuro3	0.04	0.01	0.00	0.09	0.07
Other Latino	0.26	0.09	0.01	0.38	0.32
White	0.07	0.04	0.01	0.14	0.09
Black	0.35	0.14	0.02	0.51	0.40
Other	0.22	0.07	0.04	0.45	0.37
Total	0.13	0.06	0.01	0.21	0.15

NOTE: 1 = Foreign-born children with foreign-born parents; 2 = Native-born children with at least one foreign-born parent; 3 = Native-born children with native-born parent; Missing = missing data.
SOURCE: SIPP (1986-1991 panels).

Similar to Hofferth's (this volume) methodology, AFDC, SSI, GA, and other welfare were combined to produce an indicator of cash assistance, and Medicaid, food stamps, heating assistance, housing assistance, and WIC were combined to produce an indicator of noncash assistance. Then a final indicator for receipt of any assistance, cash or noncash, was created.

FINDINGS

The data contain observations on 1,372 foreign-born children with foreign-born parents; 4,910 native-born children with at least one foreign-born parent; and 36,643 native-born children with native-born parents. There are 3,292 children of Mexican origin;

Housing	Heat	WIC	Unemployment	General Assistance	School Lunches
0.10	0.09	0.04	0.21	0.05	0.77
0.10	0.13	0.10	0.17	0.05	0.70
0.11	0.19	0.05	0.09	0.02	0.56
0.23	0.34	0.05	0.07	0.07	0.62
0.02	0.04	0.00	0.07	0.00	0.48
0.16	0.07	0.07	0.17	0.00	0.91
0.07	0.02	0.02	0.17	0.02	0.72
0.09	0.01	0.01	0.15	0.04	0.82
0.00	0.05	0.05	0.04	0.00	0.29
0.03	0.04	0.04	0.08	0.01	0.35
0.06	0.06	0.06	0.08	0.02	0.38
0.13	0.09	0.09	0.17	0.18	0.42
0.01	0.03	0.03	0.12	0.07	0.33
0.05	0.07	0.07	0.08	0.00	0.30
0.18	0.12	0.07	0.11	0.08	0.77
0.05	0.06	0.04	0.09	0.02	0.39
0.23	0.22	0.08	0.09	0.07	0.64
0.12	0.05	0.20	0.29	0.08	0.77
0.08	0.08	0.04	0.03	0.01	0.51

579 of Puerto Rican background; 85 of Cuban background; 1,184 of other Hispanic background; 835 children of Asian background; and 475 of Eastern and 6,791 of Western European backgrounds. There are 24,279 white children and 5,219 black children.

When ethnicity and generation were combined, the following numbers of foreign-born children with foreign-born parents were obtained: 399 Mexican children, 68 Puerto Rican children, 7 Cuban children,[9] 193 children of other Latino background, 64 Western European children, 26 Eastern European children, and 221

[9]Because sample sizes for foreign-born Cuban children and native-born Cuban children with foreign-born parents were too small, these groups were recombined in the regression models.

Asian children. Similarly, by combining ethnicity and generation, the following numbers of native-born children with at least one foreign-born parent were obtained: 1,509 Mexican children; 39 Puerto Rican children; 75 Cuban children; 402 children of other Latino background; 428 Western European children; 73 Eastern European children; and 431 Asian children. The numbers of native-born children with native-born parents were 1,384 Mexican children; 472 Puerto Rican children; 3 Cuban children; 589 children of other Latino background; 6,299 Western European children; 376 Eastern European children; and 183 Asian children.

Once separate person-year records were created and years in which each child was 18 or older were deleted, 125,822 person-years were observed.[10] Breaking down the sample by ethnicity and generation in *child person-years* yielded 1,145 foreign-born Mexican children and 4,455 native-born Mexican children with at least one parent born in Mexico; 200 foreign-born Puerto Rican children and 116 native-born Puerto Rican children with at least one foreign-born parent; and 1,388 native-born Puerto Rican children with native-born Puerto Rican parents. For Cuban children there were 213 native-born children with at least one parent born in Cuba (see note 9). Asian children in person-years included 595 who were foreign born; 1,261 who were native born with at least one parent born in an Asian country; and 533 native-born children. For Eastern and Western European children combined, there were 265 foreign born; 1,472 native born with a least one parent foreign born; and 19,557 native born. Finally, there were 539 other Latino children person-years; 71,284 white person-years; and 15,255 black person-years.

The sample distributions on child and family characteristics for individual child-years by ethnicity and generation are shown in Table 11A-1. On average, children in the sample were about 9 years old, and the head of the family was age 36, married, working, at least a high school graduate, and caring for 2.4 children, with the youngest about age 6.5.

[10]Owing to initial data construction of the 1986, 1987, and 1988 SIPP panels, data for SSI and GA were unavailable. Other SIPP panels still possessed large samples, however, numbering 66,465 child person-years. Models were estimated for these programs.

Foreign-born Mexican American families had the most children, 3.5 on average, with about 3 for native-born children with a foreign-born parent. Asians and Puerto Ricans have the next-largest family sizes, about 3 children. Cubans have the smallest family size, about 2 children each.

Mexicans also possessed the lowest levels of education. Among foreign-born Mexican children with foreign-born parents, 76 percent were in a family whose head had less than a high school education. Among native-born Mexican children with native-born Mexican parents, however, there were much higher levels of high school completion; 51 percent of these Mexican children were in a family whose head had at least a high school education. Puerto Rican children were in families in which about half the heads had less than a high school education. Foreign-born Eastern and Western European children were in families in which very few heads had less than a high school education. Children born in Puerto Rico were in families in which 25 percent of heads had health problems that stopped them from working. That was nearly four times higher than the number of foreign-born Asian children and over double that of foreign-born Mexican children.

Puerto Rican and black children were more likely than any other group of children to live with only one parent. Cuban and Asian children were most likely to live with two married parents. Though less apparent, among Mexican children, those who were native born were more likely to live with one parent than their foreign-born counterparts. Foreign-born Asian children with foreign-born parents and native-born Asian children with at least one foreign-born parent lived with heads who were more likely to be citizens than other groups of children, while Western European and Mexican children experienced the opposite.

Incidence of Public Assistance Receipt by Ethnicity and Generation

Table 11-3 shows the incidence of participation in public assistance programs by combining ethnicity and generation for person-years in which each child was under 18. In the table, foreign-born Mexican children are more likely than white children in native-born families to receive AFDC, food stamps, Medicaid, other welfare, school lunches, and housing and heating assistance. They are at least two times more likely than white children to live in families that receive either AFDC (17 percent compared to 7 percent) or Medicaid (24 percent in contrast to 9 percent). Use of SSI and the WIC program is equal to that of white children in native-born families. Except for other welfare, native-born Mexican children with a foreign-born parent are more likely than white children in native-born families to use all forms of public assistance. Mexican children in native-born families are also more likely than white children in native-born families to use all forms of public assistance.

Cuban children in native-born families are actually less likely than white children in native-born families to receive AFDC, other welfare, housing assistance, heating assistance, and WIC benefits. In contrast, all other Latino children, except Puerto Rican children (discussed below), are more likely to use all forms of public assistance (see Table 11-3).

According to Table 11-3, foreign-born Asian children are more likely than white children in native-born families to receive AFDC, SSI, food stamps, Medicaid, WIC, school lunches, and housing and heating assistance. They are nearly four times more likely than white children to live in families that receive either AFDC (27 percent compared to 7 percent) or Medicaid (31 percent in contrast to 9 percent). Use of other welfare is less than that of white children in native-born families. Except for WIC, other welfare, and heating assistance, native-born Asian children with a foreign-born parent are more likely than white children in native-born families to use the major public transfer programs. Asian children in native-born families also are more likely than white children in native-born families to use AFDC, SSI, other welfare, food stamps, housing, and school lunches but are less likely to use Medicaid, heating assistance, and WIC.

Among Eastern Europeans, Table 11-3 indicates that foreign-born Eastern European children are less likely than white children in native-born families to use AFDC, SSI, other welfare, and Medicaid but are more likely to receive WIC, school lunches, and housing and heating assistance. Except for WIC, Eastern European children with native-born parents are less likely than white children in native-born families to use the major public transfer programs. Eastern European children with at least one foreign-born parent are less likely than white children in native-born families to receive AFDC, SSI, other welfare, food stamps, housing assistance, heating assistance, WIC, and school lunches but are more likely to receive Medicaid benefits.

Foreign-born Western European children are less likely than white children in native-born families to receive AFDC, SSI, other welfare, assistance for housing and heating, and school lunches but are more likely to use food stamps, Medicaid, and WIC. Western European children with native-born parents and Western European children with at least one parent who is foreign born have essentially the same chances of using various forms of public assistance as white children in native-born families.

Among all groups of children, Table 11-3 shows that black children and Puerto Rican children have the highest rates of public transfer receipt, with 35 and 42 percent, respectively, receiving AFDC. Whereas 9 percent of white children received Medicaid, 40 percent of black children and 52 percent of Puerto Rican children lived in families that received Medicaid. With respect to food stamps, 51 percent of black children and 52 percent of Puerto Rican children lived in families that received them, while only 14 percent of white children lived in families that received food stamps.

Multivariate Analyses of the Determinants of Public Assistance Receipt

Comparing the prevalence of welfare receipt among foreign-born children with that of native-born children is informative but, without adjusting for the extent of disadvantage across groups, knowing whether the higher rates of receipt are due primarily to socioeconomic differences, such as education levels, or to recency of arrival in the United States remains uncertain. To resolve this uncertainty, multivariate analyses were conducted in which each type of public assistance receipt was regressed on ethnicity, generation, the combined measure, poverty status, and other demographic factors.

Tables 11A-2 through 11A-5 show the coefficients from such

regressions. The coefficients suggest that differences in receipt decline once poverty status and demographic factors are controlled and lead to the conclusion that socioeconomic characteristics of families of immigrant children, rather than recency of immigration per se, explain the higher rates of public assistance use.

The first set of multivariate results (see Table 11A-2) suggest that controlling for poverty and other socioeconomic factors, and except for SSI and school lunches, foreign-born children and native-born children with at least one foreign-born parent are less likely to be in families that receive public assistance than native-born children with native-born parents. Specifically, both groups of children are less likely to receive AFDC, food stamps, Medicaid, and housing and heating assistance but are more likely than native-born children in native-born families to receive SSI. Foreign-born children are also more likely than native-born children with native-born parents to use the federal school lunch program.

After controlling for recency of arrival, poverty status, and other factors, it is evident that Mexican children are less likely than white children with native-born parents to use SSI and other welfare, are no more likely to use AFDC or WIC, but are more likely to use food stamps, Medicaid, and housing and heat assistance. Compared to white children, only for food stamps and Medicaid were Cuban children more likely to use these programs.

Puerto Rican children, on the other hand, were more likely than white children to use AFDC, SSI, food stamps, Medicaid, school lunches, and housing and heating assistance but less likely to receive other welfare. Aside from heating assistance, Asian children exhibited exactly the same pattern as Puerto Rican children. And, both Eastern and Western European children were either less likely or no more likely than white children to use AFDC, SSI, food stamps, and the WIC program. Possibly because of refugee status, however, Eastern European children were more likely than white children to use Medicaid, housing assistance (as were Western Europeans also), and heating assistance. After controlling for poverty status, black children were much more likely than white children to use all public assistance programs.

Figure 11-1 displays the predicted probabilities of receiving AFDC, SSI, food stamps, and Medicaid. Except for SSI, where the predicted probabilities diverge less across the different genera-

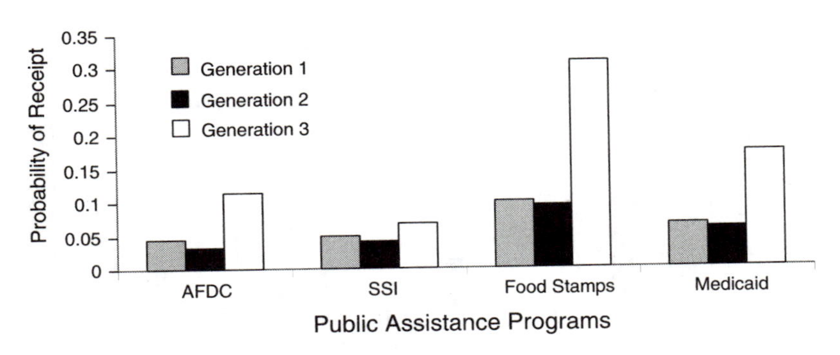

FIGURE 11-1 Predicted probability of public assistance receipt by nativity.

tions, foreign-born children with foreign-born parents and native-born children with at least one foreign-born parent are much less likely than native-born children with native-born families to receive AFDC, food stamps, and Medicaid. Moreover, the predicted probabilities shown in Table 11A-2 and Figure 11-1 suggest that foreign-born children with foreign-born parents are less likely to receive food stamps. What becomes greatly apparent from subsequent figures and tables (Figures 11-2 through 11-5) once ethnicity and generation are combined is that predicted probabilities for receipt of public assistance diminish and that differences in predicted probabilities of receipt among foreign-born children and native-born children disappear.

Table 11A-3 contains the multivariate results that combine ethnicity and generation. These results bolster the thesis that economic deprivation and other sociological factors rather than immigration status better explain the use of public assistance across ethnic groups. Foreign-born Mexican children, for example, are less likely than white children in native-born families to receive AFDC, SSI, and food stamps and are no more likely than white children in native-born families to receive Medicaid. Native-born Mexican children with a foreign-born parent are also less likely to receive AFDC and Medicaid and are no different in their use of food stamps than white children, although these children are possibly more likely than white children to receive SSI. Mexican children in native-born families are more likely to receive AFDC, food

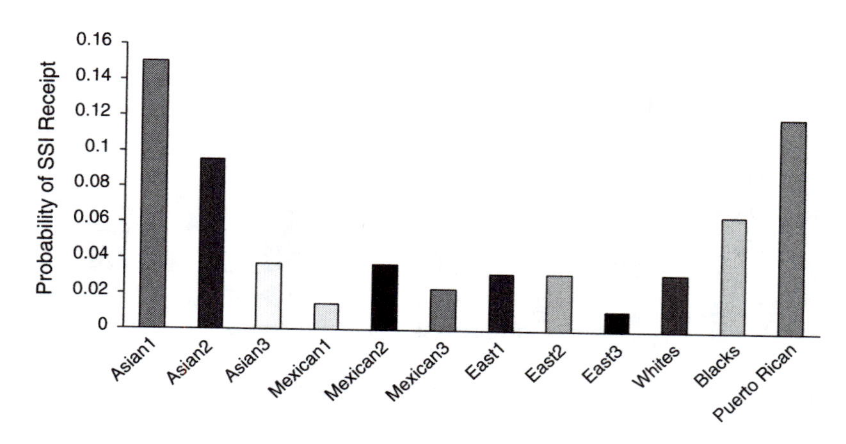

FIGURE 11-2 Predicted probability of SSI receipt by ethnicity and nativity.

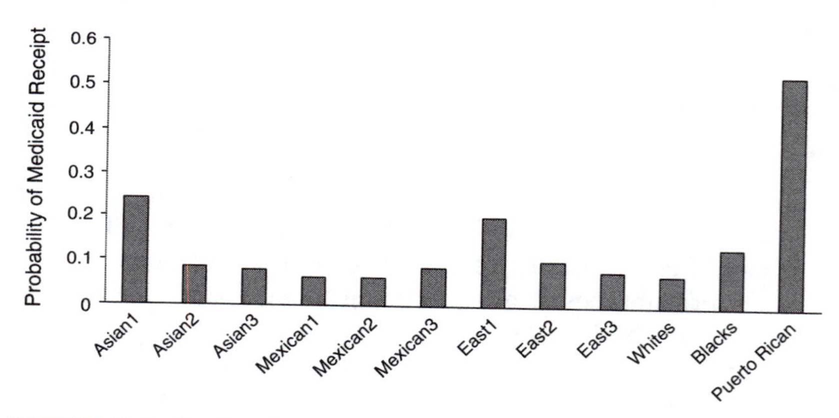

FIGURE 11-3 Predicted probability of Medicaid receipt by ethnicity and nativity.

stamps, and Medicaid when controlling for poverty but less likely than white children in native-born families to receive SSI.

For the other transfer programs, foreign-born Mexican children are less likely than white children in native-born families to receive heating assistance and WIC benefits but are more likely to receive school lunches and to live in families that receive housing assistance. Foreign-born Mexican children are no different than white children in their use of other welfare programs, again con-

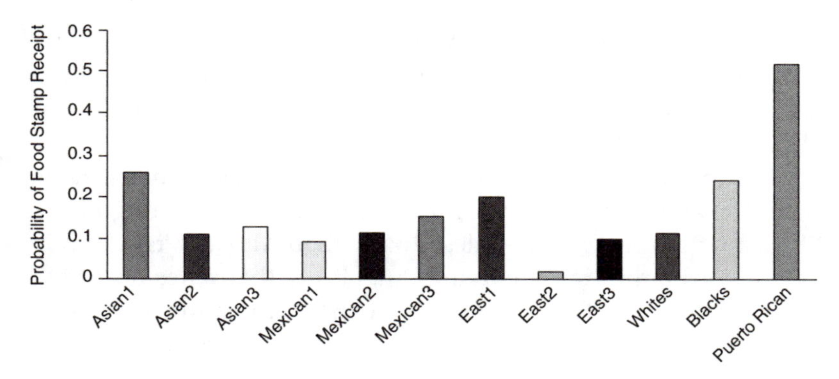

FIGURE 11-4 Predicted probability of food stamp receipt by ethnicity and generation.

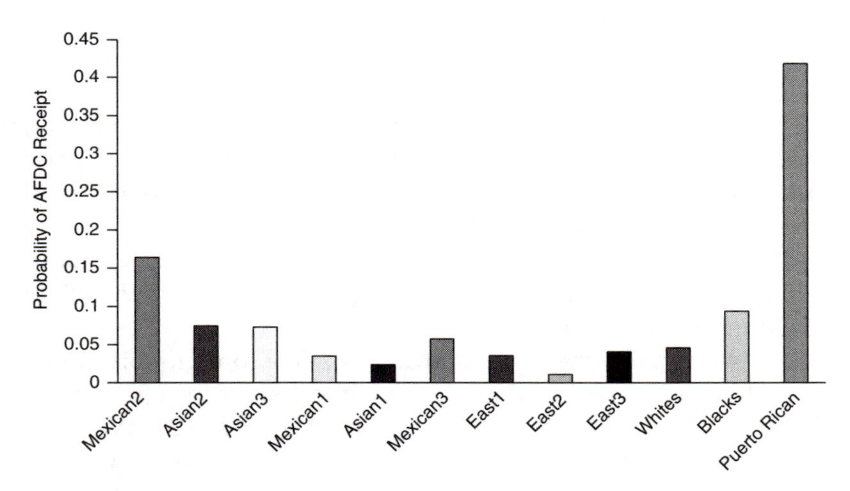

FIGURE 11-5 Predicted probability of AFDC receipt by ethnicity and nativity.

trolling for poverty status. Both native-born Mexican children with a foreign-born parent and Mexican children in native-born families are more likely than white children to receive school lunches and housing assistance. However, while the latter group of children is more likely than white children to receive heating assistance, the former group is no different than white children with respect to heating assistance. Mexican children in native-born families with at least one foreign-born parent are more likely than white children to use the WIC program when controlling for poverty, but again compared to white children in native-born families, Mexican children in native-born families are actually less likely to receive WIC benefits.

Comparing Mexican children from various generations, again with the same controls in the multivariate analyses, foreign-born Mexican children are much less likely than Mexican children in native-born families to be living in a family that relies on AFDC and food stamps. The same pattern exists for heating assistance. Only for WIC, school lunches, and housing assistance are foreign-born Mexican children more likely than Mexican children in native-born families to receive government assistance.

Overall, foreign-born Mexican children are less likely than white children in native-born families to live in families that receive AFDC, SSI, food stamps, heating assistance, and WIC while being no more likely to receive Medicaid or other types of welfare. But they are more likely to receive school lunches and housing assistance. Among Mexican children in native-born families, however, the chances of receiving AFDC, food stamps, Medicaid, and heating assistance are higher than among foreign-born Mexican children and white children in native-born families. Only with respect to other welfare are Mexican children in native-born families less likely to receive heating assistance than are white children in native-born families.

Although the proportions in Table 11-3 of foreign-born Mexican children receiving the major public transfer programs are higher for nearly every program than white children (WIC and SSI are the exceptions), the multivariate analyses suggest that, after controlling for poverty, region, and family factors, foreign-born Mexican children are actually less likely than both white and Mexican children in native-born families to receive public assistance.

Cuban children are less likely than white children in native-born families to receive AFDC and are more likely to receive food stamps and Medicaid, but they are no more likely than white children in native-born families to receive SSI, housing assistance, or heating assistance. Regarding the WIC program and other welfare, no data were available for Cubans, but data were available for the school lunch program. As with other major transfer programs, Cuban children are less likely to use the school lunch program than are white children in native-born families.

Insufficient data prohibited cross-generational comparisons among Cubans as it did among the group of Hispanics categorized as "other Latino." For the other group of Latino children, they are more likely than white children in native-born families to use every public assistance program, except for heating assistance and other welfare.

Poverty status, geographic region, and socioeconomic characteristics of families were, again, controlled for in the multivariate analyses for Asians. The results suggest that foreign-born Asian children are more likely than white children in native-born families to receive AFDC, SSI, food stamps, Medicaid, housing assistance, and school lunches. Receipt of heating assistance by foreign-born Asian children is no more likely than by white children in native-born families. Native-born Asian children with at least one foreign-born parent share the same pattern as foreign-born Asian children, albeit for a smaller set of transfer programs.

Compared to white children with native-born parents, native-born Asian children with at least one foreign-born Asian parent are more likely to receive AFDC, SSI, other welfare, Medicaid, housing assistance, and heating assistance. For three programs, though—food stamps, WIC, and school lunches—native-born Asian children with a foreign-born parent are no more likely than white children to be recipients of the three programs. Again, Asian children in native-born families are more likely than white children to receive AFDC, housing assistance, heating assistance, and school lunches, but after controlling for poverty their receipt of SSI, food stamps, other welfare, and Medicaid is no different than that of white children in native-born families.

Comparing Asian children from various generations, foreign-born Asian children are much more likely than Asian children in native-born families to be living in a family that relies on SSI, Medicaid, food stamps, and other welfare programs. On the other hand, Asian children in native-born families, like foreign-born Asian children, have higher rates of receipt of AFDC, heating assistance, housing assistance, WIC, and school lunches than white children in native-born families.

Results suggest that all Asian children, regardless of country of birth, are more likely than white children in native-born families to receive AFDC, housing assistance, and school lunches. However, only foreign-born Asian children and Asian children with at least one foreign-born parent are more likely than white children to receive Medicaid. The relatively lower use of heating assistance among native-born Asian children compared to other Asian children and white children with native-born families perhaps reflects interstate migration of subsequent generations. More meaningful comparisons would eventuate if the refugee status of Asian children's families was known and country of origin for the foreign born established.

In contrast to foreign-born Mexican children, the multivariate analyses suggest that after controlling for poverty, geographic region, and family factors, foreign-born Asian children are more likely than both white and Asian children in native-born families to receive SSI, food stamps, Medicaid, and other welfare assistance. The port of entry for foreign-born Asian children may have lowered the probability of them, compared with Asian children in native-born families, receiving heating assistance and made the chances of use no different than those of children in native-born families.

Results suggest that foreign-born Eastern European children are more likely than white children in native-born families to use some transfer programs. These particular children are more likely than white children to receive Medicaid, housing assistance, and other welfare, although they are no different in the likelihood of receiving AFDC, food stamps, heating assistance, and school lunches. Native-born Eastern European children with at least one foreign-born parent are less likely to receive AFDC and food stamps, as well as housing assistance and school lunches. Regarding other welfare, housing assistance, and the WIC program, native-born Eastern European children with a foreign-born parent are no more likely than white children to use these programs, but they are more likely to receive Medicaid. Eastern European children in native-born families are less likely than white children to receive SSI, WIC, and school lunches but are no more likely to receive Medicaid and housing assistance.

For some programs, comparisons are possible among Eastern European children. Foreign-born Eastern European children are no different in their receipt of Medicaid and housing assistance than Eastern European children in native-born families. And foreign-born Eastern European children appear to be more like white children in native-born families with respect to the federal school lunch program; both of these groups of children are less likely than Eastern European children in native-born families to participate in the school lunch program.

In contrast to foreign-born Eastern European children, foreign-born Western European children are less likely than white children in native-born families to receive AFDC, Medicaid, heating assistance, and school lunches. Moreover, these particular children are no different in their receipt of food stamps than white children in native-born families. The pattern is more distinguished for native-born Western European children with at least one foreign-born parent. They are less likely to receive food stamps, housing and heating assistance, WIC, or school lunches.

The pattern of either being less likely to receive or to receive at the same rate as white children in native-born families changes only when results for Western European children in native-born families are examined. Western European children are in fact more likely than white children to receive housing assistance and school lunches but are less likely than white children to receive SSI, food stamps, Medicaid, and heating assistance. Also, their receipt of AFDC is no different than that of white children.

For all Western European children, no great differences exist in the receipt of heating assistance. Foreign-born Western European children and those with native-born parents are actually less likely than native-born Western European children with at least one foreign-born parent to receive Medicaid, whose chances of receiving Medicaid are like that of white children. And while foreign-born Western European children are no different than white children with respect to food stamps, native-born Western European children are actually less likely than white children to receive food stamps.

Controlling for poverty and the other predictors of public assistance use, children born in Puerto Rico are more likely than white children in native-born families to participate in all of the major public assistance programs, except for WIC and other welfare. Similarly, Puerto Rican children born in the United States with at least one parent born in Puerto Rico are less likely than white children with native-born families to receive WIC benefits but are more likely to receive Medicaid and housing assistance. For this group of children, results suggest that the use of food stamps is similar to that of white children in native-born families. Puerto Rican children with both parents born in the United States are more likely than white children with native-born families to receive AFDC, food stamps, Medicaid, housing assistance, heating assistance, and school lunches. Only for use of the WIC program are Puerto Rican children with native-born families comparable to white children with native-born families.

Comparisons among groups of Puerto Rican children are less meaningful since Puerto Ricans are U.S. citizens and thus eligible for welfare. The results reflect this by showing that there are high rates of public assistance receipt across the three groups of Puerto Ricans. The one subset of results which indicate that U.S.-born Puerto Rican children with at least one parent born on the island are no different than white children in their use of AFDC, food stamps, and heating assistance may be due to smaller sample sizes that cannot properly distinguish differences.

Lastly, black children in native-born families are more likely than white children in native-born families to use all forms of public assistance, after controlling for poverty status, geographic region, and other factors. The greatest differences in the increased likelihood of their receiving some form of assistance compared to white children in native-born families occurs with food stamps, Medicaid, and housing assistance.

Overall, the analyses suggest that, after controlling for key factors, several foreign-born groups of children are typically *less likely* than white children in native-born families to use public assistance, rather than more likely as implied by Table 11-3. The results also mirror the diversity of the American welfare experience across immigrant/ethnic groupings of children. Asians display a decline, rather than an increase, in program use across generations, perhaps reflecting changes from refugee status for the first generation to comparative successes among later generations. For Eastern Europeans a similar though less clear pattern emerges as well. For them use of welfare programs declines until it is essentially no different than that of native-born whites. Mexicans, on the other hand, experience the opposite pattern. Successive generations of Mexicans—here, native-born children with native-born parents—actually become more likely than white children to use several of the major welfare programs. Their use of public assistance is still less than that of native-born Puerto Ricans and blacks but rises above that of foreign-born Mexican children. Thus, different stories arise for different generations of ethnic groups with respect to the use of public assistance.

Time Trends in Public Assistance Receipt and Other Results

The aim here was to examine the effects of immigrant status, poverty, ethnicity, race, and time of arrival in the United States on the receipt of public assistance. To keep that focus, the discussion has refrained from elaborating on other factors determining welfare receipt. The important point to note is that the other findings fully complement those findings reported by Hofferth (this volume), Tienda and Jensen (1986), and Borjas and Hilton (1996). In other words, female headship, poor health, low education, and more children raise the probability of receiving various forms of public assistance.

Further, no discernible trends were found in the use of public assistance. Nevertheless, the binary dummy variables that controlled for the five successive years predicting the probability of participating in a given program at times suggested significant differences across years. Specifically, yearly dummy variables indicate lesser use of AFDC, food stamps, and school lunches in the earlier years of SIPP (mid- to late 1980s).

To complete the analyses, separate regression analyses predicting participation for all types of public assistance programs were conducted on the 1990 and 1991 panels only. These final additional analyses assessed the sensitivity of results to smaller sample sizes and analytical sampling weights. The outcome from the analyses showed that the directions and magnitudes of the estimates remained unchanged. Occasionally, magnitudes of estimates decreased, making effects statistically insignificant, but this was the exception not the rule.

CONCLUSIONS

Findings from multivariate analyses support the economic disadvantage hypothesis rather than the immigrant status hypothesis. From the results there is evidence that foreign-born children with foreign-born parents and native-born children with foreign-born parents were less likely than white native-born children with native-born parents to receive public assistance. This result contradicts assertions that immigrant families overuse the welfare system. In fact, foreign-born immigrant children were neither more nor less likely than native-born white children with native-born parents to receive cash assistance, and native-born immigrant children with foreign-born parents were less likely to receive cash assistance. In addition, foreign-born children with foreign-born parents and native-born children with foreign-born parents were less likely than native-born white children to receive noncash forms of public assistance. After controlling for poverty and other sociodemographic factors, the association between lower use of public assistance and recency of arrival remained.

Another conclusion from the study was that, although children living in families of minority status were more likely to use public assistance programs more heavily than white children, the higher likelihood was not tied to immigration status. Indeed, receipt of public assistance significantly differed by recency of arrival for each ethnic and racial group. Among Mexican Americans, native-born Mexican American children with at least one foreign-born parent were less likely than white children to receive AFDC. In contrast, among Asian Americans, native-born Asian American children with foreign-born parents and native-born Asian American children with native-born parents were more likely than white children to live in families that received AFDC, and native-born Asian children with at least one foreign-born parent also were more likely to receive SSI, housing assistance, and Medicaid. Among Eastern European children, both native-born children with foreign-born parents and those with native-born parents were less likely than native-born white children to live in families that received AFDC, food stamps, WIC, or school lunches. Generally, there were large differences among different immigrant groups in the receipt of public assistance.

Puerto Rican children and other Latino children were more likely than white children to receive all forms of public assistance. This conclusion was not reached for Cuban children, however. Use of public assistance among Cuban children was essentially program specific. Thus, an accurate portrayal of program use according to these data is that most minority children who are beneficiaries of the U.S. welfare system live in families that are native born and therefore eligible for public assistance.

Recency of arrival in the United States is not the engine driving high receipt of public assistance among ethnic and racial minorities. Rather, poverty, truncated educational opportunities, meager job opportunities, and assimilation difficulties are the problems that need to be confronted and remedied.

REFERENCES

Blau, F.

1984 The use of transfer payments by immigrants. *Industrial and Labor Relations Review* 37(2):222-239.

1986 Immigration and the U.S. taxpayer. Pp. 89-110 in *Essays on Legal and Illegal Immigration*, S. Pozo, ed. Kalamazoo, Mich.: W.E. Upjohn Institute for Employment Research.

Borjas, G.J., and L. Hilton

1996 Immigration and the welfare state: Immigrant participation and means-tested entitlement programs. *Quarterly Journal of Economics* CVXI: 575-604.

Borjas, G.J., and S.J. Trejo

1991 Immigrant participation in the welfare system. *Industrial and Labor Relations Review* 44(2):195-211.

Bureau of the Census

1991 *SIPP Users Guide*. Various issues. Washington, D.C.: U.S. Government Printing Office.

1993 *Statistical Abstracts of the United States*. Various issues. Washington, D.C.: U.S. Government Printing Office.

Currie, J.

1997 Medicaid use by children of immigrants. *Focus* 18(2):54-57.

Edmonston, B. (ed.)

1996 *Statistics on U.S. Immigration: An Assessment of Data Needs for Future Research*. Committee on National Statistics, National Research Council. Washington, D.C.: National Academy Press.

Kao, G., and M. Tienda
1995 Optimism and achievement: The educational performance of immigrant youth. *Social Science Quarterly* 76(1):1-19.
Primus, W.
1996 Immigration provisions in the new welfare law. *Focus* 18(2).
Simon, J.
1981 What immigrants take from and give to the public coffers. *U.S. Immigration Policy and the National Interest: Appendix D to Staff Report of the Select Commission on Immigration and Refugee Policy.*
Simon, J., and A. Akbari
1996 Determinants of welfare payment use by immigrants and natives in the United States and Canada. In *Immigrants and Immigration Policy: Individual Skills, Family Ties, and Group Identities*, H. Duleep and P. Wunnava, eds. Greenwich, Conn.: JAI Press.
Tienda, M., and L. Jensen
1986 Immigration and public assistance participation: Dispelling the myth of dependency. *Social Science Research* 15(4):372-400.
U.S. House of Representatives
1993 *Background Material and Data on Programs Within the Jurisdiction of the Committee on Ways and Means (Green Book).* Various issues. Washington, D.C.: U.S. Government Printing Office.
U.S. House of Representatives, Ways and Means Committee
1996 *Overview of the Entitlement Programs: 1996 Green Book.* Washington, D.C.: U.S. Government Printing Office.

Table 11A-1 follows on next page.

TABLE 11A-1 Characteristics of Children's Years in the Survey of Income and Program Participation, 1986-1992

Generation Within Ethnicity	Age	Year	Age of Household Head	Citizen	Health	Married
Mexican1	11	1.98	36.55	0.40	0.09	0.80
Mexican2	8	1.99	35.00	0.47	0.06	0.90
Mexican3	9	1.99	35.18	1.00	0.08	0.75
Puerto Rican	10	1.99	36.94	1.00	0.12	0.56
Cuban	9	1.97	38.00	0.55	0.03	0.91
Asian1	12	1.93	42.39	0.78	0.05	0.84
Asian2	7	1.98	38.99	1.00	0.03	0.90
Asian3	8	1.98	40.56	1.00	0.08	0.79
WestEuro1	11	1.98	38.28	0.32	0.02	0.90
WestEuro2	10	1.99	37.87	0.41	0.06	0.92
WestEuro3	9	1.99	36.86	1.00	0.06	0.87
EastEuro1	11	2.00	36.34	0.44	0.00	1.00
EastEuro2	8	1.99	35.74	0.42	0.02	0.96
EastEuro3	10	1.99	37.37	1.00	0.03	0.92
Other Latino	9	1.96	39.03	0.51	0.09	0.65
White	9	1.99	36.53	1.00	0.08	0.90
Black	9	1.99	35.65	1.00	0.07	0.53
Other	8	1.99	35.29	0.96	0.09	0.77
Total	8.8	1.99	36.60	0.89	0.06	0.82

NOTE: 1 = Foreign-born children with foreign-born parents; 2 = native-born children with at least one foreign-born parent; 3 = native-born children with native-born parent.

SOURCE: SIPP (1986-1991 panels).

Age of Youngest Child	Number of Children	Completed Less than High School	High School Graduate	Some College	College Degree or Higher
5.75	3.55	0.76	0.15	0.05	0.04
4.55	3.13	0.70	0.18	0.09	0.03
5.89	2.95	0.49	0.31	0.14	0.06
7.45	2.56	0.50	0.29	0.13	0.07
6.74	2.02	0.10	0.29	0.33	0.28
8.15	2.82	0.31	0.16	0.12	0.42
4.82	2.64	0.12	0.22	0.23	0.43
5.55	3.05	0.19	0.27	0.21	0.32
7.73	2.61	0.27	0.36	0.16	0.21
6.26	2.44	0.17	0.30	0.25	0.28
7.19	2.38	0.12	0.40	0.27	0.22
8.75	2.10	0.31	0.13	0.19	0.37
5.68	2.41	0.27	0.19	0.32	0.22
7.62	2.33	0.08	0.35	0.25	0.33
6.43	2.59	0.35	0.36	0.19	0.10
6.75	2.37	0.13	0.39	0.26	0.22
6.54	2.79	0.31	0.37	0.23	0.09
5.43	2.68	0.27	0.45	0.13	0.15
6.56	2.46	0.20	0.36	0.24	0.19

TABLE 11A-2 Odds Ratios from Logistic Regressions of Program Participation on Generation

Program	AFDC	SSI[a]	Other Welfare[a]	Food Stamps
Gen1	0.83***	1.54***	0.69**	0.73***
Gen2	0.60***	1.27***	0.85*	0.69***
Mexican	1.02	0.77***	0.80**	1.31***
Puerto Rican	3.16***	1.58***	0.47***	2.25***
Cuban	0.65	1.33	Missing	3.84***
Other Latino	1.89***	1.30**	0.71**	1.69***
Black	2.15***	2.11***	1.19**	2.41***
Other	1.14	1.27	2.04***	3.00***
West Europ	0.98	0.81***	0.86*	0.88***
East Europ	0.77*	0.24***	1.21	0.74***
Asian	2.90***	2.59***	0.39***	1.68***
Year1	0.72***	Missing	Missing	0.82***
Year2	0.85***	Missing	Missing	0.98
Year3	0.84***	Missing	Missing	0.85***
Year4	1.00	0.83***	1.26***	0.92**
Agehd	0.97***	1.02***	0.99***	0.96***
Health	2.55***	4.07***	2.02***	2.69***
Married	0.16***	0.48***	0.61***	0.21***
Lths	2.26***	1.98***	1.22***	2.66***
Smec	0.82***	0.71***	0.76***	0.73***
Colp	0.21***	0.37***	0.39***	0.20***
Yngage	0.97***	1.01*	0.97***	0.98***
Nkids	1.09***	1.07***	1.01	1.26***
South	1.13***	1.35***	2.06***	1.71***
West	2.15***	1.21***	5.17***	1.48***
North	1.06	1.03	7.94***	1.09**
Belowpov	5.69***	1.35***	3.34***	6.76***

NOTES: Native-born children with native-born parents and whites omitted categories in models; N.A. = not applicable; Missing = variable dropped due to insufficient data.

SOURCE: SIPP (1986-1991 panels) except where [a].

Medicaid	Housing Assistance	Heating Assistance	WIC	School Lunch
0.80***	0.81***	0.61***	0.62***	1.06***
0.74***	0.77***	0.74***	1.02	0.76***
1.21***	1.46***	1.21***	1.04	1.90***
4.41***	2.39***	2.73***	0.79*	1.86***
3.07***	0.52	1.13	Missing	0.98
1.95***	2.49***	0.75***	1.24**	1.92***
2.10***	2.52***	1.15***	1.39***	1.80***
2.57***	1.28	0.60**	4.90***	1.26
0.90***	1.17***	0.81***	0.93	1.11***
1.39***	1.27*	1.37**	0.56***	0.84**
2.19***	2.34***	0.62***	0.91	1.60***
0.80***	0.93*	1.42***	0.85***	0.31***
0.96	0.64***	1.32***	0.81**	0.34***
0.91*	1.05	1.20***	0.78***	0.40***
0.90**	1.12***	0.58***	0.96	2.60***
0.96***	0.95***	0.98***	0.94***	1.03***
3.22***	1.49***	1.62***	1.82***	1.41***
0.17***	0.31***	0.26***	0.82***	0.43***
2.19***	1.41***	1.74***	1.54***	1.82***
0.72***	0.88***	0.85***	0.73***	0.91***
0.23***	0.47***	0.31***	0.22***	0.73***
0.95***	1.01**	1.00	0.71***	1.02***
1.09***	1.04***	1.24***	0.84***	1.59***
1.06	1.13***	0.52***	1.59***	14.20***
1.85***	1.31***	0.31***	0.95	7.79***
1.52***	1.86***	0.37***	1.26***	7.97***
5.58***	2.17***	3.95***	2.21***	2.00***

[a]Only 1990 and 1991 panels of SIPP.
*** $p < 0.01$; ** $p < 0.05$; * $p < 0.10$.

TABLE 11A-3 Odds Ratios from Logistic Regressions of Program Participation on Ethnic Groups within Generation

Program	AFDC	SSI[a]	Other Welfare[a]	Food Stamps
Mex1	0.76***	0.44***	1.08	0.78**
Mex2	0.50***	1.18	0.84	0.96
Mex3	1.28***	0.72***	0.51***	1.37***
Ric1	5.79***	4.80***	0.41**	2.24***
Ric2	1.46	Missing	Missing	0.97
Ric3	3.08***	1.19	0.50***	2.36***
Cuban	0.40***	1.66	Missing	2.72***
Other Latino	1.62***	1.44***	0.64***	1.45***
Black	2.15***	2.11***	1.18**	2.39***
Other	1.15	1.24	2.10***	3.03***
West Eur1	0.31***	Missing	Missing	1.61
West Eur2	0.85	1.10	0.17***	0.78**
West Eur3	1.00	0.81***	0.92	0.88***
East Eur1	0.77	Missing	10.46***	1.91
East Eur2	0.23***	Missing	1.81	0.14***
East Eur3	0.89	0.36***	Missing	0.85
Asian1	4.09***	5.41***	0.13***	2.64***
Asian2	1.68***	3.22***	0.24***	0.92
Asian3	1.64**	1.16	0.87	1.12
Year1	0.72***	N.A.	N.A.	0.82***
Year2	0.84***	N.A.	N.A.	0.98
Year3	0.84***	N.A.	N.A.	0.85***
Year4	1.00	0.83***	1.26***	0.93**
Agehd	0.97***	1.02***	0.99***	0.96***
Health	2.53***	4.05***	2.07***	2.70***
Married	0.16***	0.48***	0.59***	0.21***
Lths	2.26***	1.96***	1.19***	2.64***
Smec	0.81***	0.71***	0.77***	0.73***
Colp	0.20***	0.36***	0.39***	0.20***
Yngage	0.97***	1.01	0.97***	0.98***
Nkids	1.10***	1.08***	1.00	1.27***
South	1.14***	1.36***	2.06***	1.73***
West	2.21***	1.25***	4.95***	1.49***
North	1.01	1.07	7.74***	1.06
Belowpov	5.68***	1.34***	3.36***	6.74***

NOTES: Whites omitted category in models; N.A. = not applicable; Missing = variable dropped due to insufficient data.

[a]Only 1990 and 1991 panels of SIPP.

Medicaid	Housing Assistance	Heating Assistance	WIC	School Lunch
0.87	1.29**	0.48***	0.68*	2.67***
0.86**	1.38***	0.95	1.42***	2.22***
1.34***	1.23***	1.27***	0.66***	1.21***
3.75***	1.73**	4.67***	0.30**	4.09***
2.12**	2.47***	0.63	0.25***	2.72***
4.69***	2.39***	2.78***	0.90	1.71***
2.32***	0.41	0.85	Missing	0.75*
1.74***	2.28***	0.66***	1.19*	1.78***
2.10***	2.50***	1.15***	1.37***	1.79***
2.59***	1.30	0.60**	4.96***	1.28
0.34***	Missing	0.38***	Missing	0.41***
0.88	0.55***	0.50***	0.22***	0.71***
0.91***	1.22***	0.84***	0.99	1.16***
3.52***	4.61***	2.68**	Missing	0.91
1.51**	0.27***	0.51	0.52	0.68***
1.17	1.30	1.43***	0.59**	0.85**
4.31***	3.70***	1.02	0.56*	3.03***
1.23*	1.44***	0.32***	1.16	0.97
1.22	1.59***	0.22***	0.31***	2.35***
0.80***	0.93	1.43***	0.85***	0.31***
0.95	0.64***	1.31***	0.82**	0.34***
0.91**	1.04	1.20***	0.77***	0.40***
0.90**	1.12***	0.58***	0.95	2.61***
0.96***	0.95***	0.98***	0.94***	1.03***
3.23***	1.49***	1.61***	1.82***	1.42***
0.16***	0.30***	0.26***	0.79***	0.42***
2.18***	1.39***	1.73***	1.51***	1.78***
0.71***	0.88***	0.85***	0.73***	0.90***
0.23***	0.47***	0.31***	0.22***	0.73***
0.95***	1.01***	1.00	0.71***	1.02***
1.10***	1.04***	1.24***	0.84***	1.59***
1.07*	1.14***	0.53***	1.60***	14.31***
1.86***	1.29***	0.32***	0.92	7.67***
1.49***	1.83***	0.35***	1.25***	7.91***
5.57***	2.17***	3.96***	2.23***	2.01***

***$p < 0.01$; **$p < 0.05$; *$p < 0.10$.

SOURCE: SIPP (1986-1991 panels) except for [a].

TABLE 11A-4 Odds Ratios from Regression of Public Assistance on Ethnicity and Generation

	Cash	Noncash	Total
Gen1	0.87**	0.77***	0.74***
Gen2	0.68***	0.75***	0.76***
Mexican	0.99	1.40***	1.43***
Puerto Rican	2.98***	3.31***	3.31***
Cuban	0.82	3.99***	3.58***
Latino	1.82***	2.12***	2.18***
Black	2.16***	2.49***	2.56***
Other	1.33*	2.95***	3.20***
West Eur	1.00	0.94***	0.96*
East Eur	0.70***	1.16*	1.13
Asian	3.35***	1.45***	1.71***
Year1	0.67***	1.02	1.00
Year2	0.78***	0.95	0.92**
Year3	0.77***	0.88***	0.85***
Year4	1.04	0.89***	0.90***
Agehd	0.98***	0.96***	0.97***
Health	2.63***	2.59***	2.59***
Married	0.18***	0.22***	0.22***
Lths	2.30***	2.23***	2.24***
Smec	0.84***	0.70***	0.70***
Colp	0.29***	0.29***	0.29***
Ynage	0.97***	0.98***	0.99***
Nkids	1.08***	1.19***	1.17***
South	1.61***	1.49***	1.63***
West	2.67***	1.43***	1.63***
North	1.42***	1.23***	1.26***
Belowpov	4.93***	5.02***	4.84***

NOTES: Omitted categories include whites and native-born children with native-born parents. Scenario one: "Cash" is participation in either AFDC, SSI, or other welfare; "Noncash" is participation in either food stamps, Medicaid, or housing or energy assistance; "Total" is participation in any of these programs. Scenario two: "Cash" is participation in either AFDC, SSI, other welfare, unemployment assistance, or general assistance; "Noncash" is participation in either food stamps, Medicaid, housing or energy assistance, or WIC; "Total" is participation in any of these programs.

***$p < .01$; **$p < .05$; *$p < .10$.

SOURCE: SIPP (1986-1991 panels).

TABLE 11A-5 Odds Ratios from Regression of Public Assistance on Ethnicity and Generational Groups

	Cash	Noncash	Total
Mex1	0.75***	1.03	1.01
Mex2	0.57***	1.09*	1.12**
Mex3	1.22***	1.42***	1.45***
Ric1	5.94***	2.11***	2.39***
Ric2	1.38	2.96***	2.90***
Ric3	2.90***	3.42***	3.36***
Cuban	0.57*	3.06***	2.79***
Other Latino	1.62***	1.87***	1.92***
Black	2.16***	2.48***	2.55***
Other	1.33*	2.98***	3.22***
West Eur1	0.26***	1.15	1.16
West Eur2	0.90	0.81**	0.81**
West Eur3	1.02	0.94**	0.97
East Eur1	0.60	2.89***	2.65***
East Eur2	0.19***	0.76	0.72*
East Eur3	0.84	1.11	1.09
Asian1	4.57***	2.32***	2.32***
Asian2	2.19***	0.88	1.18
Asian3	2.13***	0.96	1.07
Year1	0.67***	1.02	1.00
Year2	0.78***	0.95	0.92**
Year3	0.77***	0.87***	0.85***
Year4	1.04	0.89***	0.90***
Agehd	0.98***	0.96***	0.97***
Health	2.61***	2.60***	2.60***
Married	0.18***	0.22***	0.22***
Lths	2.31***	2.21***	2.23***
Smec	0.83***	0.70***	0.70***
Colp	0.28***	0.28***	0.29***
Yngage	0.97***	0.98***	0.99***
Nkids	1.08***	1.19***	1.17***
South	1.63***	1.50***	1.64***
West	2.74***	1.43***	1.63***
North	1.37***	1.20***	1.23***
Belowpov	4.93***	5.00***	4.81***

NOTE: 1 = Foreign-born children with foreign-born parents; 2 = Native-born children with at least one foreign-born parent; 3 = Native-born children with native-born parents. Scenario one: "Cash" is participation in either AFDC, SSI, or other welfare; "Noncash" is participation in either food stamps, Medicaid, housing or energy assistance; "Total" is participation in any of these programs. Scenario two: "Cash" is participation in either AFDC, SSI, other welfare, unemployment assistance, or general assistance; "Noncash" is participation in either food stamps, Medicaid, housing or energy assistance, or WIC; "Total" is participation in any of these programs. Omitted category is white. ***$p < .01$; **$p < .05$; *$p < .10$.
SOURCE: SIPP (1986-1991 panels).

CHAPTER 12

Children in Immigrant and Nonimmigrant Farmworker Families:

Findings from the National Agricultural Workers Survey

Richard Mines

This paper reports information for the 1993 to 1995 period from the National Agricultural Workers Survey (NAWS), which interviews cropworkers across the United States annually. The NAWS collects detailed information about farmworkers as well as in-depth data about members of their families. Wherever possible the information directly describes children of interviewed farmworkers.

This paper also provides data on another (nonoverlapping) group of young people: the employed minor farmworkers (under age 18) directly interviewed by the NAWS who are living away from their parents. Information on these minor interviewees supplements the data on the children of farmworkers who live in their parents' households. These farmworker children who are unaccompanied by their parents are a small but significant group.[1]

---

[1]During the period under study (fiscal years 1993 to 1995), young (under age 18) farmworkers unaccompanied by their parents made up 3.6 percent of all interviewees. Based on a national estimate of 1,810,000 farmworkers, there were about 65,000 of these workers. The figure 1.81 million is derived from the total number of farmworkers estimated by the Commission on Agricultural Workers (2.5 million) multiplied by the proportion of cropworkers estimated by the 1990 U.S. Census of Population and Housing (72.4 percent).

Finally, first-generation Puerto Rican-born farmworkers, since they are neither immigrants nor were born in one of the 50 United States, were treated differently in the analysis. Children living in Puerto Rico were not included in the sample of U.S.-based children and were treated as a separate group in the analysis.

INTRODUCTION

The arduous fieldwork of large-scale crop agriculture in the United States has been done, in large measure, by foreign-born or domestic migrants. Many ethnic groups and nationalities have taken such jobs temporarily, only to be replaced by later-arriving groups. When U.S.-born whites and blacks were the main source of labor in the 1930s, they were internal migrants who moved from the Midwest and South to the West. As journalist Carey McWilliams (1935) put it: "Sources of cheap labor in China, Japan, the Philippine Islands, Puerto Rico, Mexico, the Deep South, and Europe have been generously tapped to recruit its ever expanding [farmworker] ranks. As one contingent of recruits after the other has been exhausted, or has mutinied, others have been assembled to take their places."

Agriculture provides or enforces on its workers a flow-through labor market with extraordinarily high rates of turnover. In recent years almost one in five farmworkers was new to U.S. agriculture in the year of the interview—a rate of influx and departure that is quite remarkable. However, the flow through for workers who have U.S.-based children has been much less; just one in 20 of the U.S.-based children has parents who were new to agriculture in the year of the NAWS interview. Among the unaccompanied children who themselves worked in agriculture the rate was much higher—over half (56 percent) were in their first year of U.S. farmwork.

Farmwork has not, for the most part, been a lifetime profession. Instead, it is a job for young workers at the beginning of their employment careers and in their prime working years. The NAWS has demonstrated that in recent years about two-thirds of all farmworkers have been younger than 35 years of age. These are also the years of childbearing and the rearing of young children for these workers. More than four in 10 (44 percent) of the children of farmworkers in the NAWS were under age 6 and three-quarters (75 percent) were younger than age 12.

Many foreign-born farmworkers go through various stages on a continuum between international back-and-forth migration and settlement. Large numbers of workers settle down in U.S. urban areas, where some find better jobs. Some settle in one farm area in the United States and live off agricultural work. Others continue migrating despite the inconvenience of transporting their families long distances at least twice a year. Finally, many find the environment north of the border inhospitable and return to their home country (see Gabbard et al., 1994).

Conditions in the farmworker community are greatly influenced by a large population of unaccompanied males (over half of all farmworkers) who have yet to bring or who will never bring their families to the United States. Many are married and have children abroad; a significant percentage are minors themselves and spend time in the United States working far from their parents.

Many other occupations depend on a high-turnover flow-through labor market that is constantly replenished by new immigrants. The garment and shoe sector, the back-of-the-house restaurant and hotel industry, the auto parts industry, the food-processing sector, the janitorial service industry, and many other sectors have been documented as relying on new immigrants (see Waldinger, 1996; U.S. Government Accounting Office, 1987; Mines and Avina, 1992; Lichtner and Waldinger, 1996). The children of these nonagricultural workers (who greatly outnumber farmworkers' children) may have living conditions similar to those of the children of farmworkers.

The study of children of immigrant farmworkers does not provide much information about children of foreign-born workers who have been living in the United States for many years. Because of the nature of this population, the focus of the present study is on the early years of immigration, settlement, and back-and-forth flows. Still, as a study of risk factors among poor immigrants struggling to survive and raise a family in their first years in the United States, the study of children of farmworkers serves as an excellent laboratory.

A Word About the NAWS

The NAWS is a random employer-based sample survey of about 2,500 farmworkers per year, gathered in three cycles—winter, summer, and fall. Data from the surveys occurring in fiscal years 1993 to 1995 are used here. There were about 7,000 interviews in total in those years. Among these, there were about 3,000 parents, who together had about 6,000 children ages 0 to 17. These parents, their spouses, and children constitute the sample for the major part of this paper. Not counting their spouses, the parent interviewees are representative of about 775,000 farmworker parents who have about 1.6 million children. Of these children, about 880,000 live in the United States and about 720,000 live abroad at any given time.[2] In addition, a small group of interviewed children living away from their parents are analyzed separately.

Organization of the Tables and Paper

The demographic and service access data are organized into two sections below. First, the basic demographics of children of farmworkers are used to describe certain obstacles they face in trying to gain access to American society. Then, some measures of the access they have achieved are reported. Finally, a separate group of children, those working in the United States without their parents, are described.

The first two sections of this paper are organized such that data can be reported and verified in stepwise fashion from Tables 12-1 to 12-4. The descriptions for the first three tables are for U.S.-

[2]The number of children is calculated by taking the ratio of weighted sampled children during fiscal years 1993 to 1995 to weighted sampled farmworker interviewees during the same years. This ratio is 0.88. This proportion of the total 1,810,000 cropworker population is approximately 1.6 million children. Fifty-five percent of the children are in the United States, 44 percent are abroad, and 1 percent are in Puerto Rico.

[3]The sample size of 4,838 in Tables 12-1 through 12-3 represents an estimated 880,000 children. These are the U.S.-based children. Adding the Puerto Rico-based children for Table 12-4, the sample size grows to 4,905, which represents an estimated population of 892,000 children. The population estimates of all cropworkers are derived from the Commission on Agricultural Workers and the U.S. Census of Population and Housing. They are lower-limit estimates.

TABLE 12-1 Circumstances of Children in Farmworker Families, for U.S.-Based Children by Child's Birthplace: 1993-1995

	U.S.-Born (%)	Foreign-Born (%)	Total U.S.-Based (%)
Interviewed Parent's Characteristics			
U.S.-born non-Hispanic	28.0	0.0	21.0
U.S.-born Hispanic	9.0	1.0	7.5
Mexican-born	60.0	94.0	69.0
Other foreign-born	2.0	5.0	2.5
Total	100.0	100.0	100.0
Parent finished 8 or more years of school	46.0	18.0	40.1
Family migrates each year	22.0	33.0	25.4
School Variables			
Enrolled in school, ages 6-11 ($N = 974$)	92.0	84.0	88.1
Enrolled in school, ages 12-17 ($N = 873$)	93.0	78.0	87.3
Behind grade level ($N = 1,848$)	13.3	23.6	16.7
Family Income			
Median family income	$12,500-$14,999	$10,000-$12,499	$10,000-$12,499
Families below the poverty line (lower-bound estimate)	61.0	86.0	67.2
Families below the poverty line (upper-bound estimate)	66.9	89.8	72.9
Extended Family Members in Household	5.0	6.0	5.6

Family Receives Federal Services	61.0	56.0	59.5
AFDC	9.0	3.0	7.7
Food stamps	40.0	31.0	38.3
Medicaid	40.0	32.0	37.7
WIC (*N* = 1,400)	43.0	20.0	40.3
Family in Poverty and Receives Federal Services	79.0	56.0	71.8
AFDC	15.0	3.0	10.7
Food stamps	57.0	35.0	50.7
Medicaid	50.0	34.0	45.0
WIC (*N* = 986)	47.0	21.0	43.4
Source of Family's Health Care			
Emergency room	20.0	37.0	27.9
Migrant health clinic	10.0	18.0	13.0
Nowhere	9.8	11.0	6.4
Private	42.0	25.0	35.6
Public	19.2	9.8	19.0
Total	100.0	100.0	100.0
Family's Perceived Difficulty in Obtaining Health Care	17.0	25.0	19.6
Parent Mixes or Handles Pesticides at Work	29.9	24.7	28.5
Total, All Children	74.1	24.9	100.0

NOTES: *N* = 4,838, except where noted. See Appendix 12A for descriptions of selected variables.

TABLE 12-2 Circumstances of Children in Farmworker Families, for U.S.-Based Children by Parental Presence in Household and Birthplace, 1993-1995

	Children in Immigrant Families	
	Two-Parent Families	
	Both Foreign Born (%)	One Foreign Born (%)
Child lives in U.S. and abroad	5.3	1.5
Child lives only in U.S.	94.7	98.5
Total (N = 2,045)	100.0	100.0
Siblings born in U.S. and abroad	43.6	5.6
Siblings all born in U.S.	56.4	94.4
Total (N = 2,045)	100.0	100.0
Child separated from one parent (N = 5,621)	59.1	10.1
Child's father came to U.S. first (N = 1,139)	71.0	X
Child's family migrates each year	29.6	31.0
Parent finished 8 or more years of school	21.0	36.0
Child enrolled in school, ages 6-11 (N = 974)	85.9	86.2
Child enrolled in school, ages 12-17 (N = 873)	84.8	91.0
Child behind grade level (N = 1,848)	15.5	11.1
Median family income	$10,000-$12,499	$10,000-$12,499
Families below the poverty line (lower-bound estimate)	76.0	68.0
Families below the poverty line (upper-bound estimate)	82.0	71.2
Extended family members in household	7.0	5.0
Nonfamily present in household	29.0	24.0
Family receiving any federal services	66.0	68.0
AFDC	44.6	40.3
Food stamps	38.0	47.0
Medicaid	41.0	43.0
WIC (N = 1,400)	31.0	33.0
Family in poverty and receives federal services	70.0	81.0
AFDC	4.0	12.0
Food stamps	46.0	65.0
Medicaid	43.0	49.0
WIC (N = 986)	34.0	36.0
Family's source of health care		
Emergency room	25.4	23.6
Migrant health clinic	11.3	17.2
Nowhere	5.7	5.0
Private	31.5	32.3
Public	19.2	19.8
Total	100.0	100.0
Family's perceived difficulty in obtaining health care	22.0	21.8
Parent mixes or applies pesticides at work	30.6	24.1
Total, all U.S.-based children	58.2	10.0

NOTES: N = 4,838, except where noted. See Appendix 12A for descriptions of selected variables.

	Children in Nonimmigrant Families		
One-Parent Family	Two-Parent Family	One-Parent Family	
Lone-Parent Foreign Born (%)	Both U.S. Born (%)	Lone-Parent U.S. Born (%)	Total U.S.-Based (%)
15.1	X	X	3.3
84.9	X	X	96.7
100.0	X	X	
36.3	X	X	26.1
63.7	X	X	73.9
100.0	X	X	
X	2.2	X	50.8
X	X	X	71.3
35.0	11.7	11.7	27.2
29.0	89.0	88.0	39.8
97.0	93.3	87.8	87.9
87.4	89.9	96.4	87.2
27.9	18.1	17.9	17.2
$10,000-$12,499	$10,000-$12,499	$10,000 - $12,499	$10,000-$12,499
86.0	31.0	80.0	67.4
87.9	36.2	82.7	73.1
6.0	3.0	4.0	5.6
33.0	10.0	30.0	26.0
62.4	27.0	79.0	59.5
41.5	16.6	68.6	42.1
43.0	20.0	71.0	37.7
40.0	16.0	59.0	37.8
22.0	7.0	38.0	26.8
60.0	60.0	92.0	71.5
21.0	20.0	52.0	10.6
47.0	52.0	82.0	50.7
46.0	35.0	69.0	45.0
23.0	14.0	39.0	31.6
40.4	16.2	23.9	25.9
13.9	2.6	2.9	9.7
9.9	0.6	3.5	4.8
10.2	58.3	34.9	35.9
24.6	20.3	35.3	23.7
100.0	100.0	100.0	100.0
31.2	9.4	14.6	19.7
21.7	331.6	15.8	28.4
6.5	18.4	6.8	100.0

TABLE 12-3 Circumstances of Children in Farmworker Families, for U.S.-Based Children by Legal Status of Child's Interviewed Parent, 1993-1995

	U.S. Citizen (%)	Legal Resident (%)	Status Pending (%)	Unauthorized (%)	Total U.S.-Based (%)
Parent is U.S.-born non-Hispanic	63.5	0.0	0.0	0.2	20.6
Parent is U.S.-born Hispanic	26.6	0.0	0.0	0.0	7.4
Parent is Mexican born	9.1	98.4	93.2	93.5	68.0
Parent is other foreign born	1.0	1.4	5.9	6.1	2.5
Total	100.0	100.0	100.0	100.0	100.0
Child is U.S. born	95.0	69.0	56.0	53.0	74.4
Child is foreign born	3.0	30.0	43.0	43.0	0.7
Child was born in Puerto Rico	2.2	10.0	0.0	4.0	24.6
Total	100.0	100.0	100.0	100.0	100.0
Child lives in U.S. and abroad	X	3.3	8.4	14.2	3.2
Child lives only in U.S.	X	96.7	91.6	85.8	96.8
Total (*N* = 2,045)	X	100.0	100.0	100.0	100.0
Siblings born in U.S. and abroad	X	34.9	52.4	45.7	26.0
Siblings all born in U.S.	X	65.1	47.7	54.3	74.0
Total (*N* = 2,045)	X	100.0	100.0	100.0	100.0

Child separated from one parent ($N = 5,621$)	16.9	40.7	56.8	77.0	50.6
Child's father came to U.S. first ($N = 1,139$)	X	81.2	77.4	77.4	75.3
Child's family migrates each year	21.5	23.1	34.7	46.7	27.2
Parent finished 8 or more years of school	79.0	22.0	15.0	25.0	40.5
Child enrolled in school, ages 6-11 ($N = 974$)	91.0	86.0	85.0	85.0	87.4
Child enrolled in school, ages 12-17 ($N = 873$)	91.0	89.0	71.0	75.0	86.9
Child behind grade level ($N = 1,848$)	19.5	12.1	26.3	25.4	17.2
Median family income	$12,500-$14,999	$12,500-$14,999	$10,000-$12,499	$7,500-$9,999	$10,000-$12,499
Families below the poverty line (lower-bound estimate)	50.0	69.0	86.0	86.0	67.2
Families below the poverty line (upper-bound estimate)	54.8	77.1	87.9	89.3	72.9
Extended family members in household	4.0	7.0	9.0	3.0	5.5
Nonfamily present in household	20.0	14.0	34.0	54.0	26.9
Family receives any federal services	46.0	64.0	70.0	64.0	59.5
AFDC	13.7	4.8	1.7	6.6	7.6
Food stamps	29.0	60.0	55.0	38.0	38.3
Medicaid	24.0	47.0	32.0	41.0	37.5
WIC ($N = 1,400$)	29.0	41.0	62.0	43.0	40.3
Total, all U.S.-based children	33.2	42.4	8.9	15.5	100.0

NOTES: N = 4,838, except where noted. See Appendix 12A for descriptions of selected variables.

TABLE 12-4 Circumstances of Children in Farmworker Families, for U.S.-Based and Puerto Rico-Based Children by Ethnicity and Birthplace of Child's Interviewed Parent, 1993-1995

	U.S.-Born Non-Hispanic (%)	U.S.-Born Hispanic (%)
Child lives in U.S. and abroad	X	0.3
Child lives only in U.S.	X	99.7
Total (N = 2,045)	X	73.0
Siblings born in U.S. and abroad	X	3.1
Siblings all born in U.S.	X	96.9
Total (N = 2,045)	X	100.0
Child separated from one parent (N = 5,621)	1.3	8.9
Child's father came to U.S. first (N = 658)	X	X
Child's family migrates each year	6.3	37.7
Parent finished 8 or more years of school	92.0	63.0
Child enrolled in school, ages 6-11 (N = 1,537)	92.2	85.4
Child enrolled in school, ages 12-17 (N = 1,310)	91.2	91.1
Child behind grade level (N = 1,892)	17.3	21.1
Median family income	$17,500-$19,999	$10,000-$12,499
Families below the poverty line (lower-bound estimate)	41.7	77.0
Families below the poverty line (upper-bound estimate)	37.0	74.0
Extended family members in household	0.0	5.0
Nonfamily present in household	14.0	22.0
Family receives any federal services	37.0	70.0
AFDC	38.5	37.5
Food stamps	28.0	60.0
Medicaid	24.0	47.0
WIC (N = 1,423)	34.0	41.0
Family in poverty and receives any federal services	73.0	81.0
TAFDC	33.0	30.0
Food stamps	62.0	74.0
Medicaid	48.0	53.0
WIC (N = 1,010)	39.0	37.0
Family's source of health care		
Emergency room	18.5	18.6
Migrant health clinic	0.0	16.1
Nowhere	1.1	3.5
Private	52.0	41.1
Public	22.0	17.6
Total	100.0	100.0
Family's perceived difficulty in obtaining health care	9.3	19.6
Parent mixes or applies pesticides	29.1	16.4
Total, all U.S.-based children	20.20	7.30

NOTES: N = 4,905, except where noted. See Appendix 12A for descriptions of selected variables.

Puerto Rican (%)	Mexico-Born (%)	Other Foreign-Born (%)	Total U.S.-Based (%)
0.0	5.4	18.3	3.3
100.0	94.6	81.7	96.8
100.0	100.0	100.0	100.0
X	38.2	52.4	26.1
X	61.8	47.6	74.0
X	100.0	100.0	100.0
86.8	55.3	78.2	50.7
X	81.7	56.4	62.9
74.4	29.7	35.4	27.2
60.0	22.0	17.0	40.5
62.4	90.2	90.0	85.9
72.5	86.1	66.0	85.9
29.7	16.1	14.2	71.2
$5,000-$7,499	$7,500-$9,999	$5,000-$7,499	$10,000-$12,499
91.8	81.3	79.3	73.6
91.0	75.0	77.0	68.3
7.0	6.0	15.0	5.7
83.0	29.0	59.0	28.2
64.0	65.0	53.0	59.5
19.9	43.3	47.4	42.2
55.0	38.0	29.0	38.3
32.0	41.0	36.0	37.5
62.0	43.0	39.0	40.3
69.0	7.1	55.0	71.2
8.0	6.0	3.0	10.5
60.0	47.0	40.0	51.0
33.0	44.0	37.0	44.3
6.0	43.0	5.0	43.2
25.8	26.7	19.2	24.3
22.2	11.4	14.5	9.9
9.0	5.9	5.7	4.9
8.2	29.7	24.5	34.2
7.4	19.9	20.3	19.7
100.0	100.0	100.0	100.0
20.2	21.3	32.2	19.0
31.6	29.7	17.7	28.3
3.40	66.60	2.50	100.00

based children only, while the fourth table includes Puerto Rico-based children as well.[3] Foreign-based children are excluded from all tables unless otherwise specified. Table 12-1 compares the groups by the birthplaces of the children, both foreign and U.S. born. Table 12-2 distinguishes the children by type of family. These include three types of two-parent families: both parents are U.S. born, both are foreign born, and one parent of each. It also includes foreign- and U.S.-born single-parent families. Table 12-3 discusses the children with regard to the legal status of their interviewee parent. The four possibilities here are U.S. citizen, legal permanent resident (green card holder), pending (waiting for status adjudication), and unauthorized. Finally, Table 12-4 discusses the children in terms of their ethnicity or birthplace. There are two U.S.-born categories (U.S. non-Hispanic and U.S. Hispanic), a Puerto Rican category, and two foreign-born categories (Mexican and other foreign born). (See Appendix 12A for further details about the tables.) Some numbers reported in the text do not appear in any of the tables. Table 12-5 accompanies the discussion of child farmworkers not accompanied by parents.

TABLE 12-5 Circumstances of Child Farmworkers Not Accompanied by Parents, 1993-1995

Median income	$1,000-$2,500
Proportion with more than 8 years of schooling	35
Proportion who migrate each year	79
Proportion who are unauthorized U.S. residents	90
Proportion who migrate each year	79
Proportion who are unauthorized to work in the U.S.	90
Proportion whose family receives food stamps	6
Proportion whose family receives Medicaid	6
Proportion whose family receives WIC	2
Proportion whose family receives AFDC	0
Proportion who mix or apply pesticides at work	15
Source of health care	
Emergency room	38
Public clinics	42
Private doctors	7
Nowhere or in Mexico	14
Total	100

NOTE: See Appendix 12A for descriptions of selected variables.

OBSTACLES TO CHILDREN'S WELL-BEING

A number of sociological factors complicate the lives of children of farmworkers and act as obstacles to their well-being. One important group relates to the foreign origin of the children and their parents and the precarious legal status of many families. These factors may act as cultural and legal barriers for parents in obtaining services for their children's needs as well as for the children in gaining access to the greater society.

In the NAWS, most U.S-based children (children who live in the United States) have foreign-born parents. The proportions of foreign-born and Hispanics among parents are higher than among the general farmworker population. This is true because a large proportion of white non-Hispanic farmworkers are young unmarried workers with short time commitments to farmwork. Also, foreign-born farmworkers on average have children at a younger age than do their U.S.-born counterparts. Overall, 72 percent of the U.S-based children in the survey have a foreign-born parent, 8 percent have a U.S.-born Hispanic parent, and only 21 percent have a non-Hispanic U.S.-born interviewee parent. Even limiting the discussion here to only children who were born and are based in the United States, 62 percent have a foreign-born parent, 9 percent a U.S.-born Hispanic parent, and 28 percent a non-Hispanic U.S.-born parent (see Table 12-1).

Moreover, non-Puerto Rican U.S.-born Hispanics should be considered with special care since they are extremely intertwined with the immigrant community. Most are of Mexican parentage and apparently mix easily with new Mexican immigrants. Among the children of U.S.-born Hispanic farmworker parents in the NAWS, 39 percent have a U.S.-born farmworker parent who is married to a foreigner, 32 percent have a farmworker parent married to a U.S.-born individual, and 29 percent have single parents. Although the parents may speak English, three-quarters (76 percent) of the children have farmworker parents who list Spanish as their first language. This is not surprising, since they live and work in Spanish-dominated environments.

Moreover, few (5 percent) of the foreign-born parents interviewed in the NAWS have become U.S. citizens. Only one in 10 of the children with citizen parents are the children of foreign-born parents. Naturally, among the other legal status categories—legal permanent resident, pending, and undocumented—all of the interviewee parents were foreign born (see Table 12-3). Of these, about 95 percent were Mexican born.

The precarious legal status of many of the farmworker parents in the NAWS may restrict the access of their children to American society; 9 percent of these children have a parent with pending status, and 16 percent are in a family with an undocumented interviewee. Based on the estimate of 880,000 U.S.-based children of cropworkers, about 140,000 children of farmworkers are living with a parent who is in this country without work-authorized status. Approximately half of these children of undocumented immigrants who now live in the United States were born here (54 percent); they, of course, are U.S. citizens, which may lower the barriers for their children.

A child's birthplace (regardless of the legal status of his or her parents) may affect his or her well-being; being born abroad may add to the negative impacts of having foreign-born parents. This factor comes into play because in the NAWS the majority of children born to U.S. farmworkers were born abroad. Looking at all children of farmworkers, 44 percent were born abroad and are still abroad, 14 percent were born abroad but have moved to the United States, 41 percent were born and live in the United States, and 1 percent were born and live in Puerto Rico. Overall, 58 percent of the children were born abroad, and 55 percent lived in the United States at the time of their NAWS interview.

Focusing on just those children living in the United States at the time of their NAWS interview, the proportion born abroad is still significant—one-quarter of the U.S.-based children of farmworkers were born abroad (see Table 12-1). Almost two-thirds (65 percent) of U.S.-based children with foreign-born parents were born in the United States.

U.S.-based children in families with some children living abroad and some living in the United States ("mixed-residence" families) and those in families with some children born abroad and some born in the United States ("mixed-birth" families) may face special problems. Few U.S.-based children live in families that also have children living abroad. Of the U.S.-based children in families in the NAWS with at least one foreign-born parent and at least one child living in the United States, only 3 percent had some children living in the United States and some elsewhere. In terms of children's birthplaces, there were many more mixed families. Twenty-six percent of the children in families with a foreign-born parent and a U.S-based child had some children who were born abroad and some who were born in the United States (see Table 12-2).

Children in single-parent foreign-born households in the NAWS have very high rates of mixed households. Fifteen percent of these children live in families with children residing in two countries, and 36 percent live in families with children who were born in two different countries. Children in two-parent foreign-born families also have high levels of mixed households. The percentages are 5 percent for mixed residence and 44 percent for mixed place of birth. Also, a few children in families with one U.S.- and one foreign-born parent have mixed households. Two percent live in mixed-residence households and 5 percent live in mixed-birth households (see Table 12-2).

Looking at this phenomenon from the viewpoint of the legal status of those with foreign nationality, children of farmworkers with undocumented or pending status have the highest percentage of mixed-status families—almost half have some children born both here and others born abroad. Children of legal permanent residents have the lowest levels; even they have 3 percent mixed-residence and 35 percent mixed-birthplace families (see Table 12-3).

Children of non-Mexican foreign-born farmworkers have higher levels of mixed residence (18 percent) and mixed birth (53 percent) than the children of Mexicans, who have a high level of mixed birth (38 percent) but not mixed residence (5 percent). Even a small number of children in U.S. Hispanic families have mixed-birth or mixed-residence families (see Table 12-4). Families with children of mixed nationality and place of residence may face special obstacles in accessing services since some of the children in these families may qualify and others may not.

The separation of children from their foreign-born farmworker parents may present another serious problem for the children. The immigrant status of the parents of most children of farmworkers may have at least one advantage—fewer of the children are in single-parent families. The number of broken marriages is lower in Latin American countries than in the United States. The foreign born bring this behavior with them when they come to the United States. In the NAWS one-quarter of the U.S.-based children from households with at least one U.S.-born parent were from a single-parent family, whereas only 9 percent of the children from households with one or more foreign-born parents lived with a single parent. Children of Puerto Rican farmworkers had an intermediate level of single parents—21 percent.

This tendency for foreign-born parents to maintain two-parent families here in the United States is, however, of less value to the children if one of the parents is habitually absent from home. To check the total rate of separation from one of the parents in two-parent families, I report on children from two-parent families living both in the United States and abroad. Overall, about half of all children of farmworkers from two-parent families are separated from one of their parents. This separation is concentrated almost entirely among children with foreign-born or Puerto Rican parents.

Looking at this phenomenon according to the different types of two-parent families, three-fifths (59 percent) of children who have two foreign-born parents are separated from one parent; for those who come from families with one U.S.-born and one foreign-born parent, 10 percent are separated; for those with two U.S.-born parents, only 2 percent are separated from one of their parents (Table 12-2). Looking at the legal status categories, all of the children of noncitizen families have separation rates over 40 percent, but the children of undocumented residents have the highest rate of separation at 77 percent (Table 12-3). Looking at this issue by ethnic/nationality groups shows that the children of Puerto Ricans (87 percent) and of non-Mexican other foreign-born parents (78 percent) have the highest rates of separation, but the children of the largest group, Mexicans, also have a very high rate of separation from one of their parents, 55 percent (Table 12-4).

The one bright spot in the separation story is that most U.S. farmworkers' children who are living abroad appear to be with their mothers in home countries. In nearly 100 percent of the cases where the child is separated from one parent, the child and mother are residing in the same country.

Studying this issue only for U.S.-based children (about 55 percent of the total), the rate of separation is much lower. Except for the children of Puerto Ricans, 54 percent of whom are separated from one parent, the other groups have relatively low rates of separation. The children of undocumented workers and those of other foreign-born parents are the groups with the most separation (8 and 12 percent, respectively). These data show several interconnected phenomena. The children of most foreign-born U.S. farmworkers are left behind in their home countries while one of their parents (usually the father) does farmwork in the United States. However, once the children come to the United States or for those who are born here, in a large majority of cases they live with both of their parents. Still, the years of separation from one parent for the children who eventually come to the United States may be a negative factor in their ability to adapt to American society.

One element of this separation that is crucial for social planning is the tendency of those family members who are living abroad to eventually come to the United States. The NAWS data imply that regrouping of families in the United States is a tendency among many of these immigrants regardless of legal status. For children with fathers in the households that were reunited in the United States, generally the fathers were the first to come to this country. Four-fifths (80 percent) had fathers who came to the United States before their children (Table 12-2). A minority had fathers (about 20 percent) who came to the United States at the same time they did. The fathers of nearly seven-tenths (69 percent) of the children came to the United States before the mothers. Most had mothers (72 percent) who came at the same time as their children. However, some children's mothers came first (28 percent). The only group with a lower rate is that of other foreign born. Only 45 percent of the children of this group came to this country after their fathers (Table 12-4). There is a strong tendency for eventual reunion of families in the United States with the male head of household for almost all groups.

In addition to separation from their parents, many children of farmworkers undergo problems associated with migration. In the

NAWS the parents of 53 percent of all children of farmworkers are migrants.[4] A smaller yet still sizable level of migrancy applies to the children of farmworkers living in the United States—26 percent of these children have parents who are migrant farmworkers.

Considering all types of migration, there is a great deal of variation across demographic groups. Children of U.S.-born non-Hispanic farmworkers have very low levels of parental migration—only 6 percent. The other ethnic groups all have high levels. U.S.-born Hispanics actually have slightly higher levels than the foreign-born groups. About 38 percent of the children of U.S. Hispanics have parents who migrate, while 30 percent of the children of Mexicans and 35 percent of the children of the other foreign born have parents who migrate. Puerto Ricans have the highest level of migration—almost three-quarters of children of Puerto Ricans have parents who migrate (Table 12-4). The overwhelming majority of the Puerto Rican parent interviewees in the NAWS were men whose families lived in Puerto Rico.

Looking at migration rates by type of family, over 30 percent of the children who have at least one foreign-born parent have a parent who migrates. Thirty-five percent of the children of foreign-born single-parent workers have a migrating parent (Table 12-2). By contrast, fewer than 12 percent of the children in households headed by U.S.-born parents have a parent who migrates. As would be expected, higher proportions of children whose parents have pending or undocumented status have a parent who migrates (35 and 47 percent, respectively) than the proportion of children whose parents are U.S. citizens or legal permanent residents (just over 20 percent migrate).

There are several types of migration that have different impacts on children, but all are disruptive to a stable lifestyle (see Figure 12-1).[5] One style of migration is to follow crops from one

---

[4]A migrant is defined by the NAWS as anyone who travels 75 miles or more to do or to look for a farmwork job in the United States.

[5]To a small extent the migration categories overlap. A migrant who shuttles back and forth between either a foreign location or a non-U.S. farmwork location and a U.S. farmwork area but also continues on to follow crops to other U.S. farmwork areas is both a follow-the-crop and a shuttle migrant.

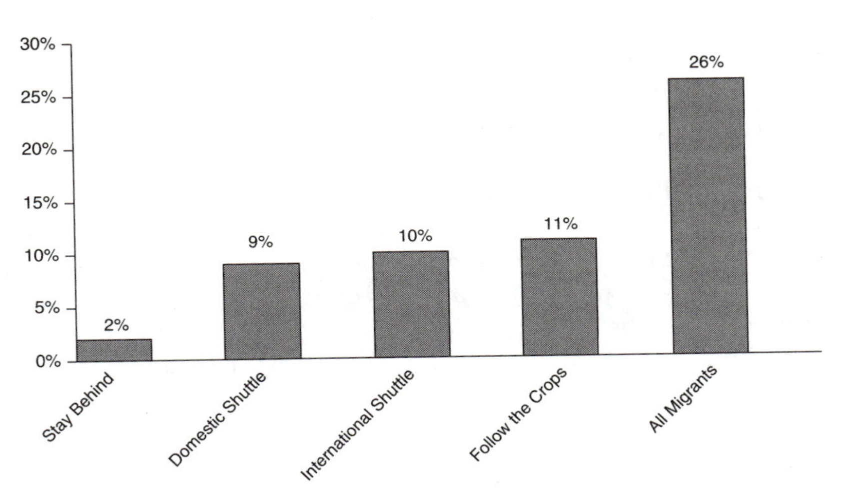

FIGURE 12-1 U.S.-based children who migrate with their farmworker parents.

area to another in the United States. In the NAWS the parents of about 11 percent of U.S.-based children participate in this type of migration. Another style is to have a home base either in the United States or abroad (where one does not do U.S. farmwork) and then each year "shuttle" migrate to a U.S. farm area. Approximately 19 percent of U.S.-based children accompany their parents in this kind of migration. About half of these children (9 percent of all U.S.-based children) migrate to and from a U.S. location, while the other half (10 percent of all U.S.-based children) have their home base abroad, which means that each year these children must travel back and forth across international borders. All together, approximately 24 percent of all the U.S.-based children of farmworkers take a trek each year on the migrant trail.[6] Since there are approximately 880,000 U.S.-based children, about 212,000 youngsters whose parents are cropworkers are in the migrant stream and about 80,000 are international shuttle migrant

[6]Since 26 percent of the children have parents who migrate and 2 percent of the children do not accompany their parents when they migrate, that leaves 24 percent who actually make the migrant trek.

children. Another 2 percent of U.S.-based children have parents who migrate while the children stay behind in their U.S. home base. Similar proportions of children in all age groups appear to participate in the different types of migration.

The low educational levels of farmworkers are another barrier for their children. The parents, especially foreign-born parents, have had little schooling. In the NAWS only 40 percent of U.S.-based children have parents who finished the eighth grade. Almost half (46 percent) of the U.S.-born children have parents who finished the eighth grade, while only 18 percent of the foreign-born children have parents who went that far in school (Table 12-1). Among the family types, less than 30 percent of children in families with one or two foreign-born parents had a parent who finished the eighth grade, while in the families with a single U.S.-born parent or two U.S.-born parents, the parents of 88 percent of the children finished the eighth grade (Table 12-2). Interestingly, the children with undocumented parents had somewhat better educated parents than the children of parents with pending status (Table 12-3). This may be explained by the fact that more recent arrivals from Mexico tend to be better educated. The clearest contrast can be seen by looking at the different ethnic groups. For the children of U.S.-born non-Hispanics, 92 percent have parents who finished the eighth grade; for the children of U.S. Hispanics and Puerto Ricans, about 60 percent have a parent who went that far in school; of children in the foreign-born groups, about 20 percent have parents who finished eight years of school (Table 12-4).

The children themselves have poor academic records. Overall, school enrollment levels are low for all groups. About 87 percent of both the young children and the adolescents are in school. The groups with particularly low levels are the foreign born over age 12—only 78 percent are enrolled. This is particularly true for the children of farmworkers with pending or undocumented immigration status—only 71 and 75 percent, respectively, of those adolescents are enrolled in school (Table 12-3). Puerto Rican children have very low levels of enrollment—only 72 percent of adolescents are enrolled in school, and only 62 percent of children ages 6 to 11 are enrolled (Table 12-4).

Many of the children are performing at least one grade level below that expected for their age. Overall, about 17 percent of U.S.-based children are below grade level. Not surprisingly, only 13 percent of U.S.-born children are below grade level, while 24 percent of the foreign born are behind. Moreover, comparing foreign-born children with U.S.-born children of foreign-born parents, children born abroad are particularly disadvantaged educationally. About one-quarter (24 percent) of U.S.-based foreign-born children of foreign-born parents are below grade level, while only 9 percent of U.S.-born children of foreign-born parents have fallen behind.

Looking at family types, children living in a foreign-born single-parent family are particularly disadvantaged—28 percent are performing below grade level, while fewer than 20 percent of children in other family types are behind (Table 12-2). The children of parents whose legal status is pending or undocumented are the farthest behind—about one-quarter are below grade level, whereas fewer than 20 percent of children of citizens and legal permanent residents are below grade level (Table 12-3). As many as 30 percent of Puerto Rican children are performing below grade level in school.

More children tend to fall behind at the higher grades than in grammar school. Nine percent of 6 to 11 year olds are behind, while 27 percent of 12 to 17 year olds are behind. This is due in part to dropout rates and in part to the fact that some children come to the United States as teenagers and begin working immediately instead of going to school. One can observe this phenomenon by comparing the proportion of adolescents falling behind who do farmwork (about 16 percent of 12 to 17 year olds work) with those who do not. Among those who do not do farmwork, 24 percent are behind; among working teenagers, 41 percent are behind.

There are other factors associated with children of farmworkers falling below grade level. The education level of their parents has an impact but only if the parents have very low educational achievement. For children with parents who have less than four years of school, 30 percent are below grade, compared to the average of 17 percent for children whose parents have had more schooling. For children whose parents have higher levels of education, no pattern emerges. Also, migration has an impact in certain circumstances. International shuttle migration has a statistically significant and negative impact on children's performance in school. Also, domestic shuttle migration and follow-the-crop migration both show a negative impact on school performance, but the effect is not statistically significant.

Probably the most serious barrier to the children of farmworkers is the extreme poverty of their families. The median annual income for such U.S.-based children's families is $10,000 to $12,500. Income differs when looking at families by parental groups. Dividing by family type, children in families with two U.S.-born parents have a median annual income of $17,500 to $20,000, while children in two-parent families with one or two foreign-born parents earn $10,000 to $12,500 annually, and those in single-parent families (either foreign or U.S. born) have a median annual income of $5,000 to $7,500 (Table 12-2). With respect to legal status, pending and undocumented workers earn less than the other groups. Children in pending status families have family incomes of $10,000 to $12,500 annually, while children of undocumented farmworkers have family earnings of $7,500 to $10,000 per year; children in families of U.S. citizens and legal permanent residents have family earnings of $12,500 to $15,000 (Table 12-3). By ethnic group, children in U.S. non-Hispanic families have family earnings much higher than the others ($17,500 to $20,000). Children of U.S. Hispanics have the next highest family earnings ($10,000 to $12,500); next are Mexicans at $7,500 to $10,000, while Puerto Ricans and the other foreign born have the lowest family earnings, at $5,000 to $7,500 per year (Table 12-4).

The extent of impoverishment among children of farmworkers becomes even clearer when looking at the proportions who fall below the poverty line adjusted by the size of the family living in the United States. Only conservative estimates for poverty are reported in Tables 12-1 through 12-5. Readers should note that these numbers represent an optimistically low estimate of poverty for children in the NAWS. These families reported a range of incomes, and the lower-bound estimate for poverty makes reference only to the top (upper end) of that income range (see Appendix 12A). The tables also report upper-bound estimates of poverty. According to the lower-bound estimate, 68 percent of U.S.-based children of farmworkers are in families that fall below the poverty line. Using the upper-bound estimate, 73 percent of the U.S.-based children are in poor families. Only conservative lower-bound estimates are presented below (see tables for upper-bound estimates).

Even among children in the United States who have both parents present in the household, in the NAWS two-thirds (65 percent) are in poor families. Children in two-parent families in which both parents are U.S. born did better—only 31 percent of these children live below poverty.[7] But over two-thirds (68 percent) of the children in mixed families and three-quarters (76 percent) of those in families with two foreign-born parents are poor. Considerably more children in the single-parent families, not surprisingly, are poorer than children in two-parent families. For children living with a single U.S.-born parent, 80 percent are poor; among children living with a single foreign-born parent, 86 percent live below the poverty line (see Table 12-2). Legal status is also a strong indicator of poverty for those with children in the United States. Half of the children living with a citizen interviewee live below the poverty line. Among those living with a legal permanent resident, 69 percent of the children live in poverty, but 86 percent of those living with a parent with pending or unauthorized status live in poverty (Table 12-3).

For children in families headed by a U.S.-born non-Hispanic, 37 percent are in families whose income puts them below the poverty line, while three-quarters of the children in families headed by a U.S. Hispanic or a foreign-born individual are in families whose income is below that minimal level (Table 12-4). Ninety-one percent of the children of Puerto Ricans lived in families whose income is below the poverty line. One group, indigenous-speaking Central Americans and Mexicans, is particularly poor—100 percent of the families with U.S.-based children are living in poverty.

Children of farmworkers also suffer some risks because of a lack of supervised child care. In the NAWS only 4 percent of the

[7]If the interviewee was an Hispanic in these two-parent U.S.-born families, 63 percent were poor; if the interviewee was a non-Hispanic, only 26 percent were poor.

children under age 12 are taken to child care centers. About the same proportion (4 percent) are left in less than safe conditions. These children are either left alone, brought with their parents to the fields, or left with other minor children. The overwhelming majority of children (92 percent) are left with a spouse, other relative, neighbor, or adult sibling. The level of unsafe child care is higher for the children of single parents than for other children. About 9 percent of the children in single-parent households are left in unsafe conditions while their parent works.

Some children experience risks by engaging in farmwork themselves. In the NAWS about 13 percent of children ages 10 to 17 who live with their farmworker parents were reported by their parent as doing farmwork. The majority (51 percent) of these children were ages 16 and 17, and 83 percent were age 14 or older. About one-third of the 16 to 17 year olds do farmwork. The proportion of 10 to 17 year olds who do farmwork is particularly high for children whose farmworker parent is a U.S.-born Hispanic. One-quarter of these young U.S. Hispanic children do farmwork, while only 12 percent of the non-Hispanic U.S. born do farmwork. The level is also particularly high among the children of single parents—22 percent of these children do farmwork. At a national level, the 13 percent figure for children ages 10 to 17 living with their farmworker parents yields an estimate of 40,000 children engaged in crop agriculture.[8] This figure does not count the young workers who are not living with their parents. They are discussed in a separate section.

Another problem facing children of farmworkers is the presence of nonnuclear family members in the household. This phenomenon is related to the large presence of solo male immigrants in farmworker communities. In fact, over half of all farmworkers are men unaccompanied by their families. (Ninety percent of them are either foreign- or U.S.-born Hispanics.) Many live in all-male arrangements, ranging from employer-owned labor camps

[8]This is calculated on the basis that about 19.2 percent of all U.S. farmworker children are U.S. based and are 10 to 17 years old (19.2 percent of 1.6 million or about 310,000). Thirteen percent of these children is about 40,000.

to apartments in rural towns. In addition, large numbers of these men double up with families of farmworkers; about one in five farmworker families has a nonrelative sharing their living space (Mines et al., 1997). Solo male agglomerations tend to lead to questionable social behaviors, such as gambling and prostitution, which can present risks to children living alongside them (see Commission on Agricultural Workers, 1993; Griffith and Kissam, 1995).

Although only a small percentage of farmworker children live in households with extended family members present (about 6 percent), over a quarter live with nonrelatives. The concentration of these nonrelatives is among the families connected with immigrants. Looking at family type, about a quarter to a third of the children living with two foreign-born parents with mixed U.S.-/foreign-born families or in single-parent families have nonrelatives living with them. However, only one in 10 of the children in families with two U.S.-born parents have nonrelatives living with them (Table 12-2). According to legal status, 34 percent of children whose parents have pending status and 54 percent of children whose parents have undocumented status have nonrelatives living with them (Table 12-3). By ethnic group, 83 percent of children with Puerto Rican parents and 59 percent of non-Mexican foreign-born parents have nonrelatives living in their households (Table 12-4).

Access to Public Resources

Having reviewed the social and economic circumstances of children in farmworker families, measures of their access to and use of social services are examined next. We look at any use of federal services first for the families of all children and then for those children whose families are below the poverty line. For all income levels, about three out of five children are in families that use some federal service. Looking at use of services by type of family shows that children in families with a single U.S. parent are the most likely to receive any service—79 percent (Table 12-2). Children in families with one or more foreign-born parents are more likely to use services (over 60 percent do) than children in families with two U.S.-born parents (27 percent do). Children in families headed by a U.S. citizen are less likely to use any service (46 percent) than are children in families headed by an immigrant (64 percent or more; Table 12-3). The children from non-Hispanic U.S.-born families are less likely to use any federal service than the other groups (37 percent use services), while children in families headed by U.S-born Hispanics are the most likely to use federal services (70 percent; Table 12-4).

Restricting the analysis to children of farmworkers whose family incomes are below the poverty line, the results change dramatically. In this poor-only group, 72 percent use some federal social services. Considerably more families of U.S.-born children use federal social services than the families of foreign-born children (79 vs. 56 percent; Table 12-1). Looking at family type, proportionately more children of U.S.-born single parents (92 percent) and mixed families with one foreign-born and one U.S.-born parent (81 percent) use federal social services than do other family types (Table 12-2). By ethnic group, children of U.S.-born Hispanics have the highest proportion of users of any social service (81 percent), followed by U.S. non-Hispanics at 73 percent, Mexicans and Puerto Rican-born families at about 70 percent, and the other foreign born at 55 percent (Table 12-4).

There is a tendency for more families with younger children to use social services. Combining the four major social services demonstrates that for all U.S.-based children about 58 percent are in families that use some service. For children under age 6, 67 percent are in families that use social services, 55 percent for children ages 6 to 11, and 48 percent for teenage children. Finally, certain regions of the country demonstrated higher service utilization rates. The regions where larger proportions of children used services were the West, Midwest, Southeast, and Western Plains areas, while the lower-utilization regions were the Northeast and Northwest.

There are four major social services used by farmworkers—Aid to Families with Dependent Children (AFDC); food stamps; Medicaid; and the supplemental food program, Women, Infants, and Children (WIC). The other federal social services are not used by many farmworkers. Social Security, veterans' pay, low-income housing, legal services, and disaster relief are used by 2 percent or less of the families with children. Disability insurance is used by 3 percent.

AFDC is a program used by fewer families headed by immigrants than those headed by U.S.-born individuals. It is also a program that is used much less in general than the other three benefits programs. For groups of all income levels in the NAWS, 8 percent of the children lived in families that received AFDC, and for the poor-only group 11 percent received AFDC benefits. There is, however, considerable variation across groups, with relatively higher proportions of certain groups receiving AFDC.

U.S.-born children live in families that are three times more likely to receive AFDC than the foreign born. Among the poor-only group, U.S.-born children's families are five times more likely (15 vs. 3 percent) to receive AFDC (Table 12-1). Looking at the use of AFDC by family type, definite utilization differences are seen. Among children in two-parent foreign-born families, the utilization rate is quite low in the poor-only group (4 percent). For children in two-parent families in which one or both parents are U.S. born, the rate is higher among the poor-only group. For mixed-nationality couples, 12 percent of the children lived in families collecting AFDC; among children in U.S.-born two-parent families, 20 percent lived in families collecting AFDC. For children in foreign-born single-parent families, the level is relatively high, at 20 percent. However, extremely high levels are found for children in single-parent U.S.-born families. Among the poor-only group, 52 percent of the children lived in families that received AFDC (Table 12-2).

Looking at the groups by ethnic type, a definite slant is seen toward higher utilization by U.S.-born groups. Among the poor-only group, for both the non-Hispanic and Hispanic U.S. born, over 30 percent of the children lived in families receiving AFDC. Among Puerto Ricans, Mexicans, and other foreign born, 8 percent or less received AFDC benefits (Table 12-4). This program is also used much more by the U.S. citizen group. Looking at all children (regardless of poverty status) in the NAWS, 14 percent of the children from U.S. citizen-headed households received AFDC, but only 5 percent of the children from legal permanent resident families did, as well as 2 percent of the children from households with a pending status head and 7 percent of those from undocumented families (Table 12-3).

With respect to the other three noncash benefits programs, the patterns of utilization are different. For children in all families in the NAWS, regardless of income levels, all programs were used at moderate levels—about 40 percent of the children lived in families that used them. For children in poor-only families, higher levels of use were recorded; 43 to 51 percent of the children lived in families that used these programs (Table 12-1).

For children in poor-only families, food stamps were the most used program; 51 percent of such children lived in families that used food stamps. A focus on children in poor-only families shows the distinctions in utilization patterns for food stamps more clearly. U.S.-born children's families were much more likely to use the program than those in foreign-born families. Looking at the groups by family type shows that the proportionately highest users were children in U.S. single-parent families—82 percent (Table 12-2). Among children with mixed-nationality parents, 65 percent received food stamps. For the other groups—children in two-parent families and single-parent foreign-born families—about half lived in families that received food stamps. Analysis by ethnic group shows similar trends. The groups with the highest proportions of food stamp use were U.S. Hispanics (74 percent) and U.S. non-Hispanics (62 percent). The families of children from the other groups received proportionately less in the way of food stamps—60 percent of children in Puerto Rican families, 47 percent of children in Mexican-born families, and 40 percent of the families of other foreign-born children (Table 12-4). In sum, moderate levels of all groups used food stamps, while higher proportions of some U.S.-born groups did so.

Medicaid was the second most frequently utilized federal program for the poor-only group. Among all farmworkers' children, 38 percent were from families using Medicaid, while in the poor-only group, 45 percent were from families receiving Medicaid benefits. Again, the focus here is strictly on the poor-only group to demonstrate clear distinctions in utilization across groups. As with the other social services, the families of U.S.-born children used Medicaid more than the families of foreign-born children. Looking at utilization by type of family, certain patterns emerge.

Sixty-nine percent of the children of a single U.S.-born parent lived in families using Medicaid. Between 43 and 49 percent of the families of children with one or more foreign-born parents used the service. However, fewer of the families of children in two-parent U.S.-born families used Medicaid than the other family types (Table 12-2). With respect to ethnic groups, there are a few small differences. Fifty-three percent of the children of U.S.-born Hispanics lived in families using this service, while fewer Puerto Ricans and other foreign born did so—about a third of the children's families in these groups used the service (Table 12-4). In sum, fewer than half of poor farmworkers' children lived in families using Medicaid. The only exceptions were children in U.S.-born single-parent families and U.S.-born Hispanic families.

The Women, Infants, and Children (WIC) program also is used to some extent by farmworker families. In the NAWS 40 percent of children age 5 and under came from families of all income brackets that utilized this benefit. For children under age 6 in families below the poverty line, the rate of receipt rose only to 43 percent. Again, I report data for the poor-only groups to show distinctions more clearly. Proportionately twice as many U.S-born children's families used WIC than the families of foreign-born children (47 vs. 21 percent; Table 12-1). Family types show that the smallest percentage of users is found in families made up of two U.S.-born parents—only 14 percent of children from that group were in families that received WIC. Again, proportionately more children in U.S.-born single-parent families used the program (69 percent) than the other groups (42 to 45 percent of the childrens' families did; Table 12-2). According to ethnic group, approximately 40 percent of the children in U.S.-born and Mexican-born families (with children under age 6) lived in families receiving WIC, while only about 5 percent of the children of Puerto Rican and other foreign-born families did so (Table 12-4).

One comment must be made about the use of these three in-kind transfer payments by legal status. Analyzing the data regardless of poverty level, the differences among the foreign-born legal status groups are not remarkable. One exception is that for food stamps higher percentages of children in the legal permanent resident and pending status families received food stamps than children in undocumented families. It is with undocumented farmworkers with children born abroad but living in the United States that the level of children receiving services drops markedly. Fewer U.S.-based children born abroad who lived with an unauthorized parent had a parent receiving federal social services than did U.S.-born children living with parents who are unauthorized U.S. residents. Only about 18 percent of these foreign-born children are in families that received food stamps, 26 percent received Medicaid, and 23 percent received WIC. It should be noted that the presence of an unauthorized interviewee in a household may not mean that the family does not qualify for services. Another adult may be a legal resident, and some services, such as emergency Medicaid, are legally available to unauthorized U.S. residents.

Turning our attention to another measure of children's well-being—use of health care services—we find that farmworker parents have some interesting access patterns. Among all children, about a third (30 percent) are in families that go to public clinics (including migrant clinics) for health care, about a quarter (24 percent) go to emergency rooms, about a third go to private doctors (34 percent), and about 5 percent either go nowhere or go back to their native country. However, among major groups there are big differences. For example, the proportion of children in U.S.-born non-Hispanic farmworker families using private doctors is relatively high—over half (52 percent). These children's families are much less likely to use emergency rooms—only 18 percent do. For children from Mexican-born households, 30 percent lived in families using private doctors and 27 percent use emergency rooms. Migrant health care centers are used almost exclusively by foreign-born residents and U.S.-born Hispanics. Children from U.S.-born Hispanic families are in households that are actually the largest relative users of migrant clinics—16 percent of these children are from families that seek health care services at these clinics. Puerto Ricans follow the pattern of the foreign-born groups—almost half use emergency care and very few private doctors (Table 12-4). Looking at family structure, another interesting finding emerges; nearly 4 out of 10 children from foreign-born single-parent families are taken to emergency rooms when they are sick, a much larger proportion than those who use other service providers (Table 12-2).

A relatively large percentage (19 percent) of farmworker parents say that it is difficult to access health care in the United States. Fewer U.S.-born children live in families experiencing difficulty than those who are foreign born. Only 9 percent of children in non-Hispanic U.S.-born families experienced difficulty; 19 percent of all the other ethnic categories lived in families that experienced difficulty obtaining health care services (Table 12-4). Among children in families headed by a non-Mexican foreign-born person, 32 percent reported difficulty accessing health care. This difficulty is experienced by twice as many children (proportionately) from families with at least one foreign parent (22 percent) than by children without a foreign-born parent (11 percent). Foreign-born single parents more often reported having a difficult time accessing health care in the United States. For 31 percent of children from this type of family, health care was perceived as hard to obtain (Table 12-2). For those who find health care services difficult to obtain, the major barriers for farmworkers' children are cost (34 percent), language (17 percent), and fear of losing one's job if one goes to the doctor (11 percent). With respect to language, only children with both foreign-born parents or a foreign-born single parent experienced this barrier; families with mixed-nationality parents, not surprisingly, had few problems of this type.

A small group of children have farmworker parents who have access to off-the-job health care—14 percent. The proportion of children with a parent who is a U.S.-born non-Hispanic with access to health care is somewhat higher (17 percent) than among children of U.S. Hispanics (8 percent) and children of foreign-born parents (14 percent). The proportion of children whose parents are unauthorized U.S. residents or have pending status who are covered by off-the-job health care is much lower—only 6 percent.

Many farmworkers mix or apply pesticides and other chemicals in their work. In the NAWS, 28 percent of all children have parents who engage in this activity. About 14 percent of such children live on a farm with their parents. Of these children, 34 percent have parents who apply or mix chemicals at work.

U.S.-born children are more likely to live with parents who apply pesticides at work (30 percent) than are foreign-born children (25 percent; Table 12-1). There are few patterns by type of family: children in two-parent families were more likely to have a head of household who applies pesticides at work than children in single-parent families. By ethnic group, the groups most likely to apply pesticides are Mexicans, Puerto Ricans, and U.S. non-Hispanics (Table 12-4). This task is more closely associated with experience and seniority than with ethnic group or family organization.

UNACCOMPANIED MINORS

In addition to the children of employed farmworkers, the NAWS collects data on another group of children—those who are themselves farmworkers and who are not living with their parents at the time of their NAWS interview. In the 1993 to 1995 surveys these employed unaccompanied children made up about 4 percent of the interviewees, or the equivalent of 65,000 workers.[9]

About two-thirds of these minors are foreign born. These young foreigners, who number perhaps 44,000 workers, are a group especially likely to experience high risk on the socioeconomic factors measured in the NAWS (see Table 12-5). They have very low personal income—the median is $1,000 to $2,500 per year. Even including the incomes of relatives with whom they share their budgets, family income averages $2,500 to $5,000 per year. Like most foreign farmworkers, these children have a low level of educational achievement—only 35 percent of the young foreign workers have gone to school beyond the eighth grade. They are also an extremely migratory group—79 percent migrated in the year prior to their interview. Almost one-quarter of them follow crops from one area of the United States to another during the year, and almost three out of five either are first-year immigrants or return to their country of origin each year. Nearly 9 out of 10 do not have documents authorizing them to work in the

[9]The weighted sample size for all unaccompanied youth for 1993 to 1995 is 248 workers. The sample size for the foreign born is 167. From these weighted sample sizes (as a proportion of all workers in the total sample) point estimates of the population were calculated. The base level of cropworkers is 1,810,000, derived from the U.S. Census of Population and Housing for the proportion of cropworkers and the Commission on Agricultural Workers for the size of the total population of farmworkers (see note 1).

United States. Almost all of them are between the ages of 14 and 17, 6 percent are married, and a large majority (85 percent) are boys.

These children often live in all-male environments, where lack of adult supervision and protection may put them at risk. There are several indicators of risk in the NAWS data. First, almost all of these children live in households without any relatives at all—only 13 percent live with a relative who is not their parent. The households they live in receive almost no social services. Despite the fact that 78 percent of such children live below the poverty line, their households receive no transfer payments; 2 percent receive WIC, 6 percent receive Medicaid, and 6 percent receive food stamps. Despite their age, 15 percent mix or apply pesticides, and few (23 percent) receive instruction on how to use the chemicals safely, as is required by law. In addition, over half say it is difficult to access health care facilities. Seventy-three percent indicate that the language barrier keeps them from finding health care services. When they do find services, 38 percent use emergency rooms, 42 percent go to public clinics, only 7 percent go to private doctors, and 14 percent go back to their native country when sick or they do not seek treatment. Finally, only 1 percent, compared to 11 percent of all farmworkers, say that they are covered by off-the-job health insurance.

The other one-third of these young unaccompanied workers are U.S. born. Apparently, these young people are better connected to family and U.S. institutions than their foreign-born counterparts, as their conditions are somewhat better. Although they earn little income themselves (the median is $1,000 to $2,500), they are associated with households whose median annual incomes are $10,000 to $12,500. About half live below the poverty line. These youth have had much more education than their foreign-born counterparts—more than half completed tenth grade or beyond. Their rates of migration are much less—only 20 percent migrate each year. More of them receive federal social services—21 percent receive food stamps, 17 percent receive Medicaid, and 4 percent receive WIC. On one issue they are at greater risk than foreign-born young people: 24 percent mix or apply pesticides in their work.

SUMMARY

This study of farmworkers' children serves as a first look at such children. Many of these children are disadvantaged by educational and linguistic handicaps, by separation from their parents, and often by periodic migration. In fact, the farmworkers' world can be seen as a sort of "foreign island" in American society, where Spanish is a first language and the proportion of newly arrived foreign born each year is extremely high.

The high flow-through labor market characterized by a high percentage of solo males is common in other labor markets but is difficult to study since household-based surveys and censuses miss many of the participants in these labor markets. The research reported here is a first such effort to describe the circumstances of children in one of these labor markets.

This paper shows that many of these children experience a variety of risks. They are "strangers in our fields"—three-quarters of U.S.-based farmworkers' children have a foreign parent and a quarter are foreign born. Although children of foreign-born parents are less likely to be from single-parent families, most are separated from one of their parents. In addition, a quarter of the children are in the migrant stream. All together, about 212,000 farmworkers' children migrate each year. Among these are about 80,000 who go back and forth across international borders. The data show that these "international shuttle" children are particularly likely to be behind in school. In fact, most farmworkers' children have parents with limited educational attainments—only 40 percent have parents who finished the eighth grade. Moreover, more than one-sixth of the U.S.-based children are behind grade level for their age. This rate is higher for teenagers, many of whom work with their parents in the fields.

The most serious difficulty for such children may be extreme poverty, especially for the foreign born and for U.S. Hispanics. Overall, 68 to 73 percent of the children come from families whose income is below the poverty line. For the foreign born and U.S. Hispanics, three-quarters live in poverty. Despite this poverty, most poor children's families do not use most federal social services. Except for food stamps, most legally authorized poor families, who clearly qualify for the programs, do not use them.

When they are sick, immigrant families tend to use emergency rooms and public clinics. Many children have parents who say they have difficulty accessing care because of language and economic barriers. In addition, many have parents who mix and apply pesticides in their work, which may be a hazard for the children. Finally, there is a small but significant group of unaccompanied children, most of whom are far from their Mexican and Central American parents. They live in all-male subgroups and face some of the most severe risks of any farmworkers be they adults or children.

ACKNOWLEDGMENTS

The author thanks Kyra Kissam, Anne Steirman, Susan Gabbard, Bea Boccalandro, Flavio Flefferman, and Victor Renteria for their contributions to the preparation of this paper. This paper reflects the opinions of the author and not necessarily those of the U.S. Department of Labor.

REFERENCES

Commission on Agricultural Workers
1993 *Report to Congress, Case Studies and Research Reports, Appendix I.* Washington, D.C.: Commission on Agricultural Workers.

Gabbard, S., R. Mines, and B. Boccalandro
1994 *Migrant Farmworkers: Pursuing Stability in an Unstable Labor Market.* Research Report No. 5. Washington, D.C.: U.S. Department of Labor.

Griffith, D., and E. Kissam
1995 *Working Poor.* Philadelphia: Temple University Press.

Lichter, M., and R. Waldinger
1996 Black/Immigrant Labor Market Competition: New Insights from a Case Study of the Hospital Industry in Los Angeles. Unpublished manuscript, UCLA.

McWilliams, C.
1935 *Factories in the Field.* Santa Barbara: Peregrine Press.

Mines, R., and J. Avina
1992 Immigrants and labor standards: The case of California janitors. In *U.S.-Mexico Relations: Labor Market Interdependence,* J. Bustamante, C. Reynolds, and R. Hinojosa, eds. Stanford, Calif.: Stanford University Press.

Mines, R., S. Gabbard, and A. Steirman
1997 *A Profile of U.S. Farmworkers: Demographics, Household Composition, Income and Use of Services*. Research Report No. 6. Washington, D.C.: U.S. Department of Labor.

U.S. Government Accounting Office
1997 *Illegal Aliens: Influence of Illegal Workers on Wages and Working Conditions of Legal Workers*. GAO/PEMD-88-13BR. Washington, D.C.: U.S. General Accounting Office.

Waldinger, R.
1996 *Still the Promised City*. Cambridge, Mass.: Harvard University Press.

APPENDIX 12A: EXPLANATION OF SELECTED VARIABLES

Child is separated from one parent:

This variable gives the percentage of children separated from one of their parents if they live in a two-parent family. It includes children based abroad and in the United States and therefore has a larger sample size than the other variables.

Child's father came to the United States first:

This variable gives the percentage of children whose fathers preceded them to the United States. It includes only U.S.-based foreign-born children who have a foreign-born parent.

Child's family migrates every year:

This variable gives the percentage of children whose interviewee parent moves 75 miles or more to look for or obtain farmwork.

Parent finished eight or more years of school:

This variable gives the percentage of children whose interviewee parent finished eight years of school.

Child is enrolled in school:

This variable gives the percentage of children enrolled in school in the year of the interview. It includes only children age 6 and older.

Child is behind in grade level:

This variable gives the percentage of children who were a full year or more behind in school for their age. For example, a 9 year old who has not reached second grade or a 17 year old who has not reached tenth grade would be classified as behind. It includes only children age 6 and older.

Median family income:

This variable gives the median income range earned by the families of farmworker children.

Poverty:

Since income is reported as a range rather than a point quantity, two calculations were made: one underestimates poverty in the groups (lower-bound estimate) and one overestimates it (upper-bound estimate). In the lower-bound estimate, the top of the range was used to estimate poverty for the family; in the upper-bound estimate, the bottom of the range was used. For example, if a family of four reported an income level of $12,500 to $15,000 and if the poverty threshold is $13,500, it is not known for sure on which side of the line the family is. As a result, two calculations were made, one assuming the family earned $12,500 and fell below the poverty line (upper-bound estimate) and one assuming it earned $15,000 and thus was not poor (lower-bound estimate). In the text the conservative lower-bound measure was used.

AFDC, food stamps, Medicaid, WIC:

These variables give the percentage of children from families that collected a given federal benefit. WIC is for children age 5 and younger.

Source of family's health care:

This variable presents the percentage of children whose families used different kinds of health care providers.

Family's perceived difficulty in obtaining health care:

This variable gives the percentage of children whose parents find it difficult to access health care.

Parent mixes or handles pesticides at work:

This variable gives the percentage of children whose interviewee parent mixes or applies pesticides.

Other Reports from the Board on Children, Youth, and Families

From Generation to Generation: The Health and Well-Being of Children in Immigrant Families (1998)

Protecting Youth at Work: Health, Safety, and Development of Working Children and Adolescents in the United States (1998)

Reducing the Odds: Preventing Perinatal Transmission of HIV in the United States (with the Division of Health Promotion and Disease Prevention of the Institute of Medicine) (1998)

America's Children: Health Insurance and Access to Care (with the Division of Health Care Services of the Institute of Medicine) (1998)

Systems of Accountability: Implementing Children's Health Insurance Programs (with the Division of Health Care Services of the Institute of Medicine) (1998)

Longitudinal Surveys of Children: Report of a Workshop (with the Committee on National Statistics of the National Research Council) (1998)

New Findings on Poverty and Child Health and Nutrition: Summary of a Research Briefing (1998)

Violence in Families: Assessing Prevention and Treatment Programs (1998)

Welfare, the Family, and Reproductive Behavior: Report of a Meeting (with the Committee on Population of the National Research Council) (1998)

Educating Language-Minority Children (1998)

Improving Schooling for Language-Minority Children: A Research Agenda (1997)

New Findings on Welfare and Children's Development: Summary of a Research Briefing (1997)

Youth Development and Neighborhood Influences: Challenges and Opportunities: Summary of a Workshop (1996)

Paying Attention to Children in a Changing Health Care System: Summaries of Workshops (1996)

Beyond the Blueprint: Directions for Research on Head Start's Families: Report of Three Roundtable Meetings (1996)

Child Care for Low-Income Families: Directions for Research: Summary of a Workshop (1996)

Service Provider Perspectives on Family Violence Interventions: Proceedings of a Workshop (1995)

"Immigrant Children and Their Families: Issues for Research and Policy" in the David and Lucile Packard Foundation's *The Future of Children* (1995)

Integrating Federal Statistics on Children (with the Committee on National Statistics of the National Research Council) (1995)

Child Care for Low-Income Families: Summary of Two Workshops (1995)

New Findings on Children, Families, and Economic Self-Sufficiency: Summary of a Research Briefing (1995)

The Impact of War on Child Health in the Countries of the Former Yugoslavia: A Workshop Summary (with the Institute of Medicine and the Office of International Affairs of the National Research Council) (1995)

Cultural Diversity and Early Education: Report of a Workshop (1994)

Benefits and Systems of Care for Maternal and Child Health: Workshop Highlights (with the Board on Health Promotion and Disease Prevention of the Institute of Medicine) (1994)

Protecting and Improving Quality of Care for Children Under Health Care Reform: Workshop Highlights (with the Board on Health Promotion and Disease Prevention of the Institute of Medicine) (1994)

America's Fathers and Public Policy: Report of a Workshop (1994)

Violence and the American Family: Report of a Workshop (1994)